TECHNOLOGY

Online Learning Center

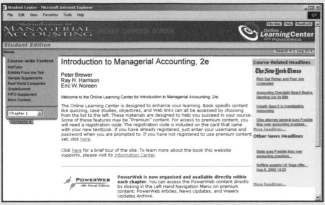

More and more students are studying online, and more and more instructors rely on the Internet to present and manage course material. That's why the **Introduction to Managerial Accounting** team has provided the most complete and up-to-date collection of Web resources—whether it be alternate problems and solutions, an online tutorial, or links to professional resources.

Whether you're an instructor building a lesson plan or a student preparing for an exam, the **Introduction to Managerial Accounting Online Learning Center** is the perfect one-stop resource. Check it out at **www.mhhe.com/bgn2e.**

Homework Manager

McGraw-Hill/Irwin's Homework Manager pulls problem structures directly from the end-of-chapter material using algorithmic technology, providing a limitless supply of online self-graded practice for students. These problem structures are easily identifiable in the text by the **Homework Manager** icon. A wealth of textbook-quality questions allows students to work on fresh problems until they have fully mastered the topic presented. Immediate feedback and scoring helps guide them through their studies. For a demonstration of McGraw-Hill/Irwin's Homework Manager, visit the Online Information Center at **www.mhhe.com/bgn2e.**

NetTutor™

For students with hectic schedules, **NetTutor™** allows one-on-one assistance completely online and at their convenience. Qualified accounting tutors work with students on specific problems or concepts from the text through the **Live Tutor Center**. Students may submit questions to the Q&A Center at any time and retrieve responses within 24 hours. Additionally, the Archive Center allows students to peruse previously asked questions and search on particular topics. For a demonstration of **NetTutor™**, visit the Online Information Center at **www.mhhe.com/bgn2e.**

Online Information Center
- Overview
- Table of Contents
- Author Biographies
- Preface
- Print and Electronic Supplements
- Link to PageOut
- Topic Tackler Demo
- NetTutor™ Demo

Online Instructor Center
- Instructor's Manual
- PowerPoint® files
- Solutions Manual
- Downloadable Images from the Text
- Excel Template Exercises and and Solutions
- Links to Professional Resources

Online Student Center
- Sample Study Guide and Working Papers
- Learning Objectives
- Chapter Overviews
- Glossary of Key Terms
- PowerPoint® files
- Internet Exercises
- Online Quizzes
- Practice Exams
- Links to URLs referenced in the Text
- Online Factory Tours

Online Tutorial
- Excel Template Exercises
- Link to ALEKS® Math Skills Assessor
- Link to NetTutor™ Live Online Tutoring
- Downloadable Images from the Text

Other updates will be added throughout the term.

Introduction to

MANAGERIAL ACCOUNTING
2nd edition

Peter C. Brewer
Associate Professor, Miami University

Ray H. Garrison
Professor Emeritus, Brigham Young University

Eric W. Noreen
Professor Emeritus, University of Washington

McGraw-Hill Irwin

Boston   Burr Ridge, IL   Dubuque, IA   Madison, WI   New York   San Francisco   St. Louis
Bangkok   Bogotá   Caracas   Kuala Lumpur   Lisbon   London   Madrid   Mexico City
Milan   Montreal   New Delhi   Santiago   Seoul   Singapore   Sydney   Taipei   Toronto

McGraw-Hill
Irwin

INTRODUCTION TO MANAGERIAL ACCOUNTING

Published by McGraw-Hill/Irwin, a business unit of The McGraw-Hill Companies, Inc., 1221 Avenue of the Americas, New York, NY, 10020. Copyright © 2005, 2002 by The McGraw-Hill Companies, Inc. All rights reserved. No part of this publication may be reproduced or distributed in any form or by any means, or stored in a database or retrieval system, without the prior written consent of The McGraw-Hill Companies, Inc., including, but not limited to, in any network or other electronic storage or transmission, or broadcast for distance learning.

Some ancillaries, including electronic and print components, may not be available to customers outside the United States.

This book is printed on acid-free paper.

2 3 4 5 6 7 8 9 0 VNH/VNH 0 9 8 7 6 5 4

ISBN 0-07-281787-9

Editorial director: *Brent Gordon*
Publisher: *Stewart Mattson*
Executive editor: *Tim Vertovec*
Developmental editor I: *Sarah Wood*
Marketing manager: *Katherine Mattison*
Senior producer, media technology: *Ed Przyzycki*
Lead project manager: *Pat Frederickson*
Production supervisor: *Debra R. Sylvester*
Lead designer: *Pam Verros*
Photo research coordinator: *Judy Kausal*
Photo researcher: *Charlotte Goldman*
Senior supplement producer: *Carol Loreth*
Senior digital content specialist: *Brian Nacik*
Cover design: *Ryan Brown*
Cover photo credit: © *Macduff Everton/Corbis*
Typeface: *10.5/12 Times New Roman*
Compositor: *GAC Indianapolis*
Printer: *Von Hoffmann Corporation*

Library of Congress Cataloging-in-Publication Data

Brewer, Peter C.
    Introduction to managerial accounting / Peter C. Brewer, Ray H. Garrison, Eric W.
Noreen.—2nd ed.
        p. cm.
    Rev. ed. of: Introduction to managerial accounting / Jeannie M. Folk, Ray H. Garrison, Eric W.
Noreen. 1st ed. 2002.
    Includes indexes.
    ISBN 0-07-281787-9 (alk. paper)
    1. Managerial accounting. I. Garrison, Ray H. II. Noreen, Eric W. III. Folk, Jeannie M.
Introduction to managerial accounting. IV. Title.
HF5657.4.F65 2005
658.15′11—dc22
                                                                                    2003059317

www.mhhe.com

DEDICATION

To our families and to our many colleagues who use this book.
—Peter C. Brewer, Ray H. Garrison, and Eric W. Noreen

Peter C. Brewer

is an associate professor in the Department of Accountancy at Miami University, Oxford, Ohio. He holds a BS degree in accounting from Penn State University, an MS degree in accounting from the University of Virginia, and a PhD from the University of Tennessee. He has published numerous articles in a variety of journals including: *Management Accounting Research, The Journal of Information Systems, The Journal of Cost Management, Strategic Finance, The Journal of Accountancy, Issues in Accounting Education, The Journal of Corporate Accounting and Finance, The Journal of Business Logistics,* and *The Supply Chain Management Review.*

Professor Brewer is a member of the editorial board of *Issues in Accounting Education* and has served on the editorial board of *The Journal of the Academy of Business Education.* He has also served as an associate editor for the *Journal of Engineering Valuation and Cost Analysis.* He has been recognized on two occasions by the Miami University Associated Student Government for "making a remarkable commitment to students and their educational development." He has taught a continuing professional education (CPE) workshop at the AAA national meeting dealing with teaching case-driven undergraduate management accounting courses and is a leading thinker in undergraduate management accounting curriculum innovation. He is a frequent presenter at various professional and academic conferences and meetings.

Prior to joining the faculty at Miami University, Professor Brewer was employed as an auditor for Touche Ross in the firm's Philadelphia office. He also worked as an internal audit manager for the Board of Pensions of the Presbyterian Church (U.S.A.). He frequently collaborates with companies such as Harris Corporation, Ethicon Endo-Surgery, Square D, Lenscrafters, and Fidelity Investments in a consulting or case writing capacity.

*the*authors

Eric W. Noreen

is a globe-trotting academic who has held appointments at institutions in the United States, Europe, and Asia. He is emeritus professor of accounting at the University of Washington.

He received his BA degree from the University of Washington and MBA and PhD degrees from Stanford University. A Certified Management Accountant, he was awarded a Certificate of Distinguished Performance by the Institute of Certified Management Accountants.

Professor Noreen has served as associate editor of *The Accounting Review* and the *Journal of Accounting and Economics*. He has numerous articles in academic journals including: the *Journal of Accounting Research; The Accounting Review;* the *Journal of Accounting and Economics; Accounting Horizons; Accounting, Organizations and Society; Contemporary Accounting Research;* the *Journal of Management Accounting Research;* and the *Review of Accounting Studies.*

Professor Noreen teaches management accounting at the undergraduate and master's levels and has won a number of awards from students for his teaching.

Ray H. Garrison

is emeritus professor of accounting at Brigham Young University, Provo, Utah. He received his BS and MS degrees from Brigham Young University and his DBA degree from Indiana University.

As a certified public accountant, Professor Garrison has been involved in management consulting work with both national and regional accounting firms. He has published articles in *The Accounting Review, Management Accounting,* and other professional journals. Innovation in the classroom has earned Professor Garrison the Karl G. Maeser Distinguished Teaching Award from Brigham Young University.

Empowering Students to Rise to New Levels

Most students question whether they will ever use managerial accounting information as managers in an organization or business. **Introduction to Managerial Accounting**, 2nd edition, by **Brewer, Garrison, and Noreen** will teach your students not only tools that everyone from accountants to marketing managers use, but also the critical thinking skills necessary to succeed in business. It is this combination of understanding, technique, and the ability to apply it in the real world that empowers students to make business decisions and ascend to new heights.

Introduction to Managerial Accounting, *2nd edition*, by **BREWER/GARRISON/NOREEN** empowers your students to rise to new levels in the following ways:

Concise

Most of your students taking this course will not be accounting majors. Your students want a text that is concise, and that presents material in a clear and readable manner. Your students' biggest concern is making sure they can solve the end-of-chapter problems after reading the chapter. Our market survey indicates that Brewer/Garrison/Noreen achieves this better than any other concise managerial accounting text on the market. Moreover, the authors write all the major supplements, so the text, study guide, test bank, and solutions manual are consistent with one another.

Decision-Making Focus

It is important for your students to understand how managerial accounting information is used to make business decisions, especially if your students plan to be future managers. Brewer/Garrison/Noreen accomplishes this with three types of pedagogy. First, the Managerial Accounting in Action scenarios place students in a real-world business problem and then walk them through how to solve it. Second, the Decision Maker and You Decide boxes put the student in real-world scenarios, both corporate and entrepreneurial, and ask them to apply what they have learned. Lastly, the Building Your Skills cases help your students build the decision-making skills they need.

Contemporary

Today's students rely on technology more than ever. Brewer/Garrison/Noreen provides them with the technological ancillaries they need to succeed in this class. McGraw-Hill/Irwin's Homework Manager uses the web and algorithmically generated problems taken from the text to develop problem-solving skills. Topic Tackler combines video, self-assessment, and PowerPoint lectures that cover the most difficult topics in each chapter. Additionally, NetTutor and the Online Learning Center provide your students with a variety of multimedia aids to help them master managerial accounting.

What makes **Brewer/Garrison/Noreen,**

Introduction to Managerial Accounting is full of pedagogy designed to make studying productive and hassle-free. On the following pages, you will see the kind of engaging, helpful pedagogical features that make Brewer/Garrison/Noreen a favorite among both teachers and students.

Opening Vignette
Each chapter opens with a two-page Chapter Opener featuring a real-world company.

Author-Written Supplements
The authors write all of the text's major supplements, ensuring a perfect fit between text and supplement. For more information on Brewer/Garrison/Noreen's supplements, see pages xxii and xxiii.

Infographics
New infographics have been included throughout the text to help students visualize key accounting concepts.

CHAPTER FOUR

Systems Design: Process Costing

A LOOK BACK
We described a basic job-order costing system in Chapter 2 that used a single plantwide overhead rate. Then, in Chapter 3, we looked at activity-based costing, a more sophisticated technique that uses a variety of allocation bases to assign overhead costs to products.

A LOOK AT THIS CHAPTER
Chapter 4 covers process costing, which is an important alternative to job-order costing. In process costing, departmental costs are applied uniformly to the products processed through the department during the period.

A LOOK AHEAD
After discussing how costs respond to changes in the level of business activity, we will introduce the contribution format income statement in Chapter 5.

CHAPTER OUTLINE

Comparison of Job-Order and Process Costing
- Similarities between Job-Order and Process Costing
- Differences between Job-Order and Process Costing

A Perspective of Process Cost Flows
- Processing Departments
- The Flow of Materials, Labor, and Overhead Costs
- Materials, Labor, and Overhead Cost Entries

Equivalent Units of Production
- Weighted-Average Method

Production Report—Weighted-Average Method
- Step 1: Prepare a Quantity Schedule and Compute the Equivalent Units
- Step 2: Compute Costs per Equivalent Unit
- Step 3: Prepare a Cost Reconciliation
- A Comment about Rounding Errors

SUPPLEMENT: FIFO METHOD (AVAILABLE ON THE WEB AT WWW.MHHE.COM/BGN2E)
Equivalent Units—FIFO Method

Comparison of Equivalent Units of Production under the Weighted-Average and FIFO Methods

Production Report—FIFO Method
- Step 1: Prepare a Quantity Schedule

- Step 2: Compute the Costs per Equivalent Unit
- Step 3: Prepare a Cost Reconciliation

A Comparison of Costing Methods

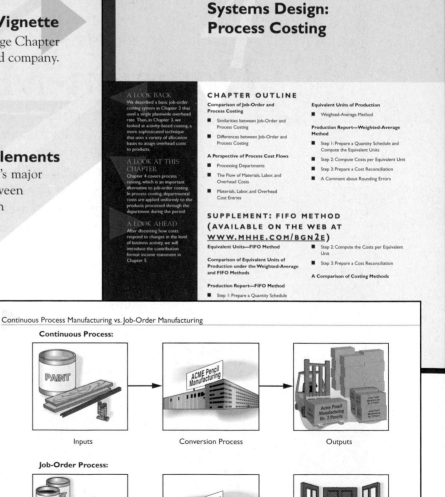

Continuous Process Manufacturing vs. Job-Order Manufacturing

Continuous Process:

Inputs — Conversion Process — Outputs

Job-Order Process:

Inputs — Conversion Process — Outputs

2nd edition, such a powerful learning tool?

based costing, we have been able to better identify the overhead costs of each product and thus derive more accurate cost data.

The pattern of cost distortion shown by the ABC team's findings is quite common. Such distortion can happen in any company that relies on direct labor-hours or machine-hours in assigning overhead cost to products and ignores other significant factors affecting overhead cost incurrence.

MANAGERIAL ACCOUNTING IN ACTION

comtek SOUND, INC.

Wrap-Up

The ABC team presented the results of its work in a meeting attended by all of the top managers of Comtek Sound including the president, Sarah Kastler; the production manager, Frank Hines; the marketing manager, Nicole Sermone; and the accounting manager, Tom Frazier. After the formal presentation by the ABC team, the following discussion took place:

Sarah: I would like to personally thank the ABC team for all the work they have done. I am now beginning to wonder about some of the decisions we have made in the past using our old cost accounting system.

Tom: I hope I don't have to remind anyone that I have been warning people about this problem for quite some time.

Sarah: No, you don't have to remind us, Tom. I guess we just didn't understand the problem before.

obvious from this activity-based costing information that we had every-
kwards. We thought the competition was pricing below cost on the CD
in fact *we* were overcharging for these units because our costs were over-
d we thought the competition was overpricing DVD units, but in fact *our*
re way too low because our costs for these units were understated. I'll bet
etition has really been laughing behind our backs!
can bet they won't be laughing when they see our next bids.

...ION FEATURE

ng Cream Soda

ris started a company that produces cream soda from an old family recipe. At first the
ruggled, but as sales increased, the company expanded rapidly. Megan soon realized that to
further, it would be necessary to borrow money. The investment in additional equipment
ge for her to finance out of the company's current cash flows.

was disappointed to find that few banks were willing to make a loan to such a small
ut she finally found a bank that would consider her loan application. However, Megan was
hat she would have to supply up-to-date financial statements with her loan application.
had never bothered with financial statements before—she felt that as long as the balance
pany's checkbook kept increasing, the company was doing fine. She was puzzled how the
o determine the value of the cream soda in the work in process and finished goods inven-
valuation of the cream soda would affect both the cost of goods sold and the inventory
her company. Megan thought of perhaps using job-order costing, which had been used at
us employer, but her company produces only one product. Raw ingredients are continually
d to make more cream soda, and more bot
g line. Megan didn't see how she could use a
d. Perhaps there was another way to accou
d you like to produce your own brand of so
ml on the Internet for a detailed discussion

LEARNING OBJECTIVES

After studying Chapter 4, you should be able to:

LO1 Record the flow of materials, labor, and overhead through a process costing system.

LO2 Compute the equivalent units of production using the weighted-average method.

LO3 Prepare a quantity schedule using the weighted-average method.

LO4 Compute the costs per equivalent unit using the

132   Chapter 3

IN BUSINESS

Is E-Tailing Really Easier?

The company art.com™ sells prints and framed prints over the web. An ABC study identified the following 12 activities carried out in the company:

1. Service customers
2. Website optimization
3. Merchandise inventory selection and management
4. Purchasing and receiving
5. Customer acquisition and retention—paid-for marketing
6. Customer acquisition and retention—revenue share marketing (affiliate group)
7. Sustain information system
8. Sustain business—administration
9. Sustain business—production
10. Maintain facility—administrative
11. Maintain facility—production
12. Sustain business—executive

For example, the activity "merchandise inventory selection and management" involves scanning, describing, classifying, and linking each inventory item to search options. "Staff must carefully manage each change to the database, which is similar to adding and removing inventory items from the shelf of a store. They annotate added inventory items and upload them into the system, as well as remove obsolete and discontinued items. . . . The number of inventory items for an e-tailer is typically much greater than for a brick-and-mortar [store], which is a competitive advantage, but experience shows managing a large inventory consumes substantial resources."

Source: Thomas L. Zeller, David R. Kublank, and Philip G. Makris, " How art.com™ Uses ABC to Succeed," *Strategic Finance*, March 2001, pp. 25–31. Reprinted with permission from the IMA, Montvale, NJ, USA, www.imanet.org.

"Managerial Accounting in Action"

These highly praised vignettes depict cross-functional teams working together in real-life settings on products and services that students recognize from their own lives. Students are shown step-by-step how accounting concepts are implemented in organizations and how these concepts are applied to solve everyday business problems. First, "The Issue" is introduced through a dialogue. The student then walks through the implementation process. Finally the "Wrap-Up" summarizes the big picture.

"In Business"

These helpful boxed features offer a glimpse into how real companies use the managerial accounting concepts discussed within the chapter. Every chapter contains from two to nine of these current examples.

Service IS

Owing to the growing number of service-based companies in business today, the second edition uses a helpful icon to distinguish service-related examples.

mayor of the city, Stephen Goldsmith, explained: "Introducing competition and privatization to government services requires real cost information. You can't compete out if you are using fake money." When city workers became aware of the costs of carrying out activities such as filling potholes in streets and were faced with the possible transfer of such tasks to the private sector, they became highly motivated to reduce costs. Instead of going out to fill potholes with a five- or six-man repair crew, plus a supervisor, they started doing the same job with a three- or four-man crew without a supervisor. The number of politically appointed supervisors, which had stood at 36 for 75 employees, was slashed by half.

Source: Robert S. Kaplan and Robin Cooper, *Cost & Effect: Using Integrated Cost Systems to Drive Profitability and Performance,* Harvard Business School Press, Boston, 1998, pp. 245–250.

The **Decision Maker** feature fosters critical thinking and decision-making skills by providing real-world business scenarios that require the resolution of a business issue. The suggested solution is located at the end of the chapter.

Legal Firm Business Manager

DECISION MAKER

You have been hired to manage the business aspects of a local legal firm with a staff of 6 attorneys, 10 paralegals, and 5 staffpersons. Clients of the firm are billed a fixed amount per hour of attorney time. The fixed hourly charge is determined each year by dividing the total cost of the legal office for the preceding year by the total billed hours of attorney time for that year. A markup of 25 percent is then added to this average cost per hour of billed attorney time to provide for a profit and for inflation.

The firm's partners are concerned because the firm has been unprofitable for several years. The firm has been losing its smaller clients to other local firms—largely because the firm's fees have become uncompetitive. And the firm has been attracting larger clients with more complex legal problems from its competitors. To serve these demanding larger clients, the firm must subscribe to expensive on-line legal reference services, hire additional paralegals and staffpersons, and lease additional office space.

What do you think might be the reason for the unprofitable operations in recent years? What might be done to improve the situation for the coming year?

CONCEPT CHECK ✓

2. Which of the following statements is false? (You may select more than one answer.)
   a. Activity-based costing systems usually shift costs from low-volume products to high-volume products.
   b. Benchmarking can be used to identify activities with the greatest potential for improvement.
   c. Activity-based costing is most valuable to companies that manufacture products

Internet assignments teach students how to find information online and apply it to managerial accounting situations.

Writing assignments encourage your students to practice critical thinking.

	(14)		
Cost of Goods Sold		5,000	
Manufacturing Overhead			5,000

Note that since the Manufacturing Overhead account has a debit balance, Manufacturing Overhead must be credited to close out the account. This has the effect of increasing Cost of Goods Sold for April to $123,500:

Unadjusted cost of goods sold [from entry (13)]	$118,500
Add underapplied overhead [entry (14) above]	5,000
Adjusted cost of goods sold	$123,500

After this adjustment has been made, Rand Company's income statement for April will appear as shown earlier in Exhibit 2–12.

The **You Decide** feature challenges students to apply the tools of analysis and make decisions. The suggested solution is found at the end of the chapter.

Remaining Balance in the Overhead Account

YOU DECIDE

The simplest method for disposing of any balance remaining in the Overhead account is to close it out to Cost of Goods Sold. If there is a debit balance (that is, overhead has been underapplied), the entry to dispose of the balance would include a debit to Cost of Goods Sold. That debit would increase the balance in the Cost of Goods Sold account. On the other hand, if there is a credit balance, the entry to dispose of the balance would include a credit to Cost of Goods Sold. That credit would decrease the balance in the Cost of Goods Sold account. If you were the company's controller, would you want a debit balance, a credit balance, or no balance in the Overhead account at the end of the period?

A General Model of Product Cost Flows

The flow of costs in a product costing system is presented in the form of a T-account model in Exhibit 2–14. This model applies as much to a process costing system as it does to a job-order costing system. Examination of this model can be very helpful in understanding how costs enter a system, flow through it, and finally end up as Cost of Goods Sold on the income statement.

Multiple Predetermined Overhead Rates

Our discussion in this chapter has assumed that there is a single predetermined overhead rate for an entire factory called a **plantwide overhead rate.** This is a fairly common practice—particularly in smaller companies. But in larger companies, *multiple predetermined overhead rates* are often used. In a **multiple predetermined overhead rate** system, each production department may have its own predetermined overhead rate. Such a system, while more complex, is considered to be more accurate, since it can reflect differences across departments in how overhead costs are incurred. For example, over-

2nd edition, such a powerful learning tool?

total cost would you expect to be incurred for direct materials? For rent on the factory building? (In preparing your answer, assume that direct materials is a variable cost and that rent is a fixed cost.)
4. Explain to the president the reason for any difference in the average cost per unit between (2) and (3) above.

BUILDING YOUR SKILLS

CHECK FIGURE
(1) Cost of goods manufactured: $450,000

ANALYTICAL THINKING (LO1, LO2, LO3, LO4)

Hickey Company, a manufacturing firm, produces a single product. The following information has been taken from the company's production, sales, and cost records for the just completed year:

Production in units	30,000
Sales in units	?
Ending finished goods inventory in units	?
Sales in dollars	$650,000
Costs:	
Advertising	$50,000
Direct labor	$80,000
Indirect labor	$60,000
Raw materials purchased	$160,000
Building rent (production uses 80% of the space; administrative and sales offices use the rest)	$50,000
Utilities, factory	$35,000
Royalty paid for use of production patent, $1 per unit produced	
Maintenance, factory	
Rent for special production equipment, $6,000 per year plus $0.10 per unit produced	
Selling and administrative salaries	
Other factory overhead costs	
Other selling and administrative expenses	

End-of-Chapter Material

Our problem and case material continues to conform to AECC and AACSB recommendations and makes a great starting point for class discussions and group projects. Other helpful features include:

Spreadsheets have become an increasingly common tool for managerial accountants; therefore, selected exhibits and data appear as Microsoft Excel® screen captures.

Problems   71

PROBLEM 1–22 Financial Statements; Cost Behavior (LO3, LO4, LO5)

Various cost and sales data for Jaskot Company for the just completed year follow:

CHECK FIGURE
(1) Cost of goods manufactured: $233,000

Microsoft Excel - Problem 1-22 screen capture.xls

	A	B
1	Finished goods inventory, beginning	$16,000
2	Finished goods inventory, ending	$14,000
3	Depreciation, factory	$21,000
4	Administrative expenses	$45,000
5	Utilities, factory	$12,000
6	Maintenance, factory	$26,000
7	Supplies, factory	$6,000
8	Insurance, factory	$7,000
9	Purchases of raw materials	$72,000
10	Raw materials inventory, beginning	$5,000
11	Raw materials inventory, ending	$8,000
12	Direct labor	$61,000
13	Indirect labor	$32,000
14	Work in process inventory, beginning	$13,000
15	Work in process inventory, ending	$14,000
16	Sales	$355,000
17	Selling expenses	$61,000
18		

CASE (LO3, LO4)

While snoozing at the controls of his Pepper Six airplane, Dunse P. Sluggard leaned heavily against the door; suddenly, the door flew open and a startled Dunse tumbled out. As he parachuted to the ground, Dunse watched helplessly as the empty plane smashed into Operex Products' plant and administrative offices.

"The insurance company will never believe this," cried Mercedes Juliet, the company's controller, as she watched the ensuing fire burn the building to the ground. "The entire company is wiped out!"

"There's no reason to even contact the insurance agent," replied Ford Romero, the company's operations manager. "We can't file a claim without records, and all we have left is this copy of last year's annual report. It shows that raw materials at the beginning of this year (January 1) totaled $30,000, work in process totaled $50,000, and finished goods totaled $90,000. But what we need is a record of these inventories as of today, and our records are up in smoke."

"All except this summary page I was working on when the plane hit the building," said Mercedes. "It shows that our sales to date this year have totaled $1,350,000 and that manufacturing overhead cost has totaled $520,000."

"Hey! This annual report is more helpful than I thought," exclaimed Ford. "I can see that our gross margin rate has been 40% of sales for years. I can also see that direct labor cost is one-quarter of the manufacturing overhead cost."

"We may have a chance after all," cried Mercedes. "My summary sheet lists the sum of direct labor and direct materials at $510,000 for the year, and it says that our goods available for sale to customers this year has totaled $960,000 at cost. Now if we just knew the amount of raw materials purchased so far this year."

"I know that figure," yelled Ford. "It's $420,000! The purchasing agent gave it to me in our planning meeting yesterday."

"Fantastic," shouted Mercedes. "We'll have our claim ready before the day is over!"

To file a claim with the insurance company, Operex Products must determine the amount of cost in its inventories as of the date of the accident. You may assume that all of the materials used in production during the year were direct materials.

Required:
Determine the amount of cost in the raw materials, work in process, and finished goods inventories as of the date of the accident. (Hint: One way to proceed would be to reconstruct the various schedules and statements that would have been affected by the company's inventory accounts during the year.)

ETHICS CHALLENGE (LO2)

The top management of General Electronics, Inc., is well known for "managing by the numbers." With an eye on the company's desired growth in overall net profit, the company's CEO (chief executive officer) sets target profits at the beginning of the year for each of the company's divisions. The CEO has stated her policy as follows: "I won't interfere with operations in the divisions. I am available for advice, but the division vice presidents are free to do anything they want so long as they hit the target profits for the year."

In November, Stan Richart, the vice president in charge of the Cellular Telephone Technologies Division, saw that making the current year's target profit for his division was going to be very difficult. Among other actions, he directed that discretionary expenditures be delayed until the beginning of the new year. On December 30, he was angered to discover that a warehouse clerk had ordered $350,000 of cellular telephone parts earlier in December even though the parts weren't really needed by the assembly department until January or February. Contrary to common accounting practice, the General Electronics, Inc., Accounting Policy Manual states that such parts are to be recorded as an expense when delivered. To avoid recording the expense, Mr. Richart asked that the order be canceled, but the purchasing department reported that the parts had already been delivered and the supplier would not accept returns. Since the bill had

of cost of goods manufactured.
statement.
...uced the equivalent of 12,000 units of product during the year just completed.
...age cost per unit for direct materials? What was the average cost per unit for
...?
...cts to produce 10,000 units of product during the coming year. What per unit cost
... would you expect the company to incur for direct materials at this level of
y depreciation? (In preparing your answer, assume that direct materials is a
...at depreciation is a fixed cost that will be the same next year as it was this year.)
...dent any difference in the average cost per unit between (3) and (4) above.

...ncial Statements; Cost Behavior (LO3, LO4, LO5)
...es for the year ended December 31 are provided below for Rolling Company:

CHECK FIGURE
(1) Cost of goods manufactured: $244,000

Selling and administrative salaries	$55,000
Insurance, factory	$6,000
Utilities, factory	$10,000
Purchases of raw materials	$76,000
Indirect labor	$3,000
Direct labor	?
Advertising expense	$26,000
Cleaning supplies, factory	$4,000
Sales commissions	$33,000
Rent, factory building	$49,000
Maintenance, factory	$15,000

Ethics assignments

serve as a reminder that good conduct is essential in business. Group projects can be assigned either as homework or as in-class discussion projects.

What's new about

the second edition?

CHAPTER 6

New in this Edition

- The CVP graph is introduced before break-even analysis to provide a better intuitive basis for the analysis.

- Many new In Business boxes have been added.

CHAPTER 7

New in this Edition

- The mechanics of how to construct the various schedules in the master budget are more thoroughly explained in the text.

- Many new In Business boxes have been added.

CHAPTER 8

New in this Edition

- A new exhibit, Exhibit 8–1, provides an overview of the variance reporting process.

- Several new In Business boxes have been added.

- The variances, and their computations, are more fully explained.

CHAPTER 9

New in this Edition

- Improved illustration of static vs. flexible budgets has been added.

- New In Business boxes have been added.

CHAPTER 10

New in this Edition

- New In Business boxes have been added.

CHAPTER 11

New in this Edition

- A new, easy-to-understand example has been added illustrating the identification of relevant and irrelevant costs.

- Material dealing with the reconciliation of the total and differential approaches has been added.

- The section dealing with equipment replacement decisions has been eliminated. This subject is more appropriately covered in the capital budgeting chapter.

- Many new In Business boxes have been added.

CHAPTER 12

New in this Edition

- Many new In Business boxes have been added.

- The present value tables have been expanded to include all rates of return between 5% and 25%.

CHAPTER 13

New in this Edition

- Many new In Business boxes have been added.

CHAPTER 14

New in this Edition

- Many new In Business boxes have been added.

Can technology *really* help students and professors in the learning process?

Today, nearly 200,000

college instructors use the Internet in their courses. Some are just getting started, while others are ready to embrace the very latest advances in educational content delivery and course management.

That's why we at McGraw-Hill/Irwin offer you a complete range of digital solutions. Your students can use **Introduction to Managerial Accounting's** complete Online Learning Center, NetTutor, and PowerWeb on their own, or we can help you create your own course website using McGraw-Hill's PageOut.

In addition to web-based assets, **Introduction to Managerial Accounting** boasts **Topic Tackler**, a CD-ROM that offers special chapter-by-chapter assistance for the most demanding managerial accounting topics. With McGraw-Hill's Presentation Manager CD-ROM, instructors have access to nearly every crucial supplement, from the instructor's resource manual to the test bank, in both print and electronic media.

McGraw-Hill is a leader in bringing helpful technology into the classroom. And with **Introduction to Managerial Accounting,** your class gets all the benefits of the digital age.

How can I easily integrate web resources into my course?

ONLINE LEARNING CENTER (OLC)

More and more students are studying online. That's why we offer an Online Learning Center (OLC) that follows **Introduction to Managerial Accounting** chapter by chapter. It doesn't require any building or maintenance on your part. It's ready to go the moment you and your students type in the URL.

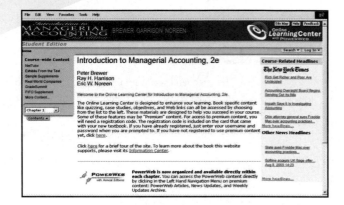

As your students study, they can refer to the OLC for such benefits as:

- Self-grading quizzes
- PowerPoint presentations
- Internet exercises
- Alternate problems
- Chapter outlines
- Practice exams
- Online tutoring (NetTutor)
- Excel spreadsheets
- Links to URLs referenced in the text

A secured Instructor Resource Center stores your essential course materials to save you prep time before class. The Instructor's Manual, Solutions, PowerPoint, and sample syllabi are now just a couple of clicks away. You will also find useful packaging information and transition notes.

The OLC also serves as a doorway to other technology solutions like PageOut, which is free to textbook adopters.

Many of my students work or have other obligations outside of class.

How can they get book-specific help at their convenience?

Net Tutor™ is a breakthrough program that allows one-on-one assistance completely online. Qualified accounting tutors equipped with **Introduction to Managerial Accounting** work online with your students on specific problems or concepts from their text.

NetTutor allows tutors and students to communicate with each other in a variety of ways:

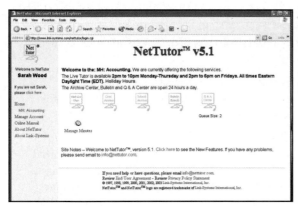

The Live Tutor Center via NetTutor's WWWhiteboard enables a tutor to hold an interactive, online tutorial session with a student or several students. The WWWhiteboard acts as a virtual chalkboard where students can view tutor-created spreadsheets, T-accounts, and written explanations during hours that work with your students' schedules.

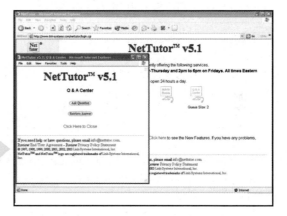

The Q&A Center allows students to submit questions at any time and retrieve answers within 24 hours.

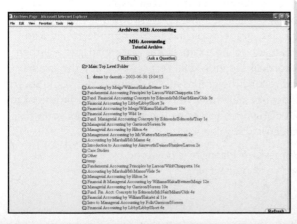

The Archive Center allows students to browse for answers to previously asked questions. They can also search for questions pertinent to a particular topic. If they encounter an answer they do not understand, they can ask a follow-up question.

Students are issued five hours of free NetTutor time when they purchase a new copy of Introduction to Managerial Accounting. Additional time may be purchased in five-hour increments. Tutors are available during the week to help students clear those afternoon and evening study hurdles.

How can my **students** *use their* study time *more effectively?*

Topic Tackler is an exciting, interactive CD created by Jeannie Folk to help students with the concepts they typically find the most difficult to learn. These concepts are highlighted in the text with the topic tackler icon, which tells students that they can refer to the CD for additional instruction. The material on the CD includes a video segment, a PowerPoint® slide show, a practice session, and a self-test for each of the 28 difficult-to-master concepts. It also contains a student tutorial.

The following are examples of the difficult-to-master topics that are included in Topic Tackler:

- Application of Overhead
- Computing Activity Rates and Product Costs
- Calculation of Equivalent Units
- Process-Costing Cost Reconciliation
- Contribution Format Income Statement
- Budgeting Process
- Flexible Budgets
- Variance Analysis (Direct Materials, Direct Labor, and Overhead)
- Adding or Dropping Product Lines or Segments
- Make or Buy Decisions
- Net Present Value Method for Capital Budgeting
- Classifying Cash Flows

McGRAW-HILL HOMEWORK MANAGER

Homework Manager is an exciting new web-based supplement available with *Introduction to Managerial Accounting.*

Homework Manager will help your students learn management accounting by allowing them to work through selected problem structures pulled from the text and powered by algorithms. Providing a wealth of these textbook-quality questions enables students to work on fresh problems with the same problem structure until they master the topics covered. Each student also receives immediate scoring and feedback from the program to guide his or her studies.

The problem structures available in Homework Manager can be easily identified in the text by the Homework Manager icon found in the margin.

Homework Manager to accompany *Introduction to Managerial Accounting* also includes problem material that will require your students to build the research, analysis, judgment, communication, and spreadsheet skills that will be required on the new Uniform CPA Exam. This provides you with an easy solution for ensuring that your students are prepared to sit the new exam.

Homework Manager may be used in practice, homework, or exam mode, as well a variety of other standard assignment modes. In the practice mode, students receive feedback and work as many iterations of each problem as they like without entering a record in the class grade book. In the homework mode, students receive a customized level of feedback, and their grades and individual responses are recorded in the class grade book. In the exam mode, faculty can create an online exam. Homework Manager will then record all the individual responses, grade the exams, and record the grades in the online grade book. So, you know not only how your class performed on the exam but also which topics or learning objectives your students struggled with.

Homework Manager is powered by Brownstone Learning.

What's the best way for my students to brush up their Accounting skills?

ALEKS®

ALEKS (Assessment and LEarning in Knowledge Spaces) is an artificial-intelligence-based system for individualized learning, available from McGraw-Hill over the World Wide Web.

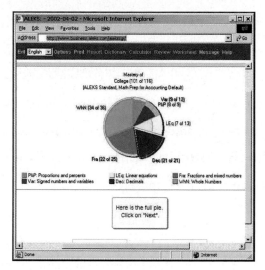

ALEKS delivers precise, qualitative diagnostic assessments of students' knowledge, guides them in the selection of appropriate new study material, and records their progress toward mastery of curricular goals in a robust classroom management system.

ALEKS interacts with the student much as a skilled human tutor would, moving between explanation and practice as needed, correcting and analyzing errors, defining terms, and changing topics on request. By sophisticated modeling of a student's knowledge state for a given subject, ALEKS can focus clearly on what the student is most ready to learn next. When students focus on exactly what they are ready to learn, they build confidence and a learning momentum that fuels success.

ALEKS Math Prep for Accounting provides coverage of the basic math skills needed to succeed in introductory accounting, including basic arithmetic, fractions, decimals, percents, and simple algebra concepts. Refreshing and improving these skills help students perform better throughout the course. Visit the ALEKS website at www.business.aleks.com for more information.

GradeSummit

GradeSummit tells your students what they need to know in order to study effectively. And it provides you, the instructor, with valuable insight into which of your students are struggling and which course topics give them the most trouble.

GradeSummit provides a series of practice tests that can be taken in various formats according to student preference: practice mode, for instance, displays the correct answer immediately, while exam mode simulates a real classroom exam and displays results at the end. There's even a smart testing engine, SummitExpress, that automatically scales the difficulty level of the questions according to the student's responses.

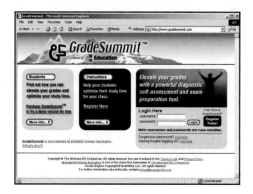

Once a student has taken a particular test, GradeSummit returns a detailed results page showing exactly where the student did well and where he or she needs to improve. Students can compare their results with those of their other classmates, or even with those of every other student using the text nationwide. With that information, students can plan their studying to focus exclusively on their weak areas, without wasting effort on material they've already mastered. And they can come back to take a retest on those subjects later, comparing their new score with their previous efforts.

As an instructor, you'll know which students are falling behind simply by consulting GradeSummit's test logs, where results for every student in your course are available for review. Because GradeSummit's results are so detailed, you'll know exactly what topics are causing difficulties—an invaluable aid when it comes to planning lectures and homework.

How can I easily

For the instructor

needing to educate students online, we offer **Introduction to Managerial Accounting** content for complete online courses. To make this possible, we have joined forces with the most popular delivery platforms currently available. These platforms are designed for instructors who want complete control over course content and how it is presented to students. You can customize the **Introduction to Managerial Accounting** Online Learning Center content and author your own course materials. It's entirely up to you.

Products like **WebCT, Blackboard,** and **eCollege** all expand the reach of your course. Online discussion and message boards complement your office hours. Thanks to a sophisticated tracking system, you will know which students need more attention—even if they don't ask for help. That's because online testing scores are recorded and automatically placed in your grade book, and if a student is struggling with coursework, a special alert message lets you know.

Remember, **Introduction to Managerial Accounting's** content is flexible enough to use with any platform currently available. If your department or school is already using a platform, we can help. For information on McGraw-Hill/Irwin's course management supplements, including Instructor Advantage and Knowledge Gateway, see "Knowledge Gateway" on the previous page.

create an online course?

Create a custom course website with **PageOut**, free to instructors using a McGraw-Hill textbook.

To learn more, contact your McGraw-Hill publisher's representative or visit www.mhhe.com/solutions.

McGraw-Hill's Course Management System

PageOut is the easiest way to create a website for your accounting course.

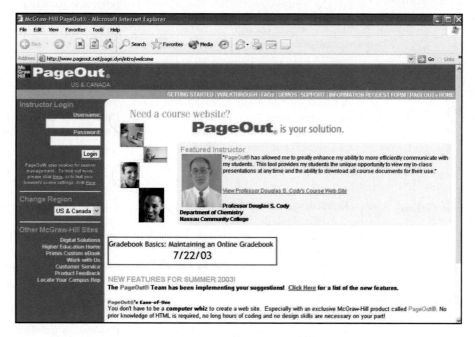

There's no need for HTML coding, graphic design, or a thick how-to book. Just fill in a series of boxes with simple English and click on one of our professional designs. In no time, your course is online with a website that contains your syllabus!

If you need assistance in preparing your website, we can help. Our team of product specialists is ready to take your course materials and build a custom website to your specifications. You simply need to call a McGraw-Hill/Irwin PageOut specialist to start the process. Best of all, PageOut is free when you adopt **Introduction to Managerial Accounting!** To learn more, please visit **http://www.pageout.net.**

Supplements

INSTRUCTOR SUPPLEMENTS

Instructor CD-ROM

ISBN 0072917466

Allowing instructors to create a customized multimedia presentation, this all-in-one resource incorporates the Test Bank, PowerPoint® Slides, Instructor's Resource Guide, Solutions Manual, Teaching Transparency Masters, links to PageOut, and the Spreadsheet Application Template Software (SPATS).

Instructor's Resource Guide and Video Manual

ISBN 0072917512

This supplement contains the teaching transparency masters and the video guide, extensive chapter-by-chapter lecture notes to help with classroom presentation, and useful suggestions for presenting key concepts and ideas.

Check Figures

These provide key answers for selected problems and cases. They are available on the text's website.

Solutions Transparencies

ISBN 0072917482

These transparencies feature completely worked-out solutions to all assignment material. The font used in the solutions is large enough for the back row of any lecture hall. Masters of these transparencies are available in the Solutions Manual.

Solutions Manual and Disk

ISBN 0072921595

This supplement contains completely worked-out solutions to all assignment material and a general discussion of the use of group exercises. In addition, the manual contains suggested course outlines and a listing of exercises, problems, and cases scaled according to difficulty. This print supplement is packaged with a CD-ROM containing the Solutions Manual in Microsoft Word® format.

Teaching Transparencies

ISBN 0072917474

Contains a comprehensive set of over 260 teaching transparencies covering every chapter that can be used for classroom lectures and discussion.

PowerPoint® Slides

Prepared by Jon Booker, Charles Caldwell, and Richard Rand, all of Tennessee Technological University, and Susan Galbreath of Lipscomb University, these slides offer a great visual complement for your lectures. A complete set of slides covers each chapter. They are only available on the Instructor CD-ROM and the text's website.

Test Bank

ISBN 0072917504

Nearly 2,000 questions are organized by chapter and include true/false, multiple-choice, and essay questions and computational problems.

Diploma Computerized Testbank

ISBN 0072917490

This test bank is now delivered in the Diploma Shell, new from Brownstone. Use it to make different versions of the same test, change the answer order, edit and add questions, and conduct online testing. Technical support for this software is available.

Excel Templates

Prepared by Jack Terry of ComSource Associates, Inc., these Excel templates offer solutions to the Student SPATS version. They are only available on the Instructor CD and the text's website.

Dallas County Community College Telecourse

These short, action-oriented videos, developed by Dallas County Community College, provide the impetus for lively classroom discussion. The focus is on the preparation, analysis, and use of accounting information for business decision making. (To acquire the complete telecourse, Accounting in Action, call Dallas TeleLearning at 972-669-6666, fax them at 972-669-6668, or visit their website at **http://telelearning.dcccd.edu.**)

STUDENT SUPPLEMENTS

Topic Tackler CD-ROM

ISBN 0072917458

Free with the text, the Topic Tackler CD-ROM helps students master difficult concepts in managerial accounting through a creative, interactive learning process. Designed for study outside the classroom, this multimedia CD delves into chapter concepts with graphical slides and diagrams, web links, video clips, and animations, all centered around engaging exercises designed to put students in control of their learning of managerial accounting topics.

Workbook/Study Guide

ISBN 0072835249

This study aid provides suggestions for studying chapter material, summarizes essential points in each chapter, and tests students' knowledge using self-test questions and exercises.

Working Papers

ISBN 0072835230

This study aid contains forms that help students organize their solutions to homework problems.

Excel Templates

Prepared by Jack Terry of ComSource Associates, Inc., this spreadsheet-based software uses Excel to solve selected problems and cases in the text. These selected problems and cases are identified in the margin of the text with an appropriate icon. The Excel Templates are only available on the text's website.

Telecourse Guide

ISBN 0072531754

This study guide ties the Dallas County Community College Telecourse directly to this text.

Ramblewood Manufacturing, Inc., CD-ROM

ISBN for instructor version 0072536357
ISBN for student version 0072536667

This computerized practice set was prepared by Leland Mansuetti and Keith Weidkamp, both of Sierra College, and has been completely updated. This software simulates the operations of a company that manufactures customized fencing.
It can be used to illustrate job-order costing systems with JIT inventory in a realistic setting. The entire simulation requires 10 to 14 hours to complete. A new feature prevents files from being transferred from one disk to another without detection. It is available on CD-ROM and runs on Microsoft Windows®.

Communication for Accountants: Effective Strategies for Students and Professionals

ISBN 0070383901

Authored by Maurice Hirsch of Southern Illinois University–Carbondale and Susan Gabriel and Rob Anderson, both of St. Louis University, this brief and inexpensive handbook addresses the need for accountants to communicate effectively through both writing and speaking.

Reviewers

Suggestions have been received from many of our colleagues throughout the world who have used the prior edition of Introduction to Managerial Accounting. This is vital feedback that we rely on in each edition. Each of those who have offered comments and suggestions has our thanks.

The efforts of many people are needed to develop and improve a text. Among these people are the reviewers and consultants who point out areas of concern, cite areas of strength, and make recommendations for change. In this regard, the following professors provided feedback that was enormously helpful in preparing the second edition of Introduction to Managerial Accounting:

Omneya Abd-Elsalam, *Aston University*
L. M. Abney, *LaSalle University*
Sol Ahiarah, *SUNY College at Buffalo*
William Ambrose, *DeVry University*
Robert Appleton, *University of North Carolina – Wilmington*
Leonard Bacon, *California State University – Bakersfield*
Roderick Barclay, *Texas A&M University*
Larry Bitner, *Hood College*
Jay Blazer, *Milwaukee Area Technical College*
Nancy Bledsoe, *Millsaps College*
William Blouch, *Loyola College*
Eugene Blue, *Governor State University*
Linda Bolduc, *Mount Wachusett Community College*
Casey Bradley, *Troy State University*
Marley Brown, *Mt. Hood Community College*
Betty Jo Browning, *Bradley University*
Myra Bruegger, *Southeastern Community College*
Francis Bush, *Virginia Military Institute*
Rebecca Butler, *Gateway Community college*
June Calahan, *Redlands Community College*
John Callister, *Cornell University*
Annhenrie Campbell, *California State University, Stanislaus*
Elizabeth Cannata, *Stonehill College*
Dennis Caplan, *Iowa State University*
Kay Carnes, *Gonzaga University*
Siew Chan, *University of Massachusetts, Boston*
John Chandler, *University of Illinois – Champaign*
Lawrence Chin, *Golden Gate University*
Carolyn Clark, *St. Joseph's University*
Joanne Collins, *California State University – Los Angeles*
Judith Cook, *Grossmont College*
Charles Croxford, *Merced College*
Richard Cummings, *Benedictine College*
Jill Cunningham, *Santa Fe Community College*
Alan Czyzewski, *Indiana State University*
Betty David, *Francis Marion University*
Deborah Davis, *Hampton University*
G. DiLorenzo, *Gloucester County College*
Keith Dusenbery, *Johnson State College*
James Emig, *Villanova University*
Michael Farina, *Cerritos College*

John Farlin, *Ohio Dominican University*

Harriet Farney, *University of Hartford*

M. A. Fekrat, *Georgetown University*

W. L. Ferrara, *Stetson University*

Jerry Ferry, *University of North Alabama*

Joan Foster, *Collge Misericordia*

James Franklin, *Troy State University Montgomery*

Joseph Galante, *Millersville University of Pennsylvania*

David Gibson, *Hampden-Sydney College*

John Gill, *Jackson State University*

Jackson Gillespie, *University of Delaware*

Joe Goetz, *Louisiana State University*

Art Goldman, *University of Kentucky*

James Gravel, *Husson College*

Linda Hadley, *University of Dayton*

Anita Hape, *Farrant County Jr. College*

Dan Hary, *Southwestern Oklahoma State University*

Susan Hass, *Simmons College*

Robert Hayes, *Tennessee State University*

James Hendricks, *Northern Illinois University*

Nancy Thorley Hill, *DePaul University*

Kathy Ho, *Niagra University*

Mary Hollars, *Vincennes University*

Norma Holter, *Towson University*

Ronald Huntsman, *Texas Lutheran University*

Wayne Ingalls, *University of Maine College*

David Jacobson, *Salem State College*

Martha Janis, *University of Wisconsin – Waukesha*

Holly Johnston, *Boston University*

Sanford Kahn, *University of Cincinnati*

Marsha Kertz, *San Jose State University*

Michael Klimesh, *Gustav Adolphus University*

Greg Kordecki, *Clayton College and State University*

Michael Kulper, *Santa Barbara City College*

Christoper Kwak, *Ohlone College*

Steven LaFave, *Augsburg College*

Thomas Largay, *Thomas College*

Robert Larson, *Penn State University*

Chor Lau, *California State University – Los Angeles*

Angela Letourneau, *Winthrop University*

Barry Lewis, *Southwest Missouri State University*

Joan Litton, *Ferrum College*

G. D. Lorenzo, *Gloucester Community College*

Bob Mahan, *Milligan College*

Leland Mansuetti, *Sierra College*

Lisa Martin, *Western Michigan University*

Jayne Mass, *Towson University*

Laura Morgan, *University of New Hampshire*

Anthony Moses, *Saint Anselm College*

Daniel Mugavero, *Lake Superior State University*

Muroki Mwaura, *William Patterson University*

Presha Neidermeyer, *Union College*

Eizabeth Nolan, *Southwestern Oklahoma State University*

Michael O'Neill, *Seattle Central Community College*

George Otto, *Truman College*

Chei Paik, *George Washington University*

Eustace Phillip, *Emmanuel College*

Anthony Piltz, *Rocky Mountain College*

H. M. Pomroy, *Elizabethtown College*

Alan Porter, *Eastern New Mexico University*

Barbara Prince, *Cambridge Community College*

Ahmad Rahman, *La Roche College*

Joan Reicosky, *University of Minnesota – Morris*

Leonardo Rodriguez, *Florida International University*

Gary Ross, *College of the Southwest*

Martha Sampsell, *Elmhurst College*

John Savash, *Elmira College*

Roger Scherser, *Edison Community College*

Henry Schwarzbach, *University of Colorado*

Eldon Schafer, *University of Arizona*

Deborah Shafer, *Temple College*

Ola Smith, *Michigan State University*

John Snyder, *Florida Technical*

Soliman Soliman, *Tulane University*

Alice Steljes, *Illinois Valley Community College*

Joseph Ugras, *LaSalle University*

Edward Walker, *University of Texas – Pan American*

Frank Walker, *Lee College*

Robert Weprin, *Lourdes College*

Brent Wickham, *Owens Community College*

Geri Wink, *University of Texas at Tyler*

James Wolfson, *Wilson College*

We are grateful

for the outstanding support from McGraw-Hill/Irwin. In particular, we would like to thank Brent Gordon, Editorial Director; Stewart Mattson, Publisher; Tim Vertovec, Executive Editor; Tracey Douglas and Sarah Wood, Developmental Editors; Katherine Mattison, Marketing Manager; Pat Frederickson, Lead Project Manager; Heather Burbridge, Manager, New Book Production; Pam Verros, Lead Designer; Carol Loreth, Senior Supplement Producer; and Judy Kausal, Photo Research Coordinator.

Finally, we would like to thank Beth Woods and Barbara Schnathorst, for working so hard to ensure an error-free second edition.

We are grateful to the Institute of Certified Management Accountants for permission to use questions and/or unofficial answers from past Certificate in Management Accounting (CMA) examinations. Likewise, we thank the American Institute of Certified Public Accountants, the Society of Management Accountants of Canada, and the Chartered Institute of Management Accountants (United Kingdom) for permission to use (or to adapt) selected problems from their examinations. These problems bear the notations CMA, CPA, SMA, and CIMA, respectively.

Peter C. BREWER

Ray H. GARRISON

Eric W. NOREEN

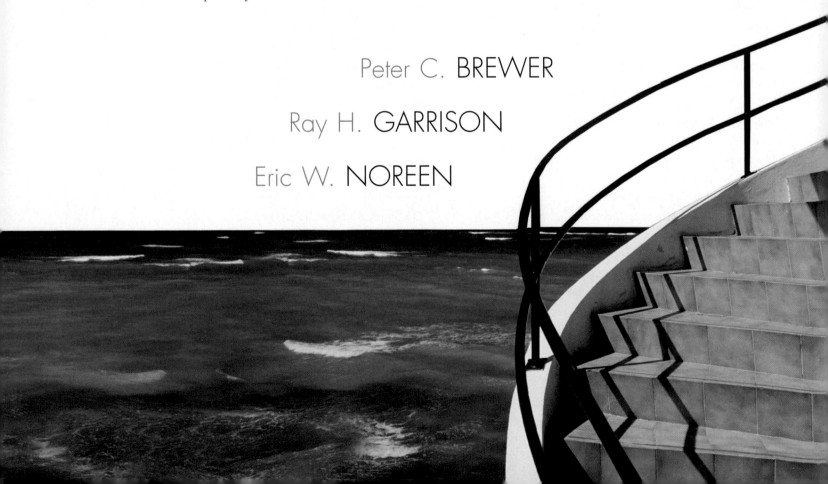

BRIEF TABLE OF CONTENTS

TABLE OF CONTENTS

CHAPTER FIVE
Cost Behavior: Analysis and Use   200

CHAPTER SIX
Cost-Volume-Profit Relationships   240

CHAPTER SEVEN
Profit Planning   286

CHAPTER EIGHT
Standard Costs 336

APPENDIX 8A
General Ledger Entries to Record Variances 364

CHAPTER NINE
Flexible Budgets and Overhead Analysis 380

Managerial Accounting and the Business Environment

A LOOK AT THE PROLOGUE

Today's managers know that their world is constantly changing and becoming even more complex. Before we get down to the basics, this Prologue will expose you to a few of the revolutionary changes that today's managers are facing.

A LOOK AHEAD

Chapter 1 describes the work performed by managers, stresses the need for managerial accounting information, contrasts managerial and financial accounting, and defines many of the cost terms that will be used throughout the textbook. You will begin to build your base there.

The last two decades have been a period of tremendous turmoil and change in the business environment including the explosive growth of the Internet. Competition in many industries has become worldwide in scope, and the pace of innovation in products and services has accelerated. This has been good news for consumers, since intensified competition has generally led to lower prices, higher quality, and more choices. However, the last two decades have been a period of wrenching change for many businesses and their employees. Many managers have learned that cherished ways of doing business do not work anymore and that major changes must be made in the way organizations are managed and work gets done. These changes are so great that some observers view them as a second industrial revolution. And to add even more dynamism, the Internet has been changing the fundamental ways of doing business in more and more industries since the mid 1990s.

These changes are having a profound effect on the practice of management accounting—as we will see throughout the rest of the text. First, however, it is necessary to have an appreciation of the ways in which organizations are transforming themselves to become more competitive. Since the early 1980s, many companies have gone through several waves of improvement programs, starting with just-in-time (JIT) and passing on to total quality management (TQM), process reengineering, and various other management programs—including in some companies the theory of constraints (TOC). When properly implemented, these improvement programs can enhance quality, reduce cost, increase output, eliminate delays in responding to customers, and ultimately increase profits. They have not, however, always been wisely implemented, and considerable controversy exists concerning the ultimate value of each of these programs. Nevertheless, the current business environment cannot be properly understood without some appreciation of what each of these approaches attempts to accomplish. Each is worthy of extended study, but we will discuss them only in the broadest terms. The details are best handled in operations management courses.

JUST-IN-TIME (JIT)

Traditionally, managers in manufacturing companies have sought to minimize the unit costs of products on the theory that in the long run only the lowest cost producer will survive and prosper. This strategy led managers to maximize production to spread the fixed costs of investments in equipment and other assets over as many units as possible. In addition, managers have traditionally felt that an important part of their job was to keep everyone busy—idleness wastes money. These traditional views, often aided and abetted by traditional management accounting practices, resulted in a number of practices that have come under severe criticism in recent years. Critics point to excessive inventories as the most visible symptom of outdated management practices. Why do excessive inventories result from the desire to maximize production and to keep everyone busy and why are they a problem?

In a traditional manufacturing company, work is *pushed* through the system. Enough materials are released to workstations to keep everyone busy, and when a workstation completes its tasks, the partially completed goods are "pushed" forward to the next workstation regardless of whether that workstation is ready to receive them. The result is that partially completed goods stack up, waiting for the next workstation to become available. They may not be completed for days, weeks, or even months. Additionally, when the units are finally completed, customers may or may not want them. If finished goods are produced faster than the market will absorb, the result is bloated finished goods inventories.

In addition, companies typically maintained large amounts of inventories as a form of insurance so that operations could proceed smoothly even if unanticipated disruptions occurred. Suppliers might be late with deliveries, so companies maintained inventories of key supplies. A workstation might be unable to operate due to a breakdown or other reason, so companies maintained inventories of partially completed goods. And customers might suddenly place big unexpected orders, so companies maintained large inventories of finished goods.

While these inventories provide some insurance against unforeseen events, they have a cost. According to experts, in addition to tying up money, maintaining inventories encourages inefficient and sloppy work, results in too many defects, and dramatically increases the amount of time required to complete a product. For example, when partially completed products are stored for long periods of time before being processed by the next workstation, defects introduced by the preceding workstation go unnoticed. If a machine is out of calibration or incorrect procedures are being followed, many defective units will be produced before the problem is discovered. And when the defects are finally discovered, it may be very difficult to track down the source of the problem. In addition, units may be obsolete or out of fashion by the time they are finally completed.

Large inventories of partially completed goods create many other operating problems that are best discussed in more advanced courses. These problems are not obvious—if they were, companies would have long ago reduced their inventories. Managers at Toyota are credited with the insight that large inventories often create many more problems than they solve, and Toyota pioneered the *JIT approach.*

The JIT Approach

In contrast to the traditional approach, companies that use the **just-in-time (JIT)** approach purchase materials and produce units only as needed to meet actual customer demand. The theory is that producing things doesn't do the company any good unless someone buys them and that excess inventories create a multitude of operating problems. In a JIT system, inventories are reduced to an absolute minimum. Under ideal conditions, a company operating a just-in-time system would purchase only enough materials each day to meet that day's needs. Moreover, the company would have no goods still in process at the end of the day, and all goods completed during the day would have been shipped immediately to customers. As this sequence suggests, "just-in-time" means that raw materials are received just in time to go into production, manufactured parts are completed just in time to be assembled into products, and products are completed just in time to be shipped to customers.

Although few companies have been able to reach this ideal, many companies have been able to reduce inventories to a fraction of their previous levels. The results have been a substantial reduction in ordering and warehousing costs and much more effective operations.

The change from a traditional to a JIT approach is more profound than it may appear to be. Among other things, producing only in response to a customer order means that workers will be idle whenever demand falls below the company's production capacity. This can be an extremely difficult cultural change for an organization to make. It challenges the core beliefs of many managers and raises anxieties in workers who have become accustomed to being kept busy all of the time. It also requires fundamental changes in managerial accounting practices, as we will see in later chapters.

Zero Defects and JIT

Defective units create big problems in a JIT environment. If a completed order contains a defective unit, the company must ship the order with less than the promised quantity or it must restart the whole production process to make just one unit. At minimum, this creates a delay in shipping the order and may generate a ripple effect that delays other orders. For this and other reasons, defects cannot be tolerated in a JIT system. Companies that are deeply involved in JIT tend to become zealously committed to a goal of *zero defects.* Even though it may be next to impossible to attain the zero defect goal, companies have found that they can come very close. For example, Motorola, Allied Signal, and many other companies now measure defects in terms of the number of defects per *million* units of product.

In a traditional company, parts and materials are inspected for defects when they are received from suppliers, and quality inspectors inspect units as they progress along the production line. In a JIT system, the company's suppliers are responsible for the quality of incoming parts and materials. And instead of using quality inspectors, the company's production workers are directly responsible for spotting defective units. A worker who discovers a defect punches an alarm button that stops the production flow line and sets off flashing lights. Supervisors and other workers go immediately to the workstation to determine the cause of the defect and correct it before any further defective units are produced. This procedure ensures that problems are quickly identified and corrected, but it does require that defects are rare—otherwise the production process would be constantly interrupted.

Adopters of the JIT Approach

Many companies—large and small—have employed JIT with great success. Among the major companies using JIT are Bose, Goodyear, Westinghouse, General Motors, Hughes Aircraft, Ford Motor Company, Black and Decker, Chrysler, Borg-Warner, John Deere, Xerox, Tektronix, and Intel.

Benefits of a JIT System

The main benefits of JIT are:

1. Funds that have been tied up in inventories can be used elsewhere.
2. Areas previously used to store inventories are made available for other, more productive uses.
3. The time required to fill an order is reduced, resulting in quicker response to customers and consequentially greater potential sales.
4. Defect rates are reduced, resulting in less waste and greater customer satisfaction.

As a result of benefits such as those cited above, more companies are embracing JIT each year. Most companies find, however, that simply reducing inventories is not enough. To remain competitive in an ever-changing and ever-more-competitive business environment, companies must strive for *continuous improvement*.

PCs Just in Time

Dell Computer Corporation has finely tuned its just-in-time (JIT) system so that an order for a customized personal computer that comes in over the Internet at 9 A.M. can be on a delivery truck to the customer by 9 P.M. the following day. In addition, Dell's low-cost production system allows it to underprice its rivals by 10% to 15%. This combination has made Dell the envy of the personal computer industry and has enabled the company to grow at five times the industry rate.

How does the company's JIT system deliver lower costs? "While machines from Compaq and IBM can languish on dealer shelves for two months, Dell doesn't start ordering components and assembling computers until an order is booked. That may sound like no biggie, but the price of PC parts can fall rapidly in just a few months. By ordering right before assembly, Dell figures its parts, on average, are 60 days newer than those in an IBM or Compaq machine sold at the same time. That can translate into a 6% profit advantage in components alone."

Source: Gary McWilliams, "Whirlwind on the Web," *Business Week*, April 7, 1997, p. 134.

TOTAL QUALITY MANAGEMENT (TQM)

The most popular approach to continuous improvement is known as *total quality management.* There are two major characteristics of **total quality management (TQM):** (1) a focus on serving customers and (2) systematic problem solving using teams made up of front-line workers. A variety of specific tools is available to aid teams in their problem solving. One of these tools, **benchmarking,** involves studying organizations that are among the best in the world at performing a particular task. For example, when Xerox wanted to improve its procedures for filling customer orders, it studied how the mail-order company L. L. Bean processes its customer orders.

The Plan-Do-Check-Act Cycle

Perhaps the most important and pervasive TQM problem-solving tool is the *plan-do-check-act (PDCA) cycle,* which is also referred to as the Deming Wheel.[1] The **plan-do-check-act cycle** is a systematic, fact-based approach to continuous improvement. The basic elements of the PDCA cycle are illustrated in Exhibit P–1. The PDCA cycle applies the scientific method to problem solving. In the Plan phase, the problem-solving team analyzes data to identify possible causes for the problem and then proposes a solution. In the Do phase, an experiment is conducted. In the Check phase, the results of the experiment are analyzed. And in the Act phase, if the results of the experiment are favorable, the plan is implemented. If the results of the experiment are not favorable, the team goes back to the original data and starts all over again.

An Example of TQM in Practice

Sterling Chemicals, Inc., a producer of basic industrial chemicals, provides a good example of the use of TQM.[2] Among many other problems, the company had been plagued by pump failures. In one year, a particular type of pump had failed 22 times at an average cost of about $10,000 per failure. The company first tried to solve the problem using a traditional, non-TQM approach. A committee of "experts"—in this case engineers and manufacturing supervisors—was appointed to solve the problem. A manager at Sterling Chemicals describes the results:

> This team immediately concluded that each of the 22 pump failures . . . was due to a special or one-of-a-kind cause. There was some finger pointing by team members trying to assign blame. Maintenance engineers claimed that production personnel didn't know how to operate the pumps, and production supervisors blamed maintenance people for poor repair work.

One year later, a TQM team was formed to tackle the same pump failure problem. The team consisted primarily of hourly workers with hands-on experience working with the pumps. The team brainstormed and came up with a list of 57 theories that could potentially explain the high pump-failure rate. Each of these theories was tested against the data and all but two were rejected. The team made recommendations to address both of these theories, and once the recommendations were implemented, there were no more pump failures.

Notice how the plan-do-check-act cycle was used to solve this pump-failure problem. Instead of bickering over who was responsible for the problem, the team began by collecting data. They then hypothesized a number of possible causes for the problem, and

---

[1]Dr. W. Edwards Deming, a pioneer in TQM, introduced many of the elements of TQM to Japanese industry after World War II. TQM was further refined and developed at Japanese companies such as Toyota.
[2]Karen Hopper Wruck and Michael C. Jensen, "Science, Specific Knowledge, and Total Quality Management," *Journal of Accounting and Economics* 18, pp. 247–287.

EXHIBIT P–I

The Plan-Do-Check-Act Cycle

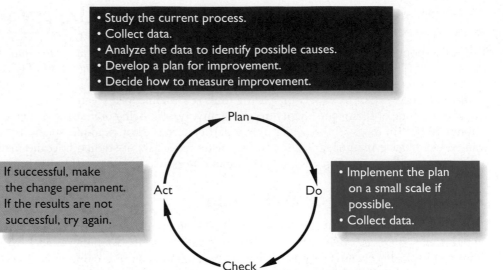

• Study the current process.
• Collect data.
• Analyze the data to identify possible causes.
• Develop a plan for improvement.
• Decide how to measure improvement.

• If successful, make the change permanent.
• If the results are not successful, try again.

• Implement the plan on a small scale if possible.
• Collect data.

• Evaluate the data collected during the Do phase.
• Did the expected improvement occur?

Plan — Do — Check — Act

these hypotheses were checked against the data. Perhaps the most important feature of TQM is that "it improves productivity by encouraging the use of science in decision-making and discouraging counterproductive defensive behavior."

IN BUSINESS

TQM Is Widely Used

Thousands of organizations have been involved in TQM and similar programs. Some of the more well-known companies are American Express, AT&T, Cadillac Motor Car, Corning, Dun & Bradstreet, Ericsson of Sweden, FedEx, GTE Directories, Bank One, Florida Power and Light, General Electric, Hospital Corporation of America, IBM, Johnson & Johnson, KLM Royal Dutch Airlines, LTV, 3M, Milliken & Company, Motorola, Northern Telecom of Canada, Phillips of the Netherlands, Ritz Carlton Hotel, Texas Instruments, Westinghouse Electric, and Xerox. As this list illustrates, TQM is international in scope and is not confined to manufacturing.

In sum, TQM provides tools and techniques for continuous improvement based on facts and analysis and, if properly implemented, it avoids counterproductive organizational infighting.

PROCESS REENGINEERING

Process reengineering is a more radical approach to improvement than TQM. Instead of tweaking the existing system by making a series of small incremental improvements, **process reengineering** diagrams a *business process* in detail, questions it, and then completely redesigns it to eliminate unnecessary steps, reduce opportunities for errors, and reduce costs. A **business process** is any series of steps that are followed to carry out some task in a business. For example, the steps followed to make a large pineapple and Canadian bacon pizza at Godfather's Pizza are a business process. The steps followed by your bank when you deposit a check are a business process. While process reengineering is similar in some respects to TQM, its proponents view it as a more sweeping approach to

Process Reengineering Illustration: The Rental Car Return Process

  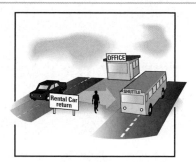

change. One difference is that while TQM emphasizes a team approach involving people who work directly in the processes, process reengineering is more likely to be imposed from above and to use outside consultants.

Process reengineering focuses on *simplification* and *elimination of wasted effort*. A central idea of process reengineering is that *all activities that do not add value to a product or service should be eliminated.* Activities that do not add value to a product or service that customers are not willing to pay for are known as **non-value-added activities.** For example, moving large batches of partially completed goods from one workstation to another is a non-value-added activity that can be eliminated by redesigning the factory layout to bring the workstations closer together.[3]

Design by Computer

One of the most time-consuming and expensive business processes is the design stage in product development, which has traditionally relied on paper and drafting tools. Dassault Systèmes has met the challenge of reengineering this process and has created Catia, the top-selling CAD/CAM software application to do it. CAD/CAM allows engineers to design and develop products on a computer. This eliminates huge amounts of paperwork and slashes the time required to design and develop a new product. Catia is used by nearly every aircraft manufacturer and was used by Boeing to design the 777. DaimlerChrysler used Catia to design the new Jeep Grand Cherokee. By debugging the production line on-screen, the company saved months and eliminated $800 million of costs.

Source: Howard Banks, "Virtually Perfect," *Forbes,* October 4, 1999, pp. 128–129.

The Problem of Employee Morale

Employee resistance is a recurrent problem in process reengineering. The cause of much of this resistance is the fear that employees may lose their jobs. Employees reason that if process reengineering succeeds in eliminating non-value-added activities, there will be less work to do and management may be tempted to reduce the payroll. Process reengineering, if carried out insensitively and without regard to such fears, can undermine morale and will ultimately fail to improve the bottom line (i.e., profits). As with other improvement projects, employees must be convinced that the end result of the improvement will be more secure, rather than less secure, jobs. Real improvement can have this effect if management uses the improvement to generate more business rather than to cut the

---

[3]Activity-based costing and activity-based management, both of which are discussed in a later chapter, can be helpful in identifying areas in the company that could benefit from process reengineering.

workforce. If by improving processes the company is able to produce a better product at lower cost, the company will have the competitive strength to prosper. And a prosperous company is a much more secure employer than a company that is in trouble.

THE THEORY OF CONSTRAINTS (TOC)

A **constraint** is anything that prevents you from getting more of what you want. Every individual and every organization faces at least one constraint. You may not have enough time to study thoroughly for every subject and to go out with your friends on the weekend, so time is your constraint. United Airlines has only a limited number of loading gates available at its busy O'Hare hub, so its constraint is loading gates. Vail Resorts has only a limited amount of land to develop as home sites and commercial lots at its ski areas, so its constraint is land.

The **theory of constraints (TOC)** focuses on effectively managing the constraint as a key to success. As an example, long waiting periods for surgery are a chronic problem in the National Health Service (NHS), the government-funded provider of health care in the United Kingdom. The diagram in Exhibit P–2 illustrates a simplified version of the steps followed by a patient who is identified for surgery and eventually treated. The number of patients that can be processed through each step in a day is indicated in the exhibit. For example, up to 100 referrals from general practitioners can be processed in a day.

The constraint, or *bottleneck,* in the system is determined by the step that has the smallest capacity—in this case surgery. The total number of patients processed through the entire system cannot exceed 15 per day—the maximum number of patients that can be treated in surgery. No matter how hard managers, doctors, and nurses try to improve the processing rate elsewhere in the system, they will never succeed in driving down the wait lists until the capacity of surgery is increased. In fact, improvements elsewhere in the system—particularly before the constraint—are likely to result in even longer waiting times and more frustrated patients and health care providers. Thus, to be effective, improvement efforts must be focused on the constraint. A business process, such as the process for serving surgery patients, is like a chain. If you want to increase the strength of a chain, what is the most effective way to do this? Should you concentrate your efforts on strengthening the strongest link, all the links, or the weakest link? Clearly, focusing your effort on the weakest link will bring the biggest benefit.

Continuing with this analogy, the procedure to follow to strengthen the chain is clear. First, identify the weakest link, which is the constraint. Second, do not place a greater strain on the system than the weakest link can handle—if you do, the chain will break. In the case of the NHS, waiting lists become unacceptably long. Third, concentrate improvement efforts on strengthening the weakest link. Find ways to increase the number of surgeries that can be performed in a day. Fourth, if the improvement efforts are successful, eventually the weakest link will improve to the point where it is no longer the weakest link. At that point, the new weakest link (i.e., the new constraint) must be identified, and improvement efforts must be shifted over to that link. This simple sequential process provides a powerful strategy for continuous improvement. The TOC approach is a perfect complement to other improvement tools such as TQM and process reengineering—it focuses improvement efforts where they are likely to be most effective.

EXHIBIT P–2   Processing Surgery Patients at an NHS Facility (simplified)*

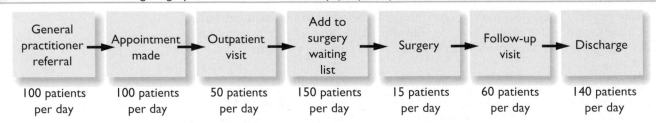

General practitioner referral	Appointment made	Outpatient visit	Add to surgery waiting list	Surgery	Follow-up visit	Discharge
100 patients per day	100 patients per day	50 patients per day	150 patients per day	15 patients per day	60 patients per day	140 patients per day

*This diagram originally appeared in the February 1999 issue of the U.K. magazine *Health Management.*

The Constraint Is the Key

The Lessines plant of Baxter International makes medical products such as sterile bags. Management of the plant is acutely aware of the necessity to actively manage its constraints. For example, when materials are the constraint, management may go to a secondary vendor and purchase materials at a higher cost than normal. When a machine is the constraint, a weekend shift is often added on the machine. If a particular machine is chronically the constraint and management has exhausted the possibilities of using it more effectively, then additional capacity is purchased. For example, when the constraint was the plastic extruding machines, a new extruding machine was ordered. However, even before the machine arrived, management had determined that the constraint would shift to the blenders once the new extruding capacity was added. Therefore, a new blender was already being planned. By thinking ahead and focusing on the constraints, management is able to increase the plant's real capacity at the lowest possible cost.

Source: Eric Noreen, Debra Smith, and James Mackey, *The Theory of Constraints and Its Implications for Management Accounting* (Montvale, NJ: The IMA Foundation for Applied Research, Inc., 1995), p. 67.

CONCEPT CHECK

1. Which of the following statements is false? (You may select more than one answer.)
   a. The plan-do-check-act cycle is an important total quality management problem-solving tool.
   b. Total quality management focuses on completely redesigning the processes that have been targeted for improvement.
   c. Just-in-time manufacturing relies on customer demand to trigger the production process.
   d. Just-in-time manufacturing is designed to reduce inventories.
2. The goals of the theory of constraints include which of the following? (You may select more than one answer.)
   a. Identifying the constraint and focusing improvement efforts on it.
   b. Increasing capacity of nonconstraining departments.
   c. Maximizing the quantity of production within all departments.
   d. Accumulating inventory in all departments.

INTERNATIONAL COMPETITION

Over the last several decades, reductions in tariffs, quotas, and other barriers to free trade; improvements in global transportation systems; and increasing sophistication in international markets have led to worldwide competition in many industries. These factors work together to reduce the costs of conducting international trade and make it possible for foreign companies to compete on a more equal footing with local firms. These changes have been most dramatic within the European Union (EU) and the North American Free Trade Association (NAFTA) free trade zones.

Managers cannot afford to be complacent. A company that is currently very successful in its local market may suddenly find itself facing competition from halfway around the globe. It is likely that this threat will become even more potent as business migrates to the Internet. As a matter of survival, even firms that are presently doing very well in their home markets must become world-class competitors. On the bright side, the freer international movement of goods and services presents tremendous export opportunities for those companies that can transform themselves into world-class competitors. And from the standpoint of consumers, heightened competition promises an even greater variety of goods, at higher quality and lower prices.

What are the implications for managerial accounting of increased global competition? It would be very difficult for a company to become world-class if it plans, directs, and controls its operations and makes decisions using a second-class management accounting system. An excellent management accounting system will not by itself guarantee success, but a poor management accounting system can stymie the best efforts of people to make the organization truly competitive.

Throughout this text we will highlight the differences between obsolete management accounting systems that get in the way of success and well-designed management accounting systems that can enhance a firm's performance. It is noteworthy that elements of well-designed management accounting systems have originated in many countries. More and more, managerial accounting has become a discipline that is worldwide in scope.

IN BUSINESS

Global Forces

Traditionally, management accounting practices have differed significantly from one country to another. For example, Spain, Italy, and Greece have relied on less formal management accounting systems than other European countries. According to Professor Norman B. Macintosh, "In Greece and Italy the predominance of close-knit, private, family firms motivated by secrecy, tax avoidance, and largesse for family members along with lack of market competition (price fixing?) mitigated the development of MACS [management accounting and control systems]. Spain also followed this pattern and relied more on personal relationships and oral inquisitions than on hard data for control." At the same time, other Western European countries such as Germany, France, and the Netherlands developed relatively sophisticated formal management accounting systems emphasizing efficient operations. In the case of France, these were codified in law. In England, management accounting practice was influenced by economists, who emphasized the use of accounting data in decision making. The Nordic countries tended to import management accounting ideas from both Germany and England.

A number of factors have been acting in recent years to make management accounting practices more similar within Europe and around the world. These forces include: intensified global competition, which makes it more difficult to continue sloppy practices; standardized information system software sold throughout the world by vendors such as SAP, PeopleSoft, Oracle, and Baan; the increasing significance and authority of multinational corporations; the global consultancy industry; the diffusion of information throughout academia; and the global use of market-leading textbooks.

Sources: Markus Granlund and Kari Lukka, "It's a Small World of Management Accounting Practices," *Journal of Management Accounting Research* 10, 1998, pp. 153–171; and Norman B. Macintosh, "Management Accounting in Europe: A View from Canada," *Management Accounting Research* 9, 1998, pp. 495–500.

E-COMMERCE

Widespread use of the Internet is a fairly new phenomenon, and the impact it will eventually have on business is far from settled. For a few brief months, it looked like dot.com start-ups would take over the business world—their stock market valuations reached astonishing heights. But, of course, the bubble burst and few of the start-ups are now in business. With the benefit of hindsight, it is now clear that the managers of the dot.com start-ups would have benefited from the use of many of the tools covered in this book, including cost concepts (Chapter 1), cost estimation (Chapter 5), cost-volume-profit analysis (Chapter 6), activity-based costing (Chapter 3), budgeting (Chapter 7), decision making (Chapter 11), and capital budgeting (Chapter 12). While applying these tools to a new company with little operational history would be difficult, it needs to be done. And the investors who plowed billions into dot.com start-ups only to see the money vanish would have been wise to pay attention to the tools covered in the chapters on the statement of cash flows (Chapter 13) and financial statement analysis (Chapter 14).

At the time of this writing, it is still not clear if a successful business model will emerge for Internet-based companies. It is generally believed that Amazon.com and eBay may have the best chances of building sustainable e-commerce businesses, but even Amazon.com has its detractors who believe it will never break even on a cash flow basis. If a successful e-commerce business model does emerge, it will be based on attracting enough profitable customers to cover the fixed expenses of the company as discussed in Chapter 6.

Established brick-and-mortar companies like General Electric, Wells Fargo, American Airlines, and Wal-Mart will undoubtedly continue to expand into cyberspace—both for business-to-business transactions and for retailing. The Internet has important advantages over more conventional marketplaces for some kinds of transactions such as mortgage banking. The financial institution does not have to tie up staff filling out forms—that can be done directly by the consumer over the Internet. And data and funds can be sent back and forth electronically—no UPS delivery truck needs to drop by the consumer's home to deliver a check. However, it is unlikely that a successful blockbuster business will ever be built around the concept of selling low-value, low-margin, and bulky items like groceries over the Internet.

ORGANIZATIONAL STRUCTURE

Since organizations are made up of people, management must accomplish its objectives by working through people. Presidents of companies with more than a few employees cannot possibly execute all of their company's strategies alone; they must rely on other people. This is done by creating an organizational structure that permits *decentralization* of management responsibilities.

Decentralization

Decentralization is the delegation of decision-making authority throughout an organization by providing managers at various operating levels with the authority to make decisions relating to their area of responsibility. Some organizations are more decentralized than others. For example, consider Good Vibrations, Inc., an international retailer of music CDs with shops in major cities scattered around the Pacific Rim. Because of Good Vibrations, Inc.'s geographic dispersion and the peculiarities of local markets, the company is highly decentralized.

Good Vibrations, Inc.'s president (also called chief executive officer, or CEO) sets the broad strategy for the company and makes major strategic decisions such as opening stores in new markets, but much of the remaining decision-making authority is delegated to managers on various levels throughout the organization. Each of the company's numerous retail stores has a store manager as well as a separate manager for each section such as international rock and classical/jazz. In addition, the company has support departments such as a central Purchasing Department and a Personnel Department. The organizational structure of the company is depicted in Exhibit P–3.

The arrangement of boxes shown in Exhibit P–3 is called an **organization chart.** The purpose of an organization chart is to show how responsibility has been divided among managers and to show formal lines of reporting and communication, or *chain of command.* Each box depicts an area of management responsibility, and the lines between the boxes show the lines of formal authority between managers. The chart tells us, for example, that the store managers are responsible to the operations vice president. In turn, the latter is responsible to the company president, who in turn is responsible to the board of directors. Following the lines of authority and communication on the organization chart, we can see that the manager of the Hong Kong store would ordinarily report to the operations vice president rather than directly to the president of the company.

Informal relationships and channels of communication often develop outside the formal reporting relationships on the organization chart as a result of personal contacts between managers. The informal structure does not appear on the organization chart, but it is often vital to effective operations.

EXHIBIT P–3 Organization Chart, Good Vibrations, Inc.

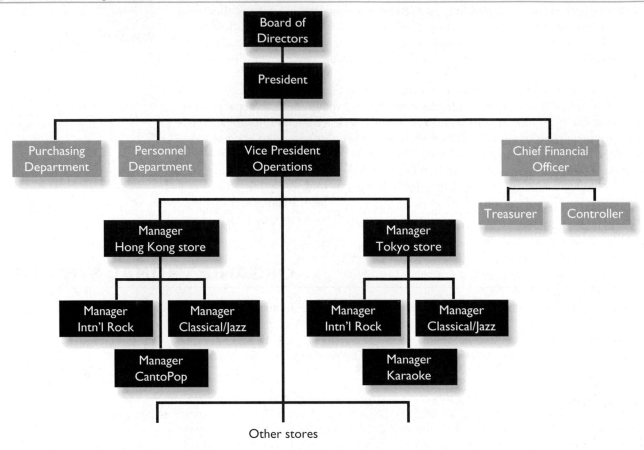

Line and Staff Relationships

An organization chart also depicts *line* and *staff* positions in an organization. A person in a **line** position is *directly* involved in achieving the basic objectives of the organization. A person in a **staff** position, by contrast, is only *indirectly* involved in achieving those basic objectives. Staff positions *support* or provide assistance to line positions or other parts of the organization, but they do not have direct authority over line positions. Refer again to the organization chart in Exhibit P–3. Since the basic objective of Good Vibrations, Inc., is to sell recorded music at a profit, those managers whose areas of responsibility are directly related to the sales effort occupy line positions. These positions, which are shown in a darker color in the exhibit, include the managers of the various music departments in each store, the store managers, the operations vice president, and members of top management.

By contrast, the manager of the central Purchasing Department occupies a staff position, since the only function of the Purchasing Department is to support and serve the line departments by doing their purchasing for them.

The Chief Financial Officer

In the United States the manager of the accounting department is often known as the *controller.* The controller in turn reports to the *Chief Financial Officer,* who usually comes from an accounting background. The **Chief Financial Officer (CFO)** is the member of the top management team who is responsible for providing timely and relevant data to support planning and control activities and for preparing financial statements for external users. An effective CFO is considered a key member of the top management team whose advice is sought in all major decisions. The CFO is a highly paid professional who has command over the technical details of accounting and finance, who can provide leadership to other professionals in his or her department, who can analyze new and evolving situations, who can communicate technical data to others in a simple and clear manner, and who is able to work well with top managers from other disciplines.

It should be noted that few of the people who are trained as accountants and who work under the Chief Financial Officer in either the treasurer's office or the controller's office think of themselves as accountants. If asked, they are likely to identify themselves as working in finance. Management accounting is not about debits and credits or recording journal entries, although some knowledge of that is necessary. Management accounting is about helping managers to pursue the organization's goals. A recent report states that:

> Growing numbers of management accountants spend the bulk of their time as internal consultants or business analysts within their companies. Technological advances have liberated them from the mechanical aspects of accounting. They spend less time preparing standardized reports and more time analyzing and interpreting information. Many have moved from the isolation of accounting departments to be physically positioned in the operating departments with which they work. Management accountants work on cross-functional teams, have extensive face-to-face communications with people throughout their organizations, and are actively involved in decision making. . . . They are trusted advisors.[4]

Beyond the Numbers

IN BUSINESS

Judy C. Lewent is the Chief Financial Officer (CFO) of Merck, a major pharmaceutical company. She is in charge of 750 people and is intimately involved in the company's most important strategic decisions. Cynthia Beach, vice president of global investment research at Goldman Sachs & Co., says this about Lewent: "From my standpoint, Merck is one of the best-managed [pharmaceutical] companies, and Judy is a key reason why." Merck's chairman, CEO, and president Raymond Gilmartin adds this about Lewent: "Many CFOs take as their prime directive the timely, accurate delivery of detailed financial data and analysis to top management. While the importance of these services cannot be overestimated, with Judy they are simply one of the many ways she contributes to the business. [Lewent and her organization] make decisions about which developmental-product projects to fund and how to structure our product franchises, acquisition possibilities, and licensing arrangements."

Source: Russ Banham, "Merck Grows from the Inside Out, Powered by the CFO's Joint Ventures," *CFO*, October 2000, pp. 69–70.

PROFESSIONAL ETHICS

A series of major financial scandals involving Enron, Tyco, Adelphia, WorldCom, Global Crossing, Arthur Andersen, Rite Aid, and others has raised deep concerns about the state of ethics in business. The managers and companies involved in these scandals have suffered mightily—from huge fines to jail terms to financial collapse. And the recognition that ethical behavior is absolutely essential for the functioning of our economy has led to

[4]Gary Siegel Organization, *Counting More, Counting Less: Transformations in the Management Accounting Profession, The 1999 Practice Analysis of Management Accounting,* Institute of Management Accountants, Montvale, NJ, August 1999, p. 3.

numerous regulatory changes and calls for new legislation. But why is ethical behavior so important? This is not a matter of just being "nice." Ethical behavior is the lubricant that keeps the economy running. Without that lubricant, the economy would operate much less efficiently—less would be available to consumers, quality would be lower, and prices would be higher. As James Surowiecki writes:

> [F]lourishing economies require a healthy level of trust in the reliability and fairness of everyday transactions. If you assumed every potential deal was a rip-off or that the products you were buying were probably going to be lemons, then very little business would get done. More important, the costs of the transactions that did take place would be exorbitant, since you'd have to do enormous work to investigate each deal and you'd have to rely on the threat of legal action to enforce every contract. For an economy to prosper, what's needed is not a Pollyanish faith that everyone else has your best interests at heart—"caveat emptor" [buyer beware] remains an important truth—but a basic confidence in the promises and commitments that people make about their products and services.[5]

Take a very simple example. Suppose that unethical farmers, distributors, and grocers knowingly tried to sell wormy apples as good apples and that grocers refused to take back wormy apples. What would you do? Go to another grocer? But what if all grocers acted in this way? What would you do then? You would probably either stop buying apples or you would spend a lot of time inspecting apples before buying them. So would everyone else. Now notice what has happened. Because farmers, distributors, and grocers could not be trusted, sales of apples would plummet and those who do buy apples would waste a lot of time inspecting them minutely. Everyone loses. Farmers, distributors, and groceries make less money, consumers enjoy fewer apples, and consumers waste time looking for worms.

The same phenomenon exists for other markets, as the accompanying In Business box illustrates.

---

[5]James Surowiecki, "A Virtuous Cycle," *Forbes,* December 23, 2002, pp. 248–256.

No Trust—No Enron

Jonathan Karpoff reports on a particularly important, but often overlooked, aspect of the Enron debacle:

> As we know, some of Enron's reported profits in the late 1990s were pure accounting fiction. But the firm also had legitimate businesses and actual assets. Enron's most important businesses involved buying and selling electricity and other forms of energy. [Using Enron as an intermediary, utilities that needed power bought energy from producers with surplus generating capacity.] Now when an electric utility contracts to buy electricity, the managers of the utility want to make darned sure that the seller will deliver the electrons exactly as agreed, at the contracted price. There is no room for fudging on this because the consequences of not having the electricity when consumers switch on their lights are dire . . .
>
> This means that the firms with whom Enron was trading electricity . . . had to trust Enron. And trust Enron they did, to the tune of billions of dollars of trades every year. But in October 2001, when Enron announced that its previous financial statements overstated the firm's profits, it undermined such trust. As everyone recognizes, the announcement caused investors to lower their valuations of the firm. Less understood, however, was the more important impact of the announcement; by revealing some of its reported earnings to be a house of cards, Enron sabotaged its reputation. The effect was to undermine even its legitimate and (previously) profitable operations that relied on its trustworthiness.

This is why Enron melted down so fast. Its core businesses relied on the firm's reputation. When that reputation was wounded, energy traders took their business elsewhere.

Energy traders lost their faith in Enron, but what if no other company could be trusted to deliver on its commitments to provide electricity as contracted? In that case, energy traders would have nowhere to turn. As a direct result, energy producers with surplus generating capacity would be unable to sell their surplus power. As a consequence, their existing customers would have to pay higher prices. And utilities that do not have sufficient capacity to meet demand on their own would have to build more capacity, which would also mean higher prices for their consumers. So a general lack of trust in companies such as Enron would ultimately result in overinvestment in energy generating capacity and higher energy prices for consumers.

Source: Jonathan M. Karpoff, "Regulation vs. Reputation in Preventing Corporate Fraud," *UW Business,* Spring 2002, pp. 28–30.

The Institute of Management Accountants (IMA) of the United States has developed a very useful ethical code called the *Standards of Ethical Conduct for Practitioners of Management Accounting and Financial Management.* Even though the standards were specifically developed for management accountants, they have much broader application.

Code of Conduct for Management Accountants

The IMA's Standards of Ethical Conduct for Practitioners of Management Accounting and Financial Management is presented in full in Exhibit P–4. The standards have two parts. The first part provides general guidelines for ethical behavior. In a nutshell, the

Practitioners of management accounting and financial management have an obligation to the public, their profession, the organization they serve, and themselves, to maintain the highest standards of ethical conduct. In recognition of this obligation, the Institute of Management Accountants has promulgated the following standards of ethical conduct for practitioners of management accounting and financial management. Adherence to these standards, both domestically and internationally, is integral to achieving the Objectives of Management Accounting. Practitioners of management accounting and financial management shall not commit acts contrary to these standards nor shall they condone the commission of such acts by others within their organizations.

Competence. Practitioners of management accounting and financial management have a responsibility to:

- Maintain an appropriate level of professional competence by ongoing development of their knowledge and skills.
- Perform their professional duties in accordance with relevant laws, regulations, and technical standards.
- Prepare complete and clear reports and recommendations after appropriate analysis of relevant and reliable information.

Confidentiality. Practitioners of management accounting and financial management have a responsibility to:

- Refrain from disclosing confidential information acquired in the course of their work except when authorized, unless legally obligated to do so.
- Inform subordinates as appropriate regarding the confidentiality of information acquired in the course of their work and monitor their activities to assure the maintenance of that confidentiality.

continued

EXHIBIT P–4

Standards of Ethical Conduct for Practitioners of Management Accounting and Financial Management

EXHIBIT P–4

(concluded)

- Refrain from using or appearing to use confidential information acquired in the course of their work for unethical or illegal advantage either personally or through third parties.

Integrity. Practitioners of management accounting and financial management have a responsibility to:

- Avoid actual or apparent conflicts of interest and advise all appropriate parties of any potential conflict.
- Refrain from engaging in any activity that would prejudice their ability to carry out their duties ethically.
- Refuse any gift, favor, or hospitality that would influence or would appear to influence their actions.
- Refrain from either actively or passively subverting the attainment of the organization's legitimate and ethical objectives.
- Recognize and communicate professional limitations or other constraints that would preclude responsible judgment or successful performance of an activity.
- Communicate unfavorable as well as favorable information and professional judgments or opinions.
- Refrain from engaging in or supporting any activity that would discredit the profession.

Objectivity. Practitioners of management accounting and financial management have a responsibility to:

- Communicate information fairly and objectively.
- Disclose fully all relevant information that could reasonably be expected to influence an intended user's understanding of the reports, comments, and recommendations presented.

Resolution of Ethical Conflict. In applying the standards of ethical conduct, practitioners of management accounting and financial management may encounter problems in identifying unethical behavior or in resolving an ethical conflict. When faced with significant ethical issues, practitioners of management accounting and financial management should follow the established policies of the organization bearing on the resolution of such conflict. If these policies do not resolve the ethical conflict, such practitioner should consider the following courses of action:

- Discuss such problems with the immediate superior except when it appears that the superior is involved, in which case the problem should be presented initially to the next higher managerial level. If a satisfactory resolution cannot be achieved when the problem is initially presented, submit the issues to the next higher managerial level.
- If the immediate superior is the chief executive officer, or equivalent, the acceptable reviewing authority may be a group such as the audit committee, executive committee, board of directors, board of trustees, or owners. Contact with levels above the immediate superior should be initiated only with the superior's knowledge, assuming the superior is not involved. Except where legally prescribed, communication of such problems to authorities or individuals not employed or engaged by the organization is not considered appropriate.
- Clarify relevant ethical issues by confidential discussion with an objective advisor (e.g., IMA Ethics Counseling Service) to obtain a better understanding of possible courses of action.
- Consult your own attorney as to legal obligations and rights concerning the ethical conflict.
- If the ethical conflict still exists after exhausting all levels of internal review, there may be no other recourse on significant matters than to resign from the organization and to submit an informative memorandum to an appropriate representative of the organization. After resignation, depending on the nature of the ethical conflict, it may also be appropriate to notify other parties.

*Institute of Management Accountants, formerly National Association of Accountants, *Statements on Management Accounting: Objectives of Management Accounting,* Statement No. 1B, New York, NY, June 17, 1982, as revised in 1997.

management accountant has ethical responsibilities in four broad areas: first, to maintain a high level of professional competence; second, to treat sensitive matters with confidentiality; third, to maintain personal integrity; and fourth, to be objective in all disclosures. The second part of the standards specifies what should be done if an individual finds evidence of ethical misconduct. We recommend that you stop at this point and read the standards in Exhibit P–4.

The ethical standards provide sound, practical advice for management accountants and managers. Most of the rules in the ethical standards are motivated by a very practical consideration—if these rules were not generally followed in business, then the economy and all of us would suffer. Consider the following specific examples of the consequences of not abiding by the standards:

- Suppose employees could not be trusted with confidential information. Then top managers would be reluctant to distribute such information within the company and, as a result, decisions would be based on incomplete information and operations would deteriorate.
- Suppose employees accepted bribes from suppliers. Then contracts would tend to go to suppliers who pay the highest bribes rather than to the most competent suppliers. Would you like to fly in aircraft whose wings were made by the subcontractor who paid the highest bribe? Would you fly as often? What would happen to the airline industry if its safety record deteriorated due to shoddy workmanship on contracted parts and assemblies?
- Suppose the presidents of companies routinely lied in their annual reports and financial statements. If investors could not rely on the basic integrity of a company's financial statements, they would have little basis for making informed decisions. Suspecting the worst, rational investors would pay less for securities issued by companies and may not be willing to invest at all. As a consequence, companies would have less money for productive investments—leading to slower economic growth, fewer goods and services, and higher prices.

As these examples suggest, if ethical standards were not generally adhered to, everyone would suffer—businesses as well as consumers. Essentially, abandoning ethical standards would lead to a lower standard of living with lower-quality goods and services, less to choose from, and higher prices. In short, following ethical rules such as those in the Standards of Ethical Conduct for Practitioners of Management Accounting and Financial Management is absolutely essential for the smooth functioning of an advanced market economy.

Character's the Thing

Personal character has become critically important to CEOs when hiring a CFO. A huge proportion (about 84%) of CEOs ranked personal integrity as second in importance only to technical expertise. The growing emphasis on character is partly driven by external pressures. The Securities and Exchange Commission is becoming more aggressive in going after companies that cook their books, and powerful shareholders are increasingly likely to demand that CFOs be beyond reproach. Moreover, CEOs agree that character is integral to the job. George Fellows, the CEO of Revlon, says: "Personal integrity is the cost of entry to this position." Frank Weise, the CEO of Toronto-based Cott Corp., agrees: "When you hire a CFO, you want that person to reek of integrity." Susan Landon, an executive recruiter with LAI Worldwide, adds: "In most executives, CEOs look for personal character; in a CFO, it is an absolute requirement."

Source: Julie Carrick Dalton, "What CEOs Want," *CFO*, July 1999, pp. 45–52.

Capitalism and Greed

Capitalism is often associated with ruthless, self-centered behavior, but is that a bum rap? Researchers have run many variations of the following experiment. Two randomly selected players who do not know each other are placed in different rooms. The individuals cannot see or hear each other and are never introduced to each other. The first player is given $100 and told to split the money with the second player in any way he or she chooses. The first player could propose a $100/$0 split, an $80/$20 split, or any other combination that adds up to $100. However, under the rules of the experiment, the second player is allowed to refuse the offer and in that case, neither player gets anything. The game is played only once for each pair of players.

What would a greedy person do? A greedy and ruthless first player would reason that the second player would accept a very low offer of perhaps $10 since $10 is better than nothing. However, in repeated experiments of this sort, people cast as player one were usually far more generous than this and people cast as player two often rejected small offers, even though that left them with nothing. Even more interestingly, responses differed among cultures. When the experiment was run with farmers from Hamilton, Missouri, player one offered on average $48—very close to a $50/$50 split. In contrast, the average offer by player one among the Quichua Indians in Peru was only $25. The Quichua Indians subsist in a slash-and-burn agricultural society with little market trading, whereas farmers from Missouri live in a fully developed capitalist market economy. This experiment has been repeated in many communities around the world and the consistent result is that greed (i.e., a low average offer by player one) is associated with nonmarket, precapitalist societies. In general, the more developed the local economy, the closer the offer by player one is to a $50/$50 split.

It is not clear what is the cause and what is the effect. Do markets make people less greedy or is suppression of greed a prerequisite to a fully developed market economy? At any rate, ruthless greed seems to be much more a hallmark of people who live in undeveloped, precapitalist societies than of those who live in fully developed market economies.

Source: David Wessel, "Capital: The Civilizing Effect of the Market," *The Wall Street Journal*, January 24, 2002, p. A1.

Company Codes of Conduct

"Those who engage in unethical behavior often justify their actions with one or more of the following reasons: (1) the organization expects unethical behavior, (2) everyone else is unethical, and/or (3) behaving unethically is the only way to get ahead."[6]

To counter the first justification for unethical behavior, many companies have adopted formal ethics codes of conduct. These codes are generally broad-based statements of a company's responsibilities to its employees, its customers, its suppliers, and the communities in which the company operates. Codes rarely spell out specific dos and don'ts or suggest proper behavior in specific situations. Instead, they give broad guidelines.

Unfortunately, the single-minded emphasis placed on short-term profits in some companies may make it seem like the only way to get ahead is to act unethically. When top managers say, in effect, that they will only be satisfied with bottom-line results and will accept no excuses, they are asking for trouble.

---

[6]Michael K. McCuddy, Karl E. Reichardt, and David Schroeder, "Ethical Pressures: Fact or Fiction?" *Management Accounting*, April 1993, pp. 57–61.

Undue Pressure Can Lead to Unethical Behavior

Top managers at Sears, Roebuck & Company created a situation in its automotive service business that led to unethical actions by its front-line employees.

> Consumers and attorneys general in more than 40 states had accused the company of misleading customers and selling them unnecessary parts and services, from brake jobs to front-end alignments. It would be a mistake, however, to see this situation . . . in terms of any one individual's moral failings. Nor did management set out to defraud Sears customers . . .
>
> In the face of declining revenues, shrinking market share, and an increasingly competitive market, . . . Sears management attempted to spur performance of its auto centers . . . The company increased minimum work quotas and introduced productivity incentives for mechanics. The automotive service advisers were given product-specific sales quotas—sell so many springs, shock absorbers, alignments, or brake jobs per shift—and paid a commission based on sales. According to advisers, failure to meet quotas could lead to a transfer or a reduction in work hours. Some employees spoke of the "pressure, pressure, pressure" to bring in sales.
>
> This pressure-cooker atmosphere created conditions under which employees felt that the only way to satisfy top management was by selling customers products and services they didn't really need.
>
> Shortly after the allegations against Sears became public, CEO Edward Brennan acknowledged management's responsibility for putting in place compensation and goal-setting systems that "created an environment in which mistakes did occur."

Source: Reprinted by permission of Harvard Business Review. Excerpt from Lynn Sharp Paine, "Managing for Organizational Integrity," *Harvard Business Review*, March–April 1994. Copyright © 1994 by the President and Fellows of Harvard College. All rights reserved.

Codes of Conduct on the International Level

The *Guideline on Ethics for Professional Accountants*, issued in July 1990 by the International Federation of Accountants (IFAC), governs the activities of *all* professional accountants throughout the world, regardless of whether they are practicing as independent CPAs, employed in government service, or employed as internal accountants.[7] In addition to outlining ethical requirements in matters dealing with competence, objectivity, independence, and confidentiality, the IFAC's code also outlines the accountant's ethical responsibilities in matters relating to taxes, fees and commissions, advertising and solicitation, the handling of monies, and cross-border activities. Where cross-border activities are involved, the IFAC ethical requirements must be followed if these requirements are stricter than the ethical requirements of the country in which the work is being performed.[8]

In addition to professional and company codes of ethical conduct, accountants and managers in the United States are subject to the legal requirements of *The Foreign Corrupt Practices Act of 1977*. The Act requires that companies devise and maintain a system of internal controls sufficient to ensure that all transactions are properly executed and recorded. The Act specifically prohibits giving bribes, even if giving bribes is common practice in the country in which the company is doing business.

---

[7]A copy of this code can be obtained on the International Federation of Accountants' website at www.ifac.org.

[8]*Guideline on Ethics for Professional Accountants* (New York: International Federation of Accountants, July 1990), p. 23.

IN BUSINESS

Are Women More Ethical than Men?

CMA Canada, the association of chartered management accountants in Canada, distributed questionnaires to Canadian business students that contained 28 questions involving ethical issues. For example, students were asked whether it would be acceptable or unacceptable to export a product that would be considered unsafe in Canada. The students responded on a six-point scale—with 1 being "acceptable" and 6 "unacceptable." Note that the scores are the students' perceptions of the acceptability of the action and not the "right" answer in any absolute sense. The average responses are revealing:

CMA Canada Business Student Survey (1 = considered by student to be acceptable; 6 = considered by student to be unacceptable)		
	Female	Male
Inflate an insurance claim?	5.09	4.18
Return worn clothing?	4.43	3.23
Purchase mismarked item for the incorrect price?	3.27	2.22
Sell a frequent flyer ticket?	3.39	2.69
Keep extra change given in error?	4.03	3.30
Misrepresent age to obtain a senior discount?	4.33	3.77
Misrepresent age to obtain a child discount?	3.95	3.33
Charge higher prices in a poorer area?	3.92	2.84
Use cheap foreign labor?	2.72	2.02
Sell an unsafe product overseas?	5.18	2.40
Charge a higher price after a tornado?	3.94	3.26
Sell an illegal pharmaceutical product?	4.64	3.99

Robert Dye, president and CEO of CMA Canada, emphasizes the importance of ethics in business: "Employees like to work for a company that they can trust. Customers like to deal with an ethically reliable business. Suppliers like to sell to firms with which they can have a real partnership. Communities are more likely to co-operate with organizations that deal honestly and fairly with them." If the business community is to function effectively, all of the players need to act ethically.

Source: Excerpted from a study by J. Fisher, "Ethics Check," appearing in *CMA Management* magazine (formerly *CMA Magazine*), April 1999, pp. 36–37, with permission of CMA Canada.

THE CERTIFIED MANAGEMENT ACCOUNTANT (CMA)

A management accountant who possesses the necessary qualifications and who passes a rigorous professional exam earns the right to be known as a *Certified Management Accountant (CMA)*. In addition to the prestige that accompanies a professional designation, CMAs are often given greater responsibilities and higher compensation than those who do not have such a designation. Information about becoming a CMA and the CMA program can be accessed on the Institute of Management Accountants' (IMA) website at www.imanet.org or by calling 1-800-638-4427.

To become a Certified Management Accountant, the following four steps must be completed:

1. File an Application for Admission and register for the CMA examination.
2. Pass all four parts of the CMA examination within a three-year period.
3. Satisfy the experience requirement of two continuous years of professional experience in management and/or financial accounting prior to or within seven years of passing the CMA examination.
4. Comply with the Standards of Ethical Conduct for Practitioners of Management Accounting and Financial Management.

How's the Pay?

The Institute of Management Accountants has made available the following table that allows an individual to estimate what his salary would be as a management accountant. (The table applies specifically to men. A similar table exists for women, who constitute about 31% of all IMA members.)

			Your Calculation
Start with this base amount		$64,625	
If you are TOP-level management	ADD	$22,970	
OR, If you are ENTRY-level management	SUBTRACT	$20,725	
Number of years in the field _____	TIMES	$521	
If you have an advanced degree	ADD	$13,737	
If you hold the CMA	ADD	$8,786	
If you hold the CPA	ADD	$8,619	
Your estimated salary level			

For example, if you make it to the top management level in ten years and have an advanced degree and a CMA, your estimated annual salary would be $115,328 (= $64,625 + $22,970 + 10 × $521 + $13,737 + $8,786).

Source: Karl E. Reichardt and David Schroeder, "Members' Salaries Are Still Going Up," *Strategic Finance*, June 2003, pp. 27–40.

SUMMARY

The business environment in recent years has been characterized by increasing competition and a relentless drive for continuous improvement. A number of approaches have been developed to assist organizations in meeting these challenges—including just-in-time (JIT), total quality management (TQM), process reengineering, and the theory of constraints (TOC).

JIT emphasizes the importance of reducing inventories to the barest minimum possible. This reduces working capital requirements, frees up space, reduces throughput time, reduces defects, and eliminates waste.

TQM involves focusing on the customer, and it employs systematic problem solving using teams made up of front-line workers. Specific TQM tools include benchmarking and the plan-do-check-act (PDCA) cycle. By emphasizing teamwork, a focus on the customer, and facts, TQM can avoid the organizational infighting that might otherwise block improvement.

Process reengineering involves completely redesigning a business process to eliminate non-value-added activities and to reduce opportunities for errors. Process reengineering relies more on outside specialists than TQM and is more likely to be imposed by top management.

The theory of constraints emphasizes the importance of managing the organization's constraints. Since the constraint is whatever is holding back the organization, improvement efforts usually must be focused on the constraint in order to be really effective.

Most organizations are decentralized to some degree. The organization chart depicts who works for whom in the organization and which units perform staff functions rather than line functions. Accountants perform a staff function—they support and provide assistance to others inside the organization.

Ethical standards serve a very important practical function in an advanced market economy. Without widespread adherence to ethical standards, living standards would fall. Ethics is the lubrication that keeps a market economy functioning smoothly. The Standards of Ethical Conduct for Practitioners of Management Accounting and Financial Management provide sound, practical guidelines for resolving ethics problems that might arise in an organization.

GUIDANCE ANSWERS TO CONCEPT CHECKS

1. **Choice b.** Process reengineering, rather than total quality management, focuses on completely redesigning processes that have been targeted for improvement.
2. **Choice a.** The theory of constraints focuses on identifying and improving the constraint. The other three choices suggest managing nonconstraining departments in a manner that is not generally consistent with the goals of the theory of constraints.

GLOSSARY

At the end of each chapter, a list of key terms for review is given, along with the definition of each term. (These terms are printed in boldface where they are defined in the chapter.) Carefully study each term to be sure you understand its meaning, since these terms are used repeatedly in the chapters that follow. The list for the Prologue follows.

Benchmarking   A study of organizations that are among the best in the world at performing a particular task. (p. 5)

Business process   A series of steps that are followed in order to carry out some task in a business. (p. 6)

Chief Financial Officer (CFO)   The member of the top management team who is responsible for providing timely and relevant data to support planning and control activities and for preparing financial statements for external users. An effective CFO is a key member of the top management team whose advice is sought in all major decisions. (p. 12)

Controller   The member of the top management team who is responsible for providing relevant and timely data to managers and for preparing financial statements for external users. (p. 12)

Constraint   Anything that prevents an organization or individual from getting more of what it wants. (p. 8)

Decentralization   The delegation of decision-making authority throughout an organization by providing managers at various operating levels with the authority to make key decisions relating to their area of responsibility. (p. 11)

Just-in-time (JIT)   A production and inventory control system in which materials are purchased and units are produced only as needed to meet actual customer demand. (p. 3)

Line   A position in an organization that is directly related to the achievement of the organization's basic objectives. (p. 12)

Non-value-added activity   An activity that consumes resources or takes time but that does not add value for which customers are willing to pay. (p. 7)

Organization chart   A visual diagram of a firm's organizational structure that depicts formal lines of reporting, communication, and responsibility between managers. (p. 11)

Plan-do-check-act (PDCA) cycle   A systematic approach to continuous improvement that applies the scientific method to problem solving. (p. 5)

Process reengineering   An approach to improvement that involves completely redesigning business processes in order to eliminate unnecessary steps, reduce errors, and reduce costs. (p. 6)

Staff   A position in an organization that is only indirectly related to the achievement of the organization's basic objectives. Such positions are supportive in nature in that they provide service or assistance to line positions or to other staff positions. (p. 12)

Theory of constraints (TOC)   A management approach that emphasizes the importance of managing constraints. (p. 8)

Total quality management (TQM)   An approach to continuous improvement that focuses on customers and using teams of front-line workers to systematically identify and solve problems. (p. 5)

CHAPTER ONE

An Introduction to Managerial Accounting and Cost Concepts

CHAPTER OUTLINE

Making Fact-Based Decisions in Real Time

Cisco Systems and Alcoa are on the leading edge of their industries and real-time management accounting is one of the keys to their success. Managers at these companies can drill down into the company's management accounting system to find the latest data on revenues, margins, order backlogs, expenses, and other data, by region, by business unit, by distribution channel, by salesperson, and so on. The Chief Financial Officer of Cisco, Larry Carter, says that with this kind of live information "you can empower all your management team to improve decision making." Richard Kelson, the Chief Financial Officer of Alcoa, says: "The earlier you get information, the easier it is to fix a problem." For example, with up-to-date data, managers at Alcoa saw softness in aerospace markets early enough to shift production from hard alloys that are used in aircraft to other products. John Chambers, the CEO of Cisco, says: "At any time in the quarter, first-line managers can look at margins and products and know exactly what the effect of their decisions will be."

Source: Thomas A. Stewart, "Making Decisions in Real Time," *Fortune,* June 26, 2000, pp. 332–333.

LEARNING OBJECTIVES

After studying Chapter 1, you should be able to:

LO1 Identify and give examples of each of the three basic manufacturing cost categories.

LO2 Distinguish between product costs and period costs and give examples of each.

LO3 Prepare an income statement including calculation of the cost of goods sold.

LO4 Prepare a schedule of cost of goods manufactured.

LO5 Define and give examples of variable costs and fixed costs.

LO6 Define and give examples of direct and indirect costs.

LO7 Define and give examples of cost classifications used in making decisions: differential costs, opportunity costs, and sunk costs.

LO8 (Appendix 1A) Identify the four types of quality costs and explain how they interact.

Managerial accounting is concerned with providing information to managers—that is, people *inside* an organization who direct and control its operations. In contrast, **financial accounting** is concerned with providing information to stockholders, creditors, and others who are *outside* an organization. Managerial accounting provides the essential data with which organizations are actually run. Financial accounting provides the scorecard by which a company's overall past performance is judged by outsiders.

Managerial accountants prepare a variety of reports. Some reports focus on how well managers or business units have performed—comparing actual results to plans and to benchmarks. Some reports provide timely, frequent updates on key indicators such as orders received, order backlog, capacity utilization, and sales. Other analytical reports are prepared as needed to investigate specific problems such as a decline in the profitability of a product line. And yet other reports analyze a developing business situation or opportunity. In contrast, financial accounting is oriented toward producing a limited set of specific prescribed annual and quarterly financial statements in accordance with generally accepted accounting principles.

THE WORK OF MANAGEMENT AND THE NEED FOR MANAGERIAL ACCOUNTING INFORMATION

Is Every organization—large and small—has managers. Someone must be responsible for making plans, organizing resources, directing personnel, and controlling operations. This is true of the Bank of America, the Peace Corps, the University of Illinois, the Catholic Church, and the Coca-Cola Corporation, as well as the local 7-Eleven convenience store. We will use a particular organization—Good Vibrations, Inc.—to illustrate the work of management. What we have to say about the management of Good Vibrations, Inc., however, is very general and can be applied to virtually any organization.

Good Vibrations runs a chain of retail outlets that sell a full range of music CDs. The chain's stores are concentrated in Pacific Rim cities such as Sydney, Singapore, Hong Kong, Beijing, Tokyo, and Vancouver, British Columbia. The company has found that the best way to generate sales, and profits, is to create an exciting shopping environment. Consequently, the company puts a great deal of effort into planning the layout and decor of its stores—which are often quite large and extend over several floors in key downtown locations. Management knows that different types of clientele are attracted to different kinds of music. The international rock section is decorated with bold, brightly colored graphics, and the aisles are purposely narrow to create a crowded feeling much like one would experience at a popular nightclub on Friday night. In contrast, the classical music section is wood-paneled and fully sound insulated, with the rich, spacious feeling of a country club meeting room.

Managers at Good Vibrations, like managers everywhere, carry out three major activities—*planning, directing and motivating,* and *controlling.* **Planning** involves selecting a course of action and specifying how the action will be implemented. **Directing and motivating** involves mobilizing people to carry out plans and run routine operations. **Controlling** involves ensuring that the plan is actually carried out and is appropriately modified as circumstances change. Management accounting information plays a vital role in these basic management activities—but most particularly in the planning and control functions.

Planning

The first step in planning is to identify alternatives and then to select from among the alternatives the one that does the best job of furthering the organization's objectives. The basic objective of Good Vibrations is to earn profits for the owners of the company by providing superior service at competitive prices in as many markets as possible. To further this objective, every year top management carefully considers a number of alternatives for expanding into new geographic markets. This year management is considering opening new stores in Shanghai, Los Angeles, and Auckland.

When making this and other choices, management must balance the opportunities against the demands made on the company's resources. Management knows from bitter experience that opening a store in a major new market is a big step that cannot be taken lightly. It requires enormous amounts of time and energy from the company's most experienced, talented, and busy professionals. When the company attempted to open stores in both Beijing and Vancouver in the same year, resources were stretched too thinly. The result was that neither store opened on schedule, and operations in the rest of the company suffered. Therefore, entering new markets is planned very, very carefully.

Among other data, top management looks at the sales volumes, profit margins, and costs of the company's established stores in similar markets. These data, supplied by the management accountant, are combined with projected sales volume data at the proposed new locations to estimate the profits that would be generated by the new stores. In general, virtually all important alternatives considered by management in the planning process have some effect on revenues or costs, and management accounting data are essential in estimating those effects.

After considering all of the alternatives, Good Vibrations, Inc.'s top management decided to open a store in the burgeoning Shanghai market in the third quarter of the year, but to defer opening any other new stores to another year. As soon as this decision was made, detailed plans were drawn up for all parts of the company that would be involved in the Shanghai opening. For example, the Personnel Department's travel budget was increased, since it would be providing extensive on-the-site training to the new personnel hired in Shanghai.

As in the Personnel Department example, the plans of management are often expressed formally in **budgets,** and the term *budgeting* is applied to generally describe this part of the planning process. Budgets are usually prepared under the direction of the controller, who is the manager in charge of the Accounting Department. Typically, budgets are prepared annually and represent management's plans in specific, quantitative terms. In addition to a travel budget, the Personnel Department will be given goals in terms of new hires, courses taught, and detailed breakdowns of expected expenses. Similarly, the manager of each store will be given a target for sales volume, profit, expenses, pilferage losses, and employee training. These data will be collected, analyzed, and summarized for management use in the form of budgets prepared by management accountants.

Directing and Motivating

In addition to planning for the future, managers must oversee day-to-day activities and keep the organization functioning smoothly. This requires the ability to motivate and effectively direct people. Managers assign tasks to employees, arbitrate disputes, answer questions, solve on-the-spot problems, and make many small decisions that affect customers and employees. In effect, directing is that part of managers' work that deals with the routine and the here and now. Managerial accounting data, such as daily sales reports, are often used in this type of day-to-day decision making.

Controlling

In carrying out the **control** function, managers seek to ensure that the plan is being followed. **Feedback,** which signals whether operations are on track, is the key to effective control. In sophisticated organizations, this feedback is provided by detailed reports of various types. One of these reports, which compares budgeted to actual results, is called a **performance report.** Performance reports suggest where operations are not proceeding as planned and where some parts of the organization may require additional attention. For example, before the opening of the new Shanghai store in the third quarter of the year, the store's manager will be given sales volume, profit, and expense targets for the fourth quarter of the year. As the fourth quarter progresses, periodic reports will be made in

EXHIBIT 1–1   The Planning and Control Cycle

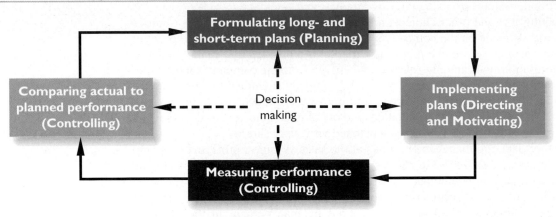

which the actual sales volume, profit, and expenses are compared to the targets. If the actual results fall below the targets, top management is alerted that the Shanghai store requires more attention. Experienced personnel can be flown in to help the new manager, or top management may come to the conclusion that plans will have to be revised. As we shall see in following chapters, providing this kind of feedback to managers is one of the central purposes of managerial accounting.

The End Results of Managers' Activities

As a customer enters one of the Good Vibrations stores, the results of management's planning, directing and motivating, and controlling activities will be evident in the many details that make the difference between a pleasant and an irritating shopping experience. The store will be clean, fashionably decorated, and logically laid out. Featured artists' videos will be displayed on TV monitors throughout the store, and the background rock music will be loud enough to send older patrons scurrying for the classical music section. Popular CDs will be in stock, and the latest hits will be available for private listening on earphones. Specific titles will be easy to find. Regional music, such as CantoPop in Hong Kong, will be prominently featured. Checkout clerks will be alert, friendly, and efficient. In short, what the customer experiences doesn't simply happen; it is the result of the efforts of managers who must visualize and fit together the processes that are needed to get the job done.

The Planning and Control Cycle

The work of management can be summarized in a model such as the one shown in Exhibit 1–1. The model, which depicts the **planning and control cycle,** illustrates the smooth flow of management activities from planning through directing and motivating, controlling, and then back to planning again. All of these activities involve decision making, so it is depicted as the hub around which the other activities revolve.

COMPARISON OF FINANCIAL AND MANAGERIAL ACCOUNTING

Financial accounting reports are prepared for the use of external parties such as shareholders and creditors, whereas managerial accounting reports are prepared for managers inside the organization. This contrast in basic orientation results in a number of major differences between financial and managerial accounting, even though both financial and managerial accounting often rely on the same underlying financial data. These differences are summarized in Exhibit 1–2.

As shown in Exhibit 1–2, in addition to the difference in who the reports are prepared for, financial and managerial accounting also differ in their emphasis between the past

EXHIBIT 1–2

Comparison of Financial and
Managerial Accounting

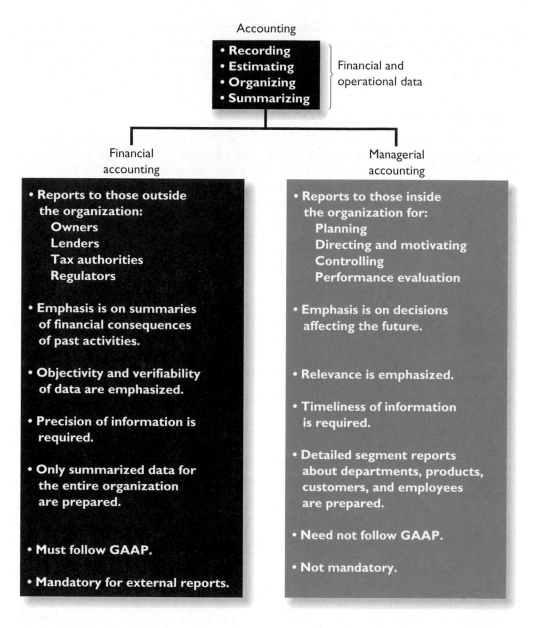

and the future, in the type of data provided to users, and in several other ways. These differences are discussed in the following paragraphs.

Emphasis on the Future

Since *planning* is such an important part of the manager's job, managerial accounting has a strong future orientation. In contrast, financial accounting primarily provides summaries of past financial transactions. These summaries may be useful in planning, but only to a point. The future is not simply a reflection of what has happened in the past. Changes are constantly taking place in economic conditions, customer needs and desires, competitive conditions, and so on. All of these changes demand that the manager's planning be based in large part on estimates of what will happen rather than on summaries of what has already happened.

Relevance of Data

Financial accounting data are expected to be objective and verifiable. However, for internal uses, the manager wants information that is relevant even if it is not completely objective or verifiable. By relevant, we mean *appropriate for the problem at hand.* For example, it is difficult to verify estimated sales volumes for a proposed new store at Good Vibrations, Inc., but this is exactly the type of information that is most useful to managers in their decision making. The managerial accounting information system should be flexible enough to provide whatever data are relevant for a particular decision.

Less Emphasis on Precision

Timeliness is often more important than precision to managers. If a decision must be made, a manager would much rather have a good estimate now than wait a week for a more precise answer. A decision involving tens of millions of dollars does not have to be based on estimates that are precise down to the penny, or even to the dollar. In fact, one authoritative source recommends that, "as a general rule, no one needs more than three significant digits."[1] This means, for example, that if a company's sales are in the hundreds of millions of dollars, then nothing on an income statement needs to be more accurate than the nearest million dollars. Estimates that are accurate to the nearest million dollars may be precise enough to make a good decision. Since precision is costly in terms of both time and resources, managerial accounting places less emphasis on precision than does financial accounting. In addition, managerial accounting places considerable weight on nonmonetary data. For example, information about customer satisfaction is of tremendous importance even though it would be difficult to express such data in a monetary form.

Segments of an Organization

Financial accounting is primarily concerned with reporting for the company as a whole. By contrast, managerial accounting focuses much more on the parts, or **segments,** of a company. These segments may be product lines, sales territories, divisions, departments, or any other categorization of the company's activities that management finds useful. Financial accounting does require some breakdowns of revenues and costs by major segments in external reports, but this is a secondary emphasis. In managerial accounting, segment reporting is the primary emphasis.

IN BUSINESS

Recordkeeping for the Future

Properly maintained corporate records have significant future benefits and, as such, should be considered an essential asset. Reviews of recordkeeping policies should be performed periodically to ensure that important information, needed for reference in the future, is documented and can be retrieved. Most of the problems uncovered in such reviews tend to relate to how the records are organized rather than how much information is being documented. There is little value in information that cannot be retrieved when it is needed for decision making.

Source: J. Edwin Dietal, "Improving Corporate Performance," *Information Management Journal,* April 2000, pp. 18–26.

Generally Accepted Accounting Principles (GAAP)

Financial accounting statements prepared for external users must be prepared in accordance with generally accepted accounting principles (GAAP). External users must have some assurance that the reports have been prepared in accordance with a common set of ground rules. These common ground rules enhance comparability and help reduce fraud

---

[1]*Statements on Management Accounting, Statement Number 5B, Fundamentals of Reporting Information to Managers,* Institute of Management Accounting, Montvale, NJ, p. 6.

and misrepresentation, but they do not necessarily lead to the type of reports that would be most useful in internal decision making. For example, GAAP requires that land be stated at its historical cost on financial reports. However, if management is considering moving a store to a new location and then selling the land the store currently sits on, management would like to know the current market value of the land—a vital piece of information that is ignored under GAAP.

Managerial accounting is not bound by generally accepted accounting principles. Managers set their own ground rules concerning the content and form of internal reports. The only constraint is that the expected benefits from using the information should outweigh the costs of collecting, analyzing, and summarizing the data. Nevertheless, as we shall see in subsequent chapters, it is undeniably true that financial reporting requirements have heavily influenced management accounting practice.

Managerial Accounting—Not Mandatory

Financial accounting is mandatory; that is, it must be done. Various outside parties such as the Securities and Exchange Commission (SEC) and the tax authorities require periodic financial statements. Managerial accounting, on the other hand, is not mandatory. A company is completely free to do as much or as little as it wishes. No regulatory bodies or other outside agencies specify what is to be done, or, for that matter, whether anything is to be done at all. Since managerial accounting is completely optional, the important question is always, "Is the information useful?" rather than, "Is the information required?"

As explained above, the work of management focuses on (1) planning, which includes setting objectives and outlining how to attain these objectives; and (2) control, which includes the steps to take to ensure that objectives are realized. To carry out these planning and control responsibilities, managers need *information* about the organization. From an accounting point of view, this information often relates to the *costs* of the organization.

In managerial accounting, the term *cost* is used in many different ways. The reason is that there are many types of costs, and these costs are classified differently according to the immediate needs of management. For example, managers may want cost data to prepare external financial reports, to prepare planning budgets, or to make decisions. Each different use of cost data demands a different classification and definition of costs. For example, the preparation of external financial reports requires the use of historical cost data, whereas decision making may require current cost data.

GENERAL COST CLASSIFICATIONS

All types of organizations incur costs—business, nonbusiness, manufacturing, retail, and service. Generally, the kinds of costs that are incurred and the way in which these costs are classified depends on the type of organization. Managerial accounting is as applicable to one type of organization as to another. For this reason, we will consider in our discussion the cost characteristics of a variety of organizations—manufacturing, merchandising, and service.

Our initial focus in this chapter is on manufacturing companies, since their basic activities include most of the activities found in other types of business organizations. Manufacturing companies such as Texas Instruments, Ford, and Kodak are involved in acquiring raw materials, producing finished goods, marketing, distributing, billing, and almost every other business activity. Therefore, an understanding of costs in a manufacturing company can be very helpful in understanding costs in other types of organizations.

In this chapter, we develop cost concepts that apply to diverse organizations. For example, these cost concepts apply to fast-food outlets such as KFC, Pizza Hut, and Taco Bell; movie studios such as Disney, Paramount, and United Artists; consulting firms such as Accenture and McKinsey; and your local hospital. The exact terms used in these

Concept 1–1

industries may not be the same as those used in manufacturing, but the same basic concepts apply. With some slight modifications, these basic concepts also apply to merchandising companies such as Wal-Mart, The Gap, 7-Eleven, Nordstrom, and Tower Records that resell finished goods acquired from manufacturers and other sources. With that in mind, let us begin our discussion of manufacturing costs.

Manufacturing Costs

LEARNING OBJECTIVE 1

Identify and give examples of each of the three basic manufacturing cost categories.

Most manufacturing companies divide manufacturing costs into three broad categories: direct materials, direct labor, and manufacturing overhead. A discussion of each of these categories follows.

Direct Materials The materials that go into the final product are called **raw materials.** This term is somewhat misleading, since it seems to imply unprocessed natural resources like wood pulp or iron ore. Actually, raw materials refer to any materials that are used in the final product; and the finished product of one company can become the raw materials of another company. One study of 37 manufacturing industries found that materials costs averaged about 55% of sales revenues.[2]

Raw materials may include both direct and indirect materials. **Direct materials** are those materials that become an integral part of the finished product and that can be physically and conveniently traced to it. This would include, for example, the seats that Boeing purchases from subcontractors to install in its commercial aircraft. Another example is the tiny electric motor Panasonic uses in its CD players to make the CD spin.

Sometimes it isn't worth the effort to trace the costs of relatively insignificant materials to the end products. Such minor items would include the solder used to make electrical connections in a Sony TV or the glue used to assemble an Ethan Allen chair. Materials such as solder and glue are called **indirect materials** and are included as part of manufacturing overhead, which is discussed later in this section.

Direct Labor The term **direct labor** is reserved for those labor costs that can be easily (i.e., physically and conveniently) traced to individual units of product. Direct labor is sometimes called *touch labor,* since direct labor workers typically touch the product while it is being made. The labor costs of assembly-line workers, for example, would be direct labor costs, as would the labor costs of carpenters, bricklayers, and machine operators.

Labor costs that cannot be physically traced to the creation of products, or that can be traced only at great cost and inconvenience, are termed **indirect labor** and treated as part of manufacturing overhead, along with indirect materials. Indirect labor includes the labor costs of janitors, supervisors, materials handlers, and night security guards. Although the efforts of these workers are essential to production, it would be either impractical or impossible to accurately trace their costs to specific units of product. Hence, such labor costs are treated as indirect labor.

In some industries, major shifts are taking place in the structure of labor costs. Sophisticated automated equipment, run and maintained by skilled indirect workers, is increasingly replacing direct labor. Indeed, in the study cited above of 37 manufacturing industries, direct labor averaged only about 10% of sales revenues. In a few companies, direct labor has become such a minor element of cost that it has disappeared altogether as a separate cost category. More is said in later chapters about this trend and about the impact it is having on cost systems. However, the vast majority of manufacturing and service companies throughout the world continue to recognize direct labor as a separate cost category.

---

[2]Germain Boer and Debra Jeter, "What's New About Modern Manufacturing? Empirical Evidence on Manufacturing Cost Changes," *Journal of Management Accounting Research*, Fall 1993, pp. 61–83.

Manufacturing Overhead   **Manufacturing overhead,** the third element of manufacturing cost, includes all costs of manufacturing except direct materials and direct labor. Manufacturing overhead includes items such as indirect materials; indirect labor; maintenance and repairs on production equipment; and heat and light, property taxes, depreciation, and insurance on manufacturing facilities. A company also incurs costs for heat and light, property taxes, insurance, depreciation, and so forth, associated with its selling and administrative functions, but these costs are not included as part of manufacturing overhead. Only those costs associated with *operating the factory* are included in the manufacturing overhead category. Several studies have found that manufacturing overhead averages about 16% of sales revenues.[3]

Various names are used for manufacturing overhead, such as *indirect manufacturing cost, factory overhead,* and *factory burden.* All of these terms mean the same thing as *manufacturing overhead.*

Manufacturing overhead combined with direct labor is called **conversion cost.** This term stems from the fact that direct labor costs and overhead costs are incurred to convert raw materials into finished products. Direct labor combined with direct materials is called **prime cost.**

Nonmanufacturing Costs

Generally, nonmanufacturing costs are subclassified into two categories:

1. Marketing or selling costs.
2. Administrative costs.

Marketing or selling costs include all costs necessary to secure customer orders and get the finished product into the hands of the customer. These costs are often called *order-getting and order-filling costs.* Examples of marketing costs include advertising, shipping, sales travel, sales commissions, sales salaries, and costs of finished goods warehouses.

Administrative costs include all executive, organizational, and clerical costs associated with the *general management* of an organization rather than with manufacturing, marketing, or selling. Examples of administrative costs include executive compensation, general accounting, secretarial, public relations, and similar costs involved in the overall, general administration of the organization *as a whole.*

Nonmanufacturing costs are often also called *selling, general, and administrative (SG&A) costs.*

Why Is Tuition So High?

Do you ever wonder why tuition costs are so high? Administrative costs can be crushing. *Forbes* magazine reports that an average of 2.5 administrators are employed for each faculty member in public colleges and 1.9 in private colleges. The worst case is Mississippi, which has four administrators for every teacher. The best case found in public colleges is Colorado, which "manages to get by with just under two administrators per teacher." Much of the administrative work results from "the mandates that accompany federal money, such as affirmative action, and the personnel needed to monitor compliance with those mandates."

Source: Peter Brimelow, "The Paper Chase," *Forbes,* May 17, 1999, pp. 78–79.

---

[3]J. Miller, A. DeMeyer, and J. Nakane, *Benchmarking Global Manufacturing* (Homewood, IL: Richard D. Irwin), 1992, Chapter 2. The Boer and Jeter article previously cited contains a similar finding concerning the magnitude of manufacturing overhead.

PRODUCT COSTS VERSUS PERIOD COSTS

LEARNING OBJECTIVE 2

Distinguish between product costs and period costs and give examples of each.

In addition to the distinction between manufacturing and nonmanufacturing costs, there are other ways to look at costs. For instance, they can also be classified as either *product costs* or *period costs*. To understand the difference between product costs and period costs, we must first refresh our understanding of the matching principle from financial accounting.

Generally, costs are recognized as expenses on the income statement in the period that benefits from the cost. For example, if a company pays for liability insurance in advance for two years, the entire amount is not considered an expense of the year in which the payment is made. Instead, one-half of the cost would be recognized as an expense each year. The reason is that both years—not just the first year—benefit from the insurance payment. The unexpensed portion of the insurance payment is carried on the balance sheet as an asset called *prepaid insurance*. You should be familiar with this type of *accrual* from your financial accounting coursework.

The *matching principle* is based on the accrual concept and states that *costs incurred to generate a particular revenue should be recognized as expenses in the same period that the revenue is recognized*. This means that if a cost is incurred to acquire or make something that will eventually be sold, then the cost should be recognized as an expense only when the sale takes place—that is, when the benefit occurs. Such costs are called *product costs*.

Product Costs

For financial accounting purposes, **product costs** include all the costs that are involved in acquiring or making a product. In the case of manufactured goods, these costs consist of direct materials, direct labor, and manufacturing overhead. Product costs are viewed as "attaching" to units of product as the goods are purchased or manufactured, and they remain attached as the goods go into inventory awaiting sale. So initially, product costs are assigned to an inventory account on the balance sheet. When the goods are sold, the costs are released from inventory as expenses (typically called *cost of goods sold*) and matched against sales revenue. Since product costs are initially assigned to inventories, they are also known as **inventoriable costs.**

We want to emphasize that product costs are not necessarily treated as expenses in the period in which they are incurred. Rather, as explained above, they are treated as expenses in the period in which the related products *are sold*. This means that a product cost such as direct materials or direct labor might be incurred during one period but not treated as an expense until a following period when the completed product is sold.

Period Costs

Period costs are all the costs that are not included in product costs. These costs are expensed on the income statement in the period in which they are incurred, using the usual rules of accrual accounting you have already learned in financial accounting. Period costs are not included as part of the cost of either purchased or manufactured goods. Sales commissions and office rent are good examples of period costs. Neither commissions nor office rent are included as part of the cost of purchased or manufactured goods. Rather, both items are treated as expenses on the income statement in the period in which they are incurred. Thus, they are said to be period costs.

As suggested above, *all selling and administrative expenses are considered to be period costs*. Therefore, advertising, executive salaries, sales commissions, public relations, and other nonmanufacturing costs discussed earlier would all be period costs. They will appear on the income statement as expenses in the period in which they are incurred.

Exhibit 1–3 contains a summary of the cost terms that we have introduced so far.

EXHIBIT 1–3 Summary of Cost Terms

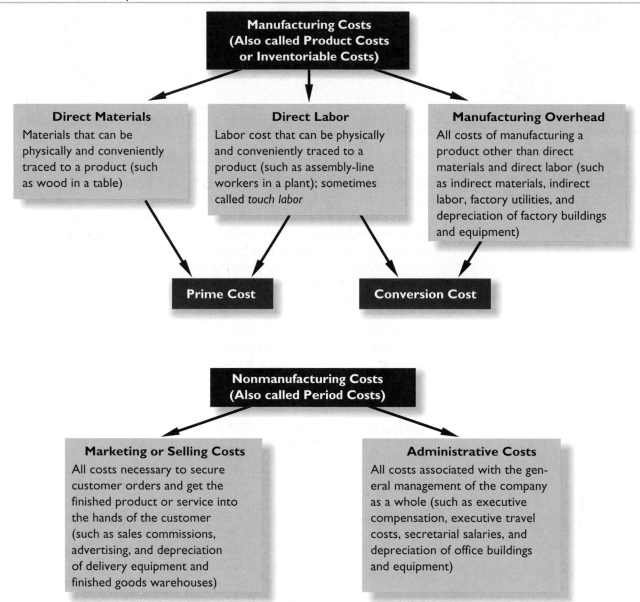

Bloated Sales and Administrative Expenses

IN BUSINESS

Selling and administrative expenses tend to creep up during economic booms—creating problems when the economy falls into recession. Ron Nicol, a partner at the Boston Consulting Group, found that selling and administrative expenses at America's 1,000 largest companies grew at an average rate of 1.7% per year between 1985 and 1996 and then exploded to an average of 10% per year between 1997 and 2000. If companies had maintained their historical balance between sales revenues on the one hand and selling and administrative expenses on the other hand, Mr. Nicol calculates that selling and administrative expenses would have been about $500 million lower in the year 2000 for the average company on his list. For example, a review of selling and administrative costs at International Paper in 2001 found layers of unproductive costs such as newsletters that no one reads.

Source: Jon E. Hilsenrath, "The Outlook: Corporate Dieting Is Far from Over," *The Wall Street Journal,* July 9, 2001, p. A1.

Raw Materials

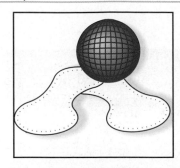

Work in Process

Finished Goods

COST CLASSIFICATIONS ON FINANCIAL STATEMENTS

In your prior accounting training, you learned that firms prepare periodic financial reports for creditors, stockholders, and others to show the financial condition of the firm and the firm's earnings performance over some specified interval. The reports you studied were probably those of merchandising companies, such as retail stores, which simply purchase goods from suppliers for resale to customers.

The financial statements prepared by a *manufacturing* company are more complex than the statements prepared by a merchandising company because a manufacturing company must produce its goods as well as market them. The production process involves many costs that do not exist in a merchandising company, and somehow these costs must be accounted for on the manufacturing company's financial statements. In this section, we focus our attention on how this accounting is carried out in the balance sheet and income statement.

The Balance Sheet

The balance sheet, or statement of financial position, of a manufacturing company is similar to that of a merchandising company. However, the inventory accounts differ between the two types of companies. A merchandising company has only one class of inventory—goods purchased from suppliers that are awaiting resale to customers. In contrast, manufacturing companies have three classes of inventories—*raw materials*, *work in process*, and *finished goods*. Raw materials, as we've noted, are the materials that are used to make a product. **Work in process** consists of units of product that are only partially complete and will require further work before they are ready for sale to a customer. **Finished goods** consist of units of product that have been completed but have not yet been sold to customers. The overall inventory figure is usually broken down into these three classes of inventories in a footnote to the financial statements.

We will use two companies—Graham Manufacturing and Reston Bookstore—to illustrate the concepts discussed in this section. Graham Manufacturing is located in Portsmouth, New Hampshire, and makes precision brass fittings for yachts. Reston Bookstore is a small bookstore in Reston, Virginia, specializing in books about the Civil War.

The footnotes to Graham Manufacturing's Annual Report reveal the following information concerning its inventories:

GRAHAM MANUFACTURING CORPORATION Inventory Accounts	Beginning Balance	Ending Balance
Raw materials	$ 60,000	$ 50,000
Work in process	90,000	60,000
Finished goods	125,000	175,000
Total inventory accounts	$275,000	$285,000

Graham Manufacturing's raw materials inventory consists largely of brass rods and brass blocks. The work in process inventory consists of partially completed brass fittings. The finished goods inventory consists of brass fittings that are ready to be sold to customers.

In contrast, the inventory account at Reston Bookstore consists entirely of the costs of books the company has purchased from publishers for resale to the public. In merchandising companies like Reston, these inventories may be called *merchandise inventory*. The beginning and ending balances in this account appear as follows:

RESTON BOOKSTORE Inventory Accounts		
	Beginning Balance	**Ending Balance**
Merchandise inventory...............	$100,000	$150,000

Concept 1–2

The Income Statement

Exhibit 1–4 compares the income statements of Reston Bookstore and Graham Manufacturing. For purposes of illustration, these statements contain more detail about cost of goods sold than you will generally find in published financial statements.

At first glance, the income statements of merchandising and manufacturing firms like Reston Bookstore and Graham Manufacturing are very similar. The only apparent difference is in the labels of some of the entries in the computation of the cost of goods sold. In

LEARNING OBJECTIVE 3

Prepare an income statement including calculation of the cost of goods sold.

EXHIBIT 1–4   Comparative Income Statements: Merchandising and Manufacturing Companies

	MERCHANDISING COMPANY Reston Bookstore		
	Sales		$1,000,000
The cost of merchandise inventory purchased from outside suppliers during the period.	Cost of goods sold:		
	Beginning merchandise inventory	$100,000	
	Add: Purchases	650,000	
	Goods available for sale	750,000	
	Deduct: Ending merchandise inventory	150,000	600,000
	Gross margin		400,000
	Less operating expenses:		
	Selling expense...............................	100,000	
	Administrative expense	200,000	300,000
	Net operating income		$ 100,000

	MANUFACTURING COMPANY Graham Manufacturing		
	Sales		$1,500,000
The manufacturing costs associated with the goods that were finished during the period. (See Exhibit 1–6 for details.)	Cost of goods sold:		
	Beginning finished goods inventory	$125,000	
	Add: Cost of goods manufactured	850,000	
	Goods available for sale	975,000	
	Deduct: Ending finished goods inventory.........	175,000	800,000
	Gross margin		700,000
	Less operating expenses:		
	Selling expense...............................	250,000	
	Administrative expense	300,000	550,000
	Net operating income		$ 150,000

the exhibit, the computation of cost of goods sold relies on the following basic equation for inventory accounts:

> ### BASIC EQUATION FOR INVENTORY ACCOUNTS
>
> $$\begin{array}{c} \text{Beginning} \\ \text{balance} \end{array} + \begin{array}{c} \text{Additions} \\ \text{to inventory} \end{array} = \begin{array}{c} \text{Ending} \\ \text{balance} \end{array} + \begin{array}{c} \text{Withdrawals} \\ \text{from inventory} \end{array}$$

The logic underlying this equation, which applies to any inventory account, is illustrated in Exhibit 1–5. At the beginning of the period, the inventory contains some beginning balance. During the period, additions are made to the inventory through purchases or other means. The sum of the beginning balance and the additions to the account is the total amount of inventory available. During the period, withdrawals are made from inventory. Whatever is left at the end of the period after these withdrawals is the ending balance.

These concepts are applied to determine the cost of goods sold for a merchandising company like Reston Bookstore as follows:

> ### COST OF GOODS SOLD IN A MERCHANDISING COMPANY
>
> $$\begin{array}{c} \text{Beginning} \\ \text{merchandise} \\ \text{inventory} \end{array} + \text{Purchases} = \begin{array}{c} \text{Ending} \\ \text{merchandise} \\ \text{inventory} \end{array} + \begin{array}{c} \text{Cost of} \\ \text{goods sold} \end{array}$$
>
> or
>
> $$\begin{array}{c} \text{Cost of} \\ \text{goods sold} \end{array} = \begin{array}{c} \text{Beginning} \\ \text{merchandise} \\ \text{inventory} \end{array} + \text{Purchases} - \begin{array}{c} \text{Ending} \\ \text{merchandise} \\ \text{inventory} \end{array}$$

EXHIBIT 1–5

Inventory Flows

Beginning balance

Beginning balance
+ Additions
= Total available

Total available
− Withdrawals
= Ending balance

To determine the cost of goods sold in a merchandising company like Reston Bookstore, we only need to know the beginning and ending balances in the Merchandise Inventory account and the purchases. Total purchases can be easily determined in a merchandising company by simply adding together all purchases from suppliers.

The cost of goods sold for a manufacturing company like Graham Manufacturing is determined as follows:

COST OF GOODS SOLD IN A MANUFACTURING COMPANY

$$\text{Beginning finished goods inventory} + \text{Cost of goods manufactured} = \text{Ending finished goods inventory} + \text{Cost of goods sold}$$

or

$$\text{Cost of goods sold} = \text{Beginning finished goods inventory} + \text{Cost of goods manufactured} - \text{Ending finished goods inventory}$$

To determine the cost of goods sold in a manufacturing company like Graham Manufacturing, we need to know the *cost of goods manufactured* and the beginning and ending balances in the Finished Goods inventory account. The **cost of goods manufactured** consists of the manufacturing costs associated with goods that were *finished* during the period. The cost of goods manufactured figure for Graham Manufacturing is derived in Exhibit 1–6, which contains a *schedule of cost of goods manufactured.*

Schedule of Cost of Goods Manufactured

At first glance, the **schedule of cost of goods manufactured** in Exhibit 1–6 appears complex and perhaps even intimidating. However, it is all quite logical. The schedule of cost of goods manufactured contains the three elements of product costs that we discussed earlier—direct materials, direct labor, and manufacturing overhead.

LEARNING OBJECTIVE 4

Prepare a schedule of cost of goods manufactured.

EXHIBIT 1–6   Schedule of Cost of Goods Manufactured

	Direct materials:		
	Beginning raw materials inventory*	$ 60,000	
	Add: Purchases of raw materials.................	400,000	
Direct Materials	Raw materials available for use.................	460,000	
	Deduct: Ending raw materials inventory...........	50,000	
	Raw materials used in production		$410,000
Direct Labor	Direct labor.....................................		60,000
	Manufacturing overhead:		
	Insurance, factory	6,000	
	Indirect labor.................................	100,000	
	Machine rental................................	50,000	
Manufacturing Overhead	Utilities, factory...............................	75,000	
	Supplies	21,000	
	Depreciation, factory...........................	90,000	
	Property taxes, factory	8,000	
	Total manufacturing overhead costs................		350,000
	Total manufacturing costs:		820,000
	Add: Beginning work in process inventory...........		90,000
Cost of Goods Manufactured			910,000
	Deduct: Ending work in process inventory..........		60,000
	Cost of goods manufactured (taken to Exhibit 1–4) ...		$850,000

*We assume in this example that the Raw Materials inventory account contains only direct materials and that indirect materials are carried in a separate Supplies account. Using a Supplies account for indirect materials is a common practice among companies. In Chapter 2, we discuss the procedure to be followed if *both* direct and indirect materials are carried in a single account.

The direct materials cost is not simply the cost of materials purchased during the period—rather it is the cost of materials *used* during the period. The purchases of raw materials are added to the beginning balance to determine the cost of the materials available for use. The ending materials inventory is deducted from this amount to arrive at the cost of the materials used in production. The sum of the three cost elements—materials, direct labor, and manufacturing overhead—is the total manufacturing cost. This is *not* the same thing, however, as the cost of goods manufactured for the period. The subtle distinction between the total manufacturing cost and the cost of goods manufactured is very easy to miss. Some of the materials, direct labor, and manufacturing overhead costs incurred during the period relate to goods that are not yet completed. As stated above, the *cost of goods manufactured* consists of the manufacturing costs associated with the goods that were *finished* during the period. Consequently, adjustments need to be made to the total manufacturing cost of the period for the partially completed goods that were in process at the beginning and at the end of the period. The costs that relate to goods that are not yet completed are shown in the work in process inventory figures at the bottom of the schedule. Note that the beginning work in process inventory must be added to the manufacturing costs of the period, and the ending work in process inventory must be deducted, to arrive at the cost of goods manufactured.

PRODUCT COSTS—A CLOSER LOOK

Earlier in the chapter, we defined product costs as those costs that are incurred to either purchase or manufacture goods. For manufactured goods, these costs consist of direct materials, direct labor, and manufacturing overhead. It will be helpful at this point to look briefly at the flow of costs in a manufacturing company. This will help us understand how product costs move through the various accounts and how they affect the balance sheet and the income statement.

Exhibit 1–7 illustrates the flow of costs in a manufacturing company. Raw materials purchases are recorded in the Raw Materials inventory account. When raw materials are used in production, their costs are transferred to the Work in Process inventory account as direct materials. Notice that direct labor cost and manufacturing overhead cost are added directly to Work in Process. Work in Process can be viewed most simply as an assembly line where workers are stationed and where products slowly take shape as they move from one end of the assembly line to the other. The direct materials, direct labor, and manufacturing overhead costs added to Work in Process in Exhibit 1–7 are the costs needed to complete these products as they move along this assembly line.

Notice from the exhibit that as goods are completed, their costs are transferred from Work in Process to Finished Goods. Here the goods await sale to customers. As goods are sold, their costs are transferred from Finished Goods to Cost of Goods Sold. At this point the various material, labor, and overhead costs required to make the product are finally treated as expenses. Until that point, these costs are in inventory accounts on the balance sheet.

Inventoriable Costs

As stated earlier, product costs are often called inventoriable costs. The reason is that these costs go directly into inventory accounts as they are incurred (first into Work in Process and then into Finished Goods), rather than going into expense accounts. Thus, they are termed *inventoriable costs. This is a key concept since such costs can end up on the balance sheet as assets if goods are only partially completed or are unsold at the end of a period.* To illustrate this point, refer again to Exhibit 1–7. At the end of the period, the materials, labor, and overhead costs that are associated with the units in the Work in Process and Finished Goods inventory accounts will appear on the balance sheet as part of the company's assets. As explained earlier, these costs will not become expenses until later when the goods are completed and sold.

EXHIBIT 1–7   Cost Flows and Classifications in a Manufacturing Company

Selling and administrative expenses are not involved in making a product. For this reason, they are not treated as product costs but rather as period costs that are expensed as they are incurred as shown in Exhibit 1–7.

Benetton and the Value Chain

United Colors of Benetton, an Italian apparel company headquartered in Ponzano, is unusual in that it is involved in all activities in the "value chain" from clothing design through manufacturing, distribution, and ultimate sale to customers in Benetton retail outlets. Most companies are involved in only one or two of these activities. Looking at this company allows us to see how costs are distributed across the entire value chain. A recent income statement from the company contained the following data:

	Millions of Euros	Percent of Revenues
Revenues.	2,125	100.0%
Cost of sales.	1,199	56.4
Selling, general, and administrative expenses:		
Payroll and related cost	126	5.9
Distribution and transport.	45	2.1
Sales commissions	102	4.8
Advertising and promotion	125	5.9
Depreciation and amortization	62	2.9
Other expenses	141	6.6
Total selling, general, and administrative expenses.	601	28.3%

Even though this company spends large sums on advertising and runs its own shops, the cost of sales is still quite high in relation to the net sales—56.4% of net sales. And despite the company's lavish advertising campaigns, advertising and promotion costs amounted to only 5.9% of net sales. (Note: One U.S. dollar was worth about 1.1218 euros at the time of this financial report.)

EXHIBIT I–8   An Example of Cost Flows in a Manufacturing Company

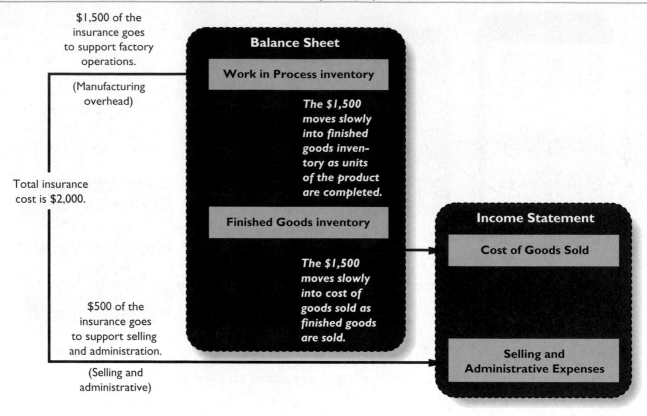

An Example of Cost Flows

To provide an example of cost flows in a manufacturing company, assume that a company's annual insurance cost is $2,000. Three-fourths of this amount ($1,500) applies to factory operations, and one-fourth ($500) applies to selling and administrative activities. Therefore, $1,500 of the $2,000 insurance cost would be a product (inventoriable) cost and would be added to the cost of the goods produced during the year. This concept is illustrated in Exhibit 1–8, where $1,500 of insurance cost is added into Work in Process. As shown in the exhibit, this portion of the year's insurance cost will not become an expense until the goods that are produced during the year are sold—which may not happen until the following year or even later. Until the goods are sold, the $1,500 will remain as part of inventory (either as part of Work in Process or as part of Finished Goods), along with the other costs of producing the goods.

By contrast, the $500 of insurance cost that applies to the company's selling and administrative activities will be expensed immediately.

Thus far, we have been mainly concerned with classifications of manufacturing costs for the purpose of determining inventory valuations on the balance sheet and cost of goods sold on the income statement of external financial reports. However, costs are used for many other purposes, and each purpose requires a different classification of costs. We will consider several different purposes for cost classifications in the remaining sections of this chapter. These purposes and the corresponding cost classifications are summarized in Exhibit 1–9. To help keep the big picture in mind, we suggest that you refer back to this exhibit frequently as you progress through the rest of this chapter.

EXHIBIT 1–9

Summary of Cost Classifications

Purpose of Cost Classification	Cost Classifications

Preparing external financial statements	• Product costs (inventoriable)
	  • Direct materials
	  • Direct labor
	  • Manufacturing overhead
	• Period costs (expensed)
	  • Nonmanufacturing costs
	    • Marketing or selling costs
	    • Administrative costs

Predicting cost behavior in response to changes in activity	• Variable cost (proportional to activity) • Fixed cost (constant in total)
Assigning costs to cost objects such as departments or products	• Direct cost (can be easily traced) • Indirect cost (cannot be easily traced; must be allocated)
Making decisions	• Differential cost (differs between alternatives) • Sunk cost (past cost not affected by a decision) • Opportunity cost (forgone benefit)
Cost of quality (Appendix 1A)	• Prevention costs • Appraisal costs • Internal failure costs • External failure costs

Product or Period Cost?—Not Just an Academic Distinction

IN BUSINESS

Whether a cost is considered a product or period cost can have an important impact on a company's financial statements and can create conflicts inside an organization. Consider the following excerpts from a conversation recorded on the Institute of Management Accountants' Ethics Hot Line:

Caller: My problem basically is that my boss, the division general manager, wants me to put costs into inventory that I know should be expensed.

Counselor: Have you expressed your doubts to your boss?

Caller: Yes, but he is basically a salesman and claims he knows nothing about GAAP. He just wants the "numbers" to back up the good news he keeps telling corporate [headquarters], which is what corporate demands. Also, he asks if I am ready to make the entries that I think are improper. It seems he wants to make it look like my idea all along. Our company had legal problems a few years ago with some government contracts, and it was the lower level people who were "hung out to dry" rather than the higher-ups who were really at fault.

Counselor: What does he say when you tell him these matters need resolution?

Caller: He just says we need a meeting, but the meetings never solve anything.

Counselor: Does your company have an ethics hot line?

Caller: Yes, but my boss would view use of the hot line as snitching or even whistle-blowing.

Counselor: If you might face reprisals for using the hot line, perhaps you should evaluate whether or not you really want to work for a company whose ethical climate is one you are uncomfortable in.

Caller: I have already asked . . . for a transfer back to the corporate office.

Source: Curtis C. Verschoor, "Using a Hot Line Isn't Whistle-Blowing," *Strategic Finance*, April 1999, pp. 27–28. Used with permission from *Strategic Finance* and the Institute of Management Accountants, Montvale, N.J., www.imanet.org.

1. Which of the following statements is false? (You may select more than one answer.)
   a. Conversion costs include direct material and direct labor.
   b. Indirect materials are included as part of manufacturing overhead.
   c. Prime costs are included as part of manufacturing overhead.
   d. Marketing/selling costs are considered period costs.
2. If the cost of goods sold is $100,000 and the ending finished goods inventory is $30,000 higher than the beginning finished goods inventory, what must be the amount of the cost of goods manufactured?
   a. $30,000
   b. $100,000
   c. $130,000
   d. $70,000

COST CLASSIFICATIONS FOR PREDICTING COST BEHAVIOR

LEARNING OBJECTIVE 5

Define and give examples of variable costs and fixed costs.

Quite frequently, it is necessary to predict how a certain cost will behave in response to a change in activity. For example, a manager at AT&T may want to estimate the impact a 5% increase in long-distance calls would have on the company's total electric bill or on the total wages the company pays its long-distance operators. **Cost behavior** is the way a cost will react or respond to changes in the level of business activity. As the activity level rises and falls, a particular cost may rise and fall as well—or it may remain constant. For planning purposes, a manager must be able to anticipate which of these will happen; and if a cost can be expected to change, the manager must be able to estimate how much it will change. To help make such distinctions, costs are often categorized as variable or fixed.

Variable Cost

A **variable cost** is a cost that varies, in total, in direct proportion to changes in the level of activity. The activity can be expressed in many ways, such as units produced, units sold, miles driven, beds occupied, lines of print, hours worked, and so forth. Direct materials is a good example of a variable cost. The cost of direct materials used during a period will vary, in total, in direct proportion to the number of units that are produced. As an example, consider the Saturn Division of GM. Each auto requires one battery. As the output of autos increases and decreases, the number of batteries used will increase and decrease proportionately. If auto production goes up 10%, then the number of batteries used will also go up 10%. The concept of a variable cost is shown in graphic form in Exhibit 1–10.

It is important to note that when we speak of a cost as being variable, we mean the *total* cost rises and falls as the activity level rises and falls. This idea is presented below, assuming that a Saturn's battery costs $24:

Number of Autos Produced	Cost per Battery	Total Variable Cost— Batteries
1	$24	$24
500	$24	$12,000
1,000	$24	$24,000

One interesting aspect of variable cost behavior is that a variable cost is constant if expressed on a *per unit* basis. Observe from the tabulation above that the per unit cost of

EXHIBIT 1-10   Variable and Fixed Cost Behavior

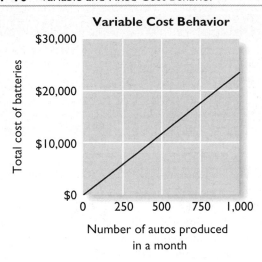

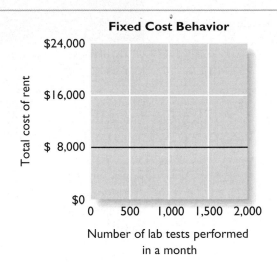

batteries remains constant at $24 even though the total cost of the batteries increases and decreases with activity.

There are many examples of costs that are variable with respect to the products and services provided by a company. In a manufacturing company, variable costs include items such as direct materials and some elements of manufacturing overhead such as lubricants, shipping costs, and sales commissions. For the present we will also assume that direct labor is a variable cost, although as we shall see in a later chapter, direct labor may act more like a fixed cost in many situations. In a merchandising company, variable costs include items such as cost of goods sold, commissions to salespersons, and billing costs. In a hospital, the variable costs of providing health care services to patients would include the costs of the supplies, drugs, meals, and perhaps nursing services.

When we say that a cost is variable, we ordinarily mean that it is variable with respect to the amount of goods or services the organization produces. However, costs can be variable with respect to other things. For example, the wages paid to employees at a Blockbuster Video outlet will depend on the number of hours the store is open and not strictly on the number of videos rented. In this case, we would say that wage costs are variable with respect to the hours of operation. Nevertheless, when we say that a cost is variable, we ordinarily mean it is variable with respect to the amount of goods and services produced. This could be how many Jeep Cherokees are produced, how many videos are rented, how many patients are treated, and so on.

Fixed Cost

A **fixed cost** is a cost that remains constant, in total, regardless of changes in the level of activity. Unlike variable costs, fixed costs are not affected by changes in activity. Consequently, as the activity level rises and falls, the fixed costs remain constant in total amount unless influenced by some outside force, such as a price change. Rent is a good example of a fixed cost. Suppose the Mayo Clinic rents a machine for $8,000 per month that tests blood samples for the presence of leukemia cells. The $8,000 monthly rental cost will be sustained regardless of the number of tests that may be performed during the month. The concept of a fixed cost is shown in graphic form in Exhibit 1-10.

Very few costs are completely fixed. Most will change if there is a large enough change in activity. For example, suppose that the capacity of the leukemia diagnostic machine at the Mayo Clinic is 2,000 tests per month. If the clinic wishes to perform more than 2,000 tests in a month, it would be necessary to rent an additional machine, which would cause a jump in the fixed costs. When we say a cost is fixed, we mean it is fixed within some *relevant range*. The **relevant range** is the range of activity within which the assumptions about variable and fixed costs are valid. For example, the assumption that the

EXHIBIT 1–11

Summary of Variable and Fixed Cost Behavior

	Behavior of the Cost (within the relevant range)	
Cost	In Total	Per Unit
Variable cost	Total variable cost increases and decreases in proportion to changes in the activity level.	Variable cost remains constant per unit.
Fixed cost	Total fixed cost is not affected by changes in the activity level within the relevant range.	Fixed cost per unit decreases as the activity level rises and increases as the activity level falls.

rent for diagnostic machines is $8,000 per month is valid within the relevant range of 0 to 2,000 tests per month.

Fixed costs can create confusion if they are expressed on a per-unit basis. This is because the average fixed cost per unit increases and decreases *inversely* with changes in activity. In the Mayo Clinic, for example, the average cost per test will fall as the number of tests performed increases. This is because the $8,000 rental cost will be spread over more tests. Conversely, as the number of tests performed in the clinic declines, the average cost per test will rise as the $8,000 rental cost is spread over fewer tests. This concept is illustrated in the table below:

Monthly Rental Cost	Number of Tests Performed	Average Cost per Test
$8,000	10	$800
$8,000	500	$16
$8,000	2,000	$4

Note that if the Mayo Clinic performs only 10 tests each month, the rental cost of the equipment will average $800 per test. But if 2,000 tests are performed each month, the average cost will drop to only $4 per test. More will be said later about the problems created for both the accountant and the manager by this variation in unit costs.

Examples of fixed costs include straight-line depreciation, insurance, property taxes, rent, supervisory salaries, administrative salaries, and advertising.

A summary of both variable and fixed cost behavior is presented in Exhibit 1–11.

The Cost of a Call

On average, the variable cost of physically transporting a telephone call is about 7% of the price a customer pays for the call. It now costs more to bill for the call than to provide it. Then why aren't telephone companies fabulously profitable? In short, they have extremely high fixed costs for equipment, buildings, and personnel. The prices the telephone companies charge to consumers must cover these fixed costs as well as the relatively small variable costs of completing a particular call for a customer.

Source: Scott Woolley, "Meltdown," *Forbes,* July 3, 2000, pp. 70–71.

Financial Analyst

You are a financial analyst for several clients who are interested in making investments in stable companies. You become aware of a privately owned airline that has been in business for 20 years and needs to raise $75 million in new capital. When you call one of your clients, she replies that she avoids investing in airlines because of the high proportion of fixed costs in this industry. How would you reply to this statement?

COST CLASSIFICATIONS FOR ASSIGNING COSTS TO COST OBJECTS

Costs are assigned to objects for a variety of purposes including pricing, profitability studies, and control of spending. A **cost object** is anything for which cost data are desired—including products, product lines, customers, jobs, and organizational subunits. For purposes of assigning costs to cost objects, costs are classified as either *direct* or *indirect.*

Direct Cost

A **direct cost** is a cost that can be easily and conveniently traced to the particular cost object under consideration. The concept of direct cost extends beyond just direct materials and direct labor. For example, if Reebok is assigning costs to its various regional and national sales offices, then the salary of the sales manager in its Tokyo office would be a direct cost of that office.

Indirect Cost

An **indirect cost** is a cost that cannot be easily and conveniently traced to the particular cost object under consideration. For example, a Campbell Soup factory may produce dozens of varieties of canned soups. The factory manager's salary would be an indirect cost of a particular variety such as chicken noodle soup. The reason is that the factory manager's salary is not caused by any one variety of soup but rather is incurred as a consequence of running the entire factory. *To be traced to a cost object such as a particular product, the cost must be caused by the cost object.* The factory manager's salary is called a *common cost* of producing the various products of the factory. A **common cost** is a cost that is incurred to support a number of costing objects but that cannot be traced to them individually. A common cost is a type of indirect cost.

A particular cost may be direct or indirect, depending on the cost object. While the Campbell Soup factory manager's salary is an *indirect* cost of manufacturing chicken noodle soup, it is a *direct* cost of the manufacturing division. In the first case, the cost object is the chicken noodle soup product. In the second case, the cost object is the entire manufacturing division.

COST CLASSIFICATIONS FOR DECISION MAKING

Costs are an important feature of many business decisions. In making decisions, it is essential to have a firm grasp of the concepts *differential cost, opportunity cost,* and *sunk cost.*

Differential Cost and Revenue

Decisions involve choosing between alternatives. In business decisions, each alternative will have certain costs and benefits that must be compared to the costs and benefits of the other available alternatives. A difference in costs between any two alternatives is known as a **differential cost.** A difference in revenues between any two alternatives is known as **differential revenue.**

A differential cost is also known as an **incremental cost,** although technically an incremental cost should refer only to an increase in cost from one alternative to another; decreases in cost should be referred to as *decremental costs.* Differential cost is a broader term, encompassing both cost increases (incremental costs) and cost decreases (decremental costs) between alternatives.

The accountant's differential cost concept can be compared to the economist's marginal cost concept. In speaking of changes in cost and revenue, the economist employs the terms *marginal cost* and *marginal revenue.* The revenue that can be obtained from selling one more unit of product is called marginal revenue, and the cost involved in producing one more unit of product is called marginal cost. The economist's marginal concept is basically the same as the accountant's differential concept applied to a single unit of output.

Differential costs can be either fixed or variable. To illustrate, assume that Nature Way Cosmetics, Inc., is thinking about changing its marketing method from distribution through retailers to distribution by door-to-door direct sale. Present costs and revenues are compared to projected costs and revenues in the following table:

	Retailer Distribution (present)	Direct Sale Distribution (proposed)	Differential Costs and Revenues
Revenues (V)...................	$700,000	$800,000	$100,000
Cost of goods sold (V)............	350,000	400,000	50,000
Advertising (F)	80,000	45,000	(35,000)
Commissions (V)	0	40,000	40,000
Warehouse depreciation (F)	50,000	80,000	30,000
Other expenses (F)	60,000	60,000	0
Total expenses	540,000	625,000	85,000
Net operating income	$160,000	$175,000	$ 15,000

V = Variable; F = Fixed.

According to the above analysis, the differential revenue is $100,000 and the differential costs total $85,000, leaving a positive differential net operating income of $15,000 under the proposed marketing plan.

The decision of whether Nature Way Cosmetics should stay with the present retail distribution or switch to door-to-door direct selling could be made on the basis of the net operating incomes of the two alternatives. As we see in the above analysis, the net operating income under the present distribution method is $160,000, whereas the net operating income under door-to-door direct selling is estimated to be $175,000. Therefore, the door-to-door direct distribution method is preferred, since it would result in $15,000 higher net operating income. Note that we would have arrived at exactly the same conclusion by simply focusing on the differential revenues, differential costs, and differential net operating income, which also show a $15,000 advantage for the direct selling method.

In general, only the differences between alternatives are relevant in decisions. Those items that are the same under all alternatives are not affected by the decision and can be ignored. For example, in the Nature Way Cosmetics example above, the "Other expenses" category, which is $60,000 under both alternatives, can be ignored, since it is not affected by the decision. If it were removed from the calculations, the door-to-door direct selling method would still be preferred by $15,000. This is an extremely important principle in management accounting that we will return to in later chapters.

Opportunity Cost

Opportunity cost is the potential benefit that is given up when one alternative is selected over another. To illustrate this important concept, consider the following examples:

Example 1
Vicki has a part-time job that pays $200 per week while she attends college. She would like to spend a week at the beach during spring break, and her employer has agreed to give her the time off, but without pay. The $200 in lost wages would be an opportunity cost of taking the week off to be at the beach.

Example 2
Suppose that Neiman Marcus is considering investing a large sum of money in land that may be a site for a future store. Rather than invest the funds in land, the company could invest the funds in high-grade securities. If the land is acquired, the

Using Those Empty Seats

Cancer patients who seek specialized or experimental treatments must often travel far from home. Flying on a commercial airline can be an expensive and grueling experience for these patients. Priscilla Blum noted that many corporate jets fly with empty seats and she wondered why these seats couldn't be used for cancer patients. Taking the initiative, she founded Corporate Angel Network (www.corpangelnetwork.org), an organization that arranges free flights on some 1,500 jets from over 500 companies. There are no tax breaks for putting cancer patients in empty corporate jet seats, but filling an empty seat with a cancer patient doesn't involve any significant incremental cost. Since its founding, Corporate Angel Network has provided over 16,000 free flights.

Sources: Scott McCormack, "Waste Not, Want Not," *Forbes,* July 26, 1999, p. 118; Roger McCaffrey, "A True Tale of Angels in the Sky," *The Wall Street Journal,* February 2002, p. A14; and Helen Gibbs, Communication Director, Corporate Angel Network, private communication.

opportunity cost will be the investment income that could have been realized if the securities had been purchased instead.

Example 3

Steve is employed with a company that pays him a salary of $30,000 per year. He is thinking about leaving the company and returning to school. Since returning to school would require that he give up his $30,000 salary, the forgone salary would be an opportunity cost of seeking further education.

Opportunity cost is not usually recorded in the accounts of an organization, but it is a cost that must be explicitly considered in every decision a manager makes. Virtually every alternative has some opportunity cost attached to it. In Example 3 above, for instance, if Steve decides to stay at his job, there is an opportunity cost: it is the greater income that could be realized in future years as a result of returning to school.

Your Decision to Attend Class

When you make the decision to attend class, what are the opportunity costs that are inherent in that decision?

Sunk Cost

A **sunk cost** is a cost *that has already been incurred* and that cannot be changed by any decision made now or in the future. Since sunk costs cannot be changed by any decision, they are not differential costs. Therefore, sunk costs can and should be ignored when making a decision.

To illustrate a sunk cost, assume that a company paid $50,000 several years ago for a special-purpose machine. The machine was used to make a product that is now obsolete and is no longer being sold. Even though in hindsight the purchase of the machine may have been unwise, the $50,000 cost has already been incurred and cannot be undone. And it would be folly to continue making the obsolete product in a misguided attempt to "recover" the original cost of the machine. In short, the $50,000 originally paid for the machine is a sunk cost that should be ignored in decisions.

CONCEPT CHECK

3. Which of the following cost behavior assumptions is false? (You may select more than one answer.)
   a. Variable costs are constant if expressed on a per unit basis.
   b. Total variable costs increase as the level of the activity increases.
   c. The average fixed cost per unit increases as the level of the activity increases.
   d. Total fixed costs decrease as the level of the activity decreases.
4. Which of the following statements is false? (You may select more than one answer.)
   a. A common cost is one type of direct cost.
   b. A sunk cost is usually a differential cost.
   c. Opportunity costs are not usually recorded in the accounts of an organization.
   d. A particular cost may be direct or indirect depending on the cost object.

IN BUSINESS

What Number Did You Have in Mind?

Caterpillar has long been at the forefront of management accounting practice. When asked by a manager for the cost of something, accountants at Caterpillar have been trained to ask "What are you going to use the cost for?" One management accountant at Caterpillar explains: "We want to make sure the information is formatted and the right elements are included. Do you need a variable cost, do you need a fully burdened cost, do you need overhead applied, are you just talking about discretionary cost? The cost that they really need depends on the decision they are making."

Source: Gary Siegel, "Practice Analysis: Adding Value," *Strategic Finance,* November 2000, pp. 89–90.

SUMMARY

LO1   Identify and give examples of each of the three basic manufacturing cost categories.
Manufacturing costs consist of two categories of costs that can be conveniently and directly traced to units of product—direct materials and direct labor—and one category that cannot be conveniently traced to units of product—manufacturing overhead.

LO2   Distinguish between product costs and period costs and give examples of each.
For purposes of valuing inventories and determining expenses for the balance sheet and income statement, costs are classified as either product costs or period costs. Product costs are assigned to inventories and are considered assets until the products are sold. A product cost becomes an expense—cost of goods sold—only when the product is sold. In contrast, period costs are taken directly to the income statement as expenses in the period in which they are incurred.

In a merchandising company, product cost is whatever the company paid for its merchandise. For external financial reports in a manufacturing company, product costs consist of all manufacturing costs. In both kinds of companies, selling and administrative costs are considered to be period costs and are expensed as incurred.

LO3   Prepare an income statement including calculation of the cost of goods sold.
See Exhibit 1–4 for examples of income statements for both a merchandising and a manufacturing company. In general, net operating income is computed by deducting the cost of goods sold and operating expenses from sales. Cost of goods sold is calculated by adding purchases to the beginning merchandise or finished goods inventory and then deducting the ending merchandise or finished goods inventory.

LO4 Prepare a schedule of cost of goods manufactured.
See Exhibit 1–6 for an example of a schedule of cost of goods manufactured. In general, the cost of goods manufactured is the sum of direct materials, direct labor, and manufacturing overhead incurred during the period.

LO5 Define and give examples of variable costs and fixed costs.
For purposes of predicting cost behavior—how costs will react to changes in activity—costs are commonly categorized as variable or fixed. Variable costs, in total, are strictly proportional to activity. Thus, the variable cost per unit is constant. Fixed costs, in total, remain at the same level for changes in activity within the relevant range. Thus, the average fixed cost per unit decreases as the number of units increases.

LO6 Define and give examples of direct and indirect costs.
A direct cost is a cost that can be easily and conveniently traced to a costing object. Direct materials is a direct cost of making a product. An indirect cost is a cost that cannot be easily and conveniently traced to a cost object. The salary of the administrator of a hospital is an indirect cost of serving a particular patient.

LO7 Define and give examples of cost classifications used in making decisions: differential costs, opportunity costs, and sunk costs.
The concepts of differential cost and revenue, opportunity cost, and sunk cost are vitally important for purposes of making decisions. Differential costs and revenues are the cost and revenue items that differ between alternatives. Opportunity cost is the benefit that is forgone when one alternative is selected over another. Sunk cost is a cost that occurred in the past and cannot be altered. Differential costs and opportunity costs should be carefully considered in decisions. Sunk costs are always irrelevant in decisions and should be ignored.

The various cost classifications discussed in this chapter are different ways of looking at costs. A particular cost, such as the cost of cheese in a taco served at Taco Bell, can be a manufacturing cost, a product cost, a variable cost, a direct cost, and a differential cost—all at the same time. Taco Bell can be considered to be a manufacturer of fast food. The cost of the cheese in a taco would be considered a manufacturing cost and, as such, it would be a product cost as well. In addition, the cost of cheese would be considered variable with respect to the number of tacos served and would be a direct cost of serving tacos. Finally, the cost of the cheese in a taco would be considered a differential cost of the taco.

GUIDANCE ANSWERS TO *DECISION MAKER* AND *YOU DECIDE*

Financial Analyst (p. 46)
Fixed and *variable* are terms used to describe cost behavior or how a given cost will react or respond to changes in the level of business activity. A fixed cost is a cost that remains constant, in total, regardless of changes in the level of activity. However, on a per unit basis, a fixed cost varies inversely with changes in activity. The cost structures of a number of industries lean toward fixed costs because of the nature of their operations. Obviously, the cost of airplanes would be fixed, and within some relevant range, such costs would not change if the number of passengers flown changed. This would also be true in other industries, such as trucking and rail transportation. You might suggest that it would be worthwhile to research the prospects for growth in this industry and for this company. If a downturn in business is not anticipated, a cost structure weighted toward fixed costs should not be used as the primary reason for turning down the investment opportunity. On the other hand, if a period of decline is anticipated, your client's initial impression might be on target. See Chapter 6 for further discussion of the impact of a company's cost structure on its profits.

Your Decision to Attend Class (p. 49)
Every alternative has some opportunity cost attached to it. If you brainstormed a bit, you probably came up with a few opportunity costs that accompany your choice to attend class. If you had trouble answering the question, think about what you could be doing instead of attending class.

- You could have been working at a part-time job; you could quantify that cost by multiplying your pay rate by the time you spend in class.
- You could have spent the time studying for another class; the opportunity cost could be measured by the improvement in the grade that would result from spending more time on that class.
- You could have slept in or taken a nap; depending on your level of sleep deprivation, this opportunity cost might be priceless.

GUIDANCE ANSWERS TO CONCEPT CHECKS

1. **Choices a and c.** Conversion costs include direct labor and manufacturing overhead. Since prime costs include direct materials and direct labor, these costs are not part of manufacturing overhead.
2. **Choice c.** The cost of goods manufactured must be sufficient to cover the cost of goods sold of $100,000 plus the increase in the inventory account of $30,000.
3. **Choices c and d.** The average fixed cost per unit decreases, rather than increases, as the level of the activity increases. Total fixed costs do not change as the level of the activity decreases (within the relevant range).
4. **Choices a and b.** A common cost is one type of indirect cost, rather than direct cost. A sunk cost is not a differential cost. Sunk costs are irrelevant to decision making.

REVIEW PROBLEM 1: COST TERMS

Many new cost terms have been introduced in this chapter. It will take you some time to learn what each term means and how to properly classify costs in an organization. Consider the following example: Porter Company manufactures furniture, including tables. Selected costs are given below:

1. The tables are made of wood that costs $100 per table.
2. The tables are assembled by workers, at a wage cost of $40 per table.
3. Workers assembling the tables are supervised by a factory supervisor who is paid $38,000 per year.
4. Electrical costs are $2 per machine-hour. Four machine-hours are required to produce a table.
5. The depreciation on the machines used to make the tables totals $10,000 per year. The machines have no resale value and do not wear out through use.
6. The salary of the president of Porter Company is $100,000 per year.
7. Porter Company spends $250,000 per year to advertise its products.
8. Salespersons are paid a commission of $30 for each table sold.
9. Instead of producing the tables, Porter Company could rent its factory space for $50,000 per year.

Required:

Classify these costs according to various cost terms used in the chapter. *Carefully study the classification of each cost.* If you don't understand why a particular cost is classified the way it is, reread the section of the chapter discussing the particular cost term. The terms *variable cost* and *fixed cost* refer to how costs behave with respect to the number of tables produced in a year.

Solution to Review Problem 1

	Variable Cost	Fixed Cost	Period (selling and administrative) Cost	Direct Materials	Direct Labor	Manufacturing Overhead	Sunk Cost	Opportunity Cost
1. Wood used in a table ($100 per table)	X			X				
2. Labor cost to assemble a table ($40 per table)	X				X			
3. Salary of the factory supervisor ($38,000 per year)		X				X		
4. Cost of electricity to produce tables ($2 per machine-hour)	X					X		

(continued)

(concluded)	Variable Cost	Fixed Cost	Period (selling and adminis-trative) Cost	Direct Materials	Direct Labor	Manufacturing Overhead	Sunk Cost	Oppor-tunity Cost
				Product Cost				
5. Depreciation of machines used to produce tables ($10,000 per year)........		X				X	X*	
6. Salary of the company president ($100,000 per year)...............		X	X					
7. Advertising expense ($250,000 per year).......		X	X					
8. Commissions paid to salespersons ($30 per table sold).............	X		X					
9. Rental income forgone on factory space ($50,000 per year)........								X†

*This is a sunk cost, since the outlay for the equipment was made in a previous period.
†This is an opportunity cost, since it represents the potential benefit that is lost or sacrificed as a result of using the factory space to produce tables. Opportunity cost is a special category of cost that is not ordinarily recorded in an organization's accounting books. To avoid possible confusion with other costs, we will not attempt to classify this cost in any other way except as an opportunity cost.

REVIEW PROBLEM 2: SCHEDULE OF COST OF GOODS MANUFACTURED AND INCOME STATEMENT

The following information has been taken from the accounting records of Klear-Seal Company for last year:

Selling expenses	$140,000
Raw materials inventory, January 1	$90,000
Raw materials inventory, December 31	$60,000
Utilities, factory	$36,000
Direct labor cost	$150,000
Depreciation, factory	$162,000
Purchases of raw materials	$750,000
Sales	$2,500,000
Insurance, factory	$40,000
Supplies, factory	$15,000
Administrative expenses	$270,000
Indirect labor	$300,000
Maintenance, factory	$87,000
Work in process inventory, January 1	$180,000
Work in process inventory, December 31	$100,000
Finished goods inventory, January 1	$260,000
Finished goods inventory, December 31	$210,000

Management wants these data organized in a better format so that financial statements can be prepared for the year.

Required:
1. Prepare a schedule of cost of goods manufactured as in Exhibit 1–6.
2. Compute the cost of goods sold.
3. Using data as needed from (1) and (2) above, prepare an income statement.

Solution to Review Problem 2

1.

KLEAR-SEAL COMPANY Schedule of Cost of Goods Manufactured For the Year Ended December 31		
Direct materials:		
Raw materials inventory, January 1	$ 90,000	
Add: Purchases of raw materials	750,000	
Raw materials available for use	840,000	
Deduct: Raw materials inventory, December 31	60,000	
Raw materials used in production		$ 780,000
Direct labor		150,000
Manufacturing overhead:		
Utilities, factory	36,000	
Depreciation, factory	162,000	
Insurance, factory	40,000	
Supplies, factory	15,000	
Indirect labor	300,000	
Maintenance, factory	87,000	
Total manufacturing overhead costs		640,000
Total manufacturing costs		1,570,000
Add: Work in process inventory, January 1		180,000
		1,750,000
Deduct: Work in process inventory, December 31		100,000
Cost of goods manufactured		$1,650,000

2. The cost of goods sold would be computed as follows:

Finished goods inventory, January 1	$ 260,000
Add: Cost of goods manufactured	1,650,000
Goods available for sale	1,910,000
Deduct: Finished goods inventory, December 31.	210,000
Cost of goods sold	$1,700,000

3.

KLEAR-SEAL COMPANY Income Statement For the Year Ended December 31		
Sales.		$2,500,000
Less cost of goods sold (above)		1,700,000
Gross margin.		800,000
Less selling and administrative expenses:		
Selling expenses.	$140,000	
Administrative expenses.	270,000	
Total selling and administrative expenses.		410,000
Net operating income.		$ 390,000

GLOSSARY

Administrative costs   All executive, organizational, and clerical costs associated with the general management of an organization rather than with manufacturing, marketing, or selling. (p. 33)

Budget   A detailed plan for the future, usually expressed in formal quantitative terms. (p. 27)

Common cost   A cost that is incurred to support a number of costing objects but cannot be traced to them individually. For example, the wage cost of the pilot of a 747 airliner is a common cost of all of the passengers on the aircraft. Without the pilot, there would be no flight and no passengers. But no part of the pilot's wage is caused by any one passenger taking the flight. (p. 47)

Control   The process of instituting procedures and then obtaining feedback to ensure that all parts of the organization are functioning effectively and moving toward overall company goals. (p. 27)

Controlling   Ensuring that the plan is actually carried out and is appropriately modified as circumstances change. (p. 26)

Conversion cost   Direct labor cost plus manufacturing overhead cost. (p. 33)

Cost behavior   The way in which a cost reacts or responds to changes in the level of activity. (p. 44)

Cost object   Anything for which cost data are desired. Examples of possible cost objects are products, product lines, customers, jobs, and organizational subunits such as departments or divisions of a company. (p. 47)

Cost of goods manufactured   The manufacturing costs associated with the goods that were finished during the period. (p. 39)

Differential cost   A difference in cost between any two alternatives. Also see *Incremental cost*. (p. 47)

Differential revenue   The difference in revenue between any two alternatives. (p. 47)

Direct cost   A cost that can be easily and conveniently traced to a specified cost object. (p. 47)

Direct labor   Those factory labor costs that can be easily traced to individual units of product. Also called *touch labor*. (p. 32)

Direct materials   Those materials that become an integral part of a finished product and can be conveniently traced to it. (p. 32)

Directing and motivating   Mobilizing people to carry out plans and run routine operations. (p. 26)

Feedback   Accounting and other reports that help managers monitor performance and focus on problems and/or opportunities that might otherwise go unnoticed. (p. 27)

Financial accounting   The phase of accounting concerned with providing information to stockholders, creditors, and others outside the organization. (p. 26)

Finished goods   Units of product that have been completed but have not yet been sold to customers. (p. 36)

Fixed cost   A cost that remains constant, in total, regardless of changes in the level of activity within the relevant range. If a fixed cost is expressed on a per unit basis, it varies inversely with the level of activity. (p. 45)

Incremental cost   An increase in cost between two alternatives. Also see *Differential cost*. (p. 47)

Indirect cost   A cost that cannot be easily and conveniently traced to a specified cost object. (p. 47)

Indirect labor   The labor costs of janitors, supervisors, materials handlers, and other factory workers that cannot be conveniently traced directly to particular products. (p. 32)

Indirect materials   Small items of material such as glue and nails. These items may become an integral part of a finished product but are traceable to the product only at great cost or inconvenience. (p. 32)

Inventoriable costs   Synonym for *product costs*. (p. 34)

Managerial accounting   The phase of accounting concerned with providing information to managers for use in planning and controlling operations and in decision making. (p. 26)

Manufacturing overhead   All costs associated with manufacturing except direct materials and direct labor. (p. 33)

Marketing or selling costs   All costs necessary to secure customer orders and get the finished product or service into the hands of the customer. (p. 33)

Opportunity cost   The potential benefit that is given up when one alternative is selected over another. (p. 48)

Performance report   A detailed report comparing budgeted data to actual data. (p. 27)

Period costs   Costs that are taken directly to the income statement as expenses in the period in which they are incurred or accrued. (p. 34)

Planning   Selecting a course of action and specifying how the action will be implemented. (p. 26)

Planning and control cycle   The flow of management activities through planning, directing and motivating, and controlling, and then back to planning again. (p. 28)

Prime cost   Direct materials cost plus direct labor cost. (p. 33)

Product costs   All costs that are involved in the purchase or manufacture of goods. In the case of manufactured goods, these costs consist of direct materials, direct labor, and manufacturing overhead. Also see *Inventoriable costs.* (p. 34)

Raw materials   Materials that are used to make a product. (p. 32)

Relevant range   The range of activity within which assumptions about variable and fixed cost behavior are valid. (p. 45)

Schedule of cost of goods manufactured   A schedule showing the direct materials, direct labor, and manufacturing overhead costs incurred for a period and assigned to Work in Process and completed goods. (p. 39)

Segment   Any part of an organization that can be evaluated independently of other parts and about which the manager seeks financial data. Examples include a product line, a sales territory, a division, or a department. (p. 30)

Sunk cost   Any cost that has already been incurred and that cannot be changed by any decision made now or in the future. (p. 49)

Variable cost   A cost that varies, in total, in direct proportion to changes in the level of activity. (p. 44)

Work in process   Units of product that are only partially complete and will require further work before they are ready for sale to a customer. (p. 36)

APPENDIX 1A   Cost of Quality

A company may have a product that has a high quality design and that uses high quality components, but if the product is defective the company will have high warranty repair costs and dissatisfied customers. People who are dissatisfied with a product won't buy it again. They are also likely to tell others about their bad experiences. One study found that "[c]ustomers who have bad experiences tell approximately 11 people about it."[1] This is the worst possible sort of advertising. To prevent such problems, companies have been expending a great deal of effort to reduce defects. The objective is to have high *quality of conformance*.

LEARNING OBJECTIVE 8

Identify the four types of quality costs and explain how they interact.

QUALITY OF CONFORMANCE

A product that meets or exceeds its design specifications and is free of defects is said to have high **quality of conformance.** Note that if an economy car is free of defects, it can have a quality of conformance that is just as high as a defect-free luxury car. The purchasers of economy cars cannot expect their cars to be as opulently equipped as luxury cars, but they can and do expect them to be free of defects.

Preventing, detecting, and correcting defects cause costs that are called *quality costs* or the *cost of quality.* The use of the term *quality cost* is confusing to some people. It does not refer to costs such as using a higher-grade leather to make a wallet or using 14K gold instead of gold-plating in jewelry. Instead, the term **quality cost** refers to all of the costs that are incurred to prevent defects or that result from the occurrence of defects.

Quality costs can be broken down into four broad groups. Two of these groups—known as *prevention costs* and *appraisal costs*—are incurred to keep defective products from falling into the hands of customers. The other two groups of costs—known as *internal failure costs* and *external failure costs*—are incurred because defects happen despite efforts to prevent them.

Prevention Costs   Generally, the most effective way to manage quality costs is to avoid having defects in the first place. It is much less costly to prevent a problem from ever happening than it is to find and correct the problem after it has occurred. **Prevention costs** support activities whose purpose is to reduce the number of defects. Companies employ many techniques to prevent defects including statistical process control, quality engineering, training, and a variety of tools from Total Quality Management.

Appraisal Costs   Any defective parts and products should be caught as early as possible in the production process. **Appraisal costs,** which are sometimes called *inspection costs,* are incurred to identify defective products *before* the products are shipped to customers. Unfortunately, performing appraisal activities doesn't keep defects from happening again, and most managers now realize that maintaining an army of inspectors is a costly (and ineffective) approach to quality control.

---

[1]Christopher W. L. Hart, James L. Heskett, and W. Earl Sasser, Jr., "The Profitable Art of Service Recovery," *Harvard Business Review,* July–August 1990, p. 153.

Cleverness Can Go a Long Way in Ensuring Quality

IN BUSINESS

Very simple and inexpensive procedures can be used to prevent defects. Yamada Electric had a persistent problem assembling a simple push-button switch. The switch has two buttons, an on button and an off button, with a small spring under each button. Assembly is very simple. A worker inserts the small springs in the device and then installs the buttons. However, the workers sometimes forget to put in one of the springs. When the customer discovers such a defective switch in a shipment from Yamada, an inspector has to be sent to the customer's plant to check every switch in the shipment. After each such incident, workers are urged to be more careful, and for a while quality improves. But eventually, someone forgets to put in a spring, and Yamada gets into trouble with the customer again. This chronic problem was very embarrassing to Yamada.

Shigeo Shingo, an expert on quality control, suggested a very simple solution. A small dish was placed next to the assembly station. At the beginning of each operation, two of the small springs are taken out of a parts box containing hundreds of springs and placed in the dish. The worker then assembles the switch. If a spring remains on the dish after assembling the switch, the worker immediately realizes a spring has been left out, and the switch is reassembled. This simple change in procedures completely eliminated the problem.

Source: Shigeo Shingo and Dr. Alan Robinson, editor-in-chief, *Modern Approaches to Manufacturing Improvement: The Shingo System* (Cambridge, MA: Productivity Press), pp. 214–216.

Professor John K. Shank of Dartmouth College has aptly stated, "The old-style approach was to say, 'We've got great quality. We have 40 quality control inspectors in the factory.' Then somebody realized that if you need 40 inspectors, it must be a lousy factory. So now the trick is to run a factory without any quality control inspectors; each employee is his or her own quality control person."[2]

Increasingly, companies are asking employees to be responsible for their own quality control. Taking this approach, along with designing products easy to manufacture properly, allows manufacturers to build quality into products rather than rely on inspection to get the defects out.

Internal Failure Costs Failure costs are incurred when a product fails to conform to its design specifications. Failure costs can be either internal or external. **Internal failure costs** result from identification of defects before they are shipped to customers. These costs include scrap, rejected products, reworking of defective units, and downtime caused by quality problems. In some companies, as little as 10% of the company's products make it through the production process without rework of some kind. Of course, the more effective a company's appraisal activities, the greater the chance of catching defects internally and the greater the level of internal failure costs. This is the price that is paid to avoid incurring external failure costs, which can be devastating.

External Failure Costs **External failure costs** result when a defective product is delivered to a customer. These costs include warranty repairs and replacements, product recalls, legal liability, and lost sales arising from a reputation for poor quality. Such costs can decimate profits.

In the past, some managers have taken the attitude, "Let's go ahead and ship everything to customers, and we'll take care of any problems under the warranty." This attitude generally results in high external failure costs, customer ill will, and declining market share and profits.

Distribution of Quality Costs

Quality costs often exceed 10% of total sales, whereas experts say that these costs should be more in the 2% to 4% range. How does a company reduce its total quality cost? The answer lies in how the quality costs are distributed.

---

[2]Robert W. Casey, "The Changing World of the CEO," *PPM World* 24, no. 2, p. 31.

When the defect rate is high, total quality cost is high and most of this cost consists of costs of internal and external failure. However, as a company spends more and more on prevention and appraisal, the percentage of defective units drops. This results in lower costs of internal and external failure. Ordinarily, total quality cost drops rapidly as the defect rate improves. Thus, a company can reduce its total quality cost by focusing its efforts on prevention and appraisal. The cost savings from reduced defects usually swamp the costs of the additional prevention and appraisal efforts. As a company's quality program becomes more refined and as its failure costs begin to fall, prevention activities usually become more effective than appraisal activities. Appraisal can only find defects, whereas prevention can eliminate them.

Quality Cost Report

As an aid to management, prevention and appraisal costs and the costs of internal and external failure can be summarized on a **quality cost report.** This report shows the type of quality costs being incurred and their significance and trends. The report helps managers understand the importance of quality costs, spot problem areas, and assess the way in which the quality costs are distributed. For further details, see Appendix 2B in Ray Garrison and Eric Noreen, *Managerial Accounting,* 10th edition, McGraw-Hill/Irwin, 2003.

Fighting Bugs

IN BUSINESS

Software bugs can have catastrophic consequences. Companies that sell products that rely on software know this, and fighting these particular defects can consume enormous resources. For example, it was once estimated that the cost of quality (i.e., the costs of preventing, detecting, and fixing bugs) at Raytheon Electronics Systems was almost 60% of the total costs of producing software for its products. That percentage has fallen to 15% due to new software management tools designed to prevent bugs from being written into the computer code in the first place.

Source: Otis Port, "Will Bugs Eat Up the U.S. Lead in Software?" *Business Week,* December 6, 1999, p. 118.

SUMMARY OF APPENDIX 1A

LO8 (Appendix 1A) Identify the four types of quality costs and explain how they interact.
Defects cause costs, which can be classified into prevention costs, appraisal costs, internal failure costs, and external failure costs. Prevention costs are incurred to keep defects from happening. Appraisal costs are incurred to ensure that defective products are not shipped to customers. Internal failure costs result from detecting defective products before they are shipped to customers. External failure costs result from delivering defective products to customers; they include the cost of repairs, servicing, and lost future business. Most experts agree that management effort should be focused on preventing defects. Small investments in prevention can lead to dramatic reductions in appraisal costs and costs of internal and external failure.

GLOSSARY FOR APPENDIX 1A

Appraisal costs Costs that are incurred to identify defective products before they are shipped to customers. (p. 57)

External failure costs Costs that are incurred when a defective product is delivered to a customer. (p. 58)

Internal failure costs Costs that are incurred as a result of identifying defective products before they are shipped to customers. (p. 58)

Prevention costs   Costs that are incurred to keep defects from happening. (p. 57)

Quality costs   Costs that are incurred to prevent defective products from falling into the hands of customers or that are incurred as a result of defective units. (p. 57)

Quality cost report   A report that details prevention costs, appraisal costs, and the costs of internal and external failures. (p. 59)

Quality of conformance   The degree to which a product or service meets or exceeds its design specifications and is free of defects or other problems that mar its appearance or degrade its performance. (p. 57)

QUESTIONS

1–1   What is the basic difference in orientation between financial and managerial accounting?

1–2   What are the three major activities of a manager?

1–3   Describe the four steps in the planning and control cycle.

1–4   Distinguish between line and staff positions in an organization.

1–5   What are the major differences between financial and managerial accounting?

1–6   What are the three major elements of product costs in a manufacturing company?

1–7   Distinguish between the following: (a) direct materials, (b) indirect materials, (c) direct labor, (d) indirect labor, and (e) manufacturing overhead.

1–8   Explain the difference between a product cost and a period cost.

1–9   Describe how the income statement of a manufacturing company differs from the income statement of a merchandising company.

1–10   Of what value is the schedule of cost of goods manufactured? How does it tie into the income statement?

1–11   Describe how the inventory accounts of a manufacturing company differ from the inventory account of a merchandising company.

1–12   Why are product costs sometimes called inventoriable costs? Describe the flow of such costs in a manufacturing company from the point of incurrence until they finally become expenses on the income statement.

1–13   Is it possible for costs such as salaries or depreciation to end up as assets on the balance sheet? Explain.

1–14   What is meant by the term *cost behavior*?

1–15   "A variable cost is a cost that varies per unit of product, whereas a fixed cost is constant per unit of product." Do you agree? Explain.

1–16   How do fixed costs create difficulties in costing units of product?

1–17   Why is manufacturing overhead considered an indirect cost of a unit of product?

1–18   Define the following terms: differential cost, opportunity cost, and sunk cost.

1–19   Only variable costs can be differential costs. Do you agree? Explain.

1–20   (Appendix 1A) Costs associated with the quality of conformance can be broken down into four broad groups. What are these four groups and how do they differ?

1–21   (Appendix 1A) In their efforts to reduce the total cost of quality, should companies generally focus on decreasing prevention costs and appraisal costs?

1–22   (Appendix 1A) What is probably the most effective way to reduce a company's total quality costs?

BRIEF EXERCISES

BRIEF EXERCISE 1–1   Classifying Manufacturing Costs   (LO1)
Your Boat, Inc., assembles custom sailboats from components supplied by various manufacturers. The company is very small and its assembly shop and retail sales store are housed in a Gig Harbor, Washington, boathouse. Below are listed some of the costs that are incurred at the company.

Required:
For each cost, indicate whether it would most likely be classified as direct labor, direct materials, manufacturing overhead, marketing and selling, or an administrative cost.

1. The wages of employees who build the sailboats.
2. The cost of advertising in the local newspapers.
3. The cost of an aluminum mast installed in a sailboat.

4. The wages of the assembly shop's supervisor.
5. Rent on the boathouse.
6. The wages of the company's bookkeeper.
7. Sales commissions paid to the company's salespeople.
8. Depreciation on power tools.

BRIEF EXERCISE 1–2   Identifying Period and Product Costs   (LO2)

Suppose that you have been given a summer job at Fairwings Avionics, a company that manufactures sophisticated radar sets for commercial aircraft. The company, which is privately owned, has approached a bank for a loan to help finance its tremendous growth. The bank requires financial statements before approving such a loan. You have been asked to help prepare the financial statements and were given the following list of costs:

1. The cost of the memory chips used in a radar set.
2. Factory heating costs.
3. Factory equipment maintenance costs.
4. Training costs for new administrative employees.
5. The cost of the solder that is used in assembling the radar sets.
6. The travel costs of the company's salespersons.
7. Wages and salaries of factory security personnel.
8. The cost of air-conditioning executive offices.
9. Wages and salaries in the department that handles billing customers.
10. Depreciation on the equipment in the fitness room used by factory workers.
11. Telephone expenses incurred by factory management.
12. The costs of shipping completed radar sets to customers.
13. The wages of the workers who assemble the radar sets.
14. The president's salary.
15. Health insurance premiums for factory personnel.

Required:
Classify the above costs as either product (inventoriable) costs or period (noninventoriable) costs for purposes of preparing the financial statements for the bank.

BRIEF EXERCISE 1–3   Constructing an Income Statement   (LO3)

Last month Mountain High, a mountain sporting goods retailer, had total sales of $3,200,000, selling expenses of $110,000, and administrative expenses of $470,000. The company had beginning merchandise inventory of $140,000, purchased additional merchandise inventory for $2,550,000, and had ending merchandise inventory of $180,000.

Required:
Prepare an income statement for the company for the month in good form.

BRIEF EXERCISE 1–4   Prepare a Schedule of Cost of Goods Manufactured   (LO4)

Mannerman Fabrication manufactures a variety of products in its factory. Data for the most recent month's operations appear below:

Beginning raw materials inventory	$55,000
Purchases of raw materials	$440,000
Ending raw materials inventory	$65,000
Direct labor	$215,000
Manufacturing overhead	$380,000
Beginning work in process inventory	$190,000
Ending work in process inventory	$220,000

Required:
Prepare in good form a schedule of cost of goods manufactured for the company for the month.

BRIEF EXERCISE 1–5   Identifying Costs as Fixed or Variable   (LO5)

Below are a number of costs that might be incurred in a variety of organizations. Copy the list of costs onto your answer sheet, and then place an X in the appropriate column for each cost to indicate whether the cost involved would be variable or fixed with respect to the goods and services produced by the organization.

	Cost Behavior	
Cost	**Variable**	**Fixed**
1. Small glass plates used for lab tests in a hospital		
2. Straight-line depreciation of a building		
3. Top-management salaries		
4. Electrical costs of running machines		
5. Advertising of products and services		
6. Batteries used in manufacturing trucks		
7. Commissions to salespersons		
8. Insurance on a dentist's office		
9. Leather used in manufacturing footballs		
10. Rent on a medical center		

BRIEF EXERCISE 1–6   Identifying Direct and Indirect Costs   (LO6)
The Four Seasons Olympic is a four-star hotel located in downtown Seattle.

Required:
For each of the following costs incurred at the Four Seasons Olympic, indicate whether it would most likely be a direct cost or an indirect cost of the specified costing object by placing an X in the appropriate column.

Cost	**Costing Object**	**Direct Cost**	**Indirect Cost**
Ex. Room service beverages	A particular hotel guest	X	
1. The salary of the head chef	The hotel's restaurant		
2. The salary of the head chef	A particular restaurant customer		
3. Room cleaning supplies	A particular hotel guest		
4. Flowers for the reception desk	A particular hotel guest		
5. The wages of the doorman	A particular hotel guest		
6. Room cleaning supplies	The housecleaning department		
7. Fire insurance on the hotel building	The hotel's gym		
8. Towels used in the gym	The hotel's gym		

BRIEF EXERCISE 1–7   Differential, Opportunity, and Sunk Costs   (LO7)
The Four Seasons Olympic is a four-star hotel located in downtown Seattle. The hotel's operations vice president would like to replace the hotel's antiquated computer terminals at the registration desk with attractive state-of-the-art flat-panel displays. The new displays would take less space, would consume less power than the old computer terminals, and would provide additional security since they can only be viewed from a restrictive angle. The new computer displays would not require any new wiring. The hotel's chef believes the funds would be better spent on a new bulk freezer for the kitchen.

Required:
For each of the items below, indicate by placing an X in the appropriate column whether it should be considered a differential cost, an opportunity cost, or a sunk cost in the decision to replace the old computer terminals with new flat-panel displays. If none of the categories applies for a particular item, leave all columns blank.

Item	**Differential Cost**	**Opportunity Cost**	**Sunk Cost**
Ex. Cost of electricity to run the terminals	X		
1. Cost of the new flat-panel displays			
2. Cost of the old computer terminals			

(continued)

(concluded) Item	Differential Cost	Opportunity Cost	Sunk Cost
3. Rent on the space occupied by the registration desk			
4. Wages of registration desk personnel			
5. Benefits from a new freezer			
6. Costs of maintaining the old computer terminals			
7. Cost of removing the old computer terminals			
8. Cost of existing registration desk wiring			

BRIEF EXERCISE 1–8   (Appendix 1A) Categorization of Quality Costs   (LO8)

Listed below are terms relating to quality management.

appraisal costs	quality circles
quality cost report	prevention costs
quality	external failure costs
internal failure costs	quality of conformance

Choose the term or terms that most appropriately complete the following statements. The terms can be used more than once. (Note that a blank can hold more than one word.)

1. When a product or service does not conform to customer expectations in terms of features or performance, it is viewed as being poor in _____.
2. A product or service will have a low _____ if it does not function the way its designers intended, or if it has many defects as a result of sloppy manufacture.
3. A company incurs _____ and _____ in an effort to keep poor quality of conformance from occurring.
4. A company incurs _____ and _____ because poor quality of conformance has occurred.
5. Of the four groups of costs associated with quality of conformance, _____ are generally the most damaging to a company.
6. Inspection, testing, and other costs incurred to keep defective products from being shipped to customers are known as _____.
7. The costs relating to defects, rejected products, and downtime caused by quality problems are known as _____.
8. When a product that is defective in some way is delivered to a customer, then _____ are incurred.
9. Over time a company's total quality costs should decrease if it redistributes its quality costs by placing its greatest emphasis on _____ and _____.
10. In many companies, small groups of employees, known as _____, meet on a regular basis to discuss ways to improve the quality of output.
11. The way to ensure that management is aware of the costs associated with quality is to summarize such costs on a _____.

EXERCISES

EXERCISE 1–9   Classification of Costs into Various Categories   (LO1, LO2, LO5, LO7)

Several years ago Medex Company purchased a small building adjacent to its manufacturing plant in order to have room for expansion when needed. Since the company had no immediate need for the extra space, the building was rented out to another company for a rental revenue of $40,000 per year. The renter's lease will expire next month, and rather than renew the lease, Medex Company has decided to use the building itself to manufacture a new product.

Direct materials cost for the new product will total $40 per unit. It will be necessary to hire a supervisor to oversee production. Her salary will be $2,500 per month. Workers will be hired to manufacture the new product, with direct labor cost amounting to $18 per unit. Manufacturing operations will occupy all of the building space, so it will be necessary to rent space in a warehouse nearby in order to store finished units of product. The rental cost will be $1,000 per month. In addition, the company will need to rent equipment for use in producing the new product; the rental cost will be $3,000 per month. The company will continue to depreciate the building on a straight-line basis, as in past years. Depreciation on the building is $10,000 per year.

Advertising costs for the new product will total $50,000 per year. Costs of shipping the new product to customers will be $10 per unit. Electrical costs of operating machines will be $2 per unit.

To have funds to purchase materials, meet payrolls, and so forth, the company will have to liquidate some temporary investments. These investments are presently yielding a return of $6,000 per year.

Required:

Prepare an answer sheet with the following column headings:

Name of the Cost	Variable Cost	Fixed Cost	Product Cost			Period (selling and administrative) Cost	Opportunity Cost	Sunk Cost
			Direct Materials	Direct Labor	Manufacturing Overhead			

List the different costs associated with the new product decision down the extreme left column (under Name of the Cost). Then place an *X* under each heading that helps to describe the type of cost involved. There may be *X*'s under several column headings for a single cost. (For example, a cost may be a fixed cost, a period cost, and a sunk cost; you would place an *X* under each of these column headings opposite the cost.)

EXERCISE 1–10   Using Cost Terms   (LO2, LO5, LO7)

Following are a number of cost terms introduced in the chapter:

period cost	fixed cost
variable cost	prime cost
opportunity cost	conversion cost
product cost	sunk cost

Choose the cost term or terms above that most appropriately describe the costs identified in each of the following situations. A cost term can be used more than once.

1. Crestline Books, Inc., prints a small book titled *The Pocket Speller*. The paper going into the manufacture of the book would be called direct materials and classified as a _____. In terms of cost behavior, the paper could also be described as a _____ with respect to the number of books printed.
2. Instead of compiling the words in the book, the author hired by the company could have earned considerable fees consulting with business organizations. The consulting fees forgone by the author would be called _____.
3. The paper and other materials used in the manufacture of the book, combined with the direct labor cost involved, would be called _____.
4. The salary of Crestline Books' president would be classified as a _____, and the salary will appear on the income statement as an expense in the time period in which it is incurred.
5. Depreciation on the equipment used to print the book would be classified by Crestline Books as a _____. However, depreciation on any equipment used by the company in selling and administrative activities would be classified as a _____. In terms of cost behavior, depreciation would probably be classified as a _____ with respect to the number of books printed.
6. A _____ is also known as an inventoriable cost, since such costs go into the Work in Process inventory account and then into the Finished Goods inventory account before appearing on the income statement as part of cost of goods sold.
7. Taken together, the direct labor cost and manufacturing overhead cost involved in the manufacture of the book would be called _____.
8. Crestline Books sells the book through agents who are paid a commission on each book sold. The company would classify these commissions as a _____. In terms of cost behavior, commissions would be classified as a _____.
9. Several hundred copies of the book were left over from the previous edition and are stored in a warehouse. The amount invested in these books would be called a _____.
10. Costs can often be classified in several ways. For example, Crestline Books pays $4,000 rent each month on the building that houses its printing press. The rent would be part of manufacturing overhead. In terms of cost behavior, it would be classified as a _____. The rent can also be classified as a _____ and as part of _____.

EXERCISE 1–11 Product Cost Flows; Product versus Period Costs (LO2, LO3)

Ryser Company was organized on May 1. On that date the company purchased 35,000 plastic emblems, each with a peel-off adhesive backing. The front of the emblems contained the company's name, accompanied by an attractive logo. Each emblem cost Ryser Company $2.

During May, 31,000 emblems were drawn from the Raw Materials inventory account. Of these, 1,000 were taken by the sales manager to an important sales meeting with prospective customers and handed out as an advertising gimmick. The remaining emblems drawn from inventory were affixed to units of the company's product that were being manufactured during May. Of the units of product having emblems affixed during May, 90% were completed and transferred from Work in Process to Finished Goods. Of the units completed during the month, 75% were sold and shipped to customers.

Required:

1. Determine the cost of emblems that would be in each of the following accounts at May 31:
   a.   Raw Materials.
   b.   Work in Process.
   c.   Finished Goods.
   d.   Cost of Goods Sold.
   e.   Advertising Expense.
2. Specify whether each of the above accounts would appear on the balance sheet or on the income statement at May 31.

EXERCISE 1–12 Classification of Costs as Variable or Fixed and as Selling and Administrative or Product   (LO2, LO5)

Below are listed various costs that are found in organizations.

1. The costs of turn signal switches used at the General Motors Saginaw, Michigan, plant. These are one of the parts installed in the steering columns assembled at the plant.
2. Interest expense on CBS's long-term debt.
3. Salespersons' commissions at Avon Products, a company that sells cosmetics door to door.
4. Insurance on one of Cincinnati Milacron's factory buildings.
5. The costs of shipping brass fittings from Graham Manufacturing's plant in New Hampshire to customers in California.
6. Depreciation on the bookshelves at Reston Bookstore.
7. The costs of X-ray film at the Mayo Clinic's radiology lab.
8. The cost of leasing an 800 telephone number at L. L. Bean. The monthly charge for the 800 number is independent of the number of calls taken.
9. The depreciation on the playground equipment at a McDonald's outlet.
10. The cost of mozzarella cheese used at a Pizza Hut outlet.

Required:

Classify each cost as either variable or fixed with respect to the volume of goods or services produced and sold by the organization. Also classify each cost as a selling and administrative cost or a product cost. Prepare your answer sheet as shown below, placing an X in the appropriate columns.

Cost Item	Cost Behavior		Selling and Administrative Cost	Product Cost
	Variable	Fixed		

EXERCISE 1–13 Preparation of a Schedule of Cost of Goods Manufactured and Cost of Goods Sold   (LO3, LO4)

The following cost and inventory data for the just completed year are taken from the accounting records of Eccles Company:

Costs incurred:

Advertising expense	$100,000
Direct labor cost	$90,000
Purchases of raw materials	$132,000
Rent, factory building	$80,000
Indirect labor	$56,300
Sales commissions	$35,000

(continued)

Costs incurred: *(concluded)*		
Utilities, factory		$9,000
Maintenance, factory equipment		$24,000
Supplies, factory		$700
Depreciation, office equipment		$8,000
Depreciation, factory equipment		$40,000

	Beginning of Year	End of Year
Inventories:		
Raw materials	$8,000	$10,000
Work in process	$5,000	$20,000
Finished goods	$70,000	$25,000

Required:
1. Prepare a schedule of cost of goods manufactured.
2. Prepare the cost of goods sold section of Eccles Company's income statement for the year.

EXERCISE 1–14   Classification of Costs as Variable or Fixed and Direct or Indirect   (LO5, LO6)
Various costs associated with manufacturing operations are given below:

1. Plastic washers used in auto production.
2. Production superintendent's salary.
3. Wages of laborers assembling a product.
4. Electricity for operation of machines.
5. Janitorial salaries.
6. Clay used in brick production.
7. Rent on a factory building.
8. Wood used in ski production.
9. Screws used in furniture production.
10. A supervisor's salary.
11. Cloth used in suit production.
12. Depreciation of cafeteria equipment.
13. Glue used in textbook production.
14. Lubricants for machines.
15. Paper used in textbook production.

Required:
Classify each cost as being either variable or fixed with respect to the number of units produced and sold. Also indicate whether each cost would typically be treated as a direct cost or an indirect cost with respect to units of product. Prepare your answer sheet as shown below:

	Cost Behavior		To Units of Product	
Cost Item	Variable	Fixed	Direct	Indirect
Example: Factory insurance		X		X

EXERCISE 1–15   (Appendix 1A) Classification of Quality Costs   (LO8)
Below are listed a number of activities that are part of a company's quality control system:

a. Repairs of goods still under warranty.
b. Customer returns due to defects.
c. Statistical process control.
d. Disposal of spoiled goods.
e. Maintaining testing equipment.
f. Inspecting finished goods.
g. Downtime caused by quality problems.
h. Debugging errors in software.
i. Recalls of defective products.

j.   Re-entering data due to typing errors.
k.   Inspecting materials received from suppliers.
l.   Supervision of testing personnel.
m.   Rework labor.

Required:

1.   Classify the costs associated with each of these activities into one of the following categories: prevention cost, appraisal cost, internal failure cost, or external failure cost.

2.   Which of the four types of costs listed in (1) above are incurred to keep poor quality of conformance from occurring? Which of the four types of costs are incurred because poor quality of conformance has occurred?

PROBLEMS

PROBLEM 1–16   Cost Identification   (LO1, LO2, LO5, LO7)

Yuko Makiyama began growing miniature bonsai trees several years ago as a hobby. Her work is quite creative, and it has been so popular with friends and others that she has decided to quit her job in the food industry and grow bonsai trees full time. The salary from Yuko's food industry job is $3,000 per month.

CHECK FIGURE
Seeds, earth, pots and
fertilizer: variable, direct
materials

Yuko will rent an airy, brightly lit loft near her home to use as a place for growing the bonsai trees. The rent will be $400 per month. She estimates that the cost of seeds, earth, fertilizers, and pots will be $7 for each finished bonsai tree. She will hire an experienced gardener to plant and water the bonsai trees at a labor rate of $12 per hour. To sell her bonsai trees, Yuko feels that she must launch an advertising campaign that focuses on hard-core gardeners. An advertising agency states that it will handle all advertising for a fee of $550 per month.

Nurseries will sell the bonsai trees on consignment and will be paid a commission of $8 for each tree sold. Production equipment will be rented at a cost of $250 per month. Yuko has already paid the legal and filing fees associated with incorporating her business in the state. These fees amounted to $300. A small room has been located in the area that Yuko will use as a sales office. The rent will be $200 per month. A phone installed in the room for taking orders will cost $30 per month.

Yuko has some money in savings that is earning interest of $3,000 per year. These savings will be withdrawn and used to get the business going. For the time being, Yuko does not intend to draw any salary from the new company.

Required:

1.   Prepare an answer sheet with the following column headings:

Name of the Cost	Variable Cost	Fixed Cost	Product Cost			Period (selling and administrative) Cost	Opportunity Cost	Sunk Cost
			Direct Materials	Direct Labor	Manufacturing Overhead			

List the different costs associated with the new company down the extreme left column (under Name of the Cost). Then place an X under each heading that helps to describe the type of cost involved. There may be X's under several column headings for a single cost. (That is, a cost may be a fixed cost, a period cost, and a sunk cost; you would place an X under each of these column headings opposite the cost.)

Under the Variable Cost column, list only those costs that would be variable with respect to the number of bonsai trees that are produced and sold.

2.   All of the costs you have listed above, except one, would be differential costs between the alternatives of Yuko producing bonsai trees or staying with the food industry. Which cost is *not* differential? Explain.

PROBLEM 1–17   Classification of Salary Cost   (LO2)

You have just been hired by Luxmor Corporation to fill a new position that was created in response to the upcoming launch of a newly developed product. It is your responsibility to design an advertising campaign for this product's debut in Mexico and Central America.

The company is unsure how to classify your annual salary of $32,100 in its cost records. The company's cost analyst says that your salary should be classified as a manufacturing (product) cost; the controller says that it should be classified as a selling expense; and the president says that it doesn't matter which way your salary cost is classified.

Required:

1. Which viewpoint is correct? Why?
2. From the point of view of the reported net operating income for the year, is the president correct in his statement that it doesn't matter which way your salary cost is classified? Explain.

CHECK FIGURE
Insurance, finished goods
warehouses: fixed,
selling cost

PROBLEM 1–18   Cost Classification   (LO2, LO5, LO6)

Listed below are a number of costs found in organizations.

1. Wood used in producing furniture.
2. Insurance, finished goods warehouses.
3. Ink used in book production.
4. Advertising costs.
5. Property taxes, factory.
6. Thread in a garment factory.
7. Wage of receptionist, executive offices.
8. Salespersons' commissions.
9. Shipping costs on merchandise sold.
10. Depreciation, executive automobiles.
11. Magazine subscriptions, factory lunchroom.
12. Wages of workers assembling computers.
13. Executive life insurance.
14. Boxes used for packaging television sets.
15. Zippers used in jeans production.
16. Fringe benefits, assembly-line workers.
17. Supervisor's salary, factory.
18. Billing costs.
19. Packing supplies for international shipments.
20. Lubricants for machines.

Required:

Prepare an answer sheet with column headings as shown below. For each cost item, indicate whether it would be variable or fixed with respect to the number of units produced and sold; and then whether it would be a selling cost, an administrative cost, or a manufacturing cost. If it is a manufacturing cost, indicate whether it would typically be treated as a direct cost or an indirect cost with respect to units of product. Three sample answers are provided for illustration.

Cost Item	Variable or Fixed	Selling Cost	Administrative Cost	Manufacturing (Product) Cost Direct	Manufacturing (Product) Cost Indirect
Direct labor	V			X	
Executive salaries	F		X		
Factory rent	F				X

CHECK FIGURE
(1) Total variable cost:
$383,000

PROBLEM 1–19   Cost Identification and Concepts   (LO2, LO5, LO6)

The Sloane Company specializes in producing a set of wood patio furniture consisting of a table and four chairs. The set enjoys great popularity, and the company has orders for 3,000 sets per year. Annual cost data at this level of production follow:

Factory labor, direct	$150,000
Advertising	$35,000
Factory supervision	$29,000
Property taxes, factory building	$4,400
Sales commissions	$95,000
Insurance, factory	$5,600
Depreciation, office equipment	$5,500
Lease cost, factory equipment	$20,000
Indirect materials, factory	$8,000
Depreciation, factory building	$23,000
General office supplies (billing)	$4,000

(continued)

> (concluded)
> General office salaries $72,000
> Direct materials used (wood, bolts, etc.) $111,000
> Utilities, factory $15,000

Required:

1. Prepare an answer sheet with the column headings shown below. Enter each cost item on your answer sheet, placing the dollar amount under the appropriate headings. As examples, this has been done already for the first two items in the list above. Note that each cost item is classified in two ways: first, as a variable or fixed cost, with respect to the number of units produced and sold; and second, as a selling and administrative cost or a product cost. (If the item is a product cost, it should also be classified as either direct or indirect as shown.)

Cost Item	Cost Behavior		Selling or Administrative Cost	Product Cost	
	Variable	Fixed		Direct	Indirect*
Factory labor, direct	$150,000			$150,000	
Advertising		$35,000	$35,000		

*To units of product.

2. Total the dollar amounts in each of the columns in (1) above. Compute the average product cost per patio set.
3. Assume that production falls to 2,800 sets annually. Would you expect the average product cost per patio set to increase, decrease, or remain unchanged? Explain. No computations are necessary.
4. Refer to the original data. The president's brother-in-law has considered making himself a patio set and has priced the necessary materials at a building supply store. The brother-in-law has asked the president if he could purchase a patio set from the Sloane Company "at cost," and the president agreed to let him do so.
   a. Would you expect any disagreement between the two men over the price the brother-in-law should pay? Explain. What price does the president probably have in mind? The brother-in-law?
   b. Since the company is operating at full capacity, what cost term used in the chapter might be justification for the president to charge the full, regular price to the brother-in-law and still be selling "at cost?"

PROBLEM 1–20 Supplying Missing Data (LO3, LO4)

Data are provided below for four cases. Each case is independent of the others.

CHECK FIGURE
Case 1: Goods available for sale = $59,500

Required:

Supply the missing data in the following cases.

	Case			
	1	2	3	4
Direct materials	$28,000	$12,000	$18,000	$22,000
Direct labor	?	11,000	10,000	18,000
Manufacturing overhead	6,000	8,000	?	5,000
Total manufacturing costs	46,000	?	35,000	?
Beginning work in process inventory	6,500	?	12,000	?
Ending work in process inventory	?	1,500	6,000	15,000
Cost of goods manufactured	$44,500	$34,000	$?	$?
Sales	$57,000	$42,000	$62,000	$58,000
Beginning finished goods inventory	15,000	9,000	?	13,000
Cost of goods manufactured	?	?	?	41,000
Goods available for sale	?	?	?	?
Ending finished goods inventory	?	10,000	17,000	16,000
Cost of goods sold	42,500	?	45,000	?
Gross margin	14,500	?	17,000	?
Operating expenses	?	6,000	?	?
Net operating income	$ 2,500	$?	$ 2,000	$ 500

PROBLEM 1–21   Preparing Financial Statements for a Manufacturer   (LO3, LO4)

Madlinx Company was organized on April 1 of the current year. After five months of start-up losses, management had expected to earn a profit during September, the most recent month. Management was disappointed, however, when the income statement for September also showed a loss. September's income statement follows:

MADLINX COMPANY		
Income Statement		
For the Month Ended September 30		
Sales.		$266,000
Less operating expenses:		
Indirect labor cost	$ 7,200	
Utilities	9,100	
Direct labor cost.	47,000	
Depreciation, factory equipment	10,000	
Raw materials purchased	95,000	
Depreciation, sales equipment	10,400	
Insurance.	2,500	
Rent on facilities	27,000	
Selling and administrative salaries.	23,000	
Advertising	39,000	270,200
Net operating loss		$ (4,200)

After seeing the $4,200 loss for September, Madlinx's president stated, "I was sure we'd be profitable within six months, but our six months are up and this loss for September is even worse than August's. I think it's time to start looking for someone to buy out the company's assets—if we don't, within a few months there won't be any assets to sell. By the way, I don't see any reason to look for a new controller. We'll just limp along with Harry for the time being."

The company's controller resigned a month ago. Harry, a new assistant in the controller's office, prepared the income statement above. Harry has had little experience in manufacturing operations. Additional information about the company follows:

a.   65% of the utilities cost and 70% of the insurance apply to factory operations. The remaining amounts apply to selling and administrative activities.

b.   Inventory balances at the beginning and end of September were:

	September 1	September 30
Raw materials	$4,600	$7,000
Work in process	$9,000	$12,000
Finished goods	$24,000	$30,000

c.   90% of the rent on facilities applies to factory operations; the remainder applies to selling and administrative activities.

The president has asked you to check over the income statement and make a recommendation as to whether the company should look for a buyer for its assets.

Required:
1. As one step in gathering data for a recommendation to the president, prepare a schedule of cost of goods manufactured in good form for September.
2. As a second step, prepare a new income statement for September.
3. Based on your statements prepared in (1) and (2) above, would you recommend that the company look for a buyer?

PROBLEM 1–22   Financial Statements; Cost Behavior   (LO3, LO4, LO5)

Various cost and sales data for Jaskot Company for the just completed year follow:

Microsoft Excel - Problem 1-22 screen capture.xls

File Edit View Insert Format Tools Data Window Help

Arial

D18

	A	B
1	Finished goods inventory,	$16,000
2	Finished goods inventory,	$14,000
3	Depreciation, factory	$21,000
4	Administrative expenses	$45,000
5	Utilities, factory	$12,000
6	Maintenance, factory	$26,000
7	Supplies, factory	$6,000
8	Insurance, factory	$7,000
9	Purchases of raw materials	$72,000
10	Raw materials inventory,	$5,000
11	Raw materials inventory,	$8,000
12	Direct labor	$61,000
13	Indirect labor	$32,000
14	Work in process inventory,	$13,000
15	Work in process inventory,	$14,000
16	Sales	$355,000
17	Selling expenses	$61,000
18		

Sheet1 / Sheet2 / Sheet3

Ready   NUM

Required:

1. Prepare a schedule of cost of goods manufactured.
2. Prepare an income statement.
3. The company produced the equivalent of 12,000 units of product during the year just completed. What was the average cost per unit for direct materials? What was the average cost per unit for factory depreciation?
4. The company expects to produce 10,000 units of product during the coming year. What per unit cost and what total cost would you expect the company to incur for direct materials at this level of activity? For factory depreciation? (In preparing your answer, assume that direct materials is a variable cost and that depreciation is a fixed cost that will be the same next year as it was this year.)
5. Explain to the president any difference in the average cost per unit between (3) and (4) above.

PROBLEM 1–23   Financial Statements; Cost Behavior   (LO3, LO4, LO5)

Selected account balances for the year ended December 31 are provided below for Rolling Company:

Selling and administrative salaries	$55,000
Insurance, factory	$6,000
Utilities, factory	$10,000
Purchases of raw materials	$76,000
Indirect labor	$3,000
Direct labor	?
Advertising expense	$26,000
Cleaning supplies, factory	$4,000
Sales commissions	$33,000
Rent, factory building	$49,000
Maintenance, factory	$15,000

Inventory balances at the beginning and end of the year were as follows:

	Beginning of the Year	End of the Year
Raw materials	$3,000	$9,000
Work in process	?	$13,000
Finished goods	$25,000	?

The total manufacturing costs for the year were $242,000; the goods available for sale totaled $269,000; and the cost of goods sold totaled $229,000.

Required:
1. Prepare a schedule of cost of goods manufactured in good form and the cost of goods sold section of the company's income statement for the year.
2. The company produced the equivalent of 7,000 units during the year. Compute the average cost per unit for direct materials used and the average cost per unit for rent on the factory building.
3. In the following year the company expects to produce 5,000 units. What average cost per unit and total cost would you expect to be incurred for direct materials? For rent on the factory building? (In preparing your answer, assume that direct materials is a variable cost and that rent is a fixed cost.)
4. Explain to the president the reason for any difference in the average cost per unit between (2) and (3) above.

BUILDING YOUR SKILLS

CHECK FIGURE
(1) Cost of goods manufactured: $450,000

ANALYTICAL THINKING   (LO1, LO2, LO3, LO4)

Hickey Company, a manufacturing firm, produces a single product. The following information has been taken from the company's production, sales, and cost records for the just completed year:

Production in units	30,000
Sales in units	?
Ending finished goods inventory in units	?
Sales in dollars	$650,000
Costs:	
Advertising	$50,000
Direct labor	$80,000
Indirect labor	$60,000
Raw materials purchased	$160,000
Building rent (production uses 80% of the space; administrative and sales offices use the rest)	$50,000
Utilities, factory	$35,000
Royalty paid for use of production patent, $1 per unit produced	?
Maintenance, factory	$25,000
Rent for special production equipment, $6,000 per year plus $0.10 per unit produced	?
Selling and administrative salaries	$140,000
Other factory overhead costs	$11,000
Other selling and administrative expenses	$20,000

	Beginning of Year	End of Year
Inventories:		
Raw materials	$20,000	$10,000
Work in process	$30,000	$40,000
Finished goods	$0	?

The finished goods inventory is being carried at the average unit production cost for the year. The selling price of the product is $25 per unit.

Required:
1. Prepare a schedule of cost of goods manufactured for the year.
2. Compute the following:
   a. The number of units in the finished goods inventory at the end of the year.
   b. The cost of the units in the finished goods inventory at the end of the year.
3. Prepare an income statement for the year.

CASE   (LO3, LO4)
While snoozing at the controls of his Pepper Six airplane, Dunse P. Sluggard leaned heavily against the door; suddenly, the door flew open and a startled Dunse tumbled out. As he parachuted to the ground,

Dunse watched helplessly as the empty plane smashed into Operex Products' plant and administrative offices.

"The insurance company will never believe this," cried Mercedes Juliet, the company's controller, as she watched the ensuing fire burn the building to the ground. "The entire company is wiped out!"

"There's no reason to even contact the insurance agent," replied Ford Romero, the company's operations manager. "We can't file a claim without records, and all we have left is this copy of last year's annual report. It shows that raw materials at the beginning of this year (January 1) totaled $30,000, work in process totaled $50,000, and finished goods totaled $90,000. But what we need is a record of these inventories as of today, and our records are up in smoke."

"All except this summary page I was working on when the plane hit the building," said Mercedes. "It shows that our sales to date this year have totaled $1,350,000 and that manufacturing overhead cost has totaled $520,000."

"Hey! This annual report is more helpful than I thought," exclaimed Ford. "I can see that our gross margin rate has been 40% of sales for years. I can also see that direct labor cost is one-quarter of the manufacturing overhead cost."

"We may have a chance after all," cried Mercedes. "My summary sheet lists the sum of direct labor and direct materials at $510,000 for the year, and it says that our goods available for sale to customers this year has totaled $960,000 at cost. Now if we just knew the amount of raw materials purchased so far this year."

"I know that figure," yelled Ford. "It's $420,000! The purchasing agent gave it to me in our planning meeting yesterday."

"Fantastic," shouted Mercedes. "We'll have our claim ready before the day is over!"

To file a claim with the insurance company, Operex Products must determine the amount of cost in its inventories as of the date of the accident. You may assume that all of the materials used in production during the year were direct materials.

Required:
Determine the amount of cost in the raw materials, work in process, and finished goods inventories as of the date of the accident. (Hint: One way to proceed would be to reconstruct the various schedules and statements that would have been affected by the company's inventory accounts during the year.)

ETHICS CHALLENGE   (LO2)

The top management of General Electronics, Inc., is well known for "managing by the numbers." With an eye on the company's desired growth in overall net profit, the company's CEO (chief executive officer) sets target profits at the beginning of the year for each of the company's divisions. The CEO has stated her policy as follows: "I won't interfere with operations in the divisions. I am available for advice, but the division vice presidents are free to do anything they want so long as they hit the target profits for the year."

In November, Stan Richart, the vice president in charge of the Cellular Telephone Technologies Division, saw that making the current year's target profit for his division was going to be very difficult. Among other actions, he directed that discretionary expenditures be delayed until the beginning of the new year. On December 30, he was angered to discover that a warehouse clerk had ordered $350,000 of cellular telephone parts earlier in December even though the parts weren't really needed by the assembly department until January or February. Contrary to common accounting practice, the General Electronics, Inc., Accounting Policy Manual states that such parts are to be recorded as an expense when delivered. To avoid recording the expense, Mr. Richart asked that the order be canceled, but the purchasing department reported that the parts had already been delivered and the supplier would not accept returns. Since the bill had not yet been paid, Mr. Richart asked the accounting department to correct the clerk's mistake by delaying recognition of the delivery until the bill is paid in January.

Required:
1. Are Mr. Richart's actions ethical? Explain why they are or are not ethical.
2. Do the general management philosophy and accounting policies at General Electronics encourage or discourage ethical behavior? Explain.

TEAMWORK IN ACTION   (LO5)

Understanding the natures of fixed and variable costs is extremely important to managers. This knowledge is used in planning, making strategic and tactical decisions, evaluating performance, and controlling operations.

Required:

Form a team consisting of four persons. Each team member will be responsible for one of the following businesses:

a. Retail store that sells music CDs
b. Dental clinic
c. Fast-food restaurant
d. Auto repair shop

1. In each business decide what single measure best reflects the overall level of activity in the business and give examples of costs that are fixed and variable with respect to small changes in the measure of activity you have chosen.
2. Explain the relationship between the level of activity in each business and each of the following: total fixed costs, fixed cost per unit of activity, total variable costs, variable cost per unit of activity, total costs, and average total cost per unit of activity.
3. Discuss and refine your answers to each of the above questions with your group. Which of the above businesses seems to have the highest ratio of variable to fixed costs? The lowest? Which of the businesses' profits would be most sensitive to changes in demand for its services? The least sensitive? Why?

TAKING IT TO THE NET

As you know, the World Wide Web is a medium that is constantly evolving. Sites come and go and change without notice. To enable periodic update of site addresses, this problem has been posted to the textbook website (www.mhhe.com/bgn2e). After accessing the site, enter the Student Center and select this chapter. Select and complete the Taking It to the Net problem.

Systems Design: Job-Order Costing

CHAPTER OUTLINE

Managing a Successful Furniture Company

Bush Industries, Inc., was included on *Forbes'* list of the 200 Best Small Companies in America. The company is now the 8th largest and the fastest-growing furniture manufacturer in the United States. The company's products include ready-to-assemble home-entertainment, bedroom, home office, and business furniture. Potential customers can view the company's online furniture showroom via a link from its home page at www.bushfurniture.com.

   Now headquartered in Jamestown, New York, the company employs 3,500. Its manufacturing and distribution centers are located in New York, North Carolina, Pennsylvania, Florida, California, and Mexico. Bush's furniture is shipped to retailers, mass merchandisers, and dealers throughout the United States and in over 40 countries throughout the world.

   The popularity of the company's products can be attributed to price and quality. The accuracy of information relating to the costs of the company's various products is critical to the company's continued success. Product costs impact a wide assortment of management decisions—from pricing and profitability to adding and dropping product lines.

———

Sources: Bush Industries, Inc., website, June 2000; "Ranking the 200 Best Small Companies in America," *Forbes,* November 3, 1997, p. 276; Tom Hartley, "Sales Growing Piece-by-Piece at Jamestown Furniture Maker," *Business First of Buffalo—Western New York,* September 23, 1996, p. 1; Stephanie Burdo, "Bush Industries: Doin' It Right," *Business First of Buffalo—Western New York,* December 12, 1994, p. 12.

LEARNING OBJECTIVES

After studying Chapter 2, you should be able to:

LO1 Distinguish between process costing and job-order costing and identify companies that would use each costing method.

LO2 Identify the documents used in a job-order costing system.

LO3 Compute predetermined overhead rates and explain why estimated overhead costs (rather than actual overhead costs) are used in the costing process.

LO4 Prepare journal entries to record costs in a job-order costing system.

LO5 Apply overhead cost to Work in Process using a predetermined overhead rate.

LO6 Prepare schedules of cost of goods manufactured and cost of goods sold.

LO7 Prepare T-accounts to show the flow of costs in a job-order costing system.

LO8 Compute under- or overapplied overhead cost and prepare the journal entry to close the balance in Manufacturing Overhead to the appropriate accounts.

As discussed in the previous chapter, product costing is the process of assigning costs to the products and services provided by a company. An understanding of this costing process is vital to managers, since the way in which a product or service is costed can have a substantial impact on reported profits, as well as on key management decisions.

The essential purpose of any managerial costing system should be to provide cost data to help managers plan, control, direct, and make decisions. Nevertheless, external financial reporting and tax reporting requirements often heavily influence how costs are accumulated and summarized on managerial reports. This is true of product costing.

In this chapter, we use an *absorption costing* approach to determine product costs. This was also the method that was used in the previous chapter. In **absorption costing,** *all* manufacturing costs, fixed and variable, are assigned to units of product—units are said to *fully absorb manufacturing costs.* The absorption costing approach is also known as the **full cost** approach. In a later chapter, we look at product costing from a different point of view called *variable costing,* which is often advocated as an alternative to absorption costing.

In one form or another, most countries—including the United States—require absorption costing for both external financial reporting and for tax reporting. In addition, the vast majority of companies throughout the world also use absorption costing for managerial accounting purposes. Since absorption costing is the most common approach to product costing, we discuss it first and then deal with alternatives in subsequent chapters.

PROCESS AND JOB-ORDER COSTING

In computing the cost of a product or a service, managers are faced with a difficult problem. Many costs (such as rent) do not change much from month to month, whereas production may change frequently, with production going up in one month and then down in another. In addition to variations in the level of production, several different products or services may be produced in a given period in the same facility. Under these conditions, how is it possible to accurately determine the cost of a product or service? In practice, assigning costs to products and services involves an averaging of some type across time periods and across products. The way in which this averaging is carried out depends heavily on the type of production process involved. Two costing systems are commonly used in manufacturing and in many service companies; these two systems are known as *process costing* and *job-order costing.*

Process Costing

A **process costing system** is used in situations where the company produces many units of a single product (such as frozen orange juice concentrate) for long periods. Examples include producing paper at Weyerhaeuser, refining aluminum ingots at Reynolds Aluminum, mixing and bottling beverages at Coca-Cola, and making wieners at Oscar Meyer. All of these industries are characterized by an essentially homogeneous product that flows through the production process on a continuous basis.

The basic approach in process costing is to accumulate costs in a particular operation or department for an entire period (month, quarter, year) and then to divide this total cost by the number of units produced during the period. The basic formula for process costing is:

$$\frac{\text{Unit product cost}}{\text{(per gallon, pound, bottle)}} = \frac{\text{Total manufacturing cost}}{\text{Total units produced (gallons, pounds, bottles)}}$$

Since one unit of product (gallon, pound, bottle) is indistinguishable from any other unit of product, each unit is assigned the same average cost as any other unit produced during the period. This costing technique results in a broad, average unit cost figure that applies to homogeneous units flowing in a continuous stream out of the production process.

Job-Order Costing

A **job-order costing system** is used in situations where many *different* products are produced each period. For example, a Levi Strauss clothing factory would typically make many different types of jeans for both men and women during a month. A particular order might consist of 1,000 stonewashed men's blue denim jeans, style number A312. This order of 1,000 jeans is called a *batch* or a *job*. In a job-order costing system, costs are traced and allocated to jobs and then the costs of the job are divided by the number of units in the job to arrive at an average cost per unit.

Other examples of situations where job-order costing would be used include large-scale construction projects managed by Bechtel International, commercial aircraft produced by Boeing, greeting cards designed and printed at Hallmark, and airline meals prepared by LSG Sky Chefs. All of these examples are characterized by diverse outputs. Each Bechtel project is unique and different from every other—the company may be simultaneously constructing a dam in Zaire and a bridge in Indonesia. Likewise, each airline orders a different type of meal from LSG Sky Chefs' catering service.

Job-order costing is also used extensively in service industries. Hospitals, law firms, movie studios, accounting firms, advertising agencies, and repair shops, for example, all use a variation of job-order costing to accumulate costs for accounting and billing purposes. Although the detailed example of job-order costing provided in the following section deals with a manufacturing firm, the same basic concepts and procedures are used by many service organizations.

The record-keeping and cost assignment problems are more complex when a company sells many different products and services than when it has only a single product.

Continuous Process Manufacturing vs. Job-Order Manufacturing

Continuous Process:

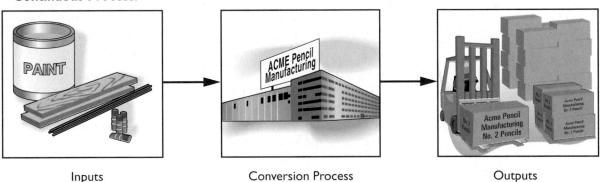

Inputs   Conversion Process   Outputs

Job-Order Process:

Inputs   Conversion Process   Outputs

Since the products are different, the costs are typically different. Consequently, cost records must be maintained for each distinct product or job. For example, an attorney in a large criminal law practice would ordinarily keep separate records of the costs of advising and defending each of her clients. And the Levi Strauss factory mentioned above would keep separate track of the costs of filling orders for particular styles, sizes, and colors of jeans. Thus, a job-order costing system requires more effort than a process-costing system. Nevertheless, job-order costing is used by over half of the manufacturers in the United States.

In this chapter, we focus on the design of a job-order costing system. In the following chapter, we focus on process costing and also look more closely at the similarities and differences between the two costing methods.

JOB-ORDER COSTING—AN OVERVIEW

LEARNING OBJECTIVE 2

Identify the documents used in a job-order costing system.

To introduce job-order costing, we will follow a specific job as it progresses through the manufacturing process. This job consists of two experimental couplings that Yost Precision Machining has agreed to produce for Loops Unlimited, a manufacturer of roller coasters. The couplings connect the cars on the roller coaster and are a critical component in the performance and safety of the ride. Before we begin our discussion, recall from the previous chapter that companies generally classify manufacturing costs into three broad categories: (1) direct materials, (2) direct labor, and (3) manufacturing overhead. As we study the operation of a job-order costing system, we will see how each of these three types of costs is recorded and accumulated.

MANAGERIAL ACCOUNTING IN ACTION

YOST☆ *PRECISION MACHINING*

The Issue

Yost Precision Machining is a small company in Michigan that specializes in fabricating precision metal parts that are used in a variety of applications ranging from deep-sea exploration vehicles to the inertial triggers in automobile air bags. The company's top managers gather every morning at 8:00 A.M. in the company's conference room for the daily planning meeting. Attending the meeting this morning are: Jean Yost, the company's president; David Cheung, the marketing manager; Debbie Turner, the production manager; and Marcus White, the company controller. The president opened the meeting:

Jean: The production schedule indicates we'll be starting job 2B47 today. Isn't that the special order for experimental couplings, David?

David: That's right, Jean. That's the order from Loops Unlimited for two couplings for their new roller coaster ride for Magic Mountain.

Debbie: Why only two couplings? Don't they need a coupling for every car?

David: That's right. But this is a completely new roller coaster. The cars will go faster and will be subjected to more twists, turns, drops, and loops than on any other existing roller coaster. To hold up under these stresses, Loops Unlimited's engineers had to completely redesign the cars and couplings. They want to thoroughly test the design before proceeding to large-scale production. So they want us to make just two of these new couplings for testing purposes. If the design works, then we'll have the inside track on the order to supply couplings for the whole ride.

Jean: We agreed to take on this initial order at our cost just to get our foot in the door. Marcus, will there be any problem documenting our cost so we can get paid?

Marcus: No problem. The contract with Loops stipulates that they will pay us an amount equal to our cost of goods sold. With our job-order costing system, I can tell you that number on the day the job is completed.

Jean: Good. Is there anything else we should discuss about this job at this time? No? Well then let's move on to the next item of business.

Measuring Direct Materials Cost

Yost Precision Machining will require four G7 Connectors and two M46 Housings to make the two experimental couplings for Loops Unlimited. If this were a standard prod-

EXHIBIT 2–1

Materials Requisition Form

Materials Requisition Number ___14873___ Date ___March 2___			
Job Number to Be Charged ___2B47___			
Department ___Milling___			

Description	Quantity	Unit Cost	Total Cost
M46 Housing	2	$124	$248
G7 Connector	4	103	_412_
			$660

Authorized
Signature ___*Bill White*___

uct, there would be a *bill of materials* for the product. A **bill of materials** is a document that lists the type and quantity of each item of materials needed to complete a unit of product. In this case, there is no established bill of materials, so Yost's production staff determined the materials requirements from the blueprints submitted by the customer. Each coupling requires two connectors and one housing, so to make two couplings, four connectors and two housings are required.

When an agreement has been reached with the customer concerning the quantities, prices, and shipment date for the order, a *production order* is issued. The Production Department then prepares a *materials requisition form* similar to the form in Exhibit 2–1. The **materials requisition form** is a detailed source document that (1) specifies the type and quantity of materials to be drawn from the storeroom, and (2) identifies the job to which the costs of the materials are to be charged. The form is used to control the flow of materials into production and also for making entries in the accounting records.

The Yost Precision Machining materials requisition form in Exhibit 2–1 shows that the company's Milling Department has requisitioned two M46 Housings and four G7 Connectors for job 2B47. This completed form is presented to the storeroom clerk who then issues the necessary raw materials. The storeroom clerk is not allowed to release materials without such a form bearing an authorized signature.

Job Cost Sheet

After being notified that the production order has been issued, the Accounting Department prepares a *job cost sheet* similar to the one presented in Exhibit 2–2. A **job cost sheet** is a form prepared for each separate job that records the materials, labor, and overhead costs charged to the job.

After direct materials are issued, the Accounting Department records their costs directly on the job cost sheet. Note from Exhibit 2–2, for example, that the $660 cost for direct materials shown earlier on the materials requisition form has been charged to job 2B47 on its job cost sheet. The requisition number 14873 is also recorded on the job cost sheet to make it easier to identify the source document for the direct materials charge.

In addition to serving as a means for charging costs to jobs, the job cost sheet also serves as a key part of a firm's accounting records. The job cost sheets form a subsidiary ledger to the Work in Process account. They are detailed records for the jobs in process that add up to the balance in Work in Process.

Concept 2–1

Measuring Direct Labor Cost

Direct labor cost is handled in much the same way as direct materials cost. Direct labor consists of labor charges that are easily traced to a particular job. Labor charges that cannot be easily traced directly to any job are treated as part of manufacturing overhead. As

EXHIBIT 2–2

Job Cost Sheet

JOB COST SHEET

Job Number __2B47__   Date Initiated ___March 2___

                                        Date Completed _____

Department __Milling__   Units Completed _____

Item __Special order coupling__

For Stock _____

Direct Materials		Direct Labor			Manufacturing Overhead		
Req. No.	Amount	Ticket	Hours	Amount	Hours	Rate	Amount
14873	$660	843	5	$45			

Cost Summary		Units Shipped		
Direct Materials	$	Date	Number	Balance
Direct Labor	$			
Manufacturing Overhead	$			
Total Cost	$			
Unit Cost	$			

discussed in the previous chapter, this latter category of labor costs is called *indirect labor* and includes tasks such as maintenance, supervision, and cleanup.

Relationship of Direct Labor to Product Cost

How much direct labor is in the products you buy? Sometimes not very much. During a visit to the Massachusetts Institute of Technology, Chinese Prime Minister Zhu Rongji claimed that, of the $120 retail cost of a pair of athletic shoes made in China, only $2 goes to the Chinese workers who assemble them. The National Labor Committee based in New York estimates that the labor cost to assemble a $90 pair of Nike sneakers is only $1.20.

Source: Robert A. Senser, letter to the editor, *Business Week,* May 24, 1999, pp. 11–12.

Workers use *time tickets* to record the time they spend on each job and task. A completed **time ticket** is an hour-by-hour summary of the employee's activities throughout the day. An example of an employee time ticket is shown in Exhibit 2–3. When working on a specific job, the employee enters the job number on the time ticket and notes the amount of time spent on that job. When not assigned to a particular job, the employee records the nature of the indirect labor task (such as cleanup and maintenance) and the amount of time spent on the task.

At the end of the day, the time tickets are gathered and the Accounting Department enters the direct labor-hours and costs on individual job cost sheets. (See Exhibit 2–2 for an example of how direct labor costs are entered on the job cost sheet.) The daily time tickets are source documents that are used as the basis for labor cost entries into the accounting records.

Time Ticket No. 843			Date	March 3		
Employee	Mary Holden		Station	4		
Started	Ended	Time Completed	Rate	Amount	Job Number	
7:00	12:00	5.0	$9	$45	2B47	
12:30	2:30	2.0	9	18	2B50	
2:30	3:30	1.0	9	9	Maintenance	
Totals		8.0		$72		
Supervisor	R.W. Pace					

EXHIBIT 2–3

Employee Time Ticket

More Productive Use of Time

IN BUSINESS

Is it always worth the trouble to fill out labor time tickets? In a word, no. United Electric Controls, Inc., located in Waterton, Massachusetts, makes temperature and pressure sensors and controls. The manufacturing vice president decided he wanted the workers to spend their time focusing on getting products out the door rather than on filling out labor time tickets. The company converted everyone to salaried workers and stopped producing labor reports.

Source: Richard L. Jenson, James W. Brackner, and Clifford Skousen. *Management Accounting in Support of Manufacturing Excellence*, 1996, The IMA Foundation for Applied Research, Inc., Montvale, New Jersey, p. 12.

Managing Diversity with Technology

IN BUSINESS

Andersen Windows, Inc., of Bayport, Minnesota, has a software program that enables it to produce just about any window configuration that a customer might order. The program, which works on most standard Microsoft® Windows platforms, allows customers to select from any of the company's large selection of standard window and door sizes and styles. Customers can add the features and options they want with an easy "point-and-click" until they've configured the desired units. Placing the order after final selections are made is just as easy. The window order can be sent electronically into Andersen's back office system where it is automatically fulfilled. The entire process is highly automated and very efficient, yet it enables the customer a high degree of flexibility.

Source: Andersen® Intelligent Quote, used by permission of Andersen Windows, Inc.

The system we have just described is a manual method for recording and posting labor costs. Many companies now rely on computerized systems and no longer record labor time by hand on sheets of paper. One computerized approach uses bar codes to enter the basic data into a computer. Each employee and each job has a unique bar code. When an employee begins work on a job, he or she scans three bar codes using a handheld device much like the bar code readers at grocery store check-out stands. The first bar code indicates that a job is being started; the second is the unique bar code on his or her identity badge; and the third is the unique bar code of the job itself. This information is fed

Concept 2–2

LEARNING OBJECTIVE 3

Compute predetermined overhead rates and explain why estimated overhead costs (rather than actual overhead costs) are used in the costing process.

automatically via an electronic network to a computer that notes the time and then records all of the data. When the employee completes the task, he or she scans a bar code indicating the task is complete, the bar code on his or her identity badge, and the bar code attached to the job. This information is relayed to the computer that again notes the time, and a time ticket is automatically prepared. Since all of the source data are already in computer files, the labor costs can be automatically posted to job cost sheets (or their electronic equivalents). Computers, coupled with technology such as bar codes, can eliminate much of the drudgery involved in routine bookkeeping activities while at the same time increasing timeliness and accuracy.

Application of Manufacturing Overhead

Manufacturing overhead must be included with direct materials and direct labor on the job cost sheet since manufacturing overhead is also a product cost. However, assigning manufacturing overhead to units of product can be a difficult task. There are three reasons for this.

1. Manufacturing overhead is an *indirect cost*. This means that it is either impossible or difficult to trace these costs to a particular product or job.
2. Manufacturing overhead consists of many different items ranging from the grease used in machines to the annual salary of the production manager.
3. Even though output may fluctuate due to seasonal or other factors, manufacturing overhead costs tend to remain relatively constant due to the presence of fixed costs.

Given these problems, about the only way to assign overhead costs to products is to use an allocation process. This allocation of overhead costs is accomplished by selecting an *allocation base* that is common to all of the company's products and services. An **allocation base** is a measure such as direct labor-hours (DLH) or machine-hours (MH) that is used to assign overhead costs to products and services.

The most widely used allocation bases are direct labor-hours and direct labor cost, with machine-hours and even units of product (where a company has only a single product) also used to some extent.

The allocation base is used to compute the **predetermined overhead rate** in the following formula:

$$\text{Predetermined overhead rate} = \frac{\text{Estimated total manufacturing overhead cost}}{\text{Estimated total units in the allocation base}}$$

Note that the predetermined overhead rate is based on *estimates* rather than actual results.[1] This is because the *predetermined* overhead rate is computed *before* the period begins and is used to *apply* overhead cost to jobs throughout the period. The process of assigning overhead cost to jobs is called **overhead application.** The formula for determining the amount of overhead cost to apply to a particular job is:

$$\begin{array}{c}\text{Overhead applied to} \\ \text{a particular job}\end{array} = \begin{array}{c}\text{Predetermined} \\ \text{overhead rate}\end{array} \times \begin{array}{c}\text{Amount of the allocation} \\ \text{base incurred by the job}\end{array}$$

For example, if the predetermined overhead rate is $8 per direct labor-hour, then $8 of overhead cost is *applied* to a job for each direct labor-hour incurred by the job. When the allocation base is direct labor-hours, the formula becomes:

$$\begin{array}{c}\text{Overhead applied to} \\ \text{a particular job}\end{array} = \begin{array}{c}\text{Predetermined} \\ \text{overhead rate}\end{array} \times \begin{array}{c}\text{Actual direct labor-hours} \\ \text{charged to the job}\end{array}$$

Using the Predetermined Overhead Rate   To illustrate the steps involved in computing and using a predetermined overhead rate, let's return to Yost Precision

---

[1]Some experts argue that the predetermined overhead rate should be based on activity at capacity rather than on estimated activity. See Appendix 3A of Ray Garrison and Eric Noreen, *Managerial Accounting,* 10th edition, for details.

EXHIBIT 2–4

A Completed Job Cost Sheet

JOB COST SHEET

Job Number __2B47__   Date Initiated __March 2__

Date Completed __March 8__

Department __Milling__

Item __Special order coupling__   Units Completed __2__

For Stock _____

Direct Materials		Direct Labor			Manufacturing Overhead		
Req. No.	Amount	Ticket	Hours	Amount	Hours	Rate	Amount
14873	$ 660	843	5	$ 45	27	$8/DLH	$216
14875	506	846	8	60			
14912	238	850	4	21			
	$1,404	851	10	54			
			27	$180			

Cost Summary		Units Shipped		
Direct Materials	$1,404	Date	Number	Balance
Direct Labor	$ 180	March 8	—	2
Manufacturing Overhead	$ 216			
Total Cost	$1,800			
Unit Cost	$ 900*			

*$1,800 ÷ 2 units = $900 per unit.

Machining. The company has estimated its total manufacturing overhead costs at $320,000 for the year and its total direct labor-hours at 40,000. Its predetermined overhead rate for the year would be $8 per direct labor-hour, as shown below:

$$\text{Predetermined overhead rate} = \frac{\text{Estimated total manufacturing overhead cost}}{\text{Estimated total units in the allocation base}}$$

$$= \frac{\$320,000}{40,000 \text{ direct labor-hours}}$$

$$= \$8 \text{ per direct labor-hour}$$

The job cost sheet in Exhibit 2–4 indicates that 27 direct labor-hours (i.e., DLHs) were charged to job 2B47. Therefore, a total of $216 of manufacturing overhead cost would be applied to the job:

$$\begin{matrix} \text{Overhead applied to} \\ \text{job 2B47} \end{matrix} = \begin{matrix} \text{Predetermined} \\ \text{overhead rate} \end{matrix} \times \begin{matrix} \text{Actual direct labor-hours} \\ \text{charged to job 2B47} \end{matrix}$$

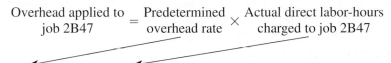

$8 per direct labor-hour × 27 direct labor-hours = $216 of overhead applied to job 2B47

This amount of overhead has been entered on the job cost sheet in Exhibit 2–4. Note that this is *not* the actual amount of overhead caused by the job. There is no attempt to trace actual overhead costs to jobs—if that could be done, the costs would be direct costs, not overhead. The overhead assigned to the job is simply a share of the total overhead that was estimated at the beginning of the year. When a company applies overhead cost to jobs as we have done—that is, by multiplying actual activity times the predetermined overhead rate—it is called a **normal cost system.**

The overhead may be applied as direct labor-hours are charged to jobs, or all of the overhead can be applied at once when the job is completed. The choice is up to the company. If a job is not completed at year-end, however, overhead should be applied to value the work in process inventory.

The Need for a Predetermined Rate   Instead of using a predetermined rate, a company could wait until the end of the accounting period to compute an actual overhead rate based on the *actual* total manufacturing costs and the *actual* total units in the allocation base for the period. However, managers cite several reasons for using predetermined overhead rates instead of actual overhead rates:

1. Managers would like to know the accounting system's valuation of completed jobs *before* the end of the accounting period. Suppose, for example, that Yost Precision Machining waits until the end of the year to compute its overhead rate. Then there would be no way for managers to know the cost of goods sold for job 2B47 until the close of the year, even though the job was completed and shipped to the customer in March. The seriousness of this problem can be reduced to some extent by computing the actual overhead more frequently, but that immediately leads to another problem as discussed below.
2. If actual overhead rates are computed frequently, seasonal factors in overhead costs or in the allocation base can produce fluctuations in the overhead rates. For example, the costs of heating and cooling a production facility in Illinois will be highest in the winter and summer months and lowest in the spring and fall. If an overhead rate were computed each month or each quarter, the predetermined overhead rate would go up in the winter and summer and down in the spring and fall. Two identical jobs, one completed in winter and one completed in the spring, would be assigned different costs if the overhead rate were computed on a monthly or quarterly basis. Managers generally feel that such fluctuations in overhead rates and costs serve no useful purpose and are misleading.
3. The use of a predetermined overhead rate simplifies record keeping. To determine the overhead cost to apply to a job, the accounting staff at Yost Precision Machining simply multiplies the direct labor-hours recorded for the job by the predetermined overhead rate of $8 per direct labor-hour.

For these reasons, most companies use predetermined overhead rates rather than actual overhead rates in their cost accounting systems.

Choice of an Allocation Base for Overhead Cost

Ideally, the allocation base used in the predetermined overhead rate should be the *cost driver* of the overhead cost. A **cost driver** is a factor, such as machine-hours, beds occupied, computer time, or flight-hours, that causes overhead costs. If a base is used to compute overhead rates that does not "drive" overhead costs, then the result will be inaccurate overhead rates and distorted product costs. For example, if direct labor-hours are used to allocate overhead, but in reality overhead has little to do with direct labor-hours, then products with high direct labor-hour requirements will shoulder an unrealistic burden of overhead and will be overcosted.

Most companies use direct labor-hours or direct labor cost as the allocation base for manufacturing overhead. However, as discussed in earlier chapters, major shifts are taking place in the structure of costs in many industries. In the past, direct labor accounted for up to 60% of the cost of many products, with overhead cost making up only a portion of the remainder. This situation has been changing—for two reasons. First, sophisticated automated equipment has taken over functions that used to be performed by direct labor workers. Since the costs of acquiring and maintaining such equipment are classified as overhead, this increases overhead while decreasing direct labor. Second, products are themselves becoming more sophisticated and complex and change more frequently. This increases the need for highly skilled indirect workers such as engineers. As a result of these two trends, direct labor is becoming less of a factor and overhead is becoming more of a factor in the cost of products in many industries.

In companies where direct labor and overhead costs have been moving in opposite directions, it would be difficult to argue that direct labor "drives" overhead costs. Accordingly, in recent years, managers in some companies have used *activity-based costing* principles to redesign their cost accounting systems. Activity-based costing is a costing technique that is designed to more accurately reflect the demands that products, customers, and other cost objects make on overhead resources. The activity-based approach is discussed in more detail in Chapter 3.

We hasten to add that although direct labor may not be an appropriate allocation base in some industries, in others it continues to be a significant driver of manufacturing overhead. Indeed, most manufacturing companies in the United States continue to use direct labor as the primary or secondary allocation base for manufacturing overhead. The key point is that the allocation base used by the company should really drive, or cause, overhead costs, and direct labor is not always an appropriate allocation base.

Computation of Unit Costs

With the application of Yost Precision Machining's $216 manufacturing overhead to the job cost sheet in Exhibit 2–4, the job cost sheet is complete except for two final steps. First, the totals for direct materials, direct labor, and manufacturing overhead are transferred to the Cost Summary section of the job cost sheet and added together to obtain the total cost for the job. Then the total cost ($1,800) is divided by the number of units (2) to obtain the unit cost ($900). As indicated earlier, *this unit cost is an average cost and should not be interpreted as the cost that would actually be incurred if another unit were produced.* Much of the actual overhead would not change at all if another unit were produced, so the incremental cost of an additional unit is something less than the average unit cost of $900.

The completed job cost sheet is now ready to be transferred to the Finished Goods inventory account, where it will serve as the basis for valuing unsold units in ending inventory and determining cost of goods sold.

Treasurer, Class Reunion Committee

DECISION
MAKER

It is hard to believe that 10 years have passed so quickly since your graduation from high school. Take a minute to reflect on what has happened in that time frame. After high school, you attended the local community college, transferred to the state university, and graduated on time. You're juggling a successful career, classes in an evening MBA program, and a new family. And now, after reminiscing with one of your high school classmates, you've somehow agreed to handle the financial arrangements for your 10-year reunion. What were you thinking? Well, at least you can fall back on those accounting skills.

You call the restaurant where the reunion will be held and jot down the most important information. The meal cost (including beverages) will be $30 per person plus a 15% gratuity. An additional $200 will be charged for a banquet room with a dance floor. A band has been hired for $500. One of the members of the reunion committee informs you that there is just enough money left in the class bank account to cover the printing and mailing costs. He mentions that at least one-half of the class of 400 will attend the reunion and wonders if he should add the 15% gratuity to the $30 per person meal cost when he drafts the invitation, which will indicate that a check must be returned with the reply card.

How should you respond? How much will you need to charge to cover the various costs? After making your decision, label your answer with the managerial accounting terms covered in this chapter. Finally, identify any issues that should be investigated further.

Summary of Document Flows

The sequence of events discussed above is summarized in Exhibit 2–5. A careful study of the flow of documents in this exhibit will provide a good overview of the overall operation of a job-order costing system.

MANAGERIAL ACCOUNTING IN ACTION

The Wrap-Up

In the 8:00 A.M. daily planning meeting on March 9, Jean Yost, the president of Yost Precision Machining, once again drew attention to job 2B47, the experimental couplings:

Jean: I see job 2B47 is completed. Let's get those couplings shipped immediately to Loops Unlimited so they can get their testing program under way. Marcus, how much are we going to bill Loops for those two units?

Marcus: Just a second, let me check the job cost sheet for that job. Here it is. We agreed to sell the experimental units at cost, so we will be charging Loops Unlimited just $900 a unit.

Jean: Fine. Let's hope the couplings work out and we make some money on the big order later.

CONCEPT CHECK ✓

1. Which of the following statements is false? (You may select more than one answer.)
   a. Absorption costing assigns fixed and variable manufacturing overhead costs to products.
   b. Job-order costing systems are used when companies produce many different types of products.
   c. A normal costing system assigns costs to products by multiplying the actual activity level by the actual overhead rate.
   d. A company such as Coca-Cola is more likely to use a process costing system than a job-order costing system.

JOB-ORDER COSTING—THE FLOW OF COSTS

LEARNING OBJECTIVE 4

Prepare journal entries to record costs in a job-order costing system.

We are now ready to take a more detailed look at the flow of costs through the company's formal accounting system. To illustrate, we shall consider a single month's activity for Rand Company, a producer of gold and silver commemorative medallions. Rand Company has two jobs in process during April, the first month of its fiscal year. Job A, a special minting of 1,000 gold medallions commemorating the invention of motion pictures, was started during March. By the end of March, $30,000 in manufacturing costs had been recorded for the job. Job B, an order for 10,000 silver medallions commemorating the fall of the Berlin Wall, was started in April.

The Purchase and Issue of Materials

On April 1, Rand Company had $7,000 in raw materials on hand. During the month, the company purchased on account an additional $60,000 in raw materials. The purchase is recorded in journal entry (1) below:

(1)

Raw Materials	60,000	
Accounts Payable		60,000

As explained in the previous chapter, Raw Materials is an asset account. Thus, when raw materials are purchased, they are initially recorded as an asset—not as an expense.

EXHIBIT 2–5 The Flow of Documents in a Job-Order Costing System

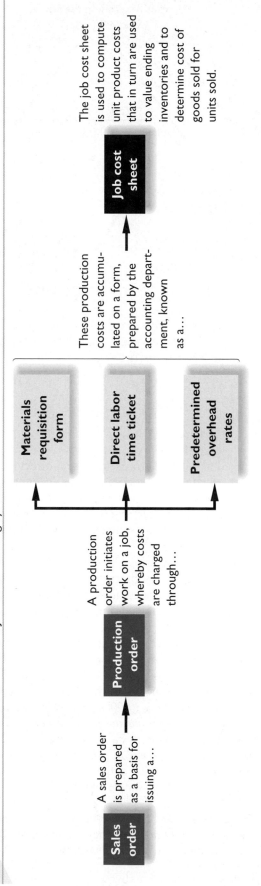

Sales order

A sales order is prepared as a basis for issuing a…

Production order

A production order initiates work on a job, whereby costs are charged through…

Materials requisition form

Direct labor time ticket

Predetermined overhead rates

These production costs are accumulated on a form, prepared by the accounting department, known as a…

Job cost sheet

The job cost sheet is used to compute unit product costs that in turn are used to value ending inventories and to determine cost of goods sold for units sold.

EXHIBIT 2–6

Raw Materials Cost Flows

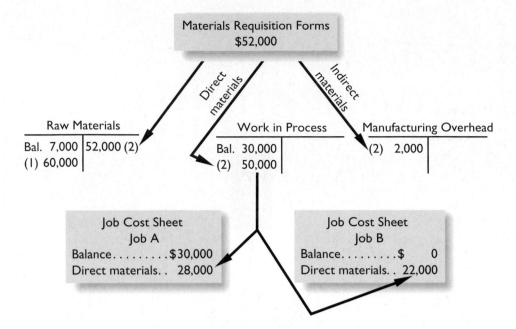

Issue of Direct and Indirect Materials

Issue of Direct and Indirect Materials   During April, $52,000 in raw materials were requisitioned from the storeroom for use in production. Entry (2) records issuing the materials to the production departments.

	(2)	
Work in Process...............................	50,000	
Manufacturing Overhead	2,000	
Raw Materials...............................		52,000

The materials charged to Work in Process represent direct materials for specific jobs. As these materials are entered into the Work in Process account, they are also recorded on the appropriate job cost sheets. This point is illustrated in Exhibit 2–6, where $28,000 of the $50,000 in direct materials is charged to job A's cost sheet and the remaining $22,000 is charged to job B's cost sheet. (In this example, all data are presented in summary form and the job cost sheet is abbreviated.)

The $2,000 charged to Manufacturing Overhead in entry (2) represents indirect materials used in production during April. Observe that the Manufacturing Overhead account is separate from the Work in Process account. The purpose of the Manufacturing Overhead account is to accumulate all manufacturing overhead costs as they are incurred during a period.

Before leaving Exhibit 2–6 we need to point out one additional thing. Notice from the exhibit that the job cost sheet for job A contains a beginning balance of $30,000. We stated earlier that this balance represents the cost of work done during March that has been carried forward to April. Also note that the Work in Process account contains the same $30,000 balance. *The reason the $30,000 appears in both places is that the Work in Process account is a control account and the job cost sheets form a subsidiary ledger. Thus, the Work in Process account contains a summarized total of all costs appearing on the individual job cost sheets for all jobs in process at any given point in time.* (Since Rand Company had only job A in process at the beginning of April, job A's $30,000 balance on that date is equal to the balance in the Work in Process account.)

Issue of Direct Materials Only

Issue of Direct Materials Only   Sometimes the materials drawn from the Raw Materials inventory account are all direct materials. In this case, the entry to record the issue of the materials into production would be as follows:

Work in Process...............................	XXX	
Raw Materials...............................		XXX

EXHIBIT 2–7

Labor Cost Flows

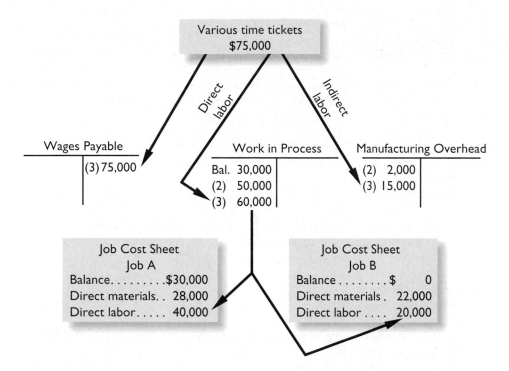

Labor Cost

As work is performed each day in various departments of Rand Company, employee time tickets are filled out by workers, collected, and forwarded to the Accounting Department. In the Accounting Department, wages are computed and the resulting costs are classified as either direct or indirect labor. This costing and classification for April resulted in the following summary entry:

	(3)	
Work in Process......................................	60,000	
Manufacturing Overhead	15,000	
Salaries and Wages Payable....................		75,000

Only direct labor is added to the Work in Process account. For Rand Company, this amounted to $60,000 for April.

At the same time that direct labor costs are added to Work in Process, they are also added to the individual job cost sheets, as shown in Exhibit 2–7. During April, $40,000 of direct labor cost was charged to job A and the remaining $20,000 was charged to job B.

The labor costs charged to Manufacturing Overhead represent the indirect labor costs of the period, such as supervision, janitorial work, and maintenance.

Manufacturing Overhead Costs

Recall that all costs of operating the factory other than direct materials and direct labor are classified as manufacturing overhead costs. These costs are entered directly into the Manufacturing Overhead account as they are incurred. To illustrate, assume that Rand Company incurred the following general factory costs during April:

Utilities (heat, water, and power)	$21,000
Rent on factory equipment	16,000
Miscellaneous factory overhead costs	3,000
Total	$40,000

The following entry records the incurrence of these costs:

(4)

| Manufacturing Overhead .... | 40,000 | |
| Accounts Payable .... | | 40,000 |

In addition, let us assume that during April, Rand Company recognized $13,000 in accrued property taxes and that $7,000 in prepaid insurance expired on factory buildings and equipment. The following entry records these items:

(5)

Manufacturing Overhead	20,000	
Property Taxes Payable.......................		13,000
Prepaid Insurance...........................		7,000

Finally, let us assume that the company recognized $18,000 in depreciation on factory equipment during April. The following entry records the accrual of this depreciation:

(6)

| Manufacturing Overhead .... | 18,000 | |
| Accumulated Depreciation.................... | | 18,000 |

In short, *all* manufacturing overhead costs are recorded directly into the Manufacturing Overhead account as they are incurred day by day throughout a period. It is important to understand that Manufacturing Overhead is a control account for many—perhaps thousands—of subsidiary accounts such as Indirect Materials, Indirect Labor, Factory Utilities, and so forth. As the Manufacturing Overhead account is debited for costs during a period, the various subsidiary accounts are also debited. In the example above and also in the assignment material for this chapter, we omit the entries to the subsidiary accounts for the sake of brevity.

The Application of Manufacturing Overhead

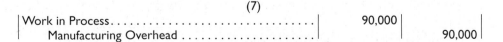

LEARNING OBJECTIVE 5

Apply overhead cost to Work in Process using a predetermined overhead rate.

Since actual manufacturing costs are charged to the Manufacturing Overhead control account rather than to Work in Process, how are manufacturing overhead costs assigned to Work in Process? The answer is, by means of the predetermined overhead rate. Recall from our discussion earlier in the chapter that a predetermined overhead rate is established at the beginning of each year. The rate is calculated by dividing the estimated total manufacturing overhead cost for the year by the estimated total units in the allocation base (measured in machine-hours, direct labor-hours, or some other base). The predetermined overhead rate is then used to apply overhead costs to jobs. For example, if direct labor-hours is the allocation base, overhead cost is applied to each job by multiplying the number of direct labor-hours charged to the job by the predetermined overhead rate.

To illustrate, assume that Rand Company has used machine-hours to compute its predetermined overhead rate and that this rate is $6 per machine-hour. Also assume that during April, 10,000 machine-hours were worked on job A and 5,000 machine-hours were worked on job B (a total of 15,000 machine-hours). Thus, $90,000 in overhead cost (15,000 machine-hours × $6 per machine-hour = $90,000) would be applied to Work in Process. The following entry records the application of Manufacturing Overhead to Work in Process:

(7)

| Work in Process................................ | 90,000 | |
| Manufacturing Overhead .... | | 90,000 |

The flow of costs through the Manufacturing Overhead account is shown in Exhibit 2–8.

The actual overhead costs in the Manufacturing Overhead account in Exhibit 2–8 are the costs that were added to the account in entries (2)–(6). Observe that the incurrence of these actual overhead costs [entries (2)–(6)] and the application of overhead to Work in Process [entry (7)] represent two separate and entirely distinct processes.

EXHIBIT 2–8

The Flow of Costs in Overhead Application

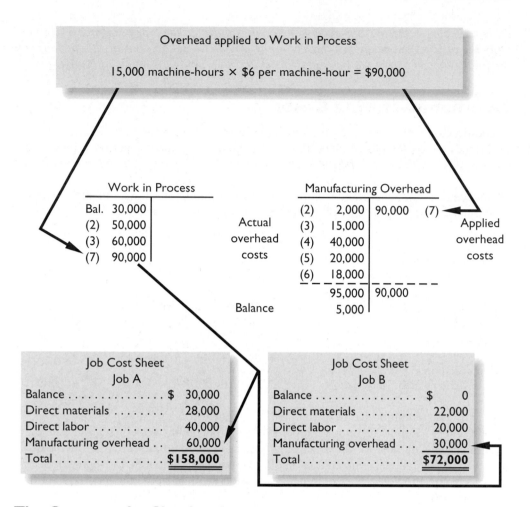

The Concept of a Clearing Account

The Manufacturing Overhead account operates as a clearing account. As we have noted, actual factory overhead costs are debited to the accounts as they are incurred day by day throughout the year. At certain intervals during the year, usually when a job is completed, overhead cost is applied to the job by means of the predetermined overhead rate, and Work in Process is debited and Manufacturing Overhead is credited. This sequence of events is illustrated below:

**Manufacturing Overhead
(a clearing account)**

Actual overhead costs are charged to this account as they are incurred throughout the period.	Overhead is removed from this account and is applied to Work in Process using the predetermined overhead rate.

As we emphasized earlier, the predetermined overhead rate is based entirely on estimates of what overhead costs are *expected* to be, and it is established before the year begins. As a result, the overhead cost applied during a year will almost certainly turn out to be more or less than the overhead cost that is actually incurred. For example, notice from Exhibit 2–8 that Rand Company's actual overhead costs for the period are $5,000 greater than the overhead cost that has been applied to Work in Process, resulting in a $5,000 debit balance in the Manufacturing Overhead account. We will reserve discussion of what to do with this $5,000 balance until the next section, Problems of Overhead Application.

For the moment, we can conclude by noting from Exhibit 2–8 that the cost of a completed job consists of the actual materials cost of the job, the actual labor cost of the job, and the overhead cost *applied* to the job. Pay particular attention to the following subtle but important point: *Actual overhead costs are not charged to jobs; actual overhead costs do not appear on the job cost sheet nor do they appear in the Work in Process account. Only the applied overhead cost, based on the predetermined overhead rate, appears on the job cost sheet and in the Work in Process account.* Study this point carefully.

Nonmanufacturing Costs

In addition to manufacturing costs, companies also incur marketing and selling costs. As explained in the previous chapter, these costs should be treated as period expenses and charged directly to the income statement. *Nonmanufacturing costs should not go into the Manufacturing Overhead account.* To illustrate the correct treatment of nonmanufacturing costs, assume that Rand Company incurred $30,000 in selling and administrative salary costs during April. The following entry records these salaries:

	(8)		
Salaries Expense................................	30,000	
Salaries and Wages Payable...................		30,000

Assume that depreciation on office equipment during April was $7,000. The entry would be:

	(9)		
Depreciation Expense	7,000	
Accumulated Depreciation...................		7,000

Pay particular attention to the difference between this entry and entry (6) where we recorded depreciation on factory equipment. In journal entry (6), depreciation on factory equipment was debited to Manufacturing Overhead and is therefore a product cost. In journal entry (9) above, depreciation on office equipment is debited to Depreciation Expense. Depreciation on office equipment is considered to be a period expense rather than a product cost.

Finally, assume that advertising was $42,000 and that other selling and administrative expenses in April totaled $8,000. The following entry records these items:

	(10)		
Advertising Expense............................	42,000	
Other Selling and Administrative Expense............	8,000	
Accounts Payable		50,000

Since the amounts in entries (8) through (10) all go directly into expense accounts, they will have no effect on the costing of Rand Company's production for April. The same will be true of any other selling and administrative expenses incurred during April, including sales commissions, depreciation on sales equipment, rent on office facilities, insurance on office facilities, and related costs.

Cost of Goods Manufactured

When a job has been completed, the finished output is transferred from the production departments to the finished goods warehouse. By this time, the accounting department will have charged the job with direct materials and direct labor cost, and manufacturing overhead will have been applied using the predetermined rate. A transfer of these costs is made within the costing system that *parallels* the physical transfer of the goods to the finished goods warehouse. The costs of the completed job are transferred out of the Work in Process account and into the Finished Goods account. The sum of all amounts transferred between these two accounts represents the cost of goods manufactured for the period.

In the case of Rand Company, let us assume that job A was completed during April. The following entry transfers the cost of job A from Work in Process to Finished Goods:

(11)

| Finished Goods.................................. | 158,000 | |
| Work in Process............................ | | 158,000 |

The $158,000 represents the completed cost of job A, as shown on the job cost sheet in Exhibit 2–8. Since job A was the only job completed during April, the $158,000 also represents the cost of goods manufactured for the month.

Job B was not completed by month-end, so its cost will remain in the Work in Process account and carry over to the next month. If a balance sheet is prepared at the end of April, the cost accumulated thus far on job B will appear as "Work in process inventory" in the assets section.

Cost of Goods Sold

As units in finished goods are shipped to fill customers' orders, their costs are transferred from the Finished Goods account into the Cost of Goods Sold account. If a complete job is shipped, as in the case where a job has been done to a customer's specifications, then it is a simple matter to transfer the entire cost appearing on the job cost sheet into the Cost of Goods Sold account. In most cases, however, only a portion of the units involved in a particular job will be immediately sold. In these situations, the unit cost must be used to determine how much product cost should be removed from Finished Goods and charged to Cost of Goods Sold.

For Rand Company, we will assume 750 of the 1,000 gold medallions in job A were shipped to customers by the end of the month for total sales revenue of $225,000. Since 1,000 units were produced and the total cost of the job from the job cost sheet was $158,000, the unit product cost was $158. The following journal entries would record the sale (all sales are on account):

(12)

| Accounts Receivable .... | 225,000 | |
| Sales .... | | 225,000 |

(13)

Cost of Goods Sold	118,500	
Finished Goods............................		118,500
($158 per unit × 750 units = $118,500)		

With entry (13), the flow of costs through our job-order costing system is completed.

Summary of Cost Flows

To pull the entire Rand Company example together, journal entries (1) through (13) are summarized in Exhibit 2–9 on page 96. The flow of costs through the accounts is presented in T-account form in Exhibit 2–10 on page 97.

Exhibit 2–11 on page 98 presents a schedule of cost of goods manufactured and a schedule of cost of goods sold for Rand Company. Note particularly from Exhibit 2–11 that the manufacturing overhead cost on the schedule of cost of goods manufactured is the overhead applied to jobs during the month—not the actual manufacturing overhead costs incurred. The reason for this can be traced back to journal entry (7) and the T-account for Work in Process that appears in Exhibit 2–10. Under a normal costing system as illustrated in this chapter, applied—not actual—overhead costs are applied to jobs and thus to Work in Process inventory. Note also the cost of goods manufactured for the month ($158,000) agrees with the amount transferred from Work in Process to Finished Goods for the month as recorded earlier in entry (11). Also note that this $158,000 figure is used in computing the cost of goods sold for the month.

An income statement for April is presented in Exhibit 2–12 on page 98. Observe that the cost of goods sold figure on this statement ($123,500) is carried down from Exhibit 2–11.

LEARNING OBJECTIVE 7

Prepare T-accounts to show the flow of costs in a job-order costing system.

EXHIBIT 2–9

Summary of Rand Company
Journal Entries

(1)		
Raw Materials...................................	60,000	
Accounts Payable............................		60,000

(2)		
Work in Process................................	50,000	
Manufacturing Overhead	2,000	
Raw Materials...............................		52,000

(3)		
Work in Process................................	60,000	
Manufacturing Overhead	15,000	
Salaries and Wages Payable....................		75,000

(4)		
Manufacturing Overhead	40,000	
Accounts Payable............................		40,000

(5)		
Manufacturing Overhead	20,000	
Property Taxes Payable.......................		13,000
Prepaid Insurance............................		7,000

(6)		
Manufacturing Overhead	18,000	
Accumulated Depreciation....................		18,000

(7)		
Work in Process................................	90,000	
Manufacturing Overhead		90,000

(8)		
Salaries Expense	30,000	
Salaries and Wages Payable....................		30,000

(9)		
Depreciation Expense	7,000	
Accumulated Depreciation....................		7,000

(10)		
Advertising Expense.............................	42,000	
Other Selling and Administrative Expense...........	8,000	
Accounts Payable............................		50,000

(11)		
Finished Goods.................................	158,000	
Work in Process.............................		158,000

(12)		
Accounts Receivable	225,000	
Sales		225,000

(13)		
Cost of Goods Sold	118,500	
Finished Goods.............................		118,500

EXHIBIT 2–10 Summary of Cost Flows—Rand Company

Accounts Receivable			
	XX*		
(12)	225,000		

Prepaid Insurance			
XX		7,000	(5)

Raw Materials			
Bal.	7,000	52,000	(2)
(1)	60,000		
Bal.	15,000		

Work in Process			
Bal.	30,000	158,000	(11)
(2)	50,000		
(3)	60,000		
(7)	90,000		
Bal.	72,000		

Finished Goods			
Bal.	10,000	118,500	(13)
(11)	158,000		
Bal.	49,500		

Accumulated Depreciation			
		XX	
		18,000	(6)
		7,000	(9)

Manufacturing Overhead			
(2)	2,000	90,000	(7)
(3)	15,000		
(4)	40,000		
(5)	20,000		
(6)	18,000		
Bal.	5,000		

Accounts Payable			
		XX	
		60,000	(1)
		40,000	(4)
		50,000	(10)

Salaries and Wages Payable			
		XX	
		75,000	(3)
		30,000	(8)

Property Taxes Payable			
		XX	
		13,000	(5)

Capital Stock			
		XX	

Retained Earnings			
		XX	

Sales			
		225,000	(12)

Cost of Goods Sold			
(13)	118,500		

Salaries Expense			
(8)	30,000		

Depreciation Expense			
(9)	7,000		

Advertising Expense			
(10)	42,000		

Other Selling and Administrative Expense			
(10)	8,000		

Explanation of entries:
(1) Raw materials purchased.
(2) Direct and indirect materials issued into production.
(3) Direct and indirect factory labor cost incurred.
(4) Utilities and other factory costs incurred.
(5) Property taxes and insurance incurred on the factory.
(6) Depreciation recorded on factory assets.
(7) Overhead cost applied to Work in Process.
(8) Administrative salaries expense incurred.
(9) Depreciation recorded on office equipment.
(10) Advertising and other expense incurred.
(11) Cost of goods manufactured transferred into finished goods.
(12) Sale of job A recorded.
(13) Cost of goods sold recorded for job A.
*XX = Normal balance in the account (for example, Accounts Receivable normally carries a debit balance).

EXHIBIT 2–11

Schedules of Cost of Goods
Manufactured and Cost of
Goods Sold

Cost of Goods Manufactured

Direct materials:

Raw materials inventory, beginning	$ 7,000	
Add: Purchases of raw materials	60,000	
Total raw materials available	67,000	
Deduct: Raw materials inventory, ending	15,000	
Raw materials used in production	52,000	
Less indirect materials included in manufacturing overhead	2,000	$ 50,000
Direct labor		60,000
Manufacturing overhead applied to work in process		90,000
Total manufacturing costs		200,000
Add: Beginning work in process inventory		30,000
		230,000
Deduct: Ending work in process inventory		72,000
Cost of goods manufactured		$158,000

Cost of Goods Sold

Finished goods inventory, beginning	$ 10,000
Add: Cost of goods manufactured	158,000
Goods available for sale	168,000
Deduct: Finished goods inventory, ending	49,500
Unadjusted cost of goods sold	118,500
Add: Underapplied overhead	5,000
Adjusted cost of goods sold	$123,500

*Note that the underapplied overhead is added to cost of goods sold. If overhead were overapplied, it would be deducted from cost of goods sold.

EXHIBIT 2–12

Income Statement

RAND COMPANY
Income Statement
For the Month Ending April 30

Sales		$225,000
Less cost of goods sold ($118,500 + $5,000)		123,500
Gross margin		101,500
Less selling and administrative expenses:		
Salaries expense	$30,000	
Depreciation expense	7,000	
Advertising expense	42,000	
Other expense	8,000	87,000
Net operating income		$ 14,500

PROBLEMS OF OVERHEAD APPLICATION

We need to consider two complications relating to overhead application. These are (1) the computation of underapplied and overapplied overhead and (2) the disposition of any balance remaining in the Manufacturing Overhead account at the end of a period.

Underapplied and Overapplied Overhead

Since the predetermined overhead rate is established before a period begins and is based entirely on estimated data, the amount of overhead cost applied to Work in Process will generally differ from the amount of overhead cost actually incurred during a period. In the case of Rand Company, for example, the predetermined overhead rate of $6 per hour resulted in $90,000 of overhead cost being applied to Work in Process, whereas actual overhead costs for April proved to be $95,000 (see Exhibit 2–8). The difference between the overhead cost applied to Work in Process and the actual overhead costs of a period is termed either **underapplied** or **overapplied overhead.** For Rand Company, overhead was underapplied because the applied cost ($90,000) was $5,000 less than the actual cost ($95,000). If the situation had been reversed and the company had applied $95,000 in overhead cost to Work in Process while incurring actual overhead costs of only $90,000, then the overhead would have been overapplied.

What is the cause of underapplied or overapplied overhead? The causes can be complex, and a full explanation will have to wait for later chapters. Nevertheless, the basic problem is that the method of applying overhead to jobs using a predetermined overhead rate assumes that actual overhead costs will be proportional to the actual amount of the allocation base incurred during the period. If, for example, the predetermined overhead rate is $6 per machine-hour, then it is assumed that actual overhead costs incurred will be $6 for every machine-hour that is actually worked. There are at least two reasons why this may not be true. First, much of the overhead often consists of fixed costs that do not grow as the number of machine-hours incurred increases. Second, spending on overhead items may or may not be under control. If individuals who are responsible for overhead costs do a good job, those costs should be less than were expected at the beginning of the period. If they do a poor job, those costs will be more than expected. As we indicated above, however, a fuller explanation of the causes of underapplied and overapplied overhead will have to wait for later chapters.

To illustrate what can happen, suppose that two companies—Turbo Crafters and Black & Howell—have prepared the following estimated data for the coming year:

LEARNING OBJECTIVE 8

Compute under- or overapplied overhead cost and prepare the journal entry to close the balance in Manufacturing Overhead to the appropriate accounts.

	Company	
	Turbo Crafters	**Black & Howell**
Predetermined overhead rate based on	Machine-hours	Direct materials cost
Estimated manufacturing overhead	$300,000 (a)	$120,000 (a)
Estimated machine-hours	75,000 (b)	—
Estimated direct materials cost	—	$80,000 (b)
Predetermined overhead rate, (a) ÷ (b)	$4 per machine-hour	150% of direct materials cost

Now assume that because of unexpected changes in overhead spending and changes in demand for the companies' products, the *actual* overhead cost and the *actual* activity recorded during the year in each company are as follows:

	Company	
	Turbo Crafters	**Black & Howell**
Actual manufacturing overhead costs	$290,000	$130,000
Actual machine-hours	68,000	—
Actual direct materials costs	—	$90,000

EXHIBIT 2–13

Summary of Overhead Concepts

At the beginning of the period:

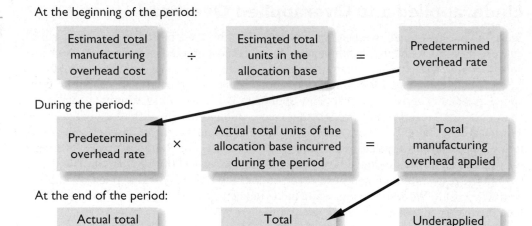

For each company, note that the actual data for both cost and activity differ from the estimates used in computing the predetermined overhead rate. This results in underapplied and overapplied overhead as follows:

	Company	
	Turbo Crafters	**Black & Howell**
Actual manufacturing overhead costs	$290,000	$130,000
Manufacturing overhead cost applied to Work in process during the year:		
68,000 *actual* machine-hours × $4 per machine-hour	272,000	
$90,000 *actual* direct materials cost × 150% of direct materials cost		135,000
Underapplied (overapplied) overhead	$ 18,000	$ (5,000)

For Turbo Crafters, notice that the amount of overhead cost that has been applied to Work in Process ($272,000) is less than the actual overhead cost for the year ($290,000). Therefore, overhead is underapplied. Also notice that the original estimate of overhead in Turbo Crafters ($300,000) is not directly involved in this computation. Its impact is felt only through the $4 predetermined overhead rate that is used.

For Black & Howell, the amount of overhead cost that has been applied to Work in Process ($135,000) is greater than the actual overhead cost for the year ($130,000), and so overhead is overapplied.

A summary of the concepts discussed above is presented in Exhibit 2–13.

Disposition of Under- or Overapplied Overhead Balances

What happens to any under- or overapplied balance remaining in the Manufacturing Overhead account at the end of a period? The simplest method is to close out the balance to Cost of Goods Sold. More complicated methods are sometimes used, but they are beyond the scope of this book. To illustrate the simplest method, recall that Rand Company had underapplied overhead of $5,000. The entry to close this underapplied overhead to Cost of Goods Sold would be:

(14)		
Cost of Goods Sold	5,000	
Manufacturing Overhead		5,000

Note that since the Manufacturing Overhead account has a debit balance, Manufacturing Overhead must be credited to close out the account. This has the effect of increasing Cost of Goods Sold for April to $123,500:

Unadjusted cost of goods sold [from entry (13)]	$118,500
Add underapplied overhead [entry (14) above]	5,000
Adjusted cost of goods sold	$123,500

After this adjustment has been made, Rand Company's income statement for April will appear as shown earlier in Exhibit 2–12.

Remaining Balance in the Overhead Account

YOU DECIDE

The simplest method for disposing of any balance remaining in the Overhead account is to close it out to Cost of Goods Sold. If there is a debit balance (that is, overhead has been underapplied), the entry to dispose of the balance would include a debit to Cost of Goods Sold. That debit would increase the balance in the Cost of Goods Sold account. On the other hand, if there is a credit balance, the entry to dispose of the balance would include a credit to Cost of Goods Sold. That credit would decrease the balance in the Cost of Goods Sold account. If you were the company's controller, would you want a debit balance, a credit balance, or no balance in the Overhead account at the end of the period?

A General Model of Product Cost Flows

The flow of costs in a product costing system is presented in the form of a T-account model in Exhibit 2–14. This model applies as much to a process costing system as it does to a job-order costing system. Examination of this model can be very helpful in understanding how costs enter a system, flow through it, and finally end up as Cost of Goods Sold on the income statement.

Multiple Predetermined Overhead Rates

Our discussion in this chapter has assumed that there is a single predetermined overhead rate for an entire factory called a **plantwide overhead rate.** This is a fairly common practice—particularly in smaller companies. But in larger companies, *multiple predetermined overhead rates* are often used. In a **multiple predetermined overhead rate** system, each production department may have its own predetermined overhead rate. Such a system, while more complex, is considered to be more accurate, since it can reflect differences across departments in how overhead costs are incurred. For example, overhead might be allocated based on direct labor-hours in departments that are relatively labor intensive and based on machine-hours in departments that are relatively machine intensive. When multiple predetermined overhead rates are used, overhead is applied in each department according to its own overhead rate as a job proceeds through the department.

EXHIBIT 2–14   A General Model of Cost Flows

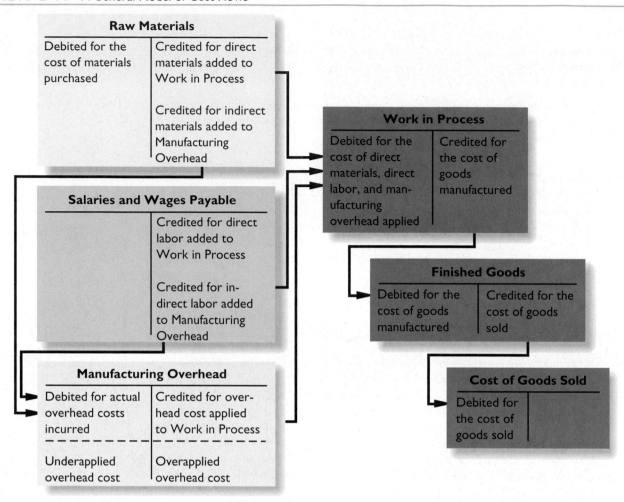

Raw Materials	
Debited for the cost of materials purchased	Credited for direct materials added to Work in Process
	Credited for indirect materials added to Manufacturing Overhead

Salaries and Wages Payable	
	Credited for direct labor added to Work in Process
	Credited for indirect labor added to Manufacturing Overhead

Manufacturing Overhead	
Debited for actual overhead costs incurred	Credited for overhead cost applied to Work in Process
Underapplied overhead cost	Overapplied overhead cost

Work in Process	
Debited for the cost of direct materials, direct labor, and manufacturing overhead applied	Credited for the cost of goods manufactured

Finished Goods	
Debited for the cost of goods manufactured	Credited for the cost of goods sold

Cost of Goods Sold	
Debited for the cost of goods sold	

CONCEPT CHECK ✓

2. Which of the following statements is false? (You may select more than one answer.)
   a. The Manufacturing Overhead account is debited when manufacturing overhead is applied to Work in Process.
   b. Job cost sheets accumulate the actual overhead costs incurred to complete a job.
   c. When products are transferred from Work in Process to Finished Goods it results in a debit to Finished Goods and a credit to Work in Process.
   d. Marketing expenses are applied to production using a predetermined overhead rate that is computed at the beginning of the period.
3. The predetermined overhead rate is $50 per machine hour, underapplied overhead is $5,000, and the actual amount of machine hours is 2,000. What is the actual amount of total manufacturing overhead incurred during the period?
   a. $105,000
   b. $95,000
   c. $150,000
   d. $110,000

JOB-ORDER COSTING IN SERVICE COMPANIES

We stated earlier in the chapter that job-order costing is also used in service organizations such as law firms, movie studios, hospitals, and repair shops, as well as in manufacturing companies. In a law firm, for example, each client is considered to be a "job," and the costs of that job are accumulated day by day on a job cost sheet as the client's case is handled by the firm. Legal forms and similar inputs represent the direct materials for the job; the time expended by attorneys represents the direct labor; and the costs of secretaries, clerks, rent, depreciation, and so forth, represent the overhead.

In a movie studio such as Columbia Pictures, each film produced by the studio is a "job," and costs for direct materials (costumes, props, film, etc.) and direct labor (actors, directors, and extras) are accounted for and charged to each film's job cost sheet. A share of the studio's overhead costs, such as utilities, depreciation of equipment, wages of maintenance workers, and so forth, is also charged to each film. However, there is considerable controversy about the methods used by some studios to distribute overhead costs among movies, and these controversies sometimes result in lawsuits. (See the accompanying In Business box.)

In sum, job-order costing is a versatile and widely used costing method that may be encountered in virtually any organization that provides diverse products or services.

A Fair Share of Profits

"Net profit participation" contracts in which writers, actors, and directors share in the net profits of movies are common in Hollywood. For example, Winston Groom, the author of the novel *Forrest Gump,* has a contract with Paramount Pictures Corp. that calls for him to receive 3% of the net profits on the movie based on his novel. However, Paramount claims that *Forrest Gump* has yet to show any profits even though it has the third-highest gross receipts of any film in history. How can this be?

Movie studios assess a variety of overhead charges including a charge of about 15% on production costs for production overhead, a charge of about 30% of gross rentals for distribution overhead, and a charge for marketing overhead that amounts to about 10% of advertising costs. After all of these overhead charges and other hotly contested accounting practices, it is a rare film that shows a profit. Fewer than 5% of released films show a profit for net profit participation purposes. Examples of "money-losing" films include *Rain Man, Batman,* and *Who Framed Roger Rabbit?* as well as *Forrest Gump.* Disgruntled writers and actors are increasingly suing studios, claiming unreasonable accounting practices that are designed to cheat them of their share of profits.

Source: Ross Engel and Bruce Ikawa, "Where's the Profit?" *Management Accounting,* January 1997, pp. 40–47.

SUMMARY

LOI   Distinguish between process costing and job-order costing and identify companies that would use each costing method.
Job-order costing and process costing are widely used to track costs. Job-order costing is used in situations where the organization offers many different products or services, such as in furniture manufacturing, hospitals, and legal firms. Process costing is used where units of product are homogeneous, such as in flour milling or cement production.

LO2   Identify the documents used in a job-order costing system.
In a job-order costing system, each job has its own job cost sheet. Materials requisition forms and labor time tickets are used to record direct materials and direct labor costs. These costs, together with manufacturing overhead, are accumulated on the job cost sheet for a job.

LO3   Compute predetermined overhead rates and explain why estimated overhead costs (rather than actual overhead costs) are used in the costing process.
Manufacturing overhead costs are assigned to jobs using a predetermined overhead rate. The rate is determined at the beginning of the period so that jobs can be costed throughout the period rather than waiting

until the end of the period. The predetermined overhead rate is determined by dividing the estimated total manufacturing cost for the period by the estimated total allocation base for the period.

LO4   Prepare journal entries to record costs in a job-order costing system.
Direct materials costs are debited to Work in Process when they are released for use in production. Direct labor costs are debited to Work in Process as incurred. Actual manufacturing overhead costs are debited to the Manufacturing Overhead control account as incurred. Manufacturing overhead costs are applied to Work in Process using the predetermined overhead rate. The journal entry that accomplishes this is a debit to Work in Process and a credit to the Manufacturing Overhead control account.

LO5   Apply overhead cost to Work in Process using a predetermined overhead rate.
Overhead is applied to jobs by multiplying the predetermined overhead rate by the actual amount of the allocation base used by the job.

LO6   Prepare schedules of cost of goods manufactured and cost of goods sold.
See Exhibit 2–11 for an example of these schedules.

LO7   Prepare T-accounts to show the flow of costs in a job-order costing system.
See Exhibit 2–14 for a summary of the cost flows through the T-accounts.

LO8   Compute under- or overapplied overhead cost and prepare the journal entry to close the balance in Manufacturing Overhead to the appropriate accounts.
The difference between the actual overhead cost incurred during a period and the amount of overhead cost applied to production is referred to as under- or overapplied overhead. Under- or overapplied overhead is closed out to Cost of Goods Sold. When overhead is underapplied, the balance in the Manufacturing Overhead control account is debited to Cost of Goods Sold. This has the effect of increasing the Cost of Goods Sold and occurs because costs assigned to products have been understated. When overhead is overapplied, the balance in the Manufacturing Overhead control account is credited to Cost of Goods Sold. This has the effect of decreasing the Cost of Goods Sold and occurs because costs assigned to products have been overstated.

GUIDANCE ANSWERS TO *DECISION MAKER* AND *YOU DECIDE*

Treasurer, Class Reunion Committee (p. 87)
You should charge $38.00 per person to cover the costs calculated as follows:

Meal cost	$30.00	Direct material cost
Gratuity ($30 × 0.15)	4.50	Direct labor cost
Room charge ($200 ÷ 200 expected attendees)	1.00	Overhead cost
Band cost ($500 ÷ 200 expected attendees)	2.50	Overhead cost
Total cost	$38.00	

The number of expected attendees (or estimated units in the allocation base) was used to allocate the band cost. Attendees who plan to leave immediately after dinner might object to this allocation. However, this personal choice probably should not override the decision to base the allocation on this very simple base.

If exactly 200 classmates attend the reunion, the $7,600 of receipts (200 @ $38) will cover the expenditures of $7,600 [meal cost of $6,000 (or 200 @ $30) plus gratuity cost of $900 (or $6,000 × 0.15) plus the $200 room charge plus the $500 band cost]. Unfortunately, if less than 200 attend, the Reunion Committee will come up short in an amount equal to the difference between the 200 estimated attendees and the actual number of attendees times $3.50 (the total per person overhead charge). As such, you should talk to the members of the Reunion Committee to ensure that (1) the estimate is as reasonable as possible, and (2) there is a plan to deal with any shortage. On the other hand, if more than 200 attend, the Reunion Committee will collect more money than it needs to disburse. The amount would be equal to the difference between the actual number of attendees and the 200 estimated attendees times $3.50. Again, a plan should be in place to deal with this situation. (Perhaps the funds could be used to cover the mailing costs for the next reunion.)

Remaining Balance in the Overhead Account (p. 101)
A quick response on your part might have been that you would prefer a credit balance in the Overhead account. The entry to dispose of the balance would decrease the balance in the Cost of Goods Sold account and would cause the company's gross margin and net operating income to be higher than might have

otherwise been expected. However, the impact on decision making during the period should be carefully considered.

Ideally, a controller would want the balance in the Overhead account to be zero. If there is no remaining balance in the Overhead account at the end of the period, that means that the actual overhead costs for the period (which are debited to the Overhead account) exactly equaled the overhead costs that were applied (or allocated to the products made by being added to the Work in Process account) during the period. As a result, the products made during the period would have had the "correct" amount of overhead assigned as they moved from the factory floor to the finished goods area to the customer. Typically, this would not be the case because the predetermined overhead rate (used to apply or allocate overhead to the products made) is developed using two estimates (the total amount of overhead expected and the total units in the allocation base expected during the period). It would be difficult, if not impossible, to accurately predict one or both estimates.

If there is a remaining balance in the Overhead account, then the products manufactured during the period either received too little overhead (if there is a debit or underapplied balance) or too much overhead (if there is a credit or overapplied balance). As such, units carried along with them inaccurate product costs as the costs flowed through system. Decisions that relied on those inaccurate product costs may have been faulty.

GUIDANCE ANSWERS TO CONCEPT CHECKS

1. **Choice c.** A predetermined overhead rate rather than an actual overhead rate is used in a normal costing system.
2. **Choices a, b, and d.** The Manufacturing Overhead account is credited when manufacturing overhead is applied to Work in Process. Job cost sheets do not accumulate actual overhead costs. They accumulate the amount of the overhead that has been applied to the job using the predetermined overhead rate. Marketing expenses are period costs. They are not applied to production.
3. **Choice a.** The amount of overhead applied to production is 2,000 hours multiplied by the $50 predetermined rate, or $100,000. If overhead is underapplied by $5,000, the actual amount of overhead is $100,000 + $5,000, or $105,000.

REVIEW PROBLEM: JOB-ORDER COSTING

Hogle Company is a manufacturing firm that uses job-order costing. On January 1, the beginning of its fiscal year, the company's inventory balances were as follows:

Raw Materials	$20,000
Work in Process	$15,000
Finished Goods	$30,000

The company applies overhead cost to jobs on the basis of machine-hours worked. For the current year, the company estimated that it would work 75,000 machine-hours and incur $450,000 in manufacturing overhead cost. The following transactions were recorded for the year:

a. Raw materials were purchased on account, $410,000.
b. Raw materials were requisitioned for use in production, $380,000 ($360,000 direct materials and $20,000 indirect materials).
c. The following costs were incurred for employee services: direct labor, $75,000; indirect labor, $110,000; sales commissions, $90,000; and administrative salaries, $200,000.
d. Sales travel costs were $17,000.
e. Utility costs in the factory were $43,000.
f. Advertising costs were $180,000.
g. Depreciation was recorded for the year, $350,000 (80% relates to factory operations, and 20% relates to selling and administrative activities).
h. Insurance expired during the year, $10,000 (70% relates to factory operations, and the remaining 30% relates to selling and administrative activities).
i. Manufacturing overhead was applied to production. Due to greater than expected demand for its products, the company worked 80,000 machine-hours during the year.

j.   Goods costing $900,000 to manufacture according to their job cost sheets were completed during the
     year.
k.   Goods were sold on account to customers during the year at a total selling price of $1,500,000. The
     goods cost $870,000 to manufacture according to their job cost sheets.

Required:
1. Prepare journal entries to record the preceding transactions.
2. Post the entries in (1) above to T-accounts (don't forget to enter the beginning balances in the
   inventory accounts).
3. Is Manufacturing Overhead underapplied or overapplied for the year? Prepare a journal entry to
   close any balance in the Manufacturing Overhead account to Cost of Goods Sold.
4. Prepare an income statement for the year.

Solution to Review Problem

1. a. Raw Materials 410,000
            Accounts Payable 410,000
   b. Work in Process 360,000
       Manufacturing Overhead 20,000
            Raw Materials 380,000
   c. Work in Process 75,000
       Manufacturing Overhead 110,000
       Sales Commissions Expense 90,000
       Administrative Salaries Expense 200,000
            Salaries and Wages Payable 475,000
   d. Sales Travel Expense 17,000
            Accounts Payable 17,000
   e. Manufacturing Overhead 43,000
            Accounts Payable 43,000
   f. Advertising Expense 180,000
            Accounts Payable 180,000
   g. Manufacturing Overhead 280,000
       Depreciation Expense 70,000
            Accumulated Depreciation 350,000
   h. Manufacturing Overhead 7,000
       Insurance Expense 3,000
            Prepaid Insurance 10,000
   i. The predetermined overhead rate for the year would be computed as follows:

$$\text{Predetermined overhead rate} = \frac{\text{Estimated total manufacturing overhead cost}}{\text{Estimated total units in the allocation base}}$$

$$= \frac{\$450,000}{75,000 \text{ machine-hours}}$$

$$= \$6 \text{ per machine-hour}$$

Based on the 80,000 machine-hours actually worked during the year, the company would have
applied $480,000 in overhead cost to production: 80,000 machine-hours $\times$ $6 per machine-hour =
$480,000. The following entry records this application of overhead cost:

       Work in Process 480,000
            Manufacturing Overhead 480,000
   j. Finished Goods 900,000
            Work in Process 900,000
   k. Accounts Receivable 1,500,000
            Sales 1,500,000
       Cost of Goods Sold 870,000
            Finished Goods 870,000

2.

Accounts Receivable		
(k)	1,500,000	

Prepaid Insurance		
		10,000	(h)

Raw Materials		
Bal.	20,000	380,000	(b)
(a)	410,000	
Bal.	50,000	

Work in Process		
Bal.	15,000	900,000	(j)
(b)	360,000	
(c)	75,000	
(i)	480,000	
Bal.	30,000	

Finished Goods		
Bal.	30,000	870,000	(k)
(j)	900,000	
Bal.	60,000	

Manufacturing Overhead			
(b)	20,000	480,000	(i)
(c)	110,000		
(e)	43,000		
(g)	280,000		
(h)	7,000		
	460,000	480,000	
		20,000	Bal.

Accumulated Depreciation		
		350,000	(g)

Accounts Payable		
		410,000	(a)
		17,000	(d)
		43,000	(e)
		180,000	(f)

Salaries and Wages Payable		
		475,000	(c)

Sales		
		1,500,000	(k)

Cost of Goods Sold		
(k)	870,000	

Commissions Expense		
(c)	90,000	

Administrative Salaries Expense		
(c)	200,000	

Sales Travel Expense		
(d)	17,000	

Advertising Expense		
(f)	180,000	

Depreciation Expense		
(g)	70,000	

Insurance Expense		
(h)	3,000	

3. Manufacturing overhead is overapplied for the year. The entry to close it out to Cost of Goods Sold is as follows:

Manufacturing Overhead	20,000	
Cost of Goods Sold		20,000

4.

HOGLE COMPANY Income Statement For the Year Ended December 31		
Sales		$1,500,000
Less cost of goods sold ($870,000 − $20,000)		850,000
Gross margin		650,000
Less selling and administrative expenses:		
Commissions expense	$ 90,000	
Administrative salaries expense	200,000	
Sales travel expense	17,000	
Advertising expense	180,000	
Depreciation expense	70,000	
Insurance expense	3,000	560,000
Net operating income		$ 90,000

GLOSSARY

Absorption costing   A costing method that includes all manufacturing costs—direct materials, direct labor, and both variable and fixed overhead—as part of the cost of a finished unit of product. This term is synonymous with *full cost*. (p. 78)

Allocation base   A measure of activity such as direct labor-hours or machine-hours that is used to assign costs to cost objects. (p. 84)

Bill of materials   A document that shows the type and quantity of each major item of materials required to make a product. (p. 81)

Cost driver   A factor, such as machine-hours, beds occupied, computer time, or flight-hours, that causes overhead costs. (p. 86)

Full cost   See *Absorption costing*. (p. 78)

Job cost sheet   A form prepared for each job that records the materials, labor, and overhead costs charged to the job. (p. 81)

Job-order costing system   A costing system used in situations where many different products, jobs, or services are produced each period. (p. 79)

Materials requisition form   A detailed source document that specifies the type and quantity of materials that are to be drawn from the storeroom and identifies the job to which the costs of materials are to be charged. (p. 81)

Multiple predetermined overhead rates   A costing system in which there are multiple overhead cost pools with a different predetermined rate for each cost pool, rather than a single predetermined overhead rate for the entire company. Frequently, each production department is treated as a separate overhead cost pool. (p. 101)

Normal cost system   A costing system in which overhead costs are applied to jobs by multiplying a predetermined overhead rate by the actual amount of the allocation base incurred by the job. (p. 85)

Overapplied overhead   A credit balance in the Manufacturing Overhead account that occurs when the amount of overhead cost applied to Work in Process is greater than the amount of overhead cost actually incurred during a period. (p. 98)

Overhead application   The process of charging manufacturing overhead cost to job cost sheets and to the Work in Process account. (p. 84)

Plantwide overhead rate   A single predetermined overhead rate that is used throughout a plant. (p. 101)

Predetermined overhead rate   A rate used to charge overhead cost to jobs in production; the rate is established in advance for each period by use of estimates of total manufacturing overhead cost and of the total allocation base for the period. (p. 84)

Process costing system   A costing system used in those manufacturing situations where a single, homogeneous product (such as cement or flour) is produced for long periods of time. (p. 78)

Time ticket   A detailed source document that is used to record the amount of time an employee spends on various activities during a day. (p. 82)

Underapplied overhead   A debit balance in the Manufacturing Overhead account that arises when the amount of overhead cost actually incurred is greater than the amount of overhead cost applied to Work in Process during a period. (p. 99)

QUESTIONS

2–1   Why aren't actual overhead costs traced to jobs just as direct materials and direct labor costs are traced to jobs?

2–2   When would job-order costing be used in preference to process costing?

2–3   What is the purpose of the job cost sheet in a job-order costing system?

2–4   What is a predetermined overhead rate, and how is it computed?

2–5   Explain how a sales order, a production order, a materials requisition form, and a labor time ticket are involved in producing and costing products.

2–6   Explain why some production costs must be assigned to products through an allocation process. Name several such costs. Would such costs be classified as *direct* or as *indirect* costs?

2–7   Why do firms use predetermined overhead rates rather than actual manufacturing overhead costs in applying overhead to jobs?

2–8   What factors should be considered in selecting a base to be used in computing the predetermined overhead rate?

2–9   If a company fully allocates all of its overhead costs to jobs, does this guarantee that a profit will be earned for the period?

2–10 What account is credited when overhead cost is applied to Work in Process? Would you expect the amount applied for a period to equal the actual overhead costs of the period? Why or why not?

2–11 What is underapplied overhead? Overapplied overhead? What disposition is made of these amounts at the end of the period?

2–12 Give two reasons why overhead might be underapplied in a given year.

2–13 What adjustment is made for underapplied overhead on the schedule of cost of goods sold? What adjustment is made for overapplied overhead?

2–14 Sigma Company applies overhead cost to jobs on the basis of direct labor cost. Job A, which was started and completed during the current period, shows charges of $5,000 for direct materials, $8,000 for direct labor, and $6,000 for overhead on its job cost sheet. Job B, which is still in process at year-end, shows charges of $2,500 for direct materials and $4,000 for direct labor. Should any overhead cost be added to job B at year-end? Explain.

2–15 A company assigns overhead cost to completed jobs on the basis of 125% of direct labor cost. The job cost sheet for job 313 shows that $10,000 in direct materials has been used on the job and that $12,000 in direct labor cost has been incurred. If 1,000 units were produced in job 313, what is the unit product cost?

2–16 What is a plantwide overhead rate? Why are multiple overhead rates, rather than a plantwide rate, used in some companies?

2–17 What happens to overhead rates based on direct labor when automated equipment replaces direct labor?

BRIEF EXERCISES

BRIEF EXERCISE 2–1   Process versus Job-Order Costing   (LO1)
Which would be more appropriate in each of the following situations—job-order costing or process costing?

a. A custom yacht builder.
b. A golf course designer.
c. A potato chip manufacturer.
d. A business consultant.
e. A plywood manufacturer.
f. A soft-drink bottler.
g. A film studio.
h. A firm that supervises bridge construction projects.
i. A manufacturer of fine custom jewelry.
j. A made-to-order garment factory.
k. A factory making one personal computer model.
l. A fertilizer factory.

BRIEF EXERCISE 2–2   Job-Order Costing Documents   (LO2)
Mountain Gearing Company has incurred the following costs on job number ES34, an order for 40 gearing wheels to be delivered at the end of next month.

> Direct materials:
>   On March 5, requisition number 870 was issued for 40 titanium blanks to be used in the special order. The blanks cost $8.00 each.
>   On March 8, requisition number 873 was issued for 960 hardened nibs also to be used in the special order. The nibs cost $0.60 each.
>
> Direct labor:
>   On March 9, Harry Kerst worked from 9:00 A.M. until 12:15 P.M. on Job ES34. He is paid $12.00 per hour.
>   On March 21, Mary Rosas worked from 2:15 P.M. until 4:30 P.M. on Job ES34. She is paid $14.00 per hour.

Required:
1. On what documents would these costs be recorded?
2. How much cost should have been recorded on each of the documents for Job ES34?

BRIEF EXERCISE 2–3   Compute the Predetermined Overhead Rate   (LO3)

Logan Products computes its predetermined overhead rate annually on the basis of direct labor hours. At the beginning of the year it estimated that its total manufacturing overhead would be $586,000 and the total direct labor would be 40,000 hours. Its actual total manufacturing overhead for the year was $713,400 and its actual total direct labor was 41,000 hours.

Required:

Compute the company's predetermined overhead rate for the year.

BRIEF EXERCISE 2–4   Prepare Journal Entries   (LO4)

Kirkaid Company recorded the following transactions for the just completed month.

a. $86,000 in raw materials were purchased on account.
b. $84,000 in raw materials were requisitioned for use in production. Of this amount, $72,000 was for direct materials and the remainder was for indirect materials.
c.   Total labor wages of $108,000 were incurred. Of this amount, $105,000 was for direct labor and the remainder was for indirect labor.
d.   Additional manufacturing overhead costs of $197,000 were incurred.

Required:

Record the above transactions in journal entries.

BRIEF EXERCISE 2–5   Apply Overhead   (LO5)

Westan Corporation uses a predetermined overhead rate of $23.10 per direct labor-hour. This predetermined rate was based on 12,000 estimated direct labor-hours and $277,200 of estimated total manufacturing overhead.

The company incurred actual total manufacturing overhead costs of $266,000 and 12,600 total direct labor-hours during the period.

Required:

Determine the amount of manufacturing overhead that would have been applied to units of product during the period.

BRIEF EXERCISE 2–6   Prepare Schedules of Cost of Goods Manufactured and Cost of Goods Sold   (LO6)

Parmitan Corporation has provided the following data concerning last month's manufacturing operations.

Purchases of raw materials	$53,000
Indirect materials included in manufacturing overhead	$8,000
Direct labor	$62,000
Manufacturing overhead applied to work in process	$41,000
Underapplied overhead	$8,000

	Beginning	Ending
Inventories:		
Raw materials	$24,000	$6,000
Work in process	$41,000	$38,000
Finished goods	$86,000	$93,000

Required:
1. Prepare a Schedule of Cost of Goods Manufactured.
2. Prepare a Schedule of Cost of Goods Sold.

BRIEF EXERCISE 2–7   Prepare T-Accounts   (LO7)

Granger Products recorded the following transactions for the just completed month. The company had no beginning inventories.

a. $75,000 in raw materials were purchased for cash.
b. $73,000 in raw materials were requisitioned for use in production. Of this amount, $67,000 was for direct materials and the remainder was for indirect materials.

c.   Total labor wages of $152,000 were incurred and paid. Of this amount, $134,000 was for direct labor and the remainder was for indirect labor.
d.   Additional manufacturing overhead costs of $126,000 were incurred and paid.
e.   Manufacturing overhead costs of $178,000 were applied to jobs using the company's predetermined overhead rate.
f.   All of the jobs in progress at the end of the month were completed and shipped to customers.
g.   The underapplied or overapplied overhead for the period was closed out to cost of goods sold.

Required:
1.   Post the above transactions to T-accounts.
2.   Determine the cost of goods sold for the period.

BRIEF EXERCISE 2–8   Under and Overapplied Overhead   (LO8)

Cretin Enterprises uses a predetermined overhead rate of $21.40 per direct labor-hour. This predetermined rate was based on 8,000 estimated direct labor-hours and $171,200 of estimated total manufacturing overhead.

The company incurred actual total manufacturing overhead costs of $172,500 and 8,250 total direct labor-hours during the period.

Required:
1.   Determine the amount of underapplied or overapplied manufacturing overhead for the period.
2.   Assuming that the entire amount of the underapplied or overapplied overhead is closed out to cost of goods sold, what would be the effect of the underapplied or overapplied overhead on the company's gross margin for the period?

EXERCISES

EXERCISE 2–9   Applying Overhead in a Service Company   (LO2, LO3, LO5)

Pearson Architectural Design began operations on January 2. The following activity was recorded in the company's Work in Process account for the first month of operations:

Work in Process

Costs of subcontracted work	90,000	570,000	To completed projects
Direct staff costs	200,000		
Studio overhead	320,000		

Pearson Architectural Design is a service firm, so the names of the accounts it uses are different from the names used in manufacturing firms. Costs of Subcontracted Work is basically the same thing as Direct Materials; Direct Staff Costs is the same as Direct Labor; Studio Overhead is the same as Manufacturing Overhead; and Completed Projects is the same as Finished Goods. Apart from the difference in terms, the accounting methods used by the company are identical to the methods used by manufacturing companies.

Pearson Architectural Design uses a job-order costing system and applies studio overhead to Work in Process on the basis of direct staff costs. At the end of January, only one job was still in process. This job (the Krimmer Corporation Headquarters project) had been charged with $13,500 in direct staff costs.

Required:
1.   Compute the predetermined overhead rate that was in use during January.
2.   Complete the following job cost sheet for the partially completed Krimmer Corporation Headquarters project.

KRIMMER CORPORATION HEADQUARTERS PROJECT	
Job Cost Sheet	
As of January 31	
Costs of subcontracted work	$?
Direct staff costs	?
Studio overhead	?
Total cost to January 31	$?

EXERCISE 2–10 Varying Predetermined Overhead Rates   (LO3, LO5)
Javadi Company makes a composting bin that is subject to wide seasonal variations in demand. Unit product costs are computed on a quarterly basis by dividing each quarter's manufacturing costs (materials, labor, and overhead) by the quarter's production in units. The company's estimated costs, by quarter, for the coming year are given below:

| | Quarter | | | |
	First	Second	Third	Fourth
Direct materials	$240,000	$120,000	$ 60,000	$180,000
Direct labor	96,000	48,000	24,000	72,000
Manufacturing overhead	228,000	204,000	192,000	216,000
Total manufacturing costs	$564,000	$372,000	$276,000	$468,000
Number of units to be produced	80,000	40,000	20,000	60,000
Estimated unit product cost	$7.05	$9.30	$13.80	$7.80

Management finds the variation in unit product costs to be confusing and difficult to work with. It has been suggested that the problem lies with manufacturing overhead, since it is the largest element of cost. Accordingly, you have been asked to find a more appropriate way of assigning manufacturing overhead cost to units of product. After some analysis, you have determined that the company's overhead costs are mostly fixed and therefore show little sensitivity to changes in the level of production.

Required:
1. The company uses a job-order costing system. How would you recommend that manufacturing overhead cost be assigned to production? Be specific, and show computations.
2. Recompute the company's unit product costs in accordance with your recommendations in (1) above.

EXERCISE 2–11 Journal Entries and T-Accounts   (LO4, LO5, LO7)
Foley Company uses a job-order costing system. The following data relate to the month of October, the first month of the company's fiscal year:

a. Raw materials purchased on account, $210,000.
b. Raw materials issued to production, $190,000 (80% direct and 20% indirect).
c. Direct labor cost incurred, $49,000; and indirect labor cost incurred, $21,000.
d. Depreciation recorded on factory equipment, $105,000.
e. Other manufacturing overhead costs incurred during October, $130,000 (credit Accounts Payable).
f. The company applies manufacturing overhead cost to production on the basis of $4 per machine-hour. There were 75,000 machine-hours recorded for October.
g. Production orders costing $510,000 according to their job cost sheets were completed during October and transferred to Finished Goods.
h. Production orders that had cost $450,000 to complete according to their job cost sheets were shipped to customers during the month. These goods were sold at 50% above cost. The goods were sold on account.

Required:
1. Prepare journal entries to record the information given above.
2. Prepare T-accounts for Manufacturing Overhead and Work in Process. Post the relevant information above to each account. Compute the ending balance in each account, assuming that Work in Process has a beginning balance of $35,000.

EXERCISE 2–12 Applying Overhead; Cost of Goods Manufactured   (LO5, LO6, LO8)
The following cost data relate to the manufacturing activities of Black Company during the just completed year:

Manufacturing overhead costs:	
Property taxes, factory	$ 3,000
Utilities, factory	5,000
Indirect labor	10,000
Depreciation, factory	24,000
Insurance, factory	6,000
Total actual manufacturing overhead costs	$48,000
Other costs incurred:	
Purchases of raw materials	$32,000
Direct labor cost	$40,000
Inventories:	
Raw materials, beginning	$8,000
Raw materials, ending	$7,000
Work in process, beginning	$6,000
Work in process, ending	$7,500

The company uses a predetermined overhead rate to apply overhead cost to production. The rate for the year was $5 per machine-hour; a total of 10,000 machine-hours was recorded for the year.

Required:
1. Compute the amount of under- or overapplied overhead cost for the year.
2. Prepare a schedule of cost of goods manufactured for the year.

EXERCISE 2–13   Applying Overhead with Various Bases   (LO3, LO5, LO8)

Estimated cost and operating data for three companies for the upcoming year are given below:

	Company		
	A	**B**	**C**
Direct labor-hours	60,000	30,000	40,000
Machine-hours	25,000	90,000	18,000
Raw materials cost	$300,000	$160,000	$240,000
Manufacturing overhead cost	$432,000	$270,000	$384,000

Predetermined overhead rates are computed using the following bases in the three companies:

Company	Overhead Rate Based on—
A	Direct labor-hours
B	Machine-hours
C	Raw materials cost

Required:
1. Compute the predetermined overhead rate to be used in each company.
2. Assume that Company A works on three jobs during the upcoming year. Direct labor-hours recorded by job are: job 308, 7,000 hours; job 309, 30,000 hours; and job 310, 21,000 hours. How much overhead cost will the company apply to Work in Process for the year? If actual costs are $420,000 for the year, will overhead be underapplied or overapplied? By how much?

EXERCISE 2–14   Applying Overhead; Journal Entries; Disposition of Underapplied or Overapplied Overhead   (LO4, LO7, LO8)

The following information is taken from the accounts of FasGrow Company. The entries in the T-accounts are summaries of the transactions that affected those accounts during the year.

Manufacturing Overhead

(a)	380,000	410,000	(b)
		30,000	Bal.

Work in Process

Bal.	105,000	760,000	(c)
	210,000		
	115,000		
(b)	410,000		
Bal.	80,000		

Finished Goods

Bal.	160,000	820,000	(d)
(c)	760,000		
Bal.	100,000		

Cost of Goods Sold

(d)	820,000	

The overhead that had been applied to production during the year is distributed among the ending balances in the accounts as follows:

Work in Process, ending	$ 32,800
Finished Goods, ending	41,000
Cost of Goods Sold	336,200
Overhead Applied	$410,000

For example, of the $80,000 ending balance in Work in Process, $32,800 was overhead that had been applied during the year.

Required:
1. Identify the reasons for entries (a) through (d).
2. Assume that the company closes any balance in the Manufacturing Overhead account directly to Cost of Goods Sold. Prepare the necessary journal entry.

EXERCISE 2–15 Applying Overhead; Journal Entries; T-Accounts   (LO3, LO4, LO5, LO7)
Custom Metal Works produces castings and other metal parts to customer specifications. The company uses a job-order costing system and applies overhead costs to jobs on the basis of machine-hours. At the beginning of the year, the company estimated that it would work 576,000 machine-hours and incur $4,320,000 in manufacturing overhead cost.

The company had no work in process at the beginning of the year. The company spent the entire month of January working on one large order—job 382, which was an order for 8,000 machined parts. Cost data for January follow:

a. Raw materials purchased on account, $315,000.
b. Raw materials requisitioned for production, $270,000 (80% direct and 20% indirect).
c. Labor cost incurred in the factory, $190,000, of which $80,000 was direct labor and $110,000 was indirect labor.
d. Depreciation recorded on factory equipment, $63,000.
e. Other manufacturing overhead costs incurred, $85,000 (credit Accounts Payable).
f. Manufacturing overhead cost was applied to production on the basis of 40,000 machine-hours actually worked during January.
g. The completed job was moved into the finished goods warehouse on January 31 to await delivery to the customer. (In computing the dollar amount for this entry, remember that the cost of a completed job consists of direct materials, direct labor, and *applied* overhead.)

Required:
1. Prepare journal entries to record items (a) through (f) above. Ignore item (g) for the moment.
2. Prepare T-accounts for Manufacturing Overhead and Work in Process. Post the relevant items from your journal entries to these T-accounts.
3. Prepare a journal entry for item (g) above.
4. Compute the unit product cost that will appear on the job cost sheet for job 382.

PROBLEM 2–16 Departmental Overhead Rates (LO2, LO3, LO5)

Meyers Company has two departments, Cutting and Finishing. The company uses a job-order cost system and computes a predetermined overhead rate in each department. The Cutting Department bases its rate on machine-hours, and the Finishing Department bases its rate on direct labor cost. At the beginning of the year, the company made the following estimates:

	Department	
	Cutting	**Finishing**
Direct labor-hours	11,000	98,000
Machine-hours	65,000	2,500
Manufacturing overhead cost	$260,000	$705,600
Direct labor cost	$66,000	$588,000

CHECK FIGURE
(2) Overhead applied to job AF-45: $980

Required:

1. Compute the predetermined overhead rate to be used in each department.
2. Assume that the overhead rates that you computed in (1) above are in effect. The job cost sheet for job AF-45, which was started and completed during the year, showed the following:

	Department	
	Cutting	**Finishing**
Direct labor-hours	11	75
Machine-hours	110	2
Materials requisitioned	$630	$760
Direct labor cost	$66	$450

    Compute the total overhead cost applied to job AF-45.

3. Would you expect substantially different amounts of overhead cost to be assigned to some jobs if the company used a plantwide overhead rate based on direct labor cost, rather than using departmental rates? Explain. No computations are necessary.

PROBLEM 2–17 Applying Overhead; T-Accounts; Journal Entries (LO3, LO4, LO5, LO7, LO8)

Natalie Lock Company is a manufacturing firm that operates a job-order costing system. Overhead costs are applied to jobs on the basis of machine-hours. At the beginning of the year, management estimated that the company would incur $248,000 in manufacturing overhead costs and work 62,000 machine-hours.

CHECK FIGURE
(3) Underapplied by $13,500

Required:

1. Compute the company's predetermined overhead rate.
2. Assume that during the year the company works only 56,000 machine-hours and incurs the following costs in the Manufacturing Overhead and Work in Process accounts:

Manufacturing Overhead			Work in Process		
(Maintenance)	21,500	?	(Direct materials)	650,000	
(Indirect materials)	15,000		(Direct labor)	67,000	
(Indirect labor)	76,000		(Overhead)	?	
(Utilities)	45,000				
(Insurance)	12,000				
(Depreciation)	68,000				

    Copy the data in the T-accounts above onto your answer sheet. Compute the amount of overhead cost that would be applied to Work in Process for the year and make the entry in your T-accounts.

3. Compute the amount of under- or overapplied overhead for the year and show the balance in your Manufacturing Overhead T-account. Prepare a general journal entry to close out the balance in this account to Cost of Goods Sold.
4. Explain why the manufacturing overhead was under- or overapplied for the year.

CHECK FIGURE
(3) Balance in WIP: $3,210

PROBLEM 2–18   Applying Overhead in a Service Firm; Journal Entries   (LO4, LO5, LO8)
Mortimer and Sons uses a job-order costing system to track the costs of its landscaping projects. The company provides garden design as well as actually carrying out the landscaping for the client. The table below provides data concerning the three landscaping projects that were in progress during May. There was no work in process at the beginning of May.

	Project		
	Alpha	Beta	Gamma
Designer-hours	30	55	15
Direct materials cost	$3,300	$5,400	$600
Direct labor cost	$5,100	$7,000	$1,500

Actual overhead costs were $7,900 for May. Overhead costs are applied to projects on the basis of designer-hours since most of the overhead is related to the costs of the garden design studio. The predetermined overhead rate is $74 per designer-hour. The Alpha and Beta projects were completed in May; the Gamma project was not completed by the end of the month.

Required:
1. Compute the amount of overhead cost that would have been charged to each project during May.
2. Prepare a journal entry showing the completion of the Alpha and Beta projects and the transfer of costs to the Completed Projects (i.e., Finished Goods) account.
3. What is the balance in the Work in Process account at the end of the month?
4. What is the balance in the Overhead account at the end of the month? What is this balance called?

CHECK FIGURE
(3) Underapplied by
    $17,500
(4) Net operating income:
    $220,500

PROBLEM 2–19   Comprehensive Problem   (LO3, LO4, LO5, LO7, LO8)
Productos Elina S.A. of Buenos Aires, Argentina, is a family-owned enterprise that makes lamps for the local market. These lamps are highly prized in the local market for their intricate ironwork and detailing. The company has been in business for over 100 years and some of its lamps have been passed down from generation to generation. Productos Elina S.A. sells through an extensive network of salesmen who receive commissions on their sales. The Argentinean currency is the peso, which is denoted by $. All of the company's transactions with customers, employees, and suppliers are conducted in cash; there is no credit.

The company uses a job-order costing system in which overhead is applied to jobs on the basis of direct labor cost. At the beginning of the year, it was estimated that the total direct labor cost for the year would be $370,000 and the total manufacturing overhead cost would be $481,000. At the beginning of the year, the inventory balances were as follows:

Raw materials	$35,000
Work in process	$25,000
Finished goods	$65,000

During the year, the following transactions were completed:

a. Raw materials purchased for cash, $400,000.
b. Raw materials requisitioned for use in production, $429,000. (Materials costing $350,000 were charged directly to jobs; the remaining materials were indirect.)
c. Costs for employee services were incurred as follows:

Direct labor	$375,000
Indirect labor	$110,000
Sales commissions	$95,000
Administrative salaries	$80,000

d. Rent for the year was $52,000. ($35,000 of this amount related to factory operations, and the remainder related to selling and administrative activities.)
e. Utility costs incurred in the factory, $98,000.
f. Advertising costs incurred, $150,000.
g. Depreciation recorded on equipment, $203,000. ($183,000 of this amount was on equipment used in factory operations; the remaining $20,000 was on equipment used in selling and administrative activities.)

h. Manufacturing overhead cost was applied to jobs, $____?____.

i. Goods that cost $1,230,000 to manufacture according to their job cost sheets were completed during the year.

j. Sales for the year totaled $1,850,000. The total cost to manufacture these goods according to their job cost sheets was $1,250,000.

Required:

1. Prepare journal entries to record the transactions for the year.

2. Prepare T-accounts for inventories, Manufacturing Overhead, and Cost of Goods Sold. Post relevant data from your journal entries to these T-accounts. (Don't forget to enter the beginning balances in your inventory accounts.) Compute an ending balance in each account.

3. Is Manufacturing Overhead underapplied or overapplied for the year? Prepare a journal entry to close any balance in the Manufacturing Overhead account to Cost of Goods Sold.

4. Prepare an income statement for the year. (Do not prepare a schedule of cost of goods manufactured; all of the information needed for the income statement is available in the journal entries and T-accounts you have prepared.)

PROBLEM 2–20   T-Account Analysis of Cost Flows   (LO3, LO6, LO8)

Selected ledger accounts of Gaynor Company are given below for the just completed year:

CHECK FIGURE
(3) Indirect labor: $20,000
(7) Underapplied: $15,000

Raw Materials					Manufacturing Overhead			
Bal. 1/1	50,000	Credits	?		Debits	765,000	Credits	?
Debits	350,000							
Bal. 12/31	40,000							

Work in Process					Factory Wages Payable			
Bal. 1/1	100,000	Credits	1,600,000		Debits	530,000	Bal. 1/1	25,000
Direct							Credits	520,000
Materials	310,000						Bal. 12/31	15,000
Direct								
Labor	500,000							
Overhead	750,000							
Bal. 12/31	?							

Finished Goods					Cost of Goods Sold		
Bal. 1/1	100,000	Credits	?		Debits	?	
Debits	?						
Bal. 12/31	200,000						

Required:

1. What was the cost of raw materials put into production during the year?

2. How much of the materials in (1) above consisted of indirect materials?

3. How much of the factory labor cost for the year consisted of indirect labor?

4. What was the cost of goods manufactured for the year?

5. What was the cost of goods sold for the year (before considering under- or overapplied overhead)?

6. If overhead is applied to production on the basis of direct labor cost, what rate was in effect during the year?

7. Was manufacturing overhead under- or overapplied? By how much?

8. Compute the ending balance in the Work in Process inventory account. Assume that this balance consists entirely of goods started during the year. If $20,000 of this balance is direct labor cost, how much of it is direct materials cost? Manufacturing overhead cost?

PROBLEM 2–21   Overhead Analysis; Schedule of Cost of Goods Manufactured   (LO3, LO5, LO6, LO8)

Timeless Products operates a job-order cost system and applies overhead cost to jobs on the basis of direct materials used in production (not on the basis of raw materials purchased). In computing a predetermined overhead rate at the beginning of the year, the company's estimates were: manufacturing overhead cost,

CHECK FIGURE
(2) COGM: $1,053,750

$360,000; and direct materials to be used in production, $288,000. The company's inventory accounts at the beginning and end of the year were:

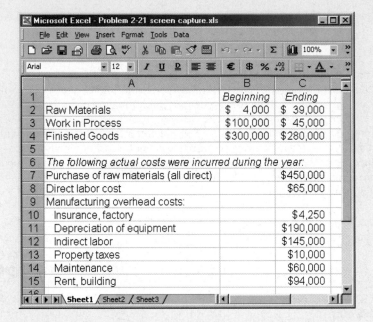

	Beginning	Ending
2 Raw Materials	$ 4,000	$ 39,000
3 Work in Process	$100,000	$ 45,000
4 Finished Goods	$300,000	$280,000
5		
6 *The following actual costs were incurred during the year:*		
7 Purchase of raw materials (all direct)		$450,000
8 Direct labor cost		$65,000
9 Manufacturing overhead costs:		
10 Insurance, factory		$4,250
11 Depreciation of equipment		$190,000
12 Indirect labor		$145,000
13 Property taxes		$10,000
14 Maintenance		$60,000
15 Rent, building		$94,000

Required:

1. a. Compute the predetermined overhead rate for the year.
    b. Compute the amount of under- or overapplied overhead for the year.
2. Prepare a schedule of cost of goods manufactured for the year.
3. Compute the Cost of Goods Sold for the year. (Do not include any under- or overapplied overhead in your Cost of Goods Sold figure.)
4. Job 576 was started and completed during the year. What price would have been charged to the customer if the job required $4,000 in direct materials and $1,500 in direct labor cost and the company priced its jobs at 12% above the job's cost according to the company's job-order costing system?
5. Direct materials made up $18,000 of the $45,000 ending Work in Process inventory balance. Supply the information missing below:

Direct materials	$18,000
Direct labor	?
Manufacturing overhead	?
Work in process inventory	$45,000

CHECK FIGURE
(3) $236.30 per unit

PROBLEM 2–22   Multiple Departments; Applying Overhead   (LO3, LO5, LO8)

Patterson Furniture makes a variety of garden furniture that it sells to retailers such as Home Depot. The company uses a job-order costing system in which predetermined overhead rates are used to apply manufacturing overhead cost to jobs. The predetermined overhead rate in the Molding Department is based on machine-hours and the rate in the Painting Department is based on direct labor cost. At the beginning of the year, the company's management made the following estimates:

	Department	
	Molding	**Painting**
Direct labor-hours	3,800	85,000
Machine-hours	60,000	2,500
Direct materials cost	$700,000	$490,000
Direct labor cost	$42,000	$595,000
Manufacturing overhead cost	$324,000	$952,000

Job 435 was started on August 10 and completed on October 2. The company's cost records show the following information concerning the job:

	Department	
	Molding	Painting
Direct labor-hours	14	230
Machine-hours	250	6
Materials placed into production	$700	$105
Direct labor cost	$150	$1,840

Required:

1. Compute the predetermined overhead rate used during the year in the Molding Department. Compute the rate used in the Painting Department.
2. Compute the total overhead cost applied to job 435.
3. What would be the total cost recorded for job 435? If the job contained 30 units, what would be the unit product cost?
4. At the end of the year, the records of Patterson Furniture revealed the following actual cost and operating data for all jobs worked on during the year:

	Department	
	Molding	Painting
Direct labor-hours	5,000	87,000
Machine-hours	62,000	3,000
Direct materials cost	$600,000	$550,000
Direct labor cost	$50,000	$602,000
Manufacturing overhead cost	$320,000	$970,000

What was the amount of under- or overapplied overhead in each department at the end of the year?

PROBLEM 2–23   T-Accounts; Applying Overhead   (LO5, LO7, LO8)

Kleinman Company's trial balance as of July 1, the beginning of the fiscal year, is given below:

CHECK FIGURE
(2) WIP balance: $16,780
(4) Net operating income: $13,080

Cash	$ 5,280	
Accounts Receivable	13,000	
Raw Materials	7,000	
Work in Process	15,600	
Finished Goods	25,000	
Prepaid Insurance	3,120	
Plant and Equipment	163,000	
Accumulated Depreciation		$ 41,000
Accounts Payable		29,000
Capital Stock		124,000
Retained Earnings		38,000
Total	$232,000	$232,000

Kleinman Company is a manufacturing firm and employs a job-order costing system. During the year, the following transactions took place:

a. Raw materials purchased on account, $31,000.
b. Raw materials were requisitioned for use in production, $29,600 (80% direct and 20% indirect).
c. Factory utility costs incurred, $15,000.
d. Depreciation was recorded on plant and equipment, $28,000 (85% of the depreciation related to factory equipment, and the remainder related to selling and administrative equipment).
e. Advertising expense incurred, $37,000.
f. Costs for salaries and wages were incurred as follows:

Direct labor	$35,100
Indirect labor	$7,800
Administrative salaries	$23,400

g. Prepaid insurance expired during the year, $2,300 (75% related to factory operations and 25% related to selling and administrative activities).
h. Miscellaneous selling and administrative expenses incurred, $7,500.
i. Manufacturing overhead was applied to production. The company applies overhead on the basis of $8 per machine-hour; 5,800 machine-hours were recorded for the year.
j. Goods that cost $104,000 to manufacture according to their job cost sheets were transferred to the finished goods warehouse.
k. Sales for the year totaled $195,000 and were all on account. The total cost to manufacture these goods according to their job cost sheets was $101,400.
l. Collections from customers during the year totaled $190,000.
m. Payments to suppliers on account during the year, $117,000; payments to employees for salaries and wages, $65,000.

Required:

1. Prepare a T-account for each account in the company's trial balance and enter the opening balances shown above.
2. Record the transactions above directly into the T-accounts. Prepare new T-accounts as needed. Key your entries to the letters (a) through (m) above. Find the ending balance in each account.
3. Is manufacturing overhead underapplied or overapplied for the year? Make an entry in the T-accounts to close any balance in the Manufacturing Overhead account to Cost of Goods Sold.
4. Prepare an income statement for the year. (Do not prepare a schedule of cost of goods manufactured; all of the information needed for the income statement is available in the T-accounts.)

CHECK FIGURE
(3) Overapplied by $3,150
(4) Net operating income: $62,000

PROBLEM 2–24   Journal Entries; T-Accounts; Cost Flows   (LO4, LO5, LO7, LO8)
Basin Products uses a job-order cost system. The company's inventory balances on January 1, the start of its fiscal year, were as follows:

Raw materials	$53,000
Work in process	$33,400
Finished goods	$81,000

During the year, the following transactions were completed:

a. Raw materials were purchased on account, $273,000.
b. Raw materials were issued from the storeroom for use in production, $320,000 (75% direct and 25% indirect).
c. Employee salaries and wages were accrued as follows: direct labor, $370,000; indirect labor, $100,000; and selling and administrative salaries $85,000.
d. Utility costs were incurred in the factory, $107,000.
e. Advertising costs were incurred, $168,000.
f. Prepaid insurance expired during the year, $43,000 (95% related to factory operations, and 5% related to selling and administrative activities).
g. Depreciation was recorded, $280,000 (80% related to factory assets, and 20% related to selling and administrative assets).
h. Manufacturing overhead was applied to jobs at the rate of 150% of direct labor cost.
i. Goods that cost $1,170,000 to manufacture according to their job cost sheets were transferred to the finished goods warehouse.
j. Sales for the year totaled $1,560,000 and were all on account. The total cost to manufacture these goods according to their job cost sheets was $1,190,000.

Required:

1. Prepare journal entries to record the transactions for the year.
2. Prepare T-accounts for Raw Materials, Work in Process, Finished Goods, Manufacturing Overhead, and Cost of Goods Sold. Post the appropriate parts of your journal entries to these T-accounts. Compute the ending balance in each account. (Don't forget to enter the beginning balances in the inventory accounts.)
3. Is Manufacturing Overhead underapplied or overapplied for the year? Prepare a journal entry to close this balance to Cost of Goods Sold.
4. Prepare an income statement for the year. (Do not prepare a schedule of cost of goods manufactured; all of the information needed for the income statement is available in the journal entries and T-accounts you have prepared.)

PROBLEM 2–25 Cost Flows; T-Accounts; Income Statement (LO3, LO5, LO7, LO8)

Videoland Corp. produces short musical videos for sale to retail outlets. The company's balance sheet accounts as of July 1, the beginning of the fiscal year, are given below.

VIDEOLAND CORP.
Balance Sheet
July 1

Assets

Current assets:		
Cash		$ 22,000
Accounts receivable		35,700
Inventories:		
Raw materials (film, costumes)	$ 10,500	
Videos in process	17,200	
Finished videos awaiting sale	40,000	67,700
Prepaid insurance		3,100
Total current assets		128,500
Studio and equipment	256,000	
Less accumulated depreciation	73,500	182,500
Total assets		$311,000

Liabilities and Stockholders' Equity

Accounts payable		$ 56,000
Capital stock	$160,500	
Retained earnings	94,500	255,000
Total liabilities and stockholders' equity		$311,000

Since the videos differ in length and in complexity of production, the company uses a job-order costing system to determine the cost of each video produced. Studio (manufacturing) overhead is charged to videos on the basis of camera-hours of activity. At the beginning of the year, the company estimated that it would work 2,500 camera-hours and incur $90,000 in studio overhead cost. The following transactions were recorded for the year:

a. Film, costumes, and similar raw materials purchased on account, $64,700.
b. Film, costumes, and other raw materials issued to production, $50,000 (80% of this material was considered direct to the videos in production, and the other 20% was considered indirect).
c. Utility costs incurred in the production studio, $16,000.
d. Depreciation recorded on the studio, cameras, and other equipment, $30,000 (85% of this depreciation related to actual production of the videos, and the remainder related to equipment used in marketing and administration).
e. Advertising expense incurred, $45,000.
f. Costs for salaries and wages were incurred as follows:

Direct labor (actors and directors)	$28,700
Indirect labor (carpenters to build sets, costume designers, and so forth)	$37,000
Administrative salaries	$35,000

g. Prepaid insurance expired during the year, $2,500 (70% related to production of videos, and 30% related to marketing and administrative activities).
h. Miscellaneous marketing and administrative expenses incurred, $2,900.
i. Studio (manufacturing) overhead was applied to videos in production. The company recorded 2,540 camera-hours of activity during the year.
j. Videos that cost $174,000 to produce according to their job cost sheets were transferred to the finished videos warehouse to await sale and shipment.
k. Sales for the year totaled $323,000 and were all on account. The total cost to produce these videos according to their job cost sheets was $210,000.

l.   Collections from customers during the year totaled $290,000.

m. Payments to suppliers on account during the year, $175,000; payments to employees for salaries and wages, $99,500.

Required:

1. Prepare a T-account for each account on the company's balance sheet and enter the opening balances.

2. Record the transactions directly into the T-accounts. Prepare new T-accounts as needed. Key your entries to the letters (a) through (m) above. Find the ending balance in each account.

3. Is the Studio (manufacturing) Overhead account underapplied or overapplied for the year? Make an entry in the T-accounts to close any balance in the Studio Overhead account to Cost of Goods Sold.

4. Prepare an income statement for the year. (Do not prepare a schedule of cost of goods manufactured; all of the information needed for the income statement is available in the T-accounts.)

BUILDING YOUR SKILLS

ANALYTICAL THINKING   (LO3, LO5)

Sharpton Fabricators Company manufactures a variety of parts for the automotive industry. The company uses a job-order costing system with a plantwide predetermined overhead rate based on direct labor-hours. On December 10, 2002, the company's controller made a preliminary estimate of the predetermined overhead rate for 2003. The new rate was based on the estimated total manufacturing overhead cost of $2,475,000 and the estimated 52,000 total direct labor-hours for 2003:

$$\text{Predetermined overhead rate} = \frac{\$2,475,000}{52,000 \text{ hours}}$$

$$= \$47.60 \text{ per direct labor-hour}$$

This new predetermined overhead rate was communicated to top managers in a meeting on December 11. The rate did not cause any comment because it was within a few pennies of the overhead rate that had been used during 2002. One of the subjects discussed at the meeting was a proposal by the production manager to purchase an automated milling machine center built by Central Robotics. The president of Sharpton Fabricators, Kevin Reynolds, agreed to meet with the regional sales representative from Central Robotics to discuss the proposal.

On the day following the meeting, Mr. Reynolds met with Jay Warner, Central Robotics' sales representative. The following discussion took place:

Reynolds: Larry Winter, our production manager, asked me to meet with you since he is interested in installing an automated milling machine center. Frankly, I am skeptical. You're going to have to show me this isn't just another expensive toy for Larry's people to play with.

Warner: That shouldn't be too difficult, Mr. Reynolds. The automated milling machine center has three major advantages. First, it is much faster than the manual methods you are using. It can process about twice as many parts per hour as your present milling machines. Second, it is much more flexible. There are some up-front programming costs, but once those have been incurred, almost no setup is required on the machines for standard operations. You just punch in the code of the standard operation, load the machine's hopper with raw material, and the machine does the rest.

Reynolds: Yeah, but what about cost? Having twice the capacity in the milling machine area won't do us much good. That center is idle much of the time anyway.

Warner: I was getting there. The third advantage of the automated milling machine center is lower cost. Larry Winters and I looked over your present operations, and we estimated that the automated equipment would eliminate the need for about 6,000 direct labor-hours a year. What is your direct labor cost per hour?

Reynolds: The wage rate in the milling area averages about $21 per hour. Fringe benefits raise that figure to about $30 per hour.

Warner: Don't forget your overhead.

Reynolds: Next year the overhead rate will be about $48 per hour.

Warner: So including fringe benefits and overhead, the cost per direct labor-hour is about $78.

Reynolds: That's right.

Warner: Since you can save 6,000 direct labor-hours per year, the cost savings would amount to about $468,000 a year.

Reynolds: That's pretty impressive, but you aren't giving away this equipment are you?

Warner: Several options are available, including leasing and outright purchase. Just for comparison purposes, our 60-month lease plan would require payments of only $300,000 per year.

Reynolds: Sold! When can you install the equipment?

Shortly after this meeting, Mr. Reynolds informed the company's controller of the decision to lease the new equipment, which would be installed over the Christmas vacation period. The controller realized that this decision would require a recomputation of the predetermined overhead rate for the year 2003 since the decision would affect both the manufacturing overhead and the direct labor-hours for the year. After talking with both the production manager and the sales representative from Central Robotics, the controller discovered that in addition to the annual lease cost of $300,000, the new machine would also require a skilled technician/programmer who would have to be hired at a cost of $45,000 per year to maintain and program the equipment. Both of these costs would be included in factory overhead. There would be no other changes in total manufacturing overhead cost, which is almost entirely fixed. The controller assumed that the new machine would result in a reduction of 6,000 direct labor-hours for the year from the levels that had initially been planned.

When the revised predetermined overhead rate for the year 2003 was circulated among the company's top managers, there was considerable dismay.

Required:
1. Recompute the predetermined rate assuming that the new machine will be installed. Explain why the new predetermined overhead rate is higher (or lower) than the rate that was originally estimated for the year 2003.
2. What effect (if any) would this new rate have on the cost of jobs that do not use the new automated milling machine?
3. Why would managers be concerned about the new overhead rate?
4. After seeing the new predetermined overhead rate, the production manager admitted that he probably wouldn't be able to eliminate all of the 6,000 direct labor-hours. He had been hoping to accomplish the reduction by not replacing workers who retire or quit, but that would not be possible. As a result, the real labor savings would be only about 2,000 hours—one worker. In the light of this additional information, evaluate the original decision to acquire the automated milling machine from Central Robotics.

COMMUNICATING IN PRACTICE   (LO1, LO3, LO5)

Look in the yellow pages or contact your local chamber of commerce or local chapter of the Institute of Certified Management Accountants to find the names of manufacturing companies in your area. Call or make an appointment to meet with the controller or chief financial officer of one of these companies.

Required:

Ask the following questions and write a brief memorandum to your instructor that addresses what you found out.
1. What are the company's main products?
2. Does the company use job-order costing, process costing, or some other method of determining product costs?
3. How is overhead assigned to products? What is the overhead rate? What is the basis of allocation? Is more than one overhead rate used?
4. Has the company recently changed its cost system or is it considering changing its cost system? If so, why? What changes were made or what changes are being considered?

ETHICS CHALLENGE   (LO3, LO5, LO8)

Cristin Madsen has recently been transferred to the Appliances Division of Solequin Corporation. Shortly after taking over her new position as divisional controller, she was asked to develop the division's predetermined overhead rate for the upcoming year. The accuracy of the rate is of some importance, since it is used throughout the year and any overapplied or underapplied overhead is closed out to Cost of Goods Sold only at the end of the year. Solequin Corporation uses direct labor-hours in all of its divisions as the allocation base for manufacturing overhead.

To compute the predetermined overhead rate, Cristin divided her estimate of the total manufacturing overhead for the coming year by the production manager's estimate of the total direct labor-hours for the coming year. She took her computations to the division's general manager for approval but was quite surprised when he suggested a modification in the base. Her conversation with the general manager of the Appliances Division, Lance Jusic, went like this:

Madsen: Here are my calculations for next year's predetermined overhead rate. If you approve, we can enter the rate into the computer on January 1 and be up and running in the job-order costing system right away this year.

Jusic: Thanks for coming up with the calculations so quickly, and they look just fine. There is, however, one slight modification I would like to see. Your estimate of the total direct labor-hours for the year is 110,000 hours. How about cutting that to about 105,000 hours?

Madsen: I don't know if I can do that. The production manager says she will need about 110,000 direct labor-hours to meet the sales projections for next year. Besides, there are going to be over 108,000 direct labor-hours during the current year and sales are projected to be higher next year.

Jusic: Cristin, I know all of that. I would still like to reduce the direct labor-hours in the base to something like 105,000 hours. You probably don't know that I had an agreement with your predecessor as divisional controller to shave 5% or so off the estimated direct labor-hours every year. That way, we kept a reserve that usually resulted in a big boost to net income at the end of the fiscal year in December. We called it our Christmas bonus. Corporate headquarters always seemed as pleased as punch that we could pull off such a miracle at the end of the year. This system has worked well for many years, and I don't want to change it now.

Required:
1. Explain how shaving 5% off the estimated direct labor-hours in the base for the predetermined overhead rate usually results in a big boost in net income at the end of the fiscal year.
2. Should Cristin Madsen go along with the general manager's request to reduce the direct labor-hours in the predetermined overhead rate computation to 105,000 direct labor-hours?

CHECK FIGURE
(3) WIP inventory: $5,300

TEAMWORK IN ACTION   (LO3, LO4, LO5, LO7, LO8)

After a dispute concerning wages, Orville Arson tossed an incendiary device into the Sparkle Company's record vault. Within moments, only a few charred fragments were readable from the company's factory ledger, as shown below:

Raw Materials		Manufacturing Overhead	
Balance 4/1 12,000		Actual costs for April 14,800	

Work in Process		Accounts Payable	
Balance 4/1 4,500			8,000 Balance 4/30

Finished Goods		Cost of Goods Sold	
Balance 4/30 16,000			

Sifting through ashes and interviewing selected employees has turned up the following additional information:

a.   The controller remembers clearly that the predetermined overhead rate was based on an estimated 60,000 direct labor-hours to be worked over the year and an estimated $180,000 in manufacturing overhead costs.

b.   The production superintendent's cost sheets showed only one job in process on April 30. Materials of $2,600 had been added to the job, and 300 direct labor-hours had been expended at $6 per hour.

c.   The accounts payable are for raw material purchases only, according to the accounts payable clerk. He clearly remembers that the balance in the account was $6,000 on April 1. An analysis of canceled checks (kept in the treasurer's office) shows that payments of $40,000 were made to suppliers during April. (All materials used during April were direct materials.)

d.   A charred piece of the payroll ledger shows that 5,200 direct labor-hours were recorded for the month. The personnel department has verified that there were no variations in pay rates among employees. (This infuriated Orville, who felt that his services were underpaid.)

e. Records maintained in the finished goods warehouse indicate that the finished goods inventory totaled $11,000 on April 1.

f. From another charred piece in the vault, you are able to discern that the cost of goods manufactured for April was $89,000.

Required:

1. Assign one of the following sets of accounts to each member of the team:
   a. Raw Materials and Accounts Payable.
   b. Work in Process and Manufacturing Overhead.
   c. Finished Goods and Cost of Goods Sold.

   Determine the types of transactions that would be posted to each account and present a summary to the other team members. When agreement is reached, the team should work together to complete steps 2 through 7.

2. Determine the company's predetermined overhead rate and the total manufacturing overhead applied for the month.

3. Determine the April 30 balance in the company's Work in Process account.

4. Prepare the company's T-accounts for the month. (It is easiest to complete the T-accounts in the following order: Accounts Payable, Work in Process, Raw Materials, Manufacturing Overhead, Finished Goods, Cost of Goods Sold.)

TAKING IT TO THE NET

As you know, the World Wide Web is a medium that is constantly evolving. Sites come and go, and change without notice. To enable periodic update of site addresses, this problem has been posted to the textbook website (www.mhhe.com/bgn2e). After accessing the site, enter the Student Center and select this chapter. Select and complete the Taking It to the Net problem.

Systems Design: Activity-Based Costing

A LOOK BACK

An overview of a job-order costing system was provided in Chapter 2. After describing the accumulation of direct materials and direct labor costs on jobs, we discussed the plantwide overhead rate approach to assigning manufacturing overhead to jobs.

A LOOK AT THIS CHAPTER

Chapter 3 continues the discussion of the allocation of overhead costs. After addressing the advantages and disadvantages of the use of a plantwide overhead rate, we provide an overview of activity-based costing, a technique that uses a number of allocation bases to assign overhead costs to products.

A LOOK AHEAD

After comparing job-order and process costing systems, we provide an overview of a process costing system in Chapter 4.

CHAPTER OUTLINE

Assigning Overhead Costs to Products

- Plantwide Overhead Rate
- Departmental Overhead Rates
- Activity-Based Costing (ABC)

Designing an Activity-Based Costing System

- Hierarchy of Activities
- An Example of an Activity-Based Costing System Design

Using Activity-Based Costing

- Comtek Sound, Inc.'s Basic Data
- Direct Labor-Hours as a Base
- Computing Activity Rates

- Computing Product Costs
- Shifting of Overhead Cost

Targeting Process Improvements

Evaluation of Activity-Based Costing

- The Benefits of Activity-Based Costing
- Limitations of Activity-Based Costing
- Activity-Based Costing and Service Industries

Cost Flows in an Activity-Based Costing System

- An Example of Cost Flows

DECISION FEATURE

Pedaling to Oblivion and Back

Claudia Post started a small bicycle-messenger service, Diamond Courier, in Philadelphia after having been unceremoniously fired by a local courier service. With her background in sales, a minimum of dollars to plunk down on starting her company, and an approach that demanded customer service every mile of the way, Claudia was looking at $1 million dollars in sales within 17 months. Tracking delivery trends and anticipating customer needs, she added truck deliveries, airfreight services, a parts-distribution division, and a legal service that served subpoenas and prepared court filings for law firms in the Philadelphia region. Within three years Diamond was booking $3.1 million dollars in annual sales and had 40 bike messengers, an office staff of 25 employees, about 50 independent drivers and one big problem. The company was losing money.

Post sold her jewelry to meet payroll and pay bills and with input from an adviser, she took a close look at the profitability of each of the company's lines of business. Post had assumed that if she charged a competitive rate, kept clients happy, and increased sales, she would make money. However, an activity-based analysis indicated that the average cost of a bike delivery, including overhead, was $9.24, but she was charging only $4.60. Recalls Post: "The bicycle division, which I thought of as Diamond's core business, was generating just 10% of total revenues and barely covered its own direct-labor and insurance costs. Worse, the division created more logistical and customer-service nightmares than any other single aspect of Diamond, therefore generating a disproportionate share of overhead costs." With smaller competitors charging as little as $3 per delivery, she decided to drop the bicycle messenger service and concentrate on other, more profitable lines of business. Further analysis later led to Post closing down the airfreight and parts distribution divisions, and the business was back on track with profits rolling in.

Today, barely 13 years after Diamond Courier made its first local messenger delivery, the company, now Diamond Transportation Group, Inc., is a leading national provider of transportation logistics management. States Post: "Today, as in 1990, Diamond delivers highly reliable and innovative solutions that meet our customers' objectives and enhance their profitability. And consistent with good business practices, we keep our eye on the numbers. Every day."

Sources: Susan Greco, "Are We Making Money Yet?" *Inc.*, July 1996, pp. 52–61; and Cheryl A. Hodolitz, Diamond Transportation Group, private communication.

As discussed in earlier chapters, direct materials and direct labor costs can be directly traced to products. Overhead costs, on the other hand, cannot be easily traced to products and some other means must be found for assigning them to products for financial reporting and other purposes. In the previous chapter, overhead costs were assigned to products using a plantwide predetermined overhead rate. This method is simpler than the other methods of assigning overhead costs to products that will be described in this chapter, but this simplicity has a cost. A plantwide predetermined overhead rate spreads overhead costs uniformly over products in proportion to whatever allocation base is used—most commonly, direct labor-hours. This procedure results in high overhead costs for products with a high direct labor-hour content and low overhead costs for products with a low direct labor-hour content. However, the real causes of overhead may have little to do with direct labor-hours and as a consequence, product costs may be distorted. Activity-based costing attempts to correct these distortions by more accurately assigning overhead costs to products.

ASSIGNING OVERHEAD COSTS TO PRODUCTS

LEARNING OBJECTIVE 1

Understand the basic approach in activity-based costing and how it differs from conventional costing.

Companies use three common approaches to assign overhead costs to products. The simplest method is to use a plantwide overhead rate. A slightly more refined approach is to use departmental overhead rates. The most complex method is activity-based costing, which is the most accurate of the three approaches to overhead cost assignment.

Plantwide Overhead Rate

Our discussion in the two preceding chapters assumed that a single overhead rate, called a *plantwide overhead rate*, was being used throughout an entire factory. This simple approach to overhead assignment can result in distorted unit product costs, as we shall see below.

When cost systems were developed in the 1800s, cost and activity data had to be collected by hand and all calculations were done with paper and pen. Consequently, the emphasis was on simplicity. Companies often established a single overhead cost pool for an entire facility or department as described in Chapter 2. Direct labor was the obvious choice as an allocation base for overhead costs. Direct labor-hours were already being recorded for purposes of determining wages and direct labor time spent on tasks was often closely monitored. In the labor-intensive production processes of that time, direct labor was a large component of product costs—larger than it is today. Moreover, managers believed direct labor and overhead costs were highly correlated. (Two variables, such as direct labor and overhead costs, are highly correlated if they tend to move together.) And finally, most companies produced a very limited variety of similar products, so in fact there was probably little difference in the overhead costs attributable to different products. Under these conditions, it was not cost-effective to use a more elaborate costing system.

Conditions have changed. Many companies now sell a large variety of products that consume significantly different overhead resources. Consequently, a costing system that assigns essentially the same overhead cost to every product may no longer be adequate. Additionally, many managers now believe that overhead costs and direct labor are no longer highly correlated and that other factors drive overhead costs.

On an economywide basis, direct labor and overhead costs have been moving in opposite directions for a long time. As a percentage of total cost, direct labor has been declining, whereas overhead has been increasing.[1] Many tasks that used to be done by hand are now done with largely automated equipment—a component of overhead. Further-

---

[1]Germain Böer provides some data concerning these trends in "Five Modern Management Accounting Myths," *Management Accounting*, January 1994, pp. 22–27. Since 1849, on average, material cost has been fairly constant at 55% of sales. Labor cost has always been less important than direct materials and has declined steadily from 23% of sales in 1849 to about 10% in 1987. Overhead has grown from about 18% of sales to about 33% of sales over the last 50 years.

more, product diversity has increased. Companies are creating new products and services at an ever-accelerating rate that differ in volume, batch size, and complexity. Managing and sustaining this product diversity requires many more overhead resources such as production schedulers and product design engineers, and many of these overhead resources have no obvious connection with direct labor. Finally, computers, bar code readers, and other technology have dramatically reduced the costs of collecting and manipulating data—making more complex (and accurate) costing systems such as activity-based costing much less expensive to build and maintain.

Nevertheless, direct labor remains a viable base for applying overhead to products in some companies—particularly for external reports. Direct labor is an appropriate allocation base for overhead when overhead costs and direct labor are highly correlated. And indeed, most companies throughout the world continue to base overhead allocations on direct labor or machine-hours. However, if factorywide overhead costs do not move in tandem with factorywide direct labor or machine-hours, some other means of assigning overhead costs must be found or product costs will be distorted.

Departmental Overhead Rates

Rather than use a plantwide overhead rate, many companies use departmental overhead rates. The nature of the work performed in a department will determine the department's allocation base. For example, overhead costs in a machining department may be allocated on the basis of the machine-hours in that department. In contrast, the overhead costs in an assembly department may be allocated on the basis of direct labor-hours in that department.

Unfortunately, even departmental overhead rates will not correctly assign overhead costs in situations where a company has a range of products and complex overhead costs. The reason is that the departmental approach usually relies on volume as the factor in allocating overhead cost to products. For example, if the machining department's overhead is applied to products on the basis of machine-hours, it is assumed that the department's overhead costs are caused by, and are directly proportional to, machine-hours. However, the department's overhead costs are probably more complex than this and are caused by a variety of factors, including the range of products processed in the department, the number of batch setups that are required, the complexity of the products, and so on. A more sophisticated method like *activity-based costing* is required to adequately account for these diverse factors.

ABC Changes the Focus

IN BUSINESS

Euclid Engineering makes parts and components for the big automobile manufacturers. As a result of an ABC study, Euclid's managers "discovered that the company was spending more in launching new products than on direct labor expenses to produce existing products. Product development and launch expenses were 10% of expenses, whereas direct labor costs were only 9%. Of course, in the previous direct labor cost system, all attention had been focused on reducing direct labor costs . . . Product development and launch costs were blended into the factory overhead rate applied to products based on direct labor cost. Now Euclid's managers realized that they had a major cost reduction opportunity by attacking the product launch cost directly."

The new information produced by the ABC study also helped Euclid in its relations with customers. The detailed breakdown of the costs of design and engineering activities helped customers to make trade-offs, with the result that they would often ask that certain activities whose costs exceeded their benefits be skipped.

Source: Robert S. Kaplan and Robin Cooper, *Cost & Effect: Using Integrated Cost Systems to Drive Profitability and Performance* (Boston: Harvard Business School Press, 1998), pp. 219–222.

Activity-Based Costing (ABC)

Activity-based costing (ABC) is a technique that attempts to assign overhead costs more accurately to products than the simpler methods discussed thus far. The basic idea underlying the activity-based costing approach is illustrated in Exhibit 3–1. A customer order triggers a number of activities. For example, if Nordstrom orders a line of women's skirts from Calvin Klein, a production order is generated, materials are ordered, patterns are created, textiles are cut to pattern and then sewn, and the finished products are packed for shipping. These activities consume resources. For example, ordering the appropriate materials consumes clerical time—a resource the company must pay for. In activity-based costing, an attempt is made to trace these costs directly to the products that cause them.

Rather than a single allocation base such as direct labor-hours or machine-hours, in activity-based costing a company uses a number of allocation bases for assigning costs to products. Each allocation base in an activity-based costing system represents a major *activity* that causes overhead costs. An **activity** in activity-based costing is an event that causes the consumption of overhead resources. Examples of activities in various organizations include the following:

- Setting up machines.
- Admitting patients to a hospital.
- Scheduling production.
- Performing blood tests at a clinic.
- Billing customers.
- Maintaining equipment.
- Ordering materials or supplies.
- Stocking shelves at a store.
- Meeting with clients at a law firm.
- Preparing shipments.
- Inspecting materials for defects.
- Opening an account at a bank.

Activity-based costing focuses on these activities. Each major activity has its own overhead cost pool (also known as an *activity cost pool*), its own *activity measure*, and its own predetermined overhead rate (also known as an *activity rate*). An **activity cost pool** is a "cost bucket" in which costs related to a particular activity measure are accumulated. The **activity measure** expresses how much of the activity is carried out and it is used as the allocation basis for applying overhead costs to products and services. For example, *the number of patients admitted* is a natural choice of an activity measure for the activity *admitting patients to the hospital.* An **activity rate** is a predetermined overhead rate in an activity-based costing system. Each activity has its own activity rate that is used to apply overhead costs.

For example, the activity *setting up machines to process a batch* would have its own activity cost pool. Products are ordinarily processed in batches. And since each product has its own machine settings, machines must be set up when changing over from a batch of one product to another. If the total cost in this activity cost pool is $150,000 and the total expected activity is 1,000 machine setups, the predetermined overhead rate (i.e., activity rate) for this activity would be $150 per machine setup ($150,000 ÷ 1,000 machine setups = $150 per machine setup). Each product that requires a machine setup would be charged $150. Note that this charge does not depend on how many units are produced after the machine is set up. A small job requiring a machine setup would be charged $150—just the same as a large job.

Taking each activity in isolation, this system works exactly like the job-order costing system described in the last chapter. A predetermined overhead rate is computed for each activity and then applied to jobs and products based on the amount of activity required by the job or product.

EXHIBIT 3–1 The Activity-Based Costing Model

Cost Objects

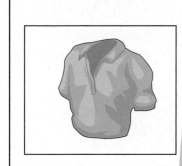 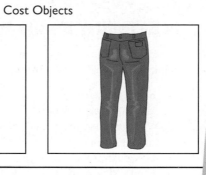 

Customer Orders Require:

Activities

Scheduling   Sewing   Inspection   Shipping

Activities Consume:

Resources

 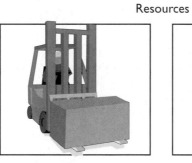  

Labor   Equipment   Energy   Supplies

Consumption of Resources Incur:

Costs

Account Title	Dr.	Cr.
Salary Expense	XX	
Depreciation	XX	

Account Title	Dr.	Cr.
Utilities Expense	XX	
Supplies Expense	XX	

Is E-Tailing Really Easier?

The company art.com™ sells prints and framed prints over the web. An ABC study identified the following 12 activities carried out in the company:

1. Service customers
2. Website optimization
3. Merchandise inventory selection and management
4. Purchasing and receiving
5. Customer acquisition and retention—paid-for marketing
6. Customer acquisition and retention—revenue share marketing (affiliate group)
7. Sustain information system
8. Sustain business—administration
9. Sustain business—production
10. Maintain facility—administrative
11. Maintain facility—production
12. Sustain business—executive

For example, the activity "merchandise inventory selection and management" involves scanning, describing, classifying, and linking each inventory item to search options. "Staff must carefully manage each change to the database, which is similar to adding and removing inventory items from the shelf of a store. They annotate added inventory items and upload them into the system, as well as remove obsolete and discontinued items . . . The number of inventory items for an e-tailer is typically much greater than for a brick-and-mortar [store], which is a competitive advantage, but experience shows managing a large inventory consumes substantial resources."

Source: Thomas L. Zeller, David R. Kublank, and Philip G. Makris, "How art.com™ Uses ABC to Succeed," *Strategic Finance*, March 2001, pp. 25–31. Reprinted with permission from the IMA, Montvale, NJ, USA, www.imanet.org.

DESIGNING AN ACTIVITY-BASED COSTING SYSTEM

The most important decisions in designing an activity-based costing system concern what activities will be included in the system and how the activities will be measured. In most companies, hundreds or even thousands of different activities cause overhead costs. These activities range from taking a telephone order to training new employees. Setting up and maintaining a complex costing system that includes all of these activities would be prohibitively expensive. The challenge in designing an activity-based costing system is to identify a reasonably small number of activities that explain the bulk of the variation in overhead costs. This is usually done by interviewing a broad range of managers in the organization to find out what activities they think are important and that consume most of the resources they manage. This often results in a long list of potential activities that could be included in the activity-based costing system. This list is refined and pruned in consultation with top managers. Related activities are frequently combined to reduce the amount of detail and record-keeping cost. For example, several actions may be involved in handling and moving raw materials, but these may be combined into a single activity titled *material handling*. The end result of this stage of the design process is an *activity dictionary* that defines each of the activities that will be included in the activity-based costing system and how the activities will be measured.

Some of the activities commonly found in activity-based costing systems in manufacturing companies are listed in Exhibit 3–2. In the exhibit, activities have been grouped into a four-level hierarchy: *unit-level activities, batch-level activities, product-level activities,* and *facility-level activities.* This cost hierarchy is useful in understanding the impact of activity-based costing. It also serves as a guide when simplifying an activity-based costing system. In general, activities and costs should be combined in the activity-based costing system only if they fall within the same level in the cost hierarchy.

Level	Activities	Activity Measures
Unit-level	Processing units on machines	Machine-hours
	Processing units by hand	Direct labor-hours
	Consuming factory supplies	Units produced
Batch-level	Processing purchase orders	Purchase orders processed
	Processing production orders	Production orders processed
	Setting up equipment	Number of setups; setup hours
	Handling material	Pounds of material handled; number of times material moved
Product-level	Testing new products	Hours of testing time
	Administering parts inventories	Number of part types
	Designing products	Hours of design time
Facility-level	General factory administration	Direct labor-hours*
	Plant building and grounds	Direct labor-hours*

*Facility-level costs cannot be traced on a cause-and-effect basis to individual products. Nevertheless, these costs are usually allocated to products using some arbitrary basis such as direct labor-hours—particularly for purposes of external reporting.

EXHIBIT 3–2

Examples of Activities and Activity Measures in Manufacturing Companies

Hierarchy of Activities

Unit-level activities are performed each time a unit is produced. The costs of unit-level activities should be proportional to the number of units produced. For example, providing power to run processing equipment would be a unit-level activity since power tends to be consumed in proportion to the number of units produced.

Batch-level activities consist of tasks that are performed each time a batch is processed, such as processing purchase orders, setting up equipment, packing shipments to customers, and handling material. Costs at the batch level depend on *the number of batches processed* rather than on the number of units produced. For example, the cost of processing a purchase order is the same no matter how many units of an item are ordered. Thus, the total cost of a batch-level activity such as purchasing is a function of the *number* of orders placed.

Product-level activities (sometimes called *product-sustaining activities*) relate to specific products and typically must be carried out regardless of how many batches or units of the product are manufactured. Product-level activities include maintaining inventories of parts for a product, issuing engineering change notices to modify a product to meet a customer's specifications, and developing special test routines when a product is first placed into production.

ABC and the Virtual Bakery

IN BUSINESS

Super Bakery, Inc., founded by former Pittsburgh Steelers' running back Franco Harris, is a "virtual corporation" that supplies donuts and other baked goods to schools, hospitals, and other institutions. "In a virtual corporation, only the core, strategic functions of the business are performed inside the company. The remaining support activities are outsourced to a network of external companies that specialize in each function." A network of independent brokers sells Super Bakery's products and the company contracts out baking, warehousing, and shipping. What does Super Bakery itself do? The company's master baker develops products and the company formulates and produces its own dry mixes from ingredients it has purchased. The contracted bakeries simply add water to the mix and follow the baking instructions. Super Bakery maintains four regional sales managers, and a small office staff processes orders and handles bookkeeping and accounting.

As much as possible, actual costs are traced to individual customer accounts. The remaining costs of the company are assigned to customer accounts using the following activity cost pools and activity measures:

Activity Description	Activity Measure
Advertising, trade shows, and bonds	Projected number of cases sold
Order department	Number of orders
Sales management	Time spent in each sales territory
Research and development (R&D)	Hours of R&D for each product line

Since the independent sales brokers are paid a flat 5% commission on sales, they have little incentive to make sure that the sales are actually profitable to Super Bakery. The brokers will slash prices if that is necessary to make a sale. Consequently, Super Bakery's regional sales managers must approve all price discounts and they use the ABC data to evaluate the profitability of the deals proposed by the brokers.

Source: Tim R. V. Davis and Bruce L. Darling, "ABC in a Virtual Corporation," *Management Accounting*, October 1996, pp. 18–26.

Facility-level activities (also called *organization-sustaining activities*) are activities that are carried out regardless of which products are produced, how many batches are run, or how many units are made. Facility-level costs include items such as factory management salaries, insurance, property taxes, and building depreciation. The costs of facility-level activities are often combined into a single cost pool and allocated to products using an arbitrary basis such as direct labor-hours. As we will see later in the book, allocating such costs to products will result in misleading data that can lead to bad decisions. However, facility-level costs must be allocated to products for external financial reports.

An Example of an Activity-Based Costing System Design

The complexity of an activity-based costing system will differ from company to company. For some companies, the structure of the activity-based costing system will be simple with only one or two activity cost pools at the unit, batch, and product levels. For other companies, the structure will be much more complex.

Exhibit 3–3 provides a graphic example of a relatively simple activity-based costing system. The purpose of this exhibit is to tie together the concepts discussed on preceding pages and also to present a bird's-eye view of an activity-based costing system.

The unallocated manufacturing overhead costs are at the top of Exhibit 3–3. These costs are ultimately allocated to products via the two-stage procedure illustrated in the exhibit. In the first stage, overhead costs are assigned to the activity cost pools. In the second stage, the costs that have been accumulated in the activity cost pools are allocated to products using activity rates and activity measures. For example, in the first stage cost assignment, various manufacturing overhead costs are assigned to the material receipts activity cost pool. These costs could include wages of workers who receive materials, wages of the clerks who handle shipping documents, and other costs that are incurred as a consequence of receiving materials. We will not go into the details of how these first-stage cost assignments are made. In all of the examples and assignments in this book, the first-stage cost assignments have already been completed. Once the amount of cost in the material receipts activity cost pool is known, procedures from Chapter 2 can be followed. The activity rate for material receipts is computed by dividing the total cost in the material receipts activity cost pool by the anticipated number of times material will be received in the upcoming year. For example, the total cost in the activity cost pool might be $50,000 and the total number of material receipts might be 2,500. In that case, the activity rate would be $20 per material receipt. If a job requires three shipments of incoming materials, it would be charged $60 for material receipts. This is really no different from the way overhead was applied to jobs in Chapter 2 except that the number of material receipts is the allocation basis rather than direct labor-hours.

EXHIBIT 3–3 Graphic Example of Activity-Based Costing

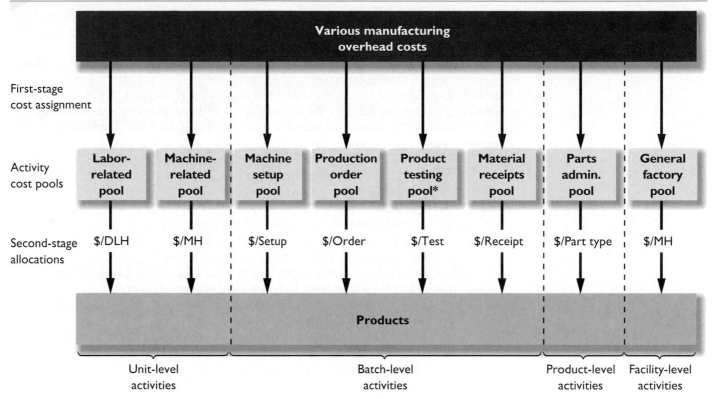

| | Unit-level activities | | Batch-level activities | | | | Product-level activities | Facility-level activities |

* Standard tests are performed on a few randomly selected units in each batch.

USING ACTIVITY-BASED COSTING

Different products place different demands on resources. This difference in demand on resources is not recognized by traditional costing systems, which assume that overhead resources are consumed in direct proportion to direct labor-hours. The following example illustrates the distortions in product costs that can result from using a traditional costing system.

Comtek Sound, Inc., makes two products, a radio with a built-in CD player (called a *CD unit*) and a radio with a built-in DVD player (called a *DVD unit*). Both of these products are sold to automobile manufacturers for installation in new vehicles. The president of the company, Sarah Kastler, recently returned from a management conference at which activity-based costing was discussed. Following the conference, she called a meeting of the top managers in the company to discuss what she had learned. Attending the meeting

MANAGERIAL ACCOUNTING IN ACTION
The Issue

comtek
SOUND, INC.

were the production manager, Frank Hines; the marketing manager, Nicole Sermone; and the accounting manager, Tom Frazier.

Sarah: I learned some things at the conference I just attended that may help resolve some long-standing puzzles here at Comtek Sound.

Frank: Did anyone at the conference explain why my equipment always breaks down at the worst possible moment?

Sarah: Sorry, Frank, I guess it must be bad karma or something.

Nicole: Did they tell you why we've been losing all those bids lately on our bread-and-butter CD units and winning every bid on our specialty DVD units?

Sarah: Nicole, you probably weren't expecting this answer, but yes, there may be a simple explanation. We may have been shooting ourselves in the foot.

Nicole: How so? I don't know about anyone else, but we have been hustling like crazy to get more business for the company.

Frank: Wait a minute, Nicole, my production people have been turning in tremendous improvements in defect rates, on-time delivery, you name it.

Sarah: Whoa, everybody. Calm down. I don't think anyone is to blame for us losing so many bids on our high-volume bread-and-butter product. Nicole, when you talk with our customers, what reasons do they give for taking their CD unit business to our competitors? Is it a problem with quality or on-time delivery?

Nicole: No, our customers readily admit that we're among the best in the business.

Sarah: Then what's the problem?

Nicole: Price. The competition is undercutting our price on the CD units and then bidding high on the DVD units. As a result, they're stealing our high-volume CD business and leaving us with just the low-volume DVD business.

Sarah: Why is our price so high for the CD units that the competition is able to undercut us?

Nicole: Our price isn't too high. Theirs is too low. Our competitors must be pricing below their costs on the CD units.

Sarah: Why do you think that?

Nicole: Well, if we charged the prices for our CD units that our competitors are quoting, we'd be pricing below *our* cost, and I know we're just as efficient as any competitor.

Frank: Nicole, why would our competitors price below their cost?

Nicole: They're out to grab market share.

Frank: Does that make any sense? What good does more market share do them if they're pricing below their cost?

Sarah: I think Frank has a point. Tom, you're the expert with the numbers. Can you suggest another explanation?

Tom: I was hoping you'd ask that. Those product cost figures my department reports to you are primarily intended to be used to value inventories and determine cost of goods sold for our external financial statements. I am awfully uncomfortable about using them for bidding. In fact, I have mentioned this several times, but no one was interested.

Sarah: Now I'm interested. Tom, are you telling us that the product cost figures we have been using for bidding may be wrong? Are you suggesting that we really don't know what the manufacturing cost is for either the CD units or the DVD units?

Tom: Yes, that could be the problem. Our cost system isn't designed to recognize that our two products place different demands on our resources. The CD units are simple to manufacture, and the DVD units are more complex. For example, both products take the same amount of labor time for assembly, but the more complex DVD units take a disproportionate amount of machine and testing time. We need a cost system that recognizes this difference in demand on resources.

Sarah: That's exactly the point made at the conference. The conference speakers suggested we recost our products using something called activity-based costing. Tom, can we do this?

Tom: You bet! But we need to do it as a team. Can each person in the room appoint one of their top people to work with me?

Sarah: Let's do it! I'd like the special ABC team to report back to this group as soon as possible. If there's a problem with our costs, we need to know it before the competition plows us under.

Comtek Sound, Inc.'s Basic Data

Tom Frazier and the ABC team immediately began gathering basic information relating to the company's two products. As a basis for its study, the team decided to use the cost and other data planned for the current year. A summary of some of this information follows. For the current year, the company's budget provides for selling 50,000 DVD units and 200,000 CD units. Both products require two direct labor-hours to complete. Therefore, the company plans to work 500,000 direct labor-hours (DLHs) during the current year, computed as follows:

	Hours
DVD units: 50,000 units × 2 DLHs per unit	100,000
CD units: 200,000 units × 2 DLHs per unit.	400,000
Total direct labor-hours.	500,000

Costs for materials and labor for one unit of each product are given below:

	DVD Units	CD Units
Direct materials	$90	$50
Direct labor (at $10 per DLH)	$20	$20

The company's estimated manufacturing overhead costs for the current year total $10,000,000. The ABC team discovered that although the same amount of direct labor time is required for each product, the more complex DVD units require more machine time, more machine setups, and more testing than the CD units. Also, the team found that it is necessary to manufacture the DVD units in smaller lots, so they require a relatively large number of production orders as compared to the CD units.

The company has always used direct labor-hours as the base for assigning overhead costs to its products.

With this data in hand, the ABC team was prepared to begin the design of the new activity-based costing system. But first, they wanted to compute the cost of each product using the company's existing cost system.

Direct Labor-Hours as a Base

Under the company's existing costing system, the company's predetermined overhead rate would be $20 per direct labor-hour. The rate is computed as follows:

$$\frac{\text{Predetermined}}{\text{overhead rate}} = \frac{\text{Estimated total manufacturing overhead}}{\text{Estimated total direct labor-hours (DLHs)}}$$

$$= \frac{\$10,000,000}{500,000 \text{ DLHs}} = \$20 \text{ per DLH}$$

Using this rate, the ABC team then computed the unit product costs as given below:

	DVD Units	CD Units
Direct materials (above)	$ 90	$ 50
Direct labor (above)	20	20
Manufacturing overhead (2 DLHs × $20 per DLH)	40	40
Unit product cost	$150	$110

Tom Frazier explained to the ABC team that the problem with this costing approach is that it relies entirely on labor time in assigning overhead cost to products and does not consider the impact of other factors—such as setups and testing—on the overhead costs of the company. Since these other factors are being ignored and the two products require equal amounts of labor time, they are assigned equal amounts of overhead cost.

Tom explained that while this method of computing costs is fast and simple, it is accurate only in those situations where other factors affecting overhead costs are not significant. Tom stated that he believed these other factors are significant in the case of Comtek Sound, Inc., and he was anxious for the team to analyze the various activities of the company to see what impact they have on costs.

Computing Activity Rates

LEARNING OBJECTIVE 2

Compute activity rates for an activity-based costing system.

Concept 3–2

The ABC team then analyzed Comtek Sound, Inc.'s operations and identified eight major activities to be included in the new activity-based costing system. (These eight activities are identical to those illustrated earlier in Exhibit 3–3.) Cost and other data relating to the activities are presented in Exhibit 3–4.

As shown in the Basic Data at the top of Exhibit 3–4, the ABC team estimated the amount of overhead cost for each activity cost pool, along with the expected amount of activity for the current year. The machine setups activity cost pool, for example, was assigned $1,600,000 in overhead cost. The company expects to complete 4,000 setups during the year, of which 3,000 will be for DVD units and 1,000 will be for CD units. Data for other activities are also shown in the exhibit.

The ABC team then computed an activity rate for each activity. (See the middle panel in Exhibit 3–4.) The rate for machine setups, for example, was computed by dividing the total estimated overhead cost in the activity cost pool, $1,600,000, by the expected amount of activity, 4,000 setups. The result was the activity rate of $400 per setup. This process was repeated for each of the other activities in the activity-based costing system.

Computing Product Costs

LEARNING OBJECTIVE 3

Compute product costs using activity-based costing.

Once the activity rates were determined, it was then an easy matter to compute the overhead cost that would be allocated to each product. (See the bottom panel of Exhibit 3–4.) For example, the amount of machine setup cost allocated to DVD units was determined by multiplying the activity rate of $400 per setup by the 3,000 expected setups for DVD units during the year. This yielded a total of $1,200,000 in machine setup costs to be assigned to the DVD units.

Note from the exhibit that the use of an activity approach has resulted in $93.20 in overhead cost being assigned to each DVD unit and $26.70 to each CD unit. The ABC team then used these amounts to determine unit product costs under activity-based costing, as presented in the table below. For comparison, the table also shows the unit costs derived earlier when direct labor was used as the base for assigning overhead costs to the products.

	Activity-Based Costing		Direct-Labor Based Costing	
	DVD Units	**CD Units**	**DVD Units**	**CD Units**
Direct materials	$ 90.00	$50.00	$ 90.00	$ 50.00
Direct labor	20.00	20.00	20.00	20.00
Manufacturing overhead	93.20	26.70	40.00	40.00
Unit product cost	$203.20	$96.70	$150.00	$110.00

EXHIBIT 3–4   Comtek Sound's Activity-Based Costing System

Basic Data

Activities and Activity Measures	Estimated Overhead Cost	Expected Activity		
		Total	DVD Units	CD Units
Labor related (direct labor-hours)	$ 800,000	500,000	100,000	400,000
Machine related (machine-hours)	2,100,000	1,000,000	300,000	700,000
Machine setups (setups)	1,600,000	4,000	3,000	1,000
Production orders (orders).	450,000	1,200	400	800
Product testing (tests).	1,700,000	20,000	16,000	4,000
Material receipts (receipts)	1,000,000	5,000	1,800	3,200
Parts administration (part types)	350,000	700	400	300
General factory (machine-hours)	2,000,000	1,000,000	300,000	700,000
	$10,000,000			

Computation of Activity Rates

Activities	(a) Estimated Overhead Cost	(b) Total Expected Activity	(a) ÷ (b) Activity Rate
Labor related	$800,000	500,000 DLHs	$1.60 per DLH
Machine related	$2,100,000	1,000,000 MHs	$2.10 per MH
Machine setups	$1,600,000	4,000 setups	$400.00 per setup
Production orders	$450,000	1,200 orders	$375.00 per order
Product testing	$1,700,000	20,000 tests	$85.00 per test
Material receipts	$1,000,000	5,000 receipts	$200.00 per receipt
Parts administration.	$350,000	700 part types	$500.00 per part type
General factory	$2,000,000	1,000,000 MHs	$2.00 per MH

Computation of the Overhead Cost per Unit of Product

Activities and Activity Rates	DVD Units		CD Units	
	Expected Activity	Amount	Expected Activity	Amount
Labor related, at $1.60 per DLH.	100,000	$ 160,000	400,000	$ 640,000
Machine related, at $2.10 per MH.	300,000	630,000	700,000	1,470,000
Machine setups, at $400 per setup	3,000	1,200,000	1,000	400,000
Production orders, at $375 per order	400	150,000	800	300,000
Product testing, at $85 per test.	16,000	1,360,000	4,000	340,000
Materials receipts, at $200 per receipt	1,800	360,000	3,200	640,000
Parts administration, at $500 per part type	400	200,000	300	150,000
General factory, at $2.00 per MH.	300,000	600,000	700,000	1,400,000
Total overhead costs assigned (a)		$4,660,000		$5,340,000
Number of units produced (b)		50,000		200,000
Overhead cost per unit (a) ÷ (b)		$93.20		$26.70

The ABC team members were shocked by their findings, which Tom Frazier summarized as follows in the team's report:

> In the past, the company has been charging $40.00 in overhead cost to a unit of either product, whereas it should have been charging $93.20 in overhead cost to each DVD unit and only $26.70 to each CD unit. Thus, as a result of using direct labor as

the base for overhead costing, unit product costs had been badly distorted. The company may even have been suffering a loss on the DVD units without knowing it because the cost of these units has been so vastly understated. Through activity-based costing, we have been able to better identify the overhead costs of each product and thus derive more accurate cost data.

The pattern of cost distortion shown by the ABC team's findings is quite common. Such distortion can happen in any company that relies on direct labor-hours or machine-hours in assigning overhead cost to products and ignores other significant factors affecting overhead cost incurrence.

MANAGERIAL ACCOUNTING IN ACTION Wrap-Up

comtek
SOUND, INC.

The ABC team presented the results of its work in a meeting attended by all of the top managers of Comtek Sound including the president, Sarah Kastler; the production manager, Frank Hines; the marketing manager, Nicole Sermone; and the accounting manager, Tom Frazier. After the formal presentation by the ABC team, the following discussion took place:

Sarah: I would like to personally thank the ABC team for all the work they have done. I am now beginning to wonder about some of the decisions we have made in the past using our old cost accounting system.

Tom: I hope I don't have to remind anyone that I have been warning people about this problem for quite some time.

Sarah: No, you don't have to remind us, Tom. I guess we just didn't understand the problem before.

Nicole: It's obvious from this activity-based costing information that we had everything backwards. We thought the competition was pricing below cost on the CD units, but in fact *we* were overcharging for these units because our costs were overstated. And we thought the competition was overpricing DVD units, but in fact *our* prices were way too low because our costs for these units were understated. I'll bet the competition has really been laughing behind our backs!

Sarah: You can bet they won't be laughing when they see our next bids.

Shifting of Overhead Cost

LEARNING OBJECTIVE 4

Contrast the product costs computed under activity-based costing and conventional costing methods.

When a company implements activity-based costing, overhead cost often shifts from high-volume products to low-volume products, with a higher unit product cost resulting for the low-volume products. We saw this happen in the example above, where overhead cost was shifted to the DVD units—the low-volume product—and their unit product cost increased from $150.00 to $203.20 per unit. This results from the existence of batch-level and product-level costs. When these costs are spread across lower volumes, higher average costs result. For example, consider the cost of issuing production orders, which is a batch activity. As shown in Exhibit 3–4, the average cost to Comtek Sound to issue a single production order is $375. This cost is assigned to a production order regardless of how many units are to be processed under that product order. The key here is to realize that fewer DVD units (the low-volume product) are processed per production order than CD units:

	DVD Units	CD Units
Number of units produced per year (a)....................	50,000	200,000
Number of production orders issued per year (b)	400	800
Number of units processed per production order (a) ÷ (b) ...	125	250

If the $375 cost to issue a production order is spread over the number of units processed per order, we get the following average cost per unit:

	DVD Units	CD Units
Cost to issue a production order (a)	$375	$375
Number of units processed per production order (above) (b) . . .	125	250
Production order cost per unit (a) ÷ (b)	$3.00	$1.50

Thus, the production order cost for a DVD unit (the low-volume product) is $3, which is *double* the $1.50 cost for a CD unit.

Product-level costs—such as parts administration—have a similar impact. In a conventional costing system, these costs are spread more or less uniformly across all units that are produced. In an activity-based costing system, these costs are assigned more appropriately to products. Since product-level costs are fixed with respect to the number of units that are processed, the average cost per unit of something like parts administration will be higher for low-volume products than for high-volume products.

TARGETING PROCESS IMPROVEMENTS

Activity-based costing can also be used to identify activities that would benefit from process improvements. Indeed, this is the most widely cited benefit of activity-based costing by managers.[2] When used in this way, activity-based costing is often called *activity-based management*. Basically, **activity-based management** involves focusing on activities to eliminate waste, decrease processing time, and reduce defects. Activity-based management is used in organizations as diverse as manufacturing companies, hospitals, and the U.S. Marine Corps. When "40 percent of the cost of running a hospital involves storing, collecting and moving information," there is obviously a great deal of room for eliminating waste.[3]

The first step in any improvement program is to decide what to improve. The Theory of Constraints approach discussed in the Prologue is a powerful tool for targeting the area in an organization whose improvement will yield the greatest benefit. Activity-based management provides another approach. The activity rates computed in activity-based costing can provide valuable clues concerning where there is waste and scope for improvement in an organization. For example, looking at the activity rates in Exhibit 3–4, Comtek's managers may wonder why it costs $375 on average to process a purchase order. That may seem like an awful lot of money for an activity that adds no value to the product. As a consequence, the purchase order processing activity may be targeted for process improvement using TQM or process reengineering as discussed in the Prologue. *Benchmarking* is often advocated as a way to leverage the information in activity rates.

Benchmarking is a systematic approach to identifying the activities with the greatest room for improvement. It is based on comparing the performance in an organization with the performance of other, similar organizations known for their outstanding performance. If a particular part of the organization performs far below the world-class standard, managers will be likely to target that area for an improvement program.

---

[2]Dan Swenson, "The Benefits of Activity-Based Cost Management to the Manufacturing Industry," *Journal of Management Accounting Research* 7 (Fall 1995), pp. 167–180.
[3]Kambiz Foroohar, "Rx: software," *Forbes*, April 7, 1997, p. 114.

Benchmarking the Back Office

The Marketing Resources Group of Qwest, the telephone company, performed an activity-based costing analysis of the activities carried out in its accounting department. Managers computed the activity rates for the activities and then compared these rates to the costs of carrying out the same activities in other companies. Two benchmarks were used: (1) a sample of Fortune 100 companies, which are the largest 100 companies in the United States and (2) "world class" companies that had been identified by a consultant as having the best accounting practices in the world. These comparisons appear below:

Activity	Activity Measure	Qwest Activity Rate	Fortune 100 Benchmark	World Class Benchmark
Processing accounts receivable	Number of invoices processed	$3.80 per invoice	$15.00 per invoice	$4.60 per invoice
Processing accounts payable	Number of invoices processed	$8.90 per invoice	$7.00 per invoice	$1.80 per invoice
Processing payroll checks	Number of checks processed	$7.30 per check	$5.00 per check	$1.72 per check
Managing customer credit	Number of customer accounts	$12.00 per account	$16.00 per account	$5.60 per account

It is clear from this analysis that Qwest does a good job of processing accounts receivables. Its average cost per invoice is $3.80, whereas the cost in other companies that are considered world class is even higher—$4.60 per invoice. On the other hand, the cost of processing payroll checks is significantly higher at Qwest than at benchmark companies. The cost per payroll check at Qwest is $7.30 versus $5.00 at Fortune 100 companies and $1.72 at world-class companies. This suggests that it may be possible to wring waste out of this activity. As a consequence, the payroll processing activity may be targeted for a TQM effort or for process reengineering.

Source: Steve Coburn, Hugh Grove, and Cynthia Fukami, "Benchmarking with ABCM," *Management Accounting*, January 1995, pp. 56–60. Reprinted with permission from the IMA, Montvale, NJ, USA, www.imanet.org.

EVALUATION OF ACTIVITY-BASED COSTING

Activity-based costing improves the accuracy of product costs, helps managers to understand the nature of overhead costs, and helps managers target areas for improvement through benchmarking and other techniques. These benefits are discussed in this section.

The Benefits of Activity-Based Costing

Activity-based costing improves the accuracy of product costs in three ways. First, activity-based costing usually increases the number of cost pools used to accumulate overhead costs. Rather than accumulating all overhead costs in a single, plantwide pool, or accumulating them in departmental pools, the company accumulates costs for each major activity. Second, the activity cost pools are more homogeneous than departmental cost pools. In principle, all of the costs in an activity cost pool pertain to a single activity. In contrast, departmental cost pools contain the costs of many different activities carried out in the department. Third, activity-based costing changes the bases used to assign overhead costs to products. Rather than assign costs on the basis of direct labor or some other measure of volume, managers assign costs on the basis of the activities that cause overhead costs.

In a traditional costing system, overhead is typically applied to products on the basis of direct labor-hours. As a consequence, it may appear that overhead costs are caused by direct labor-hours. In activity-based costing, managers see that batch setups, engineering change orders, and other activities cause overhead costs rather than just direct labor. Better understanding can lead to better decisions and better control over overhead costs.

Finally, activity-based costing can be used as part of a program to improve the overall operations in an organization. It can provide valuable clues concerning the activities that could benefit most from TQM, process reengineering, and other improvement initiatives.

Limitations of Activity-Based Costing

Any discussion of activity-based costing is incomplete without some cautionary warnings. First, the cost of implementing and maintaining an activity-based costing system may outweigh the benefits. Second, it would be naïve to assume that product costs provided even by an activity-based costing are always relevant when making decisions. These limitations are discussed below.

The Cost of Implementing Activity-Based Costing   Implementing ABC is a major project that involves a great deal of effort. First, the cost system must be designed—preferably by a cross-functional team. This requires taking valued employees away from other tasks for a major project. In addition, the data used in the activity-based costing system must be collected and verified. In some cases, this requires collecting data that has never been collected before. In short, implementing and maintaining an activity-based costing system can present a formidable challenge, and management may decide that the costs are too great to justify the expected benefits. Nevertheless, it should be kept in mind that the costs of collecting and processing data have dropped dramatically over the last several decades due to bar coding and other technologies, and these costs can be expected to continue to fall.

When are the benefits of activity-based costing most likely to be worth the cost? Companies that have some of the following characteristics are most likely to benefit from activity-based costing:

1. Products differ substantially in volume, lot size, and in the activities they require.
2. Conditions have changed substantially since the existing cost system was established.
3. Overhead costs are high and increasing and no one seems to understand why.
4. Management does not trust the existing cost system and ignores cost data from the system when making decisions.

Limitations of the ABC Model   The activity-based costing model relies on a number of critical assumptions.[4] Perhaps the most important of these assumptions is that the cost in each activity cost pool is strictly proportional to its activity measure. What little evidence we have on this issue suggests that overhead costs are less than proportional to activity.[5] Economists call this increasing returns to scale—as activity increases, the average cost drops. As a practical matter, this means that product costs will be overstated for the purposes of making decisions. The product costs generated by activity-based costing are almost certainly more accurate than those generated by a conventional costing system, but the product costs should nevertheless be viewed with caution. Managers should be particularly alert to product costs that contain allocations of facility-level costs. As we shall see later in the book, such product costs can easily lead managers astray in decisions.

---

[4]Eric Noreen, "Conditions under Which Activity-Based Cost Systems Provide Relevant Costs," *Journal of Management Accounting Research*, Fall 1991, pp. 159–168.

[5]Eric Noreen and Naomi Soderstrom, "The Accuracy of Proportional Cost Models: Evidence from Hospital Service Departments," *Review of Accounting Studies* 2, 1997; and Eric Noreen and Naomi Soderstrom, "Are Overhead Costs Proportional to Activity? Evidence from Hospital Service Departments," *Journal of Accounting and Economics*, January 1994, pp. 253–278.

Bakery Owner

YOU DECIDE

You are the owner of a bakery that makes a complete line of specialty breads, pastries, cakes, and pies for the retail and wholesale markets. A summer intern has just completed an activity-based costing study that concluded, among other things, that one of your largest recurring jobs is losing money. A local luxury hotel orders the same assortment of desserts every week for its Sunday brunch buffet for a fixed price of $975 per week. The hotel is quite happy with the quality of the desserts the bakery has been providing, but it would seek bids from other local bakeries if the price were increased.

The activity-based costing study conducted by the intern revealed that the cost to the bakery of providing these desserts is $1,034 per week, resulting in an apparent loss of $59 per week or over $3,000 per year. Scrutinizing the intern's report, you find that the weekly cost of $1,034 includes facility-level costs of $329. These facility-level costs include portions of the rent on the bakery's building, your salary, depreciation on the office personal computer, and so on. The facility-level costs were arbitrarily allocated to the Sunday brunch job on the basis of the direct labor-hours in the bakery required to produce the desserts.

Should you demand an increase in price from the luxury hotel for the Sunday brunch desserts to at least $1,034? If an increase is not forthcoming, should you withdraw from the agreement and discontinue providing the desserts?

Modifying the ABC Model   The discussion in this chapter has assumed that the primary purpose of the activity-based costing system is to provide more accurate product costs for external reports. If the product costs are to be used by managers for internal decisions, some modifications should be made. For example, for decision-making purposes, the distinction between manufacturing costs on the one hand and selling and general administrative expenses on the other hand is unimportant. Managers need to know what costs a product causes, and it doesn't matter whether the costs are manufacturing costs or selling and general administrative expenses. Consequently, for decision-making purposes, some selling and general administrative expenses should be assigned to products as well as manufacturing costs. Moreover, as mentioned above, facility-level costs should be removed from product costs when making decisions. Nevertheless, the techniques covered in this chapter provide a good basis for understanding the mechanics of activity-based costing. For a more complete coverage of the use of activity-based costing in decisions, see more advanced texts.[6]

ABC at the Bank

First Tennessee National Corporation, a regional bank holding company, used activity-based costing to analyze the profitability of its certificates of deposit (CDs). The bank found that 30% of its CD customers were responsible for 88% of the overall profit generated from CDs, while another 30% of its customers were losing the bank money. "This situation was corrected through a combination of higher minimum balances, new products, and process redesign."

Source: Robert B. Sweeney and James W. Mays, "ABM," *Management Accounting*, March 1997, pp. 20–26.

Activity-Based Costing and Service Industries

Although initially developed as a tool for manufacturing companies, activity-based costing is also being used in service industries. Successful implementation of an activity-based costing system depends on identifying the key activities that generate costs and tracking how many of those activities are performed for each service the organization

---

[6]See, for example, Chapter 8 and its appendix in Ray Garrison and Eric Noreen, *Managerial Accounting*, 10th edition, Irwin/McGraw-Hill, © 2003.

provides. Activity-based costing has been implemented in a wide variety of service industries including railroads, hospitals, banks, and data services companies.

ABC in the Public Sector

Robin Cooper and Robert S. Kaplan report that: "The U.S. Veterans Affairs Department has identified the cost of the 10 activities performed to process death benefits and uses this information to monitor and improve the underlying cost structure for performing this function. The U.S. Immigration and Naturalization Service (INS) uses its ABC cost information to set fees for all its outputs, including administering citizenship exams and issuing permanent work permits (green cards)." The City of Indianapolis made ABC a cornerstone of its privatization efforts and its drive to provide more services at lower cost to citizens. As the mayor of the city, Stephen Goldsmith, explained: "Introducing competition and privatization to government services requires real cost information. You can't compete out if you are using fake money." When city workers became aware of the costs of carrying out activities such as filling potholes in streets and were faced with the possible transfer of such tasks to the private sector, they became highly motivated to reduce costs. Instead of going out to fill potholes with a five- or six-man repair crew, plus a supervisor, they started doing the same job with a three- or four-man crew without a supervisor. The number of politically appointed supervisors, which had stood at 36 for 75 employees, was slashed by half.

Source: Robert S. Kaplan and Robin Cooper, *Cost & Effect: Using Integrated Cost Systems to Drive Profitability and Performance,* Harvard Business School Press, Boston, 1998, pp. 245–250.

Legal Firm Business Manager

DECISION MAKER

You have been hired to manage the business aspects of a local legal firm with a staff of 6 attorneys, 10 paralegals, and 5 staffpersons. Clients of the firm are billed a fixed amount per hour of attorney time. The fixed hourly charge is determined each year by dividing the total cost of the legal office for the preceding year by the total billed hours of attorney time for that year. A markup of 25 percent is then added to this average cost per hour of billed attorney time to provide for a profit and for inflation.

The firm's partners are concerned because the firm has been unprofitable for several years. The firm has been losing its smaller clients to other local firms—largely because the firm's fees have become uncompetitive. And the firm has been attracting larger clients with more complex legal problems from its competitors. To serve these demanding larger clients, the firm must subscribe to expensive on-line legal reference services, hire additional paralegals and staffpersons, and lease additional office space.

What do you think might be the reason for the unprofitable operations in recent years? What might be done to improve the situation for the coming year?

2. Which of the following statements is false? (You may select more than one answer.)

a. Activity-based costing systems usually shift costs from low-volume products to high-volume products.

b. Benchmarking can be used to identify activities with the greatest potential for improvement.

c. Activity-based costing is most valuable to companies that manufacture products that are similar in terms of their volume of production, lot size, and complexity.

d. Activity-based costing systems are based on the assumption that the costs included in each activity cost pool are strictly proportional to the cost pool's activity measure.

3. A company manufactures and sells 10,000 units of A and 5,000 units of B. The average batch sizes for A and B are 1,000 and 250 units, respectively. Which of the following statements is false? (You may select more than one answer.)
   a. A costing system that relies solely on a unit-level activity measure to assign all manufacturing overhead to products will overcost product A.
   b. A costing system that relies solely on a unit-level activity measure to assign manufacturing overhead to products will overcost product B.
   c. An activity-based costing system would assign 67 percent of the batch-level overhead costs to product B.
   d. An activity-based costing system would assign 67 percent of the unit-level overhead costs to product A.

COST FLOWS IN AN ACTIVITY-BASED COSTING SYSTEM

LEARNING OBJECTIVE 5

Record the flow of costs in an activity-based costing system.

In Chapter 2, we discussed the flow of costs in a job-order costing system. The flow of costs through Raw Materials, Work in Process, and other accounts is the same under activity-based costing. The only difference in activity-based costing is that more than one predetermined overhead rate is used to apply overhead costs to products. Our purpose in this section is to provide a detailed example of cost flows in an activity-based costing system.

An Example of Cost Flows

The company in the following example has five activity cost pools and therefore must compute five predetermined overhead rates (i.e., activity rates). Except for that detail, the journal entries, T-accounts, and general cost flows are the same as described in Chapter 2.

Basic Data   Sarvik Company uses activity-based costing for its external financial reports. The company has five activity cost pools, which are listed below along with relevant data for the coming year.

Activity Cost Pool	Activity Measure	Estimated Overhead Cost	Expected Activity
Machine related	Machine-hours	$175,000	5,000 MHs
Purchase orders	Number of orders	$63,000	700 orders
Machine setups	Number of setups	$92,000	460 setups
Product testing	Number of tests	$160,000	200 tests
General factory.	Direct labor-hours	$300,000	25,000 DLHs

At the beginning of the year, the company had inventory balances as follows:

Raw materials	$3,000
Work in process	$4,000
Finished goods	$0

Selected transactions recorded by the company during the year are given below:

a. Raw materials were purchased on account, $915,000.
b. Raw materials were requisitioned for use in production, $900,000 ($810,000 direct and $90,000 indirect).
c. Labor costs were incurred in the factory, $370,000 ($95,000 direct labor and $275,000 indirect labor).
d. Depreciation was recorded on factory assets, $180,000.
e. Miscellaneous manufacturing overhead costs were incurred, $230,000.
f. Manufacturing overhead cost was applied to production. Actual activity during the year was as follows:

Activity Cost Pool	Actual Activity
Machine related	4,600 MHs
Purchase orders	800 orders
Machine setups	500 setups
Product testing	190 tests
General factory.	23,000 DLHs

g. Goods costing $1,650,000 to manufacture according to the activity-based costing system were completed during the year.

Tracking the Flow of Costs The predetermined overhead rates (i.e., activity rates) for the activity cost pools would be computed as follows:

Activity Cost Pools	(a) Estimated Overhead Cost	(b) Total Expected Activity	(a) ÷ (b) Activity Rate
Machine related	$175,000	5,000 machine-hours	$35 per machine-hour
Purchase orders	$63,000	700 orders	$90 per order
Machine setups	$92,000	460 setups	$200 per setup
Product testing	$160,000	200 tests	$800 per test
General factory.	$300,000	25,000 direct labor-hours	$12 per direct labor-hour

The following journal entries would be used to record transactions (a) through (g) above:

a.	Raw Materials.	915,000	
	Accounts Payable		915,000
b.	Work in Process	810,000	
	Manufacturing Overhead.	90,000	
	Raw Materials		900,000
c.	Work in Process	95,000	
	Manufacturing Overhead.	275,000	
	Salaries and Wages Payable.		370,000
d.	Manufacturing Overhead.	180,000	
	Accumulated Depreciation.		180,000
e.	Manufacturing Overhead.	230,000	
	Accounts Payable		230,000

Recall from Chapter 2 the formula for computing applied overhead cost, which is:

Predetermined overhead rate × Actual activity = Applied overhead cost

In activity-based costing, this formula is applied for each activity cost pool using its own predetermined overhead rate (i.e., activity rate). The computations are as follows:

Activities	(1) Activity Rate	(2) Actual Activity	(1) × (2) Applied Overhead Cost
Machine related	$35 per MH	4,600 MHs	$161,000
Purchase orders	$90 per order	800 orders	72,000
Machine setups	$200 per setup	500 setups	100,000
Product testing	$800 per test	190 tests	152,000
General factory.	$12 per DLH	23,000 DLHs	276,000
Total			$761,000

By totaling these five applied overhead cost figures, we find that the company applied $761,000 in overhead cost to products during the year. The following entry would be used to record this application of overhead cost:

| f. | Work in Process............................ | 761,000 | |
| | Manufacturing Overhead .... | | 761,000 |

Finally, the following journal entry would be used to record the completion of work in process as described in transaction (g) above:

| g. | Finished Goods .... | 1,650,000 | |
| | Work in Process......................... | | 1,650,000 |

The T-accounts corresponding to the above journal entries appear below:

Raw Materials					Work in Process					Finished Goods		
Bal.	3,000	900,000	(b)		Bal.	4,000	1,650,000	(g)		Bal.	0	
(a)	915,000				(b)	810,000				(g)	1,650,000	
Bal.	18,000				(c)	95,000						
					(f)	761,000						
					Bal.	20,000						

Accumulated Depreciation				Accounts Payable				Salaries and Wages Payable		
	180,000	(d)			915,000	(a)			370,000	(c)
					230,000	(e)				

Manufacturing Overhead			
(b)	90,000	761,000	(f)
(c)	275,000		
(d)	180,000		
(e)	230,000		
	775,000	761,000	
Bal.	14,000		

The overhead is underapplied by $14,000. This can be determined directly, as shown below, or by reference to the balance in the Manufacturing Overhead T-account above.

Actual manufacturing overhead incurred	$775,000
Manufacturing overhead applied	761,000
Overhead underapplied	$ 14,000

SUMMARY

LO1   Understand the basic approach in activity-based costing and how it differs from conventional costing.

Activity-based costing was developed as a way of more accurately assigning overhead to products. Activity-based costing differs from conventional costing as described in Chapter 2 in two major ways. First, in activity-based costing, each major activity that consumes overhead resources has its own cost pool and its own activity rate, whereas in Chapter 2 there was only a single overhead cost pool and a single pre-determined overhead rate. Second, the allocation bases (or activity measures) in activity-based costing are diverse. They may include machine setups, purchase orders, engineering change orders, and so on, in addition to direct labor-hours or machine-hours. Nevertheless, within each activity cost pool, the mechanics of computing overhead rates and of applying overhead to products are the same as described in Chapter 2. However, the increase in the number of cost pools and the use of better measures of activity generally result in more accurate product costs.

LO2   Compute activity rates for an activity-based costing system.
Each activity in an activity-based costing system has its own cost pool and its own measure of activity. The activity rate for a particular activity is computed by dividing the total cost in the activity's cost pool by the total amount of activity.

LO3   Compute product costs using activity-based costing.
Product costs in activity-based costing, as in conventional costing systems, consist of direct materials, direct labor, and overhead. In both systems, overhead is applied to products using predetermined overhead rates. In the case of an activity-based costing system, each activity has its own predetermined overhead rate (i.e., activity rate). The activities required by a product are multiplied by their respective activity rates to determine the amount of overhead that is applied to the product.

LO4   Contrast the product costs computed under activity-based costing and conventional costing methods.
Under conventional costing methods, overhead costs are allocated to products on the basis of some measure of volume such as direct labor-hours or machine-hours. This results in most of the overhead cost being allocated to high-volume products. In contrast, under activity-based costing, some overhead costs are allocated on the basis of batch-level or product-level activities. This change in allocation bases results in shifting overhead costs from the high-volume products to low-volume products. Accordingly, product costs for high-volume products are commonly lower under activity-based costing than under conventional costing methods, and product costs for low-volume products are higher.

LO5   Record the flow of costs in an activity-based costing system.
The journal entries and general flow of costs in an activity-based costing system are the same as they are in a conventional costing system. The only difference is the use of more than one predetermined overhead rate (i.e., activity rate) to apply overhead to products.

GUIDANCE ANSWERS TO *DECISION MAKER* AND *YOU DECIDE*

Bakery Owner (p. 143)
The bakery really isn't losing money on the weekly order of desserts from the luxury hotel. By definition, facility-level costs are not affected by individual products and jobs—these costs would continue unchanged even if the weekly order were dropped. Recalling the discussion in Chapter 1 concerning decision making, only those costs and benefits that differ between alternatives in a decision are relevant. Since the facility-level costs would be the same whether the dessert order is kept or dropped, they are not relevant in this decision and should be ignored. Hence, the real cost of the job is $705 ($1,034 − $329), which reveals that the job actually yields a weekly profit of $270 ($975 − $705) rather than a loss.

No, the bakery owner should not press for a price increase—particularly if that would result in the hotel seeking bids from competitors. And no, the bakery owner certainly should not withdraw from the agreement to provide the desserts.

Legal Firm Business Manager (p. 145)
The recent problems the firm has been facing can probably be traced to its simplified system for billing for work. Rather than carefully tracing costs to clients, costs are arbitrarily allocated to clients on the basis of attorney hours. Large, demanding clients require much more overhead resources than smaller clients, but the costs of these overhead resources are arbitrarily allocated to all clients on the basis of attorney hours. This results in shifting overhead costs to the smaller, less demanding clients and increasing their charges. It also results in undercharging larger, more demanding clients. Consequently, the firm has been losing smaller clients to competitors and has been attracting larger, demanding clients. Unfortunately, this change in the mix of clients leads to much higher costs and reduced profits.

The situation can be improved by using activity-based costing to trace more costs directly to clients. This should result in shifting costs from the smaller, less demanding clients to the larger, more demanding clients that cause those costs. Smaller clients will face lower charges and hence will be more likely to stay with the firm. Larger, more demanding clients will face higher charges that will fully cover the costs they impose on the firm.

GUIDANCE ANSWERS TO CONCEPT CHECKS

1. **Choice d.** Product-level costs are unrelated to the amount of a product that is made.
2. **Choices a and c.** Activity-based costing systems usually shift costs from high-volume products to low-volume products. Activity-based costing is most valuable for companies with highly diverse products rather than with similar products.
3. **Choice b.** Relying solely on a unit-level activity measure will result in 33% of the total overhead costs being assigned to product B. While product B should be assigned 33% of the unit-level overhead costs, it should be assigned 67% of the batch-level overhead costs.

REVIEW PROBLEM: ACTIVITY-BASED COSTING

Aerodec, Inc., manufactures and sells two types of wooden deck chairs: Deluxe and Tourist. Annual sales in units, direct labor-hours (DLHs) per unit, and total direct labor-hours per year are provided below:

	Total Hours
Deluxe deck chair: 2,000 units × 5 DLHs per unit...........	10,000
Tourist deck chair: 10,000 units × 4 DLHs per unit..........	40,000
Total direct labor-hours	50,000

Costs for materials and labor for one unit of each product are given below:

	Deluxe	Tourist
Direct materials	$25	$17
Direct labor (at $12 per DLH)..............	$60	$48

Manufacturing overhead costs total $800,000 each year. The breakdown of these costs among the company's six activity cost pools is given below. The activity measures are shown in parentheses.

Activities and Activity Measures	Estimated Overhead Cost	Expected Activity		
		Total	Deluxe	Tourist
Labor related (direct labor-hours)............	$ 80,000	50,000	10,000	40,000
Machine setups (number of setups)...........	150,000	5,000	3,000	2,000
Parts administration (number of parts)........	160,000	80	50	30
Production orders (number of orders)........	70,000	400	100	300
Material receipts (number of receipts)	90,000	750	150	600
General factory (machine-hours)	250,000	40,000	12,000	28,000
	$800,000			

Required:

1. Classify each of Aerodec's activities as either a unit-level, batch-level, product-level, or facility-level activity.
2. Assume that the company applies overhead cost to products on the basis of direct labor-hours.
   a. Compute the predetermined overhead rate that would be used.
   b. Determine the unit product cost of each product, using the predetermined overhead rate computed in (2)(a) above.
3. Assume that the company uses activity-based costing to compute overhead rates.
   a. Compute the activity rate (i.e., predetermined overhead rate) for each of the six activity centers listed above.
   b. Using the rates developed in (3)(a) above, determine the amount of overhead cost that would be assigned to a unit of each product.

c.   Determine the unit product cost of each product and compare this cost to the cost computed in
(2)(b) above.

Solution to Review Problem

1.

Activity Cost Pool	Type of Activity
Labor related.	Unit level
Machine setups	Batch level
Parts administration.	Product level
Production orders.	Batch level
Material receipts	Batch level
General factory	Facility level

2. a.

$$\frac{\text{Predetermined}}{\text{overhead rate}} = \frac{\text{Estimated total manufacturing overhead}}{\text{Estimated total direct labor-hours (DLHs)}} = \frac{\$800{,}000}{50{,}000 \text{ DLHs}} = \$16 \text{ per DLH}$$

b.

	Deluxe	Tourist
Direct materials	$ 25	$ 17
Direct labor	60	48
Manufacturing overhead applied:		
Deluxe: 5 DLHs × $16 per DLH	80	
Tourist: 4 DLHs × $16 per DLH.		64
Unit product cost.	$165	$129

3. a.

Activities	(a) Estimated Overhead Cost	(b) Total Expected Activity	(a) ÷ (b) Activity Rate
Labor related	$80,000	50,000 DLHs	$1.60 per DLH
Machine setups	$150,000	5,000 setups	$30.00 per setup
Parts administration.	$160,000	80 parts	$2,000.00 per part
Production orders	$70,000	400 orders	$175.00 per order
Material receipts	$90,000	750 receipts	$120.00 per receipt
General factory	$250,000	40,000 MHs	$6.25 per MH

b.

	Deluxe		Tourist	
Activities and Activity Rates	Expected Activity	Amount	Expected Activity	Amount
Labor related, at $1.60 per DLH.	10,000	$ 16,000	40,000	$ 64,000
Machine setups, at $30 per setup	3,000	90,000	2,000	60,000
Parts administration, at $2,000 per part.	50	100,000	30	60,000
Production orders, at $175 per order	100	17,500	300	52,500
Material receipts, at $120 per receipt.	150	18,000	600	72,000
General factory, at $6.25 per MH	12,000	75,000	28,000	175,000
Total overhead cost assigned (a)		$316,500		$483,500
Number of units produced (b)		2,000		10,000
Overhead cost per unit, (a) ÷ (b).		$158.25		$48.35

c.

	Deluxe	Tourist
Direct materials.	$ 25.00	$ 17.00
Direct labor.	60.00	48.00
Manufacturing overhead (see above)	158.25	48.35
Unit product cost	$243.25	$113.35

Under activity-based costing, the unit product cost of the Deluxe deck chair is much greater than the cost computed in (2)(b) above, and the unit product cost of the Tourist deck chair is much less. Using volume (direct labor-hours) in (2)(b) as a basis for applying overhead cost to products has resulted in too little overhead cost being applied to the Deluxe deck chair (the low-volume product) and too much overhead cost being applied to the Tourist deck chair (the high-volume product).

GLOSSARY

Activity   An event that causes the consumption of overhead resources in an organization. (p. 130)

Activity-based costing (ABC)   A two-stage costing method in which overhead costs are assigned to products on the basis of the activities they require. (p. 130)

Activity-based management   A management approach that focuses on managing activities as a way of eliminating waste and reducing delays and defects. (p. 141)

Activity cost pool   A "bucket" in which costs are accumulated that relate to a single activity measure in the activity-based costing system. (p. 130)

Activity measure   An allocation base in an activity-based costing system; ideally, a measure of whatever causes the costs in an activity cost pool. (p. 130)

Activity rate   A predetermined overhead rate in activity-based costing. Each activity cost pool has its own activity rate which is used to apply overhead to products and services. (p. 130)

Batch-level activities   Activities that are performed each time a batch of goods is handled or processed, regardless of how many units are in a batch. The amount of resources consumed depends on the number of batches run rather than on the number of units in the batch. (p. 133)

Benchmarking   A systematic approach to identifying the activities with the greatest room for improvement. It is based on comparing the performance in an organization with the performance of other, similar organizations known for their outstanding performance. (p. 141)

Facility-level activities   Activities that relate to overall production and therefore can't be traced to specific products. Costs associated with these activities pertain to a plant's general manufacturing process. (p. 133)

Product-level activities   Activities that relate to specific products that must be carried out regardless of how many units are produced and sold or batches run. (p. 133)

Unit-level activities   Activities that arise as a result of the total volume of goods and services that are produced, and that are performed each time a unit is produced. (p. 133)

QUESTIONS

3–1   What are the three common approaches for assigning overhead costs to products?

3–2   Why is activity-based costing growing in popularity?

3–3   Why do departmental overhead rates sometimes result in inaccurate product costs?

3–4   What are the four hierarchical levels of activity discussed in the chapter?

3–5   Why is activity-based costing described as a "two-stage" costing method?

3–6   Why do overhead costs often shift from high-volume products to low-volume products when a company switches from a conventional costing method to activity-based costing?

3–7   What are the three major ways in which activity-based costing improves the accuracy of product costs?

3–8   What are the major limitations of activity-based costing?

BRIEF EXERCISES

BRIEF EXERCISE 3–1 ABC Cost Hierarchy (LO1)

The following activities occur at Greenwich Corporation, a company that manufactures a variety of products.

a. Various individuals manage the parts inventories.
b. A clerk in the factory issues purchase orders for a job.
c. The personnel department trains new production workers.
d. The factory's general manager uses her office in the factory building.
e. Direct labor workers assemble products.
f. Engineers design new products.
g. The materials storekeeper issues raw materials to be used in jobs.
h. The maintenance department performs periodic preventive maintenance on general-use equipment.

Required:

Classify each of the activities above as either a unit-level, batch-level, product-level, or facility-level activity.

BRIEF EXERCISE 3–2 Compute Activity Rates (LO2)

Rustafson Corporation is a diversified manufacturer of consumer goods. The company's activity-based costing system has the following seven activity cost pools:

Activity Cost Pool	Estimated Overhead Cost	Expected Activity
Labor related	$52,000	8,000 direct labor-hours
Machine related	$15,000	20,000 machine-hours
Machine setups.................	$42,000	1,000 setups
Production orders	$18,000	500 orders
Product testing................	$48,000	2,000 tests
Packaging	$75,000	5,000 packages
General factory	$108,800	8,000 direct labor-hours

Required:

1. Compute the activity rate for each activity cost pool.
2. Compute the company's predetermined overhead rate, assuming that the company uses a single plantwide predetermined overhead rate based on direct labor-hours.

BRIEF EXERCISE 3–3 Compute ABC Product Costs (LO3)

Larner Corporation is a diversified manufacturer of industrial goods. The company's activity-based costing system has the following six activity cost pools and activity rates:

Activity Cost Pool	Activity Rates
Labor related	$7.00 per direct labor-hour
Machine related	$3.00 per machine-hour
Machine setups...................	$40.00 per setup
Production orders	$160.00 per order
Shipments........................	$120.00 per shipment
General factory	$4.00 per direct labor-hour

Cost and activity data have been supplied for the following products:

	J78	B52
Direct materials cost per unit	$6.50	$31.00
Direct labor cost per unit....................	$3.75	$6.00
Number of units produced per year	4,000	100

	Total Expected Activity	
	J78	B52
Direct labor-hours	1,000	40
Machine-hours	3,200	30
Machine setups......................	5	1
Production orders	5	1
Shipments	10	1

Required:
Compute the unit product cost of each of the products listed above.

BRIEF EXERCISE 3–4   Contrast ABC and Conventional Product Costs   (LO4)
Pacifica Industrial Products Corporation makes two products, Product H and Product L. Product H is expected to sell 40,000 units next year and Product L is expected to sell 8,000 units. A unit of either product requires 0.4 direct labor-hours.
 The company's total manufacturing overhead for the year is expected to be $1,632,000.

Required:
1. The company currently applies manufacturing overhead to products using direct labor-hours as the allocation base. If this method is followed, how much overhead cost would be applied to each product? Compute both the overhead cost per unit and the total amount of overhead cost that would be applied to each product. (In other words, how much overhead cost is applied to a unit of Product H? Product L? How much overhead cost is applied in total to all the units of Product H? Product L?)
2. Management is considering an activity-based costing system and would like to know what impact this change might have on product costs. For purposes of discussion, it has been suggested that all of the manufacturing overhead be treated as a product-level cost. The total manufacturing overhead would be divided in half between the two products, with $816,000 assigned to Product H and $816,000 assigned to Product L.
    If this suggestion is followed, how much overhead cost per unit would be applied to each product?
3. Explain the impact on unit product costs of the switch in costing systems.

BRIEF EXERCISE 3–5   Cost Flows In an ABC System   (LO5)
Masters Corporation implemented activity-based costing several years ago and uses it for its external financial reports. The company has four activity cost pools, which are listed below.

Activity Cost Pool	Activity Rate
Machine related.........................	$18 per MH
Purchase orders	$78 per order
Machine setups	$63 per setup
General factory.........................	$14 per DLH

At the beginning of the year, the company had inventory balances as follows:

Raw materials	$25,000
Work in process.........	$44,000
Finished goods	$86,000

Selected transactions recorded by the company during the year are given below:

a. Raw materials were purchased on account, $928,000.
b. Raw materials were requisitioned for use in production, $931,000 ($822,000 direct and $109,000 indirect).
c. Labor costs were incurred in the factory, $468,000 ($396,000 direct labor and $72,000 indirect labor).
d. Depreciation was recorded on factory assets, $284,000.
e. Miscellaneous manufacturing overhead costs were incurred, $175,000.
f. Manufacturing overhead cost was applied to production. Actual activity during the year was as follows:

Activity Cost Pool	Actual Activity
Machine related	15,000 MHs
Purchase orders..................	900 orders
Machine setups	1,300 setups
General factory	12,000 DLHs

g. Completed products were transferred to the company's finished goods warehouse. According to the company's costing system, these products cost $1,830,000.

Required:
1. Prepare journal entries to record transactions (a) through (g) above.
2. Post the entries in (1) above to T-accounts.
3. Compute the underapplied or overapplied overhead cost in the Manufacturing Overhead account.

EXERCISES

EXERCISE 3–6   Cost Hierarchy and Activity Measures   (LO1)
Listed below are various activities that you have observed at Companhia de Textils, S.A., a manufacturing company located in Brazil. The company makes a variety of products in its plant outside Sao Paulo.

a. Preventive maintenance is performed on general-purpose production equipment.
b. Products are assembled by hand.
c. Reminder notices are sent to customers who are late in making payments.
d. Purchase orders are issued for materials to be used in production.
e. Modifications are made to product designs.
f. New employees are hired by the personnel office.
g. Machine settings are changed between batches of different products.
h. Parts inventories are maintained in the storeroom. (Each product requires its own unique parts.)
i. Insurance costs are incurred on the company's facilities.

Required:
1. Classify each of the activities as either a unit-level, batch-level, product-level, customer-level, or organization-sustaining activity.
2. Where possible, name one or more activity measures that could be used to assign costs generated by the activity to products or customers.

EXERCISE 3–7   Contrast ABC and Conventional Product Costs   (LO2, LO3, LO4)
Kunkel Company makes two products and uses a conventional costing system in which a single plantwide predetermined overhead rate is computed based on direct labor-hours. Data for the two products for the upcoming year follow:

	Mercon	Wurcon
Direct materials cost per unit	$10.00	$8.00
Direct labor cost per unit	$3.00	$3.75
Direct labor-hours per unit	0.20	0.25
Number of units produced	10,000	40,000

These products are customized to some degree for specific customers.

Required:
1. The company's manufacturing overhead costs for the year are expected to be $336,000. Using the company's conventional costing system, compute the unit product costs for the two products.
2. Management is considering an activity-based costing system in which half of the overhead would continue to be allocated on the basis of direct labor-hours and half would be allocated on the basis of engineering design time. This time is expected to be distributed as follows during the upcoming year:

	Mercon	Wurcon	Total
Engineering design time (in hours)	4,000	4,000	8,000

Compute the unit product costs for the two products using the proposed ABC system.
3. Explain why the product costs differ between the two systems.

EXERCISE 3–8 Cost Flows in Activity-Based Costing (LO2, LO5)
Sultan Company uses activity-based costing to determine product costs for external financial reports. Some of the entries have been completed to the Manufacturing Overhead account for the current year, as shown by entry (a) below:

Manufacturing Overhead

(a)	530,000	

Required:
1. What does the entry (a) above represent?
2. At the beginning of the year, the company made the following estimates of cost and activity for its five activity cost pools:

Activity Cost Pool	Activity Measure	Expected Overhead Cost	Expected Activity
Labor related.	Direct labor-hours	$156,000	26,000 DLHs
Purchase orders	Number of orders	$11,000	220 orders
Parts management.	Number of part types	$80,000	100 part types
Board etching	Number of boards	$90,000	2,000 boards
General factory.	Machine-hours	$180,000	20,000 MHs

Compute the activity rate (i.e., predetermined overhead rate) for each of the activity cost pools.
3. During the year, actual activity was recorded as follows:

Activity Cost Pool	Actual Activity
Labor related	25,000 DLHs
Purchase orders.	200 orders
Parts management.	110 part types
Board etching.	1,800 boards
General factory	22,000 MHs

Determine the amount of manufacturing overhead cost applied to production for the year.
4. Determine the amount of underapplied or overapplied overhead cost for the year.

EXERCISE 3–9 Assigning Overhead to Products in ABC (LO3)
Refer to the data in Exercise 3–8 for Sultan Company. The activities during the year were distributed across the company's four products as follows:

Activity Cost Pool	Actual Activity	Product A	Product B	Product C	Product D
Labor related	25,000 DLHs	6,000	10,000	4,000	5,000
Purchase orders.	200 orders	60	30	20	90
Parts management	110 part types	30	25	40	15
Board etching.	1,800 boards	500	900	400	0
General factory	22,000 MHs	3,000	8,000	5,000	6,000

Required:
Compute the amount of overhead cost applied to each product during the year.

EXERCISE 3–10   Computing ABC Product Costs   (LO2, LO3)

Performance Products Corporation makes two products, titanium Rims and Posts. Data regarding the two products follow:

	Direct Labor-Hours per Unit	Annual Production
Rims.	0.40	20,000 units
Posts	0.20	80,000 units

Additional information about the company follows:

a.   Rims require $17 in direct materials per unit, and Posts require $10.
b.   The direct labor wage rate is $16 per hour.
c.   Rims are more complex to manufacture than Posts, and they require special equipment.
d.   The ABC system has the following activity cost pools:

Activity Cost Pool	Activity Measure	Estimated Overhead Cost	Activity Total	Rims	Posts
Machine setups.	Number of setups	$ 21,600	180	100	80
Special processing.	Machine-hours	180,000	4,000	4,000	0
General factory	Direct labor-hours	288,000	24,000	8,000	16,000
		$489,600			

Required:
1. Compute the activity rate (i.e., predetermined overhead rate) for each activity cost pool.
2. Determine the unit product cost of each product.

PROBLEMS

PROBLEM 3–11   ABC Cost Hierarchy   (LO1)

Mitchell Corporation manufactures a variety of products in a single facility. Consultants hired by the company to do an activity-based costing analysis have identified the following activities carried out in the company on a routine basis:

a.   Milling machines are used to make components for products.
b.   A percentage of all completed goods are inspected on a random basis.
c.   Production orders are issued for jobs.
d.   The company's grounds crew maintains planted areas surrounding the factory.
e.   Employees are trained in general procedures.
f.   The human resources department screens and hires new employees.
g.   Purchase orders are issued for materials required in production.
h.   Material is received on the receiving dock and moved to the production area.
i.   The plant controller prepares periodic accounting reports.
j.   The engineering department makes modifications in the designs of products.
k.   Machines are set up between batches of different products.
l.   The maintenance crew does routine periodic maintenance on general-purpose equipment.

Required:
1. Classify each of the above activities as a unit-level, batch-level, product-level, or facility-level activity.
2. For each of the above activities, suggest an activity measure that could be used to allocate its costs to products.

PROBLEM 3–12   Contrasting ABC and Conventional Product Costs   (LO2, LO3, LO4)

Marine, Inc., manufactures a product that is available in both a flexible and a rigid model. The company has made the rigid model for years; the flexible model was introduced several years ago to tap a new segment of the market. Since introduction of the flexible model, the company's profits have steadily declined,

CHECK FIGURE
(3b) Rigid: $131.70 per unit

and management has become concerned about the accuracy of its costing system. Sales of the flexible model have been increasing rapidly.

Overhead is applied to products on the basis of direct labor-hours. At the beginning of the current year, management estimated that $600,000 in overhead costs would be incurred and the company would produce and sell 1,000 units of the flexible model and 10,000 units of the rigid model. The flexible model requires 2.0 hours of direct labor time per unit, and the rigid model requires 1.0 hours. Materials and labor costs per unit are given below:

	Flexible	Rigid
Direct materials cost per unit..............	$110.00	$80.00
Direct labor cost per unit.................	$30.00	$15.00

Required:
1. Compute the predetermined overhead rate using direct labor-hours as the basis for allocating overhead costs to products. Compute the unit product cost for one unit of each model.
2. An intern suggested that the company use activity-based costing to cost its products. A team was formed to investigate this idea. It came back with the recommendation that four activity cost pools be used. These cost pools and their associated activities are listed below:

Activity Cost Pool and Activity Measure	Estimated Overhead Cost	Activity Total	Flexible	Rigid
Purchase orders (number of orders)...........	$ 20,000	400	100	300
Rework requests (number of requests)........	10,000	200	60	140
Product testing (number of tests)	210,000	2,100	900	1,200
Machine-related (machine-hours).............	360,000	4,000	1,500	2,500
	$600,000			

Compute the activity rate (i.e., predetermined overhead rate) for each of the activity cost pools.
3. Assume that actual activity is as expected for the year. Using activity-based costing, do the following:
   a. Determine the total amount of overhead that would be applied to each model for the year.
   b. Compute the unit product cost for one unit of each model.
4. Can you identify a possible explanation for the company's declining profits? If so, what is it?

CHECK FIGURE
(2d) Total overhead over-
applied: $6,820

PROBLEM 3–13   Cost flows and Unit Product Costs in Activity-Based Costing   (LO2, LO3, LO5)
Adria Company uses activity-based costing to determine product costs for external financial reports. At the beginning of the year, management made the following estimates of cost and activity in the company's five activity cost pools:

Activity Cost Pool	Activity Measure	Estimated Overhead Cost	Expected Activity
Labor related.............	Direct labor-hours	$35,000	7,000 DLHs
Production orders.........	Number of orders	$4,000	2,000 orders
Material receipts	Number of receipts	$10,450	950 receipts
Relay assembly............	Number of relays	$7,000	1,000 relays
General factory...........	Machine-hours	$240,000	40,000 MHs

Required:
1. Compute the activity rate (i.e., predetermined overhead rate) for each of the activity cost pools.
2. During the year, actual overhead cost and activity were recorded as follows:

Activity Cost Pool	Actual Overhead Cost	Actual Activity
Labor related..............	$ 33,000	6,700 DLHs
Production orders..........	3,890	1,900 orders
		(continued)

(concluded) Activity Cost Pool	Actual Overhead Cost	Actual Activity
Material receipts	8,000	700 receipts
Relay assembly.............	6,800	930 relays
General factory	245,000	42,000 MHs
Total overhead cost.........	$296,690	

a. Prepare a journal entry to record the incurrence of actual manufacturing overhead cost for the year (credit Accounts Payable). Post the entry to the company's Manufacturing Overhead T-account.

b. Determine the amount of overhead cost applied to production during the year.

c. Prepare a journal entry to record the application of manufacturing overhead cost to work in process for the year. Post the entry to the company's Manufacturing Overhead T-account.

d. Determine the amount of underapplied or overapplied manufacturing overhead for the year.

3. The actual activity for the year was distributed among the company's four products as follows:

Activity Cost Pool	Actual Activity	Product A	Product B	Product C	Product D
Labor related	6,700 DLHs	2,400	500	3,000	800
Production orders	1,900 orders	100	350	500	950
Material receipts	700 receipts	400	200	100	0
Relay assembly........	930 relays	170	400	0	360
General factory	42,000 MHs	12,000	7,000	8,000	15,000

a. Determine the total amount of overhead cost applied to each product.

b. Does the total amount of overhead cost applied to the products above tie in to the T-accounts in any way? Explain.

PROBLEM 3–14 Contrast Activity-Based Costing and Conventional Product Costs   (LO2, LO3, LO4)

CHECK FIGURE
(2b) N 800 XL unit product cost: $404.00

Puget World, Inc., manufactures two models of television sets, the N 800 XL model and the N 500 model. Data regarding the two products follow:

	Direct Labor-Hours per Unit	Annual Production	Total Direct Labor-Hours
Model N 800 XL...	3.0	3,000 units	9,000
Model N 500......	1.0	12,000 units	12,000
			21,000

Additional information about the company follows:

a. Model N 800 XL requires $75 in direct materials per unit, and Model N 500 requires $25.

b. The direct labor wage rate is $18 per hour.

c. The company has always used direct labor-hours as the base for applying manufacturing overhead cost to products.

d. Model N 800 XL is more complex to manufacture than Model N 500 and requires the use of special equipment. Consequently, the company is considering the use of activity-based costing to apply manufacturing overhead cost to products for external financial reports. Three activity cost pools have been identified as follows:

Activity Cost Pool	Activity Measure	Estimated Overhead Cost
Machine setups............	Number of setups	$ 360,000
Special processing..........	Machine-hours	165,000
General factory	Direct labor-hours	1,260,000
		$1,785,000

Activity Measure	Expected Activity		
	Model N 800 XL	Model N 500	Total
Number of setups	100	200	300
Machine-hours	16,500	0	16,500
Direct labor-hours	9,000	12,000	21,000

Required:

1. Assume that the company continues to use direct labor-hours as the base for applying overhead cost to products.
   a. Compute the predetermined overhead rate.
   b. Compute the unit product cost of each model.
2. Assume that the company decides to use activity-based costing to apply manufacturing overhead cost to products.
   a. Compute the predetermined overhead rate for each activity cost pool and determine the amount of overhead cost that would be applied to each model using the activity-based costing system.
   b. Compute the unit product cost of each model.
3. Explain why manufacturing overhead cost shifts from Model N 500 to Model N 800 XL under activity-based costing.

CHECK FIGURE
(2d) Total overhead over-
     applied: $2,450

PROBLEM 3–15   Activity-Based Costing Cost Flows   (LO2, LO3, LO5)

Rusties Company uses activity-based costing to determine product costs for external financial reports. At the beginning of the year, management made the following estimates of cost and activity in the company's five activity cost pools:

Activity Cost Pool	Activity Measure	Estimated Overhead Cost	Expected Activity
Labor related...........	Direct labor-hours	$18,000	2,000 DLHs
Purchase orders.........	Number of orders	$1,050	525 orders
Product testing	Number of tests	$3,500	350 tests
Template etching........	Number of templates	$700	28 templates
General factory.........	Machine-hours	$50,000	10,000 MHs

Required:

1. Compute the activity rate (i.e., predetermined overhead rate) for each of the activity cost pools.
2. During the year, actual overhead cost and activity were recorded as follows:

Activity Cost Pool	Actual Overhead Cost	Actual Activity
Labor related	$20,000	2,200 DLHs
Purchase orders	1,300	1,000 orders
Product testing................	3,600	360 tests
Template etching	800	30 templates
General factory	58,000	12,000 MHs
Total overhead cost	$83,700	

   a. Prepare a journal entry to record the incurrence of actual manufacturing overhead cost for the year (credit Accounts Payable). Post the entry to the company's Manufacturing Overhead T-account.
   b. Determine the amount of overhead cost applied to production during the year.
   c. Prepare a journal entry to record the application of manufacturing overhead cost to work in process for the year. Post the entry to the company's Manufacturing Overhead T-account.
   d. Determine the amount of underapplied or overapplied manufacturing overhead for the year.
3. The actual activity for the year was distributed among the company's four products as follows:

Activity Cost Pool	Actual Activity	Product A	Product B	Product C	Product D
Labor related.........	2,200 DLHs	500	300	700	700
Purchase orders.......	1,000 orders	320	120	500	60
Product testing.......	360 tests	200	60	0	100
Template etching......	30 templates	0	14	10	6
General factory.......	12,000 MHs	3,400	2,200	1,800	4,600

a. Determine the total amount of overhead cost applied to each product.
b. Does the total amount of overhead cost applied to the products above tie in to the T accounts in any way? Explain.

PROBLEM 3–16 Activity-Based Costing Cost Flows and Income Statement   (LO2, LO5)

CHECK FIGURE
(4) Total overhead overapplied: $6,800

Flint Corporation is a manufacturing company that uses activity-based costing for its external financial reports. The company's activity cost pools and associated data for the coming year appear below:

Activity Cost Pool	Activity Measure	Estimated Overhead Cost	Expected Activity
Machining...............	Machine-hours	$52,000	13,000 MHs
Purchase orders.........	Number of orders	$24,000	3,000 orders
Parts management.......	Number of part types	$36,000	60 part types
Testing................	Number of tests	$63,000	700 tests
General factory.........	Direct labor-hours	$414,000	46,000 DLHs

At the beginning of the year, the company had inventory balances as follows:

Raw materials.........	$5,000
Work in process.......	$10,000
Finished goods........	$8,000

The following transactions were recorded for the year:

a. Raw materials were purchased on account, $415,000.
b. Raw materials were withdrawn from the storeroom for use in production, $400,000 ($220,000 direct and $180,000 indirect).
c. The following costs were incurred for employee services: direct labor, $190,000; indirect labor, $140,000; sales commissions, $36,000; and administrative salaries, $80,000.
d. Sales travel costs were incurred, $12,000.
e. Various factory overhead costs were incurred, $158,000.
f. Advertising costs were incurred, $50,000.
g. Depreciation was recorded for the year, $200,000 ($143,000 related to factory operations and $57,000 related to selling and administrative activities).
h. Manufacturing overhead was applied to products. Actual activity for the year was as follows:

Activity Cost Pool	Actual Activity
Machining.................	13,200 MHs
Purchase orders	2,950 orders
Parts management..........	100 part types
Testing	760 tests
General factory............	47,000 DLHs

i. Goods were completed and transferred to the finished goods warehouse. According to the company's activity-based costing system, these finished goods cost $1,007,800 to manufacture.
j. Goods were sold on account to customers during the year for a total of $1,480,000. According to the company's activity-based costing system, the goods cost $1,000,000 to manufacture.

Required:

1. Compute the predetermined overhead rate (i.e., activity rate) for each activity cost pool.
2. Prepare journal entries to record transactions (a) through (j) above.
3. Post the entries in (2) above to T-accounts.
4. Compute the underapplied or overapplied manufacturing overhead cost. Prepare a journal entry to close any balance in the Manufacturing Overhead account to Cost of Goods Sold. Post the entry to the appropriate T-accounts.
5. Prepare an income statement for the year.

CHECK FIGURE
(3a) LEC 40 overhead cost:
$5.06

PROBLEM 3–17   Contrasting ABC and Conventional Product Costs   (LO2, LO3, LO4)

For many years, Thomson Company manufactured a single product called a LEC 40. Then three years ago, the company automated a portion of its plant and at the same time introduced a second product called a LEC 90 that has become increasingly popular. The LEC 90 is a more complex product, requiring 0.80 hour of direct labor time per unit to manufacture and extensive machining in the automated portion of the plant. The LEC 40 requires only 0.40 hour of direct labor time per unit and only a small amount of machining. Manufacturing overhead costs are currently assigned to products on the basis of direct labor-hours.

Despite the growing popularity of the company's new LEC 90, profits have been declining steadily. Management is beginning to believe that there may be a problem with the company's costing system. Material and labor costs per unit are as follows:

	LEC 40	LEC 90
Direct materials...	$30.00	$50.00
Direct labor (0.40 hour and 0.80 hour @ $15.00 per hour)...........	$6.00	$12.00

Management estimates that the company will incur $912,000 in manufacturing overhead costs during the current year and 60,000 units of the LEC 40 and 20,000 units of the LEC 90 will be produced and sold.

Required:

1. Compute the predetermined manufacturing overhead rate assuming that the company continues to apply manufacturing overhead cost on the basis of direct labor-hours. Using this rate and other data from the problem, determine the unit product cost of each product.
2. Management is considering using activity-based costing to apply manufacturing overhead cost to products for external financial reports. The activity-based costing system would have the following four activity cost pools:

Activity Cost Pool	Activity Measure	Estimated Overhead Cost
Maintaining parts inventory ..	Number of part types	$225,000
Processing purchase orders..	Number of purchase orders	182,000
Quality control............	Number of tests run	45,000
Machine related	Machine-hours	460,000
		$912,000

	Expected Activity		
Activity Measure	LEC 40	LEC 90	Total
Number of part types	600	900	1,500
Number of purchase orders ..	2,000	800	2,800
Number of tests run	500	1,750	2,250
Machine-hours	1,600	8,400	10,000

Determine the activity rate (i.e., predetermined overhead rate) for each of the four activity cost pools.
3. Using the activity rates you computed in (2) above, do the following:
   a. Compute the total amount of manufacturing overhead cost that would be applied to each product using the activity-based costing system. After these totals have been computed, determine the amount of manufacturing overhead cost per unit of each product.
   b. Compute the unit product cost of each product.

4. From the data you have developed in (1) through (3) above, identify factors that may account for the company's declining profits.

PROBLEM 3–18   Compute and Use Activity Rates to Determine the Costs of Serving Customers (LO2, LO3, LO4)

Gino's Restaurant is a popular restaurant of Boston, Massachusetts. The owner of the restaurant has been trying to better understand costs at the restaurant and has hired a student intern to conduct an activity-based costing study. The intern, in consultation with the owner, identified the following major activities:

CHECK FIGURE
(3b) $8.65 per diner

Activity Cost Pool	Activity Measure
Serving a party of diners	Number of parties served
Serving a diner	Number of diners served
Serving drinks	Number of drinks ordered

A group of diners who ask to sit at the same table is counted as a party. Some costs, such as the costs of cleaning linen, are the same whether one person is at a table or the table is full. Other costs, such as washing dishes, depend on the number of diners served.

Data concerning these activities are displayed below.

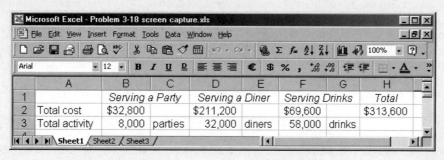

	A	B	C	D	E	F	G	H
1		Serving a Party		Serving a Diner		Serving Drinks		Total
2	Total cost	$32,800		$211,200		$69,600		$313,600
3	Total activity	8,000	parties	32,000	diners	58,000	drinks	

Prior to the activity-based costing study, the owner knew very little about the costs of the restaurant. She knew that the total cost for the month was $313,600 and that 32,000 diners had been served. Therefore, the average cost per diner was $9.80 ($313,600 ÷ 32,000 = $9.80).

Required:
1. Compute the activity rates for each of the three activities.
2. According to the activity-based costing system, what is the total cost of serving each of the following parties of diners?
   a.   A party of four diners who order three drinks in total.
   b.   A party of two diners who do not order any drinks.
   c.   A lone diner who orders two drinks.
3. Convert the total costs you computed in (1) above to costs per diner. In other words, what is the average cost per diner for serving each of the following parties of diners?
   a.   A party of four diners who order three drinks in total.
   b.   A party of two diners who do not order any drinks.
   c.   A lone diner who orders two drinks.
4. Why do the costs per diner for the three different parties differ from each other and from the overall average cost of $9.80 per diner?

BUILDING YOUR SKILLS

ANALYTICAL THINKING*   (LO2, LO3, LO4)

"Two dollars of gross margin per briefcase? That's ridiculous!" roared Roy Thurmond, president of First-Line Cases, Inc. "Why do we go on producing those standard briefcases when we're able to make over $11

CHECK FIGURE
(2) Standard briefcase unit product cost: $20.48

---

* Adapted from Harold P. Roth and Imogene Posey, "Management Accounting Case Study: CarryAll Company," *Management Accounting Campus Report*, Institute of Management Accountants, Fall 1991, p. 9. Used by permission from the IMA, Montvale, NJ, USA, www.imanet.org.

per unit on our specialty items? Maybe it's time to get out of the standard line and focus the whole plant on specialty work."

Mr. Thurmond was referring to a summary of unit costs and revenues that he had just received from the company's accounting department:

	Standard Briefcases	Specialty Briefcases
Selling price per unit..................	$26.25	$42.50
Unit manufacturing cost................	24.25	31.40
Gross margin per unit	$ 2.00	$11.10

FirstLine Cases produces briefcases from leather, fabric, and synthetic materials in a single plant. The basic product is a standard briefcase that is made from leather lined with fabric. The standard briefcase is a high-quality item and has sold well for many years.

Last year, the company decided to expand its product line and produce specialty briefcases for special orders. These briefcases differ from the standard in that they vary in size, they contain the finest leather and synthetic materials, and they are imprinted with the buyer's name. To reduce labor costs on the specialty briefcases, automated machines do most of the cutting and stitching. These machines are used to a much lesser degree in the production of standard briefcases.

"I agree that the specialty business is looking better and better," replied Beth Mersey, the company's marketing manager. "And there seems to be plenty of demand out there, particularly since the competition hasn't been able to touch our price. Did you know that Velsun Company, our biggest competitor, charges over $50 a unit for its specialty items? Now that's what I call gouging the customer!"

A breakdown of the manufacturing cost for each of FirstLine Cases' products is given below:

	Standard Briefcases	Specialty Briefcases
Units produced each month.............................	10,000	2,500
Direct materials:		
Leather	$ 8.00	$12.00
Fabric...	2.00	1.00
Synthetic	0	7.00
Total materials...	10.00	20.00
Direct labor (0.5 DLH and 0.4 DLH @ $12.00 per DLH)	6.00	4.80
Manufacturing overhead (0.5 DLH and 0.4 DLH @ $16.50 per DLH)...............	8.25	6.60
Total cost per unit.......................................	$24.25	$31.40

Manufacturing overhead is applied to products on the basis of direct labor-hours. The rate of $16.50 per hour was determined by dividing the total manufacturing overhead cost for a month by the direct labor-hours:

$$\text{Predetermined overhead rate} = \frac{\text{Manufacturing overhead}}{\text{Direct labor-hours}}$$

$$= \frac{\$99,000}{6,000 \text{ DLHs}} = \$16.50 \text{ per DLH}$$

The following additional information is available about the company and its products:

a.   Standard briefcases are produced in batches of 1,000 units, and specialty briefcases are produced in batches of 100 units. Thus, the company does 10 setups for the standard items each month and 25 setups for the specialty items. A setup for the standard items requires one hour of time, whereas a setup for the specialty items requires two hours of time.

b.   All briefcases are inspected to ensure that quality standards are met. A total of 200 hours of inspection time is spent on the standard briefcases and 400 hours of inspection time is spent on the specialty briefcases each month.

c.   A standard briefcase requires 0.5 hour of machine time, and a specialty briefcase requires 1.2 hours of machine time.

d. The company is considering the use of activity-based costing as an alternative to its traditional cost-ing system for computing unit product costs. Since these unit product costs will be used for external financial reporting, all manufacturing overhead costs are to be allocated to products and nonmanu-facturing costs are to be excluded from product costs. The activity-based costing system has already been designed and costs have been allocated to the activity cost pools. The activity cost pools and activity measures are detailed below:

Activity Cost Pool	Activity Measure	Estimated Overhead Cost
Purchasing	Number of orders	$15,000
Material handling	Number of receipts	16,000
Production orders and setups. . .	Setup-hours	6,000
Inspection	Inspection-hours	18,000
Frame assembly	Assembly-hours	12,000
Machine-related.	Machine-hours	32,000
		$99,000

	Expected Activity		
Activity Measure	Standard Briefcases	Specialty Briefcases	Total
Number of orders:			
Leather	50	10	60
Fabric.	70	20	90
Synthetic material	0	150	150
Number of receipts:			
Leather	70	10	80
Fabric.	85	20	105
Synthetic material	0	215	215
Setup-hours.	?	?	?
Inspection-hours.	200	400	600
Assembly-hours	700	800	1,500
Machine-hours	?	?	?

Required:
1. Using activity-based costing, determine the amount of manufacturing overhead cost that should be applied to each standard briefcase and each specialty briefcase.
2. Using the data computed in (1) above and other data from the case as needed, determine the unit product cost of each product line from the perspective of activity-based costing.
3. Within the limitations of the data that have been provided, evaluate the president's concern about the profitability of the two product lines. Would you recommend that the company shift its resources en-tirely to the production of specialty briefcases? Explain.
4. Beth Mersey stated that "the competition hasn't been able to touch our price on specialty business." Why do you suppose the competition hasn't been able to touch FirstLine Cases' price?

CASE (LO2, LO3, LO4)

Coffee Bean, Inc. (CBI), is a processor and distributor of a variety of blends of coffee. The company buys coffee beans from around the world and roasts, blends, and packages them for resale. CBI currently has 40 different coffees that it offers to gourmet shops in one-pound bags. The major cost of the coffee is raw ma-terials. However, the company's predominantly automated roasting, blending, and packing process requires a substantial amount of manufacturing overhead. The company uses relatively little direct labor.

Some of CBI's coffees are very popular and sell in large volumes, while a few of the newer blends have very low volumes. CBI prices its coffee at manufacturing cost plus a markup of 30%. If CBI's prices for certain coffees are significantly higher than market, adjustments are made to bring CBI's prices more into alignment with the market since customers are somewhat price conscious.

For the coming year, CBI's budget includes estimated manufacturing overhead cost of $3,000,000. CBI assigns manufacturing overhead to products on the basis of direct labor-hours. The expected direct la-bor cost totals $600,000, which represents 50,000 hours of direct labor time. Based on the sales budget and

CHECK FIGURE
(2c) Mona Loa unit product cost: $4.83

expected raw materials costs, the company will purchase and use $6,000,000 of raw materials (mostly coffee beans) during the year.

The expected costs for direct materials and direct labor for one-pound bags of two of the company's coffee products appear below.

	Mona Loa	Malaysian
Direct materials..	$4.20	$3.20
Direct labor (0.025 hours per bag)........................	0.30	0.30

CBI's controller believes that the company's traditional costing system may be providing misleading cost information. To determine whether or not this is correct, the controller has prepared an analysis of the year's expected manufacturing overhead costs, as shown in the following table:

Activity Cost Pool	Activity Measure	Expected Activity for the Year	Expected Cost for the Year
Purchasing	Purchase orders	1,710 orders	$ 513,000
Material handling	Number of setups	1,800 setups	720,000
Quality control	Number of batches	600 batches	144,000
Roasting	Roasting hours	96,100 roasting hours	961,000
Blending	Blending hours	33,500 blending hours	402,000
Packaging	Packaging hours	26,000 packaging hours	260,000
Total manufacturing overhead cost			$3,000,000

Data regarding the expected production of Mona Loa and Malaysian coffee are presented below. There will be no raw materials inventory for either of these coffees at the beginning of the year.

	Mona Loa	Malaysian
Expected sales	100,000 pounds	2,000 pounds
Batch size	10,000 pounds	500 pounds
Setups................................	3 per batch	3 per batch
Purchase order size	20,000 pounds	500 pounds
Roasting time per 100 pounds..............	1.0 hour	1.0 hour
Blending time per 100 pounds..............	0.5 hour	0.5 hour
Packaging time per 100 pounds.............	0.1 hour	0.1 hour

Required:

1. Using direct labor-hours as the base for assigning manufacturing overhead cost to products, do the following:
   a. Determine the predetermined overhead rate that will be used during the year.
   b. Determine the unit product cost of one pound of the Mona Loa coffee and one pound of the Malaysian coffee.
   c. Determine the selling price of one pound of the Mona Loa coffee and one pound of the Malaysian coffee using the company's 30% markup.
2. Using activity-based costing as the basis for assigning manufacturing overhead cost to products, do the following:
   a. Determine the total amount of manufacturing overhead cost assigned to the Mona Loa coffee and to the Malaysian coffee for the year.
   b. Using the data developed in (2a) above, compute the amount of manufacturing overhead cost per pound of the Mona Loa coffee and the Malaysian coffee. Round all computations to the nearest whole cent.
   c. Determine the unit product cost of one pound of the Mona Loa coffee and one pound of the Malaysian coffee.
3. Write a brief memo to the president of CBI explaining what you have found in (1) and (2) above and discussing the implications to the company of using direct labor as the base for assigning manufacturing overhead cost to products.

(CMA, adapted)

TEAMWORK IN ACTION (LOI)

Your team should visit and closely observe the operations at a fast food restaurant.

Required:

Identify activities and costs at the restaurant that fall into each of the following categories:

a. Unit-level activities and costs.
b. Customer-level activities and costs. (This is like a batch-level activity at a manufacturing company.)
c. Product-level activities and costs.
d. Facility-level activities and costs.

ETHICS CHALLENGE (LOI)

You and your friends go to a restaurant as a group. At the end of the meal, the issue arises of how the bill for the group should be shared. One alternative is to figure out the cost of what each individual consumed and divide up the bill accordingly. Another alternative is to split the bill equally among the individuals.

Required:

Which system for dividing the bill is more equitable? Which system is easier to use? How does this issue relate to the material covered in this chapter?

COMMUNICATING IN PRACTICE (LOI)

You often provide advice to Maria Graham, a client who is interested in diversifying her company. Maria is considering the purchase of a small manufacturing company that assembles and packages its many products by hand. She plans to automate the factory and her projections indicate that the company will once again be profitable within two to three years. During her review of the company's records, she discovered that the company currently uses direct labor-hours to allocate overhead to its products. Because of its simplicity, Maria hopes that this approach can continue to be used.

Required:

Write a memorandum to Maria that addresses whether or not direct labor should continue to be used as an allocation base for overhead.

TAKING IT TO THE NET

As you know, the World Wide Web is a medium that is constantly evolving. Sites come and go and change without notice. To enable periodic update of site addresses, this problem has been posted to the textbook website (www.mhhe.com/bgn2e). After accessing the site, enter the Student Center and select this chapter. Select and complete the Taking It to the Net problem.

Systems Design: Process Costing

Costing Cream Soda

Megan Harris started a company that produces cream soda from an old family recipe. At first the company struggled, but as sales increased, the company expanded rapidly. Megan soon realized that to expand any further, it would be necessary to borrow money. The investment in additional equipment was too large for her to finance out of the company's current cash flows.

Megan was disappointed to find that few banks were willing to make a loan to such a small company, but she finally found a bank that would consider her loan application. However, Megan was informed that she would have to supply up-to-date financial statements with her loan application.

Megan had never bothered with financial statements before—she felt that as long as the balance in the company's checkbook kept increasing, the company was doing fine. She was puzzled about how she was going to determine the value of the cream soda in the Work in Process and Finished Goods inventories. The valuation of the cream soda would affect both the cost of goods sold and the inventory balances of her company. Megan thought of perhaps using job-order costing, which had been used at her previous employer, but her company produces only one product. Raw ingredients are continually being mixed to make more cream soda, and more bottled cream soda is always coming off the end of the bottling line. Megan didn't see how she could use a job-order costing system since the job never really ended. Perhaps there was another way to account for the costs of producing the cream soda.

LEARNING OBJECTIVES

After studying Chapter 4, you should be able to:

LO1 Record the flow of materials, labor, and overhead through a process costing system.

LO2 Compute the equivalent units of production using the weighted-average method.

LO3 Prepare a quantity schedule using the weighted-average method.

LO4 Compute the costs per equivalent unit using the weighted-average method.

LO5 Prepare a cost reconciliation using the weighted-average method.

As explained in Chapter 2, either job-order costing or process costing can be used to determine unit product costs. A job-order costing system is used in situations where many different jobs or products are worked on each period. Examples of industries that would typically use job-order costing include furniture manufacture, special-order printing, shipbuilding, and many types of service organizations.

By contrast, **process costing** is most commonly used in industries that produce essentially homogenous (i.e., uniform) products on a continuous basis, such as bricks, corn flakes, or paper. Process costing is particularly used in companies that convert basic raw materials into homogenous products, such as Reynolds Aluminum (aluminum ingots), Scott Paper (toilet paper), General Mills (flour), Exxon (gasoline and lubricating oils), Coppertone (sunscreens), and Kellogg (breakfast cereals). In addition, process costing is often used in companies with assembly operations, such as Panasonic (video monitors), Compaq (personal computers), General Electric (refrigerators), Toyota (automobiles), Amana (washing machines), and Sony (CD players). A form of process costing may also be used in utilities that produce gas, water, and electricity. As suggested by the length of this list, process costing is in very wide use.

Our purpose in this chapter is to explain how product costing works in a process costing system.

COMPARISON OF JOB-ORDER AND PROCESS COSTING

In some ways process costing is very similar to job-order costing, and in some ways it is very different. In this section, we focus on these similarities and differences in order to provide a foundation for the detailed discussion of process costing that follows.

Similarities between Job-Order and Process Costing

Much of what was learned in Chapter 2 about costing and cost flows applies equally well to process costing in this chapter. That is, we are not throwing out all that we have learned about costing and starting from "scratch" with a whole new system. The similarities between job-order and process costing can be summarized as follows:

1. Both systems have the same basic purposes—to assign material, labor, and overhead cost to products and to provide a mechanism for computing unit product costs.
2. Both systems use the same basic manufacturing accounts, including Manufacturing Overhead, Raw Materials, Work in Process, and Finished Goods.
3. The flow of costs through the manufacturing accounts is basically the same in both systems.

As can be seen from this comparison, much of the knowledge that we have already acquired about costing is applicable to a process costing system. Our task now is to refine and extend this knowledge to process costing.

Differences between Job-Order and Process Costing

The differences between job-order and process costing arise from two factors. The first is that the flow of units in a process costing system is more or less continuous, and the second is that these units are indistinguishable from one another. Under process costing, it makes no sense to try to identify materials, labor, and overhead costs with a particular order from a customer (as we did with job-order costing), since each order is just one of many that are filled from a continuous flow of virtually identical units from the production line. Under process costing, we accumulate costs *by department,* rather than by order, and assign these costs uniformly to all units that pass through the department during a period.

A further difference between the two costing systems is that the job cost sheet is not used in process costing, since the focal point of process costing is on departments. Instead

EXHIBIT 4–1

Differences between Job-Order and Process Costing

Job-Order Costing	Process Costing
1. Many different jobs are worked on during each period, with each job having different production requirements.	1. A single product is produced either on a continuous basis or for long periods of time. All units of product are identical.
2. Costs are accumulated by individual job.	2. Costs are accumulated by department.
3. The *job cost sheet* is the key document controlling the accumulation of costs by a job.	3. The *department production report* is the key document showing the accumulation and disposition of costs by a department.
4. Unit costs are computed *by job* on the job cost sheet.	4. Unit costs are computed *by department* on the department production report.

EXHIBIT 4–1

Differences between Job-Order and Process Costing

of using job cost sheets, a **production report** is prepared for each production department. The production report serves several functions. It provides a summary of the number of units moving through a department during a period, and it also provides a computation of unit product costs. In addition, it shows what costs were charged to the department and what disposition was made of these costs. The department production report is the key document in a process costing system.

The major differences between job-order and process costing are summarized in Exhibit 4–1.

A Hybrid Approach

Managers of successful pharmacies understand product costs. Some pharmacies use a hybrid approach to costing drugs. For example, a hospital pharmacy may use process costing to develop the cost of formulating the base solution for parenterals (that is, drugs delivered by injection or through the blood stream), and then use job-order costing to accumulate the additional costs incurred to create specific parenteral solutions. These additional costs include the ingredients added to the base solution and the time spent by the pharmacist to prepare the specific prescribed drug solution.

Source: "Pharmaceutical Care: Cost Estimation and Cost Management," *Drug Store News*, February 16, 1998, p. CP21 (5 pages).

A PERSPECTIVE OF PROCESS COST FLOWS

Before going through a detailed example of process costing, it will be helpful to see how manufacturing costs flow through a process costing system.

Processing Departments

A **processing department** is any part of an organization where work is performed on a product and where materials, labor, or overhead costs are added to the product. For example, a potato chip factory operated by Nalley's might have three processing departments—one for preparing potatoes, one for cooking, and one for inspecting and packaging. A brick factory might have two processing departments—one for mixing and molding clay into brick form and one for firing the molded brick. A company can have as many or as few processing departments as are needed to complete a product or service.

EXHIBIT 4–2   Sequential Processing Departments

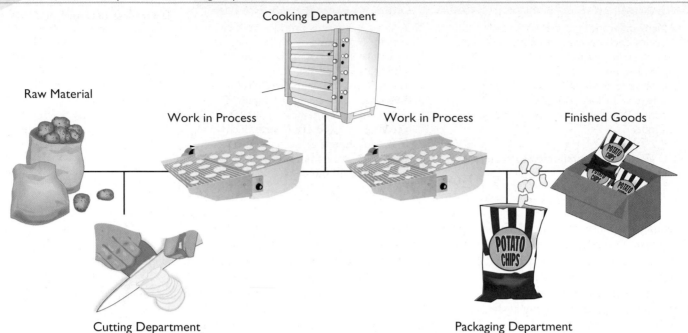

Some products and services may go through several processing departments, while others may go through only one or two. Regardless of the number of departments involved, all processing departments in a process costing system have two essential features. First, the activity in the processing department must be performed uniformly on all of the units passing through it. Second, the output of the processing department must be homogeneous.

The processing departments involved in making a product such as bricks or potato chips would probably be organized in a *sequential* pattern in which units flow in sequence from one department to another as in Exhibit 4–2.

The Flow of Materials, Labor, and Overhead Costs

Cost accumulation is simpler in a process costing system than in a job-order costing system. In a process costing system, instead of having to trace costs to hundreds of different jobs, costs are traced to only a few processing departments.

A T-account model of materials, labor, and overhead cost flows in a process costing system is presented in Exhibit 4–3. Several key points should be noted from this exhibit. First, note that a separate Work in Process account is maintained for *each processing department.* In contrast, in a job-order costing system there may be only a single Work in Process account for the entire company. Second, note that the completed production of the first processing department (Department A in the exhibit) is transferred to the Work in Process account of the second processing department (Department B), where it undergoes further work. After this further work, the completed units are then transferred to Finished Goods. (In Exhibit 4–3, we show only two processing departments, but a company can have many such departments.)

Finally, note that materials, labor, and overhead costs can be added in *any* processing department—not just the first. Costs in Department B's Work in Process account would consist of the materials, labor, and overhead costs incurred in Department B plus the costs attached to partially completed units transferred in from Department A (called **transferred-in costs**).

EXHIBIT 4–3 T-Account Model of Process Costing Flows

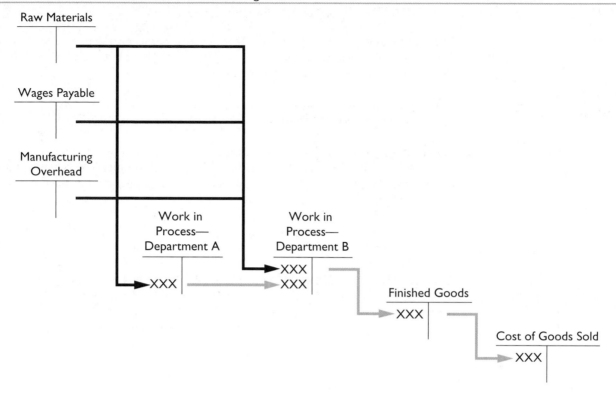

Materials, Labor, and Overhead Cost Entries

To complete our discussion of cost flows in a process costing system, in this section we show journal entries relating to materials, labor, and overhead costs at Megan's Classic Cream Soda, the company mentioned at the very beginning of this chapter. Megan's Classic Cream Soda has two processing departments—Formulating and Bottling. In the Formulating Department, the various ingredients are checked for quality and then mixed and injected with carbon dioxide to create bulk cream soda. In the Bottling Department, bottles are checked for defects, filled with cream soda, capped, visually inspected again for defects, and then packed for shipping.

Materials Costs As in job-order costing, materials are drawn from the storeroom using a materials requisition form. As stated earlier, materials can be added in any processing department, although it is not unusual for materials to be added only in the first processing department, with subsequent departments adding only labor and overhead costs as the partially completed units move along toward completion.

At Megan's Classic Cream Soda, some materials (i.e., water, flavors, sugar, and carbon dioxide) are added in the Formulating Department and some materials (i.e., bottles, caps, and packing materials) are added in the Bottling Department. The journal entry to record the materials used in the first processing department, the Formulating Department, is as follows:

Work in Process—Formulating   XXX
   Raw Materials   XXX

If other materials are subsequently added in another department, as at Megan's Classic Cream Soda, the entry is the following:

| Work in Process—Bottling . . . . | XXX | |
| Raw Materials . . . . | | XXX |

Labor Costs   In process costing, labor costs are traced to departments—not to individual jobs. The following journal entry will record the labor costs in the Formulating Department at Megan's Classic Cream Soda:

| Work in Process—Formulating . . . . | XXX | |
| Salaries and Wages Payable. . . . . | | XXX |

Overhead Costs   In process costing, as in job-order costing, predetermined overhead rates are usually used. Overhead cost is applied to units of product as they move through the department. A journal entry such as the following records the cost for the Formulating Department:

| Work in Process—Formulating . . . . | XXX | |
| Manufacturing Overhead . . . . | | XXX |

Completing the Cost Flows   Once processing has been completed in a department, the units are transferred to the next department for further processing, as illustrated earlier in the T-accounts in Exhibit 4–3. The following journal entry is used to transfer the costs of partially completed units from the Formulating Department to the Bottling Department:

| Work in Process—Bottling . . . . | XXX | |
| Work in Process—Formulating . . . . | | XXX |

After processing has been completed in the final department, the costs of the completed units are then transferred to the Finished Goods inventory account:

| Finished Goods. . . . . | XXX | |
| Work in Process—Bottling . . . . | | XXX |

Finally, when a customer's order is filled and units are sold, the cost of the units is transferred to Cost of Goods Sold:

| Cost of Goods Sold . . . . | XXX | |
| Finished Goods. . . . . | | XXX |

To summarize, the cost flows between accounts are basically the same in a process costing system as they are in a job-order costing system. The only noticeable difference at this point is that in a process costing system each department has a separate Work in Process account.

MANAGERIAL ACCOUNTING IN ACTION

The Issue

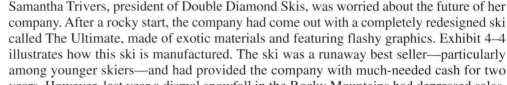

Samantha Trivers, president of Double Diamond Skis, was worried about the future of her company. After a rocky start, the company had come out with a completely redesigned ski called The Ultimate, made of exotic materials and featuring flashy graphics. Exhibit 4–4 illustrates how this ski is manufactured. The ski was a runaway best seller—particularly among younger skiers—and had provided the company with much-needed cash for two years. However, last year a dismal snowfall in the Rocky Mountains had depressed sales, and Double Diamond was once again short of cash. Samantha was worried that another bad ski season would force Double Diamond into bankruptcy.

Just before starting production of next year's model of The Ultimate, Samantha called Jerry Madison, the company controller, into her office to discuss the reports she would need in the coming year.

Wood, aluminum, plastic sheets

EXHIBIT 4–4

The Production Process at
Double Diamond Skis

Shaping and Milling Department	Computer-assisted milling machines shape the wood core and aluminum sheets that serve as the backbone of the ski.
Graphics Application Department	Graphics are applied to the back of the clear plastic top sheets using a heat-transfer process.
Molding Department	The wooden core and various layers are stacked in a mold, polyurethane foam is injected into the mold, and then the mold is placed in a press that fuses the parts together.
Grinding and Sanding Department	The semi-finished skis are tuned by stone grinding and belt sanding. The ski edges are beveled and polished.
Finishing and Pairing Department	A skilled technician selects skis to form a pair and adjusts the skis' camber.

Finished goods

Source: Adapted from Bill Gout, Jesse James Doquilo, and Studio M D, "Capped Crusaders," *Skiing*, October 1993, pp. 138–144.

Samantha: Jerry, I am going to need more frequent cost information this year. I really have to stay on top of things.

Jerry: What do you have in mind?

Samantha: I'd like reports at least once a month that detail our production costs for each department and for each pair of skis.

Jerry: That shouldn't be much of a problem. We already compile almost all of the necessary data for the annual report. The only complication is our work in process inventories. They haven't been a problem in our annual reports, since our fiscal year ends at a time when we have finished producing skis for the last model year and haven't yet started producing for the new model year. Consequently, there aren't any work in process inventories to value for the annual report. But that won't be true for monthly reports.

Samantha: I'm not sure why that is a problem, Jerry. But I'm confident you can figure out how to solve it.

EQUIVALENT UNITS OF PRODUCTION

Jerry Madison, the controller of Double Diamond Skis, was concerned with the following problem: After materials, labor, and overhead costs have been accumulated in a department, the department's output must be determined so that unit costs can be computed. The difficulty is that a department usually has some partially completed units in its ending inventory. It does not seem reasonable to count these partially completed units as equivalent to fully completed units when counting the department's output. Therefore, Jerry will mathematically convert those partially completed units into an *equivalent* number of fully completed units. In process costing, this is done using the following formula:

$$\text{Equivalent units} = \text{Number of partially completed units} \times \text{Percentage completion}$$

As the formula states, **equivalent units** is defined to be the product of the number of partially completed units and the percentage completion of those units. The equivalent units is the number of complete units that could have been obtained from the materials and effort that went into the partially complete units.

For example, suppose the Molding Department at Double Diamond has 500 units in its ending work in process inventory that are 60% complete. These 500 partially complete units are equivalent to 300 fully complete units (500 × 60% = 300). Therefore, the ending work in process inventory would be said to contain 300 equivalent units. These equivalent units would be added to any units completed during the period to determine the period's output for the department—called the *equivalent units of production*.

The equivalent units of production can be computed using either the *weighted-average method* or the *FIFO method*. The weighted-average method is a little simpler, and for that reason, it is the method used in this chapter. If you are interested in the details of the FIFO method, a supplement to this chapter on the FIFO method can be downloaded at www.mhhe.com/bgn2e. In broad terms, in the **FIFO method** the equivalent units and unit costs relate only to work done during the current period. In contrast, the **weighted-average method** blends together units and costs from the current period with units and costs from the prior period. In the weighted-average method, the **equivalent units of production** for a department are the number of units transferred to the next department (or to finished goods) plus the equivalent units in the department's ending work in process inventory.

Weighted-Average Method

Concept 4–1

Under the weighted-average method, a department's equivalent units are computed as follows:

> **Weighted-Average Method**
> **(a separate calculation is made for each cost category in each processing department)**
>
> Equivalent units of production = Units transferred to the next department or to finished goods
> + Equivalent units in ending work in process inventory

We do not have to make an equivalent units calculation for units transferred to the next department. We can assume that they would not have been transferred unless they were 100% complete with respect to the work performed in the transferring department.

Consider the Shaping and Milling Department at Double Diamond. This department uses computerized milling machines to precisely shape the wooden core and metal sheets that will be used to form the backbone of the ski. (See Exhibit 4–4 for an overview of the production process at Double Diamond.) The following activity took place in the department in May, several months into the production of the new model of The Ultimate ski:

Shaping and Milling Department			
		Percent Completed	
	Units	**Materials**	**Conversion**
Work in process, May 1	200	55%	30%
Units started into production during May	5,000		
Units completed during May and transferred to the next department	4,800	100%*	100%*
Work in process, May 31	400	40%	25%

*It is always assumed that units transferred out of a department are 100% complete with respect to the processing done in that department.

EXHIBIT 4–5

Equivalent Units of Production:
Weighted-Average Method

Shaping and Milling Department	Materials	Conversion
Units transferred to the next department	4,800	4,800
Work in process, May 31:		
400 units × 40%	160	
400 units × 25%		100
Equivalent units of production	4,960	4,900

EXHIBIT 4–6

Visual Perspective of Equivalent
Units of Production

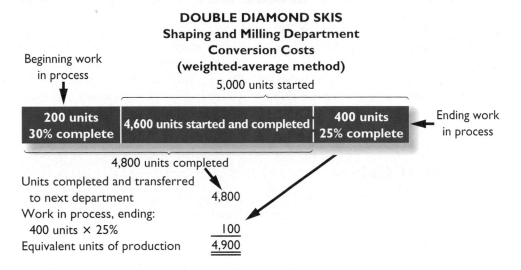

Note the use of the term *conversion* in the table on the previous page. **Conversion cost,** as defined in Chapter 1, is direct labor cost plus manufacturing overhead cost. In process costing, conversion cost is often—but not always—treated as a single element of product cost.

Also note that the May 1 beginning work in process was 55% complete with respect to materials costs and 30% complete with respect to conversion costs. This means that 55% of the materials costs required to complete the units in the department had already been incurred. Likewise, 30% of the conversion costs required to complete the units had already been incurred.

Since Double Diamond's work in process inventories are at different stages of completion in terms of the amounts of materials cost and conversion cost that have been added in the department, two equivalent unit figures must be computed. The equivalent units computations are shown in Exhibit 4–5.

Note from the computation in Exhibit 4–5 that units in the beginning work in process inventory are ignored. The weighted-average method is concerned only with the fact that there are 4,900 equivalent units for conversion cost in ending inventories and in units transferred to the next department—the method is not concerned with the additional fact that some of this work was accomplished in prior periods. This is a key point in the weighted-average method that is easy to overlook.

Computation of equivalent units of production is illustrated in Exhibit 4–6. Study this exhibit carefully before going on.

Term Paper Writer

YOU
DECIDE

Assume that all of your professors have assigned short papers this term. In fact, you have to turn in four separate five-page papers early next month. During the month, you began and finished two papers and wrote the first two and one-half pages of the other two papers. You turned in the papers that you had finished to your instructors on the last day of the month.

If instead you had focused all your efforts into starting *and* completing papers this month, how many complete papers would you have written this month? After answering that question, reconfigure your answer as a computation of equivalent units of production by (1) preparing a quantity schedule and (2) computing the number of equivalent units for labor.

PRODUCTION REPORT—WEIGHTED-AVERAGE METHOD

The production report developed in this section contains the information requested by the president of Double Diamond Skis. The purpose of the production report is to summarize for management all of the activity that takes place in a department's Work in Process account for a period. This activity includes the units and costs that flow through the Work in Process account. As illustrated in Exhibit 4–7, a separate production report is prepared for each department.

Home Runs Galore

Remember the summer of 1999? Rawlings, the ball manufacturer, was forced to open its Turrialba facility in Costa Rica to a delegation from Major League Baseball to dispel rumors that Rawlings balls were behind the record numbers of home runs.

The delegation found that the production process is unchanged from earlier years. The red pills (rubber-coated corks purchased from a company in Mississippi) are wound three times with wool yarn and then once with cotton string. The balls are weighed, measured, and inspected after each wind. The covers, cut from sheets of rawhide, are hand-stitched and then machine-rolled. After a trip through a drying room to remove the moisture that kept the leather soft during the sewing process, the balls are stamped with logos. After they are weighed, measured, and inspected once again, the balls are wrapped in tissue and packed in boxes. Balls that don't meet Major League specifications (5–5¼ ounces and 9–9¼ inches in circumference) are sold commercially.

Source: "Behind-the-Seams Look: Rawlings Throws Open Baseball Plant Door," *USA Today*, May 24, 2000, pp. 1C–2C.

Cost Analyst

Assume that you are a cost analyst in the Rawlings plant in Costa Rica that supplies baseballs to Major League Baseball. Your assignment is to identify the production departments in that facility. How many production reports will be needed?

Earlier, when we outlined the differences between job-order costing and process costing, we stated that the production report takes the place of a job cost sheet in a process costing system. The production report is a key management document. It has three separate (though highly interrelated) parts:

1. A quantity schedule, which shows the flow of units through the department and a computation of equivalent units.
2. A computation of costs per equivalent unit.
3. A reconciliation of all cost flows into and out of the department during the period.

We will use the data that follows for the May operations of the Shaping and Milling Department of Double Diamond Skis to illustrate the production report. Keep in mind that this report is only one of the five reports that would be prepared for the company since the company has five processing departments.

Shaping and Milling Department

Work in process, beginning:	
Units in process	200
Stage of completion with respect to materials	55%
Stage of completion with respect to conversion	30%
Costs in the beginning inventory:	
Materials cost	$ 9,600
Conversion cost	5,575
Total cost in the beginning inventory	$ 15,175
Units started into production during May	5,000
Units completed and transferred out	4,800
Costs added to production during May:	
Materials cost	$368,600
Conversion cost	350,900
Total cost added in the department	$719,500
Work in process, ending:	
Units in process	400
Stage of completion with respect to materials	40%
Stage of completion with respect to conversion	25%

EXHIBIT 4–7   The Position of the Production Report in the Flow of Costs

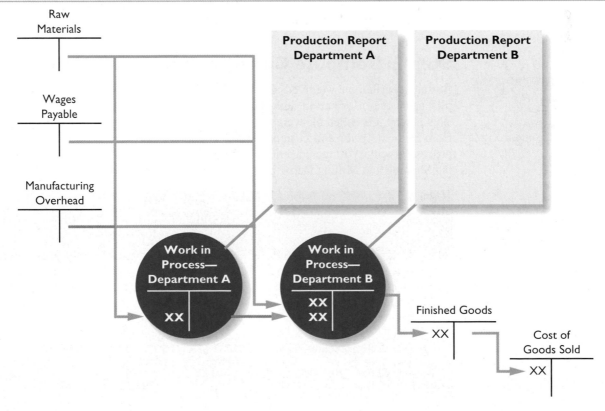

In this section, we show how a production report is prepared when the weighted-average method is used to compute equivalent units and unit costs.

Step 1: Prepare a Quantity Schedule and Compute the Equivalent Units

LEARNING OBJECTIVE 3

Prepare a quantity schedule using the weighted-average method.

The first part of a production report consists of a **quantity schedule,** which shows the flow of units through the department and a computation of equivalent units.

Shaping and Milling Department Quantity Schedule and Equivalent Units			
	Quantity Schedule		
Units to be accounted for:			
Work in process, May 1 (materials 55% complete; conversion 30% complete) . . .	200		
Started into production	5,000		
Total units to be accounted for	5,200	**Equivalent Units**	
		Materials	**Conversion**
Units accounted for as follows:			
Transferred to next department	4,800	4,800	4,800
Work in process, May 31 (materials 40% complete; conversion 25% complete) . . .	400	160*	100†
Total units accounted for	5,200	4,960	4,900

*40% × 400 units = 160 equivalent units.
†25% × 400 units = 100 equivalent units.

The quantity schedule shows how many units moved through the department during the period as well as the stage of completion of any in-process units. In addition to providing this information, the quantity schedule serves as an essential guide in preparing and tying together the remaining parts of a production report.

Step 2: Compute Costs per Equivalent Unit

LEARNING OBJECTIVE 4

Compute the costs per equivalent unit using the weighted-average method.

As stated earlier, the weighted-average method blends together the work that was accomplished in the prior period with the work that was accomplished in the current period. That is why it is called the weighted-average method; it averages together units and costs from both the prior and current periods by adding the cost in the beginning work in process inventory to the current period costs. These computations are shown below for the Shaping and Milling Department for May:

Shaping and Milling Department Costs per Equivalent Unit				
	Total Cost	Materials	Conversion	Whole Unit
Cost to be accounted for:				
Work in process, May 1	$ 15,175	$ 9,600	$ 5,575	
Cost added during the month in the Shaping and Milling Department	719,500	368,600	350,900	
Total cost to be accounted for (a)	$734,675	$378,200	$356,475	
Equivalent units (Step 1 above) (b). . . .		4,960	4,900	
Cost per equivalent unit, (a) ÷ (b). . . .		$76.25 +	$72.75 =	$149.00

EXHIBIT 4–8 Graphic Illustration of the Cost Reconciliation Part of a Production Report

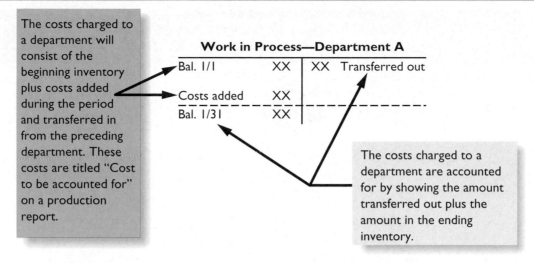

The costs charged to a department will consist of the beginning inventory plus costs added during the period and transferred in from the preceding department. These costs are titled "Cost to be accounted for" on a production report.

Work in Process—Department A

Bal. 1/1	XX	XX	Transferred out
Costs added	XX		
Bal. 1/31	XX		

The costs charged to a department are accounted for by showing the amount transferred out plus the amount in the ending inventory.

The cost per equivalent unit (EU) that we have computed for the Shaping and Milling Department will be used to apply cost to units that are transferred to the next department, Graphics Application, and will also be used to compute the cost in the ending work in process inventory. For example, each unit transferred out of the Shaping and Milling Department to the Graphics Application Department will carry with it a cost of $149. Since the costs are passed on from department to department, the unit cost of the last department, Finishing and Pairing, will represent the final cost of a completed unit of product.

Step 3: Prepare a Cost Reconciliation

The purpose of a **cost reconciliation** is to show how the costs that have been charged to a department during a period are accounted for. Typically, the costs charged to a department will consist of the following:

1. Cost in the beginning work in process inventory.
2. Materials, labor, and overhead costs added during the period.
3. Cost (if any) transferred in from the preceding department.

In a production report, these costs are titled "Cost to be accounted for." They are accounted for in a production report by computing the following amounts:

1. Cost transferred out to the next department (or to Finished Goods).
2. Cost remaining in the ending work in process inventory.

In short, when a cost reconciliation is prepared, the "Cost to be accounted for" from step 2 is reconciled with the sum of the cost transferred out during the period plus the cost in the ending work in process inventory. This concept is shown graphically in Exhibit 4–8. Study this exhibit carefully before going on to the cost reconciliation for the Shaping and Milling Department.

Example of a Cost Reconciliation To prepare a cost reconciliation, follow the quantity schedule line for line and show the cost associated with each group of units. This is done in Exhibit 4–9, where we present a completed production report for the Shaping and Milling Department.

The quantity schedule in the exhibit shows that 200 units were in process on May 1 and that an additional 5,000 units were started into production during the month. Looking at the "Cost to be accounted for" in the middle part of the exhibit, notice that the units in process on May 1 had $15,175 in cost attached to them and that the Shaping and Milling Department added another $719,500 in cost to production during the month. Thus, the department has $734,675 ($15,175 + $719,500) in cost to be accounted for.

Concept 4–2

EXHIBIT 4–9   Production Report—Weighted-Average Method

DOUBLE DIAMOND SKIS
Shaping and Milling Department Production Report
(Weighted-Average Method)

Quantity Schedule and Equivalent Units

	Quantity Schedule		
Units to be accounted for:			
Work in process, May 1 (materials 55% complete; conversion 30% complete)	200		
Started into production	5,000		
Total units to be accounted for	5,200		

	Quantity Schedule	Equivalent Units (EU)	
		Materials	**Conversion**
Units accounted for as follows:			
Transferred to next department	4,800	4,800	4,800
Work in process, May 31 (materials 40% complete; conversion 25% complete)	400	160*	100†
Total units accounted for	5,200	4,960	4,900

Costs per Equivalent Unit

	Total Cost	Materials	Conversion	Whole Unit
Cost to be accounted for:				
Work in process, May 1	$ 15,175	$ 9,600	$ 5,575	
Cost added in the department	719,500	368,600	350,900	
Total cost to be accounted for (a)	$734,675	$378,200	$356,475	
Equivalent units (b)		4,960	4,900	
Cost per EU, (a) ÷ (b)		$76.25 +	$72.75 =	$149.00

Cost Reconciliation

	Total Cost	Equivalent Units (above)	
		Materials	**Conversion**
Cost accounted for as follows:			
Transferred to the next department:			
4,800 units × $149.00 per unit	$715,200	4,800	4,800
Work in process, May 31:			
Materials, at $76.25 per EU	12,200	160	
Conversion, at $72.75 per EU	7,275		100
Total work in process, May 31	19,475		
Total cost accounted for	$734,675		

*40% × 400 units = 160 equivalent units.
†25% × 400 units = 100 equivalent units.
EU = Equivalent unit.

This cost is accounted for in two ways. As shown on the quantity schedule, 4,800 units were transferred to the Graphics Application Department, the next department in the production process. Another 400 units were still in process in the Shaping and Milling Department at the end of the month. Thus, part of the $734,675 "Cost to be accounted for" goes with the 4,800 units to the Graphics Application Department, and part of it remains with the 400 units in the ending work in process inventory in the Shaping and Milling Department.

Each of the 4,800 units transferred to the Graphics Application Department is assigned $149.00 in cost, for a total of $715,200. The 400 units still in process at the end of the month are assigned costs according to their stage of completion. To determine the stage of completion, we refer to the equivalent units computation and bring the equivalent units figures down to the cost reconciliation part of the report. We then assign costs to these units, using the cost per equivalent unit figures already computed.

After cost has been assigned to the ending work in process inventory, the total cost that we have accounted for ($734,675) agrees with the amount that we had to account for ($734,675). Thus, the cost reconciliation is complete.

CONCEPT CHECK ✓

1. Beginning work in process includes 400 units that are 20% complete with respect to conversion costs and 30% complete with respect to materials. Ending work in process includes 200 hundred units that are 40% percent complete with respect to conversion costs and 50% complete with respect materials. If 2,000 units were started during the period, what are the equivalent units of production for the period according to the weighted-average method?
   a. Conversion EU = 2,280 units; Material EU = 2,100 units
   b. Conversion EU = 1,980 units; Material EU = 2,080 units
   c. Conversion EU = 2,480 units; Material EU = 1,980 units
   d. Conversion EU = 2,280 units; Material EU = 2,300 units
2. Assume the same facts as above in Concept Check 1. Also, assume that $9,900 of material costs and $14,880 of conversion costs were in the beginning inventory and $180,080 of material and $409,200 of conversion costs were added to production during the period. What is the total cost per equivalent unit using the weighted-average method?
   a. $268.60
   b. $267.85
   c. $280.00
   d. $265.00

MANAGERIAL ACCOUNTING IN ACTION
The Wrap-Up

Jerry: Here's an example of the kind of report I can put together for you every month. This particular report is for the Shaping and Milling Department. It follows a fairly standard format for industries like ours and is called a production report. I hope this is what you have in mind.

Samantha: The quantity schedule makes sense to me. I can see we had a total of 5,200 units to account for in the department, and 4,800 of those were transferred to the next department while 400 were still in process at the end of the month. What are these "equivalent units"?

Jerry: That's the problem I mentioned earlier. The 400 units that are still in process are far from complete. When we compute the unit costs, it wouldn't make sense to count them as whole units.

Samantha: I suppose not. I see what you are driving at. Since those 400 units are only 25% complete with respect to our conversion costs, they should only be counted as 100 units when we compute the unit costs for conversion.

Jerry: That's right. Is the rest of the report clear?

Samantha: Yes, it does seem pretty clear, although I want to work the numbers through on my own to make sure I thoroughly understand the report.

Jerry: Does this report give you the information you wanted?

Samantha: Yes, it does. I can tell how many units are in process, how complete they are, what happened to them, and their costs. While I know the unit costs are averages and are heavily influenced by our volume, they still can give me some idea of how well we are doing on the cost side. Thanks, Jerry.

SUMMARY

LO1   Record the flow of materials, labor, and overhead through a process costing system.
The journal entries to record the flow of costs in process costing are basically the same as in job-order costing. Direct materials costs are debited to Work in Process when the materials are released for use in production. Direct labor costs are debited to Work in Process as incurred. Manufacturing overhead costs are applied to Work in Process by debiting Work in Process. Costs are accumulated by department in process costing and by job in job-order costing.

LO2   Compute the equivalent units of production using the weighted-average method.
To compute unit costs for a department, the department's output in terms of equivalent units must be determined. In the weighted-average method, the equivalent units for a period are the sum of the units transferred out of the department during the period and the equivalent units in ending work in process inventory at the end of the period.

LO3   Prepare a quantity schedule using the weighted-average method.
The activity in a department is summarized on a production report which has three separate (though highly interrelated) parts. The first part is a quantity schedule, which includes a computation of equivalent units and shows the flow of units through the department during the period. The quantity schedule shows the units to be accounted for—the units in beginning Work in Process inventory and the units started into production. These units are accounted for by detailing the units transferred to the next department and the units still in process in the department at the end of the period. This part of the report also shows the equivalent units of production for the units still in process.

LO4   Compute the costs per equivalent unit using the weighted-average method.
The cost per equivalent unit is computed by dividing the total cost for a particular cost category such as conversion costs by the equivalent units of production for that cost category.

LO5   Prepare a cost reconciliation using the weighted-average method.
In the cost reconciliation report, the costs of beginning Work in Process inventory and the costs added during the period are reconciled with the costs of the units transferred out of the department and the costs of ending Work in Process inventory.

GUIDANCE ANSWERS TO *DECISION MAKER* AND *YOU DECIDE*

Term Paper Writer (p. 177)
You wrote a total of 15 pages (5 + 5 + 2.5 + 2.5) this month. If you had placed all of your efforts into starting *and* completing papers, you could have written three complete five-page papers.

	Quantity Schedule
Units (papers) to be accounted for:	
Work in process, beginning of month	0
Started into production	4
Total units	4

	Quantity Schedule	Equivalent Units Labor
Units accounted for as follows:		
Transferred (handed in) to instructors	2	2
Work in process, end of month (50% of labor added this month)	2	1*
Total units and equivalent units of production	4	3

*2 units (papers) × 50% = 1

Cost Analyst (p. 178)
The Rawlings baseball production facility in Costa Rica might include the following production departments: winding, cutting, stitching, rolling, drying, stamping, inspecting, and packaging. Each department would have its own production report.

GUIDANCE ANSWERS TO CONCEPT CHECKS

1. **Choice d.** Material EU is 2,200 units completed and transferred to the next department + 100 EU in ending work in process (200 units × 50%). Conversion EU is 2,200 units completed and transferred to the next department plus 80 EU in ending work in process (200 units × 40%).
2. **Choice a.** ($189,980 ÷ 2,300 EU) + ($424,080 ÷ 2,280 EU) = $268.60.

REVIEW PROBLEM: PROCESS COST FLOWS AND REPORTS

Luxguard Home Paint Company produces exterior latex paint, which it sells in one-gallon containers. The company has two processing departments—Base Fab and Finishing. White paint, which is used as a base for all the company's paints, is mixed from raw ingredients in the Base Fab Department. Pigments are added to the basic white paint, the pigmented paint is squirted under pressure into one-gallon containers, and the containers are labeled and packed for shipping in the Finishing Department. Information relating to the company's operations for April follows:

a. Raw materials were issued for use in production: Base Fab Department, $851,000; and Finishing Department, $629,000.
b. Direct labor costs were incurred: Base Fab Department, $330,000; and Finishing Department, $270,000.
c. Manufacturing overhead cost was applied: Base Fab Department, $665,000; and Finishing Department, $405,000.
d. The cost of basic white paint was transferred from the Base Fab Department to the Finishing Department: $1,850,000.
e. Paint that had been prepared for shipping was transferred from the Finishing Department to Finished Goods. Its cost according to the company's cost system was $3,200,000.

Required:
1. Prepare journal entries to record items (a) through (e) above.
2. Post the journal entries from (1) above to T-accounts. The balance in the Base Fab Department's Work in Process account on April 1 was $150,000; the balance in the Finishing Department's Work in Process account was $70,000. After posting entries to the T-accounts, find the ending balance in each department's Work in Process account.
3. Prepare a production report for the Base Fab Department for April. The following additional information is available regarding production in the Base Fab Department during April:

Production data:	
Units (gallons) in process, April 1: materials 100% complete, labor and overhead 60% complete	30,000
Units (gallons) started into production during April	420,000
Units (gallons) completed and transferred to the Finishing Department	370,000
Units (gallons) in process, April 30: materials 50% complete, labor and overhead 25% complete	80,000
Cost data:	
Work in process inventory, April 1:	
Materials	$ 92,000
Labor	21,000
Overhead	37,000
Total cost of work in process	$ 150,000

(continued)

> (concluded)
>
> Cost added during April:
> Materials . . . . $ 851,000
> Labor   330,000
> Overhead   665,000
> Total cost added during April $1,846,000

Solution to Review Problem

1. a.

Work in Process—Base Fab Department	851,000	
Work in Process—Finishing Department	629,000	
Raw Materials		1,480,000

   b.

Work in Process—Base Fab Department	330,000	
Work in Process—Finishing Department	270,000	
Salaries and Wages Payable		600,000

   c.

Work in Process—Base Fab Department	665,000	
Work in Process—Finishing Department	405,000	
Manufacturing Overhead		1,070,000

   d.

Work in Process—Finishing Department	1,850,000	
Work in Process—Base Fab Department		1,850,000

   e.

Finished Goods	3,200,000	
Work in Process—Finishing Department		3,200,000

2.

Raw Materials				Salaries and Wages Payable		
Bal.	XXX	1,480,000	(a)		600,000	(b)

Work in Process—Base Fab Department				Manufacturing Overhead		
Bal.	150,000	1,850,000	(d)	(Various actual costs)	1,070,000	(c)
(a)	851,000					
(b)	330,000					
(c)	665,000					
Bal.	146,000					

Work in Process—Finishing Department				Finished Goods		
Bal.	70,000	3,200,000	(e)	Bal.	XXX	
(a)	629,000			(e)	3,200,000	
(b)	270,000					
(c)	405,000					
(d)	1,850,000					
Bal.	24,000					

3.

LUXGUARD HOME PAINT COMPANY
Production Report—Base Fab Department
For the Month Ended April 30

Quantity Schedule and Equivalent Units

	Quantity Schedule
Units (gallons) to be accounted for:	
Work in process, April 1 (materials 100% complete, labor and overhead 60% complete)	30,000
Started into production	420,000
Total units to be accounted for	450,000

		Equivalent Units (EU)		
		Materials	Labor	Overhead
Units (gallons) accounted for as follows:				
Transferred to Finishing Department	370,000	370,000	370,000	370,000
Work in process, April 30 (materials 50% complete, labor and overhead 25% complete)	80,000	40,000*	20,000*	20,000*
Total units accounted for	450,000	410,000	390,000	390,000

Costs per Equivalent Unit

	Total Cost	Materials	Labor	Overhead	Whole Unit
Cost to be accounted for:					
Work in process, April 1	$ 150,000	$ 92,000	$ 21,000	$ 37,000	
Cost added by the Base Fab Department	1,846,000	851,000	330,000	665,000	
Total cost to be accounted for (a)	$1,996,000	$943,000	$351,000	$702,000	
Equivalent units of production (b)		410,000	390,000	390,000	
Cost per EU, (a) ÷ (b)		$2.30 +	$0.90 +	$1.80 =	$5.00

Cost Reconciliation

	Total Cost	Equivalent Units (above)		
		Materials	Labor	Overhead
Cost accounted for as follows:				
Transferred to Finishing Department:				
370,000 units × $5.00 per unit	$1,850,000	370,000	370,000	370,000
Work in process, April 30:				
Materials, at $2.30 per EU	92,000	40,000		
Labor, at $0.90 per EU	18,000		20,000	
Overhead, at $1.80 per EU	36,000			20,000
Total work in process	146,000			
Total cost accounted for	$1,996,000			

*Materials: 80,000 units × 50% = 40,000 EUs; labor and overhead: 80,000 units × 25% = 20,000 EUs.

EU = Equivalent unit.

GLOSSARY

Conversion cost   Direct labor cost plus manufacturing overhead cost. (p. 177)

Cost reconciliation   The part of a department's production report that shows the cost to be accounted for during a period and how those costs are accounted for. (p. 181)

Equivalent units   The product of the number of partially completed units and their percentage of completion with respect to a particular cost. Equivalent units are the number of complete whole units one could obtain from the materials and effort contained in partially completed units. (p. 176)

Equivalent units of production (weighted-average method)   The units transferred to the next department (or to finished goods) during the period plus the equivalent units in the department's ending work in process inventory. (p. 176)

FIFO method   A method of accounting for cost flows in a process costing system in which equivalent units and unit costs relate only to work done during the current period. (p. 176)

Process costing   A costing method used in situations where essentially homogeneous products are produced on a continuous basis. (p. 170)

Processing department   Any part of an organization where work is performed on a product and where materials, labor, or overhead costs are added to the product. (p. 171)

Production report   A report that summarizes all activity in a department's Work in Process account during a period and that contains three parts: a quantity schedule and a computation of equivalent units, a computation of total and unit costs, and a cost reconciliation. (p. 171)

Quantity schedule   The part of a production report that shows the flow of units through a department during a period and a computation of equivalent units. (p. 180)

Transferred-in cost   The cost attached to products that have been received from a prior processing department. (p. 172)

Weighted-average method   A method of process costing that blends together units and costs from both the current and prior periods. (p. 176)

QUESTIONS

4–1   Under what conditions would it be appropriate to use a process costing system?

4–2   In what ways are job-order and process costing similar?

4–3   Costs are accumulated by job in a job-order costing system; how are costs accumulated in a process costing system?

4–4   Why is cost accumulation easier under a process costing system than it is under a job-order costing system?

4–5   How many Work in Process accounts are maintained in a company using process costing?

4–6   Assume that a company has two processing departments, Mixing and Firing. Prepare a journal entry to show a transfer of partially completed units from the Mixing Department to the Firing Department.

4–7   Assume again that a company has two processing departments, Mixing and Firing. Explain what costs might be added to the Firing Department's Work in Process account during a period.

4–8   What is meant by the term *equivalent units of production* when the weighted-average method is used?

4–9   What is a quantity schedule, and what purpose does it serve?

4–10   Under process costing, it is often suggested that a product is like a rolling snowball as it moves from department to department. Why is this an apt comparison?

BRIEF EXERCISES

BRIEF EXERCISE 4–1   Process Costing Journal Entries   (LO1)

Arizona Brick Corporation produces bricks in two processing departments—molding and firing. Information relating to the company's operations in March follows:

a.   Raw materials were issued for use in production: Molding Department, $28,000; and Firing Department, $5,000.

b.   Direct labor costs were incurred: Molding Department, $18,000; and Firing Department, $5,000.

c.   Manufacturing overhead was applied: Molding Department, $24,000; and Firing Department, $37,000.

d.   Unfired, molded bricks were transferred from the Molding Department to the Firing Department. According to the company's process costing system, the cost of the unfired, molded bricks was $67,000.

e.   Finished bricks were transferred from the Firing Department to the finished goods warehouse. According to the company's process costing system, the cost of the finished bricks was $108,000.

f.   Finished bricks were sold to customers. According to the company's process costing system, the cost of the finished bricks sold was $106,000.

Required:

Prepare journal entries to record items (a) through (f) above.

BRIEF EXERCISE 4–2   Computation of Equivalent Units—Weighted-Average Method   (LO2)

Lindex Company manufactures a product that goes through three departments. Information relating to activity in the first department during October is given below:

		Percent Completed	
	Units	Materials	Conversion
Work in process, October 1	50,000	90%	60%
Started into production	390,000		
Completed and transferred to the next department	410,000		
Work in process, October 31	30,000	70%	50%

Required:

Compute the equivalent units for the first department for October, assuming that the company uses the weighted-average method for accounting for units and costs.

BRIEF EXERCISE 4–3   Preparation of Quantity Schedule—Weighted-Average Method   (LO3)

Societe Clemeau, a company located in Lyons, France, manufactures cement for the construction industry in the immediate area. Data relating to the kilograms of cement processed through the Mixing Department, the first department in the production process, are provided below for May:

	Kilograms of Cement	Percent Completed	
		Materials	Conversion
Work in process, May 1	80,000	80%	20%
Started into production during May	300,000	—	—
Work in process, May 31	50,000	40%	10%

Required:

1.   Compute the number of kilograms of cement completed and transferred out of the Mixing Department during May.
2.   Prepare a quantity schedule for the Mixing Department for May, assuming that the company uses the weighted-average method.

BRIEF EXERCISE 4–4   Cost Per Equivalent Unit—Weighted-Average Method   (LO4)

Billinstaff Industries uses the weighted-average method in its process costing system. Data for the Assembly Department for May appear below:

	Materials	Labor	Overhead
Work in process, May 1	$14,550	$23,620	$118,100
Cost added during May	$88,350	$14,330	$71,650
Equivalent units of production	1,200	1,100	1,100

Required:

1.   Compute the cost per equivalent unit for materials, for labor, and for overhead.
2.   Compute the total cost per equivalent whole unit.

BRIEF EXERCISE 4–5   Cost Reconciliation—Weighted-Average Method   (LO5)

Kenton Industrial Corporation uses the weighted-average method in its process costing system. During January, the Delta Assembly Department completed its processing of 18,000 units and transferred them to the next department. The cost of beginning inventory and the costs added during January amounted to $855,000 in total. The ending inventory in January consisted of 1,500 units, which were 90% complete with respect to materials and 40% complete with respect to labor and overhead. The costs per equivalent unit for the month were as follows:

	Materials	Labor	Overhead
Cost per equivalent unit	$24.00	$7.00	$14.00

Required:
1. Compute the total cost per equivalent unit for the month.
2. Compute the equivalent units of material, of labor, and of overhead in the ending inventory for the month.
3. Prepare the cost reconciliation portion of the department's production report for January.

EXERCISES

EXERCISE 4–6   Process Costing Journal Entries   (LO1)

Schneider Brot is a bread-baking company located in Aachen, Germany, near the Dutch border. The company uses a process costing system for its single product—a popular pumpernickel bread. Schneider Brot has two processing departments—Mixing and Baking. The T-accounts below show the flow of costs through the two departments in April (all amounts are in the currency euros):

Work in Process—Mixing

Bal. 4/1	10,000	760,000	Transferred out
Direct materials	330,000		
Direct labor	260,000		
Overhead	190,000		

Work in Process—Baking

Bal. 4/1	20,000	980,000	Transferred out
Transferred in	760,000		
Direct labor	120,000		
Overhead	90,000		

Required:
Prepare journal entries showing the flow of costs through the two processing departments during April.

EXERCISE 4–7   Quantity Schedule and Equivalent Units—Weighted-Average Method   (LO2, LO3)

Gulf Fisheries, Inc., processes tuna for various distributors. Two departments are involved—Cleaning and Packing. Data relating to pounds of tuna processed in the Cleaning Department during May are given below:

	Pounds of Tuna	Percent Completed*
Work in process, May 1	30,000	55%
Started into processing during May	480,000	—
Work in process, May 31	20,000	90%
*Labor and overhead only.		

All materials are added at the beginning of processing in the Cleaning Department.

Required:

Prepare a quantity schedule and a computation of equivalent units for May for the Cleaning Department, assuming that the company uses the weighted-average method of accounting for units.

EXERCISE 4–8   Equivalent Units and Cost per Equivalent Unit—Weighted-Average Method   (LO2, LO4)

Solex Company produces a high-quality insulation material that passes through two production processes. A quantity schedule for June for the first process follows:

	Quantity Schedule		
Units to be accounted for:			
Work in process, June 1 (materials 75% complete; conversion 40% complete)	60,000		
Started into production	280,000		
Total units to be accounted for	340,000		

		Equivalent Units	
		Materials	**Conversion**
Units accounted for as follows:			
Transferred to the next process	300,000	?	?
Work in process, June 30 (materials 50% complete; conversion 25% complete)	40,000	?	?
Total units accounted for	340,000	?	?

Costs in the beginning work in process inventory of the first processing department were: materials, $56,600; and conversion cost, $14,900. Costs added during June were: materials, $385,000; and conversion cost, $214,500.

Required:

1. Assume that the company uses the weighted-average method of accounting for units and costs. Determine the equivalent units for June for the first process.
2. Compute the costs per equivalent unit for June for the first process.

EXERCISE 4–9   Cost Reconciliation—Weighted-Average Method   (LO5)

(This exercise should be assigned only if Exercise 4–8 is also assigned.) Refer to the data in Exercise 4–8 and to the equivalent units and costs per equivalent unit you have computed there.

Required:

Complete the following cost reconciliation for the first process:

		Equivalent Units	
	Total Cost	**Materials**	**Conversion**
Cost accounted for as follows:			
Transferred to the next process:			
_____ units × _____ each .... $?			
Work in process, June 30:			
Materials, at _____ per EU	?	?	
Conversion, at _____ per EU	?		?
Total work in process, June 30	?		
Total cost accounted for .... $?			

EXERCISE 4–10   Quantity Schedule, Equivalent Units, and Cost per Equivalent Unit—Weighted-Average Method   (LO2, LO3, LO4)

Kalox, Inc., manufactures an antacid product that passes through two departments. Data for May for the first department follow:

	Gallons	Materials	Labor	Overhead
Work in process, May 1	80,000	$68,600	$30,000	$48,000
Gallons started in process	760,000			
Gallons transferred out	790,000			
Work in process, May 31	50,000			
Cost added during May	—	$907,200	$370,000	$592,000

The beginning work in process inventory was 80% complete with respect to materials and 75% complete with respect to processing. The ending work in process inventory was 60% complete with respect to materials and 20% complete with respect to processing.

Required:
1. Assume that the company uses the weighted-average method of accounting for units and costs. Prepare a quantity schedule and a computation of equivalent units for May's activity for the first department.
2. Determine the costs per equivalent unit for May.

PROBLEMS

CHECK FIGURE
(2) April 30 WIP: $13,616

Whole Statement

PROBLEM 4–11   Equivalent Units; Cost Reconciliation—Weighted-Average Method   (LO2, LO5)
Spring Falls Products manufactures a single product. The company uses the weighted-average method in its process costing system. Activity for April has just been completed. An incomplete production report for the first processing department follows:

Quantity Schedule and Equivalent Units

	Quantity Schedule
Units to be accounted for:	
Work in process, April 1 (materials 100% complete; labor and overhead 80% complete)	5,000
Started into production	38,000
Total units	43,000

	Quantity Schedule	Equivalent Units (EU)		
		Materials	Labor	Overhead
Units accounted for as follows:				
Transferred to the next department ...	35,600	?	?	?
Work in process, April 30 (materials 80% complete, labor and overhead 60% complete)	7,400	?	?	?
Total units	43,000	?	?	?

Cost per Equivalent Unit

	Total Cost	Materials	Labor	Overhead	Whole Unit
Cost to be accounted for:					
Work in process, April 1 ....$	11,500	$ 2,500	$ 4,000	$ 5,000	
Cost added by the department	105,356	18,260	40,044	47,052	
Total cost (a)	$116,856	$20,760	$44,044	$52,052	
Equivalent units (b)		41,520	40,040	40,040	
Cost per EU, (a) ÷ (b)		$0.50 +	$1.10 +	$1.30 =	$2.90

(continued)

(concluded)
Cost Reconciliation

	Total Cost
Cost accounted for as follows:	
?	?

Required:

1. Prepare a schedule showing how the equivalent units were computed for the first processing department.
2. Complete the "Cost Reconciliation" part of the production report for the first processing department.

PROBLEM 4–12 Interpreting a Production Report—Weighted-Average Method (LO2, LO3, LO4)

Cooperative Santa Maria of southern Sonora state in Mexico makes a unique syrup using cane sugar and local herbs. The syrup is sold in small bottles and is prized as a flavoring for drinks and for use in desserts. The bottles are sold for $13 each. (The Mexican currency is the peso and is denoted by $.) The first stage in the production process is carried out in the Mixing Department, which removes foreign matter from the raw materials and mixes them in the proper proportions in large vats. The company uses the weighted-average method in its process costing system.

A hastily prepared report for the Mixing Department for May appears below:

CHECK FIGURE
(1) Materials: 102,500 equivalent units;
(2) Conversion: $2.50 per unit;
(3) 86,000 units

Quantity Schedule	
Units to be accounted for:	
Work in process, May 1 (materials 90% complete; conversion 70% complete)	6,000
Started into production	100,000
Total units	106,000
Units accounted for as follows:	
Transferred to the next department	92,000
Work in process, May 30 (materials 75% complete, conversion 50% complete)	14,000
Total units	106,000
Total Cost	
Cost to be accounted for:	
Work in process, May 1	$ 16,400
Cost added during the month	431,200
Total cost	$447,600
Cost Reconciliation	
Cost accounted for as follows:	
Transferred to the next department	$409,400
Work in process, May 30	37,975
Total cost	$447,375

Cooperative Santa Maria has just been acquired by another company, and the management of the acquiring company wants some additional information about its operations.

Required:

1. What were the equivalent units for the month?
2. What were the costs per equivalent unit for the month? The beginning inventory consisted of the following costs: materials, $5,900; and conversion cost, $10,500. The costs added during the month consisted of: materials, $194,200; and conversion cost, $237,000.
3. How many of the units transferred to the next department were started and completed during the month?

4. The manager of the Mixing Department, anxious to make a good impression on the new owner, stated, "Materials prices jumped from about $1.10 per unit in April to $2.00 per unit in May, but due to good cost control I was able to hold our materials cost to less than $2.00 per unit for the month." Should this manager be rewarded for good cost control? Explain.

CHECK FIGURE
April 30 WIP: $14,430

PROBLEM 4–13 Production Report—Weighted-Average Method   (LO2, LO3, LO4, LO5)
Tropical Break, Ltd., of Fiji makes blended tropical fruit drinks in two stages. Fruit juices are extracted from fresh fruits and blended in the Blending Department. The blended juices are then bottled and packed for shipping in the Bottling Department. The following information pertains to the operations of the Blending Department for April. (The currency in Fiji is the Fijian dollar.)

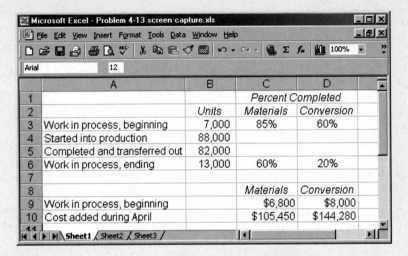

	Units	Percent Completed Materials	Percent Completed Conversion
Work in process, beginning	7,000	85%	60%
Started into production	88,000		
Completed and transferred out	82,000		
Work in process, ending	13,000	60%	20%
		Materials	Conversion
Work in process, beginning		$6,800	$8,000
Cost added during April		$105,450	$144,280

Required:
Prepare a production report for the Blending Department for April assuming that the company uses the weighted-average method.

CHECK FIGURE
(2) Materials: $0.96 per
    unit
(3) July 31 WIP: $13,480

PROBLEM 4–14 Step-by-Step Production Report—Weighted-Average Method   (LO2, LO3, LO4, LO5)
Laura Houldsworth Co. manufactures porcelain dolls that go through three processing stages prior to completion. Information on work in the first department, Molding, is given below for July:

Production data:
  Units in process, July 1 (materials 100% complete;
    labor and overhead 90% complete) 15,000
  Units started into production during July 160,000
  Units completed and transferred out 155,000
  Units in process, July 31 (materials 40% complete;
    labor and overhead 10% complete) .... ?

Cost data:
  Work in process inventory, July 1:
    Materials cost $14,100
    Labor cost $22,680
    Overhead cost $16,340
  Cost added during July:
    Materials cost $142,380
    Labor cost $237,940
    Overhead cost $178,340

Materials are added at several stages during the molding process, whereas labor and overhead costs are incurred uniformly. The company uses the weighted-average method.

Required:
Prepare a production report for the Molding Department for July. Use the following three steps in preparing your report:

1. Prepare a quantity schedule and a computation of equivalent units.
2. Compute the costs per equivalent unit for the month.
3. Using the data from (1) and (2) above, prepare a cost reconciliation.

PROBLEM 4–15 Preparation of Production Report from Analysis of Work in Process—Weighted-Average Method (LO2, LO3, LO4, LO5)

Dillon Corporation manufactures an industrial cleaning compound that goes through three processing departments—Grinding, Mixing, and Cooking. All raw materials are introduced at the start of work in the Grinding Department, with conversion costs being incurred evenly throughout the grinding process. The Work in Process T-account for the Grinding Department for a recent month is given below:

CHECK FIGURE
(1) Materials: $2.00 per unit; March 31 WIP $8,439

Work in Process—Grinding Department

Inventory, March 1 (4,500 units, ⅗ processed)	12,365	?	Completed and transferred to mixing (? units)
March costs added:			
Raw material (56,800 units)	113,475		
Labor and overhead	75,319		
Inventory, March 31 (2,900 units, ⅔ processed)	?		

The March 1 work in process inventory consists of $9,125 in materials cost and $3,240 in labor and overhead cost. The company uses the weighted-average method to account for units and costs.

Required:
1. Prepare a production report for the Grinding Department for the month.
2. What criticism can be made of the unit costs that you have computed on your production report?

PROBLEM 4–16 Costing Inventories; Journal Entries; Cost of Goods Sold—Weighted-Average Method (LO1, LO2, LO4, LO5)

You are employed by Tuff Soles Corporation, a manufacturer of boots. The company's chief financial officer is trying to verify the accuracy of the ending Work in Process and Finished Goods inventories prior to closing the books for the year. You have been asked to assist in this verification. The year-end balances shown on Tuff Soles Corporation's books are as follows:

CHECK FIGURES
(1) Labor: $0.95 per unit
(2) December 31 WIP: $86,040
(4) COGS: $1,999,830

	Units	Costs
Work in process, December 31 (labor and overhead 80% complete)	30,000	$85,000
Finished goods, December 31	12,000	$60,000

Materials are added to production at the beginning of the manufacturing process, and overhead is applied to each product at the rate of 80% of direct labor cost. There was no finished goods inventory at the beginning of the year. A review of Tuff Soles Corporation's inventory and cost records has disclosed the following data, all of which are accurate:

		Costs	
	Units	Materials	Labor
Work in process, January 1 (labor and overhead 70% complete)	15,000	$18,000	$9,555
Units started into production	650,000		
Cost added during the year:			
Materials cost		$979,500	
Labor cost			$616,495
Units completed during the year	635,000		

The company uses the weighted-average cost method.

Required:

1. Determine the equivalent units and costs per equivalent unit for materials, labor, and overhead for the year.
2. Determine the amount of cost that should be assigned to the ending Work in Process and Finished Goods inventories.
3. Prepare the necessary correcting journal entry to adjust the Work in Process and Finished Goods inventories to the correct balances as of December 31.
4. Determine the cost of goods sold for the year assuming there is no under- or overapplied overhead.

(CPA, adapted)

CHECK FIGURE
May 31 Bending
Department WIP: $34,317

PROBLEM 4–17   Comprehensive Process Costing Problem—Weighted-Average Method   (LO1, LO2, LO3, LO4, LO5)

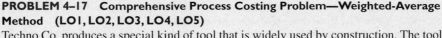

Techno Co. produces a special kind of tool that is widely used by construction. The tool is produced in two processes: bending and drilling. Raw materials are introduced at various points in the Bending Department; labor and overhead costs are incurred evenly throughout the bending operation. The bent output is then transferred to the Drilling Department.

The following incomplete Work in Process account has been provided for the Bending Department for May:

Work in Process—Bending Department

May 1 inventory (12,000 units; materials 80% complete; labor and overhead 60% complete)	45,369	?	Completed and transferred to Drilling (? units)
May costs added:			
Raw materials (270,000 units)	394,210		
Direct labor	638,144		
Overhead	493,584		
May 31 inventory (9,000; materials 90% complete; labor and overhead 60% complete)	?		

The May 1 work in process inventory in the Bending Department consists of the following cost elements: raw materials, $13,385; direct labor, $18,880; and overhead, $13,104. Costs incurred during May in the Drilling Department were: materials used, $100,800; direct labor, $250,600; and overhead cost applied to production, $189,000.

The company accounts for units and costs using the weighted-average method.

Required:

1. Prepare journal entries to record the costs incurred in both the Bending Department and Drilling Department during May. Key your entries to the items (a) through (g) below.
   a. Raw materials were issued for use in production.
   b. Direct labor costs were incurred.
   c. Manufacturing overhead costs for the entire factory were incurred, $685,000. (Credit Accounts Payable.)
   d. Manufacturing overhead cost was applied to production using a predetermined overhead rate.
   e. Units that were complete as to processing in the Bending Department were transferred to the Drilling Department, $1,536,990.
   f. Units that were complete as to processing in the Drilling Department were transferred to Finished Goods, $1,650,000.
   g. Completed units were sold on account, $2,700,000. The Cost of Goods Sold was $1,600,000.
2. Post the journal entries from (1) above to T-accounts. The following account balances existed at the beginning of May. (The beginning balance in the Bending Department's Work in Process account is given above.)

Raw Materials	$500,000
Work in Process—Drilling Department	$10,000
Finished Goods	$110,000

After posting the entries to the T-accounts, find the ending balance in the inventory accounts and the manufacturing overhead accounts.

3. Prepare a production report for the Bending Department for May.

PROBLEM 4–18 Comprehensive Process Costing Problem—Weighted-Average Method (LO1, LO2, LO3, LO4, LO5)

CHECK FIGURE
December 31 Drying
Department WIP: $44,000

Seaside Company, produces a dried fish product that goes through two departments—Drying and Salting. The company has recently hired a new assistant accountant, who has prepared the following summary of production and costs for the Drying Department for December using the weighted-average method.

Drying Department costs:	
Work in process inventory, December 1: 19,000 pounds,	
materials 90% complete and labor and overhead 80% complete	$ 97,400*
Materials added during December	540,460
Labor added during December	397,970
Overhead applied during December	208,170
Total departmental costs	$1,244,000
Drying Department costs assigned to:	
Pounds completed and transferred to the Salting Department:	
200,000 pounds at ___?___ per pound	$?
Work in process inventory, December 31: 10,000 pounds,	
materials 100% complete and labor and overhead 50% complete	?
Total departmental costs assigned	$?

*Consists of materials, $47,540; labor, $32,530; and overhead, $17,330.

The new assistant accountant has determined the cost per pound transferred to be $6.22 as follows:

$$\frac{\text{Total departmental costs}}{\text{Pounds completed and transferred}} = \frac{\$1,244,000}{200,000 \text{ pounds}} = \$6.22 \text{ per pound}$$

However, the assistant accountant is unsure how to use this unit cost figure in assigning cost to the ending work in process inventory. In addition, the company's general ledger shows only $1,200,000 in cost transferred from the Drying Department to the Salting Department, which does not agree with the $1,244,000 figure above.

The general ledger also shows the following costs incurred in the Salting Department during December: materials used, $295,000; direct labor cost incurred, $201,000; and overhead cost applied to products, $340,000.

Required:

1. Prepare journal entries as follows to record activity in the company during December. Key your entries to the letters (a) through (g) below.

   a. Raw materials were issued to the two departments for use in production.

   b. Direct labor costs were incurred in the two departments.

   c. Manufacturing overhead costs were incurred, $542,000. (Credit Accounts Payable.) The company maintains a single Manufacturing Overhead account for the entire plant.

   d. Manufacturing overhead cost was applied to production in each department using predetermined overhead rates.

   e. Units completed as to processing in the Drying Department were transferred to the Salting Department, $1,200,000.

   f. Units completed as to processing in the Salting Department were transferred to Finished Goods, $1,980,000.

   g. Units were sold on account, $2,500,000. The Cost of Goods Sold was $1,930,000.

2. Post the journal entries from (1) above to T-accounts. Balances in selected accounts on December 1 are given below:

Raw Materials	$850,000
Work in Process—Salting Department	$33,000
Finished Goods	$57,000

After posting the entries to the T-accounts, find the ending balance in the inventory accounts and the Manufacturing Overhead accounts.

3. Prepare a production report for the Drying Department for December.

BUILDING YOUR SKILLS

ANALYTICAL THINKING   (LO2, LO3, LO4, LO5)

Durall Company manufactures a plastic gasket that is used in automobile engines. The gaskets go through three processing departments: Mixing, Forming, and Stamping. The company's accountant (who is very inexperienced) has prepared a summary of production and costs for the Forming Department as follows for October:

Forming Department costs:
Work in process inventory, October 1, 8,000 units;
  materials 100% complete; conversion costs ⅞ complete . . . . $ 22,420*
Costs transferred in from the Mixing Department   81,480
Material added during October (added when processing
  is 50% complete in the Forming Department)   27,600
Conversion costs added during October   96,900
Total departmental costs $228,400

Forming Department costs assigned to:
Units completed and transferred to the Stamping
  Department, 100,000 units at $2.284 each $228,400
Work in process inventory, October 31, 5,000 units,
  conversion costs ⅖ complete   0
Total departmental costs assigned $228,400

*Consists of cost transferred in, $8,820; materials cost, $3,400; and conversion costs, $10,200.

After mulling over the data above, Durall's president commented, "I can't understand what's happening here. Despite a concentrated effort at cost reduction, our unit cost actually went up in the Forming Department last month. With that kind of performance, year-end bonuses are out of the question for the people in that department."

The company uses the weighted-average method in its process costing.

Required:

1. Prepare a revised production report for the Forming Department for October.
2. Explain to the president why the unit cost appearing on the report prepared by the accountant is so high.

ETHICS CASE   (LO2, LO4, LO5)

Thad Kostowski and Carol Lee are production managers in the Appliances Division of Mesger Corporation, which has several dozen plants scattered in locations throughout the world. Carol manages the plant located in Kansas City, Missouri, while Thad manages the plant in Roseville, Oregon. Production managers are paid a salary and get an additional bonus equal to 10% of their base salary if the entire division meets or exceeds its target profits for the year. The bonus is determined in March after the company's annual report has been prepared and issued to stockholders.

Late in February, Carol received a phone call from Thad that went like this:

Thad: How's it going, Carol?
Carol: Fine, Thad. How's it going with you?
Thad: Great! I just got the preliminary profit figures for the division for last year and we are within $62,500 of making the year's target profits. All we have to do is to pull a few strings, and we'll be over the top!
Carol: What do you mean?
Thad: Well, one thing that would be easy to change is your estimate of the percentage completion of your ending work in process inventories.

Carol: I don't know if I should do that, Thad. Those percentage completion numbers are supplied by Jean Jackson, my lead supervisor. I have always trusted her to provide us with good estimates. Besides, I have already sent the percentage completion figures to the corporate headquarters.

Thad: You can always tell them there was a mistake. Think about it, Carol. All of us managers are doing as much as we can to pull this bonus out of the hat. You may not want the bonus check, but the rest of us sure could use it.

The final processing department in Carol's production facility began the year with no work in process inventories. During the year, 270,000 units were transferred in from the prior processing department and 250,000 units were completed and sold. Costs transferred in from the prior department totaled $49,221,000. No materials are added in the final processing department. A total of $16,320,000 of conversion cost was incurred in the final processing department during the year.

Required:
1. Jean Jackson estimated that the units in ending inventory in the final processing department were 25% complete with respect to the conversion costs of the final processing department. If this estimate of the percentage completion is used, what would be the Cost of Goods Sold for the year?
2. Does Thad Kostowski want the estimated percentage completion to be increased or decreased? Explain why.
3. What percentage completion figure would result in increasing the reported net operating income by $62,500 over the net operating income that would be reported if the 25% figure were used?
4. Do you think Carol Lee should go along with the request to alter estimates of the percentage completion? Why or why not?

COMMUNICATING IN PRACTICE (LO5)

Assume that you are the cost analyst who prepared the Production Report that appears in Exhibit 4–9. You receive a call from Minesh Patel, a new hire in the company's accounting staff who is not sure what needs to be done with the cost reconciliation portion of the report. He wants to know what journal entries should be prepared and what balances need to be checked in the company's accounts.

Required:
Write a memorandum to Mr. Patel that explains the steps that should be taken. Refer to specific amounts on the Cost Reconciliation portion of the Production Report to ensure that he properly completes the steps.

TEAMWORK IN ACTION (LO2, LO3, LO4, LO5)

The Production Report includes a quantity schedule, the computation of equivalent costs and costs per equivalent units, and a cost reconciliation.

Required:
1. *Learning teams* of three (or more) members should be formed. Each team member must select one of the following sections of the Production Report (as illustrated in Exhibit 4–9) as an area of expertise (each team must have at least one expert in each section).
   a. Quantity Schedule and Equivalent Units.
   b. Costs per Equivalent Unit.
   c. Cost Reconciliation.
2. *Expert teams* should be formed from the individuals who have selected the same area of expertise. Expert teams should discuss and write up a brief summary that each expert will present to his/her learning team that addresses the following:
   a. The purpose of the section of the Production Report.
   b. The manner in which the amounts appearing in this section of the report are determined.
3. Each expert should return to his/her learning team. In rotation, each member should present his/her expert team's report to the learning team.

TAKING IT TO THE NET

As you know, the World Wide Web is a medium that is constantly evolving. Sites come and go and change without notice. To enable periodic update of site addresses, this problem has been posted to the textbook website (www.mhhe.com/bgn2e). After accessing the site, enter the Student Center and select this chapter. Select and complete the Taking It to the Net problem.

CHAPTER FIVE

Cost Behavior: Analysis and Use

CHAPTER OUTLINE

Types of Cost Behavior Patterns

- Variable Costs
- True Variable versus Step-Variable Costs
- The Linearity Assumption and the Relevant Range
- Fixed Costs
- Types of Fixed Costs
- Fixed Costs and the Relevant Range
- Mixed Costs

The Analysis of Mixed Costs

- Diagnosing Cost Behavior with a Scattergraph Plot
- The High-Low Method
- The Least-Squares Regression Method

The Contribution Format

- Why a New Income Statement Format?
- The Contribution Approach

A Costly Mistake

After spending countless hours tracking down the hardware and fixtures he needed to restore his Queen Anne–style Victorian house, Stephen Gordon recognized an opportunity. He opened Restoration Hardware, Inc., a specialty store carrying antique hardware and fixtures. The company, based in Corte Madera, California, now sells fine furniture, lighting, hardware, home accessories, garden products, and gifts. The company's products, described by some as nostalgic, old-fashioned, and obscure, appeal to wealthy baby boomers. Customers can shop at one of the 90 Restoration Hardware stores, by catalog, or online at the company's website www.restorationhardware.com.

1998 was a year of phenomenal growth and change for Restoration Hardware. Twenty-four new stores were opened, increasing the total number in the chain to 65. The company's newly launched catalog business was an instant success. Net sales approached $200 million, an increase of almost 114% from the prior year. Gordon, chairman and CEO, took the company public.

The success enjoyed by the company in 1998 did not recur in 1999. Gordon's biggest mistake was a failure to consider cost behavior when making decisions to promote the company's products. The most popular furniture items in the store were discounted during the first quarter to encourage customer interest. The company spent $1 million to advertise this big sale, which was far more "successful" than Gordon had imagined. Sales for the first quarter increased by 84% to $60 million. However, much of the increase arose from sales of discounted goods. As a result, margins (that is, differences between sale prices and the cost of the goods that were sold) were lower than usual. Further, because the items placed on sale were larger and heavier than average, the costs to move them from the distribution centers to the stores were considerably higher. The company ended up reporting a loss of $2.7 million for the quarter.

Sources: Restoration Hardware website July 2000; Stephen Gordon, "My Biggest Mistake," *Inc.*, September 1999, p. 103; and Heather Chaplin, "Past? Perfect," *American Demographics*, May 1999, pp. 68–69.

LEARNING OBJECTIVES

After studying Chapter 5, you should be able to:

LO1 Understand how fixed and variable costs behave and how to use them to predict costs.

LO2 Use a scattergraph plot to diagnose cost behavior.

LO3 Analyze a mixed cost using the high-low method.

LO4 Prepare an income statement using the contribution format.

In our discussion of cost terms and concepts in Chapter 1, we stated that one way costs can be classified is by behavior. We defined cost behavior as the way a cost reacts or changes as changes take place in the level of activity. An understanding of cost behavior is the key to many decisions in an organization. Managers who understand how costs behave are better able to predict what costs will be under various operating circumstances. Attempts at decision making without a thorough understanding of the costs involved—and how these costs may change with the activity level—can lead to disaster. For example, a decision to cut back production of a particular product line might result in far less cost savings than managers had assumed if they confuse fixed costs with variable costs. To avoid such problems, a manager must be able to accurately predict what costs will be at various activity levels. In this chapter, we shall find that the key to effective cost prediction lies in understanding variable and fixed costs.

We briefly review in this chapter the definitions of variable costs and fixed costs and then discuss the behavior of these costs in greater depth than we were able to do in Chapter 1. After this review and discussion, we turn our attention to the analysis of mixed costs. We conclude the chapter by introducing a new income statement format—called the contribution format—in which costs are organized by behavior rather than by the traditional functions of production, sales, and administration.

TYPES OF COST BEHAVIOR PATTERNS

Concept 5–1

In Chapter 1 we mentioned only variable and fixed costs. In this chapter we will discuss a third behavior pattern, known as a *mixed* or *semivariable* cost. All three cost behavior patterns—variable, fixed, and mixed—are found in most organizations. The relative proportion of each type of cost present in an organization is known as the organization's **cost structure**. For example, an organization might have many fixed costs but few variable or mixed costs. Alternatively, it might have many variable costs but few fixed or mixed costs. An organization's cost structure can have a significant impact on decisions. In this chapter we will concentrate on gaining a fuller understanding of the behavior of each type of cost. In the next chapter we will discuss more fully how cost structure impacts decisions.

Selling Online

By making investments in technology, many organizations have created cost structures radically different from those of traditional companies. John Labbett, the CFO of Onsale, an Internet auctioneer of discontinued computers, was previously employed at House of Fabrics, a traditional retailer. The two companies have roughly the same total revenues of about $250 million. However, House of Fabrics, with 5,500 employees, has a revenue per employee of about $90,000. At Onsale, with only 200 employees, the figure is $1.18 million per employee. Moreover, Internet companies are often able to grow at very little cost. If demand grows, an Internet company just adds another computer server. If demand grows at a traditional retailer, the company may have to invest in a new building and additional inventory and may have to hire additional employees.

Source: George Donnelly, "New@ttitude," *CFO*, June 1999, pp. 42–54.

Variable Costs

We explained in Chapter 1 that a variable cost is a cost whose total dollar amount varies in direct proportion to changes in the activity level. If the activity level doubles, the total dollar amount of the variable cost also doubles. If the activity level increases by only 10%, then the total dollar amount of the variable cost increases by 10% as well.

We also found in Chapter 1 that a variable cost remains constant if expressed on a *per unit* basis. To provide an example, consider Nooksack Expeditions, a small company that provides daylong whitewater rafting excursions on rivers in the North Cascade Mountains. The company provides all of the necessary equipment and experienced guides, and it serves gourmet meals to its guests. The meals are purchased from an exclusive caterer for $30 a person for a daylong excursion. If we look at the cost of the meals on a *per person* basis, the cost remains constant at $30. This $30 cost per person will not change, regardless of how many people participate in a daylong excursion. The behavior of this variable cost, on both a per unit and a total basis, is tabulated below:

LEARNING OBJECTIVE 1
Understand how fixed and variable costs behave and how to use them to predict costs.

Number of Guests	Cost of Meals per Guest	Total Cost of Meals
250	$30	$7,500
500	$30	$15,000
750	$30	$22,500
1,000	$30	$30,000

The idea that a variable cost is constant per unit but varies in total with the activity level is crucial to an understanding of cost behavior patterns. We shall rely on this concept again and again in this chapter and in chapters ahead.

Exhibit 5–1 provides a graphic illustration of variable cost behavior. Note that the graph of the total cost of the meals slants upward to the right. This is because the total cost of the meals is directly proportional to the number of guests. In contrast, the graph of the per unit cost of meals is flat. This is because the cost of the meals per guest is constant at $30 per guest.

The Activity Base For a cost to be variable, it must be variable *with respect to something*. That "something" is its *activity base*. An **activity base** is a measure of whatever causes the incurrence of variable cost. An activity base is also sometimes referred to as a *cost driver*. Some of the most common activity bases are direct labor-hours, machine-hours, units produced, and units sold. Other activity bases (cost drivers) might include the number of miles driven by salespersons, the number of pounds of laundry cleaned by a

EXHIBIT 5–1 Variable Cost Behavior

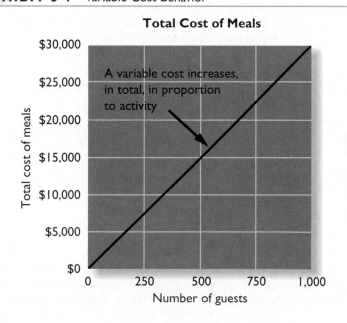

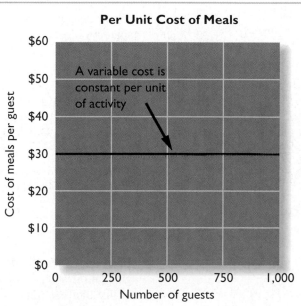

hotel, the number of calls handled by technical support staff at a software company, and the number of beds occupied in a hospital.

To plan and control variable costs, a manager must be well acquainted with the various activity bases within the firm. People sometimes get the notion that if a cost doesn't vary with production or with sales, then it is not really a variable cost. This is not correct. As suggested by the range of bases listed above, costs are caused by many different activities within an organization. Whether a cost is considered to be variable depends on whether it is caused by the activity under consideration. For example, if a manager is analyzing the cost of service calls under a product warranty, the relevant activity measure will be the number of service calls made. Those costs that vary in total with the number of service calls made are the variable costs of making service calls.

Nevertheless, unless stated otherwise, you can assume that the activity base under consideration is the total volume of goods and services provided by the organization. So, for example, if we ask whether direct materials at Ford is a variable cost, the answer is yes, since the cost of direct materials is variable with respect to Ford's total volume of output. We will specify the activity base only when it is something other than total output.

DECISION MAKER

Cost Analyst

You have been hired to analyze costs for a caterer that provides and serves refreshments for wedding receptions. Costs incurred by the caterer include administrative salaries, rental of the central kitchen, the salary of the full-time chef, wages of part-time cooks, groceries and kitchen supplies, delivery vehicle depreciation and operating expenses, the wages of part-time food servers, depreciation of silverware and dinnerware, and cleaning of table linens. Which of these costs are likely to be variable with respect to the number of guests at a wedding reception? Which are likely to be fixed? Which are likely to be mixed?

IN BUSINESS

Really Haute Cuisine

Variable costs change in proportion to changes in activity. However, they can also vary from one situation to another due to other factors. For example, as the following discussion illustrates, the variable cost per passenger of airline meals varies considerably.

In August of 2000, the air-worthiness certification of the supersonic Concorde was suspended following a fatal crash after a take-off at Paris' Charles De Gaulle airport. Prior to that time, a New York to Paris round-trip ticket on Air France's supersonic Concorde had cost as much as $10,000. At this price, passengers expected something more than standard airline food. U.S. airlines spend an average of about $3.87 to feed a passenger. Air France budgeted $55 per passenger for the Concorde flight. However, even at $55 per passenger, the meals on the Concorde were undistinguished. Tired of complaints from passengers, the airline hired superstar chef Alain Ducasse to oversee the Concorde's food service. Ducasse struggled with tiny galleys, high-speed take-offs that made a mess of carefully arranged salads, and food that had to be reheated prior to serving. Ducasse demanded, and got, a budget of $90 per passenger from Air France to upgrade the meals on the Concorde.

Source: Shelly Branch, "A Chef's Trials on the Concorde," *The Wall Street Journal,* January 13, 2000, pp. B1 and B4.

Extent of Variable Costs The number and type of variable costs present in an organization will depend in large part on the organization's structure and purpose. A public utility like Florida Power and Light, with large investments in equipment, will tend to

EXHIBIT 5–2

Examples of Variable Costs

Type of Organization	Costs that Are Normally Variable with Respect to Volume of Output
Merchandising company	Cost of goods (merchandise) sold

Manufacturing company	Manufacturing costs:
	    Direct materials
	    Direct labor*
	Variable portion of manufacturing overhead:
	    Indirect materials
	    Lubricants
	    Supplies

Both merchandising and manufacturing companies	Selling, general, and administrative costs:
	    Commissions
	    Clerical costs, such as invoicing
	    Shipping costs

Service organizations	Supplies, travel, clerical

*Direct labor may or may not be variable in practice. See the discussion later in this chapter.

have few variable costs. Most of the costs are associated with its plant, and these costs tend to be insensitive to changes in levels of service provided. A manufacturing company like Black and Decker, by contrast, will often have many variable costs; these costs will be associated with both manufacturing and distributing its products to customers.

A merchandising company like Wal-Mart or J. K. Gill will usually have a high proportion of variable costs in its cost structure. In most merchandising companies, the cost of merchandise purchased for resale, a variable cost, constitutes a very large component of total cost. Service companies, by contrast, have diverse cost structures. Some service companies, such as the Skippers restaurant chain, have fairly large variable costs because of the costs of their raw materials. On the other hand, service companies involved in consulting, auditing, engineering, dental, medical, and architectural activities have very large fixed costs in the form of expensive facilities and highly trained salaried employees.

Some of the more frequently encountered variable costs are listed in Exhibit 5–2. This exhibit is not a complete listing of all costs that can be considered variable. Moreover, some of the costs listed in the exhibit may behave more like fixed than variable costs in some organizations. We will see some examples of this later in the chapter. Nevertheless, Exhibit 5–2 provides a useful listing of many of the costs that normally would be considered variable with respect to the volume of output.

True Variable versus Step-Variable Costs

Not all variable costs have exactly the same behavior pattern. Some variable costs behave in a *true variable* or *proportionately variable* pattern. Other variable costs behave in a *step-variable* pattern.

True Variable Costs   Direct materials is a true or proportionately variable cost because the amount used during a period will vary in direct proportion to the level of production activity. Moreover, any amounts purchased but not used can be stored and carried forward to the next period as inventory.

Step-Variable Costs   The wages of maintenance workers are often considered to be a variable cost, but this labor cost doesn't behave in quite the same way as the cost of direct materials. Unlike direct materials, the time of maintenance workers can be obtained only in large chunks. Moreover, any maintenance time not utilized cannot be stored as inventory and carried forward to the next period. If the time is not used effectively, it is gone forever. Furthermore, a maintenance crew can work at a fairly leisurely pace if pressures are light but intensify its efforts if pressures build up. For this reason, small changes in the

EXHIBIT 5–3

True Variable versus
Step-Variable Costs

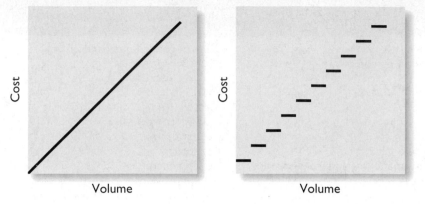

Direct Materials (true variable)   Maintenance Help (step variable)

level of production may have no effect on the number of maintenance people employed by the company.

The cost of a resource (such as the cost of maintenance workers) that is obtainable only in large chunks and increases or decreases only in response to fairly wide changes in activity level is known as a **step-variable cost.** The behavior of a step-variable cost, contrasted with the behavior of a true variable cost, is illustrated in Exhibit 5–3.

Notice that the need for maintenance help changes only with fairly wide changes in volume and that when additional maintenance time is obtained, it comes in large, indivisible chunks. Great care must be taken in working with these kinds of costs to prevent "fat" from building up in an organization. There may be a tendency to employ additional help more quickly than needed, and there is a natural reluctance to lay people off when volume declines.

IN BUSINESS

Coping with the Fallout from September 11

Costs can change for reasons having nothing to do with changes in volume. Filterfresh company services office coffee machines, providing milk, sugar, cups, and coffee. The company's operations were profoundly affected by the security measures many companies initiated after the terrorist attacks on the World Trade Center and the Pentagon on September 11, 2001. Heightened security at customer locations means that Filterfresh's 250 deliverymen can no longer casually walk through a customer's lobby with a load of supplies. Now a guard typically checks the deliveryman's identification and paperwork at the loading dock and may search the van before permitting the deliveryman access to the customer's building. These delays have added an average of about an hour per day to each route, which means that Filterfresh needs 24 more delivery people to do the same work it did prior to September 11. That's a 10% increase in cost without any increase in the amount of coffee sold.

Source: Anna Bernasek, "The Friction Economy," *Fortune*, February 18, 2002, pp. 104–112.

The Linearity Assumption and the Relevant Range

In dealing with variable costs, we have assumed a strictly linear relationship between cost and volume, except in the case of step-variable costs. Economists correctly point out that many costs that the accountant classifies as variable actually behave in a *curvilinear* fashion. The behavior of a **curvilinear cost** is shown in Exhibit 5–4.

Although many costs are not strictly linear when plotted as a function of volume, a curvilinear cost can be satisfactorily approximated with a straight line within a narrow band of activity known as the *relevant range*. The **relevant range** is that range of activity

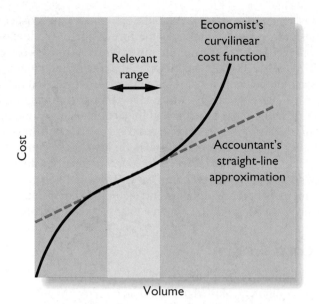

EXHIBIT 5–4

Curvilinear Costs and the
Relevant Range

within which the assumptions made about cost behavior are valid. For example, note that the dashed line in Exhibit 5–4 can be used as an approximation to the curvilinear cost with very little loss of accuracy within the shaded relevant range. However, outside of the relevant range this particular straight line is a poor approximation to the curvilinear cost relationship. Managers should always keep in mind that a particular assumption made about cost behavior may be very inappropriate if activity falls outside of the relevant range.

Fixed Costs

In our discussion of cost behavior patterns in Chapter 1, we stated that fixed costs remain constant in total dollar amount within the relevant range of activity. To continue the Nooksack Expeditions example, assume the company decides to rent a building for $500 per month to store its equipment. The *total* amount of rent paid is the same regardless of the number of guests the company takes on its expeditions during any given month. This cost behavior pattern is shown graphically in Exhibit 5–5.

EXHIBIT 5–5   Fixed Cost Behavior

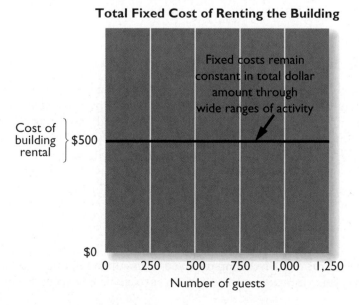

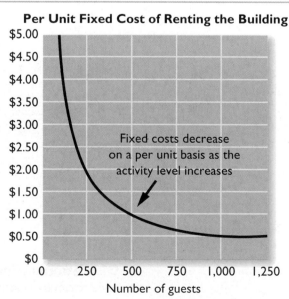

Since fixed costs remain constant in total, the amount of fixed cost computed on a *per unit* basis becomes progressively smaller as the level of activity increases. If Nooksack Expeditions has only 250 guests in a month, the $500 fixed rental cost would amount to $2 per guest. If there are 1,000 guests, the fixed rental cost would amount to only 50 cents per guest. This aspect of the behavior of fixed costs is also displayed in Exhibit 5–5. Note that as the number of guests increases, the average unit cost drops, but it drops at a decreasing rate. The first guests have the biggest impact on average unit costs.

As we noted in Chapter 1, this aspect of fixed costs can be confusing, although it is necessary in some contexts to express fixed costs on an average per unit basis. We found in Chapter 2, for example, that unit product costs for *external* financial statements contain both variable and fixed cost elements. For *internal* uses, however, fixed costs should not be expressed on a per unit basis because of the potential confusion. For internal uses, fixed costs are most easily (and most safely) dealt with on a total basis rather than on a per unit basis.

Types of Fixed Costs

Fixed costs are sometimes referred to as capacity costs, since they result from outlays made for buildings, equipment, skilled professional employees, and other items needed to provide the basic capacity for sustained operations. For planning purposes, fixed costs can be viewed as being either *committed* or *discretionary*.

Committed Fixed Costs   **Committed fixed costs** relate to the investment in facilities, equipment, and the basic organizational structure of a firm. Examples of such costs include depreciation of buildings and equipment, taxes on real estate, insurance, and salaries of top management and operating personnel.

Committed fixed costs are long term in nature and can't be reduced to zero even for short periods of time without seriously impairing the profitability or long-run goals of the organization. Even if operations are interrupted or cut back, the committed fixed costs will still continue largely unchanged. During a recession, for example, a firm won't usually discharge key executives or sell off key facilities. The basic organizational structure and facilities ordinarily are kept intact. The costs of restoring them later are likely to be far greater than any short-run savings that might be realized.

Since it is difficult to change a committed fixed cost once the commitment has been made, management should approach these decisions with particular care. Decisions to acquire major equipment or to take on other committed fixed costs involve a long planning horizon. Management should make such commitments only after careful analysis of the available alternatives. Once a decision is made to build a certain size facility, a firm becomes locked into that decision for many years to come. Decisions relating to committed fixed costs will be examined in Chapter 12.

IN BUSINESS

LS

Sharing Office Space

Even committed fixed costs may be more flexible than they would appear at first glance. Doctors in private practice have been under enormous pressure in recent years to cut costs. Dr. Edward Betz of Encino, California, reduced the committed fixed costs of maintaining his office by letting a urologist use the office on Wednesday afternoons and Friday mornings for $1,500 a month. Dr. Betz uses this time to work on paperwork at home and he makes up for the lost time in the office by treating some patients on Saturdays.

Source: Gloria Lau and Tim W. Ferguson, "Doc's Just an Employee Now," *Forbes*, May 18, 1998, pp. 162–172.

Discretionary Fixed Costs   **Discretionary fixed costs** (often referred to as *managed fixed costs*) usually arise from *annual* decisions by management to spend in certain

Committed vs. Discretionary Fixed Costs

Committed Fixed Costs:
- Multiyear Planning Horizon
- Cannot be cut for short periods of time.

Discretionary Fixed Costs:
- One-Year Planning Horizon
- Can be cut for short periods of time.

fixed cost areas. Examples of discretionary fixed costs include advertising, research, public relations, management development programs, and internships for students.

Basically, two key differences exist between discretionary fixed costs and committed fixed costs. First, the planning horizon for a discretionary fixed cost is fairly short term—usually a single year. By contrast, as we indicated earlier, committed fixed costs have a planning horizon that encompasses many years. Second, discretionary fixed costs can be cut for short periods of time with minimal damage to the long-run goals of the organization. For example, spending on management development programs can be reduced because of poor economic conditions. Although some unfavorable consequences may result from the cutback, it is doubtful that these consequences would be as great as those that would result if the company decided to economize during the year by laying off key personnel.

Whether a particular cost is regarded as committed or discretionary may depend on management's strategy. For example, during recessions when the level of home building is down, many construction companies lay off most of their workers and virtually disband operations. Other construction companies retain large numbers of employees on the payroll, even though the workers have little or no work to do. While these latter companies may be faced with short-term cash flow problems, it will be easier for them to respond quickly when economic conditions improve. And the higher morale and loyalty of their employees may give these companies a significant competitive advantage.

The most important characteristic of discretionary fixed costs is that management is not locked into a decision regarding such costs. They can be adjusted from year to year or even perhaps during the course of a year if circumstances demand such a modification.

The Trend toward Fixed Costs　The trend in many industries is toward greater fixed costs relative to variable costs. Chores that used to be performed by hand have been taken over by machines. For example, grocery clerks at Safeway and Kroger used to key in prices by hand on cash registers. Now, most stores are equipped with barcode readers that enter price and other product information automatically. In general, competition has created pressure to give customers more value for their money—a demand that often can only be satisfied by automating business processes. For example, an H & R Block employee used to fill out tax returns for customers by hand and the advice given to a customer largely depended on the knowledge of that particular employee. Now, sophisticated computer software is used to complete tax returns, and the software provides the customer with tax planning and other advice tailored to the customer's needs based on the accumulated knowledge of many experts.

As machines take over more and more of the tasks that were performed by humans, the demand for "knowledge" workers—those who work primarily with their minds rather than their muscles—has grown tremendously. And knowledge workers tend to be salaried, highly trained, and difficult to replace. As a consequence, the costs of compensating knowledge workers are often relatively fixed and are committed rather than discretionary costs.

Is Labor a Variable or a Fixed Cost?   As the preceding discussion suggests, wages and salaries may be fixed or variable. The behavior of wage and salary costs will differ from one country to another, depending on labor regulations, labor contracts, and custom. In some countries, such as France, Germany, China, and Japan, management has little flexibility in adjusting the labor force to changes in business activity. In countries such as the United States and the United Kingdom, management typically has much greater latitude. However, even in these less restrictive environments, managers may choose to treat employee compensation as a fixed cost for several reasons.

First, many companies have become much more reluctant to adjust the work force in response to short-term fluctuations in sales. Most companies realize that their employees are a very valuable asset. More and more, highly skilled and trained employees are required to run a successful business, and these workers are not easy to replace. Trained workers who are laid off may never return, and layoffs undermine the morale of those workers who remain.

In addition, managers do not want to be caught with a bloated payroll in an economic downturn. Therefore, there is an increased reluctance to add workers when sales activity picks up. Many companies are turning to temporary and part-time workers to take up the slack when their permanent, full-time employees are unable to handle all of the demand for the company's products and services. In such companies, labor costs are a mixture of fixed and variable costs.

Many major companies have undergone waves of downsizing in recent years in which large numbers of employees—particularly middle managers—have lost their jobs. It may seem that this downsizing proves that even management salaries should be regarded as variable costs, but this would not be a valid conclusion. Downsizing has largely been the result of attempts to reengineer business processes and cut costs rather than a response to a decline in sales activity. This underscores an important, but subtle, point. Fixed costs can change—they just don't change in response to small changes in activity.

In sum, we cannot provide a clear-cut answer to the question "Is labor a variable or fixed cost?" It depends on how much flexibility management has and management's strategy. Nevertheless, we will assume in this text that, unless otherwise stated, direct labor is a variable cost. This assumption is more likely to be valid for companies in the United States than in countries where employment laws permit much less flexibility.

IN BUSINESS

Labor at Southwest Airlines

Starting with a $10,000 investment in 1966, Herb Kelleher built Southwest Airlines into the most profitable airline in the United States. Prior to stepping down as president and CEO of the airline in 2001, Kelleher wrote: "The thing that would disturb me most to see after I'm no longer CEO is layoffs at Southwest. Nothing kills your company's culture like layoffs. Nobody has ever been furloughed here, and that is unprecedented in the airline industry. It's been a huge strength of ours . . . We could have furloughed at various times and been more profitable, but I always thought that was shortsighted. You want to show your people that you value them and you're not going to hurt them just to get a little money in the short run."

Because of this commitment by management to the company's employees, all wages and salaries are basically committed fixed costs at Southwest Airlines.

Source: Herb Kelleher, "The Chairman of the Board Looks Back," *Fortune*, May 28, 2001, pp. 63–76.

Fixed Costs and the Relevant Range

The concept of the relevant range, which was introduced in the discussion of variable costs, is also important in understanding fixed costs—particularly discretionary fixed costs. The levels of discretionary fixed costs are typically decided at the beginning of the year and depend on the support needs of planned programs such as advertising and training. The scope of these programs will depend, in turn, on the overall anticipated level of activity for the year. At very high levels of activity, programs are usually broadened or expanded. For example, if the company hopes to increase sales by 25%, it would probably plan for much larger advertising costs than if no sales increase were planned. So the *planned* level of activity might affect total discretionary fixed costs. However, once the total discretionary fixed costs have been budgeted, they are unaffected by the *actual* level of activity. For example, once the advertising budget has been decided on and has been spent, it will not be affected by how many units are actually sold. Therefore, the cost is fixed with respect to the *actual* number of units sold.

Discretionary fixed costs are easier to adjust than committed fixed costs. They also tend to be less "lumpy." Committed fixed costs consist of costs such as buildings, equipment, and the salaries of key personnel. It is difficult to buy half a piece of equipment or to hire a quarter of a product-line manager, so the step pattern depicted in Exhibit 5–6 is typical for such costs. The relevant range of activity for a fixed cost is the range of activity over which the graph of the cost is flat as in Exhibit 5–6. As a company expands its level of activity, it may outgrow its present facilities, or the key management team may need to be expanded. The result, of course, will be increased committed fixed costs as larger facilities are built and as new management positions are created.

One reaction to the step pattern depicted in Exhibit 5–6 is to say that discretionary and committed fixed costs are really just step-variable costs. To some extent this is true, since *almost* all costs can be adjusted in the long run. There are two major differences, however, between the step-variable costs depicted earlier in Exhibit 5–3 and the fixed costs depicted in Exhibit 5–6.

The first difference is that the step-variable costs can often be adjusted quickly as conditions change, whereas once fixed costs have been set, they often can't be changed easily. A step-variable cost such as maintenance labor, for example, can be adjusted upward or downward by hiring and laying off maintenance workers. By contrast, once a company has signed a lease for a building, it is locked into that level of lease cost for the life of the contract.

The second difference is that the *width of the steps* depicted for step-variable costs is much narrower than the width of the steps depicted for the fixed costs in Exhibit 5–6. The

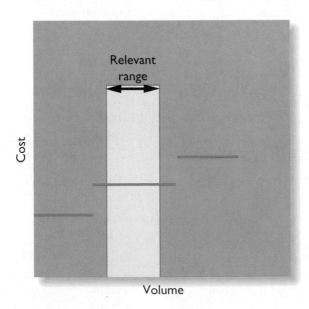

Volume

EXHIBIT 5–6

Fixed Costs and the Relevant Range

EXHIBIT 5–7

Mixed Cost Behavior

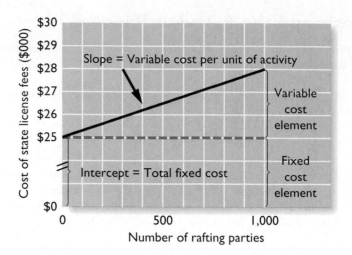

width of the steps relates to volume or level of activity. For step-variable costs, the width of a step might be 40 hours of activity or less if one is dealing, for example, with maintenance labor cost. For fixed costs, however, the width of a step might be *thousands* or even *tens of thousands* of hours of activity. In essence, the width of the steps for step-variable costs is generally so narrow that these costs can be treated essentially as variable costs for most purposes. The width of the steps for fixed costs, on the other hand, is so wide that these costs must generally be treated as being entirely fixed within the relevant range.

Mixed Costs

A **mixed cost** contains both variable and fixed cost elements. Mixed costs are also known as semivariable costs. To continue the Nooksack Expeditions example, the company must pay a license fee of $25,000 per year plus $3 per rafting party to the state's Department of Natural Resources. If the company runs 1,000 rafting parties this year, then the total fees paid to the state would be $28,000, made up of $25,000 in fixed cost plus $3,000 in variable cost. The behavior of this mixed cost is shown graphically in Exhibit 5–7.

Even if Nooksack fails to attract any customers, the company will still have to pay the license fee of $25,000. This is why the cost line in Exhibit 5–7 intersects the vertical cost axis at the $25,000 point. For each rafting party the company organizes, the total cost of the state fees will increase by $3. Therefore, the total cost line slopes upward as the variable cost element is added to the fixed cost element.

Since the mixed cost in Exhibit 5–7 is represented by a straight line, the following equation for a straight line can be used to express the relationship between mixed cost and the level of activity:

$$Y = a + bX$$

In this equation,

Y = The total mixed cost

a = The total fixed cost (the vertical intercept of the line)

b = The variable cost per unit of activity (the slope of the line)

X = The level of activity

In the case of the state fees paid by Nooksack Expeditions, the equation is written as follows:

$$Y = \$25{,}000 + \$3.00X$$

| Total mixed cost | Total fixed cost | Variable cost per unit of activity | Activity level |

This equation makes it very easy to calculate what the total mixed cost would be for any level of activity within the relevant range. For example, suppose that the company expects to organize 800 rafting parties in the next year. Then the total state fees would be $27,400 calculated as follows:

$$Y = \$25,000 + (\$3.00 \text{ per rafting party} \times 800 \text{ rafting parties})$$

$$= \$27,400$$

THE ANALYSIS OF MIXED COSTS

In practice, mixed costs are very common. For example, the cost of providing X-ray services to patients at the Harvard Medical School Hospital is a mixed cost. There are substantial fixed costs for equipment depreciation and for salaries for radiologists and technicians, but there are also variable costs for X-ray film, power, and supplies. At Southwest Airlines, maintenance costs are mixed costs. The company must incur fixed costs for renting maintenance facilities and for keeping skilled mechanics on the payroll, but the costs of replacement parts, lubricating oils, tires, and so forth are variable with respect to how often and how far the company's aircraft are flown.

The fixed portion of a mixed cost represents the basic, minimum cost of just having a service *ready and available* for use. The variable portion represents the cost incurred for *actual consumption* of the service. The variable element varies in proportion to the amount of service that is consumed.

How does management go about actually estimating the fixed and variable components of a mixed cost? The most common methods used in practice and later in this text are *account analysis* and the *engineering approach.*

In **account analysis,** each account under consideration is classified as either variable or fixed based on the analyst's prior knowledge of how the cost in the account behaves. For example, direct materials would be classified as variable and a building lease cost would be classified as fixed because of the nature of those costs. The total fixed cost of an organization is the sum of the costs for the accounts that have been classified as fixed. The variable cost per unit is estimated by dividing the sum of the costs for the accounts that have been classified as variable by the total activity.

The **engineering approach** to cost analysis involves a detailed analysis of what cost behavior should be, based on an industrial engineer's evaluation of the production methods to be used, the materials specifications, labor requirements, equipment usage, efficiency of production, power consumption, and so on. For example, Pizza Hut might use the engineering approach to estimate the cost of serving a particular take-out pizza. The cost of the pizza would be estimated by carefully costing the specific ingredients used to make the pizza, the power consumed to cook the pizza, and the cost of the container the pizza is delivered in. The engineering approach must be used in those situations where no past experience is available concerning activity and costs. In addition, it is sometimes used together with other methods to improve the accuracy of cost analysis.

Account analysis works best when analyzing costs at a fairly aggregated level, such as the cost of serving patients in the emergency room (ER) of Cook County Hospital. The costs of drugs, supplies, forms, wages, equipment, and so on can be roughly classified as variable or fixed and a mixed cost formula for the overall cost of the emergency room can be estimated fairly quickly. However, this method glosses over the fact that some of the accounts may have elements of both fixed and variable costs. For example, the cost of electricity for the ER is a mixed cost. Most of the electricity is used for heating and lighting and is a fixed cost. However, the consumption of electricity increases with activity in the ER since diagnostic equipment, operating theater lights, defibrillators, and so on all consume electricity. The most effective way to estimate the fixed and variable elements of such a mixed cost may be to analyze past records of cost and activity data. These records should reveal whether electrical costs vary significantly with the number of patients and if so, by how much. The remainder of this section will be concerned with how to conduct such an analysis of past cost and activity data.

CONCEPT CHECK ✓

1. Which of the following cost behavior assumptions is false? (You may select more than one answer.)
   a. Variable cost per unit increases as the activity level increases.
   b. The average fixed cost per unit decreases as the activity level increases.
   c. Total variable costs decrease as the activity level decreases.
   d. Total fixed costs remain the same as the activity level changes (within the relevant range).

2. Which of the following statements is false? (You may select more than one answer.)
   a. The planning horizon for discretionary fixed costs is longer than the planning horizon for committed fixed costs.
   b. Discretionary fixed costs can be cut in the short term if necessary, while committed fixed costs cannot be cut for short periods of time.
   c. As companies increasingly rely on knowledge workers, the labor cost associated with employing these workers is often committed fixed as opposed to discretionary.
   d. A mixed cost contains both committed fixed and discretionary elements.

MANAGERIAL ACCOUNTING IN ACTION
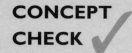
The Issue

Dr. Derek Chalmers, the chief executive officer of Brentline Hospital, motioned Kinh Nguyen, the chief financial officer of the hospital, into his office.

Derek: Kinh, come on in.

Kinh: What can I do for you?

Derek: Well for one, could you get the government to rescind the bookcase full of regulations against the wall over there?

Kinh: Sorry, that's a bit beyond my authority.

Derek: Just wishing, Kinh. Actually, I wanted to talk to you about our maintenance expenses. I don't usually pay attention to such things, but these expenses seem to be bouncing around a lot. Over the last half year or so they have been as low as $7,400 and as high as $9,800 per month.

Kinh: Actually, that's a pretty normal variation in those expenses.

Derek: Well, we budgeted a constant $8,400 a month. Can't we do a better job of predicting what these costs are going to be? And how do we know when we've spent too much in a month? Shouldn't there be some explanation for these variations?

Kinh: Now that you mention it, we are in the process right now of tightening up our budgeting process. Our first step is to break all of our costs down into fixed and variable components.

Derek: How will that help?

Kinh: Well, that will permit us to predict what the level of costs will be. Some costs are fixed and shouldn't change much. Other costs go up and down as our activity goes up and down. The trick is to figure out what is driving the variable component of the costs.

Derek: What about the maintenance costs?

Kinh: My guess is that the variations in maintenance costs are being driven by our overall level of activity. When we treat more patients, our equipment is used more intensively, which leads to more maintenance expense.

Derek: How would you measure the level of overall activity? Would you use patient-days?

Kinh: I think so. Each day a patient is in the hospital counts as one patient-day. The greater the number of patient-days in a month, the busier we are. Besides, our budgeting is all based on projected patient-days.

Derek: Okay, so suppose you are able to break the maintenance costs down into fixed and variable components. What will that do for us?

Kinh: Basically, I will be able to predict what maintenance costs should be as a function of the number of patient-days.

Derek: I can see where that would be useful. We could use it to predict costs for budgeting purposes.

Kinh: We could also use it as a benchmark. Based on the actual number of patient-days for a period, I can predict what the maintenance costs should have been. We can compare this to the actual spending on maintenance.

Derek: Sounds good to me. Let me know when you get the results.

Diagnosing Cost Behavior with a Scattergraph Plot

Kinh Nguyen began his analysis of maintenance costs by collecting cost and activity data for a number of recent months. Those data are displayed below:

LEARNING OBJECTIVE 2
Use a scattergraph plot to diagnose cost behavior.

Month	Activity Level: Patient-Days	Maintenance Cost Incurred
January	5,600	$7,900
February	7,100	$8,500
March	5,000	$7,400
April	6,500	$8,200
May	7,300	$9,100
June	8,000	$9,800
July	6,200	$7,800

The first step in analyzing the cost and activity data should be to plot the data on a scattergraph. This plot will immediately reveal any nonlinearities or other problems with the data. The scattergraph of maintenance costs versus patient-days at Brentline Hospital is reproduced in the first panel of Exhibit 5–8. Two things should be noted about this scattergraph:

1. The total maintenance cost, Y, is plotted on the vertical axis. Cost is known as the **dependent variable,** since the amount of cost incurred during a period depends on the level of activity for the period. (That is, as the level of activity increases, total cost will also ordinarily increase.)
2. The activity, X (patient-days in this case), is plotted on the horizontal axis. Activity is known as the **independent variable,** since it causes variations in the cost.

From the scattergraph, it is evident that maintenance costs do increase with the number of patient-days. In addition, the scattergraph reveals that the relation between maintenance costs and patient-days is approximately *linear*. In other words, the points lie more or less along a straight line. Such a straight line has been drawn using a ruler in the second panel of Exhibit 5–8. Cost behavior is said to be **linear** whenever a straight line is a reasonable approximation for the relation between cost and activity. Note that the data points do not fall exactly on the straight line. This will almost always happen in practice; the relation is seldom perfectly linear.

Note that the straight line in Exhibit 5–8 has been drawn through the point representing 7,300 patient-days and a total maintenance cost of $9,100. Drawing the straight line through one of the data points allows the analyst to make a quick-and-dirty estimate of variable and fixed costs. The vertical intercept where the straight line crosses the Y axis—in this case, about $3,300—is the rough estimate of the fixed cost. The variable cost can be quickly estimated by subtracting the estimated fixed cost from the total cost at the point lying on the straight line.

Total maintenance cost for 7,300 patient-days (a point falling on the straight line)	$9,100
Less estimated fixed cost (the vertical intercept)	3,300
Estimated total variable cost for 7,300 patient-days	$5,800

EXHIBIT 5–8

Scattergraph Method of
Cost Analysis

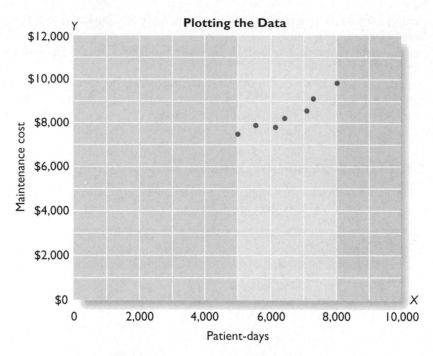

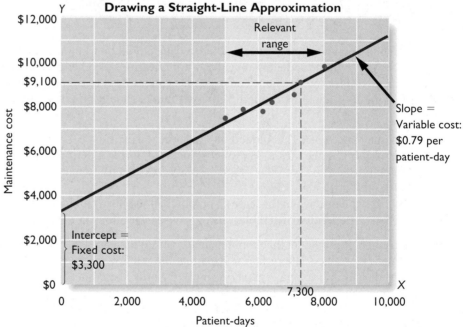

The average variable cost per unit at 7,300 patient-days is computed as follows:

$$\text{Variable cost per unit} = \$5,800 \div 7,300 \text{ patient-days}$$

$$= \$0.79 \text{ per patient-day (rounded)}$$

Combining the estimate of the fixed cost and the estimate of the variable cost per patient-day, we can write the relation between cost and activity as follows:

$$Y = \$3,300 + \$0.79X$$

where X is the number of patient-days.

EXHIBIT 5–9

More than One Relevant Range

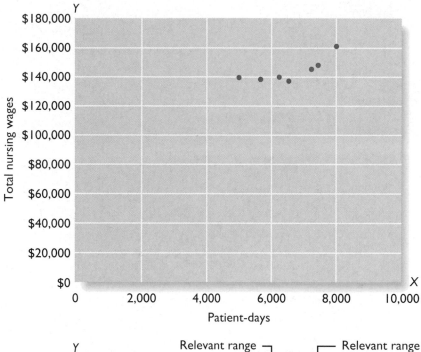

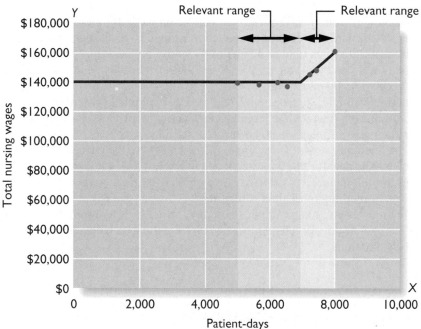

We hasten to add that this *is* a quick-and-dirty method of estimating the fixed and variable cost elements of a mixed cost; it is seldom used in practice when significant matters are at stake. However, setting aside the estimates of the fixed and variable cost elements, plotting the data on a scattergraph is an essential diagnostic step that is too often overlooked. Suppose, for example, we had been interested in the relation between total nursing wages and the number of patient-days at the hospital. The permanent, full-time nursing staff can handle up to 7,000 patient-days in a month. Beyond that level of activity, part-time nurses must be called in to help out. The cost and activity data for nurses are plotted on the scattergraph in Exhibit 5–9. Looking at that scattergraph, it is evident that two straight lines would do a much better job of fitting the data than a single straight line. Up to 7,000 patient-days, total nursing wages are essentially a fixed cost. Above 7,000 patient-days, total nursing wages are a mixed cost. This happens because, as stated above,

EXHIBIT 5–10

A Diagnostic Scattergraph Plot

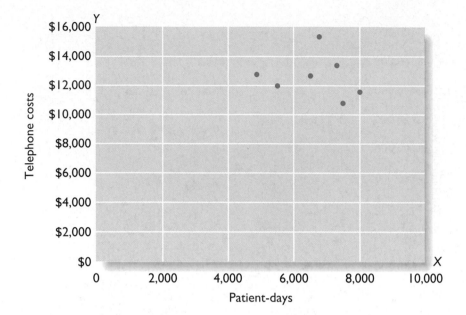

the permanent, full-time nursing staff can handle up to 7,000 patient-days in a month. Above that level, part-time nurses are called in to help, which adds to the cost. Consequently, two straight lines (and two equations) would be used to represent total nursing wages—one for the relevant range of 5,600 to 7,000 patient-days and one for the relevant range of 7,000 to 8,000 patient-days.

As another example, suppose that Brentline Hospital management is interested in the relation between the hospital's telephone costs and patient-days. Patients are billed directly for their use of telephones, so those costs do not appear on the hospital's cost records. The telephone costs of concern to management are the charges for the staff's use of telephones. The data for this cost are plotted in Exhibit 5–10. It is evident from that plot that while the telephone costs do vary from month to month, they are not related to patient-days. Something other than patient-days is driving the telephone bills. Therefore, it would not make sense to analyze this cost any further by attempting to estimate a variable cost per patient-day for telephone costs. Plotting the data helps the cost analyst to diagnose such situations.

YOU DECIDE

Choosing a Measure of Activity

You are the manager of a for-profit company that helps students prepare for standardized exams such as the SAT. You have been trying to figure out what causes variations in your monthly electrical costs. Electricity is used primarily to run office equipment such as personal computers and to provide lighting for the business office and for classrooms. Below are scattergraphs that show monthly electrical costs plotted against two different possible measures of activity—student-hours and classroom-hours. A student who takes a course involving 10 hours of classroom time would be counted as 10 student-hours. Each hour a classroom is used is counted as one classroom-hour, regardless of the number of students in the classroom at the time.

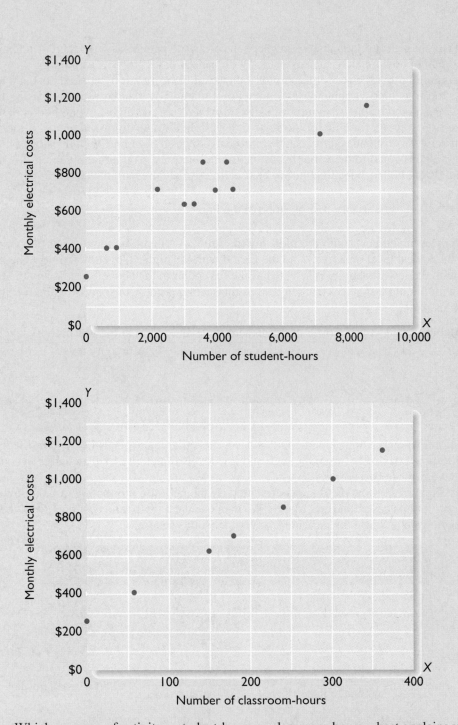

Which measure of activity—student-hours or classroom-hours—best explains variations in monthly electrical costs and should therefore be used to estimate its variable cost component?

The High-Low Method

In addition to the quick-and-dirty method described in the preceding section, more precise methods are available for estimating fixed and variable costs. However, it must be emphasized that fixed and variable costs should be computed only if a scattergraph plot confirms that the relation is approximately linear. In the case of maintenance costs at Brentline Hospital, the relation does appear to be linear. In the case of telephone costs,

LEARNING OBJECTIVE 3

Analyze a mixed cost using the high-low method.

there isn't any clear relation between telephone costs and patient-days, so there is no point in estimating how much of the cost varies with patient-days.

Assuming that the scattergraph plot indicates a linear relation between cost and activity, the fixed and variable cost elements of a mixed cost can be estimated using the *high-low method* or the *least-squares regression method*. The high-low method is based on the rise-over-run formula for the slope of a straight line. As discussed above, if the relation between cost and activity can be represented by a straight line, then the slope of the straight line is equal to the variable cost per unit of activity. Consequently, the following formula from high school algebra can be used to estimate the variable cost.

$$\text{Variable cost} = \text{Slope of the line} = \frac{\text{Rise}}{\text{Run}} = \frac{Y_2 - Y_1}{X_2 - X_1}$$

To analyze mixed costs with the **high-low method,** you begin by identifying the period with the lowest level of activity and the period with the highest level of activity. The period with the lowest activity is selected as the first point in the above formula and the period with the highest activity is selected as the second point. Consequently, the formula becomes:

$$\frac{\text{Variable}}{\text{cost}} = \frac{Y_2 - Y_1}{X_2 - X_1} = \frac{\text{Cost at the high activity level} - \text{Cost at the low activity level}}{\text{High activity level} - \text{Low activity level}}$$

or

$$\text{Variable cost} = \frac{\text{Change in cost}}{\text{Change in activity}}$$

Therefore, when the high-low method is used, the variable cost is estimated by dividing the difference in cost between the high and low levels of activity by the change in activity between those two points.

Using the high-low method, we first identify the periods with the highest and lowest *activity*—in this case, June and March. We then use the activity and cost data from these two periods to estimate the variable cost component as follows:

	Patient-Days	Maintenance Cost Incurred
High activity level (June)........	8,000	$9,800
Low activity level (March)	5,000	7,400
Change	3,000	$2,400

$$\text{Variable cost} = \frac{\text{Change in cost}}{\text{Change in activity}} = \frac{\$2,400}{3,000 \text{ patient-days}} = \$0.80 \text{ per patient-day}$$

Having determined that the variable rate for maintenance cost is 80 cents per patient-day, we can now determine the amount of fixed cost. This is done by taking total cost at *either* the high or the low activity level and deducting the variable cost element. In the computation below, total cost at the high activity level is used in computing the fixed cost element:

Fixed cost element = Total cost − Variable cost element

= $9,800 − ($0.80 per patient-day × 8,000 patient-days)

= $3,400

Both the variable and fixed cost elements have now been isolated. The cost of maintenance can be expressed as $3,400 per month plus 80 cents per patient-day.

The cost of maintenance can also be expressed in terms of the equation for a straight line as follows:

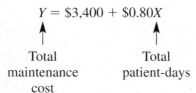

$$Y = \$3{,}400 + \$0.80X$$

Total
maintenance
cost

Total
patient-days

The data used in this illustration are shown graphically in Exhibit 5–11. Notice that a straight line has been drawn through the points corresponding to the low and high levels of activity. In essence, that is what the high-low method does—it draws a straight line through those two points.

Sometimes the high and low levels of activity don't coincide with the high and low amounts of cost. For example, the period that has the highest level of activity may not have the highest amount of cost. Nevertheless, the highest and lowest levels of *activity* are always used to analyze a mixed cost under the high-low method. The reason is that the analyst would like to use data that reflect the greatest possible variation in activity.

The high-low method is very simple to apply, but it suffers from a major (and sometimes critical) defect—it utilizes only two data points. Generally, two points are not enough to produce accurate results in cost analysis work. Additionally, periods in which the activity level is unusually low or unusually high will tend to produce inaccurate results. A cost formula that is estimated solely using data from these unusual periods may seriously misrepresent the true cost relationship that holds during normal periods. Such a distortion is evident in Exhibit 5–11. The straight line should probably be shifted down somewhat so that it is closer to more of the data points. For these reasons, other methods of cost analysis that utilize a greater number of points will generally be more accurate than the high-low method. If a manager chooses to use the high-low method, he or she should do so with a full awareness of the method's limitations.

Fortunately, modern computer software makes it very easy to use sophisticated statistical methods, such as *least-squares regression,* that use all of the data and that are capable of providing much more information than just the estimates of variable and fixed

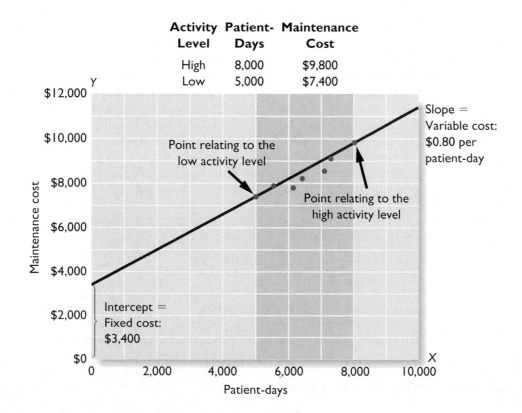

EXHIBIT 5–11

High-Low Method of Cost Analysis

Activity Level	Patient-Days	Maintenance Cost
High	8,000	$9,800
Low	5,000	$7,400

EXHIBIT 5–12

The Concept of Least-Squares
Regression

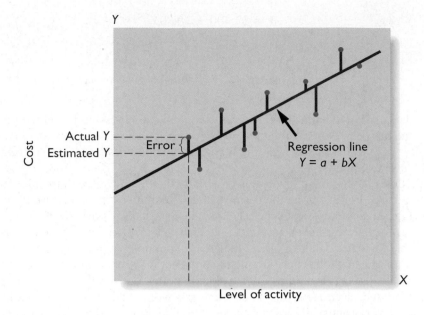

costs. The details of these statistical methods are beyond the scope of this text, but the basic approach is discussed below. Nevertheless, even if the least-squares regression approach is used, it is always a good idea to plot the data in a scattergraph. By simply looking at the scattergraph, you can quickly verify whether it makes sense to fit a straight line to the data using least-squares regression or some other method.

The Least-Squares Regression Method

The **least-squares regression method** is a method of separating a mixed cost into its fixed and variable components that, unlike the high-low method, uses all of the data. A *regression line* of the form $Y = a + bX$ is fitted to the data, where a represents the total fixed cost and b represents the variable cost per unit of activity. The basic idea underlying the least-squares regression method is illustrated in Exhibit 5–12 using hypothetical data points. Notice from the exhibit that the deviations from the plotted points to the regression line are measured vertically on the graph. These vertical deviations are called the regression errors and are the key to understanding what least-squares regression does. There is nothing mysterious about the least-squares regression method. It simply computes the regression line that minimizes the sum of these squared errors. The formulas that accomplish this are fairly complex and involve numerous calculations, but the principle is simple.

Fortunately, computers are adept at carrying out the computations required by the least-squares regression formulas. The data—the observed values of X and Y—are entered into the computer, and software does the rest. In the case of the Brentline Hospital maintenance cost data, we used a statistical software package on a personal computer to calculate the following least-squares regression estimates of the total fixed cost (a) and the variable cost per unit of activity (b):

$$a = \$3,431$$

$$b = \$0.759$$

Therefore, using the least-squares regression method, the fixed element of the maintenance cost is \$3,431 per month and the variable portion is 75.9 cents per patient-day.

In terms of the linear equation $Y = a + bX$, the cost formula can be written as

$$Y = \$3,431 + \$0.759X$$

where activity (X) is expressed in patient-days.

3. Assume a hotel rented 400, 480, and 420 rooms in the months of April, May, and June, respectively; and the total housekeeping costs for the three months in question were $6,000, $6,800, and $6,200. Using the high-low method, what is the amount of monthly fixed housekeeping costs?
   a. $1,000
   b. $1,500
   c. $2,000
   d. $2,500

CONCEPT CHECK ✓

Managing Power Consumption

IN BUSINESS

The Tata Iron Steel Company Ltd. is one of the largest companies in India. The company is faced with frequent power shortages and must carefully manage its power consumption—allocating scarce power to the most profitable uses. Estimating the power requirements of each processing station in the steel mill was the first step in building a model to better manage power consumption. Management used simple least-squares regression to estimate the fixed and variable components of the power load. Total power consumption was the dependent variable and tons of steel processed was the independent variable. The fixed component estimated from the least-squares regression was the fixed power consumption (in KWHs) per month and the variable component was the power consumption (again in KWHs) per ton of steel processed.

Source: "How Tata Steel Optimized Its Results," *The Management Accountant* (India), May 1996, pp. 372–376.

After completing the analysis of maintenance costs, Kinh Nguyen met with Dr. Derek Chalmers to discuss the results.

MANAGERIAL ACCOUNTING IN ACTION
BRENTLINE HOSPITAL
The Wrap-Up

Kinh: We used least-squares regression analysis to estimate the fixed and variable components of maintenance costs. According to the results, the fixed cost per month is $3,431 and the variable cost per patient-day is 75.9 cents.
Derek: Okay, so if we plan for 7,800 patient-days next month, what is your estimate of the maintenance costs?
Kinh: That will take just a few seconds to figure out. [Kinh wrote the following calculations on a pad of paper.]

Fixed costs.	$3,431
Variable costs:	
7,800 patient-days × $0.759 per patient-day.	5,920
Total expected maintenance costs	$9,351

Derek: Nine thousand three hundred and fifty *one* dollars; isn't that a bit *too* precise?
Kinh: Sure. I don't really believe the maintenance costs will be exactly this figure. However, based on the information we have, this is the best estimate we can come up with.
Derek: Don't let me give you a hard time. Even though it is an estimate, it will be a lot better than just guessing like we have done in the past. Thanks. I hope to see more of this kind of analysis.

THE CONTRIBUTION FORMAT

Once the manager has separated costs into fixed and variable elements, what is done with the data? We have already answered this question somewhat by showing how a cost formula can be used to predict costs. To answer this question more fully will require most of the remainder of this text, since much of what the manager does requires an understanding of cost behavior. One immediate and very significant application of the ideas we have developed, however, is found in a new income statement format known as the **contribution approach.** The unique thing about the contribution approach is that it provides the manager with an income statement geared directly to cost behavior.

Why a New Income Statement Format?

An income statement prepared using the *traditional approach,* as illustrated in Chapter 1, is not organized in terms of cost behavior. Rather, it is organized in a "functional" format—emphasizing the functions of production, administration, and sales in the classification and presentation of cost data. No attempt is made to distinguish between the behavior of costs included under each functional heading. Under the heading "Administrative expense," for example, both variable and fixed costs are lumped together.

Although an income statement prepared in the functional format may be useful for external reporting purposes, it has serious limitations when used for internal purposes. Internally, the manager needs cost data organized in a format that will facilitate planning, control, and decision making. As we shall see in chapters ahead, these tasks are much easier when cost data are available in a fixed and variable format. The contribution approach to the income statement has been developed in response to this need.

Concept 5–2

The Contribution Approach

Exhibit 5–13 illustrates the contribution approach to the income statement with a simple example, along with the traditional approach discussed in Chapter 1.

EXHIBIT 5–13   Comparison of the Contribution Income Statement with the Traditional Income Statement

Traditional Approach (costs organized by function)			Contribution Approach (costs organized by behavior)		
Sales..........................		$12,000	Sales...........................		$12,000
Less cost of goods sold..........		6,000*	Less variable expenses:		
Gross margin...................		6,000	Variable production............	$2,000	
Less operating expenses:			Variable selling...............	600	
Selling......................	$3,100*		Variable administrative	400	3,000
Administrative..............	1,900*	5,000	Contribution margin		9,000
Net operating income..........		$ 1,000			
			Less fixed expenses:		
			Fixed production..............	4,000	
			Fixed selling..................	2,500	
			Fixed administrative...........	1,500	8,000
			Net operating income............		$ 1,000

*Contains both variable and fixed expenses. This is the income statement for a manufacturing company; thus, when the income statement is placed in the contribution format, the "cost of goods sold" figure is divided between variable production costs and fixed production costs. If this were the income statement for a *merchandising* company (which simply purchases completed goods from a supplier), then the cost of goods sold would be *all* variable.

Notice that the contribution approach separates costs into fixed and variable categories, first deducting variable expenses from sales to obtain what is known as the *contribution margin*. The **contribution margin** is the amount remaining from sales revenues after variable expenses have been deducted. This amount *contributes* toward covering fixed expenses and then toward profits for the period.

The contribution approach to the income statement is used as an internal planning and decision-making tool. Its emphasis on costs by behavior facilitates cost-volume-profit analysis, such as we shall be doing in the next chapter. The approach is also very useful in appraising management performance, in segmented reporting of profit data, and in budgeting. Moreover, the contribution approach helps managers organize data pertinent to all kinds of special decisions such as product-line analysis, pricing, use of scarce resources, and make or buy analysis. All of these topics are covered in later chapters.

4. A company's contribution approach income statement showed net income, variable production expenses, and fixed expenses of $4,000, $15,000, and $10,000, respectively. How much contribution margin did the company earn?
   a. $29,000
   b. $15,000
   c. $19,000
   d. $14,000

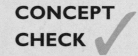
CONCEPT CHECK ✓

SUMMARY

LO1 Understand how fixed and variable costs behave and how to use them to predict costs.
A variable cost is proportional to the level of activity within the relevant range. The cost per unit of activity for a variable cost is constant as the level of activity changes.

A fixed cost is constant in total for changes of activity within the relevant range. The cost per unit of activity decreases as the level of activity increases since a constant amount is divided by a larger number.

To predict costs at a new level of activity, multiply the variable cost per unit by the new level of activity and then add to the result the constant fixed cost.

LO2 Use a scattergraph plot to diagnose cost behavior.
A scattergraph plot is an excellent means of gaining insight into the behavior of a cost. In the scattergraph, activity is plotted on the horizontal, *X,* axis and total cost is plotted on the vertical, *Y,* axis. If the relation between cost and activity appears to be linear based on the scattergraph plot, then the variable and fixed components of a mixed cost can be estimated using the quick-and-dirty method, the high-low method, or the least-squares regression method.

LO3 Analyze a mixed cost using the high-low method.
To use the high-low method, first identify the periods in which the highest and the lowest levels of activity have occurred. Second, estimate the variable cost element by dividing the change in total cost by the change in activity for these two periods. Third, estimate the fixed cost element by subtracting the total variable cost from the total cost at either the highest or the lowest level of activity.

The high-low method relies on only two, often unusual, data points rather than all of the available data and therefore may provide misleading estimates of variable and fixed costs.

LO4 Prepare an income statement using the contribution format.
Managers use costs organized by behavior in many decisions. To help managers make such decisions, the income statement can be prepared in a contribution format. The traditional income statement format emphasizes the purposes for which costs were incurred (i.e., to manufacture the product, to sell the product, or to administer the organization). In contrast, the contribution format classifies costs on the income statement by cost behavior (i.e., variable versus fixed).

GUIDANCE ANSWERS TO *DECISION MAKER* AND *YOU DECIDE*

Cost Analyst (p. 204)

Cost	Cost Behavior	Explanation
Administrative salaries	Fixed	Total administrative salaries would be unaffected by the number of guests at a wedding reception.
Rental of the central kitchen	Fixed	The cost of renting the central kitchen would be unaffected by the number of guests at a wedding reception.
Salary of the full-time chef	Fixed	The chef's salary would probably not be affected by the number of guests at a wedding reception.
Wages of part-time cooks	Variable or step-variable	More cooks must be hired to prepare meals if the number of guests increases.
Groceries and kitchen supplies	Variable	These costs should be proportional to the number of guests at a reception.
Delivery vehicle depreciation and operating expenses	Fixed or mixed	The cost of operating the vehicle may be affected if more than one trip is necessary due to the number of guests.
Wages of part-time food servers	Variable or step-variable	More food servers must be hired if the number of guests increases.
Depreciation of silverware and dinnerware	Fixed or mixed	Wear and breakage should increase with the number of guests, but not depreciation due to obsolescence.
Cleaning of table linens	Variable or step-variable	More table linens must be used if the number of guests increases.

Choosing a Measure of Activity (p. 218)

The relation between monthly electrical costs and classroom-hours seems much tighter than between monthly electrical costs and student-hours. A straight line drawn through the points on the second scatter-graph relating monthly electrical costs to classroom-hours would explain virtually all of the variation in monthly electrical costs—the fit would be almost perfect. In contrast, a straight line drawn through the first scattergraph relating monthly electrical costs to student-hours would leave a lot of unexplained variation in costs—the fit would be far from perfect. On reflection, this makes sense. The cost of lighting a classroom for an hour is the same whether the classroom contains 1 or 20 students, so if the variations in monthly electrical costs are largely due to the costs of lighting classrooms, classroom-hours would be a better measure of activity than student-hours.

GUIDANCE ANSWERS TO CONCEPT CHECKS

1. **Choice a.** Variable cost per unit is constant.
2. **Choices a and d.** The planning horizon is shorter for discretionary fixed costs relative to committed fixed costs. A mixed cost includes fixed and variable elements.
3. **Choice c.** The variable cost per room is ($6,800 − $6,000) ÷ (480 − 400) = $10. In April, the total housekeeping cost of $6,000 − (400 rooms × $10 variable cost per room) = $2,000 of fixed costs. A similar calculation can be completed for June.
4. **Choice d.** The net income of $4,000 + $10,000 of fixed expenses = Contribution margin of $14,000.

REVIEW PROBLEM I: COST BEHAVIOR

Neptune Rentals offers a boat rental service. Consider the following costs of the company over the relevant range of 5,000 to 8,000 hours of operating time for its boats:

	Hours of Operating Time			
	5,000	6,000	7,000	8,000
Total costs:				
Variable costs	$ 20,000	$?	$?	$?
Fixed costs	168,000	?	?	?
Total costs	$188,000	$?	$?	$?
Cost per hour:				
Variable cost	$?	$?	$?	$?
Fixed cost	?	?	?	?
Total cost per hour	$?	$?	$?	$?

Required:
Compute the missing amounts, assuming that cost behavior patterns remain unchanged within the relevant range of 5,000 to 8,000 hours.

Solution to Review Problem 1
The variable cost per hour can be computed as follows:

$$\$20,000 \div 5,000 \text{ hours} = \$4 \text{ per hour}$$

Therefore, in accordance with the behavior of variable and fixed costs, the missing amounts are as follows:

	Hours of Operating Time			
	5,000	6,000	7,000	8,000
Total costs:				
Variable costs	$ 20,000	$ 24,000	$ 28,000	$ 32,000
Fixed costs	168,000	168,000	168,000	168,000
Total costs	$188,000	$192,000	$196,000	$200,000
Cost per hour:				
Variable cost	$ 4.00	$ 4.00	$ 4.00	$ 4.00
Fixed cost	33.60	28.00	24.00	21.00
Total cost per hour	$37.60	$32.00	$28.00	$25.00

Observe that the total variable costs increase in proportion to the number of hours of operating time, but that these costs remain constant at $4 if expressed on a per hour basis.

In contrast, the total fixed costs do not change with changes in the level of activity. They remain constant at $168,000 within the relevant range. With increases in activity, however, the fixed costs decrease on a per hour basis, dropping from $33.60 per hour when the boats are operated 5,000 hours a period to only $21.00 per hour when the boats are operated 8,000 hours a period. *Because of this troublesome aspect of fixed costs, they are most easily (and most safely) dealt with on a total basis, rather than on a unit basis, in cost analysis work.*

REVIEW PROBLEM 2: HIGH-LOW METHOD

The administrator of Azalea Hills Hospital would like a cost formula linking the costs involved in admitting patients to the number of patients admitted during a month. The admitting department's costs and the number of patients admitted during the immediately preceding eight months are given in the following table:

Month	Number of Patients Admitted	Admitting Department Costs
May	1,800	$14,700
June	1,900	$15,200

(continued)

(concluded) Month	Number of Patients Admitted	Admitting Department Costs
July	1,700	$13,700
August	1,600	$14,000
September	1,500	$14,300
October	1,300	$13,100
November	1,100	$12,800
December	1,500	$14,600

Required:

1. Use the high-low method to establish the fixed and variable components of admitting costs.
2. Express the fixed and variable components of admitting costs as a cost formula in the linear equation form $Y = a + bX$.

Solution to Review Problem 2

1. The first step in the high-low method is to identify the periods of the lowest and highest activity. Those periods are November (1,100 patients admitted) and June (1,900 patients admitted).

    The second step is to compute the variable cost per unit using those two points:

Month	Number of Patients Admitted	Admitting Department Costs
High activity level (June)...........	1,900	$15,200
Low activity level (November)	1,100	12,800
Change	800	$ 2,400

$$\text{Variable cost} = \frac{\text{Change in cost}}{\text{Change in activity}} = \frac{\$2,400}{800 \text{ patients admitted}} = \$3 \text{ per patient admitted}$$

The third step is to compute the fixed cost element by deducting the variable cost element from the total cost at either the high or low activity. In the computation below, the high point of activity is used:

Fixed cost element = Total cost − Variable cost element

= $15,200 − ($3 per patient admitted × 1,900 patients admitted)

= $9,500

2. The cost formula expressed in the linear equation form is $Y = \$9,500 + \$3X$.

GLOSSARY

Account analysis   A method for analyzing cost behavior in which each account is classified as either variable or fixed based on the analyst's prior knowledge of how the cost in the account behaves. (p. 213)

Activity base   A measure of whatever causes the incurrence of a variable cost. For example, the total cost of X-ray film in a hospital will increase as the number of X-rays taken increases. Therefore, the number of X-rays is an activity base for explaining the total cost of X-ray film. (p. 203)

Committed fixed costs   Those fixed costs that are difficult to adjust and that relate to the investment in facilities, equipment, and the basic organizational structure of a firm. (p. 208)

Contribution approach   An income statement format that is geared to cost behavior in that costs are separated into variable and fixed categories rather than being separated according to the functions of production, sales, and administration. (p. 224)

Contribution margin   The amount remaining from sales revenues after all variable expenses have been deducted. (p. 225)

Cost structure   The relative proportion of fixed, variable, and mixed costs found within an organization. (p. 202)

Curvilinear cost   A relation between cost and activity that is a curve rather than a straight line. (p. 206)

Dependent variable   A variable that reacts or responds to some causal factor; total cost is the dependent variable, as represented by the letter Y, in the equation $Y = a + bX$. (p. 215)

Discretionary fixed costs   Those fixed costs that arise from annual decisions by management to spend in certain fixed cost areas, such as advertising and research. (p. 208)

Engineering approach   A detailed analysis of cost behavior based on an industrial engineer's evaluation of the inputs that are required to carry out a particular activity and of the prices of those inputs. (p. 213)

High-low method   A method of separating a mixed cost into its fixed and variable elements by analyzing the change in cost between the high and low levels of activity. (p. 220)

Independent variable   A variable that acts as a causal factor; activity is the independent variable, as represented by the letter X, in the equation $Y = a + bX$. (p. 215)

Least-squares regression method   A method of separating a mixed cost into its fixed and variable elements by fitting a regression line that minimizes the sum of the squared errors. (p. 222)

Linear cost behavior   Cost behavior is said to be linear when a straight line is a reasonable approximation for the relation between cost and activity. (p. 215)

Mixed cost   A cost that contains both variable and fixed cost elements. (p. 212)

Relevant range   The range of activity within which assumptions about variable and fixed cost behavior are valid. (p. 206)

Step-variable cost   The cost of a resource (such as the cost of a maintenance worker) that is obtainable only in large chunks and that increases and decreases only in response to fairly wide changes in activity. (p. 206)

QUESTIONS

5–1   Distinguish between (a) a variable cost, (b) a fixed cost, and (c) a mixed cost.

5–2   What effect does an increase in volume have on—
   a.   Unit fixed costs?
   b.   Unit variable costs?
   c.   Total fixed costs?
   d.   Total variable costs?

5–3   Define the following terms: (a) cost behavior, and (b) relevant range.

5–4   What is meant by an *activity base* when dealing with variable costs? Give several examples of activity bases.

5–5   Distinguish between (a) a variable cost, (b) a mixed cost, and (c) a step-variable cost. Chart the three costs on a graph, with activity plotted horizontally and cost plotted vertically.

5–6   Managers often assume a strictly linear relationship between cost and volume. How can this practice be defended in light of the fact that many costs are curvilinear?

5–7   Distinguish between discretionary fixed costs and committed fixed costs.

5–8   Classify the following fixed costs as normally being either committed or discretionary:
   a.   Depreciation on buildings.
   b.   Advertising.
   c.   Research.
   d.   Long-term equipment leases.
   e.   Pension payments to the firm's retirees.
   f.   Management development and training.

5–9   Does the concept of the relevant range apply to fixed costs? Explain.

5–10   What is the major disadvantage of the high-low method?

5–11   What methods are available for separating a mixed cost into its fixed and variable elements using past records of cost and activity data? Which method is considered to be most accurate? Why?

5–12   Give the general formula for a mixed cost. Which term represents the variable cost? The fixed cost?

5–13   Once a line has been drawn in the quick-and-dirty method, how does one determine the fixed cost element? The variable cost element?

5–14   What is meant by the term *least-squares regression?*

5–15   What is the difference between the contribution approach to the income statement and the traditional approach to the income statement?

5–16   What is the contribution margin?

BRIEF EXERCISES

BRIEF EXERCISE 5–1   Fixed and Variable Cost Behavior   (LO1)

Koffee Express operates a number of espresso coffee stands in busy suburban malls. The fixed weekly expense of a coffee stand is $1,100 and the variable cost per cup of coffee served is $0.26.

Required:
1. Fill in the following table with your estimates of total costs and cost per cup of coffee at the indicated levels of activity for a coffee stand. Round off the cost of a cup of coffee to the nearest tenth of a cent.

	Cups of Coffee Served in a Week		
	1,800	1,900	2,000
Fixed cost..........................	?	?	?
Variable cost.......................	?	?	?
Total cost..........................	?	?	?
Cost per cup of coffee served.........	?	?	?

2. Does the cost per cup of coffee served increase, decrease, or remain the same as the number of cups of coffee served in a week increases? Explain.

BRIEF EXERCISE 5–2   Scattergraph Analysis   (LO2)

The data below have been taken from the cost records of the Atlanta Processing Company. The data relate to the cost of operating one of the company's processing facilities at various levels of activity:

Month	Units Processed	Total Cost
January..........	8,000	$14,000
February	4,500	$10,000
March...........	7,000	$12,500
April............	9,000	$15,500
May.............	3,750	$10,000
June	6,000	$12,500
July	3,000	$8,500
August	5,000	$11,500

Required:
1. Prepare a scattergraph by plotting the above data on a graph. Plot cost on the vertical axis and activity on the horizontal axis. Fit a line to your plotted points using a ruler.
2. Using the quick-and-dirty method, what is the approximate monthly fixed cost? The approximate variable cost per unit processed? Show your computations.

BRIEF EXERCISE 5–3   High-Low Method   (LO3)

The Edelweiss Hotel in Vail, Colorado, has accumulated records of the total electrical costs of the hotel and the number of occupancy-days over the last year. An occupancy-day represents a room rented out for one day. The hotel's business is highly seasonal, with peaks occurring during the ski season and in the summer.

Month	Occupancy-Days	Electrical Costs
January..........	2,604	$6,257
February	2,856	$6,550
March...........	3,534	$7,986
April............	1,440	$4,022
May.............	540	$2,289
June	1,116	$3,591
July	3,162	$7,264
		(continued)

(concluded) Month	Occupancy-Days	Electrical Costs
August	3,608	$8,111
September	1,260	$3,707
October	186	$1,712
November	1,080	$3,321
December	2,046	$5,196

Required:

1. Using the high-low method, estimate the fixed cost of electricity per month and the variable cost of electricity per occupancy-day. Round off the fixed cost to the nearest whole dollar and the variable cost to the nearest whole cent.

2. What other factors other than occupancy-days are likely to affect the variation in electrical costs from month to month?

BRIEF EXERCISE 5–4 Contribution Format Income Statement (LO4)

Haaki Shop, Inc., is a large retailer of water sports equipment. An income statement for the company's surfboard department for a recent quarter is presented below:

THE HAAKI SHOP, INC. Income Statement—Surfboard Department For the Quarter Ended May 31		
Sales.		$800,000
Less cost of goods sold.		300,000
Gross margin.		500,000
Less operating expenses:		
Selling expenses	$250,000	
Administrative expenses.	160,000	410,000
Net operating income.		$ 90,000

The surfboards sell, on the average, for $400 each. The department's variable selling expenses are $50 per surfboard sold. The remaining selling expenses are fixed. The administrative expenses are 25% variable and 75% fixed. The company purchases its surfboards from a supplier at a cost of $150 per surfboard.

Required:

1. Prepare an income statement for the quarter using the contribution approach.
2. What was the contribution toward fixed expenses and profits from each surfboard sold during the quarter? (State this as a dollar amount per surfboard.)

EXERCISES

EXERCISE 5–5 High-Low Method; Predicting Cost (LO1, LO3)

The number of X-rays taken and X-ray costs over the last nine months in Beverly Hospital are given below:

Month	X-Rays Taken	X-Ray Costs
January.	6,250	$28,000
February	7,000	$29,000
March.	5,000	$23,000
April.	4,250	$20,000
May.	4,500	$22,000
June	3,000	$17,000
July	3,750	$18,000
August	5,500	$24,000
September	5,750	$26,000

Required:
1. Using the high-low method, estimate the cost formula for X-ray costs.
2. Using the cost formula you derived above, what X-ray costs would you expect to be incurred during a month in which 4,600 X-rays are taken?

EXERCISE 5–6   Scattergraph Analysis; High-Low Method   (LO2, LO3)
Refer to the data in Exercise 5–5.

Required:
1. Prepare a scattergraph using the data from Exercise 5–5. Plot cost on the vertical axis and activity on the horizontal axis. Using a ruler, fit a line to your plotted points.
2. Using the quick-and-dirty method, what is the approximate monthly fixed cost for X-rays? The approximate variable cost per X-ray taken?
3. Scrutinize the points on your graph, and explain why the high-low method would or would not yield an accurate cost formula in this situation.

EXERCISE 5–7   High-Low Method; Scattergraph Analysis   (LO2, LO3)
Zerbel Company, a wholesaler of large, custom-built air conditioning units for commercial buildings, has noticed considerable fluctuation in its shipping expense from month to month, as shown below:

Month	Units Shipped	Total Shipping Expense
January	4	$2,200
February	7	$3,100
March	5	$2,600
April	2	$1,500
May	3	$2,200
June	6	$3,000
July	8	$3,600

Required:
1. Using the high-low method, estimate the cost formula for shipping expense.
2. The president has no confidence in the high-low method and would like you to "check out" your results using the scattergraph method. Do the following:
   a. Prepare a scattergraph, using the data given above. Plot cost on the vertical axis and activity on the horizontal axis. Fit a straight line to your plotted points using a ruler.
   b. Using your scattergraph, estimate the approximate variable cost per unit shipped and the approximate fixed cost per month with the quick-and-dirty method.
3. What factors, other than the number of units shipped, are likely to affect the company's shipping expense? Explain.

EXERCISE 5–8   Cost Behavior; High-Low Method   (LO1, LO3)
Speedy Parcel Service operates a fleet of delivery trucks in a large metropolitan area. A careful study by the company's cost analyst has determined that if a truck is driven 120,000 miles during a year, the average operating cost is 11.6 cents per mile. If a truck is driven only 80,000 miles during a year, the average operating cost increases to 13.6 cents per mile.

Required:
1. Using the high-low method, estimate the variable and fixed cost elements of the annual cost of truck operation.
2. Express the variable and fixed costs in the form $Y = a + bX$.
3. If a truck were driven 100,000 miles during a year, what total cost would you expect to be incurred?

EXERCISE 5–9   Cost Behavior; Contribution Income Statement   (LO1, LO4)
Parker Company manufactures and sells a single product. A partially completed schedule of the company's total and per unit costs over a relevant range of 60,000 to 100,000 units produced and sold each year is given below:

	Units Produced and Sold		
	60,000	80,000	100,000
Total costs:			
Variable costs............	$150,000	?	?
Fixed costs.............	360,000	?	?
Total costs.............	$510,000	?	?
Cost per unit:			
Variable cost.............	?	?	?
Fixed cost...............	?	?	?
Total cost per unit.........	?	?	?

Required:
1. Complete the schedule of the company's total and unit costs above.
2. Assume that the company produces and sells 90,000 units during a year. The selling price is $7.50 per unit. Prepare an income statement in the contribution format for the year.

PROBLEMS

PROBLEM 5–10   High-Low Method and Predicting Cost   (LO1, LO3)

Black Forest Clinic contains 340 beds. The average occupancy rate is 85% per month. In other words, an average of 85% of the clinic's beds are occupied by patients. At this level of occupancy, the clinic's operating costs are $40 per occupied bed per day, assuming a 30-day month. This $40 cost contains both variable and fixed cost elements.

During November, the clinic's occupancy rate was only 70%. A total of $339,150 in operating cost was incurred during the month.

Required:
1. Using the high-low method, estimate:
   a.   The variable cost per occupied bed on a daily basis.
   b.   The total fixed operating costs per month.
2. Assume an occupancy rate of 80% per month. What amount of total operating cost would you expect the clinic to incur?

PROBLEM 5–11   Contribution Format Income Statement   (LO4)

The Fun Store, Inc., purchases very large and heavy toys from a manufacturer and sells them at the retail level. The toys cost, on the average, $9 each from the manufacturer. The Fun Store, Inc., sells the toys to its customers at an average price of $40 each. Because of their size and weight, the toys must be delivered to customers. The selling and administrative costs that the company incurs in a typical month are presented below:

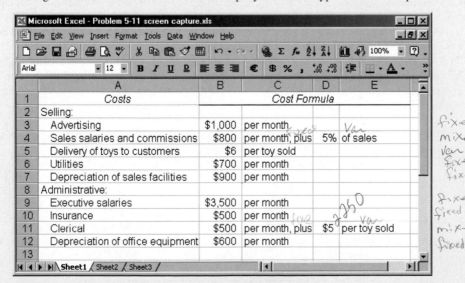

	A	B	C	D	E
1	*Costs*		*Cost Formula*		
2	Selling:				
3	Advertising	$1,000	per month		
4	Sales salaries and commissions	$800	per month, plus	5%	of sales
5	Delivery of toys to customers	$6	per toy sold		
6	Utilities	$700	per month		
7	Depreciation of sales facilities	$900	per month		
8	Administrative:				
9	Executive salaries	$3,500	per month		
10	Insurance	$500	per month		
11	Clerical	$500	per month, plus	$5	per toy sold
12	Depreciation of office equipment	$600	per month		
13					

During October, The Fun Store, Inc., sold and delivered 450 toys.

Required:

1. Prepare an income statement for The Fun Store, Inc., for October. Use the traditional format, with costs organized by function.
2. Redo (1) above, this time using the contribution format, with costs organized by behavior. Show costs and revenues on both total and a per unit basis down through contribution margin.
3. Refer to the income statement you prepared in (2) above. Why might it be misleading to show the fixed costs on a per unit basis?

PROBLEM 5–12   Scattergraph Analysis   (LO2)

Chuan Meng & Co. is a popular Chinese restaurant that owns and maintains a small fleet of motorbikes for its delivery service. All expenses of operating these motorbikes have been entered into a Motorbike Expense account on the company's books. Along with this record of expenses, the company has also kept a careful record of the number of miles the motorbikes have been driven each month.

The company's records of miles driven and total motorbike expenses over the past 10 months are given below:

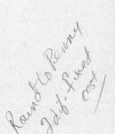

Month	Total Mileage	Total Cost
March	3,000	$1,725
April	2,500	$1,700
May	4,500	$1,820
June	1,000	$1,650
July	5,000	$2,000
August	4,000	$1,900
September	3,500	$1,815
October	1,500	$1,590
November	5,500	$1,935
December	2,000	$1,720

The company's president wants to know the cost of operating the fleet of motorbikes in terms of the fixed monthly cost and the variable cost per mile driven.

Required:

1. Prepare a scattergraph using the data given above. Place cost on the vertical axis and activity (miles driven) on the horizontal axis. Fit a straight line to the plotted points by simple visual inspection.
2. By analyzing your scattergraph, estimate fixed cost per month and the variable cost per mile driven.

CHECK FIGURE
(1) $4,590 per month plus
    $29.00 per scan

PROBLEM 5–13   High-Low and Scattergraph Analysis   (LO2, LO3)

Sinai Cedars Hospital of San Francisco has just hired a new chief administrator who is anxious to employ sound management and planning techniques in the business affairs of the hospital. Accordingly, she has directed her assistant to summarize the cost structure existing in the various departments so that data will be available for planning purposes.

The assistant is unsure how to classify the utilities costs in the Radiology Department since these costs do not exhibit either strictly variable or fixed cost behavior. Utilities costs are very high in the department due to a CAT scanner that draws a large amount of power and that is kept running at all times. The scanner can't be turned off due to the long warm-up period required for its use. When the CAT scanner is used to scan a patient, it consumes an additional burst of power. The assistant has accumulated the following data on the utilities costs and use of the CAT scanner since the first of the year.

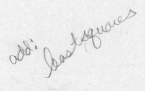

Month	Number of Scans	Utilities Cost
January	20	$5,000
February	50	$6,000
March	80	$7,000
April	60	$6,450
May	100	$7,490
June	70	$6,500

(continued)

(concluded) Month	Number of Scans	Utilities Cost
July	30	$5,500
August	10	$4,880
September	40	$5,550
October.	90	$7,000

The chief administrator has informed her assistant that the cost is probably a mixed cost that will have to be broken down into its variable and fixed cost elements using a scattergraph. The assistant feels, however, that if an analysis of this type is necessary, then the high-low method should be used, since it is easier and quicker. The controller has suggested that there may be a better approach.

Required:
1. Using the high-low method, estimate a cost formula for utilities. Express the formula in the form $Y = a + bX$. (The variable rate should be stated in terms of cost per scan.)
2. Prepare a scattergraph by plotting the above data on a graph. (The number of scans should be placed on the horizontal axis, and utilities cost should be placed on the vertical axis.) Fit a straight line to the plotted points by visual inspection and estimate a cost formula for utilities.

PROBLEM 5–14   Cost Behavior; High-Low Analysis; Contribution Format Income Statement (LO1, LO3, LO4)

Compania Maritima S.A., of Santiago de Chile, is a merchandising firm that supplies a variety of American products to the Chilean market. The company's income statements for the three most recent months follow:

CHECK FIGURE
(2) Shipping: P9,000 per month plus P9.00 per unit

COMPANIA MARITIMA S.A. Income Statements For the Three Months Ending June 30			
	April	May	June
Sales in units	6,500	7,400	7,000
Sales revenue.	P260,000	P296,000	P280,000
Less cost of goods sold.	78,000	88,800	84,000
Gross margin.	182,000	207,200	196,000
Less operating expenses:			
Advertising expense	5,000	5,000	5,000
Shipping expense.	67,500	75,600	72,000
Salaries and commissions . . .	30,800	34,400	32,800
Insurance expense	4,000	4,000	4,000
Depreciation expense.	2,500	2,500	2,500
Total operating expenses	109,800	121,500	116,300
Net operating income.	P 72,200	P 85,700	P 79,700

(Note: Compania Maritima S.A.'s Chilean-formatted income statement has been recast in the format common in the United States. The Chilean dollar is denoted by P.)

Required:
1. Identify each of the company's expenses (including cost of goods sold) as either a variable, fixed, or mixed cost.
2. Using the high-low method, separate each mixed expense into variable and fixed elements. State the cost formula for each mixed expense.
3. Redo the company's income statement at the 7,000-unit level of activity using the contribution format.

PROBLEM 5–15   Identifying Cost Behavior Patterns   (LO1)

A number of graphs displaying cost behavior patterns that might be found in a company's cost structure are shown below. The vertical axis on each graph represents total cost and the horizontal axis represents the level of activity.

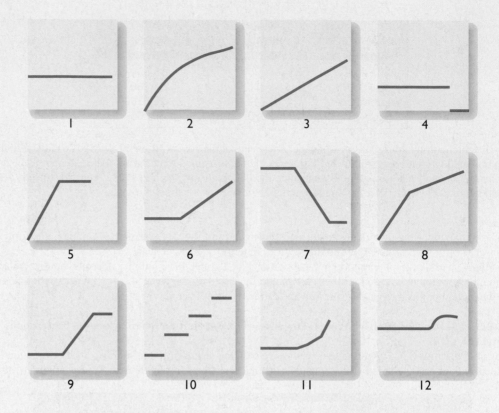

Required:

1. For each of the following situations, identify the accompanying graph that illustrates the cost pattern involved. Any graph may be used more than once.

   a. Salaries of maintenance workers, where one maintenance worker is needed for every 1,200 hours of machine-hours or less (that is, 0 to 1,200 hours requires one maintenance worker, 1,201 to 2,400 hours requires two maintenance workers, etc.).

   b. Rent on a factory building donated by the city, where the agreement calls for a fixed fee payment unless 120,000 labor-hours or more are worked, in which case no rent need be paid.

   c. Electricity bill—a flat fixed charge, plus a variable cost after a certain number of kilowatt-hours are used.

   d. Depreciation of equipment, where the amount is computed by the straight-line method. When the depreciation rate was established, it was anticipated that the obsolescence factor would be greater than the wear-and-tear factor.

   e. Use of a machine under a lease, where a minimum charge of $5,000 is paid for up to 1,000 hours of machine time. After 1,000 hours of machine time, an additional charge of $3 per hour is paid up to a maximum charge of $7,000 per period.

   f. Cost of raw materials, where the cost starts at $9 per unit and then decreases by 5 cents per unit for each of the first 100 units purchased, after which it remains constant at $6 per unit.

   g. City water bill, which is computed as follows:

First 500,000 gallons or less	$750 flat fee
Next 8,000 gallons.	$0.005 per gallon used
Next 8,000 gallons.	$0.010 per gallon used
Next 8,000 gallons.	$0.015 per gallon used
Etc.	Etc.

   h. Cost of raw materials used.

   i. Rent on a factory building donated by the county, where the agreement calls for rent of $230,000 less $1 for each direct labor-hour worked in excess of 90,000 hours, but a minimum rental payment of $45,000 must be paid.

2. How would a knowledge of cost behavior patterns such as those above be of help to a manager in analyzing the cost structure of his or her firm?

(CPA, adapted)

PROBLEM 5–16   High-Low Analysis and Cost Behavior   (LO1, LO3)

Susumi Corporation of Japan is a manufacturing company whose total factory overhead costs fluctuate considerably from year to year according to increases and decreases in the number of direct labor-hours worked in the factory. Total factory overhead costs (in Japanese yen, denoted by ¥) at high and low levels of activity for recent years are given below:

	Level of Activity	
	Low	High
Direct labor-hours	4,000	5,000
Total factory overhead costs	¥15,250,000	¥17,625,000

The factory overhead costs above consist of indirect materials, rent, and maintenance. The company has analyzed these costs at the 4,000-hour level of activity as follows:

Indirect materials (V)......................	¥ 8,000,000
Rent (F)	5,000,000
Maintenance (M)	2,250,000
Total factory overhead costs................	¥15,250,000

V = variable; F = fixed; M = mixed.

To have data available for planning, the company wants to break down the maintenance cost into its variable and fixed cost elements.

Required:
1. Estimate how much of the ¥17,625,000 factory overhead cost at the high level of activity consists of maintenance cost. (Hint: To do this, it may be helpful to first determine how much of the ¥17,625,000 consists of indirect materials and rent. Think about the behavior of variable and fixed costs!)
2. Using the high-low method of cost analysis, estimate a cost formula for maintenance.
3. What total factory overhead costs would you expect the company to incur at an operating level of 4,800 direct labor-hours?

PROBLEM 5–17   High-Low Analysis and Predicting Cost   (LO1, LO3)

Prospero Corporation's total overhead costs at various levels of activity are presented below:

Month	Machine-Hours	Total Overhead Costs
August...........	10,000	$99,500
September	15,000	$119,000
October	20,000	$138,500
November	5,000	$80,000

Assume that the total overhead costs above consist of utilities, supervisory salaries, and maintenance. The breakdown of these costs at the 5,000 machine-hour level of activity is:

Utilities (V)	$12,000
Supervisory salaries (F).......	13,000
Maintenance (M).............	55,000
Total overhead costs.........	$80,000

V = variable; F = fixed; M = mixed.

Prospero Corporation's management wants to break down the maintenance cost into its basic variable and fixed cost elements.

Required:
1. As shown above, overhead costs in October amounted to $138,500. Determine how much of this consisted of maintenance cost. (Hint: To do this, it may be helpful to first determine how much of

the $138,500 consisted of utilities and supervisory salaries. Think about the behavior of variable and fixed costs!)

2. Using the high-low method, estimate a cost formula for maintenance.
3. Express the company's *total* overhead costs in the linear equation form $Y = a + bX$.
4. What *total* overhead costs would you expect to be incurred at an operating activity level of 17,000 machine-hours?

CHECK FIGURE
(2) $83,000 per month plus
    $2.00 per unit

PROBLEM 5–18   High-Low Analysis; Cost of Goods Manufactured   (LO1, LO3)

Carlyle Company manufactures a single product. The company keeps careful records of manufacturing activities from which the following information has been extracted:

	Level of Activity	
	January—Low	**April—High**
Number of units produced..............	12,000	15,000
Cost of goods manufactured	$250,000	$300,000
Work in process inventory, beginning.......	$5,000	$16,000
Work in process inventory, ending.........	$6,000	$9,000
Direct materials cost per unit.............	$4	$4
Direct labor cost per unit................	$8	$8
Manufacturing overhead cost, total.........	?	?

The company's manufacturing overhead cost consists of both variable and fixed cost elements. To have data available for planning, management wants to determine how much of the overhead cost is variable with units produced and how much of it is fixed per month.

Required:
1. For both January and April, determine the amount of manufacturing overhead cost added to production. The company had no under- or overapplied overhead in either month. (Hint: A useful way to proceed might be to construct a schedule of cost of goods manufactured.)
2. Using the high-low method of cost analysis, estimate a cost formula for manufacturing overhead. Express the variable portion of the formula in terms of a variable rate per unit of product.
3. If 13,500 units are produced during a month, what would be the cost of goods manufactured? (Assume that work in process inventories do not change and that overhead cost is neither under- nor overapplied for the month.)

BUILDING YOUR SKILLS

ANALYTICAL THINKING CASE   (LO2)

Mapleleaf Sweepers of Toronto manufactures replacement rotary sweeper brooms for the large sweeper trucks that clear leaves and snow from city streets. The business is to some degree seasonal, with the largest demand during and just preceding the fall and winter months. Since there are so many different kinds of sweeper brooms used by its customers, Mapleleaf Sweepers makes all of its brooms to order.

The company has been analyzing its overhead accounts to determine fixed and variable components for planning purposes. Below are data for the company's janitorial labor costs over the last nine months. (Cost data are in Canadian dollars.)

	Number of Units Produced	Number of Janitorial Workdays	Janitorial Labor Cost
January	115	21	$3,840
February........	109	19	$3,648
March	102	23	$4,128
April	76	20	$3,456
May	69	23	$4,320
June............	108	22	$4,032
July	77	16	$2,784
August	71	14	$2,688
September	127	21	$3,840

The number of workdays varies from month to month due to the number of weekdays, holidays, days of vacation, and sick leave taken in the month. The number of units produced in a month varies depending on demand and the number of workdays in the month.

There are two janitors who each work an eight-hour shift each workday. They each can take up to 10 days of paid sick leave each year. Their wages on days they call in sick and their wages during paid vacations are charged to miscellaneous overhead rather than to the janitorial labor cost account.

Required:
1. Prepare a scattergraph and plot the janitorial labor cost and units produced. (Place cost on the vertical axis and units produced on the horizontal axis.)
2. Prepare a scattergraph and plot the janitorial labor cost and number of workdays. (Place cost on the vertical axis and the number of workdays on the horizontal axis.)
3. Which measure of activity—number of units produced or janitorial workdays—should be used as the activity base for explaining janitorial labor cost?

COMMUNICATING IN PRACTICE   (LO1, LO4)

Jasmine Lee owns a catering company that serves food and beverages at parties and business functions. Lee's business is seasonal, with a heavy schedule during the summer months and holidays and a lighter schedule at other times.

One of the major events requested by Lee's customers is a cocktail party. She offers a standard cocktail party and has estimated the total cost per guest as follows:

Food and beverages	$17.00
Labor (0.5 hour @ $10.00 per hour)	5.00
Overhead (0.5 hour @ $18.63 per hour)	9.32
Total cost per guest	$31.32

The standard cocktail party lasts three hours and Lee hires one worker for every six guests, which is one-half hour of labor per guest. These workers are hired only as needed and are paid only for the hours they actually work.

Lee ordinarily charges $45 per guest. She is confident about her estimates of the costs of foods and beverages and labor, but is not as comfortable with the estimate of overhead cost. The $18.63 overhead cost per labor-hour was determined by dividing the total overhead expenses for the last 12 months by the total labor-hours for the same period. Her overhead includes costs such as the annual rent for office space, administrative salaries, the costs of hiring and writing paychecks for temporary workers, and so on.

Lee has received a request to bid on a large fund-raising cocktail party to be given next month by an important local charity. (The party would last the usual three hours.) She would really like to win this contract—the guest list for this charity event includes many prominent individuals she would like to land as future clients. Other caterers have been invited to bid on the event, and she believes that one, if not more, of those companies will bid less than $45 per guest. She is not willing to lose money on the event and would like your input before making any decisions.

Required:
Write a memo to Ms. Lee that addresses her concern about the estimate of overhead costs and whether or not she should base her bid on the estimated cost of $31.32 per guest. (Hint: Start by discussing the need to consider cost behavior when estimating costs. You can assume that she will not incur any additional fixed costs if she wins the bid on the cocktail party.)   (CMA, adapted)

TEAMWORK IN ACTION   (LO1)

Assume that your team is going to form a company that will manufacture chocolate chip cookies. The team is responsible for preparing a list of all product components and costs necessary to make this product.

Required:
Prepare a list of all product components and costs necessary to manufacture your cookies and identify each of the product costs as direct materials, direct labor, or factory overhead. Identify each of those costs as variable, fixed, or mixed.

TAKING IT TO THE NET

As you know, the World Wide Web is a medium that is constantly evolving. Sites come and go, and change without notice. To enable periodic update of site addresses, this problem has been posted to the textbook website (www.mhhe.com/bgn2e). After accessing the site, enter the Student Center and select this chapter. Select and complete the Taking It to the Net problem.

Cost-Volume-Profit Relationships

DECISION FEATURE

Forget the Theater—Make Money on Cable TV

"Several years ago, Hollywood experienced a phenomenon known as the 'straight-to-cable' era. What this phrase referred to was a well used (and abused!) movie-making principle that hinted that if any-one (and many times it really was just *anyone*) could produce a movie (quality was never an issue) for under a million dollars, it'd automatically turn a profit from the sale of its cable TV rights. In essence, the 'movie' would bypass the theaters all together [sic] and still turn a profit. From a business stand-point, what this money-making scheme illustrates is [that] every product has a break-even point. Make more money than this and you turn a profit. Make less than this, and, well, you get the picture (pardon the pun)."

Source: Ben Chiu, "The Last Big-Budget Combat Sim," *Computer Games*, June 1999, p. 40.

LEARNING OBJECTIVES

After studying Chapter 6, you should be able to:

LO1 Explain how changes in activity affect contribution margin and net operating income.

LO2 Prepare and interpret a cost-volume-profit (CVP) graph.

LO3 Use the contribution margin ratio (CM ratio) to compute changes in contribution margin and net operating income resulting from changes in sales volume.

LO4 Show the effects on contribution margin of changes in variable costs, fixed costs, selling price, and volume.

LO5 Compute the break-even point.

LO6 Determine the level of sales needed to achieve a desired target profit.

LO7 Compute the margin of safety and explain its significance.

LO8 Compute the degree of operating leverage at a particular level of sales and explain how the degree of operating leverage can be used to predict changes in net operating income.

LO9 Compute the break-even point for a multiple product company and explain the effects of shifts in the sales mix on contribution margin and the break-even point.

Cost-volume-profit (CVP) analysis is one of the most powerful tools that managers have at their command. It helps them understand the relationships among cost, volume, and profit in an organization by focusing on interactions between the following five elements:

1. Prices of products.
2. Volume or level of activity.
3. Per unit variable costs.
4. Total fixed costs.
5. Mix of products sold.

Because CVP analysis helps managers understand the relationships among cost, volume, and profit, it is a vital tool in many business decisions. These decisions include what products to manufacture or sell, what pricing policy to follow, what marketing strategy to employ, and what type of production facilities to acquire. To help understand the role of CVP analysis in business decisions, consider the case of Acoustic Concepts, Inc., a company founded by Prem Narayan.

MANAGERIAL ACCOUNTING IN ACTION

The Issue

Acoustic Concepts, Inc.

Prem, who was a graduate student in engineering at the time, started Acoustic Concepts to market a radically new speaker he had designed for automobile sound systems. The speaker, called the Sonic Blaster, uses an advanced microprocessor to boost amplification to awesome levels. Prem contracted with a Taiwanese electronics manufacturer to produce the speaker. With seed money provided by his family, Prem placed an order with the manufacturer and ran advertisements in auto magazines.

The Sonic Blaster was an almost immediate success, and sales grew to the point that Prem moved the company's headquarters out of his apartment and into rented quarters in a nearby industrial park. He also hired a receptionist, an accountant, a sales manager, and a small sales staff to sell the speakers to retail stores. The accountant, Bob Luchinni, had worked for several small companies where he had acted as a business advisor as well as accountant and bookkeeper. The following discussion occurred soon after Bob was hired:

Prem: Bob, I've got a lot of questions about the company's finances that I hope you can help answer.

Bob: We're in great shape. The loan from your family will be paid off within a few months.

Prem: I know, but I am worried about the risks I've assumed by expanding operations. What would happen if a competitor entered the market and our sales slipped? How far could sales drop without putting us into the red? Another question I've been trying to resolve is how much our sales would have to increase to justify the big marketing campaign the sales staff is pushing for.

Bob: Marketing always wants more money for advertising.

Prem: And they are always pushing me to drop the selling price on the speaker. I agree with them that a lower price will boost our volume, but I'm not sure the increased volume will offset the loss in revenue from the lower price.

Bob: It sounds like these questions all are related in some way to the relationships between our selling prices, our costs, and our volume. We shouldn't have a problem coming up with some answers. I'll need a day or two, though, to gather some data.

Prem: Why don't we set up a meeting for three days from now? That would be Thursday.

Bob: That'll be fine. I'll have some preliminary answers for you as well as a model you can use for answering similar questions in the future.

Prem: Good. I'll be looking forward to seeing what you come up with.

THE BASICS OF COST-VOLUME-PROFIT (CVP) ANALYSIS

Bob Luchinni's preparation for the Thursday meeting begins where our study of cost behavior in the preceding chapter left off—with the contribution income statement. The contribution income statement emphasizes the behavior of costs and therefore is extremely helpful to a manager in judging the impact on profits of changes in selling price, cost, or volume. Bob will base his analysis on the following contribution income statement he prepared last month:

ACOUSTIC CONCEPTS, INC. Contribution Income Statement For the Month of June		
	Total	**Per Unit**
Sales (400 speakers)	$100,000	$250
Less variable expenses	60,000	150
Contribution margin.	40,000	$100
Less fixed expenses	35,000	
Net operating income	$ 5,000	

Notice that sales, variable expenses, and contribution margin are expressed on a per unit basis as well as in total on this contribution income statement. The per unit figures will be very helpful in the work we will be doing in the following pages. Note that this contribution income statement has been prepared for management's use inside the company and would not ordinarily be made available to those outside the company.

Contribution Margin

As explained in the previous chapter, contribution margin is the amount remaining from sales revenue after variable expenses have been deducted. Thus, it is the amount available to cover fixed expenses and then to provide profits for the period. Notice the sequence here—contribution margin is used *first* to cover the fixed expenses, and then whatever remains goes toward profits. If the contribution margin is not sufficient to cover the fixed expenses, then a loss occurs for the period. To illustrate with an extreme example, assume that Acoustic Concepts sells only one speaker during a particular month. Then the company's income statement will appear as follows:

LEARNING OBJECTIVE 1

Explain how changes in activity affect contribution margin and net operating income.

	Total	**Per Unit**
Sales (1 speaker)	$ 250	$250
Less variable expenses	150	150
Contribution margin	100	$100
Less fixed expenses.	35,000	
Net operating loss.	$(34,900)	

For each additional speaker that the company is able to sell during the month, $100 more in contribution margin will become available to help cover the fixed expenses. If a second speaker is sold, for example, then the total contribution margin will increase by $100 (to a total of $200) and the company's loss will decrease by $100, to $34,800:

	Total	Per Unit
Sales (2 speakers)	$ 500	$250
Less variable expenses	300	150
Contribution margin	200	$100
Less fixed expenses	35,000	
Net operating loss	$(34,800)	

If enough speakers can be sold to generate $35,000 in contribution margin, then all of the fixed costs will be covered and the company will have managed to at least *break even* for the month—that is, to show neither profit nor loss but just cover all of its costs. To reach the break-even point, the company will have to sell 350 speakers in a month, since each speaker sold yields $100 in contribution margin:

	Total	Per Unit
Sales (350 speakers)	$87,500	$250
Less variable expenses	52,500	150
Contribution margin	35,000	$100
Less fixed expenses	35,000	
Net operating income	$ 0	

Computation of the break-even point is discussed in detail later in the chapter; for the moment, note that the **break-even point** is the level of sales at which profit is zero.

Once the break-even point has been reached, net operating income will increase by the amount of the unit contribution margin for each additional unit sold. For example, if 351 speakers are sold in a month, then we can expect that the net operating income for the month will be $100, since the company will have sold 1 speaker more than the number needed to break even:

	Total	Per Unit
Sales (351 speakers)	$87,750	$250
Less variable expenses	52,650	150
Contribution margin	35,100	$100
Less fixed expenses	35,000	
Net operating income	$ 100	

If 352 speakers are sold (2 speakers above the break-even point), then we can expect that the net operating income for the month will be $200, and so forth. To know what the profits will be at various levels of activity, therefore, it is not necessary to prepare a whole series of income statements. To estimate the profit at any activity level above the break-even point, simply take the number of units to be sold over the break-even point and multiply that number by the unit contribution margin. The result represents the anticipated profits for the period. Or, to estimate the effect of a planned increase in sales on profits, simply multiply the increase in units sold by the unit contribution margin. The result will be the expected increase in profits. To illustrate, if Acoustic Concepts is currently selling 400 speakers per month and plans to increase sales to 425 speakers per month, the anticipated impact on profits can be computed as follows:

Increased number of speakers to be sold	25
Contribution margin per speaker	× $100
Increase in net operating income	$2,500

These calculations can be verified as follows:

	Sales Volume			
	400 Speakers	425 Speakers	Difference 25 Speakers	Per Unit
Sales	$100,000	$106,250	$6,250	$250
Less variable expenses.	60,000	63,750	3,750	150
Contribution margin	40,000	42,500	2,500	$100
Less fixed expenses	35,000	35,000	0	
Net operating income	$ 5,000	$ 7,500	$2,500	

To summarize these examples, if there were no sales, the company's loss would equal its fixed expenses. Each unit that is sold reduces the loss by the amount of the unit contribution margin. Once the break-even point has been reached, each additional unit sold increases the company's profit by the amount of the unit contribution margin.

CVP Relationships in Graphic Form

The relations among revenue, cost, profit, and volume can be expressed graphically by preparing a **cost-volume-profit (CVP) graph.** A CVP graph highlights CVP relationships over wide ranges of activity and can give managers a perspective that can be obtained in no other way. To help explain his analysis to Prem Narayan, Bob Luchinni decided to prepare a CVP graph for Acoustic Concepts.

LEARNING OBJECTIVE 2

Prepare and interpret a cost-volume-profit (CVP) graph.

Preparing the CVP Graph   In a CVP graph (sometimes called a *break-even chart*), unit volume is commonly represented on the horizontal (*X*) axis and dollars on the vertical (*Y*) axis. Preparing a CVP graph involves three steps. These steps are keyed to the graph in Exhibit 6–1:

1. Draw a line parallel to the volume axis to represent total fixed expenses. For Acoustic Concepts, total fixed expenses are $35,000.
2. Choose some volume of sales and plot the point representing total expenses (fixed and variable) at the activity level you have selected. In Exhibit 6–1, Bob Luchinni

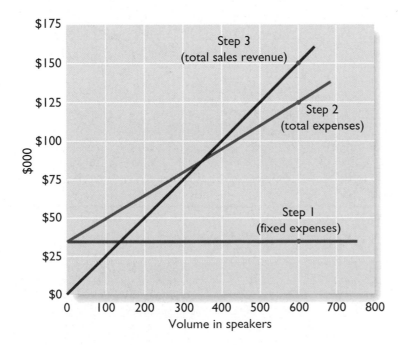

EXHIBIT 6–1

Preparing the CVP Graph

chose a volume of 600 speakers. Total expenses at that activity level would be as follows:

Fixed expenses	$ 35,000
Variable expenses (600 speakers × $150 per speaker).....	90,000
Total expenses......................................	$125,000

After the point has been plotted, draw a line through it back to the point where the fixed expenses line intersects the dollars axis.

3. Again choose some volume of sales and plot the point representing total sales dollars at the activity level you have selected. In Exhibit 6–1, Bob Luchinni again chose a volume of 600 speakers. Sales at that activity level total $150,000 (600 speakers × $250 per speaker). Draw a line through this point back to the origin.

The interpretation of the completed CVP graph is given in Exhibit 6–2. The anticipated profit or loss at any given level of sales is measured by the vertical distance between the total revenue line (sales) and the total expenses line (variable expenses plus fixed expenses).

The break-even point is where the total revenue and total expenses lines cross. The break-even point of 350 speakers in Exhibit 6–2 agrees with the break-even point computed earlier.

As discussed earlier, when sales are below the break-even point—in this case, 350 units—the company suffers a loss. Note that the loss (represented by the vertical distance between the total expense and total revenue lines) gets worse as sales decline. When sales are above the break-even point, the company earns a profit and the size of the profit (represented by the vertical distance between the total revenue and total expense lines) increases as sales increase.

EXHIBIT 6–2

The Completed CVP Graph

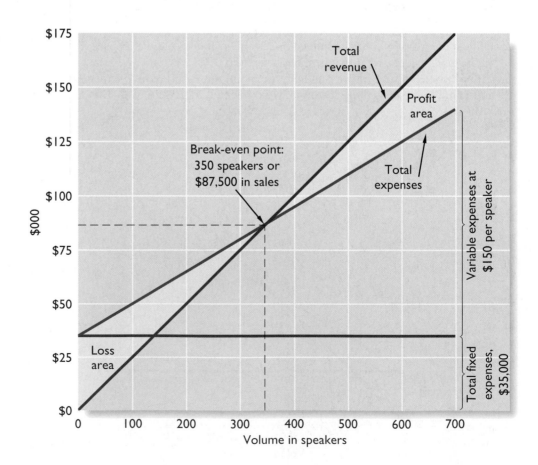

Buying Groceries Online

Online grocers such as Peapod.com (www.peapod.com), Netgrocer.com (www.netgrocer.com), and HomeGrocer.com (www.homegrocer.com) have interesting cost structures. Large investments in fixed costs are necessary to create appealing web pages and for bricks-and-mortar infrastructure such as warehouses and delivery vans. Variable costs come in at least two varieties. One kind of variable cost is related to the number of deliveries made. These variable costs include fuel, maintenance, and depreciation on vehicles. The other kind of variable cost is related to the amount of groceries ordered by a customer.

With the cost structure in this industry, and the low margins prevalent in the grocery business, it is very difficult for online grocers to break even. For example, HomeRuns.com's president Tom Furber says that the Somerville, Massachusetts–based grocer needs 8,000 orders in a week to break even. In a good week, it may get less than a third that many orders.

Source: Timothy J. Mullaney and David Leonhardt, "A Hard Sell Online? Guess Again," *Business Week*, July 12, 1999, pp. 142–143.

Contribution Margin Ratio (CM Ratio)

In the previous section, we explored how cost-volume-profit relations can be visualized. In this section we will see how the *contribution margin ratio* can be used in cost-volume-profit calculations. As the first step, we have added a column to Acoustic Concepts' contribution income statement in which sales revenues, variable expenses, and contribution margin are expressed as a percentage of sales:

	Total	Per Unit	Percent of Sales
Sales (400 speakers).................	$100,000	$250	100%
Less variable expenses...............	60,000	150	60
Contribution margin	40,000	$100	40
Less fixed expenses	35,000		
Net operating income	$ 5,000		

The contribution margin as a percentage of total sales is referred to as the **contribution margin ratio (CM ratio).** This ratio is computed as follows:

$$\text{CM ratio} = \frac{\text{Contribution margin}}{\text{Sales}}$$

For Acoustic Concepts, the computations are:

$$\text{CM ratio} = \frac{\text{Total contribution margin}}{\text{Total sales}} = \frac{\$40,000}{\$100,000} = 40\%$$

In a company such as Acoustic Concepts that has only one product, the CM ratio can also be computed as follows:

$$\text{CM ratio} = \frac{\text{Unit contribution margin}}{\text{Unit selling price}} = \frac{\$100}{\$250} = 40\%$$

The CM ratio is extremely useful since it shows how the contribution margin will be affected by a change in total sales. To illustrate, notice that Acoustic Concepts has a CM ratio of 40%. This means that for each dollar increase in sales, total contribution margin will increase by 40 cents ($1 sales × CM ratio of 40%). Net operating income will also increase by 40 cents, assuming that fixed costs do not change.

As this illustration suggests, *the impact on net operating income of any given dollar change in total sales can be computed in seconds by simply applying the CM ratio to the dollar change.* For example, if Acoustic Concepts plans a $30,000 increase in sales during the coming month, the contribution margin should increase by $12,000 ($30,000 increased sales × CM ratio of 40%). As we noted above, net operating income will also increase by $12,000 if fixed costs do not change. This is verified by the following table:

	Sales Volume			Percent of Sales
	Present	**Expected**	**Increase**	
Sales	$100,000	$130,000	$30,000	100%
Less variable expenses	60,000	78,000*	18,000	60
Contribution margin.........	40,000	52,000	12,000	40%
Less fixed expenses	35,000	35,000	0	
Net operating income	$ 5,000	$ 17,000	$12,000	

*$130,000 expected sales ÷ $250 per unit = 520 units. 520 units × $150 per unit = $78,000.

Some managers prefer to work with the CM ratio rather than the unit contribution margin. The CM ratio is particularly valuable in situations where trade-offs must be made between more dollar sales of one product versus more dollar sales of another. Generally speaking, when trying to increase sales, products that yield the greatest amount of contribution margin per dollar of sales should be emphasized.

Some Applications of CVP Concepts

Concept 6–1

Bob Luchinni, the accountant at Acoustic Concepts, wanted to demonstrate to the company's president Prem Narayan how the concepts developed on the preceding pages can be used in planning and decision making. Bob gathered the following basic data:

	Per Unit	**Percent of Sales**
Selling price	$250	100%
Less variable expenses.........	150	60
Contribution margin	$100	40%

Recall that fixed expenses are $35,000 per month. Bob Luchinni will use these data to show the effects of changes in variable costs, fixed costs, sales price, and sales volume on the company's profitability in a variety of situations.

Change in Fixed Cost and Sales Volume Acoustic Concepts is currently selling 400 speakers per month (monthly sales of $100,000). The sales manager feels that a $10,000 increase in the monthly advertising budget would increase monthly sales by $30,000 to a total of 520 units. Should the advertising budget be increased? The following table shows the effect of the proposed change in the monthly advertising budget:

	Current Sales	**Sales with Additional Advertising Budget**	**Difference**	**Percent of Sales**
Sales	$100,000	$130,000	$30,000	100%
Less variable expenses......	60,000	78,000*	18,000	60

(continued)

(concluded)	Current Sales	Sales with Additional Advertising Budget	Difference	Percent of Sales
Contribution margin	40,000	52,000	12,000	40%
Less fixed expenses	35,000	45,000†	10,000	
Net operating income	$ 5,000	$ 7,000	$ 2,000	

*520 units × $150 per unit = $78,000.
†$35,000 plus additional $10,000 monthly advertising budget = $45,000.

Assuming no other factors need to be considered, the increase in the advertising budget should be approved since it would lead to an increase in net operating income of $2,000. There are two shorter ways to present this solution. The first alternative solution follows:

Alternative Solution 1

Expected total contribution margin:	
$130,000 × 40% CM ratio	$52,000
Present total contribution margin:	
$100,000 × 40% CM ratio	40,000
Incremental contribution margin	12,000
Change in fixed expenses:	
Less incremental advertising expense.	10,000
Increased net operating income	$ 2,000

Since in this case only the fixed costs and the sales volume change, the solution can be presented in an even shorter format, as follows:

Alternative Solution 2

Incremental contribution margin:	
$30,000 × 40% CM ratio	$12,000
Less incremental advertising expense.	10,000
Increased net operating income	$ 2,000

Notice that this approach does not depend on a knowledge of previous sales. Also notice that it is unnecessary under either shorter approach to prepare an income statement. Both of the solutions above involve an **incremental analysis**—they consider only those items of revenue, cost, and volume that will change if the new program is implemented. Although in each case a new income statement could have been prepared, the incremental approach is simpler and more direct and focuses attention on the specific items involved in the decision.

Change in Variable Costs and Sales Volume   Refer to the original data. Recall that Acoustic Concepts is currently selling 400 speakers per month. Management is considering the use of higher-quality components, which would increase variable costs (and thereby reduce the contribution margin) by $10 per speaker. However, the sales manager predicts that the higher overall quality would increase sales to 480 speakers per month. Should the higher-quality components be used?

The $10 increase in variable costs will decrease the unit contribution margin by $10—from $100 down to $90.

Solution

Expected total contribution margin with higher-quality components:	
480 speakers × $90 per speaker	$43,200
Present total contribution margin:	
400 speakers × $100 per speaker	40,000
Increase in total contribution margin	$ 3,200

According to this analysis, the higher-quality components should be used. Since fixed costs will not change, the $3,200 increase in contribution margin shown above should result in a $3,200 increase in net operating income.

Change in Fixed Cost, Sales Price, and Sales Volume   Refer to the original data and recall again that the company is currently selling 400 speakers per month. To increase sales, the sales manager would like to cut the selling price by $20 per speaker and increase the advertising budget by $15,000 per month. The sales manager argues that if these two steps are taken, unit sales will increase by 50% to 600 speakers per month. Should the changes be made?

A decrease of $20 per speaker in the selling price will cause the unit contribution margin to decrease from $100 to $80.

Solution

Expected total contribution margin with lower selling price:	
600 speakers × $80 per speaker	$48,000
Present total contribution margin:	
400 speakers × $100 per speaker	40,000
Incremental contribution margin	8,000
Change in fixed expenses:	
Less incremental advertising expense.	15,000
Reduction in net operating income	$ (7,000)

According to this analysis, the changes should not be made. The same solution can be obtained by preparing comparative income statements as follows:

	Present 400 Speakers per Month		Expected 600 Speakers per Month		
	Total	Per Unit	Total	Per Unit	Difference
Sales.	$100,000	$250	$138,000	$230	$38,000
Less variable expenses . .	60,000	150	90,000	150	30,000
Contribution margin. . . .	40,000	$100	48,000	$ 80	8,000
Less fixed expenses.	35,000		50,000*		15,000
Net operating income (loss).	$ 5,000		$ (2,000)		$ (7,000)

*35,000 + Additional monthly advertising budget of $15,000 = $50,000.

Notice that the effect on net operating income is the same as that obtained by the incremental analysis above.

Change in Variable Cost, Fixed Cost, and Sales Volume   Refer to the original data. As before, the company is currently selling 400 speakers per month. The sales manager would like to pay a sales commission of $15 per speaker sold, rather than pay salespersons flat salaries that now total $6,000 per month. The sales manager is confident that the change will increase monthly sales by 15% to 460 speakers per month. Should the change be made?

Solution

Changing the sales staff from a salaried basis to a commission basis will affect both fixed and variable expenses. Fixed expenses will decrease by $6,000, from $35,000 to $29,000. Variable expenses will increase by $15, from $150 to $165, and the unit contribution margin will decrease from $100 to $85.

Expected total contribution margin with sales staff on commissions:	
460 speakers × $85 per speaker.................	$39,100
Present total contribution margin:	
400 speakers × $100 per speaker................	40,000
Decrease in total contribution margin..............	(900)
Change in fixed expenses:	
Add salaries avoided if a commission is paid........	6,000
Increase in net operating income..................	$ 5,100

According to this analysis, the changes should be made. Again, the same answer can be obtained by preparing comparative income statements:

	Present 400 Speakers per Month		Expected 460 Speakers per Month		Difference: Increase (or Decrease) in Net Operating Income
	Total	Per Unit	Total	Per Unit	
Sales......................	$100,000	$250	$115,000	$250	$15,000
Less variable expenses	60,000	150	75,900	165	(15,900)
Contribution margin	40,000	$100	39,100	$ 85	(900)
Less fixed expenses..........	35,000		29,000		6,000
Net operating income........	$ 5,000		$ 10,100		$ 5,100

Change in Regular Sales Price   Refer to the original data where Acoustic Concepts is currently selling 400 speakers per month. The company has an opportunity to make a bulk sale of 150 speakers to a wholesaler if an acceptable price can be worked out. This sale would not disturb the company's regular sales and would not affect the company's total fixed expenses. What price per speaker should be quoted to the wholesaler if Acoustic Concepts wants to increase its monthly profits by $3,000?

Solution

Variable cost per speaker	$150
Desired profit per speaker:	
$3,000 ÷ 150 speakers	20
Quoted price per speaker..........	$170

Notice that fixed expenses are not included in the computation. This is because fixed expenses are not affected by the bulk sale, so all of the additional revenue that is in excess of variable costs increases the profits of the company.

CONCEPT CHECK ✓

1. The contribution margin ratio always increases when (you may select more than one answer):
   a. Sales increase.
   b. Fixed costs decrease.
   c. Total variable costs decrease.
   d. Variable costs as a percent of sales decrease.
2. Assume the selling price per unit is $30, the contribution margin ratio 40%, and the break-even point is 5,000 units. What is the amount of total fixed costs?
   a. $20,000
   b. $30,000
   c. $50,000
   d. $60,000

The eToys Saga

The company eToys, which sells toys over the Internet, lost $190 million in 1999 on sales of $151 million. One big cost was advertising. eToys spent about $37 on advertising for each $100 of sales. (Other e-tailers were spending even more—in some cases, up to $460 on advertising for each $100 in sales!)

eToys did have some advantages relative to bricks-and-mortar stores such as Toys "R" Us. eToys had much lower inventory costs since it needed to keep on hand only one or two of a slow-moving item, whereas a traditional store has to fully stock its shelves. And bricks-and-mortar retail spaces in malls and elsewhere do cost money—on average, about 7% of sales. However, e-tailers such as eToys have their own set of disadvantages. Customers "pick and pack" their own items at a bricks-and-mortar outlet, but e-tailers have to pay employees to carry out this task. This costs eToys about $33 for every $100 in sales. And the technology to sell over the net is not free. eToys paid about $29 on its website and related technology for every $100 in sales. However, many of these costs of selling over the net are fixed. Toby Lenk, the CEO of eToys, estimated that the company would pass its break-even point somewhere between $750 and $900 million in sales—representing less than 1% of the market for toys. eToys didn't make it and laid off 70% of its employees in January 2001. Subsequently, eToys was acquired by KBkids.com.

Sources: Erin Kelly, "The Last e-Store on the Block," *Fortune,* September 18, 2000, pp. 214–220; and Jennifer Couzin, *The Industry Standard,* January 4, 2001.

BREAK-EVEN ANALYSIS

Concept 6–2

CVP analysis is sometimes referred to simply as break-even analysis. This is unfortunate because break-even analysis is only one element of CVP analysis—although an important element. Break-even analysis is designed to answer questions such as how far sales could drop before the company begins to lose money.

Break-Even Computations

Earlier in the chapter we defined the break-even point to be the level of sales at which the company's profit is zero. The break-even point can be computed using either the *equation method* or the *contribution margin method*—the two methods are equivalent.

The Equation Method   The **equation method** centers on the contribution approach to the income statement illustrated earlier in the chapter. The format of this income statement can be expressed in equation form as follows:

$$\text{Profits} = (\text{Sales} - \text{Variable expenses}) - \text{Fixed expenses}$$

Rearranging this equation slightly yields the following equation, which is widely used in CVP analysis:

$$\text{Sales} = \text{Variable expenses} + \text{Fixed expenses} + \text{Profits}$$

At the break-even point, profits are zero. Therefore, the break-even point can be computed by finding that point where sales just equal the total of the variable expenses plus the fixed expenses. For Acoustic Concepts, the break-even point in unit sales, Q, can be computed as follows:

$$\text{Sales} = \text{Variable expenses} + \text{Fixed expenses} + \text{Profits}$$

$$\$250Q = \$150Q + \$35,000 + \$0$$
$$\$100Q = \$35,000$$
$$Q = \$35,000 \div \$100 \text{ per speaker}$$
$$Q = 350 \text{ speakers}$$

where:

Q = Number (quantity) of speakers sold

$\$250$ = Unit sales price

$\$150$ = Unit variable expenses

$\$35,000$ = Total fixed expenses

The break-even point in sales dollars can be computed by multiplying the break-even level of unit sales by the selling price per unit:

$$350 \text{ speakers} \times \$250 \text{ per speaker} = \$87,500$$

The break-even in total sales dollars, X, can also be directly computed as follows:

$$\text{Sales} = \text{Variable expenses} + \text{Fixed expenses} + \text{Profits}$$

$$X = 0.60X + \$35,000 + \$0$$
$$0.40X = \$35,000$$
$$X = \$35,000 \div 0.40$$
$$X = \$87,500$$

where:

X = Total sales dollars

0.60 = Variable expense ratio (Variable expenses $\div$ Sales)

$\$35,000$ = Total fixed expenses

Firms often have data available only in percentage or ratio form, and the approach we have just illustrated must then be used to find the break-even point. Notice that use of ratios in the equation yields a break-even point in sales dollars rather than in units sold. The break-even point in units sold is the following:

$$\$87,500 \div \$250 \text{ per speaker} = 350 \text{ speakers}$$

Recruit

Assume that you are being recruited by the ConneXus Corp. and have an interview scheduled later this week. You are interested in working for this company for a variety of reasons. In preparation for the interview, you did some research at your local library and gathered the following information about the company. ConneXus is a company set up by two young engineers, George Searle and Humphrey Chen, to allow consumers to order music CDs on their mobile phones. Suppose you hear on the radio a cut from a CD that you would like to own. If you subscribe to their service, you would pick up your cell phone, punch "*CD," and enter the radio station's frequency and the time you heard the song, and the CD would be on its way to you.

ConneXus charges about $17 for a CD, including shipping. The company pays its supplier about $13, leaving a contribution margin of $4 per CD. Because of the fixed costs of running the service (about $1,850,000 a year), Searle expects the company to lose about $1.5 million in its first year of operations on sales of 88,000 CDs.

What are your initial impressions of this company based on the information you gathered? What other information would you want to obtain during the job interview?

Source: Adapted from Peter Kafka, "Play It Again," *Forbes*, July 26, 1999, p. 94.

The Contribution Margin Method The **contribution margin method** is actually just a shortcut version of the equation method already described. The approach centers on the idea discussed earlier that each unit sold provides a certain amount of contribution margin that goes toward covering fixed costs. To find how many units must be sold to break even, divide the total fixed expenses by the unit contribution margin:

$$\text{Break-even point in units sold} = \frac{\text{Fixed expenses}}{\text{Unit contribution margin}}$$

Each speaker generates a contribution margin of $100 ($250 selling price, less $150 variable expenses). Since the total fixed expenses are $35,000, the break-even point is computed as follows:

$$\frac{\text{Fixed expenses}}{\text{Unit contribution margin}} = \frac{\$35,000}{\$100 \text{ per speaker}} = 350 \text{ speakers}$$

A variation of this method uses the CM ratio instead of the unit contribution margin. The result is the break-even in total sales dollars rather than in total units sold.

$$\text{Break-even point in total sales dollars} = \frac{\text{Fixed expenses}}{\text{CM ratio}}$$

In the Acoustic Concepts example, the calculations are as follows:

$$\frac{\text{Fixed expenses}}{\text{CM ratio}} = \frac{\$35,000}{0.40} = \$87,500$$

This approach, based on the CM ratio, is particularly useful in those situations where a company has multiple product lines and wishes to compute a single break-even point for the company as a whole. More is said on this point in a later section titled The Concept of Sales Mix.

Operating on a Shoestring

Hesh Kestin failed in his attempt at publishing an English-language newspaper in Israel in the 1980s. His conclusion: "Never start a business with too many people or too much furniture." Kestin's newest venture is *The American,* a Sunday-only newspaper for overseas

Americans. His idea is to publish *The American* on the one day of the week that the well-established *International Herald Tribune* (circulation, 190,000 copies) does not publish. But following what he learned from his first failed venture, he is doing it on a shoestring.

In contrast to the Paris-based *International Herald Tribune* with its eight-story office tower and staff of 250, Kestin has set up business in a small clapboard building on Long Island. Working at desks purchased from a thrift shop, Kestin's staff of 12 assembles the tabloid from stories pulled off wire services. The result of this frugality is that *The American*'s break-even point is only 14,000 copies. Sales topped 20,000 copies just two months after the paper's first issue.

Source: Jerry Useem, "American Hopes to Conquer the World—from Long Island," *Inc,* December 1996, p. 23.

Target Profit Analysis

CVP formulas can be used to determine the sales volume needed to achieve a target profit. Suppose that Prem Narayan of Acoustic Concepts would like to earn a target profit of $40,000 per month. How many speakers would have to be sold?

The CVP Equation   One approach is to use the equation method. Instead of solving for the unit sales where profits are zero, you instead solve for the unit sales where profits are $40,000.

$$\text{Sales} = \text{Variable expenses} + \text{Fixed expenses} + \text{Profits}$$
$$\$250Q = \$150Q + \$35,000 + \$40,000$$
$$\$100Q = \$75,000$$
$$Q = \$75,000 \div \$100 \text{ per speaker}$$
$$Q = 750 \text{ speakers}$$

where:

Q = Number of speakers sold

250 = Unit sales price

150 = Unit variable expenses

$35,000$ = Total fixed expenses

$40,000$ = Target profit

Thus, the target profit can be achieved by selling 750 speakers per month, which represents $187,500 in total sales ($250 per speaker × 750 speakers).

The Contribution Margin Approach   A second approach involves expanding the contribution margin formula to include the target profit:

$$\text{Unit sales to attain the target profit} = \frac{\text{Fixed expenses} + \text{Target profit}}{\text{Unit contribution margin}}$$

$$= \frac{\$35,000 + \$40,000}{\$100 \text{ per speaker}}$$

$$= 750 \text{ speakers}$$

This approach gives the same answer as the equation method since it is simply a shortcut version of the equation method. Similarly, the dollar sales needed to attain the target profit can be computed as follows:

$$\text{Dollar sales to attain target profit} = \frac{\text{Fixed expenses} + \text{Target profit}}{\text{CM ratio}}$$

$$= \frac{\$35,000 + \$40,000}{0.40}$$

$$= \$187,500$$

The Margin of Safety

LEARNING OBJECTIVE 7

Compute the margin of safety and explain its significance.

The **margin of safety** is the excess of budgeted (or actual) sales over the break-even volume of sales. It states the amount by which sales can drop before losses begin to be incurred. The higher the margin of safety, the lower the risk of not breaking even. The formula for its calculation is:

Margin of safety = Total budgeted (or actual) sales − Break-even sales

The margin of safety can also be expressed in percentage form. This percentage is obtained by dividing the margin of safety in dollar terms by total sales:

$$\text{Margin of safety percentage} = \frac{\text{Margin of safety in dollars}}{\text{Total budgeted (or actual) sales}}$$

The calculations for the margin of safety for Acoustic Concepts are as follows:

Sales (at the current volume of 400 speakers) (a)	$100,000
Break-even sales (at 350 speakers)	87,500
Margin of safety (in dollars) (b)	$ 12,500
Margin of safety as a percentage of sales, (b) ÷ (a)	12.5%

This margin of safety means that at the current level of sales and with the company's current prices and cost structure, a reduction in sales of $12,500, or 12.5%, would result in just breaking even.

In a single-product firm like Acoustic Concepts, the margin of safety can also be expressed in terms of the number of units sold by dividing the margin of safety in dollars by the selling price per unit. In this case, the margin of safety is 50 speakers ($12,500 ÷ $250 per speaker = 50 speakers).

DECISION MAKER

Loan Officer

Pak Melwani and Kumar Hathiramani, former silk merchants from Bombay, opened a soup store in Manhattan after watching a Seinfeld episode featuring the "soup Nazi." The episode parodied a real-life soup vendor, Ali Yeganeh, whose loyal customers put up with hour-long lines and "snarling customer service." Melwani and Hathiramani approached Yeganeh about turning his soup kitchen into a chain, but they were gruffly rebuffed. Instead of giving up, the two hired a French chef with a repertoire of 500 soups and opened a store called Soup Nutsy. For $6 per serving, Soup Nutsy offers 12 homemade soups each day, such as sherry crab bisque and Thai coconut shrimp. Melwani and Hathiramani report that in their first year of operation, they netted $210,000 on sales of $700,000. They report that it costs about $2 per serving to make the soup.

Assume that Melwani and Hathiramani have approached your bank for a loan. As the loan officer, you should consider a variety of factors, including the company's margin of safety. Assuming that other information about the company is favorable, would you consider Soup Nutsy's margin of safety to be comfortable enough to extend the loan?

Source: Adapted from Silva Sansoni, "The Starbucks of Soup?" *Forbes*, July 7, 1997, pp. 90–91.

It is Thursday morning, and Prem Narayan and Bob Luchinni are discussing the results of Bob's analysis.

Prem: Bob, everything you have shown me is pretty clear. I can see what impact some of the sales manager's suggestions would have on our profits. Some of those suggestions are quite good and some are not so good. I also understand that our break-even is 350 speakers, so we have to make sure we don't slip below that level of sales. What really bothers me is that we are only selling 400 speakers a month now. What did you call the 50-speaker cushion?

Bob: That's the margin of safety.

Prem: Such a small cushion makes me very nervous. What can we do to increase the margin of safety?

Bob: We have to increase total sales or decrease the break-even point or both.

Prem: And to decrease the break-even point, we have to either decrease our fixed expenses or increase our unit contribution margin?

Bob: Exactly.

Prem: And to increase our unit contribution margin, we must either increase our selling price or decrease the variable cost per unit?

Bob: Correct.

Prem: So what do you suggest?

Bob: Well, the analysis doesn't tell us which of these to do, but it does indicate we have a potential problem here.

Prem: If you don't have any immediate suggestions, I would like to call a general meeting next week to discuss ways we can work on increasing the margin of safety. I think everyone will be concerned about how vulnerable we are to even small downturns in sales.

Bob: I agree. This is something everyone will want to work on.

---

3. Assume a company produces one product that sells for $55, has a variable cost per unit of $35, and has fixed costs of $100,000. How many units must the company sell to earn a target profit of $50,000?
   a. 7,500 units
   b. 10,000 units
   c. 12,500 units
   d. 15,000 units
4. Given the same facts as in question 3 above, if the company exactly meets its target profit, what will be its margin of safety in sales revenue?
   a. $110,000
   b. $127,500
   c. $137,500
   d. $150,000

CONCEPT CHECK ✓

CVP CONSIDERATIONS IN CHOOSING A COST STRUCTURE

As stated in the preceding chapter, cost structure refers to the relative proportion of fixed and variable costs in an organization. An organization often has some latitude in trading off between these two types of costs. For example, fixed investments in automated equipment can reduce variable labor costs. In this section, we discuss the choice of a cost structure. We focus on the impact of cost structure on profit stability, in which *operating leverage* plays a key role.

Cost Structure and Profit Stability

When a manager has some latitude in trading off between fixed and variable costs, which cost structure is better—high variable costs and low fixed costs, or the opposite? No single answer to this question is possible; there may be advantages either way, depending on the specific circumstances. To show what we mean by this statement, refer to the income statements given below for two blueberry farms. Bogside Farm depends on migrant workers to pick its berries by hand, whereas Sterling Farm has invested in expensive berry-picking machines. Consequently, Bogside Farm has higher variable costs, but Sterling Farm has higher fixed costs:

	Bogside Farm		Sterling Farm	
	Amount	Percent	Amount	Percent
Sales	$100,000	100%	$100,000	100%
Less variable expenses	60,000	60	30,000	30
Contribution margin.	40,000	40%	70,000	70%
Less fixed expenses	30,000		60,000	
Net operating income	$ 10,000		$ 10,000	

The question as to which farm has the better cost structure depends on many factors, including the long-run trend in sales, year-to-year fluctuations in the level of sales, and the attitude of the owners toward risk. If sales are expected to be above $100,000 in the future, then Sterling Farm probably has the better cost structure. The reason is that its CM ratio is higher, and its profits will therefore increase more rapidly as sales increase. To illustrate, assume that each farm experiences a 10% increase in sales without any increase in fixed costs. The new income statements would be as follows:

	Bogside Farm		Sterling Farm	
	Amount	Percent	Amount	Percent
Sales	$110,000	100%	$110,000	100%
Less variable expenses	66,000	60	33,000	30
Contribution margin	44,000	40%	77,000	70%
Less fixed expenses	30,000		60,000	
Net operating income	$ 14,000		$ 17,000	

Sterling Farm has experienced a greater increase in net operating income due to its higher CM ratio even though the increase in sales was the same for both farms.

What if sales drop below $100,000 from time to time? What are the break-even points of the two farms? What are their margins of safety? The computations needed to answer these questions are carried out below using the contribution margin method:

	Bogside Farm	Sterling Farm
Fixed expenses.	$ 30,000	$ 60,000
Contribution margin ratio	÷ 40%	÷ 70%
Break-even in total sales dollars	$ 75,000	$ 85,714
Total current sales (a)	$100,000	$100,000
Break-even sales.	75,000	85,714
Margin of safety in sales dollars (b)	$ 25,000	$ 14,286
Margin of safety as a percentage of sales, (b) ÷ (a)	25.0%	14.3%

This analysis makes it clear that Bogside Farm is less vulnerable to downturns than Sterling Farm. We can identify two reasons why it is less vulnerable. First, due to its lower fixed expenses, Bogside Farm has a lower break-even point and a higher margin of safety, as shown by the computations above. Therefore, it will not incur losses as quickly as Sterling Farm in periods of sharply declining sales. Second, due to its lower CM ratio, Bogside Farm will not lose contribution margin as rapidly as Sterling Farm when sales fall off. Thus, Bogside Farm's income will be less volatile. We saw earlier that this is a drawback when sales increase, but it provides more protection when sales drop.

To summarize, without knowing the future, it is not obvious which cost structure is better. Both have advantages and disadvantages. Sterling Farm, with its higher fixed costs and lower variable costs, will experience wider swings in net operating income as changes take place in sales, with greater profits in good years and greater losses in bad years. Bogside Farm, with its lower fixed costs and higher variable costs, will enjoy greater stability in net operating income and will be more protected from losses during bad years, but at the cost of lower net operating income in good years.

Cost Structure in an E-Business

IN BUSINESS

Career Central (later renamed Cruel World), is an employment agency located in Palo Alto, California, on the outskirts of Silicon Valley. The company was founded by Jeffrey Hyman, an MBA from Northwestern University, who was dissatisfied with his own job search in the San Francisco Bay area.

Jobseekers pay nothing to register on the company's website. They provide detailed information about their experience, salary expectations, willingness to travel, geographic preferences, and so on. Employers pay. For a fee of $2,995 per search, employers submit their specifications to a Career Central staffer who searches the database for possible matches. When a possible candidate for the job is found, he or she is sent an e-mail describing the job opening. If the jobseeker is interested, Career Central prints out the individual's résumé and sends it to the potential employer. Career Central promises to deliver the names of at least 10 qualified, interested candidates within five business days of a search request.

Note that the potential employer does not directly search the database of jobseekers. Hyman feels that this is a critical aspect of the business plan. He wants to encourage professionals who are already employed, but who might be interested in a better job, to register at the Career Central website. If potential employers could directly access the database, confidentiality would be compromised. For example, the human resources department of a jobseeker's own company might tap into the database and discover that the jobseeker is looking for another job. At best, this would be embarrassing. By having a Career Central staffer handle all database searches, confidentiality for jobseekers is assured. However, this confidentiality comes at a high price. More calls from potential employers require more staffers to handle the calls. Hence, Career Central has added a layer of variable costs to its cost structure, which has decreased the contribution margin per search and increased the level of sales at which the break-even point will occur.

Source: Jerry Useem, *Inc.*, December 1998, pp. 71–83.

Operating Leverage

A lever is a tool for multiplying force. Using a lever, a massive object can be moved with only a modest amount of force. In business, *operating leverage* serves a similar purpose. **Operating leverage** is a measure of how sensitive net operating income is to percentage changes in sales. Operating leverage acts as a multiplier. If operating leverage is high, a small percentage increase in sales can produce a much larger percentage increase in net operating income.

Operating leverage can be illustrated by returning to the data given above for the two blueberry farms. We previously showed that a 10% increase in sales (from $100,000 to

LEARNING OBJECTIVE 8

Compute the degree of operating leverage at a particular level of sales and explain how the degree of operating leverage can be used to predict changes in net operating income.

$110,000 in each farm) results in a 70% increase in the net operating income of Sterling Farm (from $10,000 to $17,000) and only a 40% increase in the net operating income of Bogside Farm (from $10,000 to $14,000). Thus, for a 10% increase in sales, Sterling Farm experiences a much greater percentage increase in profits than does Bogside Farm. Therefore, Sterling Farm has greater operating leverage than Bogside Farm.

The **degree of operating leverage** at a given level of sales is computed by the following formula:

$$\text{Degree of operating leverage} = \frac{\text{Contribution margin}}{\text{Net operating income}}$$

The degree of operating leverage is a measure, at a given level of sales, of how a percentage change in sales volume will affect profits. To illustrate, the degree of operating leverage for the two farms at a $100,000 sales level would be computed as follows:

$$\text{Bogside Farm: } \frac{\$40,000}{\$10,000} = 4$$

$$\text{Sterling Farm: } \frac{\$70,000}{\$10,000} = 7$$

Since the degree of operating leverage for Bogside Farm is 4, the farm's net operating income grows four times as fast as its sales. Similarly, Sterling Farm's net operating income grows seven times as fast as its sales. Thus, if sales increase by 10%, then we can expect the net operating income of Bogside Farm to increase by four times this amount, or by 40%, and the net operating income of Sterling Farm to increase by seven times this amount, or by 70%.

	(1) Percent Increase in Sales	(2) Degree of Operating Leverage	(3) Percent Increase in Net Operating Income (1) × (2)
Bogside Farm	10%	4	40%
Sterling Farm	10%	7	70%

What is responsible for the higher operating leverage at Sterling Farm? The only difference between the two farms is their cost structure. If two companies have the same total revenue and same total expense but different cost structures, then the company with the higher proportion of fixed costs in its cost structure will have higher operating leverage. Referring back to the original example on page 258, when both farms have sales of $100,000 and total expenses of $90,000, one-third of Bogside Farm's costs are fixed but two-thirds of Sterling Farm's costs are fixed. As a consequence, Sterling's degree of operating leverage is higher than Bogside's.

The degree of operating leverage is not constant; it is greatest at sales levels near the break-even point and decreases as sales and profits rise. This can be seen from the tabulation below, which shows the degree of operating leverage for Bogside Farm at various sales levels. (Data used earlier for Bogside Farm are shown in color.)

Sales	$75,000	$80,000	$100,000	$150,000	$225,000
Less variable expenses	45,000	48,000	60,000	90,000	135,000
Contribution margin (a)	30,000	32,000	40,000	60,000	90,000
Less fixed expenses	30,000	30,000	30,000	30,000	30,000
Net operating income (b).	$ 0	$ 2,000	$ 10,000	$ 30,000	$ 60,000
Degree of operating leverage, (a) ÷ (b)	∞	16	4	2	1.5

Thus, a 10% increase in sales would increase profits by only 15% (10% $\times$ 1.5) if the company were operating at a $225,000 sales level, as compared to the 40% increase we computed earlier at the $100,000 sales level. The degree of operating leverage will continue to decrease the farther the company moves from its break-even point. At the break-even point, the degree of operating leverage is infinitely large ($30,000 contribution margin $\div$ $0 net operating income $= \infty$).

A manager can use the degree of operating leverage to quickly estimate what impact various percentage changes in sales will have on profits, without the necessity of preparing detailed income statements. As shown by our examples, the effects of operating leverage can be dramatic. If a company is near its break-even point, then even small percentage increases in sales can yield large percentage increases in profits. *This explains why management will often work very hard for only a small increase in sales volume.* If the degree of operating leverage is 5, then a 6% increase in sales would translate into a 30% increase in profits.

Fan Appreciation   IN BUSINESS

Operating leverage can be a good thing when business is booming but can turn the situation ugly when sales slacken. Jerry Colangelo, the managing partner of the Arizona Diamondbacks professional baseball team, spent over $100 million to sign six free agents—doubling the team's payroll cost—on top of the costs of operating and servicing the debt on the team's new stadium. With annual expenses of about $100 million, the team needs to average 40,000 fans per game to just break even.

Faced with a financially risky situation, Colangelo decided to raise ticket prices by 12%. And he did it during Fan Appreciation Weekend! Attendance for the season dropped by 15%, turning what should have been a $20 million profit into a loss of over $10 million for the year. Note that a drop of attendance of 15% did not cut profit by just 15%—that's the magic of operating leverage at work.

Source: Mary Summers, "Bottom of the Ninth, Two Out," *Forbes*, November 1, 1999, pp. 69–70.

STRUCTURING SALES COMMISSIONS

Companies generally compensate salespeople by paying them either a commission based on sales or a salary plus a sales commission. Commissions based on sales dollars can lead to lower profits. To illustrate, consider Pipeline Unlimited, a producer of surfing equipment. Salespeople for the company sell the company's product to retail sporting goods stores throughout North America and the Pacific Basin. Data for two of the company's surfboards, the XR7 and Turbo models, appear below:

	Model	
	XR7	**Turbo**
Selling price....................	$695	$749
Less variable expenses	344	410
Contribution margin..............	$351	$339

Which model will salespeople push hardest if they are paid a commission of 10% of sales revenue? The answer is the Turbo, since it has the higher selling price and hence the larger commission. On the other hand, from the standpoint of the company, profits will be greater if salespeople steer customers toward the XR7 model since it has the higher contribution margin.

To eliminate such conflicts, commissions can be based on contribution margin rather than on selling price alone. If this is done, the salespersons will want to sell the mix of products that will maximize contribution margin. Providing that fixed costs are not affected by the sales mix, maximizing the contribution margin will also maximize the company's profit. In effect, by maximizing their own compensation, salespersons will also maximize the company's profit.

THE CONCEPT OF SALES MIX

Before concluding our discussion of CVP concepts, we need to consider the impact of changes in *sales mix* on a company's profit.

The Definition of Sales Mix

LEARNING OBJECTIVE 9

Compute the break-even point for a multiple product company and explain the effects of shifts in the sales mix on contribution margin and the break-even point.

The term **sales mix** refers to the relative proportions in which a company's products are sold. The idea is to achieve the combination, or mix, that will yield the greatest amount of profits. Most companies have many products, and often these products are not equally profitable. Hence, profits will depend to some extent on the company's sales mix. Profits will be greater if high-margin rather than low-margin items make up a relatively large proportion of total sales.

Changes in the sales mix can cause perplexing variations in a company's profits. A shift in the sales mix from high-margin items to low-margin items can cause total profits to decrease even though total sales may increase. Conversely, a shift in the sales mix from low-margin items to high-margin items can cause the reverse effect—total profits may increase even though total sales decrease. It is one thing to achieve a particular sales volume; it is quite a different thing to sell the most profitable mix of products.

IN BUSINESS

Kodak: Going Digital

Kodak dominates the film industry in the U.S., selling two out of every three rolls of film. It also processes 40% of all film dropped off for developing. Unfortunately for Kodak, this revenue stream is threatened by digital cameras, which do not use film at all. To counter this threat, Kodak has moved into the digital market with its own line of digital cameras and various services, but sales of digital products undeniably cut into the company's film business. "Chief Financial Officer Robert Brust has 'stress-tested' profit models based on how quickly digital cameras may spread. If half of homes go digital by 2005, . . . Kodak's sales would rise 10% a year—but profits would go up only 8% a year. Cost cuts couldn't come fast enough to offset a slide in film sales and the margin pressure from selling cheap digital cameras." The sales mix is moving in the wrong direction, given the company's current cost structure and competitive prices.

Source: Bruce Upbin, "Kodak's Digital Moment," *Forbes*, August 21, 2000, pp. 106–112.

Sales Mix and Break-Even Analysis

If a company sells more than one product, break-even analysis is somewhat more complex than discussed earlier in this chapter. The reason is that different products will have different selling prices, different costs, and different contribution margins. Consequently, the break-even point will depend on the mix in which the various products are sold. To illustrate, consider Sound Unlimited, a small company that imports CDs from France for use in personal computers. At present, the company distributes the following CDs to retail computer stores: the Le Louvre CD, a multimedia free-form tour of the famous art museum in Paris; and the Le Vin CD, which features the wines and wine-growing regions

EXHIBIT 6–3 Multiple-Product Break-Even Analysis

	Le Louvre CD		Le Vin CD		Total	
SOUND UNLIMITED **Contribution Income Statement** **For the Month of September**						
	Amount	Percent	Amount	Percent	Amount	Percent
Sales........................	$20,000	100%	$80,000	100%	$100,000	100%
Less variable expenses	15,000	75	40,000	50	55,000	55
Contribution margin..............	$ 5,000	25%	$40,000	50%	45,000	45%
Less fixed expenses..............					27,000	
Net operating income					$ 18,000	

Overall CMR

Computation of the break-even point:

$$\frac{\text{Fixed expenses}}{\text{Overall CM ratio}} = \frac{\$27,000}{0.45} = \$60,000$$ *B.E. Sales*

Verification of the break-even:

	Le Louvre CD	Le Vin CD	Total
Current dollar sales	$20,000	$80,000	$100,000
Percentage of total dollar sales	20%	80%	100%
Sales at break-even	$12,000	$48,000	$ 60,000

	Le Louvre CD		Le Vin CD		Total	
	Amount	Percent	Amount	Percent	Amount	Percent
Sales........................	$12,000	100%	$48,000	100%	$ 60,000	100%
Less variable expenses	9,000	75	24,000	50	33,000	55
Contribution margin..............	$ 3,000	25%	$24,000	50%	27,000	45%
Less fixed expenses..............					27,000	
Net operating income					$ 0	

of France. Both multimedia products have sound, photos, video clips, and sophisticated software. The company's September sales, expenses, and break-even point are shown in Exhibit 6–3.

As shown in the exhibit, the break-even point is $60,000 in sales. This is computed by dividing the fixed costs by the company's *overall* CM ratio of 45%. The sales mix is currently 20% for the Le Louvre CD and 80% for the Le Vin CD. If this sales mix is constant, then at the break-even total sales of $60,000, the sales of the Le Louvre CD would be $12,000 (20% of $60,000) and the sales of the Le Vin CD would be $48,000 (80% of $60,000). As shown in Exhibit 6–3, at these levels of sales the company would indeed break even. But $60,000 in sales represents the break-even point for the company only so long as the sales mix does not change. *If the sales mix changes, then the break-even point will also change.* This is illustrated by the results for October in which the sales mix shifted away from the more profitable Le Vin CD (which has a 50% CM ratio) toward the less profitable Le Louvre CD (which has only a 25% CM ratio). These results appear in Exhibit 6–4.

Although sales have remained unchanged at $100,000, the sales mix is exactly the reverse of what it was in Exhibit 6–3, with the bulk of the sales now coming from the less profitable Le Louvre CD. Notice that this shift in the sales mix has caused both the overall CM ratio and total profits to drop sharply from the prior month—the overall CM ratio

EXHIBIT 6–4   Multiple-Product Break-Even Analysis: A Shift in Sales Mix (see Exhibit 6–3)

SOUND UNLIMITED
Contribution Income Statement
For the Month of October

	Le Louvre CD		Le Vin CD		Total	
	Amount	Percent	Amount	Percent	Amount	Percent
Sales............................	$80,000	100%	$20,000	100%	$100,000	100%
Less variable expenses	60,000	75	10,000	50	70,000	70
Contribution margin..............	$20,000	25%	$10,000	50%	30,000	30%
Less fixed expenses...............					27,000	
Net operating income					$ 3,000	

Computation of the break-even point:

$$\frac{\text{Fixed expenses}}{\text{Overall CM ratio}} = \frac{\$27,000}{0.30} = \$90,000$$

has dropped from 45% in September to only 30% in October, and net operating income has dropped from $18,000 to only $3,000. In addition, with the drop in the overall CM ratio, the company's break-even point is no longer $60,000 in sales. Since the company is now realizing less average contribution margin per dollar of sales, it takes more sales to cover the same amount of fixed costs. Thus, the break-even point has increased from $60,000 to $90,000 in sales per year.

In preparing a break-even analysis, some assumption must be made concerning the sales mix. Usually the assumption is that it will not change. However, if the sales mix is expected to change, then this must be explicitly considered in any CVP computations.

Benefiting from a Shift in Sales Mix

Roger Maxwell grew up near a public golf course where he learned the game and worked as a caddie. After attending Oklahoma State University on a golf scholarship, he became a golf pro and eventually rose to become vice president at Marriott, responsible for Marriott's golf courses in the United States. Sensing an opportunity to serve a niche market, Maxwell invested his life savings in opening his own golfing superstore, In Celebration of Golf (ICOG), in Scottsdale, Arizona. Maxwell says, "I'd rather sacrifice profit up front for sizzle . . . [P]eople are bored by malls. They're looking for something different." Maxwell has designed his store to be a museum-like mecca for golfing fanatics. For example, maintenance work is done in a replica of a turn-of-the-century club maker's shop.

Maxwell's approach seems to be working. In the second year of operation, Maxwell projected a profit of $81,000 on sales of $2.4 million as follows:

	Projected	Percent of Sales
Sales	$2,400,000	100 %
Cost of sales..................	1,496,000	62⅓
Other variable expenses	296,000	12⅓
Contribution margin	608,000	25⅓%
Fixed expenses................	527,000	
Net operating income	$ 81,000	

Happily for Maxwell, sales for the year were even better than expected—reaching $3.0 million. In the absence of any other changes, the net operating income should have been approximately $233,000, computed as follows:

	Projected	Percent of Sales
Sales	$3,000,000	100 %
Cost of sales..................	1,870,000	62⅓
Other variable expenses	370,000	12⅓
Contribution margin	760,000	25⅓%
Fixed expenses................	527,000	
Net operating income	$ 233,000	

However, net operating income for the year was actually $289,000—apparently because of a favorable shift in the sales mix toward higher margin items. A 25% increase in sales over the projections at the beginning of the year resulted in a 356% increase in net operating income. That's leverage!

Source: Edward O. Welles, "Going for the Green," *Inc,* July 1996, pp. 68–75.

ASSUMPTIONS OF CVP ANALYSIS

A number of assumptions underlie CVP analysis:

1. Selling price is constant. The price of a product or service will not change as volume changes.
2. Costs are linear and can be accurately divided into variable and fixed elements. The variable element is constant per unit, and the fixed element is constant in total over the entire relevant range.
3. In multiproduct companies, the sales mix is constant.
4. In manufacturing companies, inventories do not change. The number of units produced equals the number of units sold.

While some of these assumptions may be violated in practice, the violations are usually not serious enough to call into question the basic validity of CVP analysis. For example, in most multiproduct companies, the sales mix is constant enough so that the results of CVP analysis are reasonably valid.

Perhaps the greatest danger lies in relying on simple CVP analysis when a manager is contemplating a large change in volume that lies outside of the relevant range. For example, a manager might contemplate increasing the level of sales far beyond what the company has ever experienced before. However, even in these situations a manager can adjust the model as we have done in this chapter to take into account anticipated changes in selling prices, fixed costs, and the sales mix that would otherwise violate the assumptions. For example, in a decision that would affect fixed costs, the change in fixed costs can be explicitly taken into account as illustrated earlier in the chapter in the Acoustic Concepts example on page 248.

VARIABLE COSTING

The last assumption, that inventories do not change, is important when a company uses absorption costing to compute its unit product costs. Under absorption costing, fixed manufacturing overhead costs are absorbed by the products made during the period. If some of these products are not sold (i.e., inventories increase), then the fixed manufacturing

Assumptions of CVP Analysis

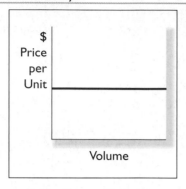

Selling Price is Constant

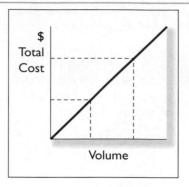

Variable Cost per Unit
is Constant

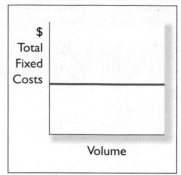

Fixed Costs are Constant

Sales Mix is Constant

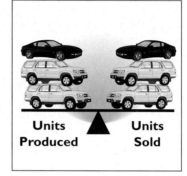

Inventory Levels are Constant

overhead costs absorbed by these products will appear as a part of ending inventories on the balance sheet rather than as an expense as shown on the contribution format income statement illustrated in this chapter.

Variable costing is an alternative approach to computing unit product costs. In contrast to absorption costing, under **variable costing** only the *variable* manufacturing costs are assigned to products. Fixed manufacturing costs under variable costing are considered to be period costs and go directly to the income statement as expenses of the current period. Consequently, under variable costing none of the fixed manufacturing overhead costs are on the balance sheet in the form of ending inventories.

Variable costing has a number of advantages over absorption costing including simplicity, compatibility with CVP analysis, and freedom from distortions caused by changes in ending inventories. For further discussion of variable costing, see Chapter 7 of Garrison & Noreen, *Managerial Accounting*, 10th edition, McGraw-Hill/Irwin.

SUMMARY

LO1   Explain how changes in activity affect contribution margin and net operating income.
The unit contribution margin, which is the difference between a unit's selling price and its variable cost, indicates how net operating income will change as the result of selling one more or one fewer unit. For example, if a product's unit contribution margin is $10, then selling one more unit will add $10 to the company's profit.

LO2   Prepare and interpret a cost-volume-profit (CVP) graph.
A cost-volume-profit graph displays sales revenues and expenses as a function of unit sales. Revenue is depicted as a straight line slanting upward to the right from the origin. Total expenses consist of both a fixed element and a variable element. The fixed element is flat on the graph. The variable element slants upward

to the right. The break-even point is the point at which the total sales revenue and total expenses lines intersect on the graph.

LO3　Use the contribution margin ratio (CM ratio) to compute changes in contribution margin and net operating income from changes in sales volume.

The contribution margin ratio is computed by dividing the unit contribution margin by the unit selling price, or by dividing the total contribution margin by the total sales.

The contribution margin shows by how much a dollar increase in sales will affect the total contribution margin and net operating income. For example, if a product has a 40% contribution margin ratio, then a $100 increase in sales should result in a $40 increase in contribution margin and in net operating income.

LO4　Show the effects on contribution margin of changes in variable costs, fixed costs, selling price, and volume.

Contribution margin concepts can be used to estimate the effects of changes in various parameters such as variable costs, fixed costs, selling prices, and volume on the total contribution margin and net operating income.

LO5　Compute the break-even point.

The break-even point is the level of sales at which profits are zero. It can be computed using several methods. The break-even point in units can be determined by dividing total fixed expenses by the unit contribution margin. The break-even point in sales dollars can be determined by dividing total fixed expenses by the contribution margin ratio.

LO6　Determine the level of sales needed to achieve a desired target profit.

The sales, in units, required to attain a desired target profit can be determined by summing the total fixed expenses and the desired target profit and then dividing the result by the unit contribution margin.

LO7　Compute the margin of safety and explain its significance.

The margin of safety is the difference between the total budgeted (or actual) sales of a period and the break-even sales. It expresses how much cushion there is in the current level of sales above the break-even point.

LO8　Compute the degree of operating leverage at a particular level of sales and explain how the degree of operating leverage can be used to predict changes in net operating income.

The degree of operating leverage is computed by dividing the total contribution margin by net operating income. The degree of operating leverage can be used to determine the impact a given percentage change in sales would have on net operating income. For example, if a company's degree of operating leverage is 2.5, then a 10% increase in sales from current levels of sales should result in a 25% increase in net operating income.

LO9　Compute the break-even point for a multiple product company and explain the effects of shifts in the sales mix on contribution margin and the break-even point.

The break-even point for a multiproduct company can be computed by dividing the company's total fixed expenses by the overall contribution margin ratio.

This method for computing the break-even point assumes that the sales mix is constant. If the sales mix shifts toward products with a lower contribution margin ratio, then more total sales are required to attain any given level of profits.

GUIDANCE ANSWERS TO *DECISION MAKER* AND *YOU DECIDE*

Recruit (p. 254)

You can get a feel for the challenges that this company will face by determining its break-even point.

$$\text{Sales} = \text{Variable expenses} + \text{Fixed expenses} + \text{Profits}$$

$$\$17Q = \$13Q + \$1,850,000 + \$0$$

$$\$4Q = \$1,850,000$$

$$Q = 462,500$$

Assuming that its cost structure stays the same, ConneXus needs to increase its sales by 426%—from 88,000 to 462,500 CDs—just to break even. After it reaches that break-even point, net operating income will increase by $4 (the contribution margin) for each additional CD that it sells. Joining the company would be a risky proposition; you should be prepared with some probing questions when you arrive for your interview. (For example, what steps does the company plan to take to increase sales? How might the company reduce its fixed and/or variable expenses so as to lower its break-even point?)

Loan Officer (p. 256)

To determine the company's margin of safety, you need to determine its break-even point. Start by estimating the company's variable expense ratio:

$$\text{Variable cost per unit} \div \text{Selling price per unit} = \text{Variable expense ratio}$$

$$\$2 \div \$6 = 33.3\% \text{ or } \tfrac{1}{3}$$

Then, estimate the company's variable expenses:

$$\text{Sales} \times \text{Variable expense ratio} = \text{Estimated amount of variable expenses}$$

$$\$700,000 \times \tfrac{1}{3} = \$233,333$$

Next, put the contribution format income statement into an equation format to estimate the company's current level of fixed expenses:

$$\text{Sales} = \text{Variable expenses} + \text{Fixed expenses} + \text{Profits}$$

$$\$700,000 = \$233,333 + X + \$210,000$$

$$X = \$700,000 - \$233,333 - \$210,000$$

$$X = \$256,667$$

Use the equation approach to estimate the company's break-even point:

$$\text{Sales} = \text{Variable expenses} + \text{Fixed expenses} + \text{Profits}$$

$$X = \tfrac{1}{3}X + \$256,667 + \$0$$

$$\tfrac{2}{3}X = \$256,667$$

$$X = \$385,000$$

Finally, compute the company's margin of safety:

$$\text{Margin of safety} = (\text{Sales} - \text{Break-even sales}) \div \text{Sales}$$

$$= (\$700,000 - \$385,000) \div \$700,000$$

$$= 45\%$$

The margin of safety appears to be adequate, so if the other information about the company is favorable, a loan would seem to be justified.

GUIDANCE ANSWERS TO CONCEPT CHECKS

1. **Choice d.** The contribution margin ratio is (1.0 − Variable costs as a percent of sales).
2. **Choice d.** The contribution margin per unit is $12. Therefore, 5,000 units × $12 contribution margin per unit = Fixed costs of $60,000.
3. **Choice a.** ($100,000 + $50,000) ÷ $20 contribution margin per unit = 7,500 units.
4. **Choice c.** 7,500 units is 2,500 units above the break-even point. Therefore, the margin of safety is 2,500 units × $55 per unit = $137,500.

REVIEW PROBLEM: CVP RELATIONSHIPS

Voltar Company manufactures and sells a telephone answering machine. The company's contribution format income statement for the most recent year is given below:

	Total	Per Unit	Percent of Sales
Sales (20,000 units)	$1,200,000	$60	100%
Less variable expenses	900,000	45	?
Contribution margin	300,000	$15	? %
Less fixed expenses	240,000		
Net operating income	$ 60,000		

Management is anxious to improve the company's profit performance and has asked for an analysis of a number of items.

Required:

1. Compute the company's CM ratio and variable expense ratio.
2. Compute the company's break-even point in both units and sales dollars. Use the equation method.
3. Assume that sales increase by $400,000 next year. If cost behavior patterns remain unchanged, by how much will the company's net operating income increase? Use the CM ratio to determine your answer.
4. Refer to the original data. Assume that next year management wants the company to earn a minimum profit of $90,000. How many units will have to be sold to meet this target profit figure?
5. Refer to the original data. Compute the company's margin of safety in both dollar and percentage form.
6. a. Compute the company's degree of operating leverage at the present level of sales.
   b. Assume that through a more intense effort by the sales staff the company's sales increase by 8% next year. By what percentage would you expect net operating income to increase? Use the operating leverage concept to obtain your answer.
   c. Verify your answer to (b) by preparing a new income statement showing an 8% increase in sales.
7. In an effort to increase sales and profits, management is considering the use of a higher quality speaker. The higher quality speaker would increase variable costs by $3 per unit, but management could eliminate one quality inspector who is paid a salary of $30,000 per year. The sales manager estimates that the higher quality speaker would increase annual sales by at least 20%.
   a. Assuming that changes are made as described above, prepare a projected income statement for next year. Show data on a total, per unit, and percentage basis.
   b. Compute the company's new break-even point in both units and dollars of sales. Use the contribution margin method.
   c. Would you recommend that the changes be made?

Solution to Review Problem

1.
$$\text{CM ratio} = \frac{\text{Contribution margin}}{\text{Selling price}} = \frac{\$15}{\$60} = 25\%$$

$$\text{Variable expense ratio} = \frac{\text{Variable expense}}{\text{Selling price}} = \frac{\$45}{\$60} = 75\%$$

2.
$$\text{Sales} = \text{Variable expenses} + \text{Fixed expenses} + \text{Profits}$$

$$\$60Q = \$45Q + \$240,000 + \$0$$

$$\$15Q = \$240,000$$

$$Q = \$240,000 \div \$15 \text{ per unit}$$

$$Q = 16,000 \text{ units; or at } \$60 \text{ per unit, } \$960,000$$

Alternative solution:

$$X = 0.75X + \$240,000 + \$0$$

$$0.25X = \$240,000$$

$$X = \$240,000 \div 0.25$$

$$X = \$960,000; \text{ or at } \$60 \text{ per unit, } 16,000 \text{ units}$$

3.

Increase in sales	$400,000
Multiply by the CM ratio	× 25%
Expected increase in contribution margin	$100,000

Since the fixed expenses are not expected to change, net operating income will increase by the entire $100,000 increase in contribution margin computed above.

4. Equation method:

$$\text{Sales} = \text{Variable expenses} + \text{Fixed expenses} + \text{Profits}$$

$$\$60Q = \$45Q + \$240,000 + \$90,000$$

$$\$15Q = \$330,000$$

$$Q = \$330,000 \div \$15 \text{ per unit}$$

$$Q = 22,000 \text{ units}$$

Contribution margin method:

$$\frac{\text{Fixed expenses} + \text{Target profit}}{\text{Contribution margin per unit}} = \frac{\$240,000 + \$90,000}{\$15 \text{ per unit}} = 22,000 \text{ units}$$

5.　　　　Margin of safety in dollars = Total sales − Break-even sales

$$= \$1,200,000 - \$960,000 = \$240,000$$

$$\text{Margin of safety percentage} = \frac{\text{Margin of safety in dollars}}{\text{Total sales}} = \frac{\$240,000}{\$1,200,000} = 20\%$$

6. a.　　　$$\text{Degree of operating leverage} = \frac{\text{Contribution margin}}{\text{Net operating income}} = \frac{\$300,000}{\$60,000} = 5$$

b.

Expected increase in sales	8%
Degree of operating leverage.	× 5
Expected increase in net operating income.	40%

c.　If sales increase by 8%, then 21,600 units (20,000 × 1.08 = 21,600) will be sold next year. The new income statement will be as follows:

	Total	Per Unit	Percent of Sales
Sales (21,600 units)	$1,296,000	$60	100%
Less variable expenses	972,000	45	75
Contribution margin	324,000	$15	25%
Less fixed expenses.	240,000		
Net operating income.	$　84,000		

Thus, the $84,000 expected net operating income for next year represents a 40% increase over the $60,000 net operating income earned during the current year:

$$\frac{\$84,000 - \$60,000}{\$60,000} = \frac{\$24,000}{\$60,000} = 40\% \text{ increase}$$

Note from the income statement above that the increase in sales from 20,000 to 21,600 units has resulted in increases in *both* total sales and total variable expenses. It is a common error to overlook the increase in variable expenses when preparing a projected income statement.

7. a.　A 20% increase in sales would result in 24,000 units being sold next year: 20,000 units × 1.20 = 24,000 units.

	Total	Per Unit	Percent of Sales
Sales (24,000 units)	$1,440,000	$60	100%
Less variable expenses	1,152,000	48*	80
Contribution margin	288,000	$12	20%
Less fixed expenses.	210,000†		
Net operating income.	$　78,000		

*$45 + $3 = $48; $48 ÷ $60 = 80%.
†$240,000 − $30,000 = $210,000.

Note that the change in per unit variable expenses results in a change in both the per unit contribution margin and the CM ratio.

b.

$$\text{Break-even point in unit sales} = \frac{\text{Fixed expenses}}{\text{Contribution margin per unit}}$$

$$= \frac{\$210,000}{\$12 \text{ per unit}} = 17,500 \text{ units}$$

$$\text{Break-even point in dollar sales} = \frac{\text{Fixed expenses}}{\text{CM ratio}}$$

$$= \frac{\$210,000}{0.20} = \$1,050,000$$

c. Yes, based on these data the changes should be made. The changes will increase the company's net operating income from the present $60,000 to $78,000 per year. Although the changes will also result in a higher break-even point (17,500 units as compared to the present 16,000 units), the company's margin of safety will actually be wider than before:

$$\text{Margin of safety in dollars} = \text{Total sales} - \text{Break-even sales}$$

$$= \$1,440,000 - \$1,050,000 = \$390,000$$

As shown in (5) above, the company's present margin of safety is only $240,000. Thus, several benefits will result from the proposed changes.

GLOSSARY

Break-even point   The level of sales at which profit is zero. The break-even point can also be defined as the point where total sales equals total expenses or as the point where total contribution margin equals total fixed expenses. (p. 244)

Contribution margin method   A method of computing the break-even point in which the fixed expenses are divided by the contribution margin per unit. (p. 254)

Contribution margin ratio (CM ratio)   The contribution margin as a percentage of total sales. (p. 247)

Cost-volume-profit (CVP) graph   The relationships between revenues, costs, and level of activity in an organization presented in graphic form. (p. 245)

Degree of operating leverage   A measure, at a given level of sales, of how a percentage change in sales volume will affect profits. The degree of operating leverage is computed by dividing contribution margin by net operating income. (p. 260)

Equation method   A method of computing the break-even point that relies on the equation Sales = Variable expenses + Fixed expenses + Profits. (p. 253)

Incremental analysis   An analytical approach that focuses only on those items of revenue, cost, and volume that will change as a result of a decision. (p. 249)

Margin of safety   The excess of budgeted (or actual) sales over the break-even volume of sales. (p. 256)

Operating leverage   A measure of how sensitive net operating income is to a given percentage change in sales. It is computed by dividing the contribution margin by net operating income. (p. 259)

Sales mix   The relative proportions in which a company's products are sold. Sales mix is computed by expressing the sales of each product as a percentage of total sales. (p. 262)

Variable costing   A method of determining unit product costs in which only the variable manufacturing costs are assigned to products and fixed manufacturing overhead costs are considered to be period expenses. (p. 266)

QUESTIONS

6–1   What is meant by a product's contribution margin (CM) ratio? How is this ratio useful in planning business operations?

6–2   Often the most direct route to a business decision is to make an incremental analysis based on the information available. What is meant by an *incremental analysis?*

6–3   Company A's cost structure includes costs that are mostly variable, whereas Company B's cost structure includes costs that are mostly fixed. In a time of increasing sales, which company will tend to realize the most rapid increase in profits? Explain.

6–4 What is meant by the term *operating leverage?*

6–5 A 10% decrease in the selling price of a product will have the same impact on net operating income as a 10% increase in the variable expenses. Do you agree? Why or why not?

6–6 What is meant by the term *break-even point?*

6–7 Name three approaches to break-even analysis. Briefly explain how each approach works.

6–8 In response to a request from your immediate supervisor, you have prepared a CVP graph portraying the cost and revenue characteristics of your company's product and operations. Explain how the lines on the graph and the break-even point would change if (a) the selling price per unit decreased, (b) the fixed cost increased throughout the entire range of activity portrayed on the graph, and (c) the variable cost per unit increased.

6–9 Al's Auto Wash charges $4 to wash a car. The variable cost of washing a car is 15% of sales. Fixed expenses total $1,700 monthly. How many cars must be washed each month for Al to break even?

6–10 What is meant by the margin of safety?

6–11 What is meant by the term *sales mix?* What assumption is usually made concerning sales mix in CVP analysis?

6–12 Explain how a shift in the sales mix could result in both a higher break-even point and a lower net operating income.

6–13 How do absorption costing and variable costing differ in how they treat fixed manufacturing overhead costs?

BRIEF EXERCISES

BRIEF EXERCISE 6–1 Preparing a Contribution Margin Format Income Statement (LO1)

Wheeler Corporation's most recent income statement is shown below:

	Total	Per Unit
Sales (8,000)	$208,000	$26.00
Less variable expenses	144,000	18.00
Contribution margin	64,000	$ 8.00
Less fixed expenses	56,000	
Net operating income	$ 8,000	

Required:

Prepare a new income statement under each of the following conditions (consider each case independently):

1. The sales volume increases by 50 units.
2. The sales volume declines by 50 units.
3. The sales volume is 7,000 units.

BRIEF EXERCISE 6–2 Prepare a Cost-Volume-Profit (CVP) Graph (LO2)

Katara Enterprises has a single product whose selling price is $36 and whose variable cost is $24 per unit. The company's monthly fixed expense is $12,000.

Required:

1. Prepare a cost-volume-profit graph for the company up to a sales level of 2,000 units.
2. Estimate the company's break-even point in unit sales using your cost-volume-profit graph.

BRIEF EXERCISE 6–3 Computing and Using the CM (LO3)

Last month when Harrison Creations, Inc., sold 40,000 units, total sales were $300,000, total variable expenses were $240,000, and total fixed expenses were $45,000.

Required:

1. What is the company's contribution margin (CM) ratio?
2. Estimate the change in the company's net income if it were to increase its total sales by $1,500.

BRIEF EXERCISE 6–4 Show the Effects on the Contribution Margin of Changes in Variable Costs, Fixed Costs, Selling Price, and Volume (LO4)

Data for Herron Corporation are shown below:

	Per Unit	Percent of Sales
Selling price..............	$75	100%
Less variable expenses	45	60
Contribution margin..........	$30	40%

Fixed expenses are $75,000 per month and the company is selling 3,000 units per month.

Required:
1. The marketing manager argues that a $8,000 increase in the monthly advertising budget would increase monthly sales by $15,000. Should the advertising budget be increased?
2. Refer to the original data. Management is considering using higher quality components that would increase the variable cost by $3 per unit. The marketing manager believes the higher quality product would increase sales by 15% per month. Should the higher quality components be used?

BRIEF EXERCISE 6–5   Compute the Break-Even Point   (LO5)
Maxson Products has a single product, a woven basket whose selling price is $8 and whose variable cost is $6 per unit. The company's monthly fixed expense is $5,500.

Required:
1. Solve for the company's break-even point in unit sales using the equation method.
2. Solve for the company's break-even point in sales dollars using the equation method and the CM ratio.
3. Solve for the company's break-even point in unit sales using the contribution margin method.
4. Solve for the company's break-even point in sales dollars using the contribution margin method and the CM ratio.

BRIEF EXERCISE 6–6   Compute the Level of Sales Required to Attain a Target Profit   (LO6)
Liman Corporation has a single product whose selling price is $140 and whose variable cost is $60 per unit. The company's monthly fixed expense is $40,000.

Required:
1. Using the equation method, solve for the unit sales that are required to earn a target profit of $6,000.
2. Using the contribution margin approach, solve for the dollar sales that are required to earn a target profit of $8,000.

BRIEF EXERCISE 6–7   Compute the Margin of Safety   (LO7)
Mohan Corporation sells a sun umbrella used at resort hotels. Data concerning the next month's budget appear below:

Selling price	$25 per unit
Variable expense	$15 per unit
Fixed expense..........	$8,500 per month
Unit sales	1,000 units per month

Required:
1. Compute the company's margin of safety.
2. Compute the company's margin of safety as a percentage of its sales.

BRIEF EXERCISE 6–8   Compute and Use the Degree of Operating Leverage   (LO8)
Eneliko Company's most recent monthly income statement appears below:

	Amount	Percent of Sales
Sales	$120,000	100%
Less variable expenses	84,000	70
Contribution margin..........	36,000	30%
Less fixed expenses	24,000	
Net operating income	$ 12,000	

Required:

1. Compute the company's degree of operating leverage.
2. Using the degree of operating leverage, estimate the impact on net operating income of a 10% increase in sales.
3. Verify your estimate from part (2) above by constructing a new income statement for the company assuming a 10% increase in sales.

BRIEF EXERCISE 6–9   Compute the Break-Even Point for a Multiproduct Company   (LO9)

Lucky Products markets two computer games: Predator and Runway. A contribution margin income statement for a recent month for the two games appears below:

	Predator	Runway	Total
Sales....................	$100,000	$50,000	$150,000
Less variable expenses	25,000	5,000	30,000
Contribution margin........	$ 75,000	$45,000	120,000
Less fixed expenses.........			90,000
Net operating income.......			$ 30,000

Required:

1. Compute the overall contribution margin (CM) ratio for the company.
2. Compute the overall break-even point for the company in sales dollars.
3. Verify the overall break-even point for the company by constructing an income statement showing the appropriate levels of sales for the two products.

EXERCISES

EXERCISE 6–10   Using a Contribution Format Income Statement   (LO1, LO4)

Porter Company's most recent income statement is shown below:

	Total	Per Unit
Sales (30,000 units)..........	$150,000	$5
Less variable expenses	90,000	3
Contribution margin.........	60,000	$2
Less fixed expenses..........	50,000	
Net operating income........	$ 10,000	

Required:

Prepare a new income statement under each of the following conditions (consider each case independently):

1. The sales volume increases by 15%.
2. The selling price decreases by 50 cents per unit, and the sales volume increases by 20%.
3. The selling price increases by 50 cents per unit, fixed expenses increase by $10,000, and the sales volume decreases by 5%.
4. Variable expenses increase by 20 cents per unit, the selling price increases by 12%, and the sales volume decreases by 10%.

EXERCISE 6–11   Break-Even Analysis and CVP Graphing   (LO2, LO4, LO5)

Chi Omega Sorority is planning its annual Riverboat Extravaganza. The Extravaganza committee has assembled the following expected costs for the event:

Dinner (per person)........................	$7
Favors and program (per person)	$3
Band	$1,500
Tickets and advertising......................	$700
Riverboat rental	$4,800
Floorshow and strolling entertainers	$1,000

Required:

The committee members would like to charge $30 per person for the evening's activities.

1. Compute the break-even point for the Extravaganza (in terms of the number of persons that must attend).
2. Assume that only 250 persons attended the Extravaganza last year. If the same number attend this year, what price per ticket must be charged to break even?
3. Refer to the original data ($30 ticket price per person). Prepare a CVP graph for the Extravaganza from a zero level of activity up to 600 tickets sold. Number of persons should be placed on the horizontal (X) axis, and dollars should be placed on the vertical (Y) axis.

EXERCISE 6–12 Break-Even Analysis; Target Profit; Margin of Safety; CM Ratio   (LO1, LO3, LO5, LO6, LO7)

Pringle Company sells a single product. The company's sales and expenses for a recent month follow:

	Total	Per Unit
Sales....................	$600,000	$40
Less variable expenses	420,000	28
Contribution margin.........	180,000	$12
Less fixed expenses..........	150,000	
Net operating income........	$ 30,000	

Required:

1. What is the monthly break-even point in units sold and in sales dollars?
2. Without resorting to computations, what is the total contribution margin at the break-even point?
3. How many units would have to be sold each month to earn a minimum target profit of $18,000? Use the contribution margin method. Verify your answer by preparing a contribution income statement at the target level of sales.
4. Refer to the original data. Compute the company's margin of safety in both dollar and percentage terms.
5. What is the company's CM ratio? If monthly sales increase by $80,000 and there is no change in fixed expenses, by how much would you expect monthly net operating income to increase?

EXERCISE 6–13 Break-Even and Target Profit Analysis   (LO3, LO4, LO5, LO6)

Super Sales Company is the exclusive distributor for a revolutionary bookbag. The product sells for $60 per unit and has a CM ratio of 40%. The company's fixed expenses are $360,000 per year.

Required:

1. What are the variable expenses per unit?
2. Using the equation method:
   a. What is the break-even point in units and in sales dollars?
   b. What sales level in units and in sales dollars is required to earn an annual profit of $90,000?
   c. Assume that through negotiation with the manufacturer the Super Sales Company is able to reduce its variable expenses by $3 per unit. What is the company's new break-even point in units and in sales dollars?
3. Repeat (2) above using the contribution margin method.

EXERCISE 6–14 Multiproduct Break-Even Analysis   (LO1, LO9)

Okabee Enterprises sells two products, Model A100 and Model B900. Monthly sales and the contribution margin ratios for the two products follow:

	Product		
	Model A100	Model B900	Total
Sales....................	$700,000	$300,000	$1,000,000
Contribution margin ratio...	60%	70%	?

The company's fixed expenses total $598,500 per month.

Required:
1. Prepare an income statement for the company as a whole. Use the format shown in Exhibit 6–3.
2. Compute the break-even point for the company based on the current sales mix.
3. If sales increase by $50,000 per month, by how much would you expect net operating income to increase? What are your assumptions?

EXERCISE 6–15   Operating Leverage   (LO4, LO8)

Superior Door Company sells prehung doors to home builders. The doors are sold for $60 each. Variable costs are $42 per door, and fixed costs total $450,000 per year. The company is currently selling 30,000 doors per year.

Required:
1. Prepare a contribution format income statement for the company at the present level of sales and compute the degree of operating leverage.
2. Management is confident that the company can sell 37,500 doors next year (an increase of 7,500 doors, or 25%, over current sales). Compute the following:
   a.   The expected percentage increase in net operating income for next year.
   b.   The expected total dollar net operating income for next year. (Do not prepare an income statement; use the degree of operating leverage to compute your answer.)

EXERCISE 6–16   Break-Even and Target Profit Analysis   (LO4, LO5, LO6)

Reveen Products sells camping equipment. One of the company's products, a camp lantern, sells for $90 per unit. Variable expenses are $63 per lantern, and fixed expenses associated with the lantern total $135,000 per month.

Required:
1. Compute the company's break-even point in number of lanterns and in total sales dollars.
2. If the variable expenses per lantern increase as a percentage of the selling price, will it result in a higher or a lower break-even point? Why? (Assume that the fixed expenses remain unchanged.)
3. At present, the company is selling 8,000 lanterns per month. The sales manager is convinced that a 10% reduction in the selling price will result in a 25% increase in the number of lanterns sold each month. Prepare two contribution income statements, one under present operating conditions, and one as operations would appear after the proposed changes. Show both total and per unit data on your statements.
4. Refer to the data in (3) above. How many lanterns would have to be sold at the new selling price to yield a minimum net operating income of $72,000 per month?

EXERCISE 6–17   Interpretive Questions on the CVP Graph   (LO2, LO5)

A CVP graph, as illustrated below, is a useful technique for showing relationships between costs, volume, and profits in an organization.

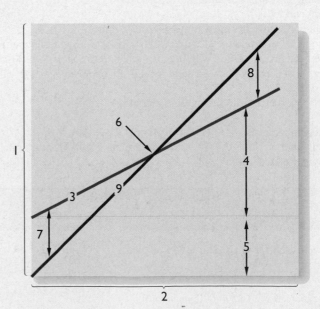

Required:
1. Identify the numbered components in the CVP graph.
2. State the effect of each of the following actions on line 3, line 9, and the break-even point. For line 3 and line 9, state whether the action will cause the line to:

> Remain unchanged.
> Shift upward.
> Shift downward.
> Have a steeper slope (i.e., rotate upward).
> Have a flatter slope (i.e., rotate downward).
> Shift upward *and* have a steeper slope.
> Shift upward *and* have a flatter slope.
> Shift downward *and* have a steeper slope.
> Shift downward *and* have a flatter slope.

In the case of the break-even point, state whether the action will cause the break-even point to:

> Remain unchanged.
> Increase.
> Decrease.
> Probably change, but the direction is uncertain.

Treat each case independently.

x. *Example.* Fixed costs are increased by $20,000 each period.
> *Answer* (see choices above): Line 3: Shift upward.
> > Line 9: Remain unchanged.
> > Break-even point: Increase.

a. The unit selling price is decreased from $30 to $27.
b. The per unit variable costs are increased from $12 to $15.
c. The total fixed costs are reduced by $40,000.
d. Five thousand fewer units are sold during the period than were budgeted.
e. Due to purchasing a robot to perform a task that was previously done by workers, fixed costs are increased by $25,000 per period, and variable costs are reduced by $8 per unit.
f. As a result of a decrease in the cost of materials, both unit variable costs and the selling price are decreased by $3.
g. Advertising costs are increased by $50,000 per period, resulting in a 10% increase in the number of units sold.
h. Due to paying salespersons a commission rather than a flat salary, fixed costs are reduced by $21,000 per period, and unit variable costs are increased by $6.

PROBLEMS

PROBLEM 6–18 Basic CVP Analysis   (LO1, LO3, LO4, LO5, LO6, LO8)
Marjolein & Co. makes a designer alarm clock that sells for $20 per unit. Variable costs are $6 per unit, and fixed costs total $210,000 per year.

CHECK FIGURE
(2) Break-even: $300,000

Required:
Answer the following independent questions:

1. What is the product's CM ratio?
2. Use the CM ratio to determine the break-even point in sales dollars.
3. Due to an increase in demand, the company estimates that sales will increase by $200,000 during the next year. By how much should net operating income (or net operating loss) change, assuming that fixed costs do not change?
4. Assume that the operating results for last year were:

Sales	$320,000
Less variable expenses	96,000
Contribution margin	224,000
Less fixed expenses	210,000
Net operating income	$ 14,000

a. Compute the degree of operating leverage at the current level of sales.
b. The president expects sales to increase by 5% next year. By what percentage should net operating income increase?

5. Refer to the original data. Assume that the company sold 20,000 units last year. The sales manager is convinced that an 8% reduction in the selling price, combined with a $24,000 increase in advertising, would cause annual sales in units to increase by one-fourth. Prepare two contribution income statements, one showing the results of last year's operations and one showing the results of operations if these changes are made. Would you recommend that the company do as the sales manager suggests?

6. Refer to the original data. Assume again that the company sold 20,000 units last year. The president does not want to change the selling price. Instead, he wants to increase the sales commission by $1.50 per unit. He thinks that this move, combined with some increase in advertising, would increase annual sales by 20%. By how much could advertising be increased with profits remaining unchanged? Do not prepare an income statement; use the incremental analysis approach.

CHECK FIGURE
(3) Net operating loss:
     $3,000
(5a) Break-even: 31,500
     units

PROBLEM 6–19   Basic CVP Analysis; Cost Structure   (LO3, LO4, LO5, LO6)
Due to erratic sales of its sole product—a disposable pocket camera—Markline Company has been experiencing difficulty for some time. The company's income statement for the most recent month is given below:

Sales (30,000 units × $20.00 per unit)........	$600,000
Less variable expenses	360,000
Contribution margin......................	240,000
Less fixed expenses.......................	250,000
Net operating loss........................	$(10,000)

Required:
1. Compute the company's CM ratio and its break-even point in both units and dollars.
2. The president believes that a $20,000 increase in the monthly advertising budget, combined with an intensified effort by the sales staff, will result in a $90,000 increase in monthly sales. If the president is right, what will be the effect on the company's monthly net operating income or loss? (Use the incremental approach to prepare your answer.)
3. Refer to the original data. The sales manager is convinced that a 14% reduction in the selling price, combined with an increase of $65,000 in the monthly advertising budget, will cause unit sales to increase by 100%. What will the new income statement look like if these changes are adopted?
4. Refer to the original data. The Marketing Department thinks that a redesigned package for the camera would help sales. The new package would increase packaging costs by $0.75 per unit. Assuming no other changes, how many units would have to be sold each month to earn a profit of $9,200?
5. Refer to the original data. By automating certain operations, the company could reduce variable costs by $2 per unit. However, fixed costs would increase by $65,000 each month.
    a. Compute the new CM ratio and the new break-even point in both units and dollars.
    b. Assume that the company expects to sell 40,000 units next month. Prepare two income statements, one assuming that operations are not automated and one assuming that they are. (Show data on a per unit and percentage basis, as well as in total, for each alternative.)
    c. Would you recommend that the company automate its operations? Explain.

CHECK FIGURE
(1) 9,375 watches
(3) $2,800 net operating loss

PROBLEM 6–20   Basic CVP Analysis; Graphing   (LO1, LO2, LO4, LO5)
Mystery Company operates a chain of watch shops around the country. The shops carry many styles of watches that are all sold at the same price. Sales personnel in the shops are paid a substantial commission on each watch sold (in addition to a small basic salary) in order to encourage them to be aggressive in their sales efforts.

The following cost and revenue data relate to Shop 30 and are typical of one of the company's many outlets:

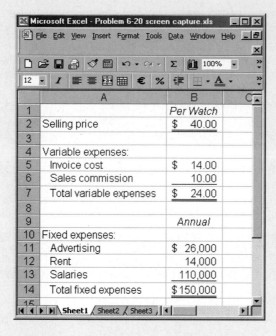

Required:

1. Calculate the annual break-even point in dollar sales and in unit sales for Shop 30.
2. Prepare a CVP graph showing cost and revenue data for Shop 30 from a zero level of activity up to 20,000 watches sold each year. Clearly indicate the break-even point on the graph.
3. If 9,200 watches are sold in a year, what would be Shop 30's net operating income or loss?
4. The company is considering paying the store manager of Shop 30 an incentive commission of $1 per watch (in addition to the salesperson's commission). If this change is made, what will be the new break-even point in dollar sales and in unit sales?
5. Refer to the original data. As an alternative to (4) above, the company is considering paying the store manager a $2 commission on each watch sold in excess of the break-even point. If this change is made, what will be the shop's net operating income or loss if 11,600 watches are sold?
6. Refer to the original data. The company is considering eliminating sales commissions entirely in its shops and increasing fixed salaries by $45,000 annually. If this change is made, what will be the new break-even point in dollar sales and in unit sales for Shop 30? Would you recommend that the change be made? Explain.

PROBLEM 6–21   Multiproduct Break-Even Analysis   (LO1, LO9)

Fill in the missing amounts in each of the eight case situations below. Each case is independent of the others. (Hint: One way to find the missing amounts would be to prepare a contribution income statement for each case, enter the known data, and then compute the missing items.)

a. Assume that only one product is being sold in each of the four following case situations:

Case	Units Sold	Sales	Variable Expenses	Contribution Margin per Unit	Fixed Expenses	Net Income (Loss)
1......	12,000	$360,000	$144,000	$?	$190,000	$?
2......	?	$50,000	$?	$6	$25,000	$5,000
3......	2,000	$?	$16,000	$12	$?	$(6,000)
4......	7,000	$280,000	$?	$?	$120,000	$34,000

b. Assume that more than one product is being sold in each of the four following case situations:

Case	Sales	Variable Expenses	Average Contribution Margin (percent)	Fixed Expenses	Net Income (Loss)
1.....	$100,000	$?	40	$?	$ (2,000)
2.....	$300,000	$165,000	?	$85,000	$?
3.....	$?	$?	15	$20,000	$10,000
4.....	$460,000	$138,000	?	$?	$62,000

PROBLEM 6–22 Sales Mix; Multiproduct Break-Even Analysis (LO1, LO5, LO9)

Mamma's Pasta, Ltd., of Italy exports Italian pasta throughout North America. The company produces three varieties of pasta—spaghetti, tortellini, and fettuccini. (The currency in Italy is the euro, which is denoted by €.) Budgeted sales by product and in total for the coming month are shown below:

	Product								
	Spaghetti		**Tortellini**		**Fettuccini**		**Total**	
Percentage of total sales..........	14%		28%		58%		100%	
Sales.................	€84,000	100%	€168,000	100%	€348,000	100%	€600,000	100.0%
Less variable expenses...	67,200	80	126,000	75	208,800	60	402,000	67.0
Contribution margin	€16,800	20%	€ 42,000	25%	€139,200	40%	198,000	33.0%
Less fixed expenses							188,100	
Net operating income ...							€ 9,900	

$$\text{Break-even sales} = \frac{\text{Fixed expenses}}{\text{CM ratio}} = \frac{€188,100}{0.330} = €570,000$$

As shown by these data, net operating income is budgeted at €9,900 for the month and break-even sales at €570,000.

Assume that actual sales for the month total €600,000 as planned. Actual sales by product are: spaghetti, €120,000; tortellini, €168,000; and fettuccini, €312,000.

Required:

1. Prepare a contribution income statement for the month based on actual sales data. Present the income statement in the format shown above.
2. Compute the break-even sales for the month based on your actual data.
3. Considering the fact that the company met its €600,000 sales budget for the month, the president is shocked at the results shown on your income statement in (1) above. Prepare a brief memo for the president explaining why both the operating results and break-even sales are different from what was budgeted.

PROBLEM 6–23 Break-Even and Target Profit Analysis (LO5, LO6)

Mugs and More sells a large variety of coffee mugs. Larry Hooper, the owner, is thinking of expanding his sales by hiring local high school students, on a commission basis, to sell coffee mugs bearing the name and mascot of the local high school.

These coffee mugs would have to be ordered from the manufacturer six weeks in advance, and they could not be returned because of the unique printing required. The coffee mugs would cost Mr. Hooper $3 each with a minimum order of 50 coffee mugs. Any additional coffee mugs would have to be ordered in increments of 50.

Since Mr. Hooper's plan would not require any additional facilities, the only costs associated with the project would be the costs of the coffee mugs and the costs of the sales commissions. The selling price of the coffee mugs would be $6 each. Mr. Hooper would pay the students a commission of $1 for each mug sold.

Required:

1. To make the project worthwhile, Mr. Hooper would require a $700 profit for the first three months of the venture. What level of sales in units and in dollars would be required to reach this target net operating income? Show all computations.

2. Assume that the venture is undertaken and an order is placed for 50 coffee mugs. What would be Mr. Hooper's break-even point in units and in sales dollars? Show computations and explain the reasoning behind your answer.

PROBLEM 6–24   Changes in Fixed and Variable Costs; Break-Even and Target Profit Analysis (LO4, LO5, LO6)

CHECK FIGURE
(1) Break-even: 32,000 units

Toujours Belle produces skin care products for men and women. An incredibly smooth moisturizing cream has come onto the market that the company is anxious to produce and sell. Enough capacity exists in the company's plant to produce 28,000 units of the cream each month. Variable costs to manufacture and sell one unit would be $12, and fixed costs associated with the cream would total $240,000 per month.

The company's Marketing Department predicts that demand for the new cream will exceed the 28,000 units that the company is able to produce. Additional manufacturing space can be rented from another company at a fixed cost of $12,000 per month. Variable costs in the rented facility would total $13 per unit, due to somewhat less efficient operations than in the main plant. The new cream will sell for $20 per unit.

Required:
1. Compute the monthly break-even point for the new cream in units and in total dollar sales. Show all computations in good form.
2. How many units must be sold each month to make a monthly profit of $14,000?
3. If the sales manager receives a bonus of $1 for each unit sold in excess of the break-even point, how many units must be sold each month to earn a return of 5.0% on the monthly investment in fixed costs?

PROBLEM 6–25   Sales Mix; Break-Even Analysis; Margin of Safety   (LO1, LO5, LO7, LO9)

CHECK FIGURE
(1b) Break-even: $756,000
(2b) Margin of safety: 65.0%

Jean Leeman & Co. of Texas makes two products, Mini and Giga. Present revenue, cost, and sales data on the two products follow:

	Mini	Giga
Selling price per unit.	$5.00	$60.00
Variable expenses per unit.	$2.00	$36.00
Number of units sold annually	108,000	9,000

Fixed expenses total $378,000 per year.

Required:
1. Assuming the sales mix given above, do the following:
   a. Prepare a contribution income statement showing both dollar and percent columns for each product and for the company as a whole.
   b. Compute the break-even point in dollars for the company as a whole and the margin of safety in both dollars and percent.
2. The company has just developed a new product, Mega. Assume that the company could sell 36,000 units at $50 each. The variable expenses would be $35 each. The company's fixed expenses would not change.
   a. Prepare another contribution income statement, including sales of Mega (sales of the other two products would not change). Carry percentage computations to one decimal place.
   b. Compute the company's new break-even point in dollars and the new margin of safety in both dollars and percent.
3. The president of the company examines your figures and says, "There's something strange here. Our fixed costs haven't changed and you show greater total contribution margin if we add the new product, but you also show our break-even point going up. With greater contribution margin, the break-even point should go down, not up. You've made a mistake somewhere." Explain to the president what has happened.

PROBLEM 6–26   Graphing; Incremental Analysis; Operating Leverage   (LO2, LO4, LO5, LO6, LO8)

CHECK FIGURE
(1) Break-even: 7,500 swimsuits
(5a) Leverage: 4.00

Jimmy Paker has recently opened Pacific Dreams in California, a store that specializes in sport swimwear. Jimmy has just received a degree in business and he is anxious to apply the principles he has learned to his business. In time, he hopes to open a chain of swimwear shops. As a first step, he has prepared the following analysis for his new store:

IS

Selling price per swimsuit.	$20.00
Variable expenses per swimsuit.	12.00
Contribution margin per swimsuit. . . .	$ 8.00
Fixed expenses per year:	
Building rental.	$18,000
Equipment depreciation	6,000
Selling	24,000
Administrative	12,000
Total fixed expenses.	$60,000

Required:

1. How many swimsuits must be sold each year to break even? What does this represent in total dollar sales?
2. Prepare a CVP graph for the store from a zero level of activity up to 10,000 swimsuits sold each year. Indicate the break-even point on your graph.
3. Jimmy has decided that he must earn at least $20,000 the first year to justify his time and effort. How many swimsuits must be sold to reach this target profit?
4. Jimmy now has one salesperson working in the store part time. It will cost him an additional $10,000 per year to convert the part-time position to a full-time position. Jimmy believes that the change would bring in an additional $60,000 in sales each year. Should he convert the position? Use the incremental approach (do not prepare an income statement).
5. Refer to the original data. During the first year, the store sold 10,000 swimsuits and reported the following operating results:

Sales (10,000 swimsuits)	$200,000
Less variable expenses.	120,000
Contribution margin	80,000
Less fixed expenses	60,000
Net operating income	$ 20,000

   a. What is the store's degree of operating leverage?
   b. Jimmy is confident that with a more intense sales effort and with a more creative advertising program he can increase sales by 15% next year. What would be the expected percentage increase in net operating income? Use the degree of operating leverage to compute your answer.

BUILDING YOUR SKILLS

CHECK FIGURE
(2) 14,320 patient-days

SKILLS CHALLENGER   (LO5, LO6)

The Cardiac Care Department at St. Andrew's General Hospital has a capacity of 70 beds and operates 24 hours a day year-around. The measure of activity in the department is patient-days, where one patient-day represents one patient occupying a bed for one day. The average revenue per patient-day is $240 and the average variable cost per patient-day is $90. The fixed cost of the department (not including personnel costs) is $1,370,000.

The only personnel directly employed by the Cardiac Care Department are aides, nurses, and supervising nurses. The hospital has minimum staffing requirements for the department based on total annual patient-days in Cardiac Care. Hospital requirements, beginning at the minimum expected level of activity, follow:

Annual Patient-Days	Aides	Nurses	Supervising Nurses
10,000–12,000	7	15	3
12,001–13,750	8	15	3
13,751–16,500	9	16	4
16,501–18,250	10	16	4
18,251–20,750	10	17	5
20,751–23,000	11	18	5

These staffing levels represent full-time equivalents, and it should be assumed that the Cardiac Care Department always employs only the minimum number of required full-time equivalent personnel.

Average annual salaries for each class of employee are: aides, $18,000; nurses, $29,000; and supervising nurses, $38,000.

Required:

1. Compute the total fixed costs (including the salaries of aides, nurses, and supervising nurses) in the Cardiac Care Department for each level of activity shown above (i.e., total fixed costs at the 10,000–12,000 patient-day level of activity, total fixed costs at the 12,001–13,750 patient-day level of activity, etc.).
2. Compute the minimum number of patient-days required for the Cardiac Care Department to break even.
3. Determine the minimum number of patient-days required for the Cardiac Care Department to earn an annual "profit" of $360,000.

(CPA, adapted)

ANALYTICAL THINKING   (LO5, LO9)

Jasmine Park encountered her boss, Bubba Gompers, at the pop machine in the lobby. Bubba is the vice president of marketing at Down South Lures Corporation. Jasmine was puzzled by some calculations she had been doing, so she asked him:

Jasmine: "Bubba, I'm not sure how to go about answering the questions that came up at the meeting with the president yesterday."
Bubba: "What's the problem?"
Jasmine: "The president wanted to know the break-even for each of the company's products, but I am having trouble figuring them out."
Bubba: "I'm sure you can handle it, Jasmine. And, by the way, I need your analysis on my desk tomorrow morning at 8:00 sharp so I can look at it before the follow-up meeting at 9:00."

Down South Lures makes three fishing lures in its manufacturing facility in Alabama. Data concerning these products appear below.

	Frog	Minnow	Worm
Normal annual sales volume	100,000	200,000	300,000
Unit selling price	$2.00	$1.40	$0.80
Variable cost per unit.	$1.20	$0.80	$0.50

Total fixed expenses for the entire company are $282,000 per year.

All three products are sold in highly competitive markets, so the company is unable to raise its prices without losing unacceptable numbers of customers.

The company has no work in process or finished goods inventories due to an extremely effective just-in-time manufacturing system.

Required:

1. What is the company's overall break-even in total sales dollars?
2. Of the total fixed costs of $282,000, $18,000 could be avoided if the Frog lure product were dropped, $96,000 if the Minnow lure product were dropped, and $60,000 if the Worm lure product were dropped. The remaining fixed costs of $108,000 consist of common fixed costs such as administrative salaries and rent on the factory building that could be avoided only by going out of business entirely.
   a. What is the break-even quantity of each product?
   b. If the company sells exactly the break-even quantity of each product, what will be the overall profit of the company? Explain this result.

COMMUNICATING IN PRACTICE   (LO4, LO5, LO6)

CHECK FIGURE
(2a) $28,333,333

Marston Corporation manufactures disposable thermometers that are sold to hospitals through a network of independent sales agents located in the United States and Canada. These sales agents sell a variety of products to hospitals in addition to Marston's disposable thermometer. The sales agents are currently paid an 18% commission on sales, and this commission rate was used when Marston's management prepared the following budgeted income statement for the upcoming year.

MARSTON CORPORATION Budgeted Income Statement		
Sales......................................		$30,000,000
Cost of goods sold:		
Variable	$17,400,000	
Fixed	2,800,000	20,200,000
Gross profit............................		9,800,000
Selling and administrative expenses:		
Commissions........................	5,400,000	
Fixed advertising expense..............	800,000	
Fixed administrative expense	3,200,000	9,400,000
Net operating income....................		$ 400,000

Since the completion of the above statement, Marston's management has learned that the independent sales agents are demanding an increase in the commission rate to 20% of sales for the upcoming year. This would be the third increase in commissions demanded by the independent sales agents in five years. As a result, Marston's management has decided to investigate the possibility of hiring its own sales staff to replace the independent sales agents.

Marston's controller estimates that the company will have to hire eight salespeople to cover the current market area, and the total annual payroll cost of these employees will be about $700,000, including fringe benefits. The salespeople will also be paid commissions of 10% of sales. Travel and entertainment expenses are expected to total about $400,000 for the year. The company will also have to hire a sales manager and support staff whose salaries and fringe benefits will come to $200,000 per year. To make up for the promotions that the independent sales agents had been running on behalf of Marston, management believes that the company's budget for fixed advertising expenses should be increased by $500,000.

Required:
1. Assuming sales of $30,000,000, construct a budgeted contribution format income statement for the upcoming year for each of the following alternatives:
   a. The independent sales agents' commission rate remains unchanged at 18%.
   b. The independent sales agents' commission rate increases to 20%.
   c. The company employs its own sales force.
2. Calculate Marston Corporation's break-even point in sales dollars for the upcoming year assuming the following:
   a. The independent sales agents' commission rate remains unchanged at 18%.
   b. The independent sales agents' commission rate increases to 20%.
   c. The company employs its own sales force.
3. Refer to your answer to (1)(b) above. If the company employs its own sales force, what volume of sales would be necessary to generate the net income the company would realize if sales are $30,000,000 and the company continues to sell through agents (at a 20% commission rate)?
4. Determine the volume of sales at which net income would be equal regardless of whether Marston Corporation sells through agents (at a 20% commission rate) or employs its own sales force.
5. Prepare a graph on which you plot the profits for both of the following alternatives.
   a. The independent sales agents' commission rate increases to 20%.
   b. The company employs its own sales force.
   On the graph, use total sales revenue as the measure of activity.
6. Write a memo to the president of Marston Corporation in which you make a recommendation as to whether the company should continue to use independent sales agents (at a 20% commission rate) or employ its own sales force. Fully explain the reasons for your recommendation in the memo.

(CMA, adapted)

 TEAMWORK IN ACTION (LO1, LO4)

Revenue from major intercollegiate sports is an important source of funds for many colleges. Most of the costs of putting on a football or basketball game may be fixed and may increase very little as the size of the crowd increases. Thus, the revenue from every extra ticket sold may be almost pure profit.

Choose a sport played at your college or university, such as football or basketball, that generates significant revenue. Talk with the business manager of your college's sports programs before answering the following questions:

Required:

1. What is the maximum seating capacity of the stadium or arena in which the sport is played? During the past year, what was the average attendance at the games? On average, what percentage of the stadium or arena capacity was filled?

2. The number of seats sold often depends on the opponent. The attendance for a game with a traditional rival (e.g., Nebraska vs. Colorado, University of Washington vs. Washington State, or Texas vs. Texas A&M) is usually substantially above the average. Also, games against conference foes may draw larger crowds than other games. As a consequence, the number of tickets sold for a game is somewhat predictable. What implications does this have for the nature of the costs of putting on a game? Are most of the costs really fixed with respect to the number of tickets sold?

3. Estimate the variable cost per ticket sold.

4. Estimate the total additional revenue that would be generated in an average game if all of the tickets were sold at their normal prices. Estimate how much profit is lost because these tickets are not sold.

5. Estimate the ancillary revenue (parking and concessions) per ticket sold. Estimate how much profit is lost in an average game from these sources of revenue as a consequence of not having a sold-out game.

6. Estimate how much additional profit would be generated for your college if every game were sold out for the entire season.

TAKING IT TO THE NET

As you know, the World Wide Web is a medium that is constantly evolving. Sites come and go and change without notice. To enable periodic update of site addresses, this problem has been posted to the textbook website (www.mhhe.com/bgn2e). After accessing the site, enter the Student Center and select this chapter. Select and complete the Taking It to the Net problem.

CHAPTER SEVEN

Profit Planning

CHAPTER OUTLINE

The Basic Framework of Budgeting

- Personal Budgets
- Difference between Planning and Control
- Advantages of Budgeting
- Responsibility Accounting
- Choosing a Budget Period
- The Self-Imposed Budget
- The Matter of Human Relations
- Zero-Based Budgeting
- The Budget Committee
- An Overview of the Master Budget
- Sales Forecasting—A Critical Step

Preparing the Master Budget

- The Sales Budget
- The Production Budget
- Inventory Purchases—Merchandising Firm
- The Direct Materials Budget
- The Direct Labor Budget
- The Manufacturing Overhead Budget
- The Ending Finished Goods Inventory Budget
- The Selling and Administrative Expense Budget
- The Cash Budget
- The Budgeted Income Statement
- The Budgeted Balance Sheet

DECISION FEATURE

A Looming Financial Crisis

The Repertory Theatre of St. Louis is a not-for-profit professional theater that is supported by contributions from donors and by ticket sales. Financially, the theater appeared to be doing well. However, a five-year budget revealed that within a few years, expenses would exceed revenues and the theater would be facing a financial crisis. Realistically, additional contributions from donors would not fill the gap. Cutting costs would not work because of the theater's already lean operations; cutting costs even more would jeopardize the quality of the theater's productions. Raising ticket prices was ruled out due to competitive pressures and to the belief that this would be unpopular with many donors. The solution was to build a second mainstage performing space that would allow the theater to put on more performances and thereby sell more tickets. By developing a long-range budget, the management of The Repertory Theatre of St. Louis was able to identify in advance a looming financial crisis and to develop a solution that would avert the crisis in time.

See the theater's website at www.repstl.org for information concerning the current season.

Source: Lawrence P. Carr, ed., "The Repertory Theatre of St. Louis (B): Strategic Budgeting," *Cases from Management Accounting Practice: Volumes 10 and 11,* Institute of Management Accountants, Montvale, NJ, 1997.

LEARNING OBJECTIVES

After studying Chapter 7, you should be able to:

LO1 Understand why organizations budget and the processes they use to create budgets.

LO2 Prepare a sales budget, including a schedule of expected cash receipts.

LO3 Prepare a production budget.

LO4 Prepare a direct materials budget, including a schedule of expected cash disbursements for purchases of materials.

LO5 Prepare a direct labor budget.

LO6 Prepare a manufacturing overhead budget.

LO7 Prepare a selling and administrative expense budget.

LO8 Prepare a cash budget.

LO9 Prepare a budgeted income statement.

LO10 Prepare a budgeted balance sheet.

In this chapter, we focus on the steps taken by businesses to achieve their desired levels of profits—a process called *profit planning*. We shall see that profit planning is accomplished through the preparation of a number of budgets, which, when brought together, form an integrated business plan known as the *master budget*. The master budget is an essential management tool that communicates management's plans throughout the organization, allocates resources, and coordinates activities.

THE BASIC FRAMEWORK OF BUDGETING

LEARNING OBJECTIVE 1

Understand why organizations budget and the processes they use to create budgets.

A **budget** is a detailed plan for acquiring and using financial and other resources over a specified time period. It represents a plan for the future expressed in formal quantitative terms. The act of preparing a budget is called *budgeting*. The use of budgets to control an organization's activities is known as *budgetary control*.

The **master budget** is a summary of a company's plans that sets specific targets for sales, production, distribution, and financing activities. It generally culminates in a cash budget, a budgeted income statement, and a budgeted balance sheet. In short, it represents a comprehensive expression of management's plans for the future and how these plans are to be accomplished.

Personal Budgets

Nearly everyone budgets to some extent, even though many of the people who use budgets do not recognize what they are doing as budgeting. For example, most people make estimates of their income and plan expenditures for food, clothing, housing, and so on. As a result of this planning, people restrict their spending to some predetermined, allowable amount. While they may not be conscious of the fact, these people clearly go through a budgeting process. Income is estimated, expenditures are planned, and spending is restricted in accordance with the plan. Individuals also use budgets to forecast their future financial condition for purposes such as purchasing a home, financing college education, or setting aside funds for retirement. These budgets may exist only in the mind of the individual, but they are budgets nevertheless.

The budgets of a business or other organization serve much the same functions as the budgets prepared informally by individuals. Business budgets tend to be more detailed and to involve more work, but they are similar to the budgets prepared by individuals in most other respects. Like personal budgets, they assist in planning and controlling expenditures; they also assist in predicting operating results and financial condition in future periods.

Concept 7–1

Difference between Planning and Control

The terms *planning* and *control* are often confused, and occasionally these terms are used in such a way as to suggest that they mean the same thing. Actually, planning and control are two quite distinct concepts. **Planning** involves developing objectives and preparing various budgets to achieve these objectives. **Control** involves the steps taken by management to increase the likelihood that the objectives set down at the planning stage are attained and that all parts of the organization are working together toward that goal. To be completely effective, a good budgeting system must provide for *both* planning and control. Good planning without effective control is time wasted.

Advantages of Budgeting

Companies realize many benefits from a budgeting program. Among these benefits are the following:

1. Budgets *communicate* management's plans throughout the organization.
2. Budgets force managers to *think about* and plan for the future. In the absence of the necessity to prepare a budget, too many managers would spend all of their time dealing with daily emergencies.
3. The budgeting process provides a means of *allocating resources* to those parts of the organization where they can be used most effectively.
4. The budgeting process can uncover potential *bottlenecks* before they occur.
5. Budgets *coordinate* the activities of the entire organization by *integrating* the plans of the various parts. Budgeting helps to ensure that everyone in the organization is pulling in the same direction.
6. Budgets define goals and objectives that can serve as *benchmarks* for evaluating subsequent performance.

Responsibility Accounting

Most of what we say in this chapter and in the next three chapters is concerned with *responsibility accounting*. The basic idea underlying **responsibility accounting** is that a manager should be held responsible for those items—and *only* those items—that the manager can actually control to a significant extent. Each line item (i.e., revenue or cost) in the budget is made the responsibility of a manager, and that manager is held responsible for subsequent deviations between budgeted goals and actual results. In effect, responsibility accounting *personalizes* accounting information by looking at costs from a *personal control* standpoint. This concept is central to any effective profit planning and control system. Someone must be held responsible for each cost or else no one will be responsible, and the cost will inevitably grow out of control.

Being held responsible for costs does not mean that the manager is penalized if the actual results do not measure up to the budgeted goals. However, the manager should take the initiative to correct any unfavorable discrepancies, should understand the source of significant favorable or unfavorable discrepancies, and should be prepared to explain the reasons for discrepancies to higher management. The point of an effective responsibility system is to make sure that nothing "falls through the cracks," that the organization reacts quickly and appropriately to deviations from its plans, and that the organization learns

Planning and Control

Planning   **Control**

from the feedback it gets by comparing budgeted goals to actual results. The point is *not* to penalize individuals for missing targets.

Choosing a Budget Period

Operating budgets ordinarily cover the company's fiscal year. Many companies divide their budget year into four quarters. The first quarter is then subdivided into months, and monthly budgets are developed. The last three quarters are carried in the budget at quarterly totals only. As the year progresses, the figures for the second quarter are broken down into monthly amounts, then the third-quarter figures are broken down, and so forth. This approach has the advantage of requiring periodic review and reappraisal of budget data throughout the year.

In this chapter, we will focus on one-year operating budgets. However, using basically the same techniques, operating budgets can be prepared for periods that extend over many years. It may be difficult to accurately forecast sales and required data much beyond a year, but even rough estimates can be invaluable in uncovering potential problems and opportunities that would otherwise be overlooked.

The Self-Imposed Budget

The success of a budget program will be determined in large part by the way in which the budget is developed. In the most successful budget programs, managers with cost control responsibilities actively participate in preparing their own budgets. This is in contrast to the approach in which budgets are imposed from above. The participative approach to preparing budgets is particularly important if the budget is to be used to control and evaluate a manager's performance. If a budget is imposed on a manager from above, it will probably generate resentment and ill will rather than cooperation and commitment.

This budgeting approach in which managers prepare their own budget estimates—called a *self-imposed budget*—is generally considered to be the most effective method of budget preparation. A **self-imposed budget** or **participative budget** is a budget that is prepared with the full cooperation and participation of managers at all levels. Exhibit 7–1 illustrates this approach to budget preparation.

EXHIBIT 7–1

The Initial Flow of Budget Data in a Participative Budgeting System

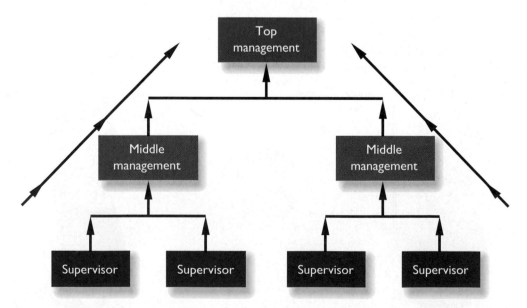

The initial flow of budget data in a participative system is from lower levels of responsibility to higher levels of responsibility. Each person with responsibility for cost control will prepare his or her own budget estimates and submit them to the next higher level of management. These estimates are reviewed and consolidated as they move upward in the organization.

A number of advantages are commonly cited for such self-imposed budgets:

1. Individuals at all levels of the organization are recognized as members of the team whose views and judgments are valued by top management.
2. Budget estimates prepared by front-line managers can be more accurate and reliable than estimates prepared by top managers who are more remote from day-to-day activities and who have less intimate knowledge of markets and operating conditions.
3. Motivation is generally higher when an individual participates in setting his or her own goals than when management imposes the goals. Self-imposed budgets create commitment.
4. A manager who is not able to meet a budget that has been imposed from above can always say that the budget was unreasonable or unrealistic to start with, and therefore was impossible to meet. With a self-imposed budget, this excuse is not available.

Once self-imposed budgets are prepared, are they subject to any kind of review? The answer is yes. Budget estimates prepared by lower-level managers should be scrutinized by higher levels of management. Without such a review, self-imposed budgets may be too loose and allow too much "budgetary slack." The result will be inefficiency and waste. Therefore, before budgets are accepted, they must be carefully reviewed by immediate superiors. If changes from the original budget seem desirable, the items in question are discussed and modified as necessary.

In essence, all levels of an organization should work together to produce the budget. Since top management is generally unfamiliar with detailed, day-to-day operations, it should rely on subordinates to provide detailed budget data. On the other hand, top management has an overall strategic perspective that is also vital. Each level of responsibility in an organization should contribute its unique knowledge and perspective in a *cooperative* effort to develop an integrated budget.

We have described an ideal budgetary process that involves self-imposed budgets prepared by the managers who are directly responsible for revenues and costs. Most companies deviate from this ideal. Typically, top managers initiate the budget process by issuing broad guidelines in terms of overall target profits or sales. Lower-level managers are directed to prepare budgets that meet those targets. The difficulty is that the targets set by top managers may be unrealistically high or may allow too much slack. If the targets are too high and employees know they are unrealistic, motivation will suffer. If the targets allow too much slack, waste will occur. And unfortunately top managers are often not in a position to know whether the targets they have set are appropriate. Admittedly, however, a pure self-imposed budgeting system may lack sufficient strategic direction and lower-level managers may be tempted to build into their budgets a great deal of budgetary slack. Nevertheless, because of the motivational advantages of self-imposed budgets, top managers should be cautious about imposing inflexible targets from above.

Human Factors in Budgeting

The success of a budget program also depends on: (1) the degree to which top management accepts the budget program as a vital part of the company's activities, and (2) the way in which top management uses budgeted data.

If a budget program is to be successful, it must have the complete acceptance and support of the persons who occupy key management positions. If lower or middle management personnel sense that top management is lukewarm about budgeting, or if they sense that top management simply tolerates budgeting as a necessary evil, then their own attitudes will reflect a similar lack of enthusiasm. Budgeting is hard work, and if top management is not enthusiastic about and committed to the budget program, then it is unlikely that anyone else in the organization will be either.

In administering the budget program, it is particularly important that top management not use the budget as a club to pressure employees or as a way to find someone to blame if something goes wrong. Using budgets in such negative ways will simply breed hostility, tension, and mistrust rather than greater cooperation and productivity. Unfortunately, the budget is too often used as a pressure device and great emphasis is placed on "meeting the budget" under all circumstances.

Rather than being used as a weapon, the budget should be used as a positive instrument to assist in establishing goals, in measuring operating results, and in isolating areas that are in need of extra effort or attention. Any misgivings that employees have about a budget program can be overcome by meaningful involvement at all levels and by proper use of the program over time. Administration of a budget program requires a great deal of insight and sensitivity on the part of management. The budget program should be designed to be a positive aid in achieving both individual and company goals.

Management must keep clearly in mind that the human aspects of budgeting are of key importance. It is easy to become preoccupied with the technical aspects of the budget to the exclusion of the human aspects. Indeed, the use of budget data in a rigid and inflexible manner is the greatest single complaint of persons whose performance is evaluated using budgets. Management should remember that the purposes of the budget are to motivate employees and to coordinate efforts. Preoccupation with the dollars and cents in the budget, or being rigid and inflexible, is usually counterproductive.

Zero-Based Budgeting

In the traditional approach to budgeting, the manager starts with last year's budget and adds to it (or subtracts from it) according to anticipated needs. This is an incremental approach to budgeting in which the previous year's budget is taken for granted as a baseline.

Zero-based budgeting is an alternative approach. Under a **zero-based budget,** managers are required to justify *all* budgeted expenditures, not just changes in the budget from the previous year. The baseline is zero rather than last year's budget.

A zero-based budget requires considerable documentation. In addition to all of the schedules in the usual master budget, the manager must prepare a series of "decision packages" in which all of the activities of the department are ranked according to their relative importance and their costs are identified. Higher-level managers can then review the decision packages and cut back in those areas that appear to be less critical or whose costs do not appear to be justified.

Zero-based budgeting sounds like a good idea. However, critics of zero-based budgeting charge that properly executed zero-based budgeting is too time-consuming and too costly to justify on an annual basis. In addition, it is argued that annual reviews soon become mechanical and that the whole purpose of zero-based budgeting is then lost.

Whether or not a company should use an annual review is a matter of judgment. In some situations, annual zero-based reviews may be justified; in other situations, they may not because of the time and cost involved. However, most managers would at least agree that occasional zero-based reviews can be very helpful.

The Budget Committee

A standing **budget committee** usually is responsible for overall policy matters relating to the budget program and for coordinating the preparation of the budget itself. This committee generally consists of the president; vice presidents in charge of various functions such as sales, production, and purchasing; and the controller. Difficulties and disputes within the organization in matters relating to the budget are resolved by the budget committee. In addition, the budget committee approves the final budget and receives periodic reports on the progress of the company in attaining budgeted goals.

Disputes can (and do) erupt over budget matters. Because budgets allocate resources, the budgeting process to a large extent determines which departments get relatively more resources and which get less. Also, the budget sets the benchmarks by which managers and their departments will be at least partially evaluated. Therefore, it should not be surprising that managers take the budgeting process very seriously and invest considerable energy and even emotion in ensuring that their interests, and those of their departments, are protected. Because of this, the budgeting process can easily degenerate into an interoffice brawl in which the ultimate goal of working together toward common goals is forgotten.

Running a successful budgeting program that avoids interoffice battles requires considerable interpersonal skills in addition to purely technical skills. But even the best interpersonal skills will fail if, as discussed earlier, top management uses the budget process inappropriately as a club or as a way to find blame.

The Politics of Budgeting

Budgeting is often an intensely political process in which managers jockey for resources and relaxed goals for the upcoming year. One group of consultants describes the process in this way: Annual budgets "have a particular urgency in that they provide the standard and most public framework against which managers are assessed and judged. It is, therefore, not surprising that budget-setting is taken seriously . . . Often budgets are a means for managers getting what they want. A relaxed budget will secure a relatively easy twelve months, a tight one means that their names will constantly be coming up in the monthly management review meeting. Far better to shift the burden of cost control and financial discipline to someone else. Budgeting is an intensely political exercise conducted with all the sharper managerial skills not taught at business school, such as lobbying and flattering superiors, forced haste, regretted delay, hidden truth, half-truths, and lies."

Source: Michael Morrow, ed., *Activity-Based Management* (New York: Woodhead-Faulkner), p. 91.

An Overview of the Master Budget

The master budget consists of a number of separate but interdependent budgets. Exhibit 7–2 provides an overview of the various parts of the master budget and how they are related.

The Sales Budget   A **sales budget** is a detailed schedule showing the expected sales for the budget period; typically, it is expressed in both dollars and units. An accurate sales budget is the key to the entire budgeting process. All of the other parts of the master budget are dependent on the sales budget in some way, as illustrated in Exhibit 7–2. Thus, if the sales budget is sloppily done, then the rest of the budgeting process is largely a waste of time.

The sales budget will help determine how many units will have to be produced. Thus, the production budget is prepared after the sales budget. The production budget in turn is used to determine the budgets for manufacturing costs including the direct materials budget, the direct labor budget, and the manufacturing overhead budget. These budgets are then combined with data from the sales budget and the selling and administrative expense budget to determine the cash budget. In essence, the sales budget triggers a chain reaction that leads to the development of the other budgets.

As shown in Exhibit 7–2, the selling and administrative expense budget is both dependent on and a determinant of the sales budget. This reciprocal relationship arises because sales will in part be determined by the funds committed for advertising and sales promotion.

The Cash Budget   Once the operating budgets (sales, production, and so on) have been established, the cash budget and other financial budgets can be prepared. A **cash budget** is a detailed plan showing how cash resources will be acquired and used over some specified time period. Observe from Exhibit 7–2 that all of the operating budgets have an impact on the cash budget. In the case of the sales budget, the impact comes from the planned cash receipts to be received from sales. In the case of the other budgets, the impact comes from the planned cash expenditures within the budgets themselves.

Sales Forecasting—A Critical Step

The sales budget is usually based on the company's *sales forecast*. Sales from prior years are commonly used as a starting point in preparing the sales forecast. In addition, the manager may examine the company's unfilled back orders, the company's pricing policy

EXHIBIT 7–2

The Master Budget
Interrelationships

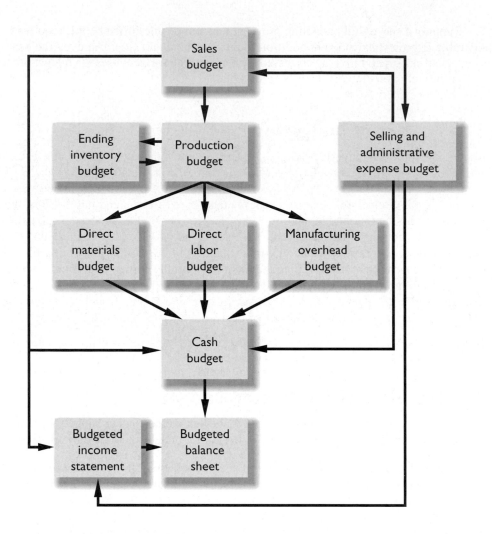

and marketing plans, trends in the industry, and general economic conditions. Sophisticated statistical tools may be used to analyze the data and to build models that are helpful in predicting key factors influencing the company's sales. Some companies use computer simulations to enhance their marketing strategies and sales forecasts. We will not, however, go into the details of how sales forecasts are made. This is a subject that is more appropriately covered in marketing courses.

IN BUSINESS

Biasing Forecasts

A manager's compensation is often tied to the budget. Typically, no bonus is paid unless a minimum performance hurdle such as 80% of the budget target is attained. Once that hurdle is passed, the manager's bonus increases until a cap is reached. That often occurs when 120% of the budget target is attained.

This common method of tying a manager's compensation to the budget has some serious negative side effects. For example, a marketing manager for a big beverage company intentionally grossly understated demand for the company's products for an upcoming major holiday so that the budget target for revenues would be low and easy to beat. Unfortunately, the company tied its production to the biased forecast and ran out of products to sell during the height of the holiday selling season.

Source: Michael C. Jensen, "Corporate Budgeting Is Broken—Let's Fix It," *Harvard Business Review*, November 2001.

Predicting Demand

O'Reilly Auto Parts uses sophisticated demand software from Nonstop Solutions to fore-cast seasonal variations in sales. For example, monthly sales of windshield wiper blades vary from 25,000 in the summer to 50,000 in the winter. Demand software uses weather data, economic trends, and other information to make forecasts and can even learn from its past mistakes.

Source: Chana R. Schoenberger, "The Weakest Link," *Forbes*, October 1, 2001, pp. 114–115.

PREPARING THE MASTER BUDGET

MANAGERIAL ACCOUNTING IN ACTION

The Issue

Hampton Freeze, Inc.

Tom Wills is the majority stockholder and chief executive officer of Hampton Freeze, Inc., a company he started in 2001. The company makes premium popsicles using only natural ingredients and featuring exotic flavors such as tangy tangerine and minty mango. The company's business is highly seasonal, with most of the sales occurring in spring and summer.

In 2002, the company's second year of operations, a major cash crunch in the first and second quarters almost forced the company into bankruptcy. In spite of this cash crunch, 2002 turned out to be a very successful year in terms of both overall cash flow and net income. Partly as a result of that harrowing experience, Tom decided toward the end of 2002 to hire a professional financial manager. Tom interviewed several promising candidates for the job and settled on Larry Giano, who had considerable experience in the packaged foods industry. In the job interview, Tom questioned Larry about the steps he would take to prevent a recurrence of the 2002 cash crunch:

Tom: As I mentioned earlier, we are going to end 2002 with a very nice profit. What you may not know is that we had some very big financial problems this year.

Larry: Let me guess. You ran out of cash sometime in the first or second quarter.

Tom: How did you know?

Larry: Most of your sales are in the second and third quarter, right?

Tom: Sure, everyone wants to buy popsicles in the spring and summer, but nobody wants them when the weather turns cold.

Larry: So you don't have many sales in the first quarter?

Tom: Right.

Larry: And in the second quarter, which is the spring, you are producing like crazy to fill orders?

Tom: Sure.

Larry: Do your customers, the grocery stores, pay you the day you make your deliveries?

Tom: Are you kidding? Of course not.

Larry: So in the first quarter, you don't have many sales. In the second quarter, you are producing like crazy, which eats up cash, but you aren't paid by your customers until long after you have paid your employees and suppliers. No wonder you had a cash problem. I see this pattern all the time in food processing because of the seasonality of the business.

Tom: So what can we do about it?

Larry: The first step is to predict the magnitude of the problem before it occurs. If we can predict early in the year what the cash shortfall is going to be, we can go to the bank and arrange for credit before we really need it. Bankers tend to be leery of panicky people who show up begging for emergency loans. They are much more likely to make the loan if you look like you know what you are doing, you have done your homework, and you are in control of the situation.

Tom: How can we predict the cash shortfall?

Larry: You can put together a cash budget. While you're at it, you might as well do a master budget. You'll find it is well worth the effort.

Tom: I don't like budgets. They are too confining. My wife budgets everything at home, and I can't spend what I want.

Larry: Can I ask a personal question?

Tom: What?

Larry: Where did you get the money to start this business?

Tom: Mainly from our family's savings. I get your point. We wouldn't have had the money to start the business if my wife hadn't been forcing us to save every month.

Larry: Exactly. I suggest you use the same discipline in your business. It is even more important here because you can't expect your employees to spend your money as carefully as you would.

With the full backing of Tom Wills, Larry Giano set out to create a master budget for the company for the year 2003. In his planning for the budgeting process, Larry drew up the following list of documents that would be a part of the master budget:

1. A sales budget, including a schedule of expected cash collections.
2. A production budget (a merchandise purchases budget would be used in a merchandising company).
3. A direct materials budget, including a schedule of expected cash disbursements for raw materials.
4. A direct labor budget.
5. A manufacturing overhead budget.
6. An ending finished goods inventory budget.
7. A selling and administrative expense budget.
8. A cash budget.
9. A budgeted income statement.
10. A budgeted balance sheet.

Larry felt it was important to have everyone's cooperation in the budgeting process, so he asked Tom to call a companywide meeting in which the budgeting process would be explained. At the meeting there was initially some grumbling, but Tom was able to convince nearly everyone of the necessity for planning and getting better control over spending. It helped that the cash crisis earlier in the year was still fresh in everyone's minds. As much as some people disliked the idea of budgets, they liked their jobs even more.

In the months that followed, Larry worked closely with all of the managers involved in the master budget, gathering data from them and making sure that they understood and fully supported the parts of the master budget that would affect them. In subsequent years, Larry hoped to turn the whole budgeting process over to the managers and to take a more advisory role.

The interdependent documents that Larry Giano prepared for Hampton Freeze are Schedules 1 through 10 of his company's master budget. In this section, we will study these schedules.

The Sales Budget

LEARNING OBJECTIVE 2

Prepare a sales budget, including a schedule of expected cash receipts.

The sales budget is the starting point in preparing the master budget. As shown earlier in Exhibit 7–2, all other items in the master budget, including production, purchases, inventories, and expenses, depend on it in some way.

The sales budget is constructed by multiplying the budgeted sales in units by the selling price. Schedule 1 on the next page contains the sales budget for Hampton Freeze for the year 2003, by quarters. Notice from the schedule that the company plans to sell 100,000 cases of popsicles during the year, with sales peaking in the third quarter.

A schedule of expected cash collections, such as the one that appears in Schedule 1 for Hampton Freeze, is prepared after the sales budget. This schedule will be needed later

SCHEDULE I

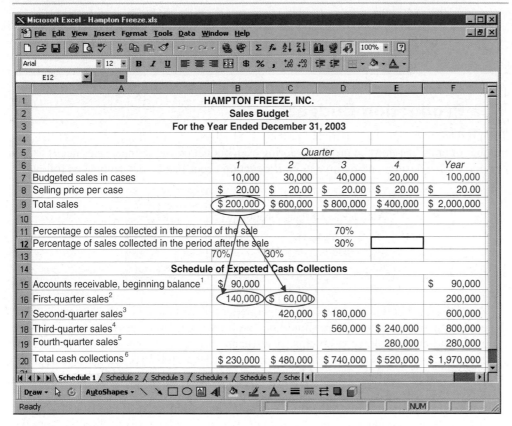

[1]Cash collections from last year's fourth-quarter sales. See the beginning-of-year balance sheet on page 311.
[2]$200,000 × 70%; $200,000 × 30%.
[3]$600,000 × 70%; $600,000 × 30%.
[4]$800,000 × 70%; $800,000 × 30%.
[5]$400,000 × 70%.
[6]Uncollected fourth-quarter sales appear as accounts receivable on the company's end-of-year balance sheet (see Schedule 10 on page 310).

to prepare the cash budget. Cash collections consist of collections on sales made to customers in prior periods plus collections on sales made in the current budget period. At Hampton Freeze, experience has shown that 70% of sales are collected in the quarter in which the sale is made and the remaining 30% are collected in the following quarter. For example, 70% of the first quarter sales of $200,000 (or $140,000) are collected during the first quarter and 30% (or $60,000) are collected during the second quarter.

The Importance of Ownership

Jack Stack, the president and CEO of Springfield Manufacturing, advises managers to accept the sales forecasts made by salespeople. He says that the forecasts should be substantiated, but that the forecasts should be accepted even when the manager disagrees with the forecasts. He admits that accepting a sales forecast that you disagree with can be very difficult, but he says that you have to do it. Why?

> Because if you don't, you let your salespeople off the hook. You take away their ownership of the forecast. It's not theirs anymore; it's yours—and so is the responsibility for hitting it. Oh, sure, your salespeople will go out and do their jobs, but

something will be missing . . . The pride, the desire to win that makes them dig deep down and pull off the big play when you need it. What you lose is passion—which is, ironically, the one thing you must have to achieve a reliable forecast.

Source: Jack Stack, "A Passion for Forecasting," *Inc.*, November 1997, pp. 37–38.

The Production Budget

LEARNING OBJECTIVE 3

Prepare a production budget.

The production budget is prepared after the sales budget. The **production budget** lists the number of units that must be produced during each budget period to meet sales needs and to provide for the desired ending inventory. Production needs can be determined as follows:

Budgeted sales in units	XXXX
Add desired ending inventory.	XXXX
Total needs	XXXX
Less beginning inventory.	XXXX
Required production.	XXXX

Note that production requirements for a quarter are influenced by the desired level of the ending inventory. Inventories should be carefully planned. Excessive inventories tie up funds and create storage problems. Insufficient inventories can lead to lost sales or crash production efforts in the following period. At Hampton Freeze, management believes that an ending inventory equal to 20% of the next quarter's sales strikes the appropriate balance.

Schedule 2 contains the production budget for Hampton Freeze. The first row in the production budget contains the budgeted sales, which have been taken directly from the sales budget (Schedule 1). The total needs for the first quarter are determined by adding together the budgeted sales of 10,000 cases for the quarter and the desired ending inventory

SCHEDULE 2

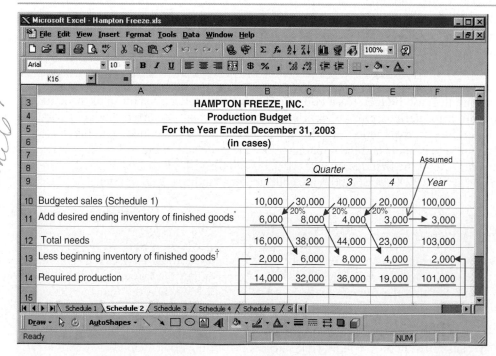

*Twenty percent of the next quarter's sales. The ending inventory of 3,000 cases is assumed.
†The beginning inventory in each quarter is the same as the prior quarter's ending inventory.

of 6,000 cases. As discussed above, the ending inventory is intended to provide some cushion in case problems develop in production or sales increase unexpectedly. Since the budgeted sales for the second quarter are 30,000 cases and management would like the ending inventory in each quarter to be equal to 20% of the following quarter's sales, the desired ending inventory is 6,000 cases (20% of 30,000 cases). Consequently, the total needs for the first quarter are 16,000 cases. However, since the company already has 2,000 cases in beginning inventory, only 14,000 cases need to be produced in the first quarter.

Pay particular attention to the Year column to the right of the production budget in Schedule 2. In some cases (e.g., budgeted sales and required production), the amount listed for the year is the sum of the quarterly amounts for the item. In other cases (e.g., desired inventory of finished goods and beginning inventory of finished goods), the amount listed for the year is not simply the sum of the quarterly amounts. From the standpoint of the entire year, the beginning inventory of finished goods is the same as the beginning inventory of finished goods for the first quarter—it is *not* the sum of the beginning inventories of finished goods for all quarters. Similarly, from the standpoint of the entire year, the ending inventory of finished goods is the same as the ending inventory of finished goods for the fourth quarter—it is *not* the sum of the ending inventories of finished goods for all four quarters. It is important to pay attention to such distinctions in all of the schedules that follow.

Inventory Purchases—Merchandising Firm

Hampton Freeze prepares a production budget, since it is a *manufacturing* firm. If it were a *merchandising* firm, it would instead prepare a **merchandise purchases budget** showing the amount of goods to be purchased from its suppliers during the period. The merchandise purchases budget follows the same basic format as the production budget, as shown below:

Budgeted cost of goods sold (in units or in dollars)	XXXXX
Add desired ending merchandise inventory	XXXXX
Total needs	XXXXX
Less beginning merchandise inventory.	XXXXX
Required purchases (in units or in dollars)	XXXXX

A merchandising firm would prepare an inventory purchases budget such as the one above for each item carried in stock.

The Direct Materials Budget

Returning to Hampton Freeze, after the production requirements have been computed, a *direct materials budget* can be prepared. The **direct materials budget** details the raw materials that must be purchased to fulfill the production budget and to provide for adequate inventories. The required purchases of raw materials are computed as follows:

Raw materials needed to meet the production schedule	XXXXX
Add desired ending inventory of raw materials.	XXXXX
Total raw materials needs.	XXXXX
Less beginning inventory of raw materials.	XXXXX
Raw materials to be purchased	XXXXX

LEARNING OBJECTIVE 4

Prepare a direct materials budget, including a schedule of expected cash disbursements for purchases of materials.

Schedule 3 contains the direct materials budget for Hampton Freeze. The only raw material included in that budget is high fructose sugar, which is the major ingredient in popsicles other than water. The remaining raw materials are relatively insignificant and are included in variable manufacturing overhead. As with finished goods, management

SCHEDULE 3

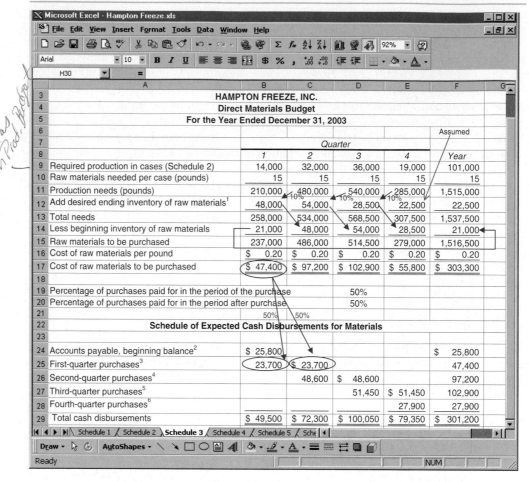

	A	B	C	D	E	F
3		HAMPTON FREEZE, INC.				
4		Direct Materials Budget				
5		For the Year Ended December 31, 2003				
6						Assumed
7		Quarter				
8		1	2	3	4	Year
9	Required production in cases (Schedule 2)	14,000	32,000	36,000	19,000	101,000
10	Raw materials needed per case (pounds)	15	15	15	15	15
11	Production needs (pounds)	210,000	480,000	540,000	285,000	1,515,000
12	Add desired ending inventory of raw materials[1]	48,000	54,000	28,500	22,500	22,500
13	Total needs	258,000	534,000	568,500	307,500	1,537,500
14	Less beginning inventory of raw materials	21,000	48,000	54,000	28,500	21,000
15	Raw materials to be purchased	237,000	486,000	514,500	279,000	1,516,500
16	Cost of raw materials per pound	$ 0.20	$ 0.20	$ 0.20	$ 0.20	$ 0.20
17	Cost of raw materials to be purchased	$ 47,400	$ 97,200	$ 102,900	$ 55,800	$ 303,300
18						
19	Percentage of purchases paid for in the period of the purchase		50%			
20	Percentage of purchases paid for in the period after purchase		50%			
21		50%	50%			
22	Schedule of Expected Cash Disbursements for Materials					
23						
24	Accounts payable, beginning balance[2]	$ 25,800				$ 25,800
25	First-quarter purchases[3]	23,700	$ 23,700			47,400
26	Second-quarter purchases[4]		48,600	$ 48,600		97,200
27	Third-quarter purchases[5]			51,450	$ 51,450	102,900
28	Fourth-quarter purchases[6]				27,900	27,900
29	Total cash disbursements	$ 49,500	$ 72,300	$ 100,050	$ 79,350	$ 301,200

[1]Ten percent of the next quarter's production needs. For example, the second-quarter production needs are 480,000 pounds. Therefore, the desired ending inventory for the first quarter would be 10% × 480,000 pounds = 48,000 pounds. The ending inventory of 22,500 pounds for the fourth quarter is assumed.

[2]Cash payments for last year's fourth-quarter material purchases. See the beginning-of-year balance sheet on page 311.

[3]$47,500 × 50%; $47,500 × 50%.

[4]$97,200 × 50%; $97,200 × 50%.

[5]$102,900 × 50%; $102,900 × 50%.

[6]$55,800 × 50%. Unpaid fourth-quarter purchases appear as accounts payable on the company's end-of-year balance sheet.

would like to maintain some minimum inventories of raw materials as a cushion. In this case, management would like to maintain ending inventories of sugar equal to 10% of the following quarter's production needs.

The first line in the direct materials budget contains the required production for each quarter, which is taken directly from the production budget (Schedule 2). Looking at the first quarter, since the production schedule calls for production of 14,000 cases of popsicles and each case requires 15 pounds of sugar, the total production needs are for 210,000 pounds of sugar (14,000 cases × 15 pounds per case). In addition, management wants to have ending inventories of 48,000 pounds of sugar, which is 10% of the following quarter's needs of 480,000 pounds. Consequently, the total needs are for 258,000 pounds (210,000 pounds for the current quarter's production plus 48,000 pounds for the desired ending inventory). However, since the company already has 21,000 pounds in beginning inventory, only 237,000 pounds of sugar (258,000 pounds − 21,000 pounds) will need to be purchased. Finally, the cost of the raw materials purchases is determined by multiplying the amount of raw material to be purchased by the cost per unit of the raw material. In this case, since 237,000 pounds of sugar will have to be purchased during the first quarter and sugar costs $0.20 per pound, the total cost will be $47,400 (237,000 pounds × $0.20 per pound).

As with the production budget, the amounts listed under the Year column are not always just the sum of the quarterly amounts. The desired ending inventory of raw materials for the year is the same as the desired ending inventory of raw materials for the fourth quarter. Likewise, the beginning inventory of raw materials for the year is the same as the beginning inventory of raw materials for the first quarter.

The direct materials budget is usually accompanied by a schedule of expected cash disbursements for raw materials. This schedule is needed to prepare the overall cash budget. Disbursements for raw materials consist of payments for purchases on account in prior periods plus any payments for purchases in the current budget period. Schedule 3 contains such a schedule of cash disbursements. Ordinarily, companies do not immediately pay their suppliers. At Hampton Freeze, the policy is to pay for 50% of purchases in the quarter in which the purchase is made and 50% in the following quarter, so while the company intends to purchase $47,400 worth of sugar in the first quarter, the company will only pay for half, $23,700, in the first quarter and the other half will be paid in the second quarter. The company will also pay $25,800 for sugar acquired in the previous quarter, but not yet paid for. This is the beginning balance in the accounts payable. Therefore, the total cash disbursements for sugar in the first quarter are $49,500—the $25,800 payment for sugar acquired in the previous quarter plus the $23,700 payment for sugar acquired during the first quarter.

The Direct Labor Budget

The **direct labor budget** is also developed from the production budget. Direct labor requirements must be computed so that the company will know whether sufficient labor time is available to meet production needs. By knowing in advance how much labor time will be needed throughout the budget year, the company can develop plans to adjust the labor force as the situation requires. Companies that neglect to budget run the risk of facing labor shortages or having to hire and lay off workers at awkward times. Erratic labor policies lead to insecurity, low morale, and inefficiency.

The direct labor budget for Hampton Freeze is shown in Schedule 4. The first line in the direct labor budget consists of the required production for each quarter, which is taken directly from the production budget (Schedule 2). The direct labor requirement for each quarter is computed by multiplying the number of units to be produced in that quarter by the number of direct labor-hours required to make a unit. For example, 14,000 cases are to be produced in the first quarter and each case requires 0.40 direct labor-hour, so a total of 5,600 direct labor-hours (14,000 cases × 0.40 direct labor-hour per case) will be required in the first quarter. The direct labor requirements can then be translated into budgeted direct labor costs. How this is done will depend on the company's labor policy. In Schedule 4, the management of Hampton Freeze has assumed that the direct labor force will be adjusted as the work requirements change from quarter to quarter. In that case, the direct labor cost is computed by simply multiplying the direct labor-hour requirements by the direct labor rate per hour. For example, the direct labor cost in the first quarter is $84,000 (5,600 direct labor-hours × $15 per direct labor-hour).

However, many companies have employment policies or contracts that prevent them from laying off and rehiring workers as needed. Suppose, for example, that Hampton Freeze has 25 workers who are classified as direct labor and each of them is guaranteed at least 480 hours of pay each quarter at a rate of $15 per hour. In that case, the minimum direct labor cost for a quarter would be as follows:

$$25 \text{ workers} \times 480 \text{ hours per worker} \times \$15 \text{ per hour} = \$180,000$$

LEARNING OBJECTIVE 5

Prepare a direct labor budget.

SCHEDULE 4

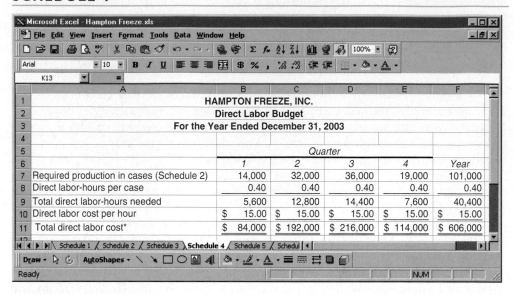

	1	2	3	4	Year
			Quarter		
Required production in cases (Schedule 2)	14,000	32,000	36,000	19,000	101,000
Direct labor-hours per case	0.40	0.40	0.40	0.40	0.40
Total direct labor-hours needed	5,600	12,800	14,400	7,600	40,400
Direct labor cost per hour	$ 15.00	$ 15.00	$ 15.00	$ 15.00	$ 15.00
Total direct labor cost*	$ 84,000	$ 192,000	$ 216,000	$ 114,000	$ 606,000

*This schedule assumes that the direct labor work force will be fully adjusted to the total direct labor-hours needed each quarter.

Note that in Schedule 4 the direct labor costs for the first and fourth quarters would have to be increased to a $180,000 level if Hampton Freeze's labor policy did not allow it to adjust the workforce at will.

The Manufacturing Overhead Budget

The **manufacturing overhead budget** provides a schedule of all costs of production other than direct materials and direct labor. Schedule 5 shows the manufacturing overhead budget for Hampton Freeze. At Hampton Freeze the manufacturing overhead is separated into variable and fixed components. The variable component is $4 per direct labor-hour and the fixed component is $60,600 per quarter. Because the variable component of the manufacturing overhead depends on direct labor, the first line in the manufacturing overhead budget consists of the budgeted direct labor-hours from the direct labor budget (Schedule 4). The budgeted direct labor-hours in each quarter are multiplied by the variable rate to determine the variable component of manufacturing overhead. For example, the variable manufacturing overhead for the first quarter is $22,400 (5,600 direct labor-hours × $4.00 per direct labor-hour). This is added to the fixed manufacturing overhead for the quarter to determine the total manufacturing overhead for the quarter. For example, the total manufacturing overhead for the first quarter is $83,000 ($22,400 + $60,600).

A few words about fixed costs and the budgeting process are in order. In most cases, fixed costs are the costs of supplying capacity to do things like make products, process purchase orders, handle customer calls, and so on. The amount of capacity that will be required depends on the expected level of activity for the period. If the expected level of activity is greater than the company's current capacity, then fixed costs may have to be increased. Or, if the expected level is appreciably below the company's current capacity, then it may be desirable to decrease fixed costs if that is possible. However, once the level of the fixed costs has been determined in the budget, the costs really are fixed. The time to adjust fixed costs is during the budgeting process. To determine the appropriate level of fixed costs at budget time, an activity-based costing system can be very helpful. It can help answer questions like, "How many clerks will we need to hire to process the anticipated number of purchase orders next year?" For simplicity, we assume in all of the budgeting

SCHEDULE 5

HAMPTON FREEZE, INC.
Manufacturing Overhead Budget
For the Year Ended December 31, 2003

	Quarter				
	1	2	3	4	Year
Budgeted direct labor-hours (Schedule 4)	5,600	12,800	14,400	7,600	40,400
Variable overhead rate	$ 4.00	$ 4.00	$ 4.00	$ 4.00	$ 4.00
Variable manufacturing overhead	$ 22,400	$ 51,200	$ 57,600	$ 30,400	$ 161,600
Fixed manufacturing overhead	60,600	60,600	60,600	60,600	242,400
Total manufacturing overhead	83,000	111,800	118,200	91,000	404,000
Less depreciation	15,000	15,000	15,000	15,000	60,000
Cash disbursement for manufacturing overhead	$ 68,000	$ 96,800	$ 103,200	$ 76,000	$ 344,000
Total manufacturing overhead (a)					$ 404,000
Budgeted direct labor-hours (b)					40,400
Predetermined overhead rate for the year (a) ÷ (b)					$ 10.00

examples in this book that the appropriate levels of fixed costs have already been determined for the budget with the aid of activity-based costing or some other method.

The last line of Schedule 5 for Hampton Freeze shows its budgeted cash disbursements for manufacturing overhead. Since some of the overhead costs are not cash outflows, the total budgeted manufacturing overhead costs must be adjusted to determine the cash disbursements for manufacturing overhead. At Hampton Freeze, the only significant noncash manufacturing overhead cost is depreciation, which is $15,000 per quarter. These noncash depreciation charges are deducted from the total budgeted manufacturing overhead to determine the expected cash disbursements. Hampton Freeze pays all overhead costs involving cash disbursements in the quarter incurred. Note that the company's predetermined overhead rate for the year will be $10 per direct labor-hour, which is determined by dividing the total budgeted manufacturing overhead for the year by the total budgeted direct labor-hours for the year.

The Ending Finished Goods Inventory Budget

After completing Schedules 1–5, Larry Giano had all of the data he needed to compute unit product costs. This computation was needed for two reasons: first, to determine cost of goods sold on the budgeted income statement; and second, to know what amount to put on the balance sheet inventory account for unsold units. The carrying cost of the unsold units is computed on the **ending finished goods inventory budget.**

Larry Giano considered using variable costing in preparing Hampton Freeze's budget statements, but he decided to use absorption costing instead since the bank would very likely require that absorption costing be used. He also knew that it would be easy to convert the absorption costing financial statements to a variable costing basis later. At this point, the primary concern was to determine what financing, if any, would be required in the year 2003 and then to arrange for that financing from the bank.

The unit product cost computations are shown in Schedule 6. For Hampton Freeze, the absorption costing unit product cost is $13 per case of popsicles—consisting of $3 of direct materials, $6 of direct labor, and $4 of manufacturing overhead. Manufacturing overhead is applied to units of product on the basis of direct labor-hour at the rate of $10 per direct labor-hour. The budgeted carrying cost of the expected ending inventory is $39,000.

SCHEDULE 6

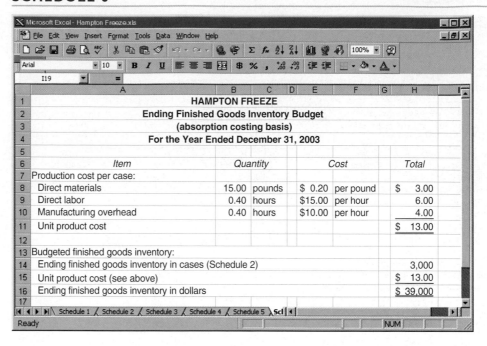

The Selling and Administrative Expense Budget

The **selling and administrative expense budget** lists the budgeted expenses for areas other than manufacturing. In large organizations, this budget would be a compilation of many smaller, individual budgets submitted by department heads and other persons responsible for selling and administrative expenses. For example, the marketing manager in a large organization would submit a budget detailing the advertising expenses for each budget period.

Schedule 7 contains the selling and administrative expense budget for Hampton Freeze. Like the manufacturing overhead budget, the selling and administrative budget is divided into variable and fixed cost components. In the case of Hampton Freeze, the variable selling and administrative expense is $1.80 per case. Consequently, budgeted sales in cases for each quarter are entered at the top of the schedule. These data are taken from the sales budget (Schedule 1). The budgeted variable selling and administrative expenses are determined by multiplying the budgeted sales in cases by the variable selling and administrative expense per case. For example, the budgeted variable selling and administrative expense for the first quarter is $18,000 (10,000 cases × $1.80 per case). The fixed selling and administrative expenses (all given data) are then added to the variable selling and administrative expenses to arrive at the total budgeted selling and administrative expenses. Finally, to determine the cash disbursements for selling and administrative items, the total budgeted selling and administrative expense is adjusted by adding back any noncash selling and administrative expenses (in this case, just depreciation).

YOU DECIDE

Budget Analyst

You have been hired as a budget analyst by a regional chain of Italian restaurants with attached bars. Management has had difficulty in the past predicting some of its costs; the assumption has always been that all operating costs are variable with respect to gross restaurant sales. What would you suggest doing to improve the accuracy of the budget forecasts?

SCHEDULE 7

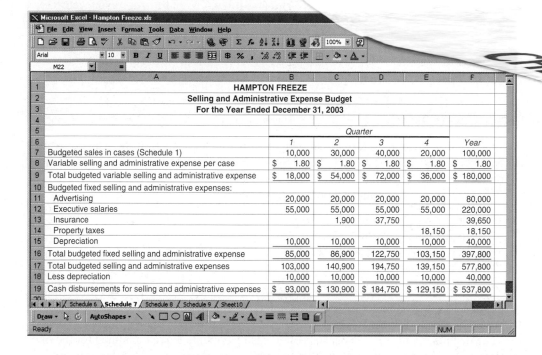

Microsoft Excel - Hampton Freeze.xls

File Edit View Insert Format Tools Data Window Help

	A	B	C	D	E	F
1	HAMPTON FREEZE					
2	Selling and Administrative Expense Budget					
3	For the Year Ended December 31, 2003					
4						
5				Quarter		
6		1	2	3	4	Year
7	Budgeted sales in cases (Schedule 1)	10,000	30,000	40,000	20,000	100,000
8	Variable selling and administrative expense per case	$ 1.80	$ 1.80	$ 1.80	$ 1.80	$ 1.80
9	Total budgeted variable selling and administrative expense	$ 18,000	$ 54,000	$ 72,000	$ 36,000	$ 180,000
10	Budgeted fixed selling and administrative expenses:					
11	Advertising	20,000	20,000	20,000	20,000	80,000
12	Executive salaries	55,000	55,000	55,000	55,000	220,000
13	Insurance		1,900	37,750		39,650
14	Property taxes				18,150	18,150
15	Depreciation	10,000	10,000	10,000	10,000	40,000
16	Total budgeted fixed selling and administrative expense	85,000	86,900	122,750	103,150	397,800
17	Total budgeted selling and administrative expenses	103,000	140,900	194,750	139,150	577,800
18	Less depreciation	10,000	10,000	10,000	10,000	40,000
19	Cash disbursements for selling and administrative expenses	$ 93,000	$ 130,900	$ 184,750	$ 129,150	$ 537,800

Schedule 6 / Schedule 7 / Schedule 8 / Schedule 9 / Sheet10

Ready

---

1. If a company has a beginning merchandise inventory of $50,000, a desired ending merchandise inventory of $30,000, and a budgeted cost of goods sold of $300,000, what is the amount of required inventory purchases?
   a. $320,000
   b. $280,000
   c. $380,000
   d. $300,000

2. Budgeted unit sales for March, April, and May are 75,000, 80,000, and 90,000 units. Management desires to maintain an ending inventory equal to 30% of the next month's unit sales. How many units should be produced in April?
   a. 80,000 units
   b. 83,000 units
   c. 77,000 units
   d. 85,000 units

CONCEPT CHECK ✓

Letting the Business Take Care of Itself

IN BUSINESS

Harlan Accola turned his interests in flying and photography into a money-making pursuit by selling aerial photos of farms and homes. Sales were so good that what started out as a way to finance a hobby soon became a full-scale business. He paid an outside accountant to prepare financial statements, which he admits he didn't understand. "I didn't think it was important. I thought a financial statement was just something you had to give to the bank to keep your loan OK. So I took it, looked at the bottom line, and tossed it into a desk drawer."

Accola's casual approach worked for a while. However, within a few years he had lost control of his cash flows. Unpaid creditors were hounding him, and the Internal Revenue Service was demanding overdue taxes. The bank, alarmed by the cash flow situation, demanded to be repaid the $240,000 loan it had extended to the company. Accola

confesses that "I thought if I made enough sales, everything else would take care of itself. But I confused profits with cash flow." The good news is that the company recovered from its near-brush with bankruptcy, instituted formal financial planning procedures, and is now very successful.

Source: Jay Finnegan, "Everything According to Plan," *Inc.,* March 1995, pp. 78–85.

The Cash Budget

LEARNING OBJECTIVE 8

Prepare a cash budget.

Concept 7–2

As illustrated in Exhibit 7–2, the cash budget pulls together much of the data developed in the preceding steps. It is a good idea to review Exhibit 7–2 to get the big picture firmly in mind before moving on.

The cash budget is composed of four major sections:

1. The receipts section.
2. The disbursements section.
3. The cash excess or deficiency section.
4. The financing section.

The receipts section consists of a listing of all of the cash inflows, except for financing, expected during the budget period. Generally, the major source of receipts will be from sales.

The disbursements section consists of all cash payments that are planned for the budget period. These payments will include raw materials purchases, direct labor payments, manufacturing overhead costs, and so on, as contained in their respective budgets. In addition, other cash disbursements such as equipment purchases and dividends are listed.

The cash excess or deficiency section is computed as follows:

Cash balance, beginning	XXXX
Add receipts	XXXX
Total cash available	XXXX
Less disbursements	XXXX
Excess (deficiency) of cash available over disbursements	XXXX

If there is a cash deficiency during any budget period, the company will need to borrow funds. If there is a cash excess during any budget period, funds borrowed in previous periods can be repaid or the excess funds can be invested.

The financing section details the borrowings and repayments projected to take place during the budget period. It also lists interest payments that will be due on money borrowed.[1]

Generally speaking, the cash budget should be broken down into time periods that are as short as feasible. Considerable fluctuations in cash balances may be hidden by looking at a longer time period. While a monthly cash budget is most common, some organizations budget cash on a weekly or even daily basis. Larry Giano has prepared a quarterly cash budget for Hampton Freeze that can be further refined as necessary. This budget appears in Schedule 8. The cash budget builds on the earlier schedules and on additional data that are provided below:

- The beginning cash balance is $42,500.
- Management plans to spend $130,000 during the year on equipment purchases: $50,000 in the first quarter; $40,000 in the second quarter; $20,000 in the third quarter; and $20,000 in the fourth quarter.

---

[1]The format for the statement of cash flows, which is discussed in Chapter 13, may also be used for the cash budget.

- The board of directors has approved cash dividends of $8,000 per quarter.
- Management would like to have a cash balance of at least $40,000 at the beginning of each quarter for contingencies.
- Assume Hampton Freeze will be able to get agreement from a bank for an open line of credit. This would enable the company to borrow at an interest rate of 10% per year. All borrowing and repayments would be in round $1,000 amounts. All borrowing would occur at the beginning of quarters and all repayments would be made at the end of quarters. Interest would be due when repayments are made and only on the amount of principal that is repaid.

The cash budget is prepared one quarter at a time, starting with the first quarter. Larry began the cash budget by entering the beginning balance of cash for the first quarter of $42,500—a number that is given above. Receipts—in this case, just the $230,000 in cash collections from customers—are added to the beginning balance to arrive at the total cash available of $272,500. Since the total disbursements are $352,500 and the total cash available is only $272,500, there is a shortfall of $80,000. Since management would like to

SCHEDULE 8

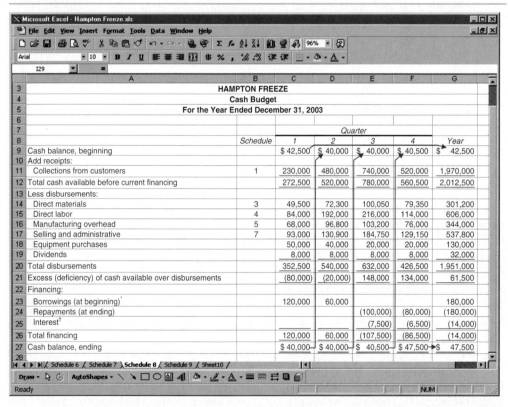

*The company requires a minimum cash balance of $40,000. Therefore, borrowing must be sufficient to cover the cash deficiency of $80,000 in quarter 1 and to provide for the minimum cash balance of $40,000. All borrowings and repayments of principal are in round $1,000 amounts.
†The interest payments relate only to the principal being repaid at the time it is repaid. For example, the interest in quarter 3 relates only to the interest due on the $100,000 principal being repaid from quarter 1 borrowing: $100,000 × 10% per year × ¾ year = $7,500. The interest paid in quarter 4 is computed as follows:

$$\begin{array}{ll}
\$20,000 \times 10\% \text{ per year} \times 1 \text{ year} \ldots\ldots & \$2,000 \\
\$60,000 \times 10\% \text{ per year} \times \tfrac{3}{4} \text{ year} \ldots\ldots & 4,500 \\
\hline
\text{Total interest paid} \ldots\ldots\ldots\ldots\ldots\ldots & \$6,500
\end{array}$$

have a beginning cash balance of at least $40,000 for the second quarter, the company will need to borrow $120,000.

Required Borrowings at the End of the First Quarter	
Desired ending cash balance	$ 40,000
Plus deficiency of cash available over disbursements	80,000
Required borrowings.	$120,000

The second quarter of the cash budget is handled similarly. Note that the ending cash balance for the first quarter is brought forward as the beginning cash balance for the second quarter. Also note that additional borrowing is required in the second quarter because of the continued cash shortfall.

Required Borrowings at the End of the Second Quarter	
Desired ending cash balance	$40,000
Plus deficiency of cash available over disbursements	20,000
Required borrowings.	$60,000

In the third quarter, the cash flow situation improves dramatically and the excess of cash available over disbursements is $148,000. This makes it possible for the company to repay part of its loan from the bank, which now totals $180,000. How much can be repaid? The total amount of the principal *and* interest that can be repaid is determined as follows:

Total Maximum Feasible Loan Payments at the End of the Third Quarter	
Excess of cash available over disbursements	$148,000
Less desired ending cash balance	40,000
Maximum feasible principal and interest payment	$108,000

The next step—figuring out the exact amount of the loan payment—is tricky since interest must be paid on the principal amount that is repaid. In this case, the principal amount that is repaid must be less than $108,000, so we know that we would be paying off part of the loan that was taken out at the beginning of the first quarter. Since the repayment would be made at the end of the third quarter, interest would have accrued for three quarters. So the interest owed would be ¾ of 10%, or 7.5%. Either a trial-and-error or an algebraic approach will lead to the conclusion that the maximum principal repayment that can be made is $100,000.[2] The interest payment would be 7.5% of this amount, or $7,500—making the total payment $107,500.

In the fourth quarter, all of the loan and accumulated interest are paid off. If all loans are not repaid at the end of the year and budgeted financial statements are prepared, then interest must be accrued on the unpaid loans. This interest will not appear on the cash budget (since it has not yet been paid), but it will appear as interest expense on the budgeted income statement and as a liability on the budgeted balance sheet.

---

[2]The algebraic approach to determining the amount that can be repaid on the loan follows:
Let X be the amount of the principal repayment. Then $10\% \times \frac{3}{4} \times X$ is the amount of interest owed on that principal amount. Since the company can afford to pay at most $108,000 to the bank, the sum of the principal repayment and the interest payment cannot exceed $108,000.

$$X + 10\% \times \tfrac{3}{4} \times X \leq \$108{,}000, \text{ or}$$

$$X \leq \$100{,}465$$

Since all repayments must be in round $1,000 amounts, the appropriate principal repayment is $100,000.

As with the production and raw materials budgets, the amounts under the Year column in the cash budget are not always the sum of the amounts for the four quarters. In particular, the beginning cash balance for the year is the same as the beginning cash balance for the first quarter and the ending cash balance for the year is the same as the ending cash balance for the fourth quarter. Also note the beginning cash balance in any quarter is the same as the ending cash balance for the previous quarter.

Concentrating on the Cash Flow

Burlington Northern Santa Fe (BNSF) operates the second largest railroad in the United States. The company's senior vice president, CFO, and treasurer is Tom Hunt, who reports that "As a general theme, we've become very cash-flow-oriented." After the merger of the Burlington Northern and Santa Fe railroads, the company went through a number of years in which they were investing heavily and consequently had negative cash flows. To keep on top of the company's cash position, Hunt has a cash forecast prepared every month. "Everything falls like dominoes from free cash flow," Hunt says. "It provides us with alternatives. Right now, the alternative of choice is buying back our own stock . . . [b]ut it could be increasing dividends or making acquisitions. All those things are not even on the radar screen if you don't have free cash flow."

Source: Randy Myers, "Cash Crop: The 2000 Working Capital Survey," *CFO*, August 2000, pp. 59–82.

The Budgeted Income Statement

A budgeted income statement can be prepared from the data developed in Schedules 1–8. *The budgeted income statement is one of the key schedules in the budget process.* It shows the company's planned profit for the upcoming budget period, and it serves as a benchmark against which subsequent company performance can be measured.

Schedule 9 contains the budgeted income statement for Hampton Freeze.

LEARNING OBJECTIVE 9

Prepare a budgeted income statement.

SCHEDULE 9

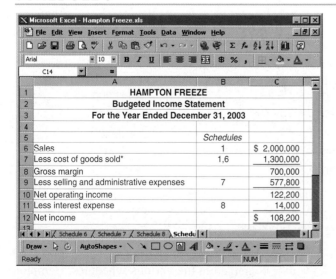

		Schedules	
6	Sales	1	$ 2,000,000
7	Less cost of goods sold*	1,6	1,300,000
8	Gross margin		700,000
9	Less selling and administrative expenses	7	577,800
10	Net operating income		122,200
11	Less interest expense	8	14,000
12	Net income		$ 108,200

HAMPTON FREEZE
Budgeted Income Statement
For the Year Ended December 31, 2003

*100,000 cases sold × $13 per case = $1,300,000.

SCHEDULE 10

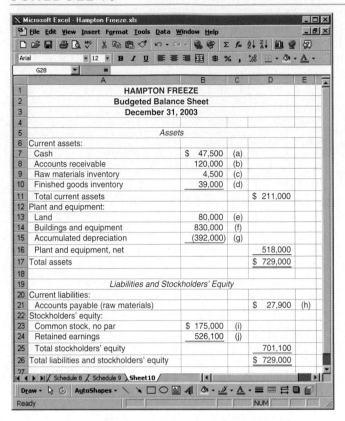

Explanation of December 31, 2003, balance sheet figures:

(a) The ending cash balance, as projected by the cash budget in Schedule 8.

(b) Thirty percent of fourth-quarter sales, from Schedule 1 ($400,000 × 30% = $120,000).

(c) From Schedule 3, the ending raw materials inventory will be 22,500 pounds. This material costs $0.20 per pound. Therefore, the ending inventory in dollars will be 22,500 pounds × $0.20 = $4,500.

(d) From Schedule 6.

(e) From the December 31, 2002, balance sheet (no change).

(f) The December 31, 2002, balance sheet indicated a balance of $700,000. During 2003, $130,000 of additional equipment will be purchased (see Schedule 8), bringing the December 31, 2003, balance to $830,000.

(g) The December 31, 2002, balance sheet indicated a balance of $292,000. During 2003, $100,000 of depreciation will be taken ($60,000 on Schedule 5 and $40,000 on Schedule 7), bringing the December 31, 2003, balance to $392,000.

(h) One-half of the fourth-quarter raw materials purchases, from Schedule 3.

(i) From the December 31, 2002, balance sheet (no change).

(j)

	December 31, 2002, balance	$449,900
	Add net income, from Schedule 9	108,200
		558,100
	Deduct dividends paid, from Schedule 8	32,000
	December 31, 2003, balance	$526,100

The Budgeted Balance Sheet

The budgeted balance sheet is developed from the balance sheet from the beginning of the budget period and is adjusted for the data contained in the various schedules. Hampton Freeze's budgeted balance sheet is presented in Schedule 10. Some of the data on the budgeted balance sheet have been taken from the company's previous end-of-year balance sheet, which appears below:

HAMPTON FREEZE, INC.		
Balance Sheet		
December 31, 2002		
Assets		
Current assets:		
Cash..	$ 42,500	
Accounts receivable	90,000	
Raw materials inventory (21,000 pounds)	4,200	
Finished goods inventory (2,000 cases)	26,000	
Total current assets...................................		$162,700
Plant and equipment:		
Land..	80,000	
Buildings and equipment............................	700,000	
Accumulated depreciation...........................	(292,000)	
Plant and equipment, net.............................		488,000
Total assets...		$650,700
Liabilities and Stockholders' Equity		
Current liabilities:		
Accounts payable (raw materials)......................		$ 25,800
Stockholders' equity:		
Common stock, no par..............................	$175,000	
Retained earnings	449,900	
Total stockholders' equity.............................		624,900
Total liabilities and stockholders' equity..................		$650,700

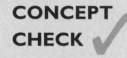

3. March, April, and May sales are $100,000, $120,000, and $125,000, respectively. A total of 80% of all sales are credit sales and 20% are cash sales. A total of 60% of credit sales are collected in the month of the sale and 40% are collected in the next month. There are no bad debt expenses. What is the amount of cash receipts for April?
   a. $89,600
   b. $111,600
   c. $113,600
   d. $132,600
4. Referring to the facts in question 3 above, what is the accounts receivable balance at the end of May?
   a. $40,000
   b. $50,000
   c. $72,000
   d. $80,000

After completing the master budget, Larry Giano took the documents to Tom Wills, chief executive officer of Hampton Freeze, for his review.

Larry: Here's the budget. Overall, the net income is excellent, and the net cash flow for the entire year is positive.

Tom: Yes, but I see on this cash budget that we have the same problem with negative cash flows in the first and second quarters that we had last year.

MANAGERIAL
ACCOUNTING
IN ACTION

The Wrap-Up

Hampton
Freeze, Inc.

Larry: That's true. I don't see any way around that problem. However, there is no doubt in my mind that if you take this budget to the bank today, they'll approve an open line of credit that will allow you to borrow enough to make it through the first two quarters without any problem.

Tom: Are you sure? They didn't seem very happy to see me last year when I came in for an emergency loan.

Larry: Did you repay the loan on time?

Tom: Sure.

Larry: I don't see any problem. You won't be asking for an emergency loan this time. The bank will have plenty of warning. And with this budget, you have a solid plan that shows when and how you are going to pay off the loan. Trust me, they'll go for it.

Tom: Fantastic! It would sure make life a lot easier this year.

DECISION MAKER

Bank Manager

You are the manager of a branch of a state bank located in a medium-sized community. The owner of a small manufacturing company in the community wants to apply for an unsecured line of credit for the upcoming year. The company has been in business for several years but has experienced seasonal cash shortages as it has grown. What documents would you request from the owner to back up the loan request and what tests would you apply to the documents to ensure that they are realistic?

IN BUSINESS

Automating the Budgeting Process

A number of companies, including Texaco, Fujitsu, Sprint, Nationwide Financial Services, Nortel Networks, Owens Corning, and Xilinx have been attempting to reengineer and automate the budgeting process. The goal is to eliminate the conventional iterative budgeting process that often finds preliminary budgets being passed up and down the management hierarchy many times before final agreement is reached—wasting much time and resulting in budgets that often don't reconcile. Apart from the tremendous technical challenges of integrating diverse budgets from many different operations, automation faces a high behavioral hurdle. As Greg Vesey of Texaco states, "Planning is the most political of all processes to fall under the finance function." Consequently, as many as half of all automation efforts fail. Companies such as National Semiconductor Corp. have given up entirely and have returned to their old budgeting methods.

Source: Russ Banham, "The Revolution in Planning," *CFO*, August 1999, pp. 46–56.

SUMMARY

LO1   Understand why organizations budget and the processes they use to create budgets.

The purpose in this chapter has been to present an overview of the budgeting process and to show how the various budgets relate to each other.

Organizations budget for a variety of reasons, including to communicate management's plans throughout the organization, to force managers to think about and plan for the future, to allocate resources within the organization, to identify bottlenecks before they occur, to coordinate activities, and to provide benchmarks for evaluating subsequent performance.

Budgets should be developed with the full participation of all managers who will be subject to budgetary controls.

LO2   Prepare a sales budget, including a schedule of expected cash receipts.

The sales budget forms the foundation for the master budget. It provides details concerning the anticipated unit and dollar sales for each budget period.

The schedule of expected cash receipts is based on the sales budget, the expected breakdown between cash and credit sales, and the expected pattern of collections on credit sales.

LO3   Prepare a production budget.

The production budget details how many units must be produced each budget period to satisfy expected sales and to provide for adequate levels of finished goods inventories.

LO4   Prepare a direct materials budget, including a schedule of expected cash disbursements for purchases of materials.

The direct materials budget shows the materials that must be purchased each budget period to meet anticipated production requirements and to provide for adequate levels of materials inventories.

Cash disbursements for purchases of materials will depend on the amount of materials purchased in each budget period and the company's policies concerning payments to suppliers for materials acquired on credit.

LO5   Prepare a direct labor budget.

The direct labor budget shows the direct labor-hours that are required to meet the production schedule as detailed in the production budget. The direct labor-hour requirements are used to determine the direct labor cost in each budget period.

LO6   Prepare a manufacturing overhead budget.

Manufacturing overhead consists of both variable and fixed manufacturing overhead. The variable manufacturing overhead ultimately depends on the number of units produced from the production budget. The variable and fixed manufacturing overheads are combined to determine the total manufacturing overhead. Any noncash manufacturing overhead such as depreciation is deducted from the total manufacturing overhead to determine the cash disbursements for manufacturing overhead.

LO7   Prepare a selling and administrative expense budget.

Like manufacturing overhead, selling and administrative expenses consist of both variable and fixed expenses. The variable expenses depend on the number of units sold or some other measure of activity. The variable and fixed expenses are combined to determine the total selling and administrative expense. Any noncash selling and administrative expenses such as depreciation are deducted from the total to determine the cash disbursements for selling and administrative expenses.

LO8   Prepare a cash budget.

The cash budget is a critical element of the master budget. It permits managers to anticipate and plan for cash shortfalls.

The cash budget is organized into a receipts section, a disbursements section, a cash excess or deficiency section, and a financing section. The cash budget draws on information taken from nearly all of the other budgets and schedules including the schedule of cash receipts, the schedule of cash disbursements for materials, the direct labor budget, the manufacturing overhead budget, and the selling and administrative expense budget.

LO9   Prepare a budgeted income statement.

The budgeted income statement is constructed using data from the sales budget, the ending finished goods budget, the manufacturing overhead budget, the selling and administrative budget, and the cash budget.

LO10   Prepare a budgeted balance sheet.

The budgeted balance sheet is constructed using data from virtually all of the other parts of the master budget.

GUIDANCE ANSWERS TO *DECISION MAKER* AND *YOU DECIDE*

Budget Analyst (p. 304)

Not all costs are variable with respect to gross restaurant sales. For example, assuming no change in the number of restaurant sites, rental costs are probably fixed. To more accurately forecast costs for the budget, costs should be separated into variable and fixed components. Furthermore, more appropriate activity measures should be selected for the variable costs. For example, gross restaurant sales may be divided into food sales and bar sales—each of which could serve as an activity measure for some costs. In addition, some costs (such as the costs of free dinner rolls) may be variable with respect to the number of diners rather than with respect to food or bar sales. Other activity measures may permit even more accurate predictions of costs.

Bank Manager (p. 312)

At minimum, you should request a cash budget with supporting documents including a sales budget, production budget, direct materials budget, direct labor budget, manufacturing overhead budget, selling and administrative expense budget, budgeted income statement, and budgeted balance sheet. You should check that the cash budget provides for repayment of the loan, plus interest, and that it leaves the company with sufficient cash reserves to start the new year. You should also check that assumptions concerning sales growth and fixed and variable costs are consistent with the company's recent experience.

GUIDANCE ANSWERS TO CONCEPT CHECKS

1. **Choice b.** Required inventory purchases are calculated as follows: Cost of goods sold of $300,000 + Ending inventory of $30,000 − Beginning inventory of $50,000 = $280,000.
2. **Choice b.** 80,000 units sold in April + 27,000 units of desired ending inventory − 24,000 units of beginning inventory = 83,000 units.
3. **Choice c.** Cash receipts for April are calculated as follows: ($100,000 × 80% × 40%) + ($120,000 × 20%) + ($120,000 × 80% × 60%) = $113,600.
4. **Choice a.** The May 31 accounts receivable balance is $125,000 × 80% × 40% = $40,000.

REVIEW PROBLEM: BUDGET SCHEDULES

Mylar Company manufactures and sells a product that has seasonal variations in demand, with peak sales coming in the third quarter. The following information concerns operations for Year 2—the coming year—and for the first two quarters of Year 3:

a. The company's single product sells for $8 per unit. Budgeted sales in units for the next six quarters are as follows:

	Year 2 Quarter				Year 3 Quarter	
	1	**2**	**3**	**4**	**1**	**2**
Budgeted sales in units . . .	40,000	60,000	100,000	50,000	70,000	80,000

b. Sales are collected in the following pattern: 75% in the quarter the sales are made, and the remaining 25% in the following quarter. On January 1, Year 2, the company's balance sheet showed $65,000 in accounts receivable, all of which will be collected in the first quarter of the year. Bad debts are negligible and can be ignored.

c. The company desires an ending inventory of finished units on hand at the end of each quarter equal to 30% of the budgeted sales for the next quarter. On December 31, Year 1, the company had 12,000 units on hand.

d. Five pounds of raw materials are required to complete one unit of product. The company requires an ending inventory of raw materials on hand at the end of each quarter equal to 10% of the production needs of the following quarter. On December 31, Year 1, the company had 23,000 pounds of raw materials on hand.

e. The raw material costs $0.80 per pound. Purchases of raw material are paid for in the following pattern: 60% paid in the quarter the purchases are made, and the remaining 40% paid in the following quarter. On January 1, Year 2, the company's balance sheet showed $81,500 in accounts payable for raw material purchases, all of which will be paid for in the first quarter of the year.

Required:

Prepare the following budgets and schedules for the year, showing both quarterly and total figures:

1. A sales budget and a schedule of expected cash collections.
2. A production budget.
3. A direct materials purchases budget and a schedule of expected cash payments for material purchases.

Solution to Review Problem

1. The sales budget is prepared as follows:

	Year 2 Quarter				
	1	2	3	4	Year
Budgeted sales in units......	40,000	60,000	100,000	50,000	250,000
Selling price per unit........	× $8	× $8	× $8	× $8	× $8
Total sales................	$320,000	$480,000	$800,000	$400,000	$2,000,000

Based on the budgeted sales above, the schedule of expected cash collections is prepared as follows:

	Year 2 Quarter				
	1	2	3	4	Year
Accounts receivable, beginning balance	$ 65,000				$ 65,000
First-quarter sales ($320,000 × 75%, 25%)........	240,000	$ 80,000			320,000
Second-quarter sales ($480,000 × 75%, 25%)......		360,000	$120,000		480,000
Third-quarter sales ($800,000 × 75%, 25%).......			600,000	$200,000	800,000
Fourth-quarter sales ($400,000 × 75%)..........				300,000	300,000
Total cash collections	$305,000	$440,000	$720,000	$500,000	$1,965,000

2. Based on the sales budget in units, the production budget is prepared as follows:

	Year 2 Quarter					Year 3 Quarter	
	1	2	3	4	Year	1	2
Budgeted sales (units).........................	40,000	60,000	100,000	50,000	250,000	70,000	80,000
Add desired ending inventory of finished goods* ...	18,000	30,000	15,000	21,000†	21,000	24,000	
Total needs	58,000	90,000	115,000	71,000	271,000	94,000	
Less beginning inventory of finished goods	12,000	18,000	30,000	15,000	12,000	21,000	
Required production...........................	46,000	72,000	85,000	56,000	259,000	73,000	

*30% of the following quarter's budgeted sales in units.
†30% of the budgeted Year 3 first-quarter sales.

3. Based on the production budget, raw materials will need to be purchased as follows during the year:

	Year 2 Quarter					Year 3 Quarter
	1	2	3	4	Year 2	1
Required production (units)	46,000	72,000	85,000	56,000	259,000	73,000
Raw materials needed per unit (pounds)	× 5	× 5	× 5	× 5	× 5	× 5
Production needs (pounds)...............	230,000	360,000	425,000	280,000	1,295,000	365,000
Add desired ending inventory of raw materials (pounds)*	36,000	42,500	28,000	36,500†	36,500	
Total needs (pounds)...................	266,000	402,500	453,000	316,500	1,331,500	
Less beginning inventory of raw materials (pounds).....................	23,000	36,000	42,500	28,000	23,000	
Raw materials to be purchased (pounds)	243,000	366,500	410,500	288,500	1,308,500	

*Ten percent of the following quarter's production needs in pounds.
†Ten percent of the Year 3 first-quarter production needs in pounds.

Based on the raw material purchases above, expected cash payments are computed as follows:

	Year 2 Quarter				
	1	2	3	4	Year
Cost of raw materials to be purchased at $0.80 per pound	$194,400	$293,200	$328,400	$230,800	$1,046,800
Accounts payable, beginning balance...............	$ 81,500				$ 81,500
First-quarter purchases ($194,400 × 60%, 40%).....	116,640	$ 77,760			194,400
Second-quarter purchases ($293,200 × 60%, 40%)...		175,920	$117,280		293,200
Third-quarter purchases ($328,400 × 60%, 40%)....			197,040	$131,360	328,400
Fourth-quarter purchases ($230,800 × 60%).......				138,480	138,480
Total cash disbursements	$198,140	$253,680	$314,320	$269,840	$1,035,980

GLOSSARY

Budget   A detailed plan for acquiring and using financial and other resources over a specified time period. (p. 288)

Budget committee   A group of key managers who are responsible for overall policy matters relating to the budget program and for coordinating the preparation of the budget. (p. 292)

Cash budget   A detailed plan showing how cash resources will be acquired and used over some specific time period. (p. 293)

Control   Those steps taken by management to increase the likelihood that the objectives set down at the planning stage are attained and that all parts of the organization are working together toward that goal. (p. 288)

Direct labor budget   A detailed plan showing labor requirements over some specific time period. (p. 301)

Direct materials budget   A detailed plan showing the amount of raw materials that must be purchased during a period to meet both production and inventory needs. (p. 299)

Ending finished goods inventory budget   A budget showing the cost expected to appear on the balance sheet for unsold units at the end of a period. (p. 303)

Manufacturing overhead budget   A detailed plan showing the production costs, other than direct materials and direct labor, that will be incurred over a specified time period. (p. 302)

Master budget   A summary of a company's plans in which specific targets are set for sales, production, distribution, and financing activities and that generally culminates in a cash budget, budgeted income statement, and budgeted balance sheet. (p. 288)

Merchandise purchases budget   A budget used by a merchandising company that shows the amount of goods that must be purchased from suppliers during the period. (p. 299)

Participative budget   See *self-imposed budget*. (p. 290)

Planning   Developing objectives and preparing budgets to achieve these objectives. (p. 288)

Production budget   A detailed plan showing the number of units that must be produced during a period in order to meet both sales and inventory needs. (p. 298)

Responsibility accounting   A system of accountability in which managers are held responsible for those items of revenue and cost—and only those items—over which the manager can exert significant control. The managers are held responsible for differences between budgeted goals and actual results. (p. 289)

Sales budget   A detailed schedule showing the expected sales for coming periods; these sales are typically expressed in both dollars and units. (p. 293)

Self-imposed budget   A method of preparing budgets in which managers prepare their own budgets. These budgets are then reviewed by the manager's supervisor, and any issues are resolved by mutual agreement. (p. 290)

Selling and administrative expense budget   A detailed schedule of planned expenses that will be incurred in areas other than manufacturing during a budget period. (p. 304)

Zero-based budget   A method of budgeting in which managers are required to justify all costs as if the programs involved were being proposed for the first time. (p. 292)

QUESTIONS

7–1 What is a budget? What is budgetary control?

7–2 What are some of the major benefits to be gained from budgeting?

7–3 What is meant by the term *responsibility accounting?*

7–4 What is a master budget? Briefly describe its contents.

7–5 Why is the sales forecast the starting point in budgeting?

7–6 "As a practical matter, planning and control mean exactly the same thing." Do you agree? Explain.

7–7 What is a self-imposed budget? What are the major advantages of self-imposed budgets? What caution must be exercised in their use?

7–8 How can budgeting assist a firm in its employment policies?

7–9 "The principal purpose of the cash budget is to see how much cash the company will have in the bank at the end of the year." Do you agree? Explain.

BRIEF EXERCISES

BRIEF EXERCISE 7–1   Budget Process   (LO1)

The following terms pertain to the budgeting process:

Benchmarks	Bottlenecks
Budget	Budget committee
Control	Imposed from above
Motivation	Planning
Responsibility accounting	Self-imposed budget

Required:

Fill in the blanks with the most appropriate word or phrase from the above list.

1. _____ involves the steps taken by management to increase the likelihood that the objectives set down at the planning stage are attained.

2. _____ is generally higher when an individual participates in setting his or her own goals than when the goals are imposed from above.

3. In _____, a manager is held accountable for those items, and only those items, over which he or she has significant control.

4. If a manager is not able to meet the budget and it has been _____, the manager can always say that the budget was unreasonable or unrealistic to start with and therefore was impossible to meet.

5. _____ involves developing objectives and preparing various budgets to achieve those objectives.

6. A _____ is a detailed plan for acquiring and using financial and other resources over a specified time period.

7. A _____ is usually responsible for overall policy matters relating to the budget program and for coordinating the preparation of the budget itself.

8. The budgeting process can uncover potential _____ before they occur.

9. A _____ is one that is prepared with the full cooperation and participation of managers at all levels of the organization.

10. Budgets define goals and objectives that can serve as _____ for evaluating subsequent performance.

BRIEF EXERCISE 7–2   Schedule of Expected Cash Collections   (LO2)

Peak sales for Midwest Products, Inc., occur in August. The company's sales budget for the third quarter showing these peak sales is given below:

	July	August	September	Total
Budgeted sales..........	$600,000	$900,000	$500,000	$2,000,000

From past experience, the company has learned that 20% of a month's sales are collected in the month of sale, that another 70% is collected in the month following sale, and that the remaining 10% is collected in the second month following sale. Bad debts are negligible and can be ignored. May sales totaled $430,000, and June sales totaled $540,000.

Required:
1. Prepare a schedule of expected cash collections from sales, by month and in total, for the third quarter.
2. Assume that the company will prepare a budgeted balance sheet as of September 30. Compute the accounts receivable as of that date.

BRIEF EXERCISE 7–3 Production Budget (LO3)

Crystal Telecom has budgeted the sales of its innovative mobile phone over the next four months as follows:

Sales in Units	
July	30,000
August	45,000
September	60,000
October	50,000

The company is now in the process of preparing a production budget for the third quarter. Past experience has shown that end-of-month inventories of finished goods must equal 10% of the next month's sales. The inventory at the end of June was 3,000 units.

Required:
Prepare a production budget for the third quarter showing the number of units to be produced each month and for the quarter in total.

BRIEF EXERCISE 7–4 Materials Purchases Budget (LO4)

Micro Products, Inc., has developed a very powerful electronic calculator. Each calculator requires three small "chips" that cost $2 each and are purchased from an overseas supplier. Micro Products has prepared a production budget for the calculator by quarters for Year 2 and for the first quarter of Year 3, as follows:

	Year 2				Year 3
	First	Second	Third	Fourth	First
Budgeted production, in calculators....	60,000	90,000	150,000	100,000	80,000

The chip used in production of the calculator is sometimes hard to get, so it is necessary to carry large inventories as a precaution against stockouts. For this reason, the inventory of chips at the end of a quarter must be equal to 20% of the following quarter's production needs. Some 36,000 chips will be on hand to start the first quarter of Year 2.

Required:
Prepare a materials purchases budget for chips, by quarter and in total, for Year 2. At the bottom of your budget, show the dollar amount of purchases for each quarter and for the year in total.

BRIEF EXERCISE 7–5 Direct Labor Budget (LO5)

The production department of Junnen Corporation has submitted the following forecast of units to be produced by quarter for the upcoming fiscal year.

	1st Quarter	2nd Quarter	3rd Quarter	4th Quarter
Units to be produced	5,000	4,400	4,500	4,900

Each unit requires 0.40 direct labor-hours, and direct labor-hour workers are paid $11 per hour.

Required:
1. Construct the company's direct labor budget for the upcoming fiscal year, assuming that the direct labor workforce is adjusted each quarter to match the number of hours required to produce the forecasted number of units produced.
2. Construct the company's direct labor budget for the upcoming fiscal year, assuming that the direct labor workforce is not adjusted each quarter. Instead, assume that the company's direct labor workforce consists of permanent employees who are guaranteed to be paid for at least 1,800 hours of work each quarter. If the number of required direct labor-hours is less than this number, the workers are paid for 1,800 hours anyway. Any hours worked in excess of 1,800 hours in a quarter are paid at the rate of 1.5 times the normal hourly rate for direct labor.

BRIEF EXERCISE 7–6 Manufacturing Overhead Budget (LO6)

The direct labor budget of Krispin Corporation for the upcoming fiscal year contains the following details concerning budgeted direct labor-hours:

	1st Quarter	2nd Quarter	3rd Quarter	4th Quarter
Budgeted direct labor-hours..	5,000	4,800	5,200	5,400

The company's variable manufacturing overhead rate is $1.75 per direct labor-hour and the company's fixed manufacturing overhead is $35,000 per quarter. The only noncash item included in the fixed manufacturing overhead is depreciation, which is $15,000 per quarter.

Required:
1. Construct the company's manufacturing overhead budget for the upcoming fiscal year.
2. Compute the company's manufacturing overhead rate (including both variable and fixed manufacturing overhead) for the upcoming fiscal year. Round off to the nearest whole cent.

BRIEF EXERCISE 7–7 Selling and Administrative Budget (LO7)

The budgeted unit sales of Haerve Company for the upcoming fiscal year are provided below:

	1st Quarter	2nd Quarter	3rd Quarter	4th Quarter
Budgeted unit sales	12,000	14,000	11,000	10,000

The company's variable selling and administrative expense per unit is $2.75. Fixed selling and administrative expenses include advertising expenses of $12,000 per quarter, executive salaries of $40,000 per quarter, and depreciation of $16,000 per quarter. In addition, the company makes insurance payments of $6,000 in the second quarter and $6,000 in the fourth quarter. Finally, property taxes of $6,000 are paid in the third quarter.

Required:
Prepare the company's selling and administrative expense budget for the upcoming fiscal year.

BRIEF EXERCISE 7–8 Cash Budget (LO8)

Forest Outfitters is a retailer that is preparing its budget for the upcoming fiscal year. Management has prepared the following summary of its budgeted cash flows:

	1st Quarter	2nd Quarter	3rd Quarter	4th Quarter
Total cash receipts.........	$340,000	$670,000	$410,000	$470,000
Total cash disbursements ...	$530,000	$450,000	$430,000	$480,000

The company's beginning cash balance for the upcoming fiscal year will be $50,000. The company requires a minimum cash balance of $30,000 and may borrow any amount needed from a local bank at an annual interest rate of 12%. The company may borrow any amount at the beginning of any quarter and may repay its loans, or any part of its loans, at the end of any quarter. Interest payments are due on any principal at the time it is repaid.

Required:
Prepare the company's cash budget for the upcoming fiscal year.

BRIEF EXERCISE 7–9   Budgeted Income Statement   (LO9)

Seattle Cat is the wholesale distributor of a small recreational catamaran sailboat. Management has prepared the following summary data to use in its annual budgeting process:

Budgeted sales (in units)	380
Selling price per unit	$1,850
Cost per unit	$1,425
Variable selling and administrative expenses (per unit)	$85
Fixed selling and administrative expenses (per year)	$105,000
Interest expense for the year	$11,000

Required:
Prepare the company's budgeted income statement.

BRIEF EXERCISE 7–10   Budgeted Balance Sheet   (LO10)

The management of Academic Copy, a photocopying center located on University Avenue, has compiled the following data to use in preparing its budgeted balance sheet for next year:

	Ending Balances
Cash.	?
Accounts receivable	$6,500
Supplies inventory	$2,100
Equipment	$28,000
Accumulated depreciation	$9,000
Accounts payable	$1,900
Common stock	$4,000
Retained earnings	?

The beginning balance of retained earnings was $21,000, net income is budgeted to be $8,600, and dividends are budgeted to be $3,500.

Required:
Prepare the company's budgeted balance sheet.

EXERCISES

EXERCISE 7–11   Schedules of Expected Cash Collections and Disbursements   (LO2, LO4, LO8)

Calgon Products, a distributor of organic beverages, needs a cash budget for September. The following information is available:

a. The cash balance at the beginning of September is $9,000.
b. Actual sales for July and August and expected sales for September are as follows:

	July	August	September
Cash sales	$ 6,500	$ 5,250	$ 7,400
Sales on account	20,000	30,000	40,000
Total sales	$26,500	$35,250	$47,400

Sales on account are collected over a three-month period in the following ratio: 10% collected in the month of sale, 70% collected in the month following sale, and 18% collected in the second month following sale. The remaining 2% is uncollectible.

c. Purchases of inventory will total $25,000 for September. Twenty percent of a month's inventory purchases are paid for during the month of purchase. The accounts payable remaining from August's inventory purchases total $16,000, all of which will be paid in September.

d. Selling and administrative expenses are budgeted at $13,000 for September. Of this amount, $4,000 is for depreciation.

e. Equipment costing $18,000 will be purchased for cash during September, and dividends totaling $3,000 will be paid during the month.

f. The company must maintain a minimum cash balance of $5,000. An open line of credit is available from the company's bank to bolster the cash position as needed.

Required:

1. Prepare a schedule of expected cash collections for September.
2. Prepare a schedule of expected cash disbursements during September for inventory purchases.
3. Prepare a cash budget for September. Indicate in the financing section any borrowing that will be needed during September.

EXERCISE 7–12   Sales and Production Budgets   (LO2, LO3)

The marketing department of Graber Corporation has submitted the following sales forecast for the upcoming fiscal year.

	1st Quarter	2nd Quarter	3rd Quarter	4th Quarter
Budgeted sales (units)	16,000	15,000	14,000	15,000

The selling price of the company's product is $22 per unit. Management expects to collect 75% of sales in the quarter in which the sales are made, 20% in the following quarter, and 5% of sales are expected to be uncollectible. The beginning balance of accounts receivable, all of which is expected to be collected in the first quarter, is $66,000.

The company expects to start the first quarter with 3,200 units in finished goods inventory. Management desires an ending finished goods inventory in each quarter equal to 20% of the next quarter's budgeted sales. The desired ending finished goods inventory for the fourth quarter is 3,400 units.

Required:

1. Prepare the company's sales budget and schedule of expected cash collections.
2. Prepare the company's production budget for the upcoming fiscal year.

EXERCISE 7–13   Production and Direct Materials Budgets   (LO3, LO4)

The marketing department of Farber Industries has submitted the following sales forecast for the upcoming fiscal year.

	1st Quarter	2nd Quarter	3rd Quarter	4th Quarter
Budgeted sales (units)	5,000	6,000	4,000	3,000

The company expects to start the first quarter with 1,500 units in finished goods inventory. Management desires an ending finished goods inventory in each quarter equal to 30% of the next quarter's budgeted sales. The desired ending finished goods inventory for the fourth quarter is 1,600 units.

In addition, the beginning raw materials inventory for the first quarter is budgeted to be 2,650 pounds and the beginning accounts payable for the first quarter is budgeted to be $28,980.

Each unit requires 5 pounds of raw material that costs $6 per pound. Management desires to end each quarter with an inventory of raw materials equal to 10% of the following quarter's production needs. The desired ending inventory for the fourth quarter is 2,670 pounds. Management plans to pay for 75% of raw material purchases in the quarter acquired and 25% in the following quarter.

Required:

1. Prepare the company's production budget for the upcoming fiscal year.
2. Prepare the company's direct materials budget and schedule of expected cash disbursements for materials for the upcoming fiscal year.

EXERCISE 7–14   Direct Materials and Direct Labor Budgets   (LO4, LO5)

The production department of Priston Company has submitted the following forecast of units to be produced by quarter for the upcoming fiscal year.

	1st Quarter	2nd Quarter	3rd Quarter	4th Quarter
Units to be produced	6,000	7,000	8,000	5,000

In addition, the beginning raw materials inventory for the first quarter is budgeted to be 3,600 pounds and the beginning accounts payable for the first quarter is budgeted to be $11,775.

Each unit requires 3 pounds of raw material that costs $2.50 per pound. Management desires to end each quarter with an inventory of raw materials equal to 20% of the following quarter's production needs. The desired ending inventory for the fourth quarter is 3,700 pounds. Management plans to pay for 70% of raw material purchases in the quarter acquired and 30% in the following quarter. Each unit requires 0.50 direct labor-hours and direct labor-hour workers are paid $12 per hour.

Required:
1. Prepare the company's direct materials budget and schedule of expected cash disbursements for materials for the upcoming fiscal year.
2. Prepare the company's direct labor budget for the upcoming fiscal year, assuming that the direct labor workforce is adjusted each quarter to match the number of hours required to produce the forecasted number of units produced.

EXERCISE 7–15   Direct Labor and Manufacturing Overhead Budgets   (LO5, LO6)
The production department of Harveton Corporation has submitted the following forecast of units to be produced by quarter for the upcoming fiscal year.

	1st Quarter	2nd Quarter	3rd Quarter	4th Quarter
Units to be produced	16,000	15,000	14,000	15,000

Each unit requires 0.80 direct labor-hours and direct labor-hour workers are paid $11.50 per hour.

In addition, the variable manufacturing overhead rate is $2.50 per direct labor-hour. The fixed manufacturing overhead is $90,000 per quarter. The only noncash element of manufacturing overhead is depreciation, which is $34,000 per quarter.

Required:
1. Prepare the company's direct labor budget for the upcoming fiscal year, assuming that the direct labor workforce is adjusted each quarter to match the number of hours required to produce the forecasted number of units produced.
2. Prepare the company's manufacturing overhead budget.

EXERCISE 7–16   Cash Budget Analysis   (LO8)
A cash budget, by quarters, is given below for a retail company (000 omitted). The company requires a minimum cash balance of $5,000 to start each quarter.

	Quarter				
	1	2	3	4	Year
Cash balance, beginning....................	$ 9	$?	$?	$?	$?
Add collections from customers	?	?	125	?	391
Total cash available	85	?	?	?	?
Less disbursements:					
Purchase of inventory...................	40	58	?	32	?
Operating expenses	?	42	54	?	180
Equipment purchases	10	8	8	?	36
Dividends.............................	2	2	2	2	?
Total disbursements	?	110	?	?	?
Excess (deficiency) of cash available over disbursements....................	(3)	?	30	?	?
Financing:					
Borrowings	?	20	—	—	?
Repayments (including interest)*	—	—	(?)	(7)	(?)
Total financing	?	?	?	?	?
Cash balance, ending......................	$?	$?	$?	$?	$?

*Interest will total $4,000 for the year.

Required:
Fill in the missing amounts in the table above.

PROBLEM 7–17   Schedule of Expected Cash Collections; Cash Budget   (LO2, LO8)
Eye Care Company, a distributor of eye care products, is ready to begin its third quarter, in which peak sales occur. The company has requested a $20,000, 90-day loan from its bank to help meet cash requirements during the quarter. Since Eye Care Company has experienced difficulty in paying off its loans in the past, the loan officer at the bank has asked the company to prepare a cash budget for the quarter. In response to this request, the following data have been assembled:

CHECK FIGURE
(1) July: $227,000
(2) July 31 cash balance:
    $12,000

a. On July 1, the beginning of the third quarter, the company will have a cash balance of $30,000.
b. Actual sales for the last two months and budgeted sales for the third quarter follow:

May (actual)	$180,000
June (actual)	$220,000
July (budgeted)	$300,000
August (budgeted)	$380,000
September (budgeted)	$350,000

Past experience shows that 25% of a month's sales are collected in the month of sale, 65% in the month following sale, and 5% in the second month following sale. The remainder is uncollectible.

c. Budgeted merchandise purchases and budgeted expenses for the third quarter are given below:

	July	August	September
Merchandise purchases	$180,000	$228,000	$210,000
Salaries and wages	$30,000	$32,000	$32,000
Advertising	$80,000	$80,000	$70,000
Rent payments	$6,000	$6,000	$6,000
Depreciation	$5,000	$5,000	$5,000

Merchandise purchases are paid in full during the month following purchase. Accounts payable for merchandise purchases on June 30, which will be paid during July, total $135,000.
d. Equipment costing $14,000 will be purchased for cash during July.
e. In preparing the cash budget, assume that the $20,000 loan will be made in July and repaid in September. Interest on the loan will total $600.

Required:
1. Prepare a schedule of expected cash collections for July, August, and September and for the quarter in total.
2. Prepare a cash budget, by month and in total, for the third quarter.
3. If the company needs a minimum cash balance of $10,000 to start each month, can the loan be repaid as planned? Explain.

PROBLEM 7–18   Production and Purchases Budgets   (LO3, LO4)
Giovinazzo of Milan, Italy, manufactures and distributes perfume throughout Europe. Each unit of Conquer, one of the company's products, requires 10 cc (cubic centimeters) of alcohol. The company is now planning raw materials needs for the third quarter, the quarter in which peak sales of Conquer occur. To keep production and sales moving smoothly, the company has the following inventory requirements:

CHECK FIGURE
(1) July: 13,880 units

a. The finished goods inventory on hand at the end of each month must be equal to 2,000 units of Conquer plus 30% of the next month's sales. The finished goods inventory on June 30 is budgeted to be 6,020 units.
b. The raw materials inventory on hand at the end of each month must be equal to 60% of the following month's production needs for raw materials. The raw materials inventory on June 30 is budgeted to be 83,280 cc of alcohol.
c. The company maintains no work in process inventories.

A sales budget for Conquer for the last six months of the year follows.

Budgeted Sales in Units	
July................	13,400
August.............	15,000
September..........	20,000
October	14,000
November..........	13,600
December..........	12,200

Required:

1. Prepare a production budget for Conquer for the months of July through October.
2. Examine the production budget that you prepared in (1) above. Why will the company produce more units than it sells in July and August, and fewer units than it sells in September and October?
3. Prepare a budget showing the quantity of alcohol to be purchased for July, August, and September, and for the quarter in total.

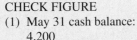

CHECK FIGURE
(1) May 31 cash balance: 4,200
(2) Net income: $15,800

PROBLEM 7–19   Cash Budget; Income Statement; Balance Sheet   (LO4, LO8, LO9, LO10)

Quinten Company is a wholesale distributor of soft drinks. The company's balance sheet as of April 30 is given below:

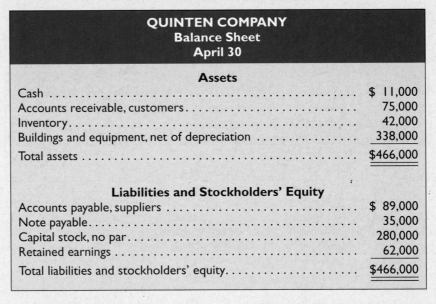

QUINTEN COMPANY Balance Sheet April 30	
Assets	
Cash	$ 11,000
Accounts receivable, customers...........................	75,000
Inventory...	42,000
Buildings and equipment, net of depreciation	338,000
Total assets	$466,000
Liabilities and Stockholders' Equity	
Accounts payable, suppliers	$ 89,000
Note payable..	35,000
Capital stock, no par.......................................	280,000
Retained earnings	62,000
Total liabilities and stockholders' equity....................	$466,000

The company is in the process of preparing budget data for May. A number of budget items have already been prepared, as stated below:

a. Sales are budgeted at $300,000 for May. Of these sales, $120,000 will be for cash; the remainder will be credit sales. 35% of a month's credit sales are collected in the month the sales are made, and the remainder are collected in the following month. All of the April 30 receivables will be collected in May.

b. Purchases of inventory are expected to total $216,000 during May. These purchases will all be on account. 60% of all purchases are paid for in the month of purchase; the remainder are paid in the following month. All of the April 30 accounts payable to suppliers will be paid during May.

c. The May 31 inventory balance is budgeted at $50,000.

d. Operating expenses for May are budgeted at $71,000, exclusive of depreciation. These expenses will be paid in cash. Depreciation is budgeted at $5,000 for the month.

e. The note payable on the April 30 balance sheet will be paid during May, with $200 in interest. (All of the interest relates to May.)

f. New refrigerating equipment costing $10,000 will be purchased for cash during May.

g. During May, the company will borrow $70,000 from its bank by giving a new note payable to the bank for that amount. The new note will be due in one year.

Required:
1. Prepare a cash budget for May. Support your budget with schedules showing budgeted cash receipts from sales and budgeted cash payments for inventory purchases.
2. Prepare a budgeted income statement for May. Use the traditional income statement format.
3. Prepare a budgeted balance sheet as of May 31.

PROBLEM 7–20 Integration of the Sales, Production, and Purchases Budgets (LO2, LO3, LO4)

CHECK FIGURE
(2) July: 17,800 units

Helsen, Inc., manufactures lamp shades. The company is now preparing detailed budgets for the third quarter and has assembled the following information to assist in the budget preparation:

a. The Marketing Department has estimated sales as follows for the remainder of the year (in units):

July 16,000	October....... 18,000
August 22,000	November 20,000
September 24,000	December 16,000

The selling price of the lamp shades is $30 per unit.

b. All sales are on account. Based on past experience, sales are collected in the following pattern:

20%	in the month of sale
76%	in the month following sale
4%	uncollectible

Sales for June totaled $420,000.

c. The company maintains finished goods inventories equal to 30% of the following month's sales. This requirement will be met at the end of June.

d. Each lamp shade requires 2.0 feet of PTX, a material that is sometimes hard to get. Therefore, the company requires that the inventory of PTX on hand at the end of each month be equal to 40% of the following month's production needs. The inventory of PTX on hand at the beginning and end of the quarter will be:

June 30 .... 14,240 feet
September 30 ..... ? feet

e. The PTX costs $5 per foot. 50% of a month's purchases of PTX is paid for in the month of purchase; the remainder is paid for in the following month. The accounts payable on July 1 for purchases of PTX during June will be $91,000.

Required:
1. Prepare a sales budget, by month and in total, for the third quarter. (Show your budget in both units and dollars.) Also prepare a schedule of expected cash collections, by month and in total, for the third quarter.
2. Prepare a production budget for each of the months of July through October.
3. Prepare a materials purchases budget for PTX, by month and in total, for the third quarter. Also prepare a schedule of expected cash payments for PTX, by month and in total, for the third quarter.

PROBLEM 7–21 Cash Budget with Supporting Schedules (LO2, LO4, LO8)

CHECK FIGURE
(2a) May purchases:
      $395,500
(3) June 30 cash balance:
      $42,070

Fowkes & Sons sells bicycles. Management is planning its cash needs for the second quarter. The company usually has to borrow money during this quarter to support peak sales of dirt bikes, which occur during May. The following information has been assembled to assist in preparing a cash budget for the quarter:

a. Budgeted monthly income statements for April–July are:

	April	May	June	July
Sales........................	$550,000	$580,000	$520,000	$480,000
Cost of goods sold	385,000	406,000	364,000	336,000

(continued)

(concluded)	April	May	June	July
Gross margin.	165,000	174,000	156,000	144,000
Less operating expenses:				
Selling expense	72,000	74,000	75,000	73,000
Administrative expense*	53,000	54,000	56,000	55,000
Total expenses.	125,000	128,000	131,000	128,000
Net operating income.	$ 40,000	$ 46,000	$ 25,000	$ 16,000

*Includes $14,000 depreciation each month.

b. Sales are 30% for cash and 70% on account.
c. Sales on account are collected over a three-month period as follows: 20% collected in the month of sale; 60% collected in the first month following the month of sale; and the remaining 20% collected in the second month following the month of sale. February sales totaled $340,000, and March sales totaled $380,000.
d. Inventory purchases are paid for as follows: 40% of a month's inventory purchases are paid for in the month of purchase; the remaining 60% are paid in the following month. Accounts payable at March 31 for inventory purchases during March total $177,450.
e. At the end of each month, inventory must be on hand equal to 25% of the cost of the merchandise to be sold in the following month. The merchandise inventory at March 31 is $96,250.
f. Dividends of $39,000 will be declared and paid in April.
g. Land costing $60,000 will be purchased for cash in May.
h. The cash balance at March 31 is $52,000; the company must maintain a cash balance of at least $30,000 at all times.
i. The company can borrow from its bank as needed to bolster the Cash account. Borrowings and repayments must be in multiples of $1,000. All borrowings take place at the beginning of a month, and all repayments are made at the end of a month. The annual interest rate is 12%. Compute interest on whole months ($\frac{1}{12}$, $\frac{2}{12}$, and so forth).

Required:
1. Prepare a schedule of expected cash collections from sales for each of the months April, May, and June, and for the quarter in total.
2. Prepare the following for merchandise inventory:
   a. An inventory purchases budget for each of the months April, May, and June.
   b. A schedule of expected cash disbursements for inventory for each of the months April, May, and June, and for the quarter in total.
3. Prepare a cash budget for the third quarter, by month as well as in total for the quarter. Show borrowings from the company's bank and repayments to the bank as needed to maintain the minimum cash balance.

CHECK FIGURE
(2) First-quarter net payments: $117,000
(3) First-quarter ending cash balance: $23,975

PROBLEM 7–22   Cash Budget with Supporting Schedules   (LO2, LO4, LO7, LO8)
Colormania is a wholesale distributor of dyes and pigments. When the treasurer of Colormania approached the company's bank in late 2002 seeking short-term financing, he was told that money was very tight and that any borrowing over the next year would have to be supported by a detailed statement of cash receipts and disbursements. The treasurer also was told that it would be very helpful to the bank if borrowers would indicate the quarters in which they would be needing funds, as well as the amounts that would be needed, and the quarters in which repayments could be made.
    Since the treasurer is unsure as to the particular quarters in which the bank financing will be needed, he has assembled the following information to assist in preparing a detailed cash budget:

a. Budgeted sales and merchandise purchases for the year 2003, as well as actual sales and purchases for the last quarter of 2002, are:

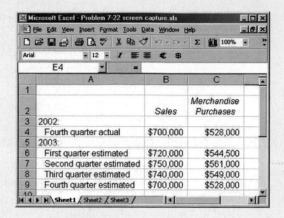

b. The company normally collects 80% of a quarter's sales before the quarter ends and another 15% in the following quarter. The remainder is uncollectible. This pattern of collections is now being experienced in the 2002 fourth-quarter actual data.

c. 85% of a quarter's merchandise purchases are paid for within the quarter. The remainder is paid in the following quarter.

d. Operating expenses for the year 2003 are budgeted quarterly at $60,000 plus 10% of sales. Of the fixed amount, $15,000 each quarter is depreciation.

e. The company will pay $18,000 in dividends each quarter.

f. Land purchases of $20,000 will be made in the second quarter, and purchases of $18,000 will be made in the third quarter. These purchases will be for cash.

g. The Cash account contained $20,000 at the end of 2002. The treasurer feels that this represents a minimum balance that must be maintained.

h. Any borrowing will take place at the beginning of a quarter, and any repayments will be made at the end of a quarter at an annual interest rate of 12%. Interest is paid only when principal is repaid. All borrowings and all repayments of principal must be in round $1,000 amounts. Interest payments can be in any amount. (Compute interest on whole months, e.g., $\frac{1}{12}$, $\frac{2}{12}$.)

i. At present, the company has no loans outstanding.

Required:

1. Prepare the following by quarter and in total for the year 2003:
   a. A schedule of expected cash collections.
   b. A schedule of budgeted cash disbursements for merchandise purchases.
2. Compute the expected cash payments for operating expenses, by quarter and in total, for the year 2003.
3. Prepare a cash budget, by quarter and in total, for the year 2003. Show clearly in your budget the quarter(s) in which borrowing will be necessary and the quarter(s) in which repayments can be made, as requested by the company's bank.

PROBLEM 7–23   Comprehensive Master Budget   (LO2, LO4, LO7, LO8, LO9, LO10)

Spektra Company, a home furnishings store, prepares its master budget on a quarterly basis. The following data have been assembled to assist in preparation of the master budget for the first quarter:

a. As of December 31 (the end of the prior quarter), the company's general ledger showed the following account balances:

	Debits	Credits
Cash	$ 26,000	
Accounts Receivable	50,000	
Inventory	86,400	
Property and Equipment (net)	80,000	
Accounts Payable		$102,000
Capital Stock		45,000
Retained Earnings		95,400
	$242,400	$242,400

CHECK FIGURE
(2a) February purchases: $159,000
(4) February ending cash balance: $5,200

b. Actual sales for December and budgeted sales for the next four months are as follows:

December (actual)	$200,000
January	$240,000
February	$250,000
March	$275,000
April	$260,000

c. Sales are 75% for cash and 25% on credit. All payments on credit sales are collected in the month following sale. The accounts receivable at December 31 are a result of December credit sales.
d. The company's gross profit margin is 40% of sales.
e. Monthly expenses are budgeted as follows: salaries and wages, $14,000 per month: advertising, $25,000 per month; shipping, 5% of sales; other expense, 15% of sales. Depreciation for the quarter will be $8,000.
f. At the end of each month, inventory is to be on hand equal to 60% of the following month's sales needs, stated at cost.
g. 30% of a month's inventory purchases are paid for in the month of purchase; the remainder is paid for in the following month.
h. During February, the company will purchase land for $8,000 cash. During March, land will be purchased for cash at a cost of $2,000.
i. During January, the company will declare and pay $30,000 in cash dividends.
j. The company must maintain a minimum cash balance of $5,000. An open line of credit is available at a local bank for any borrowing that may be needed during the quarter. All borrowing is done at the beginning of a month, and all repayments are made at the end of a month. Borrowing and repayment of principal must be in multiples of $1,000. Interest is paid only at the time of payment of principal. The annual interest rate is 18%. (Figure interest on whole months, e.g., $\frac{1}{12}$, $\frac{2}{12}$.)

Required:
Using the data above, complete the following statements and schedules for the first quarter:

1. Schedule of expected cash collections:

	January	February	March	Quarter
Cash sales.	$180,000			
Credit sales	50,000			
Total cash collections.	$230,000			

2. a. Inventory purchases budget:

	January	February	March	Quarter
Budgeted cost of goods sold	$144,000*	$150,000		
Add desired ending inventory	90,000†			
Total needs.	234,000			
Less beginning inventory	86,400			
Required: purchases.	$147,600			

*For January sales: $240,000 sales × 60% cost ratio = $144,000
†$150,000 × 60% = $90,000

b. Schedule of cash disbursements for purchases:

	January	February	March	Quarter
December purchases.	$102,000			$102,000
January purchases ($147,600)	44,280	$103,320		147,600

(continued)

(concluded)	January	February	March	Quarter
February purchases				
March purchases				
Total cash disbursements for purchases	$146,280			

3. Schedule of cash disbursements for expenses:

	January	February	March	Quarter
Salaries and wages	$14,000			
Advertising.	25,000			
Shipping	12,000			
Other expenses	36,000			
Total cash disbursements for operating expenses	$87,000			

4. Cash budget:

	January	February	March	Quarter
Cash balance, beginning	$ 26,000			
Add cash collections	230,000			
Total cash available	256,000			
Less disbursements:				
Purchases of inventory	146,280			
Operating expenses	87,000			
Purchases of land	0			
Cash dividends	30,000			
Total disbursements	263,280			
Excess (deficiency) of cash	(7,280)			
Financing:				
Etc.				

5. Prepare an income statement for the quarter ending March 31 as shown in Schedule 9 in the chapter.
6. Prepare a balance sheet as of March 31.

PROBLEM 7–24 Comprehensive Master Budget   (LO2, LO4, LO7, LO8, LO9, LO10)
The following are selected data relating to the operations of Andros Company, a magazine distributor:

Current assets as of March 31:	
Cash	$15,200
Accounts Receivable.	$40,000
Inventory.	$20,125
Buildings and Equipment (net)	$120,000
Accounts Payable	$62,250
Capital Stock.	$40,000
Retained Earnings	$93,075

Cost of Goods Sold 70% *(handwritten)*

a. Gross profit is 30% of sales.
b. Actual and budgeted sales data:

CHECK FIGURE
(2) May purchases: $83,825
(4) May 31 cash balance: $15,810

March (actual)	$100,000
April	$115,000
May	$118,000
June	$125,000
July	$130,000

c.   Sales are 60% for cash and 40% on credit. Credit sales are collected in the month following sale. The accounts receivable at March 31 are the result of March credit sales.

d.   At the end of each month, inventory is to be on hand equal to 25% of the following month's sales needs, stated at cost (75%)

e.   20% of a month's inventory purchases are paid for in the month of purchase; the remainder is paid for in the following month. The accounts payable at March 31 are a result of March purchases of inventory.

f.   Monthly expenses are as follows: salaries and wages $17,000; rent, $6,000; other expenses (excluding depreciation), 3% of sales. These expenses are paid monthly. Depreciation is $4,000 per month and includes depreciation on new assets.

g.   Equipment costing $22,000 will be purchased for cash in April.

h.   The company must maintain a minimum cash balance of $15,000. An open line of credit is available at a local bank. All borrowing is done at the beginning of a month, and all repayments are made at the end of a month; borrowing must be in multiples of $1,000. The annual interest rate is 12%. Interest is paid only at the time of repayment of principal; figure interest on whole months (1/12, 2/12, and so forth).

Required:

Using the above data:

1.   Complete the following schedule:

Schedule of Expected Cash Collections				
	April	**May**	**June**	**Quarter**
Cash sales......................	$ 69,000			
Credit sales	40,000			
Total collections.................	$109,000			

2.   Complete the following:

Inventory Purchases Budget				
	April	**May**	**June**	**Quarter**
Budgeted cost of goods sold*......	$ 80,500	$82,600		
Add desired ending inventory†	20,650			
Total needs.....................	101,150			
Less beginning inventory	20,125			
Required: purchases..............	$ 81,025			

*For April sales: $115,000 sales × 70% cost ratio = $80,500
†$82,600 × 25% = $20,650

Schedule of Expected Cash Disbursements—Purchases				
	April	**May**	**June**	**Quarter**
March purchases	$62,250			$62,250
April purchases	16,205	$64,820		81,025
May purchases				
June purchases				
Total disbursements.............	$78,455			

3. Complete the following:

Schedule of Expected Cash Disbursements—Operating Expenses				
	April	May	June	Quarter
Salaries and wages	$17,000			
Rent	6,000			
Other expenses	3,450			
Total disbursements	$26,450			

4. Complete the following cash budget:

Cash Budget				
	April	May	June	Quarter
Cash balance, beginning	$ 15,200			
Add cash collections	109,000			
Total cash available	124,200			
Less cash disbursements:				
For inventory	78,455			
For expenses	26,450			
For equipment	22,000			
Total disbursements	126,905			
Excess (deficiency) of cash	(2,705)			
Financing:				
Etc.				

5. Prepare an income statement for the quarter ending June 30. (Use the functional format in preparing your income statement, as shown in Schedule 9 in the text.)

6. Prepare a balance sheet as of June 30.

BUILDING YOUR SKILLS

ETHICS CHALLENGE   (LO1)

Granger Stokes, managing partner of the venture capital firm of Halston and Stokes, was dissatisfied with the top management of PrimeDrive, a manufacturer of computer disk drives. Halston and Stokes had invested $20 million in PrimeDrive, and the return on their investment had been below par for several years. In a tense meeting of the board of directors of PrimeDrive, Stokes exercised his firm's rights as the major equity investor in PrimeDrive and fired PrimeDrive's chief executive officer (CEO). He then quickly moved to have the board of directors of PrimeDrive appoint himself as the new CEO.

Stokes prided himself on his hard-driving management style. At the first management meeting, he asked two of the managers to stand and fired them on the spot, just to show everyone who was in control of the company. At the budget review meeting that followed, he ripped up the departmental budgets that had been submitted for his review and yelled at the managers for their "wimpy, do nothing targets." He then ordered everyone to submit new budgets calling for at least a 40% increase in sales volume and announced that he would not accept excuses for results that fell below budget.

Keri Kalani, an accountant working for the production manager at PrimeDrive, discovered toward the end of the year that her boss had not been scrapping defective disk drives that had been returned by customers. Instead, he had been shipping them in new cartons to other customers to avoid booking losses. Quality control had deteriorated during the year as a result of the push for increased volume, and returns of defective TRX drives were running as high as 15% of the new drives shipped. When she confronted her boss with her discovery, he told her to mind her own business. And then, in the way of a justification for his actions, he said, "All of us managers are finding ways to hit Stokes' targets."

Required:

1. Is Granger Stokes using budgets as a planning and control tool?

2. What are the behavioral consequences of the way budgets are being used at PrimeDrive?

3. What, if anything, do you think Keri Kalani should do?

CHECK FIGURE
(1d) April cash disburse-
       ments: $195,750
(2)   June ending cash
       balance: $10,732

CASE   (LO2, LO4, LO8, LO9, LO10)

You have just been hired as a management trainee by Cravat Sales Company, a nationwide distributor of a designer's silk ties. The company has an exclusive franchise on the distribution of the ties, and sales have grown so rapidly over the last few years that it has become necessary to add new members to the management team. You have been given direct responsibility for all planning and budgeting. Your first assignment is to prepare a master budget for the next three months, starting April 1. You are anxious to make a favorable impression on the president and have assembled the information below.

The company desires a minimum ending cash balance each month of $10,000. The ties are sold to retailers for $8 each. Recent and forecasted sales in units are as follows:

January (actual)	20,000	June	60,000
February (actual)	24,000	July	40,000
March (actual)	28,000	August	36,000
April	35,000	September	32,000
May	45,000		

The large buildup in sales before and during June is due to Father's Day. Ending inventories are supposed to equal 90% of the next month's sales in units. The ties cost the company $5 each.

Purchases are paid for as follows: 50% in the month of purchase and the remaining 50% in the following month. All sales are on credit, with no discount, and payable within 15 days. The company has found, however, that only 25% of a month's sales are collected by month-end. An additional 50% is collected in the month following, and the remaining 25% is collected in the second month following. Bad debts have been negligible.

The company's monthly operating expenses are given below:

Variable:	
Sales commissions	$1 per tie
Fixed:	
Wages and salaries	$22,000
Utilities	$14,000
Insurance expired	$1,200
Depreciation	$1,500
Miscellaneous	$3,000

All operating expenses are paid during the month, in cash, with the exception of depreciation and insurance expired. Land will be purchased during May for $25,000 cash. The company declares dividends of $12,000 each quarter, payable in the first month of the following quarter. The company's balance sheet at March 31 is given below:

Assets	
Cash	$ 14,000
Accounts receivable ($48,000 February sales; $168,000 March sales)	216,000
Inventory (31,500 units)	157,500
Unexpired insurance	14,400
Fixed assets, net of depreciation	172,700
Total assets	$574,600

Liabilities and Stockholders' Equity	
Accounts payable, purchases	$ 85,750
Dividends payable	12,000
Capital stock, no par	300,000
Retained earnings	176,850
Total liabilities and stockholders' equity	$574,600

The company can borrow money from its bank at 12% annual interest. All borrowing must be done at the beginning of a month, and repayments must be made at the end of a month. Repayments of principal must be in round $1,000 amounts. Borrowing (and payments of interest) can be in any amount.

Interest is computed and paid at the end of each quarter on all loans outstanding during the quarter. Round all interest payments to the nearest whole dollar. Compute interest on whole months ($\frac{1}{12}$, $\frac{2}{12}$, and so forth). The company wishes to use any excess cash to pay loans off as rapidly as possible.

Required:

Prepare a master budget for the three-month period ending June 30. Include the following detailed budgets:
1. a. A sales budget by month and in total.
    b. A schedule of expected cash collections from sales and accounts receivable, by month and in total.
    c. A purchases budget in units and in dollars. Show the budget by month and in total.
    d. A schedule of budgeted cash disbursements for purchases, by month and in total.
2. A cash budget. Show the budget by month and in total.
3. A budgeted income statement for the three-month period ending June 30. Use the contribution approach.
4. A budgeted balance sheet as of June 30.

TEAMWORK IN ACTION   (LO2, LO4, LO6, LO8)

Roller, Ltd., of Melbourne, Australia, is the exclusive distributor in Australia and the South Pacific of a popular brand of in-line skates manufactured in Mexico. The company is in the process of putting together its cash budget for the second quarter—April, May, and June—of next year. The president of the company suspects that some financing will be required in the second quarter because sales are expanding and the company intends to make several major equipment purchases in that quarter. The president is confident that the company will be able to meet or exceed the following budgeted sales figures (all in Australian dollars) next year:

CHECK FIGURE
June excess of cash available over disbursements:
$41,800

January	$158,000	July	$190,000
February	$160,000	August	$192,000
March	$164,000	September	$210,000
April	$172,000	October	$230,000
May	$176,000	November	$260,000
June	$184,000	December	$180,000

The following additional information will be used in formulating the cash budget:

a. All of the company's sales are on credit terms. The company collects 30% of its billings in the month after the sale and the remaining 70% in the second month after the sale. Uncollectible accounts are negligible.

b. The cost of sales is 75% of sales. Because of the shipping time from Mexico, the company orders skates from the manufacturer one month in advance of their expected sale. Roller, Ltd., desires to maintain little or no inventory.

c. The company orders the skates on credit terms from the manufacturer. The company pays half of the bill in the month after it orders the skates and the other half in the second month after it places the order.

d. Operating expenses, other than cost of sales, are budgeted to be $178,800 for the year. The composition of these expenses is given below. All of these expenses are incurred evenly throughout the year except for the property taxes. Property taxes are paid in four equal installments in the last month of each quarter.

Salaries and wages	$120,000
Advertising and promotion	12,000
Property taxes	18,000
Insurance	4,800
Utilities	6,000
Depreciation	18,000
Total operating expenses	$178,800

e.   Income tax payments are made by the company in the first month of each quarter based on the taxable income for the prior quarter. The income tax payment due in April is $16,000.

f.   Because of expanding sales, the company plans to make equipment purchases of $22,300 in April and $29,000 in May. These purchases will not affect depreciation for the year.

g.   The company has a policy of maintaining an end-of-month cash balance of $20,000. Cash is borrowed or invested monthly, as needed, to maintain this balance. All borrowing is done at the beginning of the month, and all investments and repayments are made at the end of the month. As of March 31, there are no investments of excess cash and no outstanding loans.

h.   The annual interest rate on loans from the bank is 12%. Compute interest on whole months ($\frac{1}{12}$, $\frac{2}{12}$, and so forth). The company will pay off any loans, including accumulated interest, at the end of the second quarter if sufficient cash is available.

Required:

The team should discuss and then respond to the following two questions:

1.   Prepare a cash budget for Roller, Ltd., by month and in total for the second quarter.
2.   Discuss why cash budgeting is particularly important for an expanding company like Roller, Ltd.

  COMMUNICATING IN PRACTICE   (LOI)

In the late 1980s and early 1990s, public universities found that they were no longer immune to the financial stress faced by their private sister institutions and corporate America. Budget cuts were in the air across the land. When the budget ax hit, the cuts often came without warning and their size was sometimes staggering. State support for some institutions dropped by 40% or more. Most university administrators had only experienced budget increases, never budget cuts. Also, the budget setbacks usually occurred at the most inopportune time—during the school year when contractual commitments with faculty and staff had been signed, programs had been planned, and students were enrolled and taking classes.

Required:

1.   Should the administration be "fair" to all affected and institute a round of across-the-board cuts whenever the state announces another subsidy reduction?
2.   If not across-the-board cutbacks in programs, then would you recommend more focused reductions, and if so, what priorities would you establish for bringing spending in line with revenues?
3.   Since these usually are not one-time-only cutbacks, how would you manage continuous, long-term reductions in budgets extending over a period of years?
4.   Should the decision-making process be top-down (centralized with top administrators) or bottom-up (participative)? Why?
5.   How should issues such as protect-your-turf mentality, resistance to change, and consensus building be dealt with?

TAKING IT TO THE NET

As you know, the World Wide Web is a medium that is constantly evolving. Sites come and go and change without notice. To enable periodic update of site addresses, this problem has been posted to the textbook website (www.mhhe.com/bgn2e). After accessing the site, enter the Student Center and select this chapter. Select and complete the Taking It to the Net problem.

Standard Costs

CHAPTER OUTLINE

Controlling the Costs of Visual Effects

Special effects, such as the computed-generated action shots of dinosaurs in *Jurassic Park,* are expensive to produce. A single visual effect, lasting three to seven seconds, can cost up to $50,000, and a high-profile film may contain hundreds of these shots. Since visual effects are produced under fixed-price contracts, visual-effects companies must carefully estimate their costs. Once a bid has been accepted, costs must be zealously monitored to make sure they do not spin out of control.

Buena Vista Visual Effects, a part of Walt Disney Studios, uses a standard cost system to estimate and control costs. A "storyboard" is created for each special effects shot. The storyboard sketches the visual effect, details the length of the shot, which is measured in frames (24 frames equals one second of film), and describes the work that will need to be done to create the effect. A detailed budget is then prepared using standard costs. For example, a shot may require a miniature model maker working full time for 12 weeks at a specified weekly wage. As the project progresses, actual costs are compared to the standard cost, and significant cost overruns are investigated.

Source: Ray Scalice, "Lights! Cameras! . . . Accountants," *Management Accounting,* June 1996, pp. 42–46. Reprinted with permission from *Management Accounting.*

LO1 Explain how direct materials standards and direct labor standards are set.

LO2 Compute the direct materials price and quantity variances and explain their significance.

LO3 Compute the direct labor rate and efficiency variances and explain their significance.

LO4 Compute the variable manufacturing overhead spending and efficiency variances.

LO5 (Appendix 8A) Prepare journal entries to record standard costs and variances.

In this chapter we begin our study of management control and performance measures. As explained in the following quotation, performance measurement serves a vital function in both personal life and in organizations:

> Imagine you want to improve your basketball shooting skill. You know that practice will help, so you [go] to the basketball court. There you start shooting toward the hoop, but as soon as the ball gets close to the rim your vision goes blurry for a second, so that you cannot observe where the ball ended up in relation to the target (left, right, in front, too far back, inside the hoop?). It would be pretty difficult to improve under those conditions . . . (And by the way, how long would [shooting baskets] sustain your interest if you couldn't observe the outcome of your efforts?)
>
> Or imagine someone engaging in a weight loss program. A normal step in such programs is to purchase a scale to be able to track one's progress: Is this program working? Am I losing weight? A positive answer would be encouraging and would motivate me to keep up the effort, while a negative answer might lead me to reflect on the process: Am I working on the right diet and exercise program? Am I doing everything I am supposed to? etc. Suppose you don't want to set up a sophisticated measurement system and decide to forgo the scale. You would still have some idea of how well you are doing from simple methods such as clothes feeling looser, a belt that fastens at a different hole, or simply via observation in a mirror! Now, imagine trying to sustain a weight loss program without *any* feedback on how well you are doing.
>
> In these . . . examples, availability of quantitative measures of performance can yield two types of benefits: First, performance feedback can help improve the "production process" through a better understanding of what works and what doesn't; e.g., shooting this way works better than shooting that way. Secondly, feedback on performance can sustain motivation and effort, because it is encouraging and/or because it suggests that more effort is required for the goal to be met.[1]

In the same way, performance measurement can be helpful in an organization. It can provide feedback concerning what works and what does not work, and it can help motivate people to sustain their efforts.

Companies in highly competitive industries like FedEx, Southwest Airlines, Dell Computer, Shell Oil, and Toyota must be able to provide high-quality goods and services at low cost. If they do not, they will perish. Stated in the starkest terms, managers must obtain inputs such as raw materials and electricity at the lowest possible prices and must use them as effectively as possible—while maintaining or increasing the quality of the output. If inputs are purchased at prices that are too high or more input is used than is really necessary, higher costs will result.

How do managers control the prices that are paid for inputs and the quantities that are used? They could examine every transaction in detail, but this obviously would be an inefficient use of management time. For many companies, the answer to this control problem lies at least partially in *standard costs.*

STANDARD COSTS—MANAGEMENT BY EXCEPTION

A *standard* is a benchmark or "norm" for measuring performance. Standards are found everywhere. Your doctor evaluates your weight using standards that have been set for individuals of your age, height, and gender. The food we eat in restaurants must be prepared under specified standards of cleanliness. The buildings we live in must conform to standards set in building codes. Standards are also widely used in managerial accounting where they relate to the *quantity* and *cost* of inputs used in manufacturing goods or providing services.

[1]Soumitra Dutta and Jean-François Manzoni, *Process Reengineering, Organizational Change and Performance Improvement* (New York: McGraw-Hill, 1999), Chapter IV.

Standards in the Spanish Royal Tobacco Factory

Standards have been used for centuries in commercial enterprises. For example, the Spanish Royal Tobacco Factory in Seville used standards to control costs in the 1700s. The Royal Tobacco Factory had a monopoly over snuff and cigar production in Spain and was the largest industrial building in Europe. Employee theft of tobacco was a particular problem, due to its high value. Careful records were maintained for each worker of the amount of tobacco leaf issued to the worker, the number of cigars expected to be made based on standards, and the actual production. The worker was not paid if the actual production was less than expected. To minimize theft, tobacco was weighed after each production step to determine the amount of wastage.

Source: Salvador Carmona, Mahmoud Ezzamel, and Fernando Gutiérrez, "Control and Cost Accounting Practices in the Spanish Royal Tobacco Factory," *Accounting Organizations and Society,* Vol. 22, pp. 411–446, 1997.

Managers—often assisted by engineers and accountants—set quantity and cost standards for each major input such as raw materials and labor time. *Quantity standards* specify how much of an input should be used to make a product or provide a service. *Cost (price) standards* specify how much should be paid for each unit of the input. Actual quantities and actual costs of inputs are compared to these standards. If either the quantity or the cost of inputs departs significantly from the standards, managers investigate the discrepancy. The purpose is to find the cause of the problem and then eliminate it so that it does not recur. This process is called **management by exception.**

In our daily lives, we operate in a management by exception mode most of the time. Consider what happens when you sit down in the driver's seat of your car. You put the key in the ignition, you turn the key, and your car starts. Your expectation (standard) that the car will start is met; you do not have to open the car hood and check the battery, the connecting cables, the fuel lines, and so on. If you turn the key and the car does not start, then you have a discrepancy (variance). Your expectations are not met, and you need to investigate why. Note that even if the car starts after a second try, it would be wise to investigate anyway. The fact that the expectation was not met should be viewed as an opportunity to uncover the cause of the problem rather than as simply an annoyance. If the underlying cause is not discovered and corrected, the problem may recur and become much worse.

Management by Exception

EXHIBIT 8–1

The Variance Analysis Cycle

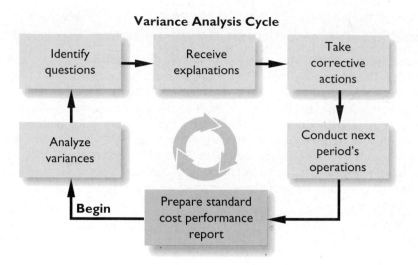

Variance Analysis Cycle

This basic approach to identifying and solving problems is exploited in the *variance analysis cycle*, which is illustrated in Exhibit 8–1. The cycle begins with the preparation of standard cost performance reports in the accounting department. These reports highlight the *variances*, which are the differences between actual results and what should have occurred according to the standards. The variances raise questions. Why did this variance occur? Why is this variance larger than it was last period? The significant variances are investigated to discover their root causes. Corrective actions are taken. And then next period's operations are carried out. The cycle then begins again with the preparation of a new standard cost performance for the latest period. The emphasis should be on flagging problems for attention, finding their root causes, and then taking corrective action. The goal is to improve operations—not to find blame.

Standard Costing at Parker Brass

The Brass Products Division at Parker Hannifin Corporation, known as Parker Brass, is a world-class manufacturer of tube and brass fittings, valves, hose, and hose fittings. Management at the company uses variances from its standard costing system to target problem areas for improvement. If a production variance exceeds 5% of sales, the responsible manager is required to explain the variance and to propose a plan of action to correct the detected problems. In the past, variances were reported at the end of the month—often several weeks after a particular job had been completed. Now, a variance report is generated the day after a job is completed and summary variance reports are prepared weekly. These more frequent reports permit managers to take more timely action.

Source: David Johnsen and Parvez Sopariwala, "Standard Costing Is Alive and Well at Parker Brass," *Management Accounting Quarterly*, Winter 2000, pp. 12–20.

Who Uses Standard Costs?

Manufacturing, service, food, and not-for-profit organizations all make use of standards to some extent. Auto service centers like Firestone and Sears, for example, often set specific labor time standards for the completion of certain work tasks, such as installing a carburetor or doing a valve job, and then measure actual performance against these standards. Fast-food outlets such as McDonald's have exacting standards for the quantity of meat going into a sandwich, as well as standards for the cost of the meat. Hospitals have standard costs (for food, laundry, and other items) for each occupied bed per day, as well as standard time allowances for certain routine activities, such as laboratory tests. In short, you are likely to run into standard costs in virtually any line of business that you enter.

Manufacturing companies often have highly developed standard costing systems in which standards relating to materials, labor, and overhead are created for each separate product. These standards are listed on a **standard cost card** that provides the manager with a great deal of information concerning the inputs that are required to produce a unit and their costs. In the following section, we provide a detailed example of the setting of standard costs and the preparation of a standard cost card.

SETTING STANDARD COSTS

Setting price and quantity standards requires the combined expertise of all persons who have responsibility for purchasing and using inputs. In a manufacturing setting, this might include accountants, purchasing managers, engineers, production supervisors, line managers, and production workers. Past records of purchase prices and of input usage can be helpful in setting standards. However, the standards should be designed to encourage efficient *future* operations, not a repetition of past inefficient operations.

Ideal versus Practical Standards

Should standards be attainable all of the time, should they be attainable only part of the time, or should they be so tight that they become, in effect, "the impossible dream"? Opinions among managers vary, but standards tend to fall into one of two categories—either ideal or practical.

Ideal standards are those that can be attained only under the best circumstances. They allow for no machine breakdowns or other work interruptions, and they call for a level of effort that can be attained only by the most skilled and efficient employees working at peak effort 100% of the time. Some managers feel that such standards have a motivational value. These managers argue that even though employees know they will rarely meet the standard, it is a constant reminder of the need for ever-increasing efficiency and effort. Few firms use ideal standards. Most managers feel that ideal standards tend to discourage even the most diligent workers. Moreover, variances from ideal standards are difficult to interpret. Large variances from the ideal are normal and it is difficult to "manage by exception."

Practical standards are defined as standards that are "tight but attainable." They allow for normal machine downtime and employee rest periods, and they can be attained through reasonable, though highly efficient, efforts by the average worker. Variances from such a standard represent deviations that fall outside of normal operating conditions and signal a need for management attention. Furthermore, practical standards can serve multiple purposes. In addition to signaling abnormal conditions, they can also be used in forecasting cash flows and in planning inventory. By contrast, ideal standards cannot be used in forecasting and planning; they do not allow for normal inefficiencies, and therefore they result in unrealistic planning and forecasting figures.

Throughout the remainder of this chapter, we will assume the use of practical rather than ideal standards.

Owner of a Painting Company

YOU DECIDE

Having painted a relative's house last summer, you have decided to start your own house-painting company this summer and have hired several of your friends. An uncle who is in the construction business has suggested that you use the time standards for various tasks such as preparing wood siding, painting wood trim, and painting wood siding. A table of such standards for professional painters has been published in a recent issue of a trade magazine for painting contractors. What advantages and disadvantages do you see in using such standards? How do you think they should be used in your business, if at all?

The Colonial Pewter Company was organized a year ago. The company's only product is a reproduction of an 18th-century pewter bookend. The bookend is made largely by hand, using traditional metal-working tools. Consequently, the manufacturing process is labor intensive and requires a high level of skill.

Colonial Pewter has recently expanded its workforce to take advantage of unexpected demand for the bookends as gifts. The company started with a small cadre of experienced pewter workers but has had to hire less experienced workers as a result of the expansion. The president of the company, J. D. Wriston, has called a meeting to discuss production problems. Attending the meeting are Tom Kuchel, the production manager; Janet Warner, the purchasing manager; and Terry Sherman, the corporate controller.

J. D.: I've got a feeling that we aren't getting the production we should out of our new people.

Tom: Give us a chance. Some of the new people have been with the company for less than a month.

Janet: Let me add that production seems to be wasting an awful lot of material—particularly pewter. That stuff is very expensive.

Tom: What about the shipment of defective pewter you bought a couple of months ago—the one with the iron contamination? That caused us major problems.

Janet: That's ancient history. How was I to know it was off-grade? Besides, it was a great deal.

J. D.: Calm down, everybody. Let's get the facts before we start sinking our fangs into each other.

Tom: I agree. The more facts the better.

J. D.: Okay, Terry, it's your turn. Facts are the controller's department.

Terry: I'm afraid I can't provide the answers off the top of my head, but it won't take me too long to set up a system that can routinely answer questions relating to worker productivity, material waste, and input prices.

J. D.: How long is "not too long"?

Terry: I will need all of your cooperation, but how about a week from today?

J. D.: That's okay with me. What about everyone else?

Tom: Sure.

Janet: Fine with me.

J. D.: Let's mark it on our calendars.

Setting Direct Materials Standards

Terry Sherman's first task was to prepare price and quantity standards for the company's only significant raw material, pewter ingots. The **standard price per unit** for direct materials should reflect the final, delivered cost of the materials, net of any discounts taken. After consulting with purchasing manager Janet Warner, Terry prepared the following documentation for the standard price of a pound of pewter in ingot form:

Purchase price, top-grade pewter ingots, in 40-pound ingots	$3.60
Freight, by truck, from the supplier's warehouse	0.44
Receiving and handling	0.05
Less purchase discount.	(0.09)
Standard price per pound.	$4.00

Notice that the standard price reflects a particular grade of material (top grade), purchased in particular lot sizes (40-pound ingots), and delivered by a particular type of carrier (truck). Allowances have also been made for handling and discounts. If everything proceeds according to these expectations, the net cost of a pound of pewter should therefore be $4.00.

The **standard quantity per unit** for direct materials should reflect the amount of material required for each unit of finished product, as well as an allowance for unavoidable waste, spoilage, and other normal inefficiencies. After consulting with the production manager, Tom Kuchel, Terry Sherman prepared the following documentation for the standard quantity of pewter in a pair of bookends:

Material requirements as specified in the bill of materials for a pair of bookends, in pounds	2.7
Allowance for waste and spoilage, in pounds	0.2
Allowance for rejects, in pounds	0.1
Standard quantity per pair of bookends, in pounds.................	3.0

A **bill of materials** is a list that shows the quantity of each type of material going into a unit of finished product. It is a handy source for determining the basic material input per unit, but it should be adjusted for waste and other factors, as shown above, when determining the standard quantity per unit of product. "Waste and spoilage" in the table above refers to materials that are wasted as a normal part of the production process or that spoil before they are used. "Rejects" refers to the direct material contained in units that are defective and must be scrapped.

"Allowable" Waste

IN BUSINESS

After many years of operating a standard cost system, a major wood products company reviewed the materials standards for its products. The company discovered that a 20% waste factor was built into the standard cost for every product. Management was dismayed to learn that the "allowable" waste was so large. Since the quantity standards had not been reviewed for many years, management was unaware of the existence of this significant cost improvement potential in the company.

Source: James M. Reeve, "The Impact of Variation on Operating System Performance," *Performance Excellence* (Sarasota, FL: American Accounting Association), p. 77.

Although allowances for waste, spoilage, and rejects are often built into standards, this practice is now coming into question. Those involved in TQM (total quality management) and similar improvement programs argue that no amount of waste or defects should be tolerated. If allowances for waste, spoilage, and rejects *are* built into the standard cost, the levels of those allowances should be periodically reviewed and reduced over time to reflect improved processes, better training, and better equipment.

Once the price and quantity standards have been set, the standard cost of material per unit of finished product can be computed as follows:

$$3.0 \text{ pounds per unit} \times \$4.00 \text{ per pound} = \$12 \text{ per unit}$$

This $12 cost will appear as one item on the product's standard cost card.

Setting Direct Labor Standards

Direct labor price and quantity standards are usually expressed in terms of a labor rate and labor-hours. The **standard rate per hour** for direct labor should include not only wages earned but also fringe benefits and other labor costs. Using last month's wage records and in consultation with the production manager, Terry determined the standard rate per hour at the Colonial Pewter Company as follows:

Basic wage rate per hour.........................	$10
Employment taxes at 10% of the basic rate	1
Fringe benefits at 30% of the basic rate	3
Standard rate per direct labor-hour	$14

Many companies prepare a single standard rate for all employees in a department. This standard rate reflects the expected "mix" of workers, even though the actual wage rates may vary somewhat from individual to individual due to differing skills or seniority. A single standard rate simplifies the use of standard costs and also permits the manager to monitor the use of employees within departments. More is said on this point a little later. According to the standard computed above, the direct labor rate for Colonial Pewter should average $14 per hour.

The standard direct labor time required to complete a unit of product (called the **standard hours per unit**) is perhaps the single most difficult standard to determine. One approach is to break down each operation performed on the product into elemental body movements (such as reaching, pushing, and turning over). Published tables of standard times for such movements are available. These times can be applied to the movements and then added together to determine the total standard time allowed per operation. Another approach is for an industrial engineer to do a time and motion study, actually clocking the time required for certain tasks. As stated earlier, the standard time should include allowances for breaks, personal needs of employees, cleanup, and machine downtime.

After consulting with the production manager, Terry Sherman prepared the following documentation for the standard hours per unit:

Basic labor time per unit, in hours...........................	1.9
Allowance for breaks and personal needs....................	0.1
Allowance for cleanup and machine downtime...............	0.3
Allowance for rejects......................................	0.2
Standard labor-hours per unit of product....................	2.5

Once the rate and time standards have been set, the standard labor cost per unit of product can be computed as follows:

$$2.5 \text{ hours per unit} \times \$14 \text{ per hour} = \$35 \text{ per unit}$$

This $35 per unit standard labor cost appears along with direct materials on the standard cost card of the product.

IN BUSINESS

Watching the Pennies

Industrie Natuzzi SpA, founded and run by Pasquale Natuzzi, produces handmade leather furniture for the world market in Santaeramo Del Colle in southern Italy. Natuzzi is export-oriented and has about 25% of the U.S. leather furniture market. The company's furniture is handmade by craftsmen, each of whom has a networked computer at his or her workstation. The computer provides precise instructions on how to accomplish a particular task and keeps track of how quickly the craftsman completes the task. If the craftsman beats the standard time for the task, the computer adds a bonus to the craftsman's pay.

The company's computers know exactly how much thread, screws, foam, leather, labor, and so on is required for every model. "Should the price of Argentinean hides or German dyes rise one day, employees in Santaeramo enter the new prices into the computer, and the costs for all sofas with that leather and those colors are immediately recalculated. 'Everything has to be clear for me,' says Natuzzi. 'Why this penny? Where is it going?'"

Source: Richard C. Morais, "A Methodical Man," *Forbes,* August 11, 1997, pp. 70–72.

EXHIBIT 8–2

Standard Cost Card—Variable
Production Cost

Inputs	(1) Standard Quantity or Hours	(2) Standard Price or Rate	(3) Standard Cost (1) × (2)
Direct materials	3.0 pounds	$ 4.00	$12.00
Direct labor	2.5 hours	14.00	35.00
Variable manufacturing overhead	2.5 hours	3.00	7.50
Total standard cost per unit			$54.50

Setting Variable Manufacturing Overhead Standards

As with direct labor, the price and quantity standards for variable manufacturing overhead are usually expressed in terms of rate and hours. The rate represents *the variable portion of the predetermined overhead rate* discussed in Chapter 2; the hours represent whatever base is used to apply overhead to units of product (usually machine-hours or direct labor-hours, as we learned in Chapter 2). At Colonial Pewter, the variable portion of the predetermined overhead rate is $3 per direct labor-hour. Therefore, the standard variable manufacturing overhead cost per unit is computed as follows:

$$2.5 \text{ hours per unit} \times \$3 \text{ per hour} = \$7.50 \text{ per unit}$$

This $7.50 per unit cost for variable manufacturing overhead appears along with direct materials and direct labor on the standard cost card in Exhibit 8–2. Observe that the **standard cost per unit** is computed by multiplying the standard quantity or hours by the standard price or rate.

Are Standards the Same as Budgets?

Standards and budgets are very similar. The major distinction between the two terms is that a standard is a *unit* amount, whereas a budget is a *total* amount. The standard cost for materials at Colonial Pewter is $12 per pair of bookends. If 1,000 pairs of bookends are to be made during a budgeting period, then the budgeted cost of materials would be $12,000. In effect, *a standard can be viewed as the budgeted cost for one unit of product.*

A GENERAL MODEL FOR VARIANCE ANALYSIS

An important reason for separating standards into two categories—price and quantity—is that different managers are usually responsible for buying and for using inputs and these two activities occur at different points in time. In the case of raw materials, for example, the purchasing manager is responsible for the price, and this responsibility is exercised at the time of purchase. In contrast, the production manager is responsible for the amount of the raw material used, and this responsibility is exercised when the materials are used in production, which may occur considerably after the purchase date. It is important, therefore, that deviations from price standards are clearly separated from those due to deviations from quantity standards. Differences between *standard* prices and *actual* prices and between *standard* quantities and *actual* quantities are called **variances.** The act of computing and interpreting variances is called *variance analysis.*

Price and Quantity Variances

A general model for computing standard cost variances for variable costs is presented in Exhibit 8–3. This model isolates price variances from quantity variances and shows how each of these variances is computed.[2] We will be using this model throughout the chapter to compute variances for direct materials, direct labor, and variable manufacturing overhead.

---

[2]Variance analysis of fixed costs is discussed in the next chapter.

EXHIBIT 8–3

A General Model for Variance
Analysis—Variable Production
Costs

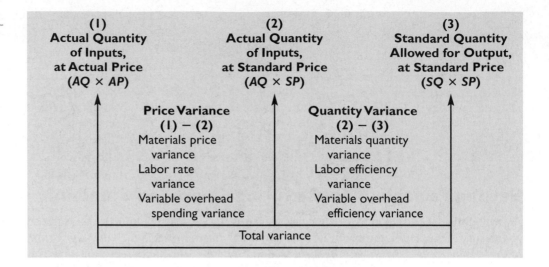

Three things should be noted from Exhibit 8–3. First, note that a price variance and a quantity variance can be computed for all three variable cost elements—direct materials, direct labor, and variable manufacturing overhead—even though the variances have different names. For example, a price variance is called a *materials price variance* in the case of direct materials but a *labor rate variance* in the case of direct labor and an *overhead spending variance* in the case of variable manufacturing overhead.

Second, note that even though a price variance may be called by different names, it is computed in exactly the same way regardless of whether one is dealing with direct materials, direct labor, or variable manufacturing overhead. The same is true of the quantity variance.

Third, the inputs represent the actual quantity of direct materials, direct labor, and variable manufacturing overhead used; the output represents the good production of the period, expressed in terms of the *standard quantity (or the standard hours) allowed for the actual output* (see column 3 in Exhibit 8–3). By **standard quantity allowed** or **standard hours allowed,** we mean the amount of direct materials, direct labor, or variable manufacturing overhead *that should have been used* to produce the actual output of the period. This could be more or could be less than the actual materials, labor, or overhead, depending on the efficiency or inefficiency of operations. The standard quantity allowed is computed by multiplying the actual output in units by the standard input allowed per unit.

With this general model as a foundation, we will now examine the price and quantity variances in more detail.

USING STANDARD COSTS—DIRECT MATERIALS VARIANCES

LEARNING OBJECTIVE 2

Compute the direct materials
price and quantity variances
and explain their significance.

Concept 8–1

After determining Colonial Pewter Company's standard costs for direct materials, direct labor, and variable manufacturing overhead, Terry Sherman's next step was to compute the company's variances for June, the most recent month. As discussed in the preceding section, variances are computed by comparing standard costs to actual costs. To facilitate this comparison, Terry referred to the standard cost data contained in Exhibit 8–2. This exhibit shows that the standard cost of direct materials per unit of product is as follows:

3.0 pounds per unit $\times$ \$4.00 per pound = \$12 per unit

Colonial Pewter's purchasing records for June showed that 6,500 pounds of pewter were purchased at a cost of \$3.80 per pound. This cost included freight and handling and was net of the quantity discount. All of the material purchased was used during June to

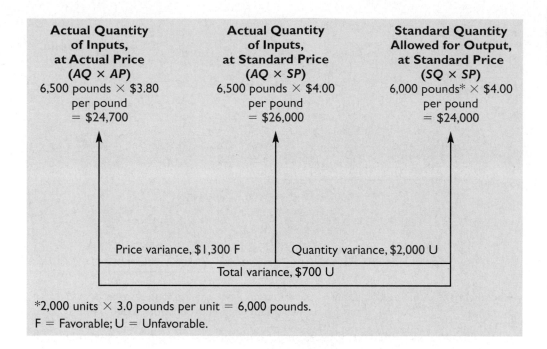

EXHIBIT 8–4

Variance Analysis—Direct Materials

manufacture 2,000 pairs of pewter bookends. Using these data and the standard costs from Exhibit 8–2, Terry computed the price and quantity variances shown in Exhibit 8–4.

The three arrows in Exhibit 8–4 point to three different total cost figures. The first, $24,700, refers to the actual total cost of the pewter that was purchased during June. The second, $26,000, refers to what the pewter would have cost if it had been purchased at the standard price of $4.00 a pound rather than the actual price of $3.80 a pound. The difference between these two amounts, $1,300 ($26,000 − $24,700), is the price variance. It exists because the actual purchase price was $0.20 per pound less than the standard purchase price. Since 6,500 pounds were purchased, the total amount of the variance is $1,300 ($0.20 per pound × 6,500 pounds). This variance is labeled favorable (denoted by F), since the actual purchase price was less than the standard purchase price. A price variance is labeled unfavorable (denoted by U) if the actual price exceeds the standard price.

The third arrow in Exhibit 8–4 points to $24,000—the cost if the pewter had been purchased at the standard price *and* only the amount allowed by the standard quantity had been used. The standards call for 3 pounds of pewter per unit. Since 2,000 units were produced, 6,000 pounds of pewter should have been used. This is referred to as the standard quantity allowed for the output. If this 6,000 pounds of pewter had been purchased at the standard price of $4.00 per pound, the company would have spent $24,000. The difference between this amount, $24,000, and the amount at the end of the middle arrow in Exhibit 8–4, $26,000, is the quantity variance of $2,000.

To understand this quantity variance, note that the actual amount of pewter used in production was 6,500 pounds. However, the standard amount of pewter allowed for the actual output is 6,000 pounds. Therefore, a total of 500 pounds too much pewter was used to produce the actual output. To express this in dollar terms, the 500 pounds is multiplied by the standard price of $4.00 per pound to yield the quantity variance of $2,000. Why is the standard price, rather than the actual price, of the pewter used in this calculation? The production manager is ordinarily responsible for the quantity variance. If the actual price were used in the calculation of the quantity variance, the production manager would be held responsible for the efficiency or inefficiency of the purchasing manager. Apart from being unfair, fruitless arguments between the production manager and purchasing manager would occur every time the actual price of an input is above its standard price. To avoid these arguments, the standard price is used when computing the quantity variance.

EXHIBIT 8–5

Variance Analysis—Direct
Materials, When the Amount
Purchased Differs from the
Amount Used

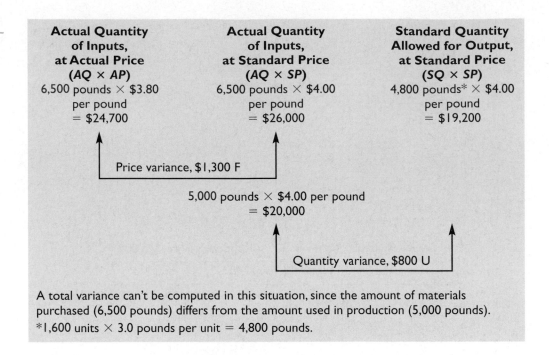

Actual Quantity of Inputs, at Actual Price (AQ × AP)	Actual Quantity of Inputs, at Standard Price (AQ × SP)	Standard Quantity Allowed for Output, at Standard Price (SQ × SP)
6,500 pounds × $3.80 per pound = $24,700	6,500 pounds × $4.00 per pound = $26,000	4,800 pounds* × $4.00 per pound = $19,200

Price variance, $1,300 F

5,000 pounds × $4.00 per pound = $20,000

Quantity variance, $800 U

A total variance can't be computed in this situation, since the amount of materials purchased (6,500 pounds) differs from the amount used in production (5,000 pounds).
*1,600 units × 3.0 pounds per unit = 4,800 pounds.

The quantity variance in Exhibit 8–4 is labeled unfavorable (denoted by U). This is because more pewter was used to produce the actual output than the standard allows. A quantity variance is labeled unfavorable (U) if the actual quantity exceeds the standard quantity and is labeled favorable (F) if the actual quantity is less than the standard quantity.

The computations in Exhibit 8–4 reflect the fact that all of the material purchased during June was also used during June. How are the variances computed if a different amount of material is purchased than is used? To illustrate, assume that during June the company purchased 6,500 pounds of materials, as before, but that it used only 5,000 pounds of material during the month and produced only 1,600 units. In this case, the price variance and quantity variance would be as shown in Exhibit 8–5.

Most companies compute the materials price variance when materials are *purchased* rather than when they are used in production. There are two reasons for this practice. First, delaying the computation of the price variance until the materials are used would result in less timely variance reports. Second, by computing the price variance when the materials are purchased, the materials can be carried in the inventory accounts at their standard cost. This greatly simplifies bookkeeping. (See Appendix 8A at the end of the chapter for an explanation of how the bookkeeping works in a standard costing system.)

Note from the exhibit that the price variance is computed on the entire amount of material purchased (6,500 pounds), as before, whereas the quantity variance is computed only on the portion of this material used in production during the month (5,000 pounds). What about the other 1,500 pounds of material that were purchased during the period, but that have not yet been used? When those materials are used in future periods, a quantity variance will be computed. However, a price variance will not be computed when the materials are finally used since the price variance was computed when the materials were purchased. The situation illustrated in Exhibit 8–5 is common for companies that purchase materials well in advance of when they are used in production.

Materials Price Variance—A Closer Look

A **materials price variance** measures the difference between what is paid for a given quantity of materials and what should have been paid according to the standard that has been set. From Exhibit 8–4, this difference can be expressed by the following formula:

$$\text{Materials price variance} = (AQ \times AP) - (AQ \times SP)$$

Actual   Actual   Standard
quantity   price   price

The formula can be factored into simpler form as follows:

$$\text{Materials price variance} = AQ(AP - SP)$$

Some managers prefer this simpler formula, since it permits variance computations to be made very quickly. Using the data from Exhibit 8–4 in this formula, we have the following:

$$6{,}500 \text{ pounds } (\$3.80 \text{ per pound} - \$4.00 \text{ per pound}) = \$1{,}300 \text{ F}$$

Notice that the answer is the same as that yielded in Exhibit 8–4. Also note that using this formula approach, a negative variance is always labeled as favorable (F) and a positive variance is always labeled as unfavorable (U). This will be true of all variance formulas in this and later chapters.

Variance reports are often issued in a tabular format. An example of such a report follows, along with an explanation for the materials price variance that has been provided by the purchasing manager.

COLONIAL PEWTER COMPANY
Performance Report—Purchasing Department

Item Purchased	(1) Quantity Purchased	(2) Actual Price	(3) Standard Price	(4) Difference in Price (2) − (3)	(5) Total Price Variance (1) × (4)	Explanation
Pewter	6,500 pounds	$3.80	$4.00	$0.20	$1,300 F	Bargained for an especially good price

F = Favorable; U = Unfavorable.

Isolation of Variances   At what point should variances be isolated and brought to the attention of management? The answer is, the earlier the better. The sooner deviations from standard are brought to the attention of management, the sooner problems can be evaluated and corrected.

Once a performance report has been prepared, what does management do with the price variance data? The most significant variances should be viewed as "red flags," calling attention to the fact that an exception has occurred that will require some explanation and perhaps follow-up effort. The performance report itself may contain some explanation of the reason for the variance, as shown above. In the case of Colonial Pewter Company, the purchasing manager, Janet Warner, said that the favorable price variance resulted from bargaining for an especially good price.

Responsibility for the Variance   Who is responsible for the materials price variance? Generally speaking, the purchasing manager has control over the price paid for goods and is therefore responsible for any price variances. Many factors influence the prices paid for goods, including how many units are ordered in a lot, how the order is delivered, whether the order is a rush order, and the quality of materials purchased. A deviation in any of these factors from what was assumed when the standards were set can result in a price variance. For example, purchase of second-grade materials rather than top-grade materials may result in a favorable price variance, since the lower-grade materials would generally be less costly (but perhaps less suitable for production).

However, someone other than the purchasing manager could be responsible for a materials price variance. Production may be scheduled in such a way, for example, that the purchasing manager must request express delivery. In these cases, the production manager should be held responsible for the resulting price variances.

A word of caution is in order. Variance analysis should not be used as an excuse to conduct witch-hunts or as a means of beating line managers and workers over the head. The emphasis must be on *supporting* the line managers and *assisting* them in meeting the goals that they have participated in setting for the company. In short, the emphasis should be positive rather than negative. Excessive dwelling on what has already happened, particularly in terms of trying to find someone to blame, can destroy morale and kill any cooperative spirit.

Materials Quantity Variance—A Closer Look

The **materials quantity variance** measures the difference between the quantity of materials used in production and the quantity that should have been used according to the standard that has been set. Although the variance is concerned with the physical usage of materials, it is generally stated in dollar terms to help judge its importance, as shown in Exhibit 8–4. The formula for the materials quantity variance is as follows:

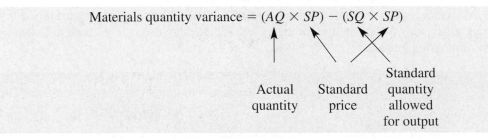

$$\text{Materials quantity variance} = (AQ \times SP) - (SQ \times SP)$$

| | Actual quantity | Standard price | Standard quantity allowed for output |

Again, the formula can be factored into simpler terms:

$$\text{Materials quantity variance} = SP(AQ - SQ)$$

Using the data from Exhibit 8–4 in the formula, we have the following:

$$\$4.00 \text{ per pound}(6{,}500 \text{ pounds} - 6{,}000 \text{ pounds}^*) = \$2{,}000 \text{ U}$$

*2,000 units × 3.0 pounds per unit = 6,000 pounds.

The answer, of course, is the same as that yielded in Exhibit 8–4. The data might appear as follows if a formal performance report were prepared:

COLONIAL PEWTER COMPANY Performance Report—Production Department						
Type of Materials	(1) Standard Price	(2) Actual Quantity	(3) Standard Quantity Allowed	(4) Difference in Quantity (2) − (3)	(5) Total Quantity Variance (1) × (4)	Explanation
Pewter	$4.00	6,500 pounds	6,000 pounds	500 pounds	$2,000 U	Low-quality materials unsuitable for production
F = Favorable; U = Unfavorable.						

The materials quantity variance is best isolated when materials are used in production. Materials are drawn for the number of units to be produced, according to the standard bill of materials for each unit. Any additional materials are usually drawn with an excess materials requisition slip, which is different in color from the normal requisition slips. This procedure calls attention to the excessive usage of materials *while production is still in process* and provides an opportunity to correct any developing problem.

Excessive usage of materials can result from many factors, including faulty machines, inferior quality of materials, untrained workers, and poor supervision. Generally speaking, it is the responsibility of the production department to see that material usage is kept in line with standards. There may be times, however, when the *purchasing* department may be responsible for an unfavorable materials quantity variance. If the purchasing department obtains inferior quality materials in an effort to economize on price, the materials may be unsuitable for use and may result in excessive waste. Thus, purchasing rather than production would be responsible for the quantity variance. At Colonial Pewter, the production manager, Tom Kuchel, claimed that low-quality materials were the cause of the unfavorable materials quantity variance for June.

1. The standard and actual prices per pound of raw material are $4.00 and $4.50, respectively. A total of 10,500 pounds of raw material was purchased and then used to produce 5,000 units. The quantity standard allows two pounds of the raw material per unit produced. What was the materials quantity variance?
   a. $5,000 unfavorable
   b. $5,000 favorable
   c. $2,000 favorable
   d. $2,000 unfavorable
2. Referring to the facts in question 1 above, what was the material price variance?
   a. $5,250 favorable
   b. $5,250 unfavorable
   c. $5,000 unfavorable
   d. $5,000 favorable

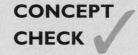

CONCEPT CHECK

USING STANDARD COSTS—DIRECT LABOR VARIANCES

Terry's next step in determining Colonial Pewter's variances for June was to compute the direct labor variances for the month. Recall from Exhibit 8–2 that the standard direct labor cost per unit of product is $35, computed as follows:

LEARNING OBJECTIVE 3
Compute the direct labor rate and efficiency variances and explain their significance.

2.5 hours per unit × $14.00 per hour = $35 per unit

During June, the company paid its direct labor workers $74,250, including employment taxes and fringe benefits, for 5,400 hours of work. This was an average of $13.75 per hour. Using these data and the standard costs from Exhibit 8–2, Terry computed the direct labor rate and efficiency variances that appear in Exhibit 8–6.

Notice that the column headings in Exhibit 8–6 are the same as those used in the prior two exhibits, except that in Exhibit 8–6 the terms *hours* and *rate* are used in place of the terms *quantity* and *price*.

Concept 8–2

Labor Rate Variance—A Closer Look

As explained earlier, the price variance for direct labor is commonly termed a **labor rate variance.** This variance measures any deviation from standard in the average hourly rate paid to direct labor workers. The formula for the labor rate variance is expressed as follows:

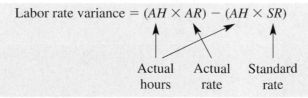

$$\text{Labor rate variance} = (AH \times AR) - (AH \times SR)$$

Actual   Actual   Standard
hours   rate   rate

EXHIBIT 8–6

Variance Analysis—Direct Labor

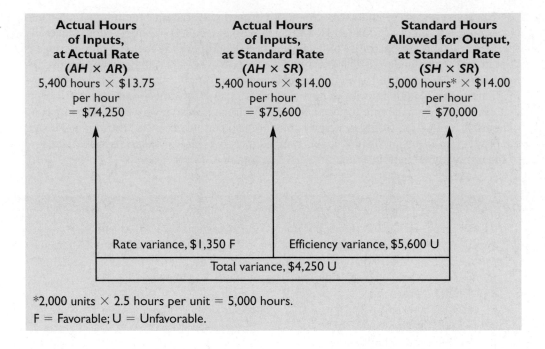

Actual Hours of Inputs, at Actual Rate (AH × AR)	Actual Hours of Inputs, at Standard Rate (AH × SR)	Standard Hours Allowed for Output, at Standard Rate (SH × SR)
5,400 hours × $13.75 per hour = $74,250	5,400 hours × $14.00 per hour = $75,600	5,000 hours* × $14.00 per hour = $70,000

Rate variance, $1,350 F   Efficiency variance, $5,600 U

Total variance, $4,250 U

*2,000 units × 2.5 hours per unit = 5,000 hours.
F = Favorable; U = Unfavorable.

The formula can be factored into simpler form as follows:

$$\text{Labor rate variance} = AH(AR - SR)$$

Using the data from Exhibit 8–6 in the formula, the labor rate variance can be computed as follows:

$$5{,}400 \text{ hours } (\$13.75 \text{ per hour} - \$14.00 \text{ per hour}) = \$1{,}350 \text{ F}$$

In most companies, the wage rates paid to workers are quite predictable. Nevertheless, rate variances can arise because of the way labor is used. Skilled workers with high hourly rates of pay may be given duties that require little skill and call for low hourly rates of pay. This will result in an unfavorable labor rate variance, since the actual hourly rate of pay will exceed the standard rate specified for the particular task. In contrast, a favorable rate variance would result when workers who are paid at a rate lower than specified in the standard are assigned to the task. However, the lower paid workers may not be as efficient. Finally, overtime work at premium rates will result in an unfavorable rate variance if the overtime premium is charged to the direct labor account.

Who is responsible for controlling the labor rate variance? Since rate variances generally arise as a result of how labor is used, production supervisors bear responsibility for seeing that labor rate variances are kept under control.

Labor Efficiency Variance—A Closer Look

The quantity variance for direct labor, more commonly called the **labor efficiency variance,** measures the productivity of labor time. No variance is more closely watched by management, since it is widely believed that increasing the productivity of direct labor time is vital to reducing costs. The formula for the labor efficiency variance is expressed as follows:

$$\text{Labor efficiency variance} = (AH \times SR) - (SH \times SR)$$

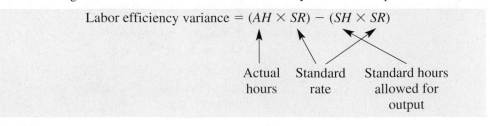

Actual hours   Standard rate   Standard hours allowed for output

Factored into simpler terms, the formula is as follows:

Labor efficiency variance $= SR(AH - SH)$

Using the data from Exhibit 8–6 in the formula, we have the following:

$14.00 per hour (5,400 hours $-$ 5,000 hours*) $=$ $5,600 U

*2,000 units $\times$ 2.5 hours per unit $=$ 5,000 hours.

Possible causes of an unfavorable labor efficiency variance include poorly trained or motivated workers; poor quality materials, requiring more labor time in processing; faulty equipment, causing breakdowns and work interruptions; poor supervision of workers; and inaccurate standards. The managers in charge of production would generally be responsible for control of the labor efficiency variance. However, purchasing could be held responsible if acquisition of poor materials resulted in excessive labor processing time.

Another important cause of an unfavorable labor efficiency variance may be insufficient demand for the company's products. Managers in some companies argue that it is difficult, and perhaps unwise, to constantly adjust the workforce in response to changes in the amount of work that needs to be done. In such companies, the direct labor workforce is essentially fixed in the short run. If demand is insufficient to keep everyone busy, workers are not laid off. In this case, if demand falls below the level needed to keep everyone busy, an unfavorable labor efficiency variance will often be recorded.

If customer orders are insufficient to keep the workers busy, the work center manager has two options—either accept an unfavorable labor efficiency variance or build inventory.[3] A central lesson of just-in-time (JIT) is that building inventory with no immediate prospect of sale is a bad idea. Inventory—particularly work in process inventory—leads to high defect rates, obsolete goods, and generally inefficient operations. As a consequence, when the workforce is basically fixed in the short term, managers must be cautious about how labor efficiency variances are used. Some experts advocate dispensing with labor efficiency variances entirely in such situations—at least for the purposes of motivating and controlling workers on the shop floor.

Department Resources Manager

DECISION MAKER

LS

You are the manager of the computer-generated special effects department for a company that produces special effects for high-profile films. You receive a copy of this month's performance report for your department and discover a large labor efficiency variance that is unfavorable. What factors might have contributed to this unfavorable variance?

USING STANDARD COSTS—VARIABLE MANUFACTURING OVERHEAD VARIANCES

The final step in Terry's analysis of Colonial Pewter's variances for June was to compute the variable manufacturing overhead variances. The variable portion of manufacturing overhead can be analyzed using the same basic formulas that are used to analyze direct materials and direct labor. Recall from Exhibit 8–2 that the standard variable manufacturing overhead is $7.50 per unit of product, computed as follows:

LEARNING OBJECTIVE 4

Compute the variable manufacturing overhead spending and efficiency variances.

2.5 hours per unit $\times$ $3.00 per hour $=$ $7.50 per unit

Colonial Pewter's cost records showed that the total actual variable manufacturing overhead cost for June was $15,390. Recall from the earlier discussion of the direct labor

---

[3]For further discussion, see Eliyahu M. Goldratt and Jeff Cox, *The Goal,* 2nd rev. ed. (Croton-on-Hudson, NY: North River Press, 1992).

EXHIBIT 8–7

Variance Analysis—Variable
Manufacturing Overhead

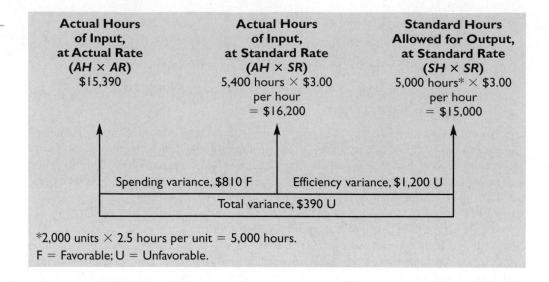

Actual Hours of Input, at Actual Rate (AH × AR)	Actual Hours of Input, at Standard Rate (AH × SR)	Standard Hours Allowed for Output, at Standard Rate (SH × SR)
$15,390	5,400 hours × $3.00 per hour = $16,200	5,000 hours* × $3.00 per hour = $15,000

Spending variance, $810 F   Efficiency variance, $1,200 U

Total variance, $390 U

*2,000 units × 2.5 hours per unit = 5,000 hours.
F = Favorable; U = Unfavorable.

variances that 5,400 hours of direct labor time were recorded during the month and that the company produced 2,000 pairs of bookends. Terry's analysis of this overhead data appears in Exhibit 8–7.

Notice the similarities between Exhibits 8–6 and 8–7. These similarities arise from the fact that direct labor-hours are being used as the base for allocating overhead cost to units of product; thus, the same hourly figures appear in Exhibit 8–7 for variable manufacturing overhead as in Exhibit 8–6 for direct labor. The main difference between the two exhibits is in the standard hourly rate being used, which in this company is much lower for variable manufacturing overhead than for direct labor.

Manufacturing Overhead Variances—A Closer Look

The formula for the **variable overhead spending variance** is expressed as follows:

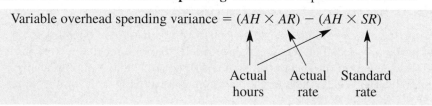

Variable overhead spending variance = (AH × AR) − (AH × SR)

Actual hours   Actual rate   Standard rate

Or, factored into simpler terms:

Variable overhead spending variance = AH(AR − SR)

Using the data from Exhibit 8–7 in the formula, the variable overhead spending variance can be computed as follows:

5,400 hours ($2.85 per hour* − $3.00 per hour) = $810 F

*$15,390 ÷ 5,400 hours = $2.85 per hour.

The formula for the **variable overhead efficiency variance** is expressed as follows:

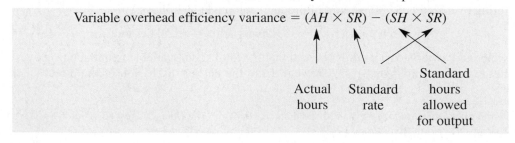

Variable overhead efficiency variance = (AH × SR) − (SH × SR)

Actual hours   Standard rate   Standard hours allowed for output

Or, factored into simpler terms:

Variable overhead efficiency variance = $SR(AH - SH)$

Again using the data from Exhibit 8–7, the variance can be computed as follows:

$3.00 per hour (5,400 hours $-$ 5,000 hours*) = \$1,200 U

*2,000 units $\times$ 2.5 hours per unit = 5,000 hours.

We will reserve further discussion of the variable overhead spending and efficiency variances until the next chapter, where overhead analysis is discussed in depth.

Before proceeding further, we suggest that you pause at this point and go back and review the data contained in Exhibits 8–2 through 8–7. These exhibits and the accompanying text discussion provide a comprehensive, integrated illustration of standard setting and variance analysis.

3. The actual direct labor wage rate is $8.50 and 4,500 direct labor hours were actually worked during the month. The standard direct labor wage rate is $8.00 and the standard quantity of hours allowed for the actual level of output was 5,000 direct labor hours. What was the direct labor efficiency variance?
   a. $4,000 favorable
   b. $4,000 unfavorable
   c. $4,500 unfavorable
   d. $4,500 favorable
4. Referring to the facts in question 3 above, what is the variable overhead efficiency variance if the standard variable overhead per direct labor hour is $5.00?
   a. $5,000 favorable
   b. $5,000 unfavorable
   c. $2,500 unfavorable
   d. $2,500 favorable

CONCEPT CHECK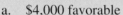

In preparation for the scheduled meeting to discuss his analysis of Colonial Pewter's standard costs and variances, Terry distributed Exhibits 8–2 through 8–7 to the management group of Colonial Pewter. This included J. D. Wriston, the president of the company; Tom Kuchel, the production manager; and Janet Warner, the purchasing manager. J. D. Wriston opened the meeting with the following question:

MANAGERIAL ACCOUNTING IN ACTION
The Wrap-Up

J. D.: Terry, I think I understand the report you distributed, but just to make sure, would you mind summarizing the highlights of what you found?
Terry: As you can see, the biggest problems are the unfavorable materials quantity variance of $2,000 and the unfavorable labor efficiency variance of $5,600.
J. D.: Tom, you're the production boss. What do you think is responsible for the unfavorable labor efficiency variance?
Tom: It pretty much has to be the new production workers. Our experienced workers shouldn't have much problem meeting the standard of 2.5 hours per unit. We all knew that there would be some inefficiency for a while as we brought new people on board.
J. D.: No one is disputing that, Tom. However, $5,600 is a lot of money. Is this problem likely to go away very soon?
Tom: I hope so. If we were to contrast the last two weeks of June with the first two weeks, I'm sure we would see some improvement.
J. D.: I don't want to beat up on you, Tom, but this is a significant problem. Can you do something to accelerate the training process?

Tom: Sure. I could pair up each of the new guys with one of our old-timers and have them work together for a while. It would slow down our older guys a bit, but I'll bet the new workers would learn a lot.

J. D.:   Let's try it. Now, what about that $2,000 unfavorable materials quantity variance?

Tom: Are you asking me?

J. D.:   Well, I would like someone to explain it.

Tom: Don't look at me. It's that iron-contaminated pewter that Janet bought on her "special deal."

Janet: We got rid of that stuff months ago.

J. D.:   Hold your horses. We're not trying to figure out who to blame here. I just want to understand what happened. If we can understand what happened, maybe we can fix it.

Terry: Tom, are the new workers generating a lot of scrap?

Tom: Yeah, I guess so.

J. D.:   I think that could be part of the problem. Can you do anything about it?

Tom: I can watch the scrap real closely for a few days to see where it's being generated. If it is the new workers, I can have the old-timers work with them on the problem when I team them up.

J. D.:   Good. Let's reconvene in a few weeks and see what has happened. Hopefully, we can get those unfavorable variances under control.

VARIANCE ANALYSIS AND MANAGEMENT BY EXCEPTION

Variance analysis and performance reports are important elements of *management by exception*. Simply put, management by exception means that the manager's attention should be directed toward those parts of the organization where plans are not working for one reason or another. Time and effort should not be wasted focusing on those parts of the organization where things are going smoothly.

The budgets and standards discussed in this chapter and in the preceding chapter reflect management's plans. If all goes according to plan, there will be little difference between actual results and the results that would be expected according to the budgets and standards. If this happens, managers can concentrate on other issues. However, if actual results do not conform to the budget and to standards, the performance reporting system sends a signal to the manager that an "exception" has occurred. This signal is in the form of a variance from the budget or standards.

However, are all variances worth investigating? The answer is no. Differences between actual results and what was expected will almost always occur. If every variance were investigated, management would waste a great deal of time tracking down nickel-and-dime differences. Variances may occur for any of a variety of reasons—only some of which are significant and warrant management attention. For example, hotter-than-normal weather in the summer may result in higher-than-expected electrical bills for air conditioning. Or, workers may work slightly faster or slower on a particular day. Because of unpredictable random factors, one can expect that virtually every cost category will produce a variance of some kind.

How should managers decide which variances are worth investigating? One clue is the size of the variance. A variance of $5 is probably not big enough to warrant attention, whereas a variance of $5,000 might well be worth tracking down. Another clue is the size of the variance relative to the amount of spending. A variance that is only 0.1% of spending on an item is likely to be well within the bounds one would normally expect due to random factors. On the other hand, a variance of 10% of spending is much more likely to be a signal that something is basically wrong.

In addition to watching for unusually large variances, the pattern of the variances should be monitored. For example, a run of steadily mounting variances should trigger an investigation even though none of the variances is large enough by itself to warrant investigation.

EVALUATION OF CONTROLS BASED ON STANDARD COSTS

Advantages of Standard Costs

Standard cost systems have a number of advantages.

1. As stated earlier, the use of standard costs is a key element in a management by exception approach. If costs remain within the standards, managers can focus on other issues. When costs fall significantly outside the standards, managers are alerted that there may be problems requiring attention. This approach helps managers focus on important issues.
2. Standards that are viewed as reasonable by employees can promote economy and efficiency. They provide benchmarks that individuals can use to judge their own performance.
3. Standard costs can greatly simplify bookkeeping. Instead of recording actual costs for each job, the standard costs for materials, labor, and overhead can be charged to jobs.
4. Standard costs fit naturally in an integrated system of "responsibility accounting." The standards establish what costs should be, who should be responsible for them, and whether actual costs are under control.

Potential Problems with the Use of Standard Costs

The use of standard costs can present a number of potential problems. Most of these problems result from improper use of standard costs and the management by exception principle or from using standard costs in situations in which they are not appropriate.

1. Standard cost variance reports are usually prepared on a monthly basis and often are released days or even weeks after the end of the month. As a consequence, the information in the reports may be so stale that it is almost useless. Timely, frequent reports that are approximately correct are better than infrequent reports that are very precise but out of date by the time they are released. Some companies are now reporting variances and other key operating data daily or even more frequently.
2. If managers are insensitive and use variance reports as a club, morale may suffer. Employees should receive positive reinforcement for work well done. Management by exception, by its nature, tends to focus on the negative. If variances are used as a club, subordinates may be tempted to cover up unfavorable variances or take actions that are not in the best interests of the company to make sure the variances are favorable. For example, workers may put on a crash effort to increase output at the end of the month to avoid an unfavorable labor efficiency variance. In the rush to produce output, quality may suffer.
3. Labor quantity standards and efficiency variances make two important assumptions. First, they assume that the production process is labor-paced; if labor works faster, output will go up. However, output in many companies is no longer determined by how fast labor works; rather, it is determined by the processing speed of machines. Second, the computations assume that labor is a variable cost. However, direct labor may be essentially fixed. If labor is fixed, then an undue emphasis on labor efficiency variances creates pressure to build excess work in process and finished goods inventories.
4. In some cases, a "favorable" variance can be as bad or worse than an "unfavorable" variance. For example, McDonald's has a standard for the amount of hamburger meat that should be in a Big Mac. A "favorable" variance would mean that less meat was used than the standard specifies. The result is a substandard Big Mac and possibly a dissatisfied customer.
5. There may be a tendency with standard cost reporting systems to emphasize meeting the standards to the exclusion of other important objectives such as maintaining and improving quality, on-time delivery, and customer satisfaction. This tendency

can be reduced by using supplemental performance measures that focus on these other objectives.

6. Just meeting standards may not be sufficient; continual improvement may be necessary to survive in a competitive environment. For this reason, some companies focus on the trends in the standard cost variances—aiming for continual improvement rather than just meeting the standards. In other companies, engineered standards are being replaced either by a rolling average of actual costs, which is expected to decline, or by very challenging target costs.

In sum, managers should exercise considerable care in their use of a standard cost system. It is particularly important that managers go out of their way to focus on the positive, rather than just on the negative, and to be aware of possible unintended consequences.

Nevertheless, standard costs are still found in the vast majority of manufacturing companies and in many service companies, although their use is changing. For evaluating performance, standard cost variances may be supplanted in the future by a particularly interesting development known as the *balanced scorecard,* which is discussed in the next section. The balanced scorecard concept has been eagerly embraced by a wide variety of organizations including Analog Devices, KPMG Peat Marwick, Tenneco, Allstate, AT&T, Elf Atochem, Conair-Franklin, CIGNA Corporation, London Life Insurance Co., Southern Gardens Citrus Processing, Duke Children's Hospital, JP Morgan Chase, 3COM, Rockwater, Apple Computer, Advanced Micro Devices (AMD), FMC, the Bank of Montreal, the Massachusetts Special Olympics, and United Way of Southeastern New England.

IN BUSINESS

When Improvement Isn't Better

Mark Graham Brown, a performance-measurement consultant, warns managers to focus on the right metrics when measuring performance. He relates the following story: "A fast-food chain gave lip service to many objectives, but what senior managers watched most rigorously was how much chicken its restaurants had to throw away . . . What happened? As one restaurant operator explained, it was easy to hit your . . . targets: just don't cook any chicken until somebody orders it. Customers might have to wait 20 minutes for their meal, and would probably never come back—but you'd sure make your numbers. Moral: a measurement may look good on paper, but you need to ask what behavior it will drive."

Source: "Using Measurement to Boost Your Unit's Performance," *Harvard Management Update*, October 1998.

BALANCED SCORECARD

A **balanced scorecard** consists of an integrated set of performance measures that are derived from the company's strategy and that support the company's strategy throughout the organization.[4, 5] A strategy is essentially a theory about how to achieve the organization's goals. For example, Southwest Airlines' strategy is to offer passengers low prices and fun

---

[4]The balanced scorecard concept was developed by Robert Kaplan and David Norton. For further details, see their articles "The Balanced Scorecard—Measures that Drive Performance," *Harvard Business Review,* January/February 1992, pp. 71–79; "Using the Balanced Scorecard as a Strategic Management System," *Harvard Business Review,* January/February 1996, pp. 75–85; "Why Does a Business Need a Balanced Scorecard?" *Journal of Cost Management,* May/June 1997, pp. 5–10; and their book *Translating Strategy into Action: The Balanced Scorecard* (Boston, MA: Harvard Business School Press, 1996).

[5]In the 1960s, the French developed a concept similar to the balanced scorecard called Tableau de Bord or "dashboard." For details, see Michel Lebas, "Managerial Accounting in France: Overview of Past Tradition and Current Practice," *The European Accounting Review,* 1994, 3, no. 3, pp. 471–487; and Marc Epstein and Jean-François Manzoni, "The Balanced Scorecard and the Tableau de Bord: Translating Strategy into Action," *Management Accounting,* August 1997, pp. 28–36.

on short-haul jet service. The low prices result from the absence of costly frills such as meals, assigned seating, and interline baggage checking. The fun is provided by flight attendants who go out of their way to entertain passengers with their antics. This is an interesting strategy. Southwest Airlines consciously hires people who have a sense of humor and who enjoy their work. Hiring and retaining such employees probably costs no more—and may cost less—than retaining grumpy flight attendants who view their jobs as a chore. Southwest Airlines' strategy is to build loyal customers through a combination of "fun"—which does not cost anything to provide—and low prices that are possible because of the lack of costly frills offered by competing airlines. The theory is that low prices and fun will lead to loyal customers, which, in combination with low costs, will lead to high profits. So far, this theory has worked.

Under the balanced scorecard approach, top management translates its strategy into performance measures that employees can understand and can do something about. For example, the amount of time passengers have to wait in line to have their baggage checked might be a performance measure for the supervisor in charge of the Southwest Airlines check-in counter at the Phoenix airport. This performance measure is easily understood by the supervisor and can be improved by the supervisor's actions. Under the balanced scorecard approach, nonfinancial measures of performance—such as the amount of time passengers must wait to check bags—are used in addition to financial measures of performance such as standard cost variances. Nonfinancial measures of performance of quality and customer satisfaction are particularly important since they typically tie directly to the company's strategy in a cause-and-effect manner and they serve as leading indicators of the company's success. The details of the balanced scorecard approach are covered in more advanced texts.

The Balanced Scorecard at the City of Charlotte

IN BUSINESS

Governmental and nonprofit organizations as well as businesses can use the balanced scorecard approach to performance measurement. The City of Charlotte, North Carolina, developed a balanced scorecard with four major goals: (1) increase perception of safety; (2) strengthen neighborhoods; (3) promote economic opportunity; and (4) improve service quality. To strengthen neighborhoods, the city's managers set goals to: (a) promote safe, decent housing; (b) increase home ownership; and (c) increase job placements. The corresponding performance measures are: (a) the number of code compliances in housing; (b) the number of assisted purchases of homes; and (c) the number of adult job placements.

Pam Syfert, Charlotte's City Manager, states: "The Scorecard is a communication, information, and learning system. Building a scorecard helps managers link today's actions with the achievement of today's priorities. It encourages accountability. And, today, we define accountability by results."

Source: Robert S. Kaplan, *City of Charlotte (A)*, Harvard Business School case 9-199-036, December 15, 1998.

SUMMARY

LO1   Explain how direct materials standards and direct labor standards are set.
Each direct cost has both a price and a quantity standard. The standard price for an input is the price that should be paid for a single unit of the input. In the case of direct materials, the price should include shipping and receiving costs and should be net of quantity and other discounts. In the case of direct labor, the standard rate should include wages, fringe benefits, and employment taxes.

LO2   Compute the direct materials price and quantity variances and explain their significance.
The materials price variance is the difference between the actual price paid for materials and the standard price, multiplied by the quantity purchased. An unfavorable variance occurs whenever the actual price

exceeds the standard price. A favorable variance occurs when the actual price is less than the standard price for the input.

The materials quantity variance is the difference between the amount of materials actually used and the amount that should have been used to produce the actual good output of the period, multiplied by the standard price per unit of the input. An unfavorable materials quantity variance occurs when the amount of materials actually used exceeds the amount that should have been used according to the materials quantity standard. A favorable variance occurs when the amount of materials actually used is less than the amount that should have been used according to the standard.

LO3   Compute the direct labor rate and efficiency variances and explain their significance.
The direct labor rate variance is the difference between the actual wage rate paid and the standard wage rate, multiplied by the hours worked. An unfavorable variance occurs whenever the actual wage rate exceeds the standard wage rate. A favorable variance occurs when the actual wage rate is less than the standard wage rate.

The labor efficiency variance is the difference between the hours actually worked and the hours that should have been used to produce the actual good output of the period, multiplied by the standard wage rate. An unfavorable labor efficiency variance occurs when the hours actually worked exceed the hours allowed for the actual output. A favorable variance occurs when the hours actually worked are less than hours allowed for the actual output.

LO4   Compute the variable manufacturing overhead spending and efficiency variances.
The variable manufacturing overhead spending variance is the difference between the actual variable manufacturing overhead cost incurred and the actual hours worked multiplied by the variable manufacturing overhead rate. The variable manufacturing overhead efficiency variance is the difference between the hours actually worked and the hours that should have been used to produce the actual good output of the period, multiplied by the standard variable manufacturing overhead rate.

GUIDANCE ANSWERS TO *DECISION MAKER* AND *YOU DECIDE*

Owner of a Painting Company   (p. 341)
The standards published in the trade magazine are for professional painters; at least initially, they would not be realistic for your painting crew, which is inexperienced. Therefore, the standards would not be particularly useful for bidding on jobs or for setting budgets. Nevertheless, the standards would provide important feedback information about how well the painting crew is performing relative to the professional competition. Setting a goal of beating the professional painters (as represented by the standards) might energize your painting crew and motivate them to work harder and to think of innovative ways of improving the painting process.

Psychologically, it might be best not to use the labels *unfavorable* and *favorable* for the variances since almost all of them will initially be unfavorable. Instead, you might focus on the ratio of the actual time to the standard time, with the idea that this ratio should decline over time and eventually should be less than 1.0. This ratio could be plotted on a weekly or daily basis and displayed in a prominent location so that everyone in the painting crew can see how well the crew is doing relative to professional painters.

Department Resources Manager   (p. 353)
An unfavorable labor efficiency variance in the computer-generated special effects department might have been caused by inexperienced, poorly trained, or unmotivated employees, faulty hardware and/or software that may have caused work interruptions, and/or poor supervision of the employees in this department. In addition, it is possible that there was insufficient demand for the output of this department—resulting in idle time—or that the standard (or benchmark) for this department is inaccurate.

GUIDANCE ANSWERS TO CONCEPT CHECKS

1. **Choice d.** The materials quantity variance is (10,500 pounds used − 10,000 pounds allowed) × $4.00 per pound = $2,000 unfavorable.
2. **Choice b.** The materials price variance is ($4.50 actual price per pound − $4.00 standard price per pound) × 10,500 pounds purchased = $5,250 unfavorable.
3. **Choice a.** The direct labor efficiency variance is (4,500 hours − 5,000 hours) × $8.00 standard hourly rate = $4,000 favorable.
4. **Choice d.** The variable overhead efficiency variance is (5,000 hours − 4,500 hours) × $5.00 per hour = $2,500 favorable.

REVIEW PROBLEM: STANDARD COSTS

Xavier Company produces a single product. Variable manufacturing overhead is applied to products on the basis of direct labor-hours. The standard costs for one unit of product are as follows:

Direct material: 6 ounces at $0.50 per ounce..........................	$ 3
Direct labor: 1.8 hours at $10 per hour...............................	18
Variable manufacturing overhead: 1.8 hours at $5 per hour	9
Total standard variable cost per unit.................................	$30

During June, 2,000 units were produced. The costs associated with June's operations were as follows:

Material purchased: 18,000 ounces at $0.60 per ounce.................	$10,800
Material used in production: 14,000 ounces.........................	—
Direct labor: 4,000 hours at $9.75 per hour	$39,000
Variable manufacturing overhead costs incurred	$20,800

Required:

Compute the materials, labor, and variable manufacturing overhead variances.

Solution to Review Problem

Materials Variances

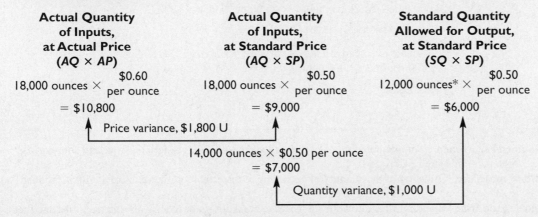

*2,000 units × 6 ounces per unit = 12,000 ounces.

Using the formulas in the chapter, the same variances would be computed as follows:

$$\text{Materials price variance} = AQ(AP - SP)$$
$$18{,}000 \text{ ounces } (\$0.60 \text{ per ounce} - \$0.50 \text{ per ounce}) = \$1{,}800 \text{ U}$$

$$\text{Materials quantity variance} = SP(AQ - SQ)$$
$$\$0.50 \text{ per ounce } (14{,}000 \text{ ounces} - 12{,}000 \text{ ounces}) = \$1{,}000 \text{ U}$$

Labor Variances

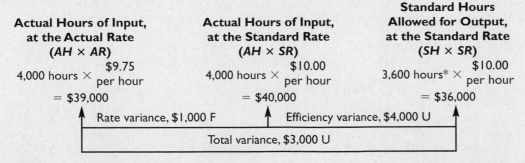

*2,000 units × 1.8 hours per unit = 3,600 hours.

Using the formulas in the chapter, the same variances would be computed as follows:

$$\text{Labor rate variance} = AH(AR - SR)$$
$$4{,}000 \text{ hours } (\$9.75 \text{ per hour} - \$10.00 \text{ per hour}) = \$1{,}000 \text{ F}$$

$$\text{Labor efficiency variance} = SR(AH - SH)$$
$$\$10.00 \text{ per hour } (4{,}000 \text{ hours} - 3{,}600 \text{ hours}) = \$4{,}000 \text{ U}$$

Variable Manufacturing Overhead Variances

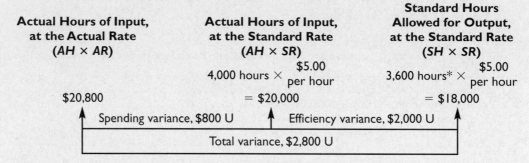

Actual Hours of Input, at the Actual Rate (AH × AR)	Actual Hours of Input, at the Standard Rate (AH × SR)	Standard Hours Allowed for Output, at the Standard Rate (SH × SR)
	$4{,}000$ hours $\times \dfrac{\$5.00}{\text{per hour}}$	$3{,}600$ hours* $\times \dfrac{\$5.00}{\text{per hour}}$
$\$20{,}800$	$= \$20{,}000$	$= \$18{,}000$

Spending variance, $800 U   Efficiency variance, $2,000 U

Total variance, $2,800 U

*2,000 units × 1.8 hours per unit = 3,600 hours.

Using the formulas in the chapter, the same variances would be computed as:

$$\text{Variable overhead spending variance} = AH(AR - SR)$$
$$4{,}000 \text{ hours } (\$5.20 \text{ per hour*} - \$5.00 \text{ per hour}) = \$800 \text{ U}$$

*$20,800 ÷ 4,000 hours = $5.20 per hour.

$$\text{Variable overhead efficiency variance} = SR(AH - SH)$$
$$\$5.00 \text{ per hour } (4{,}000 \text{ hours} - 3{,}600 \text{ hours}) = \$2{,}000 \text{ U}$$

GLOSSARY

Balanced scorecard   An integrated set of performance measures that is derived from and supports the organization's strategy. (p. 358)

Bill of materials   A listing of the quantity of each type of material required to make a unit of product. (p. 343)

Ideal standards   Standards that allow for no machine breakdowns or other work interruptions and that require peak efficiency at all times. (p. 341)

Labor efficiency variance   A measure of the difference between the actual hours taken to complete a task and the standard hours allowed, multiplied by the standard hourly labor rate. (p. 352)

Labor rate variance   A measure of the difference between the actual hourly labor rate and the standard rate, multiplied by the number of hours worked during the period. (p. 351)

Management by exception   A system of management in which standards are set for various operating activities, with actual results then compared to these standards. Any differences that are deemed significant are brought to the attention of management as "exceptions." (p. 339)

Materials price variance   A measure of the difference between the actual unit price paid for an item and the standard price, multiplied by the quantity purchased. (p. 348)

Materials quantity variance   A measure of the difference between the actual quantity of materials used in production and the standard quantity allowed, multiplied by the standard price per unit of materials. (p. 350)

Practical standards   Standards that allow for normal machine downtime and other work interruptions and that can be attained through reasonable, though highly efficient, efforts by the average worker. (p. 341)

Standard cost card   A detailed listing of the standard amounts of materials, labor, and overhead that should go into a unit of product, multiplied by the standard price or rate that has been set for each cost element. (p. 341)

Standard cost per unit   The standard cost of a unit of product as shown on the standard cost card; it is computed by multiplying the standard quantity or hours by the standard price or rate for each cost element. (p. 345)

Standard hours allowed   The time that should have been taken to complete the period's output as computed by multiplying the actual number of units produced by the standard hours per unit. (p. 346)

Standard hours per unit   The amount of labor time that should be required to complete a single unit of product, including allowances for breaks, machine downtime, cleanup, rejects, and other normal inefficiencies. (p. 344)

Standard price per unit   The price that should be paid for a single unit of materials, including allowances for quality, quantity purchased, shipping, receiving, and other such costs, net of any discounts allowed. (p. 342)

Standard quantity allowed   The amount of materials that should have been used to complete the period's output as computed by multiplying the actual number of units produced by the standard quantity per unit. (p. 346)

Standard quantity per unit   The amount of materials that should be required to complete a single unit of product, including allowances for normal waste, spoilage, rejects, and similar inefficiencies. (p. 343)

Standard rate per hour   The labor rate that should be incurred per hour of labor time, including employment taxes, fringe benefits, and other such labor costs. (p. 343)

Variable overhead efficiency variance   The difference between the actual activity (direct labor-hours, machine-hours, or some other base) of a period and the standard activity allowed, multiplied by the variable part of the predetermined overhead rate. (p. 354)

Variable overhead spending variance   The difference between the actual variable overhead cost incurred during a period and the standard cost that should have been incurred based on the actual activity of the period. (p. 354)

Variance   The difference between standard prices and quantities on the one hand and actual prices and quantities on the other hand. (p. 345)

General Ledger Entries to Record Variances

Although standard costs and variances can be computed and used by management without being formally entered into the accounting records, many organizations prefer to make formal entries. Formal entry tends to give variances a greater emphasis than informal, off-the-record computations. This emphasis gives a clear signal of management's desire to keep costs within the limits that have been set. In addition, formal use of standard costs simplifies the bookkeeping process enormously. Inventories and cost of goods sold can be valued at their standard costs—eliminating the need to keep track of the actual cost of each unit.

Direct Materials Variances

To illustrate the general ledger entries needed to record standard cost variances, we will return to the data contained in the review problem at the end of the chapter. The entry to record the purchase of direct materials would be as follows:

Raw Materials (18,000 ounces at $0.50 per ounce).	9,000	
Materials Price Variance (18,000 ounces at $0.10 per ounce U)	1,800	
Accounts Payable (18,000 ounces at $0.60 per ounce)		10,800

Notice that the price variance is recognized when purchases are made, rather than when materials are actually used in production. This permits the price variance to be isolated immediately, and it also permits the materials to be carried in the inventory account at standard cost. As direct materials are later drawn from inventory and used in production, the quantity variance is isolated as follows:

Work in Process (12,000 ounces at $0.50 per ounce).	6,000	
Materials Quantity Variance (2,000 ounces U at $0.50 per ounce). . .	1,000	
Raw Materials (14,000 ounces at $0.50 per ounce).		7,000

Thus, direct materials are added to the Work in Process account at the standard cost of the materials that should have been used to produce the actual output.

Notice that both the price variance and the quantity variance above are unfavorable and are debit entries. If these variances had been favorable, they would have appeared as credit entries.

Direct Labor Variances

Referring again to the cost data in the review problem at the end of the chapter, the general ledger entry to record the incurrence of direct labor cost would be:

Work in Process (3,600 hours at $10.00 per hour).	36,000	
Labor Efficiency Variance (400 hours U at $10.00 per hour).	4,000	
Labor Rate Variance (4,000 hours at $0.25 per hour F).		1,000
Wages Payable (4,000 hours at $9.75 per hour)		39,000

Thus, as with direct materials, direct labor costs enter into the Work in Process account at standard, both in terms of the rate and in terms of the hours allowed for the actual production of the period.

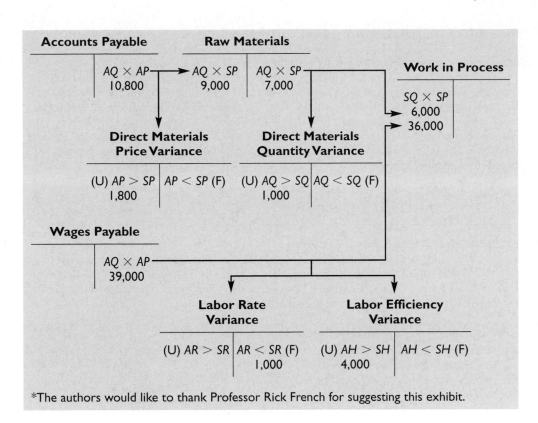

EXHIBIT 8A–1

Cost Flows in a Standard Cost System*

*The authors would like to thank Professor Rick French for suggesting this exhibit.

Variable Manufacturing Overhead Variances

Variable manufacturing overhead variances are not usually recorded in the accounts separately but rather are determined as part of the general analysis of overhead, which is discussed in the next chapter.

Cost Flows in a Standard Cost System

The flows of costs through the company's accounts are illustrated in Exhibit 8A–1. Note that entries into the various inventory accounts are made at standard cost—not actual cost. The differences between actual and standard costs are entered into special accounts that accumulate the various standard cost variances. Ordinarily, these standard cost variance accounts are closed out to Cost of Goods Sold at the end of the period. Unfavorable variances increase Cost of Goods Sold, and favorable variances decrease Cost of Goods Sold.

SUMMARY FOR APPENDIX 8A

LO5   (Appendix 8A) Prepare journal entries to record standard costs and variances.
Raw materials and work in process and finished goods inventories are all carried at their standard costs. Differences between actual and standard costs are recorded as variances. Favorable variances are credit entries and unfavorable variances are debit entries.

QUESTIONS

8–1   What is a quantity standard? What is a price standard?
8–2   Distinguish between ideal and practical standards.
8–3   What is meant by the term *variance*?
8–4   What is meant by the term *management by exception*?
8–5   Who is generally responsible for the materials price variance? The materials quantity variance? The labor efficiency variance?

8–6   The materials price variance can be computed at what two different points in time? Which point is better? Why?

8–7   What are the dangers of using standards as punitive tools?

8–8   What effect, if any, would you expect poor quality materials to have on direct labor variances?

8–9   If variable manufacturing overhead is applied to production on the basis of direct labor-hours and the direct labor efficiency variance is unfavorable, will the variable overhead efficiency variance be favorable or unfavorable, or could it be either? Explain.

8–10   Why can undue emphasis on labor efficiency variances lead to excess work in process inventories?

8–11   (Appendix 8A) What are the advantages of making formal journal entries in the accounting records for variances?

BRIEF EXERCISES

BRIEF EXERCISE 8–1   Setting Standards   (LO1)

Czar Nicholas Chocolatier, Ltd., makes premium handcrafted chocolate confections in London. The owner of the company is setting up a standard cost system and has collected the following data for one of the company's products, the Imperial Truffle. This product is made with the finest white chocolate and various fillings. The data below pertain only to the white chocolate used in the product:

Material requirements, kilograms of white chocolate per dozen truffles. . . .	0.80 kilograms
Allowance for waste, kilograms of white chocolate per dozen truffles	0.02 kilograms
Allowance for rejects, kilograms of white chocolate per dozen truffles	0.03 kilograms
Purchase price, finest grade white chocolate	£9.00 per kilogram
Purchase discount	5% of purchase price
Shipping cost from the supplier in Belgium	£0.20 per kilogram
Receiving and handling cost	£0.05 per kilogram

Required:
1. Determine the standard price of a kilogram of white chocolate.
2. Determine the standard quantity of white chocolate for a dozen truffles.
3. Determine the standard cost of the white chocolate in a dozen truffles.

BRIEF EXERCISE 8–2   Material Variances   (LO2)

Harmon Household Products, Inc., manufactures a number of consumer items for general household use. One of these products, a chopping block, requires an expensive hardwood. During a recent month, the company manufactured 4,000 chopping blocks using 11,000 board feet of hardwood. The hardwood cost the company $18,700.

     The company's standards for one chopping block are 2.5 board feet of hardwood, at a cost of $1.80 per board foot.

Required:
1. What cost for wood should have been incurred to make 4,000 chopping blocks? How much greater or less is this than the cost that was incurred?
2. Break down the difference computed in (1) above into a materials price variance and a materials quantity variance.

BRIEF EXERCISE 8–3   Direct Labor Variances   (LO3)

AirMeals, Inc., prepares in-flight meals for a number of major airlines. One of the company's products is stuffed cannelloni with roasted pepper sauce, fresh baby corn, and spring salad. During the most recent week, the company prepared 6,000 of these meals using 1,150 direct labor-hours. The company paid these direct labor workers a total of $11,500 for this work, or $10 per hour.

     According to the standard cost card for this meal, it should require 0.20 direct labor-hours at a cost of $9.50 per hour.

Required:
1. What direct labor cost should have been incurred to prepare the 6,000 meals? How much greater or less is this than the direct labor cost that was incurred?
2. Break down the difference computed in (1) above into a labor rate variance and a labor efficiency variance.

BRIEF EXERCISE 8–4   Variable Overhead Variances   (LO4)

Order Up, Inc., provides order fulfillment services for dot.com merchants. The company maintains warehouses that stock items carried by its dot.com clients. When a client receives an order from a customer, the order is forwarded to Order Up, which pulls the item from storage, packs it, and ships it to the customer. The company uses a predetermined variable overhead rate based on direct labor-hours.

In the most recent month, 140,000 items were shipped to customers using 5,800 direct labor-hours. The company incurred a total of $15,950 in variable overhead costs.

According to the company's standards, 0.04 direct labor-hours are required to fulfill an order for one item and the variable overhead rate is $2.80 per direct labor-hour.

Required:

1. What variable overhead cost should have been incurred to fill the orders for the 140,000 items? How much greater or less is this than the variable overhead cost that was incurred?
2. Break down the difference computed in (1) above into a variable overhead spending variance and a variable overhead efficiency variance.

BRIEF EXERCISE 8–5   (Appendix 8A) Recording Variances in the General Ledger   (LO5)

Kinkel Corporation makes a product with the following standard costs for direct material and direct labor:

Direct material: 1.50 meters at $5.40 per meter	$8.10
Direct labor: 0.25 hours at $14.00 per hour	$3.50

During the most recent month, 8,000 units were produced. The costs associated with the month's production of this product were as follows:

Material purchased: 15,000 meters at $5.60 per meter	$84,000
Material used in production: 11,900 meters	—
Direct labor: 1,950 hours at $14.20 per hour	$27,690

The standard cost variances for direct material and direct labor have been computed to be:

Materials price variance: 15,000 meters at $0.20 per meter U	$3,000 U
Materials quantity variance: 100 meters at $5.40 per meter F	$540 F
Labor rate variance: 1,950 hours at $0.20 per hour U	$390 U
Labor efficiency variance: 50 hours at $14.00 per hour F	$700 F

Required:

1. Prepare the general ledger entry to record the purchase of materials on account for the month.
2. Prepare the general ledger entry to record the use of materials for the month.
3. Prepare the general ledger entry to record the incurrence of direct labor cost for the month.

EXERCISES

EXERCISE 8–6   Setting Standards; Preparing a Standard Cost Card   (LO1)

Svenska Pharmicia, a Swedish pharmaceutical company, makes an anticoagulant drug. The main ingredient in the drug is a raw material called Alpha SR40. Information concerning the purchase and use of Alpha SR40 follows:

a. *Purchase of Alpha SR40:* The raw material Alpha SR40 is purchased in 2-kilogram containers at a cost of 3,000 Kr per kilogram. (The Swedish currency is the krona, which is abbreviated as Kr.) A discount of 2% is offered by the supplier for payment within 10 days and Svenska Pharmicia takes all discounts. Shipping costs, which Svenska Pharmicia must pay, amount to 1,000 Kr for an average shipment of ten 2-kilogram containers.

b. *Use of Alpha SR40:* The bill of materials calls for 6 grams of Alpha SR40 per capsule of the anticoagulant drug. (A kilogram equals 1,000 grams.) About 4% of all Alpha SR40 purchased is rejected as unsuitable before being used to make the anticoagulant drug. In addition, after the addition of Alpha SR40, about 1 out of every 26 capsules is rejected at final inspection, due to defects of one sort or another in the capsule.

Required:
1. Compute the standard purchase price for one gram of Alpha SR40.
2. Compute the standard quantity of Alpha SR40 (in grams) per capsule that passes final inspection. (Carry computations to two decimal places.)
3. Using the data from (1) and (2) above, prepare a standard cost card showing the standard cost of Alpha SR40 per capsule of the anticoagulant drug.

EXERCISE 8–7   Material and Labor Variances   (LO2, LO3)

Sonne Company produces a perfume called Whim. The direct materials and direct labor standards for one bottle of Whim are given below:

	Standard Quantity or Hours		Standard Price or Rate		Standard Cost
Direct materials..............	7.2 ounces	×	$2.50 per ounce	=	$18
Direct labor.................	0.4 hours	×	$10.00 per hour	=	$4

During the most recent month, the following activity was recorded:

a.   Twenty thousand ounces of material were purchased at a cost of $2.40 per ounce.
b.   All of the material was used to produce 2,500 bottles of Whim.
c.   Nine hundred hours of direct labor time were recorded at a total labor cost of $10,800.

Required:
1. Compute the direct materials price and quantity variances for the month.
2. Compute the direct labor rate and efficiency variances for the month.

EXERCISE 8–8   Material Variances   (LO2)

Refer to the data in Exercise 8–7. Assume that instead of producing 2,500 bottles of Whim during the month, the company produced only 2,000 bottles using 16,000 ounces of material. (The rest of the material purchased remained in inventory.)

Required:
Compute the direct materials price and quantity variances for the month.

EXERCISE 8–9   Labor and Variable Overhead Variances   (LO3, LO4)

Hollowell Audio, Inc., manufactures military-specification compact discs. The company uses standards to control its costs. The labor standards that have been set for one disc are as follows:

Standard Hours	Standard Rate per Hour	Standard Cost
24 minutes	$6.00	$2.40

During July, 8,500 hours of direct labor time were recorded to make 20,000 discs. The direct labor cost totaled $49,300 for the month.

Required:
1. What direct labor cost should have been incurred to make the 20,000 discs? By how much does this differ from the cost that was incurred?
2. Break down the difference in cost from (1) above into a labor rate variance and a labor efficiency variance.
3. The budgeted variable manufacturing overhead rate is $4 per direct labor-hour. During July, the company incurred $39,100 in variable manufacturing overhead cost. Compute the variable overhead spending and efficiency variances for the month.

EXERCISE 8–10   Material and Labor Variances   (LO2, LO3)

Topper Toys has developed a new toy called the Brainbuster. The company has a standard cost system to help control costs and has established the following standards for the Brainbuster toy:

Direct materials: 8 diodes per toy at $0.30 per diode
Direct labor: 1.2 hours per toy at $7 per hour

During August, the company produced 5,000 Brainbuster toys. Production data on the toy for August follow:

a. *Direct materials:* 70,000 diodes were purchased for use in production at a cost of $0.28 per diode. Some 20,000 of these diodes were still in inventory at the end of the month.
b. *Direct labor:* 6,400 direct labor-hours were worked at a cost of $48,000.

Required:
1. Compute the following variances for August:
    a.   Direct materials price and quantity variances.
    b.   Direct labor rate and efficiency variances.
2. Prepare a brief explanation of the significance and possible causes of each variance.

EXERCISE 8–11   (Appendix 8A) Material and Labor Variances; Journal Entries   (LO2, LO3, LO5)
Aspen Products, Inc., began production of a new product on April 1. The company uses a standard cost system and has established the following standards for one unit of the new product:

	Standard Quantity	Standard Price or Rate	Standard Cost
Direct materials.......	3.5 feet	$6 per foot	$21
Direct labor	0.4 hours	$10 per hour	$4

During April, the following activity was recorded relative to the new product:

a. Purchased 7,000 feet of material at a cost of $5.75 per foot.
b. Used 6,000 feet of material to produce 1,500 units of the new product.
c. Worked 725 direct labor-hours on the new product at a cost of $8,120.

Required:
1. For materials:
    a.   Compute the direct materials price and quantity variances.
    b.   Prepare journal entries to record the purchase of materials and the use of materials in production.
2. For direct labor:
    a.   Compute the direct labor rate and efficiency variances.
    b.   Prepare journal entries to record the incurrence of direct labor cost for the month.
3. Post the entries you have prepared to the T-accounts below:

Raw Materials	Work in Process	Labor Rate Variance
? ?	Materials used ?	
Bal. ?	Labor cost ?	

Materials Price Variance	Accounts Payable	Labor Efficiency Variance
	40,250	

Materials Quantity Variance	Wages Payable
	8,120

PROBLEMS

PROBLEM 8–12   Variance Analysis in a Hospital   (LO2, LO3, LO4)
Joan Cortez, chief administrator for Ocean Crest Hospital, is concerned about costs for tests in the hospital's lab. Charges for lab tests are consistently higher at Ocean Crest than at other hospitals and have resulted in many complaints. Also, because of strict regulations on amounts reimbursed for lab tests, payments received from insurance companies and governmental units have not been high enough to provide an acceptable level of income for the lab.

CHECK FIGURE
(1)   Materials quantity variance: $7,150 U
(2a)   Labor rate variance: $3,000 F

Ms. Cortez has asked you to evaluate costs in the hospital's lab for the past month. The following information is available:

a. Basically, two types of tests are performed in the lab—blood tests and smears. During the past month, 1,500 blood tests and 1,900 smears were performed in the lab.
b. Small glass plates are used in both types of tests. During the past month, the hospital purchased 11,450 plates at a cost of $24,045. This cost is net of a $0.10 per plate quantity discount. A total of 1,400 of these plates were still on hand unused at the end of the month; no plates were on hand at the beginning of the month.
c. During the past month, 1,200 hours of labor time were recorded in the lab. The cost of this labor time was $11,400.
d. Variable overhead cost last month in the lab for utilities and supplies totaled $6,840.

Ocean Crest Hospital has never used standard costs. By searching industry literature, however, you have determined the following nationwide averages for hospital labs:

a. *Plates:* Two plates are required per lab test. These plates cost $2.20 each and are disposed of after the test is completed.
b. *Labor:* Each blood test should require 0.40 hour to complete, and each smear should require 0.10 hour to complete. The average cost of this lab time is $12 per hour.
c. *Overhead:* Overhead cost is based on direct labor-hours. The average rate for variable overhead is $5.50 per hour.

Ms. Cortez would like a complete analysis of the cost of plates, labor, and overhead in the lab for the last month so that she can get to the root of the lab's cost problem.

Required:
1. Compute a materials price variance for the plates purchased last month and a materials quantity variance for the plates used last month.
2. For labor cost in the lab:
   a. Compute a labor rate variance and a labor efficiency variance.
   b. In most hospitals, one-half of the workers in the lab are senior technicians and one-half are assistants. In an effort to reduce costs, Ocean Crest Hospital employs only one-fourth senior technicians and three-fourths assistants. Would you recommend that this policy be continued? Explain.
3. Compute the variable overhead spending and efficiency variances. Is there any relationship between the variable overhead efficiency variance and the labor efficiency variance? Explain.

CHECK FIGURE
(1a) Materials price
     variance: $16,100 F
(2a) Labor efficiency
     variance: $3,600 U

PROBLEM 8–13   Basic Variance Analysis   (LO2, LO3, LO4)
Riley Labs produces various chemical compounds for industrial use. One compound, called Lundor, is prepared by means of an elaborate distilling process. The company has developed standard costs for one unit of Lundor as follows:

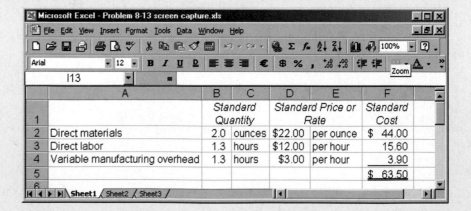

	Standard Quantity		Standard Price or Rate		Standard Cost
Direct materials	2.0	ounces	$22.00	per ounce	$ 44.00
Direct labor	1.3	hours	$12.00	per hour	15.60
Variable manufacturing overhead	1.3	hours	$3.00	per hour	3.90
					$ 63.50

During November, the following activity was recorded by the company relative to production of Lundor:

a. Materials purchased, 11,500 ounces at a cost of $236,900.
b. There was no beginning inventory of materials on hand to start the month; at the end of the month, 3,000 ounces of material remained in the warehouse unused.
c. The company employs 36 lab technicians to work on the production of Lundor. During November, they worked an average of 160 hours each at an average rate of $11.90 per hour.

d.　Variable manufacturing overhead is assigned to Lundor on the basis of direct labor-hours. Variable manufacturing overhead costs during November totaled $16,416.

e.　During November, 4,200 good units of Lundor were produced.

The company's management is anxious to determine the efficiency of the activities surrounding the production of Lundor.

Required:

1. For materials used in the production of Lundor:
   a.　Compute the price and quantity variances.
   b.　The materials were purchased from a new supplier who is anxious to enter into a long-term purchase contract. Would you recommend that the company sign the contract? Explain.
2. For direct labor employed in the production of Lundor:
   a.　Compute the rate and efficiency variances.
   b.　In the past, the 36 technicians employed in the production of Lundor consisted of 21 senior technicians and 15 assistants. During November, the company experimented with only 15 senior technicians and 21 assistants in order to save costs. Would you recommend that the new labor mix be continued? Explain.
3. Compute the variable overhead spending and efficiency variances. What relationship can you see between this efficiency variance and the labor efficiency variance?

PROBLEM 8–14　Comprehensive Variance Analysis　(LO2, LO3, LO4)

Kramer Toy Company manufactures a plastic swimming pool at its East Crest Plant. The plant has been experiencing problems for some time as shown by its September income statement below:

CHECK FIGURE
(1a) Materials price variance: $3,100 F
(2)　Net variance: $7,070 U

	Budgeted	Actual
Sales (15,000 pools).............	$495,000	$495,000
Less variable expenses:		
Variable cost of goods sold*	220,050	227,120
Variable selling expenses	24,000	24,000
Total variable expenses	244,050	251,120
Contribution margin	250,950	243,880
Less fixed expenses:		
Manufacturing overhead	128,000	128,000
Selling and administrative.......	85,000	85,000
Total fixed expenses.............	213,000	213,000
Net operating income...........	$ 37,950	$ 30,880

*Contains direct materials, direct labor, and variable manufacturing overhead.

Janet Wilson, who has just been appointed general manager of the East Crest Plant, has been given instructions to "get things under control." Upon reviewing the plant's income statement, Ms. Wilson has concluded that the major problem lies in the variable cost of goods sold. She has been provided with the following standard cost per swimming pool:

3.2 × 1.8 = $5.76

	Standard Quantity or Hours	Standard Price or Rate	Standard Cost
Direct materials	3.2 pounds	$1.80 per pound	$ 5.76
Direct labor	0.8 hours	$9.20 per hour	7.36
Variable manufacturing overhead.....	0.5 hours*	$3.10 per hour	1.55
Total standard cost...............			$14.67

*Based on machine-hours.

Ms. Wilson has determined that during September the plant produced 15,000 pools and incurred the following costs:

a. Purchased 62,000 pounds of materials at a cost of $1.75 per pound.

b. Used 51,000 pounds of materials in production. (Finished goods and work in process inventories are insignificant and can be ignored.)

c. Worked 11,800 direct labor-hours at a cost of $10.10 per hour.

d. Incurred variable manufacturing overhead cost totaling $19,240 for the month. A total of 7,400 machine-hours was recorded. It is the company's policy to close all variances to cost of goods sold on a monthly basis.

Required:

1. Compute the following variances for September:
    a. Direct materials price and quantity variances.
    b. Direct labor rate and efficiency variances.
    c. Variable overhead spending and efficiency variances.

2. Summarize the variances that you computed in (1) above by showing the net overall favorable or unfavorable variance for the month. What impact did this figure have on the company's income statement? Show computations.

3. Pick out the two most significant variances that you computed in (1) above. Explain to Ms. Wilson possible causes of these variances.

CHECK FIGURE
(2a) Labor rate variance:
      $5,880 U

PROBLEM 8–15   (Appendix 8A) Comprehensive Variance Analysis; Journal Entries   (LO2, LO3, LO4, LO5)

Pemberly Athletics produces a broad line of sports equipment and uses a standard cost system for control purposes. Last year the company produced 8,400 of its varsity basketballs. The standard costs associated with this basketball, along with the actual costs incurred last year, are given below (per basketball):

	Standard Cost	Actual Cost
Direct materials:		
Standard: 3.8 feet at $5.00 per foot	$19.00	
Actual: 4.0 feet at $4.90 per foot		$19.60
Direct labor:		
Standard: 1.1 hours at $7.50 per hour	8.25	
Actual: 1.0 hours at $8.20 per hour		8.20
Variable manufacturing overhead:		
Standard: 1.1 hours at $2.60 per hour	2.86	
Actual: 1.0 hours at $2.80 per hour		2.80
Total cost per basketball	$30.11	$30.60

The president was elated when he saw that actual costs exceeded standard costs by only $0.49 per basketball. He stated, "I was afraid that our unit cost might get out of hand when we gave out those raises last year in order to stimulate output. But it's obvious our costs are well under control."

There was no inventory of materials on hand to start the year. During the year, 33,600 feet of materials were purchased and used in production.

Required:

1. For direct materials:
    a. Compute the price and quantity variances for the year.
    b. Prepare journal entries to record all activity relating to direct materials for the year.
2. For direct labor:
    a. Compute the rate and efficiency variances.
    b. Prepare a journal entry to record the incurrence of direct labor cost for the year.
3. Compute the variable overhead spending and efficiency variances.
4. Was the president correct in his statement that "our costs are well under control"? Explain.
5. State possible causes of each variance that you have computed.

CHECK FIGURE
(1) Oxotate: 24.0 kilograms
(3) Standard cost: $119.40

PROBLEM 8–16   Setting Standards   (LO1)

Brighton Labs is a chemical manufacturer that supplies various products to industrial users. The company plans to introduce a new chemical solution, called Toric, for which it needs to develop a standard product cost. The following information is available on the production of Toric:

a. Toric is made by combining a chemical compound (Oxotate) and a solution (Mayol), and boiling the mixture. A 30% loss in volume occurs for both the Mayol and the Oxotate during boiling. After boiling, the mixture consists of 9.1 liters of Mayol and 14.0 kilograms of Oxotate per 12-liter batch of Toric.

b. After the boiling process is complete, the solution is cooled slightly before 6 kilograms of Gretat are added per 12-liter batch of Toric. The addition of this ingredient does not affect the total liquid volume. The resulting solution is then bottled in 12-liter containers.

c. The finished product is highly unstable, and one 12-liter batch out of 6 is rejected at final inspection. Rejected batches have no commercial value and are thrown out.

d. It takes a worker 35 minutes to process one 12-liter batch of Toric. Employees work an 8-hour day, including 1 hour per day for rest breaks and cleanup.

Required:

1. Determine the standard quantity for each of the raw materials needed to produce an acceptable 12-liter batch of Toric.

2. Determine the standard labor time to produce an acceptable 12-liter batch of Toric.

3. Assuming the following purchase prices and costs, prepare a standard cost card for materials and labor for one acceptable 12-liter batch of Toric:

Mayol	$1.50 per liter
Oxotate	$2.80 per kilogram
Gretat	$3.00 per kilogram
Direct labor cost	$9.00 per hour

(CMA, adapted)

PROBLEM 8–17   Working Backwards from Labor Variances   (LO3)

The auto repair shop of Mechanics World uses standards to control the labor time and labor cost in the shop. The standard labor cost for a motor tune-up is given below:

Job	Standard Hours	Standard Rate	Standard Cost
Motor tune-up	3.0	$9.50	$28.50

The record showing the time spent in the shop last week on motor tune-ups has been misplaced. However, the shop supervisor recalls that 60 tune-ups were completed during the week, and the controller recalls the following variance data relating to tune-ups:

Labor rate variance	$90 F
Total labor variance	$100 U

Required:

1. Determine the number of actual labor-hours spent on tune-ups during the week.
2. Determine the actual hourly rate of pay for tune-ups last week.

(Hint: A useful way to proceed would be to work from known to unknown data either by using the variance formulas or by using the columnar format shown in Exhibit 8–6.)

PROBLEM 8–18   Comprehensive Variance Problem   (LO1, LO2, LO3, LO4)

Celtron Inc. produces a lightweight backpack that is popular with college students. Standard variable costs relating to a single backpack are given below:

	Standard Quantity or Hours	Standard Price or Rate	Standard Cost
Direct materials	?	$6.50 per yard	$?
Direct labor	?	?	?
Variable manufacturing overhead	?	$2.80 per hour	?
Total standard cost			?

CHECK FIGURE
(1) Actual hours: 200

CHECK FIGURE
(1) Standard cost: $33.75
(3) 2.70 yards per backpack

During September 1,000 backpacks were manufactured and sold. Selected information relating to the month's production is given below:

	Materials Used	Direct Labor	Variable Manufacturing Overhead
Total standard cost allowed for the month's production............................	$17,550	$12,000	$4,200
Actual costs incurred	$14,700	?	$3,500
Materials price variance............................	?		
Materials quantity variance	$650 U		
Labor rate variance............................		?	
Labor efficiency variance............................		?	
Variable overhead spending variance			?
Variable overhead efficiency variance			?

The following additional information is available for September's production:

Actual direct labor-hours............................	1,600
Difference between standard and actual cost per backpack produced during September.........	$2.15 F

Overhead is applied to production on the basis of direct labor-hours. There were no beginning or ending inventories of raw materials.

Required:
1. What is the standard cost of a single backpack?
2. What was the actual cost per backpack produced during September?
3. How many yards of material are required at standard per backpack?
4. What was the materials price variance for September?
5. What is the standard direct labor rate per hour?
6. What was the labor rate variance for September? The labor efficiency variance?
7. What was the variable overhead spending variance for September? The variable overhead efficiency variance?
8. Prepare a standard cost card for one backpack.

CHECK FIGURE
(1a) Actual cost: $7.90 per foot
(2a) Standard labor rate: $7.50 per hour

PROBLEM 8–19   Computations from Incomplete Data   (LO2, LO3)
Cramer Company manufactures a product for which the following standards have been set:

	Standard Quantity or Hours	Standard Price or Rate	Standard Cost
Direct materials	2.00 feet	$8.00 per foot	$16.00
Direct labor	? hours	? per hour	?

During June, the company purchased direct materials at a cost of $49,770, all of which were used in the production of 3,000 units of product. There were no beginning inventories of raw materials. In addition, 5,400 hours of direct labor time were worked on the product during the month. The cost of this labor time was $38,340. The following variances have been computed for the month:

Materials quantity variance	$2,400 U
Total labor variance	$90 U
Labor efficiency variance	$2,250 U

Required:
1. For direct materials:
   a.   Compute the actual cost per foot for materials for June.
   b.   Compute the materials price variance and a total variance for materials.

2. For direct labor:
   a. Compute the standard direct labor rate per hour.
   b. Compute the standard hours allowed for the month's production.
   c. Compute the standard hours allowed per unit of product.

(Hint: In completing the problem, it may be helpful to move from known to unknown data either by using the columnar format shown in Exhibits 8–4 and 8–6 or by using the variance formulas.)

PROBLEM 8–20 Variance Analysis with Multiple Lots   (LO2, LO3)

Leary Fabrication manufactures men's clothing. The company has a single line of slacks that is produced in lots, with each lot representing an order from a customer. As a lot is completed, the customer's store label is attached to the slacks before shipment.

Leary has a standard cost system and has established the following standards for a dozen slacks:

	Standard Quantity or Hours	Standard Price or Rate	Standard Cost
Direct materials	24.0 yards	$3.60 per yard	$86.40
Direct labor	3.6 hours	$9.00 per hour	$32.40

During October, Leary worked on three orders for slacks. The company's job cost records for the month reveal the following:

Lot	Units in Lot (dozens)	Materials Used (yards)	Hours Worked
62	1,400	34,500	5,090
63	1,600	38,300	5,720
64	1,800	42,900	5,940

The following additional information is available:

a. Leary purchased 120,000 yards of material during October at a cost of $425,200.
b. Direct labor cost incurred during the month for production of slacks amounted to $153,700.
c. There was no work in process inventory on October 1. During October, lots 62 and 63 were completed, and lot 64 was 100% complete with respect to materials and 90% complete with respect to labor.

Required:
1. Compute the materials price variance for the materials purchased during October.
2. Determine the materials quantity variance for October in both yards and dollars:
   a. For each lot worked on during the month.
   b. For the company as a whole.
3. Compute the labor rate variance for October.
4. Determine the labor efficiency variance for the month in both hours and dollars:
   a. For each lot worked on during the month.
   b. For the company as a whole.
5. In what situations might it be better to express variances in units (hours, yards, and so on) rather than in dollars? In dollars rather than in units?

(CPA, adapted)

PROBLEM 8–21   (Appendix 8A) Comprehensive Variance Analysis with Incomplete Data (LO1, LO2, LO3, LO4, LO5)

Far North Sporting, Ltd., manufactures a premium hockey stick. The standard cost of one hockey stick is:

	Standard Quantity or Hours	Standard Price or Rate	Standard Cost
Direct materials	? feet	$5.00 per foot	$?
Direct labor	1.5 hours	? per hour	?
Variable manufacturing overhead	? hours	$2.50 per hour	?
Total standard cost			$45.75

Last year, 12,000 hockey sticks were produced and sold. Selected cost data relating to last year's operations follow:

	Dr.	Cr.
Accounts payable—direct materials purchased (62,000 feet)........		$297,600
Wages payable (? hours)......................................		236,640*
Work in process—direct materials	$288,000	
Direct labor rate variance		8,160
Variable overhead efficiency variance...........................	6,000	

*Relates to the actual direct labor cost for the year.

The following additional information is available for last year's operations:

a. No materials were on hand at the start of last year. Some of the materials purchased during the year were still on hand in the warehouse at the end of the year.
b. The variable manufacturing overhead rate is based on direct labor-hours. Total actual variable manufacturing overhead cost for last year was $46,920.
c. Actual direct materials usage for last year exceeded the standard by 0.2 feet per stick.

Required:
1. For direct materials:
    a. Compute the price and quantity variances for last year.
    b. Prepare journal entries to record all activities relating to direct materials for last year.
2. For direct labor:
    a. Verify the rate variance given above and compute the efficiency variance for last year.
    b. Prepare a journal entry to record activity relating to direct labor for last year.
3. Compute the variable overhead spending variance for last year and verify the variable overhead efficiency variance given above.
4. State possible causes of each variance that you have computed.
5. Prepare a completed standard cost card for one hockey stick.

CHECK FIGURE
(1) Standard cost: $37.17

PROBLEM 8–22   Developing Standard Costs   (LO1)
FlashFresh Corporation is a small producer of fruit-flavored frozen desserts. For many years, FlashFresh's products have had strong regional sales on the basis of brand recognition; however, other companies have begun marketing similar products in the area, and price competition has become increasingly important. Becky Nomura, the company's controller, is planning to implement a standard cost system for FlashFresh and has gathered considerable information on production and material requirements for FlashFresh's products. Nomura believes that the use of standard costing will allow FlashFresh to improve cost control and make better pricing decisions.

FlashFresh's most popular product is strawberry sherbet. The sherbet is produced in 10-gallon batches, and each batch requires 5 quarts of good strawberries. (If you are unfamiliar with gallons and quarts as measures, one gallon equals four quarts.) The fresh strawberries are sorted by hand before they enter the production process. Because of imperfections in the strawberries and normal spoilage, 1 quart of berries is discarded for every 9 quarts of acceptable berries. The standard direct labor time for the sorting to obtain 1 quart of acceptable strawberries is 3 minutes. The acceptable strawberries are then blended with the other ingredients; blending requires 10 minutes of direct labor time per batch. After blending, the sherbet is packaged in quart containers. Nomura has gathered the following pricing information:

a. FlashFresh purchases strawberries at a cost of $0.90 per quart. All other ingredients cost a total of $1.60 per gallon.
b. Direct labor is paid at the rate of $10.00 per hour.
c. The total cost of material and labor required to package the sherbet is $0.30 per quart.

Required:
1. Develop the standard cost for the direct cost components (materials, labor, and packaging) of a 10-gallon batch of strawberry sherbet. The standard cost should identify the standard quantity, standard rate, and standard cost per batch for each direct cost component of a batch of strawberry sherbet.
2. As part of the implementation of a standard cost system at FlashFresh, Becky Nomura plans to train those responsible for maintaining the standards on how to use variance analysis. Nomura is particularly concerned with the causes of unfavorable variances.

a.　Discuss possible causes of unfavorable materials price variances and identify the individual(s) who should be held responsible for these variances.

b.　Discuss possible causes of unfavorable labor efficiency variances and identify the individual(s) who should be held responsible for these variances.

(CMA, adapted)

BUILDING YOUR SKILLS

ETHICS CASE　(LOI)

Stacy Cummins, the newly hired controller at Merced Home Products, Inc., was disturbed by what she had discovered about the standard costs at the Home Security Division. In looking over the past several years of quarterly earnings reports at the Home Security Division, she noticed that the first-quarter earnings were always poor, the second-quarter earnings were slightly better, the third-quarter earnings were again slightly better, and then the fourth quarter and the year always ended with a spectacular performance in which the Home Security Division always managed to meet or exceed its target profit for the year. She also was concerned to find letters from the company's external auditors to top management warning about an unusual use of standard costs at the Home Security Division.

When Ms. Cummins ran across these letters, she asked the assistant controller, Gary Farber, if he knew what was going on at the Home Security Division. Gary said that it was common knowledge in the company that the vice president in charge of the Home Security Division, Preston Lansing, had rigged the standards at the Home Security Division in order to produce the same quarterly earnings pattern every year. According to company policy, variances are taken directly to the income statement as an adjustment to cost of goods sold.

Favorable variances have the effect of increasing net income, and unfavorable variances have the effect of decreasing net income. Lansing had rigged the standards so that there were always large favorable variances. Company policy was a little vague about when these variances have to be reported on the divisional income statements. While the intent was clearly to recognize variances on the income statement in the period in which they arise, nothing in the company's accounting manuals explicitly required this. So for many years Lansing had followed a practice of saving up the favorable variances and using them to create a smooth pattern of earnings growth in the first three quarters, followed by a big "Christmas present" of an extremely good fourth quarter. (Financial reporting regulations forbid carrying variances forward from one year to the next on the annual audited financial statements, so all of the variances must appear on the divisional income statement by the end of the year.)

Ms. Cummins was concerned about these revelations and attempted to bring up the subject with the president of Merced Home Products but was told that "we all know what Lansing's doing, but as long as he continues to turn in such good reports, don't bother him." When Ms. Cummins asked if the board of directors was aware of the situation, the president somewhat testily replied, "Of course they are aware."

Required:

1.　How did Preston Lansing probably "rig" the standard costs—are the standards set too high or too low? Explain.

2.　Should Preston Lansing be permitted to continue his practice of managing reported earnings?

3.　What should Stacy Cummins do in this situation?

COMMUNICATING IN PRACTICE　(LOI)

Make an appointment to meet with the manager of an auto repair shop that uses standards. In most cases, this would be an auto repair shop that is affiliated with a national chain such as Firestone or Sears or the service department of a new-car dealer.

Required:

At the scheduled meeting, find out the answers to the following questions and write a memo to your instructor describing the information obtained during your meeting.

1.　How are standards set?

2.　Are standards practical or ideal?

3.　Is the actual time taken to complete a task compared to the standard time?

4.　What are the consequences of unfavorable variances? Of favorable variances?

5.　Do the standards and variances create any potential problems?

TEAMWORK IN ACTION   (LO1)

Terry Travers is the manufacturing supervisor of Aurora Manufacturing Company, which produces a variety of plastic products. Some of these products are standard items that are listed in the company's catalog, while others are made to customer specifications. Each month, Travers receives a performance report showing the budget for the month, the actual activity, and the variance between budget and actual. Part of Travers' annual performance evaluation is based on his department's performance against budget. Aurora's purchasing manager, Sally Christensen, also receives monthly performance reports and she, too, is evaluated in part on the basis of these reports.

The monthly reports for June had just been distributed when Travers met Christensen in the hallway outside their offices. Scowling, Travers began the conversation, "I see we have another set of monthly performance reports hand-delivered by that not very nice junior employee in the budget office. He seemed pleased to tell me that I'm in trouble with my performance again."

Christensen: I got the same treatment. All I ever hear about are the things I haven't done right. Now I'll have to spend a lot of time reviewing the report and preparing explanations. The worst part is that it's now the 21st of July so the information is almost a month old, and we have to spend all this time on history.

Travers: My biggest gripe is that our production activity varies a lot from month to month, but we're given an annual budget that's written in stone. Last month we were shut down for three days when a strike delayed delivery of the basic ingredient used in our plastic formulation, and we had already exhausted our inventory. You know about that problem, though, because we asked you to call all over the country to find an alternate source of supply. When we got what we needed on a rush basis, we had to pay more than we normally do.

Christensen: I expect problems like that to pop up from time to time—that's part of my job—but now we'll both have to take a careful look at our reports to see where the charges are reflected for that rush order. Every month I spend more time making sure I should be charged for each item reported than I do making plans for my department's daily work. It's really frustrating to see charges for things I have no control over.

Travers: The way we get information doesn't help, either. I don't get copies of the reports you get, yet a lot of what I do is affected by your department, and by most of the other departments we have. Why do the budget and accounting people assume that I should be told only about my operations even though the president regularly gives us pep talks about how we all need to work together as a team?

Christensen: I seem to get more reports than I need, and I am never asked to comment on them until top management calls me on the carpet about my department's shortcomings. Do you ever hear comments when your department shines?

Travers: I guess they don't have time to review the good news. One of my problems is that all the reports are in dollars and cents. I work with people, machines, and materials. I need information to help me *this* month to solve *this* month's problems—not another report of the dollars expended *last* month or the month before.

Required:

Your team should discuss and then respond to the following questions. All team members should agree with and understand the answers and be prepared to report on those answers in class. (Each teammate can assume responsibility for a different part of the presentation.)

1. Based on the conversation between Terry Travers and Sally Christensen, describe the likely motivation and behavior of these two employees as a result of the standard cost and variance reporting system that is used by Aurora Manufacturing Company.
2. List the recommendations that your team would make to Aurora Manufacturing Company to enhance employee motivation as it relates to the company's standard cost and variance reporting system.

(CMA, adapted)

CHECK FIGURE
(1)   80 batches
(4a)   200 hours

ANALYTICAL THINKING   (Appendix 8A)   (LO2, LO3, LO4, LO5)

You have just been hired by Esprix Company, which manufactures cough syrup. The syrup requires two materials, A and B, in its manufacture, and it is produced in batches. The company uses a standard cost system, with the controller preparing variances on a weekly basis. These variances are discussed at a meeting attended by all relevant managers. The meeting to discuss last week's variances is tomorrow. Since you will be working initially in the planning and control area, the president thinks that this would be a good chance for you to get acquainted with the company's control system and has asked that you attend and be prepared to participate fully in the discussion. Accordingly, you have taken home the controller's worksheet containing last week's variances, as well as the ledger pages from which these variances were derived. You are sure that with a little study you will be able to make a great impression and be launched into a bright and successful career.

After completing your study that night, the weather being warm and humid, you leave your windows open upon retiring, only to arise the next morning horrified to discover that a sudden shower has obliterated most of the controller's figures (left lying on a table by an open window). Only the following fragments are readable:

Raw Materials—A			Accounts Payable	Material B—Quantity Variance	
Bal. 6/1	720		4,240	40	
Bal. 6/7	1,500				

Raw Materials—B			Wages Payable	Labor Efficiency Variance	
Bal. 6/1	0	600	1,725	240	
Bal. 6/7	200				

Work in Process			Material A—Price Variance	
Bal. 6/1	0		220	
Material A	2,400			
Bal. 6/7	0			

Not wanting to admit your carelessness to either the president or the controller, you have decided that your only alternative is to reproduce the obliterated data. From your study last night, you recall the following:

a. The wages payable are only for direct labor.
b. The accounts payable are for purchases of both material A and material B.
c. The standard cost of material A is $6 per gallon, and the standard quantity is 5 gallons per batch of syrup.
d. Purchases last week were: material A, 550 gallons; and material B, 200 pounds.
e. The standard rate for direct labor is $8 per hour; a total of 230 actual hours were worked last week.

Required:
1. How many batches of syrup were produced last week? (Double-check this figure before going on!)
2. For material A:
   a. How many gallons were used in production last week?
   b. What was the quantity variance?
   c. What was the cost of material A purchased during the week?
   d. Prepare journal entries to record all activity relating to material A during the week.
3. For material B:
   a. What is the standard cost per pound of material B?
   b. How many pounds of material B were used in production last week? How many pounds should have been used at standard?
   c. What is the standard quantity of material B per batch?
   d. What was the price variance for material B?
   e. Prepare journal entries to record all activity relating to material B during the week.
4. For direct labor:
   a. What were the standard hours allowed for last week's production?
   b. What are the standard hours per batch?
   c. What was the direct labor rate variance?
   d. Prepare a journal entry to record all activity relating to direct labor during the week.
5. In terms of materials and labor, compute the standard cost of one batch of syrup.

TAKING IT TO THE NET
As you know, the World Wide Web is a medium that is constantly evolving. Sites come and go and change without notice. To enable periodic update of site addresses, this problem has been posted to the textbook website (www.mhhe.com/bgn2e). After accessing the site, enter the Student Center and select this chapter. Select and complete the Taking It to the Net problem.

Flexible Budgets and Overhead Analysis

NASA Reduces Its Overhead Costs

NASA (www.nasa.gov) is the agency responsible for all civilian aeronautical and space activities sponsored by the United States. An online newsletter (today@nasa.gov) provides daily updates about the activities of NASA. During the six-year period from 1994 to 2000, NASA's budget decreased from $14.5 billion to $13.6 billion. Comparing fiscal 1990 through 1994 to fiscal 1995 through 1999, the average spacecraft development cost declined by 65%, the average development time decreased from 8 to 5 years, and the number of flights per year increased from 2 to 7.

NASA was able to achieve more with less during the 1990s by significantly reducing its overhead costs. By way of illustration, it took a crew of 1,000 to send Viking to Mars. Just under 20 years later, a crew of 50 sent the Pathfinder to Mars. Part of NASA's success can be attributed to its decision to outsource support activities. Contractors aggressively bid against each other to perform the work. This example of NASA's determination to control its overhead costs relates to a cost management program that was instituted by NASA in 1995.

The multiyear initiative encompasses NASA's management, budgeting, and accounting processes. In part, the program is expected to reduce the cost of missions, inspire the agency's managers to perform efficiently, benchmark activities, support the decision-making process, provide justification for NASA's budget requests, and further enhance NASA's accountability to the taxpayers.

Sources: NASA website; and John Rhea, "Cutting the Fat: DOD Can Learn How from NASA," *Military & Aerospace Electronics,* March 1998, p. 3 (3 pages).

LEARNING OBJECTIVES

After studying Chapter 9, you should be able to:

LO1 Prepare a flexible budget and explain the advantages of the flexible budget approach over the static budget approach.

LO2 Prepare a performance report for both variable and fixed overhead costs using the flexible budget approach.

LO3 Use the flexible budget to prepare a variable overhead performance report containing only a spending variance.

LO4 Use the flexible budget to prepare a variable overhead performance report containing both a spending and an efficiency variance.

LO5 Compute the predetermined overhead rate and apply overhead to products in a standard cost system.

LO6 Compute and interpret the fixed overhead budget and volume variances.

ontrolling overhead costs is a major preoccupation of managers in business, in government, and in not-for-profit organizations. Overhead is a major cost, if not *the* major cost, in many organizations. It costs Microsoft very little to download copies of its software onto hard disks and to provide purchasers with software manuals; almost all of Microsoft's costs are in research and development and marketing—elements of overhead. Or consider Disney World. The only direct cost of serving a particular guest is the cost of the food the guest consumes at the park; virtually all of the other costs of running the amusement park are overhead. Boeing has huge amounts of overhead in the form of engineering salaries, buildings, insurance, administrative salaries, and marketing costs.

Controlling overhead costs poses special problems. Costs like direct materials and direct labor are usually easier to understand, and therefore to control, than overhead, which can include everything from the disposable coffee cup in the visitors' waiting area to the president's salary. Overhead is usually made up of many separate costs—many of which may be small. This makes it impractical to control them in the same way that costs such as direct materials and direct labor are controlled. And some overhead costs are variable, some are fixed, and some are a mixture of fixed and variable. These particular problems can be largely overcome by the use of flexible budgets. In this chapter, we study flexible budgets in detail and learn how they can be used to control costs. We also expand the study of overhead variances that we started in Chapter 8.

FLEXIBLE BUDGETS

Characteristics of a Flexible Budget

Concept 9–1

The budgets that we studied in Chapter 7 were *static budgets.* A **static budget** is prepared at the beginning of the budgeting period and is valid for only the planned level of activity. A static budget approach is suitable for planning purposes, but it is inadequate for evaluating how well costs are controlled. If the actual activity during a period differs from what was planned, it would be misleading to simply compare actual costs to the static budget. If activity is higher than expected, variable costs should be higher than expected; and if activity is lower than expected, variable costs should be lower than expected.

Flexible budgets take into account changes in costs that should occur as a consequence of changes in activity. A **flexible budget** provides estimates of what costs should be for any level of activity within a specified range. When a flexible budget is used in performance evaluation, actual costs are compared to what the *costs should have been for the actual level of activity during the period* rather than to the budgeted costs from the original budget. This is a very important distinction—particularly for variable costs. If adjustments for the level of activity are not made, it is very difficult to interpret discrepancies between budgeted and actual costs.

Static vs. Flexible Budgets

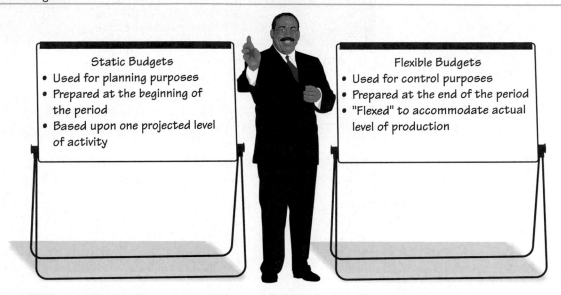

Static Budgets
- Used for planning purposes
- Prepared at the beginning of the period
- Based upon one projected level of activity

Flexible Budgets
- Used for control purposes
- Prepared at the end of the period
- "Flexed" to accommodate actual level of production

Deficiencies of the Static Budget

To illustrate the difference between a static budget and a flexible budget, consider the case of Rick's Hairstyling, an upscale hairstyling salon located in Beverly Hills that is owned and managed by Rick Manzi. The salon has very loyal customers—many of whom are associated with the film industry. Despite the glamour associated with his salon, Rick is a very shrewd businessman. Recently he has been attempting to get better control over his overhead, and at the urging of his accounting and business adviser Victoria Kho, he has begun to prepare monthly budgets. Victoria Kho is a certified public accountant and certified management accountant in independent practice who specializes in small service-oriented businesses like Rick's Hairstyling.

At the end of February, Rick carefully prepared the March budget for overhead items that appears in Exhibit 9–1. Rick believes that the number of customers served in a month is the best way to measure the overall level of activity in his salon. Rick refers to these visits as client-visits. A customer who comes into the salon and has his or her hair styled is counted as one client-visit. After some discussion with Victoria Kho, Rick identified three major categories of variable overhead costs—hairstyling supplies, client gratuities, and electricity—and four major categories of fixed costs—support staff wages and salaries, rent, insurance, and utilities other than electricity. Client gratuities consist of flowers, candies, and glasses of champagne that Rick gives to his customers while they are in the salon. Rick considers electricity to be a variable cost, since almost all of the electricity in the salon is consumed in running blow-dryers, curling irons, and other hairstyling equipment.

To develop the budget for variable overhead, Rick estimated that the average cost per client-visit should be $1.20 for hairstyling supplies, $4.00 for client gratuities, and $0.20 for electricity. Based on his estimate of 5,000 client-visits in March, Rick budgeted for $6,000 ($1.20 per client-visit $\times$ 5,000 client-visits) in hairstyling supplies, $20,000 ($4.00 per client-visit $\times$ 5,000 client-visits) in client gratuities, and $1,000 ($0.20 per client-visit $\times$ 5,000 client-visits) in electricity.

The budget for fixed overhead items was based on Rick's records of how much he had spent on these items in the past. The budget included $8,000 for support staff wages and salaries, $12,000 for rent, $1,000 for insurance, and $500 for utilities other than electricity.

At the end of March, Rick prepared a report comparing actual to budgeted costs. That report appears in Exhibit 9–2. The problem with that report, as Rick immediately realized, is that it compares costs at one level of activity (5,200 client-visits) to costs at a different

EXHIBIT 9–1

RICK'S
hairstyling salon

RICK'S HAIRSTYLING Static Budget For the Month Ended March 31	
Budgeted number of client-visits	5,000
Budget variable overhead costs:	
Hairstyling supplies (@ $1.20 per client-visit)	$ 6,000
Client gratuities (@ $4.00 per client-visit)	20,000
Electricity (@ $0.20 per client-visit)	1,000
Total variable overhead cost	27,000
Budgeted fixed overhead costs:	
Support staff wages and salaries	8,000
Rent	12,000
Insurance	1,000
Utilities other than electricity	500
Total fixed overhead cost	21,500
Total budgeted overhead cost	$48,500

EXHIBIT 9–2

RICK'S HAIRSTYLING Static Budget Performance Report For the Month Ended March 31	Actual	Budgeted	Variance
Client-visits	5,200	5,000	200 F
Variable overhead costs:			
Hairstyling supplies	$ 6,400	$ 6,000	$ 400 U*
Client gratuities	22,300	20,000	2,300 U*
Electricity	1,020	1,000	20 U*
Total variable overhead cost	29,720	27,000	2,720 U*
Fixed overhead costs:			
Support staff wages and salaries	8,100	8,000	100 U
Rent	12,000	12,000	0
Insurance	1,000	1,000	0
Utilities other than electricity	470	500	30 F
Total fixed overhead cost	21,570	21,500	70 U
Total overhead cost	$51,290	$48,500	$2,790 U*

*The cost variances for variable costs and for total overhead are useless for evaluating how well costs were controlled since they have been derived by comparing actual costs at one level of activity to budgeted costs at a different level of activity.

level of activity (5,000 client-visits). Since Rick had 200 more client-visits than expected, his variable costs *should* be higher than budgeted. The static budget performance report confuses control over activity and control over costs. From Rick's standpoint, the increase in activity was good and should be counted as a favorable variance, but the increase in activity has an apparently negative impact on the costs in the report. Rick knew that something would have to be done to make the report more meaningful, but he was unsure of what to do. So he made an appointment to meet with Victoria Kho to discuss the next step.

MANAGERIAL
ACCOUNTING
IN ACTION
The Issue

RICK'S
hairstyling salon

Victoria: How is the budgeting going?
Rick: Pretty well. I didn't have any trouble putting together the overhead budget for March. I also made out a report comparing the actual costs for March to the budgeted costs, but that report isn't giving me what I really want to know.
Victoria: Because your actual level of activity didn't match your budgeted activity?

EXHIBIT 9–3 Illustration of the Flexible Budgeting Concept

RICK'S HAIRSTYLING Flexible Budget For the Month Ended March 31					
Budgeted number of client-visits 5,000					

Overhead Costs	Cost Formula (per client-visit)	Activity (in client-visits)			
		4,900	5,000	5,100	5,200
Variable overhead costs:					
Hairstyling supplies	$1.20	$ 5,880	$ 6,000	$ 6,120	$ 6,240
Client gratuities	4.00	19,600	20,000	20,400	20,800
Electricity (variable)	0.20	980	1,000	1,020	1,040
Total variable overhead cost	$5.40	26,460	27,000	27,540	28,080
Fixed overhead costs:					
Support staff wages and salaries		8,000	8,000	8,000	8,000
Rent		12,000	12,000	12,000	12,000
Insurance		1,000	1,000	1,000	1,000
Utilities other than electricity		500	500	500	500
Total fixed overhead cost		21,500	21,500	21,500	21,500
Total overhead cost		$47,960	$48,500	$49,040	$49,580

Rick: Right. I know that the level of activity shouldn't affect my fixed costs, but we had a lot more client-visits than I had expected and that had to affect my variable costs.

Victoria: So you want to know whether the actual costs are justified by the actual level of activity you had in March?

Rick: Precisely.

Victoria: If you leave your reports and data with me, I can work on it later today, and by tomorrow I'll have a report to show to you. Actually, I have a styling appointment for later this week. Why don't I move my appointment up to tomorrow, and I will bring along the analysis so we can discuss it.

Rick: That's great.

How a Flexible Budget Works

The basic idea of the flexible budget approach is that a budget does not have to be static. Depending on the actual level of activity, a budget can be adjusted to show what costs *should be* for that specific level of activity. A master budget summarizes a company's plans and indicates how the plans will be accomplished. To simplify the discussion of the budgeting process, only one level of activity was assumed when each of the components of the master budget was illustrated in Chapter 7. However, a master budget can also be developed using a flexible budget approach. Because management places a great deal of significance on the control of overhead costs, the overhead budget is used in this chapter to illustrate the concept of flexible budgeting. However, the flexible budget approach is equally applicable to each of the components of the master budget.

To illustrate how flexible budgets work, Victoria prepared the report in Exhibit 9–3. It shows how overhead costs can be expected to change, depending on the monthly level of activity. Within the activity range of 4,900 to 5,200 client-visits, the fixed costs are expected to remain the same. For the variable overhead costs, Victoria multiplied Rick's per client costs ($1.20 for hairstyling supplies, $4.00 for client gratuities, and $0.20 for electricity) by the appropriate number of client-visits in each column. For example, the $1.20 cost of hairstyling supplies was multiplied by 4,900 client-visits to give the total cost of $5,880 for hairstyling supplies at that level of activity.

LEARNING OBJECTIVE 2

Prepare a performance report for both variable and fixed overhead costs using the flexible budget approach.

EXHIBIT 9–4

RICK'S HAIRSTYLING **Flexible Budget Performance Report** **For the Month Ended March 31**				
Budgeted number of client-visits . . . . 5,000 Actual number of client-visits 5,200				
Overhead Costs	**Cost Formula (per client-visit)**	**Actual Costs Incurred for 5,200 Client-Visits**	**Budget Based on 5,200 Client-Visits**	**Variance**
Variable overhead costs:				
Hairstyling supplies	$1.20	$ 6,400	$ 6,240	$ 160 U
Client gratuities	4.00	22,300	20,800	1,500 U
Electricity (variable)	0.20	1,020	1,040	20 F
Total variable overhead cost	$5.40	29,720	28,080	1,640 U
Fixed overhead costs:				
Support staff wages and salaries		8,100	8,000	100 U
Rent		12,000	12,000	0
Insurance		1,000	1,000	0
Utilities other than electricity		470	500	30 F
Total fixed overhead cost		21,570	21,500	70 U
Total overhead cost		$51,290	$49,580	$1,710 U

Using the Flexible Budgeting Concept in Performance Evaluation

To get a better idea of how well Rick's variable overhead costs were controlled in March, Victoria applied the flexible budgeting concept to create a new performance report (Exhibit 9–4). Using the flexible budget approach, Victoria constructed a budget based on the *actual* number of client-visits for the month. The budget is prepared by multiplying the actual level of activity by the cost formula for each of the variable cost categories. For example, using the $1.20 per client-visit for hairstyling supplies, the total cost for this item *should be* $6,240 for 5,200 client-visits ($1.20 per client-visit × 5,200 client-visits). Since the actual cost for hairstyling supplies was $6,400, the unfavorable variance was $160.

Contrast the performance report in Exhibit 9–4 with the static budget approach in Exhibit 9–2. The variance for hairstyling supplies was $400 unfavorable using the static budget approach. In that exhibit, apples were being compared to oranges in the case of the variable cost items. Actual costs at one level of activity were being compared to budgeted costs at a different level of activity. Because actual activity was higher by 200 client-visits than budgeted activity, the total cost of hairstyling supplies *should* have been $240 ($1.20 per client-visit × 200 client-visits) higher than budgeted. As a result, $240 of the $400 "unfavorable" variance in the static budget performance report in Exhibit 9–2 was spurious.

In contrast, the flexible budget performance report in Exhibit 9–4 provides a more valid assessment of performance. Apples are compared to apples. Actual costs are compared to what costs should have been at the actual level of activity. When this is done, we see that the variance is $160 unfavorable rather than $400 unfavorable as it was in the original static budget performance report. In some cases, as with electricity in Rick's report, an unfavorable variance may be transformed into a favorable variance when an increase in activity is properly taken into account in a performance report.

CONCEPT CHECK ✓

1. Which of the following statements is false? (You may select more than one answer.)
   a. A flexible budget is used for control purposes and a static budget is used for planning purposes.
   b. A flexible budget is prepared at the end of the period and a static budget is prepared at the beginning of the period.
   c. A flexible budget is most useful for controlling fixed costs.
   d. A static budget provides budgeted estimates for one level of activity.
2. A company's static budget estimate of total overhead costs was $100,000 based on the assumption that 10,000 units would be produced and sold. The company estimates that 30% of its overhead is variable and the remainder is fixed. What would be the total overhead cost according to the flexible budget if 12,000 units were produced and sold?
   a. $96,000
   b. $100,000
   c. $106,000
   d. $116,000

Focus on Opportunities

IN BUSINESS

Legendary management guru Peter F. Drucker cautions managers that "almost without exception, the first page of the [monthly] report presents the areas in which results fall below expectations or in which expenditures exceed the budget. It focuses on problems. Problems cannot be ignored. But . . . enterprises have to focus on opportunities. That requires a small but fundamental procedural change: a new first page to the monthly report, one that precedes the page that shows the problems. The new page should focus on where results are better than expected. As much time should be spent on that new first page as traditionally was spent on the problem page."

Source: Peter F. Drucker, "Change Leaders," *Inc.*, June 1999, pp. 65–72.

The following discussion took place the next day at Rick's salon.

MANAGERIAL ACCOUNTING IN ACTION
The Wrap-Up

Victoria: Let me show you what I've got. [Victoria shows the report contained in Exhibit 9–4.] All I did was multiply the costs per client-visit by the number of client-visits you actually had in March for the variable costs. That allowed me to come up with a better benchmark for what the variable costs should have been.

Rick: That's what you labeled the "budget based on 5,200 client-visits"?

Victoria: That's right. Your original budget was based on 5,000 client-visits, so it understated what the variable overhead costs should be when you actually serve 5,200 customers.

Rick: That's clear enough. These variances aren't quite as shocking as the variances on my first report.

Victoria: Yes, but you still have an unfavorable variance of $1,500 for client gratuities.

Rick: I know how that happened. In March there was a big Democratic Party fundraising dinner that I forgot about when I prepared the March budget. Everyone in the film industry was there.

Victoria: Even Arnold Schwarzenegger?

Rick: Well, all the Democrats were there. At any rate, to fit all of our regular clients in, we had to push them through here pretty fast. Everyone still got top-rate service, but I felt pretty bad about not being able to spend as much time with each customer. I wanted to give my customers a little extra something to compensate them for the less personal service, so I ordered a lot of flowers which I gave away by the bunch.

Victoria: With the prices you charge, Rick, I am sure the gesture was appreciated.

Rick: One thing bothers me about the report. Why are some of my actual fixed costs different from what I budgeted? Doesn't fixed mean that they are not supposed to change?

Victoria: We call these costs *fixed* because they shouldn't be affected by *changes in the level of activity*. However, that doesn't mean that they can't change for other reasons. For example, your utilities bill, which includes natural gas for heating, varies with the weather.

Rick: I can see that. March was warmer than normal, so my utilities bill was lower than I had expected.

Victoria: The use of the term *fixed* also suggests to people that the cost can't be controlled, but that isn't true. It is often easier to control fixed costs than variable costs. For example, it would be fairly easy for you to change your insurance bill by adjusting the amount of insurance you carry. It would be much more difficult for you to have much of an impact on the variable electric bill, which is a necessary part of serving customers.

Rick: I think I understand, but it *is* confusing.

Victoria: Just remember that a cost is called variable if it is proportional to activity; it is called fixed if it does not depend on the level of activity. However, fixed costs can change for reasons having nothing to do with changes in the level of activity. And controllability has little to do with whether a cost is variable or fixed. Fixed costs are often more controllable than variable costs.

Using the flexible budget approach, Rick Manzi now has a much better way of assessing whether overhead costs are under control. The analysis is not so simple, however, in companies that provide a variety of products and services. The number of units produced or customers served may not be an adequate measure of overall activity. For example, does it make sense to count a Sony floppy diskette, worth less than a dollar, as equivalent to a large-screen Sony TV? If the number of units produced is used as a measure of overall activity, then the floppy diskette and the large-screen TV would be counted as equivalent. Clearly, the number of units produced (or customers served) may not be appropriate as an overall measure of activity when the organization has a variety of products or services; a common denominator may be needed.

The Measure of Activity—A Critical Choice

What should be used as the measure of activity when the company produces a variety of products and services? At least three factors are important in selecting an activity base for an overhead flexible budget:

1. The variable overhead costs should be related to the activity base on a cause-and-effect basis. Changes in the activity base should cause, or at least be highly correlated with, changes in the variable overhead costs in the flexible budget. Ideally, the variable overhead costs in the flexible budget should vary in direct proportion to changes in the activity base. For example, in a carpentry shop specializing in handmade wood furniture, the costs of miscellaneous supplies such as glue, wooden

dowels, and sandpaper can be expected to vary with the number of direct labor-hours. Direct labor-hours would therefore be a good measure of activity to use in a flexible budget for the costs of such supplies.

2. The activity base should not be expressed in dollars or other currency. For example, direct labor cost is usually a poor choice for an activity base in flexible budgets. Changes in wage rates affect the activity base but do not usually result in a proportionate change in overhead. For example, we would not ordinarily expect to see a 5% increase in the consumption of glue in a carpentry shop if the workers receive a 5% increase in pay. Therefore, it is normally best to use physical rather than financial measures of activity in flexible budgets.

3. The activity base should be simple and easily understood. A base that is not easily understood will probably result in confusion and misunderstanding. It is difficult to control costs if people don't understand the reports or do not accept them as valid.

Gas Stations

IN BUSINESS

IS

Generally, convenience store and car wash sales are directly related to the volume of gas sold by a gas station. Consequently, the gas sales budget would be the starting point for the entire budgeting process. Factors that should be considered when forecasting gas sales might include: the prior year's sales, changes in the volume of traffic in the area, changes in the environment that impact access to the station (for example, road construction or the installation of median barriers that impede access), and changes in the number or type of gas stations that are operating in the immediate vicinity.

When a flexible budgeting approach is used, the manager of a gas station might choose to prepare one overhead budget or separate overhead budgets for each of its segments (gas station, convenience store, and car wash). The decision would be based on whether or not the same activity base could be used for the three segments.

Source: Steven P. Smalley, "Measuring the Convenience of Gas Stations," *Appraisal Journal,* October 1999, p. 339.

VARIABLE OVERHEAD VARIANCES—A CLOSER LOOK

A special problem arises when the flexible budget is based on *hours* of activity (such as direct labor-hours) rather than on units of product or number of customers served. The problem relates to whether actual hours or standard hours should be used to develop the flexible budget on the performance report.

Concept 9–2

The Problem of Actual versus Standard Hours

The nature of the problem can best be seen through a specific example. MicroDrive Corporation makes precision computer disk-drive motors for military applications. Data concerning the company's variable manufacturing overhead costs are shown in Exhibit 9–5.

MicroDrive Corporation uses machine-hours as the activity base in its flexible budget because the company's managers believe most of the overhead costs are driven by machine-hours. Based on the budgeted production of 25,000 motors and the standard of 2 machine-hours per motor, the budgeted level of activity was 50,000 machine-hours. However, actual production for the year was only 20,000 motors, and 42,000 hours of machine time were used to produce these motors. According to the standard, only 40,000 hours of machine time should have been used (40,000 machine-hours = 2 machine-hours per motor × 20,000 motors).

In preparing an overhead performance report for the year, MicroDrive could use the 42,000 machine-hours actually worked during the year *or* the 40,000 machine-hours that should have been worked according to the standard. If the actual hours are used, only a

EXHIBIT 9–5

MicroDrive Corporation Data

Budgeted production	25,000 motors
Actual production	20,000 motors
Standard machine-hours per motor	2 machine-hours per motor
Budgeted machine-hours (2 × 25,000)	50,000 machine-hours
Standard machine-hours allowed for the actual production (2 × 20,000)	40,000 machine-hours
Actual machine-hours	42,000 machine-hours
Variable overhead costs per machine-hour:	
Indirect labor	$0.80 per machine-hour
Lubricants	$0.30 per machine-hour
Power	$0.40 per machine-hour
Actual total variable overhead costs:	
Indirect labor	$36,000
Lubricants	11,000
Power	24,000
Total actual variable overhead cost	$71,000

spending variance will be computed. If the standard hours are used, both a spending *and* an efficiency variance will be computed. Both of these approaches are illustrated in the following sections.

Spending Variance Alone

LEARNING OBJECTIVE 3

Use the flexible budget to prepare a variable overhead performance report containing only a spending variance.

If MicroDrive Corporation bases its overhead performance report on the 42,000 machine-hours actually worked during the year, then the performance report will show only a spending variance for variable overhead. A performance report prepared in this way is shown in Exhibit 9–6.

The formula for the spending variance was introduced in the preceding chapter. That formula is:

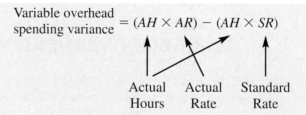

Or, in factored form:

$$\text{Variable overhead spending variance} = AH(AR - SR)$$

The report in Exhibit 9–6 is structured around the first, or unfactored, format.

Interpreting the Spending Variance   The variable overhead spending variance is useful only if the cost driver for variable overhead really is the actual hours worked. Then the flexible budget based on the actual hours worked is a valid benchmark that tells us how much *should* have been spent in total on variable overhead items during the period. The actual overhead costs would be larger than this benchmark, resulting in an unfavorable variance, if either (1) the variable overhead items cost more to purchase than the standards allow or (2) more variable overhead items were used than the standards allow. So the spending variance includes both price and quantity variances. In principle, these variances could be separately reported, but this is seldom done. Ordinarily, the price element in this variance will be small, so the variance will mainly be influenced by how efficiently variable overhead resources such as production supplies are used.

EXHIBIT 9–6

MICRODRIVE CORPORATION Variable Overhead Performance Report For the Year Ended December 31				

Budget allowances are based on 42,000 machine-hours actually worked

Comparing the budget against actual overhead cost yields only a spending variance

Budgeted machine-hours 50,000
Actual machine-hours 42,000
Standard machine-hours allowed 40,000

Overhead Costs	Cost Formula (per machine-hour)	Actual Costs Incurred 42,000 Machine-Hours (AH × AR)	Budget Based on 42,000 Machine-Hours (AH × SR)	Spending Variance
Variable overhead costs:				
Indirect labor	$0.80	$36,000	$33,600*	$2,400 U
Lubricants	0.30	11,000	12,600	1,600 F
Power	0.40	24,000	16,800	7,200 U
Total variable overhead cost	$1.50	$71,000	$63,000	$8,000 U

*42,000 machine-hours × $0.80 per machine-hour = $33,600. Other budget allowances are computed in the same way.

Both Spending and Efficiency Variances

If management of MicroDrive Corporation wants both a spending and an efficiency variance for variable overhead, then it should compute budget allowances for *both* the 40,000 machine-hour and the 42,000 machine-hour levels of activity. A performance report prepared in this way is shown in Exhibit 9–7.

Note from Exhibit 9–7 that the spending variance is the same as the spending variance shown in Exhibit 9–6. The performance report in Exhibit 9–7 has simply been expanded to include an efficiency variance as well. Together, the spending and efficiency variances make up the total variance.

Interpreting the Efficiency Variance   Like the variable overhead spending, the variable overhead efficiency variance is useful only if the cost driver for variable overhead really is the actual hours worked. Then any increase in hours actually worked should result in additional variable overhead costs. Consequently, if too many hours were used to create the actual output, this is likely to result in an increase in variable overhead. The variable overhead efficiency variance is an estimate of the effect on variable overhead costs of inefficiency in the use of the base (i.e., hours). In a sense, the term *variable overhead efficiency variance* is a misnomer. It seems to suggest that it measures the efficiency with which variable overhead resources were used. It does not. It is an estimate of the indirect effect on variable overhead costs of inefficiency in the use of the activity base.

Recall from the preceding chapter that the variable overhead efficiency variance is a function of the difference between the actual hours incurred and the hours that should have been used to produce the period's output:

LEARNING OBJECTIVE 4

Use the flexible budget to prepare a variable overhead performance report containing both a spending and an efficiency variance.

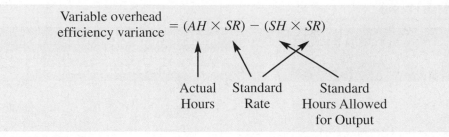

$$\text{Variable overhead efficiency variance} = (AH \times SR) - (SH \times SR)$$

Or, in factored form:

$$\text{Variable overhead efficiency variance} = SR(AH - SH)$$

If more hours are worked than are allowed at standard, then the overhead efficiency variance will be unfavorable. However, as discussed above, the inefficiency is not in the use of overhead *but rather in the use of the base itself.*

This point can be illustrated by looking again at Exhibit 9–7. Two thousand more machine-hours were used during the period than should have been used to produce the period's output. Each of these hours presumably required the incurrence of $1.50 of variable overhead cost, resulting in an unfavorable variance of $3,000 (2,000 machine-hours × $1.50 per machine-hour = $3,000). Although this $3,000 variance is called an overhead efficiency variance, it could better be called a machine-hours efficiency variance, since it results from using too many machine-hours rather than from inefficient use of overhead

EXHIBIT 9–7

						Breakdown of the Total Variance	

MICRODRIVE CORPORATION
Variable Overhead Performance Report
For the Year Ended December 31

Budget allowances are based on 40,000 machine-hours— the time it *should have taken* to produce the year's output of 20,000 motors—as well as on the 42,000 *actual* machine-hours worked

This approach yields both a spending and an efficiency variance

Budgeted machine-hours 50,000
Actual machine-hours 42,000
Standard machine-hours allowed 40,000

		(1)	(2)	(3)	(4)		
Overhead Costs	**Cost Formula (per machine-hour)**	**Actual Costs Incurred 42,000 Machine-Hours (AH × AR)**	**Budget Based on 42,000 Machine-Hours (AH × SR)**	**Budget Based on 40,000 Machine-Hours (SH × SR)**	**Total Variance (1) – (3)**	**Spending Variance (1) – (2)**	**Efficiency Variance (2) – (3)**
Variable overhead costs:							
Indirect labor	$0.80	$36,000	$33,600*	$32,000	$ 4,000 U	$2,400 U	$1,600 U
Lubricants	0.30	11,000	12,600	12,000	1,000 F	1,600 F	600 U
Power	0.40	24,000	16,800	16,000	8,000 U	7,200 U	800 U
Total variable overhead cost	$1.50	$71,000	$63,000	$60,000	$11,000 U	$8,000 U	$3,000 U

*42,000 machine-hours × $0.80 per machine-hour = $33,600. Other budget allowances are computed in the same way.

resources. However, the term *overhead efficiency variance* is so firmly ingrained in practice that a change is unlikely. Even so, be careful to interpret the variance with a clear understanding of what it really measures.

Control of the Efficiency Variance   Who is responsible for control of the overhead efficiency variance? Since the variance really reflects efficiency in the utilization of the base underlying the flexible budget, whoever is responsible for control of this base is responsible for control of the variance. If the base is direct labor-hours, then the supervisor responsible for the use of labor time will be responsible for any overhead efficiency variance.

Activity-Based Costing and the Flexible Budget

It is unlikely that all of the variable overhead in a complex organization is driven by a single factor such as the number of units produced or the number of labor-hours or machine-hours. Activity-based costing provides a way of recognizing a variety of overhead cost drivers and thereby increasing the accuracy of the costing system. In activity-based costing, each overhead cost pool has its own measure of activity. The actual spending in each overhead cost pool can be independently evaluated using the techniques discussed in this chapter. The only difference is that the cost formulas for variable overhead costs will be stated in terms of different kinds of activities instead of all being stated in terms of units or a common measure of activity such as direct labor-hours or machine-hours. If done properly, activity-based costing can greatly enhance the usefulness of overhead performance reports by recognizing multiple causes of overhead costs. But the usefulness of overhead performance reports depends on how carefully the reports are done. In particular, managers must take care to separate the variable from the fixed costs in the flexible budgets.[1]

Pools within Pools

Caterpillar, Inc., a manufacturer of heavy equipment and a pioneer in the development and use of activity-based costing, separates its overhead costs into three large pools—the logistics cost pool, the manufacturing cost pool, and the general cost pool. In turn, these three cost pools are subdivided into scores of activity centers, with each center having its own flexible budget from which variable and fixed overhead rates are developed. "The many manufacturing cost center rates are the unique elements that set Caterpillar's system apart from simple cost systems."

Source: Lou F. Jones, "Product Costing at Caterpillar," *Management Accounting* 72, no. 8, p. 39.

[1]See Mak and Roush, "Managing Activity Costs with Flexible Budgeting and Variance Analysis," *Accounting Horizons,* September 1996, pp. 141–146, for an insightful discussion of activity-based costing and overhead variance analysis.

OVERHEAD RATES AND FIXED OVERHEAD ANALYSIS

The detailed analysis of fixed overhead differs considerably from the analysis of variable overhead, simply because of the difference in the nature of the costs involved. To provide a background for our discussion, we will first review briefly the need for, and computation of, predetermined overhead rates. This review will be helpful, since the predetermined overhead rate plays a major role in fixed overhead analysis. We will then show how fixed overhead variances are computed and make some observations as to their usefulness to managers.

Flexible Budgets and Overhead Rates

Fixed costs come in large, indivisible pieces that by definition do not change with changes in the level of activity within the relevant range. This creates a problem in product costing, since a given amount of fixed overhead cost spread over a small number of units will result in a higher cost per unit than if the same amount of cost is spread over a large number of units. Consider the data in the following table:

Month	(1) Total Fixed Overhead Cost	(2) Number of Units Produced	(3) Average Fixed Cost per Unit (1) ÷ (2)
January	$6,000	1,000	$6.00
February	$6,000	1,500	$4.00
March	$6,000	800	$7.50

Notice that the large number of units produced in February results in a low unit cost ($4.00), whereas the small number of units produced in March results in a high unit cost ($7.50). This problem arises only in connection with the fixed portion of overhead, since by definition the variable portion of overhead remains constant on a per unit basis, rising and falling in total proportionately with changes in the activity level. Most managers feel that the fixed portion of unit cost should be stabilized so that a single unit cost can be used throughout the year. As we learned in Chapter 2, this stability can be accomplished through use of the predetermined overhead rate.

Throughout the remainder of this chapter, we will be analyzing the fixed overhead costs of MicroDrive Corporation. To assist us in that task, the flexible budget of the company—including fixed costs—is displayed in Exhibit 9–8. Note that the total fixed overhead costs amount to $300,000 within the range of activity in the flexible budget.

Denominator Activity   The formula that we used in Chapter 2 to compute the predetermined overhead rate was:

$$\text{Predetermined overhead rate} = \frac{\text{Estimated total manufacturing overhead cost}}{\text{Estimated total units in the base (MH, DLH, etc.)}}$$

The estimated total units in the base in the formula for the predetermined overhead rate is called the **denominator activity.** Recall from our discussion in Chapter 2 that once an estimated activity level (denominator activity) has been chosen, it remains unchanged throughout the year, even if the actual activity turns out to be different from what was estimated. The reason for not changing the denominator is to maintain stability in the amount of overhead applied to each unit of product regardless of when it is produced during the year.

Computing the Overhead Rate   When we discussed predetermined overhead rates in Chapter 2, we didn't explain how the estimated total manufacturing cost was

EXHIBIT 9–8

Overhead Costs	Cost Formula (per machine-hour)	Activity (in machine-hours)			
		40,000	45,000	50,000	55,000
MICRODRIVE CORPORATION Flexible Budgets at Various Levels of Activity					
Variable overhead costs:					
Indirect labor	$0.80	$ 32,000	$ 36,000	$ 40,000	$ 44,000
Lubricants	0.30	12,000	13,500	15,000	16,500
Power	0.40	16,000	18,000	20,000	22,000
Total variable overhead cost	$1.50	60,000	67,500	75,000	82,500
Fixed overhead costs:					
Depreciation		100,000	100,000	100,000	100,000
Supervisory salaries		160,000	160,000	160,000	160,000
Insurance		40,000	40,000	40,000	40,000
Total fixed overhead cost		300,000	300,000	300,000	300,000
Total overhead cost		$360,000	$367,500	$375,000	$382,500

determined. This figure can be derived from the flexible budget. Once the denominator level of activity has been chosen, the flexible budget can be used to determine the total amount of overhead cost that should be incurred at that level of activity. The predetermined overhead rate can then be computed using the following variation on the basic formula for the predetermined overhead rate:

$$\text{Predetermined overhead rate} = \frac{\text{Overhead from the flexible budget at the denominator level of activity}}{\text{Denominator level of activity}}$$

To illustrate, refer to MicroDrive Corporation's flexible budget for manufacturing overhead in Exhibit 9–8. Suppose that the budgeted activity level for the year is 50,000 machine-hours and that this will be used as the denominator activity in the formula for the predetermined overhead rate. The numerator in the formula is the estimated total overhead cost of $375,000 when the activity is 50,000 machine-hours. This figure is taken from the flexible budget in Exhibit 9–8. Thus, the predetermined overhead rate for Micro-Drive Corporation will be computed as follows:

$$\frac{\$375,000}{50,000 \text{ MHs}} = \$7.50 \text{ per machine-hour (MH)}$$

Or the company can break its predetermined overhead rate down into variable and fixed elements rather than using a single combined figure:

$$\text{Variable element:} \frac{\$75,000}{50,000 \text{ MHs}} = \$1.50 \text{ per machine-hour (MH)}$$

$$\text{Fixed element:} \frac{\$300,000}{50,000 \text{ MHs}} = \$6 \text{ per machine-hour (MH)}$$

For every standard machine-hour of operation, work in process will be charged with $7.50 of overhead, of which $1.50 will be variable overhead and $6.00 will be fixed overhead. If a disk-drive motor should take two machine-hours to complete, then its cost will include $3 of variable overhead and $12 of fixed overhead, as shown on the following standard cost card:

Standard Cost Card—Per Motor	
Direct materials (assumed)	$14
Direct labor (assumed)	6
Variable overhead (2 machine-hours at $1.50 per machine-hour)	3
Fixed overhead (2 machine-hours at $6 per machine-hour)	12
Total standard cost per motor	$35

In sum, the flexible budget provides the estimated overhead cost needed to compute the predetermined overhead rate. Thus, the flexible budget plays a key role in determining the amount of fixed and variable overhead cost that will be charged to units of product.

Know Your Costs

Understanding the difference between fixed and variable costs can be critical. Kennard T. Wing, of OMG Center for Collaborative Learning, reports that a large health care system made the mistake of classifying all its costs as variable. As a consequence, when volume dropped, managers felt that costs should be cut proportionately and more than 1,000 people were laid off—even though "the workload of most of them had no direct relation to patient volume. The result was that morale of the survivors plummeted and within a year the system was scrambling to replace not only those it had let go, but many others who had quit. The point is, the accounting systems we design and implement really do affect management decisions in significant ways. A system built on a bad model of the business will either not be used or, if used, will lead to bad decisions."

Source: Kennard T. Wing, "Using Enhanced Cost Models in Variance Analysis for Better Control and Decision Making," *Management Accounting Quarterly*, Winter 2000, pp. 27–35.

Overhead Application in a Standard Cost System

To understand the fixed overhead variances, it is necessary first to understand how overhead is applied to work in process in a standard cost system. Recall from Chapter 2 that we applied overhead to work in process on the basis of actual hours of activity (multiplied by the predetermined overhead rate). This procedure was correct, since at the time we were dealing with a normal cost system.[2] However, we are now dealing with a standard cost system. In such a system, overhead is applied to work in process on the basis of the *standard hours allowed for the output of the period* rather than on the basis of the actual number of hours worked. This point is illustrated in Exhibit 9–9. In a standard cost system, every unit of product bears the same amount of overhead cost, regardless of how much time the unit actually requires for processing.

The Fixed Overhead Variances

To illustrate the computation of fixed overhead variances, we will refer again to the data for MicroDrive Corporation.

Denominator activity in machine-hours	50,000	
Budgeted fixed overhead costs	$300,000	
Fixed portion of the predetermined overhead rate (computed earlier)		$6 per machine-hour

---

[2]Normal cost systems are discussed in Chapter 2.

Normal Cost System		Standard Cost System	
Manufacturing Overhead		Manufacturing Overhead	
Actual overhead costs incurred	Applied overhead costs: Actual hours × Predetermined overhead rate	Actual overhead costs incurred	Applied overhead costs: Standard hours allowed for output × Predetermined overhead rate
Under- or overapplied overhead		Under- or overapplied overhead	

EXHIBIT 9–10

Computation of the Fixed
Overhead Variances

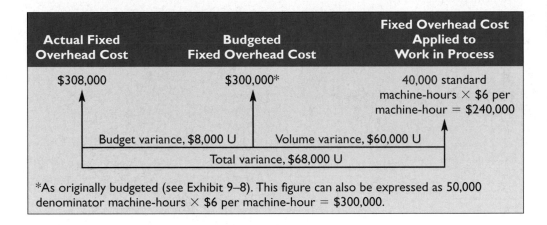

Actual Fixed Overhead Cost	Budgeted Fixed Overhead Cost	Fixed Overhead Cost Applied to Work in Process
$308,000	$300,000*	40,000 standard machine-hours × $6 per machine-hour = $240,000
	Budget variance, $8,000 U	Volume variance, $60,000 U
	Total variance, $68,000 U	

*As originally budgeted (see Exhibit 9–8). This figure can also be expressed as 50,000 denominator machine-hours × $6 per machine-hour = $300,000.

Let us assume that the following actual operating results were recorded for the year:

Actual machine-hours	42,000
Standard machine-hours allowed*	40,000
Actual fixed overhead costs:	
Depreciation	$100,000
Supervisory salaries	172,000
Insurance	36,000
Total actual fixed overhead cost	$308,000

*For the actual production of the year.

From these data, two variances can be computed for fixed overhead—a *budget variance* and a *volume variance*. The variances are shown in Exhibit 9–10.

Notice from the exhibit that overhead has been applied to work in process on the basis of 40,000 standard hours allowed for the output of the year rather than on the basis of 42,000 actual hours worked. As stated earlier, this keeps unit costs from being affected by variations in efficiency.

The Budget Variance—A Closer Look

The **budget variance** is the difference between the actual fixed overhead costs incurred during the period and the original budgeted fixed overhead costs for the period. It can be computed as shown in Exhibit 9–10 or by using the following formula:

$$\text{Budget variance} = \text{Actual fixed overhead cost} - \text{Budgeted fixed overhead cost}$$

EXHIBIT 9–11

Fixed Overhead Costs on the
Overhead Performance Report

	MICRODRIVE CORPORATION Overhead Performance Report For the Year Ended December 31			
Budgeted machine-hours .... 50,000 Actual machine-hours .... 42,000 Standard machine-hours allowed 40,000				
Overhead Costs	**Cost Formula (per machine-hour)**	**Actual Costs 42,000 Machine-Hours**	**Budget Based on 42,000 Machine-Hours**	**Spending or Budget Variance**
Variable overhead costs:				
Indirect labor	$0.80	$ 36,000	$ 33,600	$ 2,400 U
Lubricants	0.30	11,000	12,600	1,600 F
Power	0.40	24,000	16,800	7,200 U
Total variable overhead cost	$1.50	71,000	63,000	8,000 U
Fixed overhead costs:				
Depreciation		100,000	100,000	0
Supervisory salaries		172,000	160,000	12,000 U
Insurance		36,000	40,000	4,000 F
Total fixed overhead cost		308,000	300,000	8,000 U
Total overhead cost		$379,000	$363,000	$16,000 U

Applying this formula to MicroDrive Corporation, the budget variance would be as follows:

$$\$308,000 - \$300,000 = \$8,000 \text{ U}$$

The variances computed for the fixed costs at Rick's Hairstyling in Exhibit 9–4 are all budget variances, since they represent the difference between the actual fixed overhead cost and the budgeted fixed overhead cost.

An expanded overhead performance report for MicroDrive Corporation appears in Exhibit 9–11. This report now includes the budget variances for fixed overhead as well as the spending variances for variable overhead that were in Exhibit 9–6.

The budget variances for fixed overhead can be very useful, since they represent the difference between how much *should* have been spent (according to the original budget) and how much was actually spent. For example, supervisory salaries has a $12,000 unfavorable variance. There should be some explanation for this large variance. Was it due to an increase in salaries? Was it due to overtime? Was another supervisor hired? If so, why was another supervisor hired?

IN BUSINESS

The Value of Safety

Companies in the trucking industry have an average profit margin of only about 2%. Safety Solutions, Inc., a company that provides loss prevention and safety consulting services, claims that trucking companies can increase their profit margins to 5% by incurring *additional* overhead costs. How can this be?

Safety Solutions, Inc., claims that trucking companies with effective safety programs are less likely to receive large fines and often incur lower insurance costs. In addition, drivers are more likely to remain with companies with safer records, thus reducing hiring and training costs. Further, a reputation for safety may attract additional customers. Safety Solutions recommends investing in a formal safety program. In addition to ensuring ongoing compliance with government regulations, the safety program should include monitoring equipment and extensive preventative maintenance.

Source: "The Operating Margin of Safety (Safety in the Trucking Industry)," *Oregon Business,* August 1999, p. 22.

The Volume Variance—A Closer Look

The **volume variance** is a measure of facility utilization. The variance arises whenever the standard hours allowed for the output of a period are different from the denominator activity level that was planned when the period began. It can be computed as shown in Exhibit 9–10 or using the following formula:

$$\text{Volume variance} = \begin{matrix}\text{Fixed portion of}\\ \text{the predetermined}\\ \text{overhead rate}\end{matrix} \times \left(\begin{matrix}\text{Denominator}\\ \text{hours}\end{matrix} - \begin{matrix}\text{Standard hours}\\ \text{allowed}\end{matrix}\right)$$

Applying this formula to MicroDrive Corporation, the volume variance would be computed as follows:

$$\$6 \text{ per MH } (50,000 \text{ MHs} - 40,000 \text{ MHs}) = \$60,000 \text{ U}$$

Note that this computation agrees with the volume variance as shown in Exhibit 9–10. As stated earlier, the volume variance is a measure of utilization of facilities. An unfavorable variance, as above, means that the company operated at an activity level *below* that planned for the period. A favorable variance would mean that the company operated at an activity level *greater* than that planned for the period.

It is important to note that the volume variance does not measure over- or underspending. A company normally would incur the same dollar amount of fixed overhead cost regardless of whether the period's activity was above or below the planned (denominator) level. In short, the volume variance is an activity-related variance. It is explainable only by activity and is controllable only through activity.

To summarize:

1. If the denominator activity and the standard hours allowed for the output of the period are the same, then there is no volume variance.
2. If the denominator activity is greater than the standard hours allowed for the output of the period, then the volume variance is unfavorable, signifying a lower utilization of available facilities than was planned.
3. If the denominator activity is less than the standard hours allowed for the output of the period, then the volume variance is favorable, signifying a higher utilization of available facilities than was planned.

Vice President of Production

DECISION MAKER

One of the company's factories produces a single product. The factory recently reported a significant unfavorable volume variance for the year. Sales for that product were less than anticipated. What should you do?

Graphic Analysis of Fixed Overhead Variances

Graphic analysis can provide insights into the budget and volume variances. A graph containing these variances is presented in Exhibit 9–12.

As shown in the graph, fixed overhead cost is applied to work in process at the predetermined rate of $6 for each standard hour of activity. (The applied-cost line is the

EXHIBIT 9–12

Graphic Analysis of Fixed
Overhead Variances

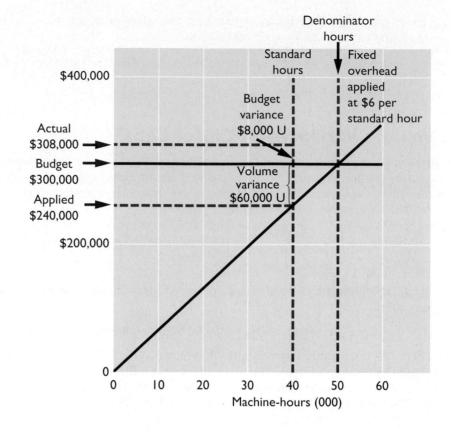

upward-sloping line on the graph.) Since a denominator level of 50,000 machine-hours was used in computing the $6 rate, the applied-cost line crosses the budget-cost line at exactly the 50,000 machine-hour point. If the denominator hours and the standard hours allowed for the output are the same, there can be no volume variance. It is only when the standard hours differ from the denominator hours that a volume variance can arise.

In the case at hand, the standard hours allowed for the actual output (40,000 hours) are less than the denominator hours (50,000 hours). The result is an unfavorable volume variance, since less cost was applied to production than was originally budgeted. If the situation had been reversed and the standard hours allowed for the actual output had exceeded the denominator hours, then the volume variance on the graph would have been favorable.

CONCEPT CHECK ✓

3. A company's actual and budgeted fixed overhead are $220,000 and $200,000, respectively. The fixed portion of the predetermined overhead rate is $8 per unit. How many units was the predetermined overhead rate based on?
   a.   20,000 units
   b.   25,000 units
   c.   30,000 units
   d.   35,000 units
4. Referring to the facts in question 3 above, what is the fixed overhead volume variance if 32,000 units were actually produced?
   a. $56,000 favorable
   b. $56,000 unfavorable
   c. $75,000 unfavorable
   d. $75,000 favorable

Cautions in Fixed Overhead Analysis

A volume variance for fixed overhead arises because when applying the costs to work in process, we act *as if* the fixed costs were variable and depended on activity. This point can be seen from the graph in Exhibit 9–12. Notice from the graph that the fixed overhead costs are applied to work in process at a rate of $6 per hour *as if* they were variable. Treating these costs as if they were variable is necessary for product costing purposes, but some real dangers lurk here. Managers can easily be misled into thinking of the fixed costs as if they were *in fact* variable.

Keep clearly in mind that fixed overhead costs come in large, indivisible pieces. Expressing fixed costs on a unit or per hour basis, though necessary for product costing for external reports, is artificial. Increases or decreases in activity in fact have no effect on total fixed costs within the relevant range of activity. Even though fixed costs are expressed on a unit or per hour basis, they are *not* proportional to activity. In a sense, the volume variance is the error that occurs as a result of treating fixed costs as variable costs in the costing system.

Overhead Variances and Under- or Overapplied Overhead Cost

Four variances relating to overhead cost have been computed for MicroDrive Corporation in this chapter. These four variances are as follows:

Variable overhead spending variance (p. 391)	$ 8,000 U
Variable overhead efficiency variance (p. 392)	3,000 U
Fixed overhead budget variance (p. 397)	8,000 U
Fixed overhead volume variance (p. 397)	60,000 U
Total overhead variance	$79,000 U

Recall from Chapter 2 that under- or overapplied overhead is the difference between the amount of overhead applied to products and the actual overhead costs incurred during a period. Basically, the overhead variances we have computed in this chapter break the under- or overapplied overhead down into variances that can be used by managers for control purposes. *The sum of the overhead variances equals the under- or overapplied overhead cost for a period.*

Furthermore, in a standard cost system, unfavorable variances are equivalent to underapplied overhead and favorable variances are equivalent to overapplied overhead. Unfavorable variances occur because more was spent on overhead than the standards allow. Underapplied overhead occurs when more was spent on overhead than was applied to products during the period. But in a standard costing system, the standard amount of overhead allowed is exactly the same amount of overhead applied to products. Therefore, in a standard costing system, unfavorable variances and underapplied overhead are the same thing, as are favorable variances and overapplied overhead.

For MicroDrive Corporation, the total overhead variance was $79,000 unfavorable. Therefore, its overhead cost was underapplied by $79,000 for the year. To solidify this point in your mind, *carefully study the review problem at the end of the chapter!* This review problem provides a comprehensive summary of overhead analysis, including the computation of under- or overapplied overhead cost in a standard cost system.

Budget Analyst

Your company is in the process of implementing an activity-based costing program and plans to use the flexible approach to budgeting. To aid in the analysis of the factory overhead once these plans are in place, how should the under- or overapplied overhead be analyzed? Who should be held responsible for each of the variances?

YOU DECIDE

SUMMARY

LO1   Prepare a flexible budget and explain the advantages of the flexible budget approach over the static budget approach.

A flexible budget shows what costs should be as a function of the level of activity. A flexible budget provides a better benchmark for evaluating how well costs have been controlled than the static budget approved at the beginning of the period. Some costs should be different from the amounts budgeted at the beginning of the period simply because the level of activity is different from what was expected. The flexible budget takes this fact into account, whereas the static budget does not.

LO2   Prepare a performance report for both variable and fixed overhead costs using the flexible budget approach.

A flexible budget performance report compares actual costs to what the costs should have been, given the actual level of activity for the period. Variable costs are flexed (i.e., adjusted) for the actual level of activity. This is done by multiplying the cost per unit of activity by the actual level of activity. Fixed costs, at least within the relevant range, are not adjusted for the level of activity. The total cost for a fixed cost item is carried over from the static budget without adjustment.

LO3   Use the flexible budget to prepare a variable overhead performance report containing only a spending variance.

The spending variance for a variable overhead item is computed by comparing the actual cost incurred to the amount that should have been spent, based on the actual direct labor-hours or machine-hours of the period.

LO4   Use the flexible budget to prepare a variable overhead performance report containing both a spending and an efficiency variance.

As stated above, the spending variance for a variable overhead item is computed by comparing the actual cost incurred to the amount that should have been spent, based on the actual direct labor-hours or machine-hours of the period. The efficiency variance is computed by comparing the cost that should have been incurred for the actual direct labor-hours or machine-hours of the period to the cost that should have been incurred for the actual level of *output* of the period.

LO5   Compute the predetermined overhead rate and apply overhead to products in a standard cost system.

In a standard cost system, overhead is applied to products based on the standard hours allowed for the actual output of the period. This differs from a normal cost system in which overhead is applied to products based on the actual hours of the period.

LO6   Compute and interpret the fixed overhead budget and volume variances.

The fixed overhead budget variance is the difference between the actual total fixed overhead costs incurred for the period and the budgeted total fixed overhead costs. This variance measures how well fixed overhead costs were controlled.

The fixed overhead volume variance is the difference between the fixed overhead applied to production using the predetermined overhead rate and the budgeted total fixed overhead. A favorable variance occurs when the standard hours allowed for the actual output exceed the hours assumed when the predetermined overhead rate was computed. An unfavorable variance occurs when the standard hours allowed for the actual output is less than the hours assumed when the predetermined overhead rate was computed.

GUIDANCE ANSWERS TO *DECISION MAKER* AND *YOU DECIDE*

Vice President of Production (p. 399)

An unfavorable fixed overhead volume variance means that the factory is operating below the activity level that was planned for the year. You should meet with the vice president of sales to determine why demand was less than planned. Was production part of the problem? Were orders delivered late? Were customers quoted lead times that were too long? Could production help increase demand by improving the quality of the product and the services provided to customers? If sales are declining and are not expected to rebound, you should consider how to make use of the excess capacity in this factory. You might consider whether the factory could be reconfigured to produce another product or if a section of the factory could be leased to another company.

Budget Analyst (p. 401)

The under- or overapplied overhead should be broken into its four components: (1) the variable overhead spending variance, (2) the variable overhead efficiency variance, (3) the fixed overhead budget variance, and (4) the fixed overhead volume variance.

The person who purchases the variable overhead items (such as lubricants) and the supervisor who directs and/or controls the employees who are classified as indirect labor are responsible for the variable overhead spending variance. Whoever is responsible for the control of the activity base that is used to apply overhead should be responsible for the control of the variable overhead efficiency variance. The person responsible for negotiating the purchase of the fixed overhead items (such as rent and insurance) and the supervisor who directs and/or controls the support staff are responsible for the fixed overhead budget variance. The fixed overhead volume variance does not indicate that the company has overspent or underspent; it is a measure of utilization of available plant facilities. As such, the person responsible for determining the level of activity for the plant would be responsible for this variance.

GUIDANCE ANSWERS TO CONCEPT CHECKS

1. **Choice c.** A flexible budget is most useful for controlling variable costs, not fixed costs.
2. **Choice c.** The flexible budget at 12,000 units would be (12,000 units × $3 per unit variable overhead) + $70,000 of fixed overhead = $106,000.
3. **Choice b.** Budgeted fixed overhead of $200,000 ÷ $8 per unit fixed overhead rate = 25,000 units.
4. **Choice a.** The fixed overhead volume variance is (32,000 units − 25,000 units) × $8 per unit = $56,000 favorable.

REVIEW PROBLEM: OVERHEAD ANALYSIS

(This problem provides a comprehensive review of Chapter 9, including the computation of under- or overapplied overhead and its breakdown into the four overhead variances.)

Data for the manufacturing overhead of Aspen Company are given below:

Overhead Costs	Cost Formula (per machine-hour)	Machine-Hours		
		5,000	6,000	7,000
Variable overhead costs:				
Supplies	$0.20	$ 1,000	$ 1,200	$ 1,400
Indirect labor	0.30	1,500	1,800	2,100
Total variable overhead cost	$0.50	2,500	3,000	3,500
Fixed overhead costs:				
Depreciation		4,000	4,000	4,000
Supervision		5,000	5,000	5,000
Total fixed overhead cost		9,000	9,000	9,000
Total overhead cost		$11,500	$12,000	$12,500

Five hours of machine time are required per unit of product. The company has set denominator activity for the coming period at 6,000 machine-hours (or 1,200 units). The computation of the predetermined overhead rate would be as follows:

$$\text{Total: } \frac{\$12,000}{6,000 \text{ MHs}} = \$2.00 \text{ per machine-hour}$$

$$\text{Variable element: } \frac{\$3,000}{6,000 \text{ MHs}} = \$0.50 \text{ per machine-hour}$$

$$\text{Fixed element: } \frac{\$9,000}{6,000 \text{ MHs}} = \$1.50 \text{ per machine-hour}$$

Assume the following *actual* results for the period:

Number of units produced	1,300 units
Actual machine-hours	6,800 machine-hours
Standard machine-hours allowed*	6,500 machine-hours
Actual variable overhead cost	$4,200
Actual fixed overhead cost	$9,400

*1,300 units × 5 machine-hours per unit.

Therefore, the company's Manufacturing Overhead account would appear as follows at the end of the period:

Manufacturing Overhead

Actual overhead costs	13,600*	13,000†	Applied overhead costs
Underapplied overhead	600		

*$4,200 variable + $9,400 fixed = $13,600.
†6,500 standard machine-hours × $2 per machine-hour = $13,000.
In a standard cost system, overhead is applied on the basis of standard hours, not actual hours.

Required:

Analyze the $600 underapplied overhead in terms of:

1. A variable overhead spending variance.
2. A variable overhead efficiency variance.
3. A fixed overhead budget variance.
4. A fixed overhead volume variance.

Solution to Review Problem

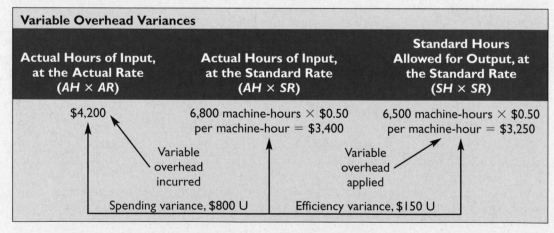

These same variances in the alternative format would be as follows:

Variable overhead spending variance:

$$\text{Spending variance} = (AH \times AR) - (AH \times SR)$$
$$(\$4,200^*) - (6,800 \text{ machine-hours} \times \$0.50 \text{ per machine-hour}) = \$800 \text{ U}$$

*$AH \times AR$ equals the total actual cost for the period.

Variable overhead efficiency variance:

$$\text{Efficiency variance} = SR(AH - SH)$$
$$\$0.50 \text{ per machine-hour } (6,800 \text{ machine-hours} - 6,500 \text{ machine-hours}) = \$150 \text{ U}$$

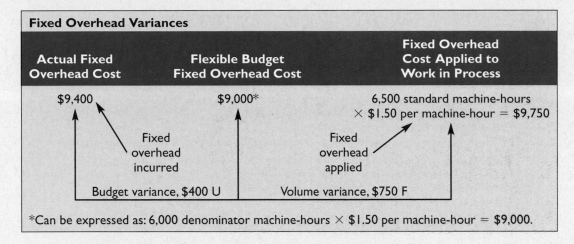

Fixed Overhead Variances

Actual Fixed Overhead Cost	Flexible Budget Fixed Overhead Cost	Fixed Overhead Cost Applied to Work in Process
$9,400	$9,000*	6,500 standard machine-hours × $1.50 per machine-hour = $9,750
	Fixed overhead incurred	Fixed overhead applied
Budget variance, $400 U		Volume variance, $750 F

*Can be expressed as: 6,000 denominator machine-hours × $1.50 per machine-hour = $9,000.

These same variances in the alternative format would be as follows:

Fixed overhead budget variance:

$$\frac{\text{Budget}}{\text{variance}} = \frac{\text{Actual fixed}}{\text{overhead cost}} - \frac{\text{Budgeted}}{\text{fixed overhead cost}}$$
$$\$9,400 - \$9,000 = \$400 \text{ U}$$

Fixed overhead volume variance:

$$\text{Volume variance} = \frac{\text{Fixed portion}}{\text{of the predetermined}} \times \left(\frac{\text{Denominator}}{\text{hours}} - \frac{\text{Standard}}{\text{hours}} \right)$$
$$\text{overhead rate}$$
$$\$1.50 \text{ per machine-hour } (6,000 \text{ machine-hours} - 6,500 \text{ machine-hours}) = \$750 \text{ F}$$

Summary of Variances

A summary of the four overhead variances is given below:

Variable overhead:	
Spending variance	$800 U
Efficiency variance	150 U
Fixed overhead:	
Budget variance	400 U
Volume variance	750 F
Underapplied overhead	$600

Notice that the $600 summary variance figure agrees with the underapplied balance in the company's Manufacturing Overhead account. This agreement verifies the accuracy of our variance analysis.

GLOSSARY

Budget variance   A measure of the difference between the actual fixed overhead costs incurred during the period and budgeted fixed overhead costs as contained in the flexible budget. (p. 397)

Denominator activity   The activity figure used to compute the predetermined overhead rate. (p. 394)

Flexible budget   A budget that is designed to cover a range of activity and that can be used to develop budgeted costs at any point within that range to compare to actual costs incurred. (p. 382)

Static budget   A budget created at the beginning of the budgeting period that is valid only for the planned level of activity. (p. 382)

Volume variance   The variance that arises whenever the standard hours allowed for the output of a period are different from the denominator activity level that was used to compute the predetermined overhead rate. (p. 399)

QUESTIONS

9–1   What is a static budget?

9–2   What is a flexible budget and how does it differ from a static budget?

9–3   In comparing flexible budget data with actual data in a performance report for variable overhead, what variance(s) will be produced if the flexible budget data are based on actual hours worked? On both actual hours worked and standard hours allowed?

9–4   What is meant by the term *standard hours allowed?*

9–5   How does the variable manufacturing overhead spending variance differ from the materials price variance?

9–6   Why is the term *overhead efficiency variance* a misnomer?

9–7   What is meant by the term *denominator level of activity?*

9–8   Why do we apply overhead to work in process on the basis of standard hours allowed in this chapter when we applied it on the basis of actual hours in Chapter 2? What is the difference in costing systems between the two chapters?

9–9   What does the fixed overhead budget variance measure?

9–10 Under what circumstances would you expect the volume variance to be favorable? Unfavorable? Does the variance measure deviations in spending for fixed overhead items? Explain.

9–11 The under- or overapplied overhead can be broken down into what four variances?

9–12 If factory overhead is overapplied for August, would you expect the total of the overhead variances to be favorable or unfavorable?

BRIEF EXERCISES

BRIEF EXERCISE 9–1   Preparing a Flexible Budget   (LO1)

An incomplete flexible budget for overhead is given below for AutoPutz, Gmbh, a German company that owns and operates a large automatic carwash facility near Köln. The German currency is the euro, which is denoted by €.

Overhead Costs	Cost Formula (per car)	Activity (cars) 7,000	8,000	9,000
AUTOPUTZ, GMBH Flexible Budget				
Variable overhead costs:				
Cleaning supplies	?	?	€ 6,000	?
Electricity	?	?	4,800	?
Maintenance	?	?	1,200	?
Total variable overhead costs	?	?	?	?
Fixed overhead costs:				
Operator wages		?	10,000	?
Depreciation		?	20,000	?
Rent		?	8,000	?
Total fixed overhead costs		?	?	?
Total overhead costs		?	?	?

Required:
Fill in the missing data in the flexible budget.

BRIEF EXERCISE 9–2   Using a Flexible Budget   (LO1)

Refer to the data in Brief Exercise 9–1. AutoPutz, Gmbh's owner-manager would like to prepare a budget for August assuming an activity level of 8,200 cars.

Required:
Prepare a static budget for August. Use Exhibit 9–1 in the chapter as your guide.

BRIEF EXERCISE 9–3   Flexible Budget Performance Report   (LO2)

Refer to the data in Brief Exercise 9–1. AutoPutz, Gmbh's actual level of activity during August was 8,300 cars, although the owner had constructed his static budget for the month assuming the level of activity would be 8,200 cars. The actual overhead costs incurred during August are given below:

	Actual Costs Incurred for 8,300 Cars
Variable overhead costs:	
Cleaning supplies	€6,350
Electricity	€4,865
Maintenance	€1,600
Fixed overhead costs:	
Operator wages	€10,050
Depreciation	€20,200
Rent	€8,000

Required:
Prepare a flexible budget performance report for both the variable and fixed overhead costs for August. Use Exhibit 9–4 in the chapter as your guide.

BRIEF EXERCISE 9–4   Variable Overhead Performance Report with Just a Spending Variance   (LO3)

Jessel Corporation bases its variable overhead performance report on the actual direct labor-hours of the period. Data concerning the most recent year that ended on December 31 appear below:

Budgeted direct labor-hours	42,000
Actual direct labor-hours	44,000
Standard direct labor-hours allowed	45,000
Cost formula (per direct labor-hour):	
Indirect labor	$0.90
Supplies	$0.15
Electricity	$0.05
Actual costs incurred:	
Indirect labor	$42,000
Supplies	$6,900
Electricity	$1,800

Required:
Prepare a variable overhead performance report using the format in Exhibit 9–6. Compute just the variable overhead spending variances; do not compute the variable overhead efficiency variances.

BRIEF EXERCISE 9–5   Variable Overhead Performance Report with Both Spending and Efficiency Variances   (LO4)

Refer to the data in Brief Exercise 9–4 for Jessel Corporation. Management would like to compute both spending and efficiency variances for variable overhead in the company's variable overhead performance report.

Required:
Prepare a variable overhead performance report using the format in Exhibit 9–7. Compute both the variable overhead spending variances and the overhead efficiency variances.

BRIEF EXERCISE 9–6   Applying Overhead in a Standard Costing System   (LO5)

Mosbach Corporation has a standard cost system in which it applies overhead to products based on the standard direct labor-hours allowed for the actual output of the period. Data concerning the most recent year appear below:

Variable overhead cost per direct labor-hour	$3.50
Total fixed overhead cost per year	$600,000
Budgeted standard direct labor-hours (denominator level of activity)	80,000
Actual direct labor-hours	84,000
Standard direct labor-hours allowed for the actual output	82,000

Required:
1. Compute the predetermined overhead rate for the year.
2. Determine the amount of overhead that would be applied to the output of the period.

BRIEF EXERCISE 9–7   Fixed Overhead Variances   (LO6)
Lusive Corporation has a standard cost system in which it applies overhead to products based on the standard direct labor-hours allowed for the actual output of the period. Data concerning the most recent year appear below:

Total budgeted fixed overhead cost for the year	$400,000
Actual fixed overhead cost for the year	$394,000
Budgeted standard direct labor-hours (denominator level of activity)	50,000
Actual direct labor-hours	51,000
Standard direct labor-hours allowed for the actual output	48,000

Required:
1. Compute the fixed portion of the predetermined overhead rate for the year.
2. Compute the fixed overhead budget variance and volume variance.

EXERCISES

EXERCISE 9–8   Prepare a Flexible Budget   (LO1)
The cost formulas for Swan Company's manufacturing overhead costs are given below. The costs cover a range of 8,000 to 10,000 machine-hours.

Overhead Costs	Cost Formula
Supplies	$0.20 per machine-hour
Indirect labor	$10,000 plus $0.25 per machine-hour
Utilities	$0.15 per machine-hour
Maintenance	$7,000 plus $0.10 per machine-hour
Depreciation	$8,000

(handwritten: var, mix, var, mix, fix)

Required:
Prepare a flexible budget in increments of 1,000 machine-hours. Include all costs in your flexible budget.

EXERCISE 9–9   Variable Overhead Performance Report   (LO2, LO3)
The variable portion of Whaley Company's flexible budget for manufacturing overhead is given below:

Overhead Costs	Cost Formula (per machine-hour)	Machine-Hours		
		10,000	18,000	24,000
Utilities	$1.20	$12,000	$21,600	$ 28,800
Supplies	0.30	3,000	5,400	7,200
Maintenance	2.40	24,000	43,200	57,600
Rework time	0.60	6,000	10,800	14,400
Total variable overhead costs	$4.50	$45,000	$81,000	$108,000

During a recent period, the company recorded 16,000 machine-hours of activity. The variable overhead costs incurred were as follows:

Utilities	$20,000
Supplies	$4,700
Maintenance	$35,100
Rework time	$12,300

The budgeted activity for the period had been 18,000 machine-hours.

Required:
1. Prepare a variable overhead performance report for the period. Indicate whether variances are favorable (F) or unfavorable (U). Show only a spending variance on your report.
2. Discuss the significance of the variances. Might some variances be the result of others? Explain.

EXERCISE 9–10   Variable Overhead Performance Report with Both Spending and Efficiency Variances   (LO4)

The check-clearing office of San Juan Bank is responsible for processing all checks that come to the bank for payment. Managers at the bank believe that variable overhead costs are essentially proportional to the number of labor-hours worked in the office, so labor-hours are used as the activity base for budgeting and for performance reports for variable overhead costs in the department. Data for October, the most recent month, appear below:

Budgeted labor-hours	865
Actual labor-hours	860
Standard labor-hours allowed for the actual number of checks processed	880

	Cost Formula (per labor-hour)	Actual Costs Incurred in October
Variable overhead costs:		
Office supplies	$0.15	$ 146
Staff coffee lounge	0.05	124
Indirect labor	3.25	2,790
Total variable overhead cost	$3.45	$3,060

Required:
Prepare a variable overhead performance report for October for the check-clearing office that includes both spending and efficiency variances. Use Exhibit 9–7 as a guide.

EXERCISE 9–11   Predetermined Overhead Rates   (LO5)

Operating at a normal level of 24,000 direct labor-hours, Trone Company produces 8,000 units of product. The direct labor wage rate is $12.60 per hour. Two pounds of raw materials go into each unit of product at a cost of $4.20 per pound. A flexible budget is used to plan and control overhead costs:

Flexible Budget Data				
	Cost Formula (per direct labor-hour)	Direct Labor-Hours		
Overhead Costs		20,000	22,000	24,000
Variable costs	$1.60	$ 32,000	$ 35,200	$ 38,400
Fixed costs		84,000	84,000	84,000
Total overhead costs		$116,000	$119,200	$122,400

Required:

1. Using 24,000 direct labor-hours as the denominator activity, compute the predetermined overhead rate and break it down into fixed and variable elements.
2. Complete the standard cost card below for one unit of product:

> Direct materials, 2 pounds at $4.20 per pound $8.40
> Direct labor, ? . . . .   ?
> Variable overhead, ? . . . .   ?
> Fixed overhead, ? . . . .   ?
> Total standard cost per unit . . . . $?

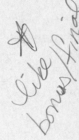

EXERCISE 9–12   Predetermined Overhead Rate; Overhead Variances   (LO4, LO5, LO6)

Weller Company's flexible budget for manufacturing overhead (in condensed form) follows:

Overhead Costs	Cost Formula (per machine-hour)	Machine-Hours		
		8,000	9,000	10,000
Variable costs	$1.05	$ 8,400	$ 9,450	$10,500
Fixed costs		24,800	24,800	24,800
Total overhead costs		$33,200	$34,250	$35,300

The following information is available for a recent period:

a.   The denominator activity of 8,000 machine-hours was chosen to compute the predetermined overhead rate.
b.   At the 8,000 standard machine-hours level of activity, the company should produce 3,200 units of product.
c.   The company's actual operating results were as follows:

> Number of units produced   3,500
> Actual machine-hours   8,500
> Actual variable overhead costs $9,860
> Actual fixed overhead costs $25,100

Required:

1. Compute the predetermined overhead rate and break it down into variable and fixed cost elements.
2. What were the standard hours allowed for the year's output?
3. Compute the variable overhead spending and efficiency variances and the fixed overhead budget and volume variances.

EXERCISE 9–13   Fixed Overhead Variances   (LO6)

Selected operating information on three different companies for a recent period is given below:

	Company		
	X	Y	Z
Full-capacity direct labor-hours	20,000	9,000	10,000
Budgeted direct labor-hours*	19,000	8,500	8,000
Actual direct labor-hours	19,500	8,000	9,000
Standard direct labor-hours allowed for actual output	18,500	8,250	9,500

*Denominator activity for computing the predetermined overhead rate.

Required:
For each company, state whether the volume variance would be favorable or unfavorable; also, explain in each case *why* the volume variance would be favorable or unfavorable.

EXERCISE 9–14   Variable Overhead Performance Report   (LO4)
Ronson Products, Ltd., an Australian company, has the following cost formulas (expressed in Australian dollars) for variable overhead costs in one of its machine shops:

Variable Overhead Cost	Cost Formula (per machine-hour)
Supplies	$0.70
Power	1.20
Lubrication	0.50
Wearing tools	3.10
Total	$5.50

During July, the machine shop was scheduled to work 3,200 machine-hours and to produce 16,000 units of product. The standard machine time per unit of product is 0.2 hours. A severe storm during the month forced the company to close for several days, which reduced the level of output for the month. Actual results for July were as follows:

Actual machine-hours worked	2,700
Actual number of units produced	14,000

Actual costs for July were as follows:

Variable Overhead Cost	Total Actual Cost	Per Machine-Hour
Supplies	$ 1,836	$0.68
Power	3,348	1.24
Lubrication	1,485	0.55
Wearing tools	8,154	3.02
Total	$14,823	$5.49

Required:
Prepare an overhead performance report for the machine shop for July. Use column headings in your report as shown below:

Overhead Item	Cost Formula (per MH)	Actual Costs Incurred, 2,700 MHs	Budget Based on ? MHs	Budget Based on ? MHs	Total Variance	Spending Variance	Efficiency Variance

PROBLEMS

PROBLEM 9–15   Preparing a Performance Report   (LO2, LO3, LO6)
Several years ago, Edwards Inc. developed a comprehensive budgeting system for profit planning and control purposes. The line supervisors have been very happy with the system and with the reports being prepared on their performance, but both middle and upper management have expressed considerable dissatisfaction with the information being generated by the system.

A typical manufacturing overhead performance report for a recent period is shown on the following page:

CHECK FIGURE
(3) Total of spending and budget variances: $6,300 U

Static

EDWARDS INC.
Overhead Performance Report—Machining Department
For the Quarter Ended June 30

	Actual	Budget	Variance
Machine-hours	20,000	24,000	
Variable overhead costs:			
Indirect materials	$ 15,200 *14,000*	$ 16,800	$1,600 F
Rework time	4,200	4,800	600 F
Utilities	34,200	36,000	1,800 F
Machine setup	9,400	9,600	200 F
Total variable overhead cost	63,000	67,200	4,200 F
Fixed overhead costs:			
Maintenance	64,300	65,000	700 F
Inspection	54,000	54,000	0
Total fixed overhead cost	118,300	119,000	700 F
Total overhead cost	$181,300	$186,200	$4,900 F

.70 per m/H

After receiving a copy of this overhead performance report, the supervisor of the Machining Department stated, "These reports are super. It makes me feel really good to see how well things are going in my department. I can't understand why those people upstairs complain so much."

The budget data above are for the original planned level of activity for the quarter.

Required:
1. The company's vice president is uneasy about the performance reports being prepared and would like you to evaluate their usefulness to the company.
2. What changes, if any, would you recommend be made in the overhead performance report above in order to give better insight into how well the supervisor is controlling costs?
3. Prepare a new overhead performance report for the quarter, incorporating any changes you suggested in (2) above. (Include both the variable and the fixed costs in your report.)

CHECK FIGURE

(1) Flexible budget total cost at 950 liters: $56,810

PROBLEM 9–16   Preparing a Performance Report   (LO2, LO3)

The Antigua Blood Bank, a private charity partly supported by government grants, is located on the Caribbean island of Antigua. The Blood Bank has just finished its operations for September, which was a particularly busy month due to a powerful hurricane that hit neighboring islands causing many injuries. The hurricane largely bypassed Antigua, but residents of Antigua willingly donated their blood to help people on other islands. As a consequence, the Blood Bank collected and processed over 10% more blood than had been originally planned for the month.

A report prepared by a government official comparing actual costs to budgeted costs for the Blood Bank appears below. (The currency on Antigua is the East Caribbean dollar.) Continued support from the government depends on the Blood Bank's ability to demonstrate control over their costs.

ANTIGUA BLOOD BANK
Cost Control Report
For the Month Ended September 30

	Actual	Budget	Variance
Liters of blood collected	950	820	130
Variable costs:			
Medical supplies	$12,500	$10,660	$1,840 U
Lab tests	7,900	7,790	110 U
Refreshments for donors	6,700	5,740	960 U
Administrative supplies	2,300	2,050	250 U
Total variable cost	29,400	26,240	3,160 U

(continued)

(concluded)	Actual	Budget	Variance
Fixed costs:			
Staff salaries	15,000	15,000	0
Equipment depreciation	6,800	6,600	200 U
Rent	4,000	4,000	0
Utilities	880	810	70 U
Total fixed cost	26,680	26,410	270 U
Total cost	$56,080	$52,650	$3,430 U

The managing director of the Blood Bank was very unhappy with this report, claiming that his costs were higher than expected due to the emergency on the neighboring islands. He also pointed out that the additional costs had been fully covered by payments from grateful recipients on the other islands. The government official who prepared the report countered that all of the figures had been submitted by the Blood Bank to the government; he was just pointing out that actual costs were a lot higher than promised in the budget.

Required:

1. Prepare a new performance report for September using the flexible budget approach. (Note: Even though some of these costs might be classified as direct costs rather than as overhead, the flexible budget approach can still be used to prepare a flexible budget performance report.)
2. Do you think any of the variances in the report you prepared should be investigated? Why?

PROBLEM 9–17 Comprehensive Standard Cost (LO4, LO6)

Luque Corporation uses a standard cost system and sets predetermined overhead rates on the basis of direct labor-hours. The following data are taken from the company's budget for the current year:

CHECK FIGURE
(1) Standard cost: $94.60
(3) Volume variance: $17,850 F

Denominator activity (direct labor-hours)	65,000
Variable manufacturing overhead cost	$143,000
Fixed manufacturing overhead cost	$341,250

The standard cost card for the company's only product is given below:

Direct materials, 4 yards @ $7.80 per yard	$31.20
Direct labor, 4 DLHs @ $8.40 per DLH	33.60
Manufacturing overhead	29.80
Standard cost per unit	$94.60

During the year, the company produced 17,100 units of product and incurred the following costs:

Materials purchased 69,200 yards @ $8.00 per yard	$553,600
Materials used in production (in yards)	69,000
Direct labor cost incurred 66,500 DLHs @ $8.60 per DLH	$571,900
Variable manufacturing overhead cost incurred	$141,800
Fixed manufacturing overhead cost incurred	$345,700

Required:

1. Redo the standard cost card in a clearer, more usable format by detailing the variable and fixed overhead cost elements.
2. Prepare an analysis of the variances for materials and labor for the year.
3. Prepare an analysis of the variances for variable and fixed overhead for the year.
4. What effect, if any, does the choice of a denominator activity level have on unit standard costs? Is the volume variance a controllable variance from a spending point of view? Explain.

PROBLEM 9–18 Applying Overhead; Overhead Variances (LO4, LO5, LO6)

Pawdewski, S.A., of Cracow, Poland, is a major producer of classic Polish sausage. The company uses a standard cost system to help control costs. Overhead is applied to production on the basis of labor-hours. According to the company's flexible budget, the following manufacturing overhead costs should be incurred at an activity level of 74,000 labor-hours (the denominator activity level):

Variable overhead costs	PZ 229,400
Fixed overhead costs	414,400
Total overhead cost	PZ 643,800

(handwritten: LH 3.10 V 5.60 F PZ 8.70)

The currency in Poland is the zloty, which is denoted here by PZ.

During the most recent year, the following operating results were recorded:

Activity:	
Actual labor-hours worked	66,000
Standard labor-hours allowed for output	68,000
Cost:	
Actual variable overhead cost incurred	PZ 210,300
Actual fixed overhead cost incurred	PZ 401,200

At the end of the year, the company's Manufacturing Overhead account contained the following data:

Manufacturing Overhead

Actual	611,500	591,600	Applied
	19,900		

Management would like to determine the cause of the PZ 19,900 underapplied overhead.

Required:

1. Compute the predetermined overhead rate. Break the rate down into variable and fixed cost elements.
2. Show how the PZ 591,600 applied in the Manufacturing Overhead account was computed.
3. Analyze the PZ 19,900 underapplied overhead in terms of the variable overhead spending and efficiency variances and the fixed overhead budget and volume variances.
4. Explain the meaning of each variance that you computed in (3) above.

PROBLEM 9–19 Comprehensive Standard Cost Variances (LO4, LO6)

"Wonderful! Not only did our salespeople do a good job in meeting the sales budget this year, but our production people did a good job in controlling costs as well," said Anna Jones, president of Hess Inc. "Our $34,110 overall manufacturing cost variance is only 1.47% of the $2,320,000 standard cost of products sold during the year. That's well within the 3% limit set by management for acceptable variances. It looks like everyone will be in line for a bonus this year."

The company produces and sells a single product. A standard cost card for the product follows:

Standard Cost Card—per Unit of Product	
Direct materials, 1.3 feet at $8.00 per foot	$10.40
Direct labor, 1.5 DLHs at $13.00 per DLH	19.50
Variable overhead, 1.5 DLHs at $1.20 per DLH	1.80
Fixed overhead, 1.5 DLHs at $3.30 per DLH	4.95
Standard cost per unit	$36.65

The following additional information is available for the year just completed:

a. The company manufactured 64,000 units of product during the year.
b. A total of 87,400 feet of material was purchased during the year at a cost of $8.05 per foot. All of this material was used to manufacture the 64,000 units. There were no beginning or ending inventories for the year.

c. The company worked 99,800 direct labor-hours during the year at a cost of $12.80 per direct labor-hour.

d. Overhead is applied to products on the basis of direct labor-hours. Data relating to manufacturing overhead costs follow:

Denominator activity level (direct labor-hours)	84,500
Budgeted fixed overhead costs (from the overhead flexible budget)	$278,850
Actual variable overhead costs incurred	$117,300
Actual fixed overhead costs incurred	$281,400

Required:

1. Compute the direct materials price and quantity variances for the year.
2. Compute the direct labor rate and efficiency variances for the year.
3. For manufacturing overhead compute:
    a. The variable overhead spending and efficiency variances for the year.
    b. The fixed overhead budget and volume variances for the year.
4. Total the variances you have computed, and compare the net amount with the $34,110 mentioned by the president. Do you agree that bonuses should be given to everyone for good cost control during the year? Explain.

PROBLEM 9–20   Using Fixed Overhead Variances   (LO6)

The standard cost card for the single product manufactured by Bailey Industries is given below:

CHECK FIGURE
(1) Standard DLHs
    allowed: 48,500 DLHs

Standard Cost Card—per Unit	
Direct materials, 80.0 yards at $0.50 per yard	$ 40.00
Direct labor, 5.0 DLHs at $12.50 per DLH	62.50
Variable overhead, 5.0 DLHs at $8.50 per DLH	42.50
Fixed overhead, 5.0 DLHs at $12.00 per DLH	60.00
Total standard cost per unit	$205.00

Manufacturing overhead is applied to production on the basis of direct labor-hours. During the year, the company worked 95,000 direct labor-hours and manufactured 9,700 units of product. Selected data relating to the company's fixed manufacturing overhead cost for the year are shown below:

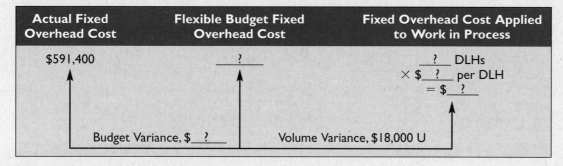

Required:

1. What were the standard direct labor-hours allowed for the year's production?
2. What was the amount of fixed overhead cost contained in the flexible budget for the year?
3. What was the fixed overhead budget variance for the year?
4. What denominator activity level did the company use in setting the predetermined overhead rate for the year?

PROBLEM 9–21   Relations Among Fixed Overhead Variances   (LO6)

Selected information relating to East Shore Inc.'s operations for the most recent year is given below:

CHECK FIGURE
(3) Volume variance:
    $5,600 U

Activity:	
Denominator activity (machine-hours)	84,000
Standard machine-hours allowed per unit	8.0
Number of units produced	10,400

(continued)

> (concluded)
> Costs:
>   Actual fixed overhead costs incurred $584,000
>   Fixed overhead budget variance .... $4,000 F

The company applies overhead cost to products on the basis of machine-hours.

Required:
1. What were the standard machine-hours allowed for the actual production?
2. What was the fixed portion of the predetermined overhead rate?
3. What was the volume variance?

CHECK FIGURE
(2) Total of spending and
    budget variances:
    $400 F

PROBLEM 9–22   Flexible Budget and Overhead Performance Report   (LO1, LO2, LO3)
You have just been hired by Seward Corporation, the manufacturer of a revolutionary new garage door opening device. Sam Ballard, the president, has asked that you review the company's costing system and "do what you can to help us get better control of our manufacturing overhead costs." You find that the company has never used a flexible budget, and you suggest that preparing such a budget would be an excellent first step in overhead planning and control.

After much effort and analysis, you are able to determine the following cost formulas for the company's normal operating range of 15,000 to 25,000 machine-hours each month:

Overhead Costs	Cost Formula
Utilities	$2.40 per machine-hour
Maintenance	$1.20 per machine-hour plus $65,000 per month
Machine setup...............	$0.50 per machine-hour
Indirect labor	$1.10 per machine-hour plus $210,000 per month
Depreciation................	$60,000 per month

To show the president how the flexible budget concept works, you have gathered the following actual cost data for the most recent month, June, in which the company worked 18,000 machine-hours and produced 32,000 units:

Utilities	$ 42,600
Maintenance	88,100
Machine setup	9,200
Indirect labor	228,100
Depreciation	60,200
Total cost	$428,200

The only variance in the fixed costs for the month was for depreciation, which was increased as a result of a purchase of new equipment.

The company had originally planned to work 25,000 machine-hours during June.

Required:
1. Prepare a flexible budget for the company in increments of 5,000 hours.
2. Prepare an overhead performance report for the company for June. (Use the format illustrated in Exhibit 9–11.)
3. What additional information would you need to compute an overhead efficiency variance for the company?

CHECK FIGURE
(2) Total variance:
    $8,900 F

PROBLEM 9–23   Overhead Performance Report   (LO2, LO4)
Debra Herman, supervisor of the Assembly Department for Greenlake Industries, was visibly upset after being reprimanded for her department's poor performance over the prior month. The department's performance report is given on the following page:

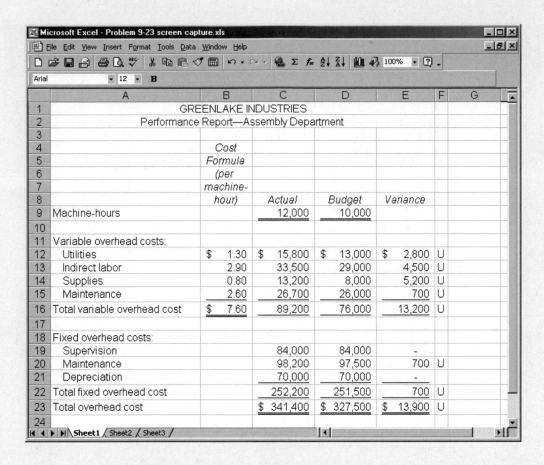

The spreadsheet shows:

Microsoft Excel - Problem 9-23 screen capture.xls

	A	B	C	D	E	F	G
1			GREENLAKE INDUSTRIES				
2			Performance Report—Assembly Department				
3							
4		Cost					
5		Formula					
6		(per					
7		machine-					
8		hour)	Actual	Budget	Variance		
9	Machine-hours		12,000	10,000			
10							
11	Variable overhead costs:						
12	Utilities	$ 1.30	$ 15,800	$ 13,000	$ 2,800 U		
13	Indirect labor	2.90	33,500	29,000	4,500 U		
14	Supplies	0.80	13,200	8,000	5,200 U		
15	Maintenance	2.60	26,700	26,000	700 U		
16	Total variable overhead cost	$ 7.60	89,200	76,000	13,200 U		
17							
18	Fixed overhead costs:						
19	Supervision		84,000	84,000	-		
20	Maintenance		98,200	97,500	700 U		
21	Depreciation		70,000	70,000	-		
22	Total fixed overhead cost		252,200	251,500	700 U		
23	Total overhead cost		$ 341,400	$ 327,500	$ 13,900 U		
24							

"I just can't understand all the red ink," said Debra Herman to Keith Johnson, supervisor of another department. "When the boss called me in, I thought he was going to give me a pat on the back because I know for a fact that my department worked more efficiently last month than it has ever worked before. Instead, he tore me apart. I thought for a minute that it might be over the supplies that were stolen out of our warehouse last month. But they only amounted to a couple of thousand dollars, and just look at this report. *Everything* is unfavorable, and I don't even know why."

The budget for the Assembly Department had called for production of 2,000 units last month, which is equal to a budgeted activity level of 10,000 machine-hours (at a standard time of 5.0 hours per unit). Actual production in the Assembly Department for the month was 2,600 units.

Required:
1. Evaluate the overhead performance report given above and explain why the variances are all unfavorable.
2. Prepare a new overhead performance report that will help managers assess how well Debra Herman was able to control costs and enhance efficiency in the Assembly Department. (Hint: Exhibit 9–7 may be helpful in structuring your report; however, the report you prepare should include both variable and fixed costs.)
3. Would the supplies stolen out of the warehouse be included as part of the variable overhead spending variance or as part of the variable overhead efficiency variance for the month? Explain.

PROBLEM 9–24   Applying Overhead; Overhead Variances   (LO4, LO5, LO6)
Thomas Corporation manufactures a single product that requires a great deal of hand labor. Overhead cost is applied on the basis of direct labor-hours. The company's condensed flexible budget for manufacturing overhead is given below:

CHECK FIGURE
(2) Standard cost: $216.00
(4) Volume variance: $20,000 F

Overhead Costs	Cost Formula (per direct labor-hour)	Direct Labor-Hours		
		16,000	24,000	32,000
Variable costs	$6.00	$ 96,000	$144,000	$192,000
Fixed costs		120,000	120,000	120,000
Total overhead cost		$216,000	$264,000	$312,000

The company's product requires 4 pounds of material that has a standard cost of $8 per pound and 8 hours of direct labor time that has a standard rate of $12 per hour.

The company planned to operate at a denominator activity level of 24,000 direct labor-hours and to produce 3,000 units of product during the most recent year. Actual activity and costs for the year were as follows:

Number of units produced	3,500
Actual direct labor-hours worked	29,600
Actual variable overhead cost incurred	$168,800
Actual fixed overhead cost incurred	$124,000

Required:

1. Compute the predetermined overhead rate for the year. Break the rate down into variable and fixed elements.
2. Prepare a standard cost card for the company's product; show the details for all manufacturing costs on your standard cost card.
3. Do the following:
   a. Compute the standard hours allowed for the year's production
   b. Complete the following Manufacturing Overhead T-account for the year:

Manufacturing Overhead

?	?
?	?

4. Determine the reason for any under- or overapplied overhead for the year by computing the variable overhead spending and efficiency variances and the fixed overhead budget and volume variances.
5. Suppose the company had chosen 30,000 direct labor-hours as the denominator activity rather than 24,000 hours. State which, if any, of the variances computed in (4) above would have changed and explain how the variance(s) would have changed. No computations are necessary.

BUILDING YOUR SKILLS

TEAMWORK IN ACTION   (LO1, LO2)

Obtain a copy of your college or university's budget and actual results for the most recently completed year.

Required:

1. Determine the major assumptions used in the last budget (e.g., number of students; tuition per student; number of employees; increases in wages, salaries, benefits; changes in occupancy costs; etc.).
2. Compare the budgeted revenue amounts with the actual results. Try to determine the reasons for any differences.

3. Compare budgeted expenses with the actual results using the basic approach shown in Exhibit 9–4. Try to determine the reasons for any differences.

ANALYTICAL THINKING (LO4, LO5, LO6)

CHECK FIGURE
(5) $72,000 fixed
(16) $6,700 overapplied

A company that uses a standard cost system has provided the following data. The company's flexible budget for manufacturing overhead is based on standard machine-hours.

Item	
1. Denominator activity in machine-hours	18,000
2. Standard machine-hours allowed for units produced	?
3. Actual machine-hours worked	?
4. Flexible budget variable overhead per machine-hour	$1.60
5. Flexible budget fixed overhead (total)	?
6. Actual variable overhead cost	$30,000
7. Actual fixed overhead cost	$72,500
8. Variable overhead cost applied to production*	$31,200
9. Fixed overhead cost applied to production*	?
10. Variable overhead spending variance	?
11. Variable overhead efficiency variance	$800 U
12. Fixed overhead budget variance	$500 U
13. Fixed overhead volume variance	?
14. Variable portion of the predetermined overhead rate	?
15. Fixed portion of the predetermined overhead rate	?
16. Underapplied (or overapplied) overhead	?

*Based on standard machine-hours allowed for units produced.

Required:
Compute the unknown amounts. (Hint: One way to proceed would be to use the format for variance analysis found in Exhibit 8–7 for variable overhead and in Exhibit 9–10 for fixed overhead.)

COMMUNICATING IN PRACTICE   (LO1)

Use an online yellow pages directory such as www.comfind.com or www.athand.com to find a manufacturer in your area that has a website. Make an appointment with the controller or chief financial officer of the company. Before your meeting, find out as much as you can about the organization's operations from its website.

Required:
After asking the following questions, write a brief memorandum to your instructor that summarizes the information obtained from the company's website and addresses what you found out during your interview.

1. Are actual overhead costs compared to a static budget, to a flexible budget, or to something else?
2. Does the organization distinguish between variable and fixed overhead costs in its performance reports?
3. What are the consequences of unfavorable variances? Of favorable variances?

ETHICS CASE   (LO2)

Lance Prating is the controller of the Colorado Springs manufacturing facility of Advance Macro, Incorporated. Among the many reports that must be filed with corporate headquarters is the annual overhead performance report. The report covers an entire fiscal year, which ends on December 31, and is due at corporate headquarters shortly after the beginning of the new year. Prating does not like putting work off to the last minute, so just before Christmas he put together a preliminary draft of the overhead performance report. Some adjustments would later be required for the few transactions that occur between Christmas and New Year's Day. A copy of the preliminary draft report, which Prating completed on December 21, follows:

COLORADO SPRINGS MANUFACTURING FACILITY
Overhead Performance Report
December 21 Preliminary Draft

Budgeted machine-hours 100,000
Actual machine-hours 90,000

Overhead Costs	Cost Formula (per machine-hour)	Actual Costs for 90,000 Machine-Hours	Budget Based on 90,000 Machine-Hours	Spending or Budget Variance
Variable overhead costs:				
Power	$0.03	$ 2,840	$ 2,700	$ 140 U
Supplies	0.86	79,060	77,400	1,660 U
Abrasives	0.34	32,580	30,600	1,980 U
Total variable overhead cost	$1.23	114,480	110,700	3,780 U
Fixed overhead costs:				
Depreciation		228,300	226,500	1,800 U
Supervisory salaries		187,300	189,000	1,700 F
Insurance		23,000	23,000	0
Industrial engineering		154,000	160,000	6,000 F
Factory building lease		46,000	46,000	0
Total fixed overhead cost		638,600	644,500	5,900 F
Total overhead cost		$753,080	$755,200	$2,120 F

Tab Kapp, the general manager at the Colorado Springs facility, asked to see a copy of the preliminary draft report at 4:45 P.M. on December 23. Prating carried a copy of the report to Kapp's office where the following discussion took place:

Kapp: Ouch! Almost all of the variances on the report are unfavorable. The only thing that looks good at all are the favorable variances for supervisory salaries and for industrial engineering. How did we have an unfavorable variance for depreciation?

Prating: Do you remember that milling machine that broke down because the wrong lubricant was used by the machine operator?

Kapp: Only vaguely.

Prating: It turned out we couldn't fix it. We had to scrap the machine and buy a new one.

Kapp: This report doesn't look good. I was raked over the coals last year when we had just a few unfavorable variances.

Prating: I'm afraid the final report is going to look even worse.

Kapp: Oh?

Prating: The line item for industrial engineering on the report is for work we hired Sanchez Engineering to do for us on a contract basis. The original contract was for $160,000, but we asked them to do some additional work that was not in the contract. Under the terms of the contract, we have to reimburse Sanchez Engineering for the costs of the additional work. The $154,000 in actual costs that appear on the preliminary draft report reflects only their billings through December 21. The last bill they had sent us was on November 28, and they completed the project just last week. Yesterday I got a call from Maria over at Sanchez and she said they would be sending us a final bill for the project before the end of the year. The total bill, including the reimbursements for the additional work, is going to be . . .

Kapp: I am not sure I want to hear this.

Prating: $176,000.

Kapp: Ouch! Ouch! Ouch!

Prating: The additional work we asked them to do added $16,000 to the cost of the project.

Kapp: No way can I turn in a performance report with an overall unfavorable variance. They'll kill me at corporate headquarters. Call up Maria at Sanchez and ask her not to send the bill until after the first of the year. We have to have that $6,000 favorable variance for industrial engineering on the performance report.

Required:

What should Lance Prating do? Explain.

TAKING IT TO THE NET

As you know, the World Wide Web is a medium that is constantly evolving. Sites come and go and change without notice. To enable periodic update of site addresses, this problem has been posted to the textbook website (www.mhhe.com/bgn2e). After accessing the site, enter the Student Center and select this chapter. Select and complete the Taking It to the Net problem.

CHAPTER TEN

Decentralization

Centralizing Communications

Ingersoll-Rand, a global conglomerate that traces its roots to the early 1870s, has about 46,000 employees. The company has received numerous recognitions and awards, including being named the *Industryweek* Best Managed Company for several years in a row. Even so, the company decided that it needed to restructure its organization to effectively compete in the current economic environment.

Previously comprising 8 autonomous companies, Ingersoll-Rand now operates as 13 separate business units. To improve communications, its computer systems were integrated to provide information to managers and headquarters in real time. The company continues to operate in a decentralized fashion. Even though many of its functions have been centralized, such as purchasing, payroll, and accounts receivable and payable, decision making is still spread throughout the organization. For example, factory managers continue to be responsible for deciding what must be purchased. However, instead of directly issuing purchase orders to vendors, requisitions are communicated to headquarters, which then issues the purchase orders. As a result of this centralized approach to purchasing, the company has been able to negotiate better discounts with suppliers.

Analysts estimate the cost of the restructuring at $50 million. Don Janson, director of common administrative resources implementations at Ingersoll-Rand, predicts that the changes will pay for themselves within three years.

Sources: Ingersoll-Rand Company website; and Steve Konicki, "A Company Merges Its Many Units—Successfully," *Informationweek*, May 8, 2000, pp. 174–178.

LEARNING OBJECTIVES

After studying Chapter 10, you should be able to:

LO1 Compute the return on investment (ROI) and show how changes in sales, expenses, and assets affect an organization's ROI.

LO2 Compute residual income and understand the strengths and weaknesses of this method of measuring performance.

Once an organization grows beyond a few people, it becomes impossible for the top manager to make decisions about everything. For example, the CEO of the Hyatt Hotel chain cannot be expected to decide whether a particular hotel guest at the Hyatt Hotel on Maui should be allowed to check out later than the normal checkout time. To some degree, managers have to delegate decisions to those who are at lower levels in the organization. However, the degree to which decisions are delegated varies from organization to organization.

DECENTRALIZATION IN ORGANIZATIONS

A **decentralized organization** is one in which decision making is not confined to a few top executives but rather is spread throughout the organization, with managers at various levels making key operating decisions relating to their sphere of responsibility. Decentralization is a matter of degree, since all organizations are decentralized to some extent out of necessity. At one extreme, a strongly decentralized organization is one in which even the lowest-level managers and employees are empowered to make decisions. At the other extreme, in a strongly centralized organization, lower-level managers have little freedom to make a decision. Although most organizations fall somewhere between these two extremes, the trend is toward more and more decentralization.

Advantages and Disadvantages of Decentralization

Decentralization has many benefits, including:

1. Top management is relieved of much day-to-day problem solving and is left free to concentrate on strategy, on higher-level decision making, and on coordinating activities.
2. Decentralization provides lower-level managers with vital experience in making decisions. Without such experience, they would be ill-prepared to make decisions when they are promoted into higher-level positions.
3. Added responsibility and decision-making authority often results in increased job satisfaction. Responsibility, and the authority that goes with it, makes the job more interesting and provides greater incentives for people to put out their best efforts.
4. Lower-level managers generally have more detailed and up-to-date information about local conditions than top managers do. Therefore, the decisions of lower-level managers are often based on better information.
5. It is difficult to evaluate a manager's performance if the manager is not given much latitude in what he or she can do.

Decentralization has four major disadvantages:

1. Lower-level managers may make decisions without fully understanding the "big picture." While top-level managers typically have less detailed information about local operations than the lower-level managers, they usually have more information about the company as a whole and should have a better understanding of the company's strategy.
2. In a truly decentralized organization, there may be a lack of coordination among autonomous managers. This problem can be reduced by clearly defining the company's strategy and communicating it effectively throughout the organization.
3. Lower-level managers may have objectives that are different from the objectives of the entire organization. For example, some managers may be more interested in increasing the sizes of their departments than in increasing the profits of the

company.[1] To some degree, this problem can be overcome by designing performance evaluation systems that motivate managers to make decisions that are in the best interests of the company.

4. In a strongly decentralized organization, it may be more difficult to effectively spread innovative ideas. Someone in one part of the organization may have a terrific idea that would benefit other parts of the organization, but without strong central direction the idea may not be shared with, and adopted by, other parts of the organization.

Decentralization and Segment Reporting

Effective decentralization requires *segmental reporting*. In addition to the companywide income statement, reports are needed for individual segments of the organization. A **segment** is a part or activity of an organization about which managers would like cost, revenue, or profit data. Examples of segments include divisions of a company, sales territories, individual stores, service centers, manufacturing plants, marketing departments, individual customers, and product lines. A company's operations can be segmented in many ways. For example, a grocery store chain like Safeway or Kroger can segment its business by geographic region, by individual store, by the nature of the merchandise (i.e., green groceries, canned goods, paper goods), by brand name, and so on.

Cost, Profit, and Investment Centers

Decentralized companies typically categorize their business segments into cost centers, profit centers, and investment centers—depending on the responsibilities of the managers of the segments.[2]

Cost Center A **cost center** is a business segment whose manager has control over costs but not over revenue or investment funds. Service departments such as accounting, finance, general administration, legal, personnel, and so on are usually considered to be cost centers. In addition, manufacturing facilities are often considered to be cost centers. The managers of cost centers are expected to minimize cost while providing the level of services or the amount of products demanded by the other parts of the organization. For example, the manager of a production facility would be evaluated at least in part by comparing actual costs to how much the costs should have been for the actual number of units produced during the period. Standard cost variances and flexible budget variances such as those described in the preceding two chapters are often used to evaluate the performance of cost centers.

---

[1]There is a similar problem with top-level managers as well. The shareholders of the company have, in effect, decentralized by delegating their decision-making authority to the top managers. Unfortunately, top managers may abuse that trust by spending too much company money on palatial offices, rewarding themselves and their friends too generously, and so on. The issue of how to ensure that top managers act in the best interests of the owners of the company continues to puzzle experts. To a large extent, the owners rely on performance evaluation using return on investment and residual income measures as discussed later in the chapter and on bonuses and stock options. The stock market is also an important disciplining mechanism. If top managers squander the company's resources, the price of the company's stock will almost surely fall—resulting in a loss of prestige, bonuses, and possibly a job.

[2]Some companies classify business segments that are responsible mainly for generating revenue, such as an insurance sales office, as *revenue centers*. Other companies would consider this to be just another type of profit center, since costs of some kind (salaries, rent, utilities) are usually deducted from the revenues in the segment's income statement.

Segmenting a Company

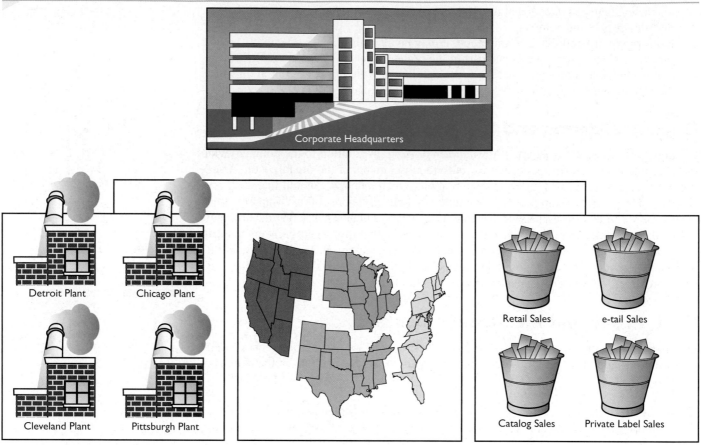

Corporate Headquarters

Detroit Plant   Chicago Plant

Cleveland Plant   Pittsburgh Plant

Segmenting by Plant

Segmenting by Geographic Territory

Retail Sales   e-tail Sales

Catalog Sales   Private Label Sales

Segmenting by Customer Channel

Profit Center In contrast to a cost center, a **profit center** is any business segment whose manager has control over both cost and revenue. Like a cost center, however, a profit center generally does not have control over investment funds. For example, the manager in charge of one of the Six Flags amusement parks would be responsible for both the revenues and costs, and hence the profits, of the amusement park but may not have control over major investments in the park. Profit center managers are often evaluated by comparing actual profit to targeted or budgeted profit.

Investment Center An **investment center** is any segment of an organization whose manager has control over cost, revenue, and investments in operating assets. For example, the vice president of the Truck Division at General Motors would have a great deal of discretion over investments in the division. The vice president of the Truck Division would be responsible for initiating investment proposals, such as funding research into more fuel-efficient engines for sport-utility vehicles. Once the proposal has been approved by the top level of managers at General Motors and the board of directors, the vice president of the Truck Division would then be responsible for making sure that the investment pays off. Investment center managers are usually evaluated using return on investment or residual income measures as discussed later in the chapter.

Responsibility Centers

A **responsibility center** is any part of an organization whose manager has control over cost, revenue, or investment funds. Cost centers, profit centers, and investment centers are *all* known as responsibility centers.

EXHIBIT 10–1   Business Segments Classified as Cost, Profit, and Investment Centers

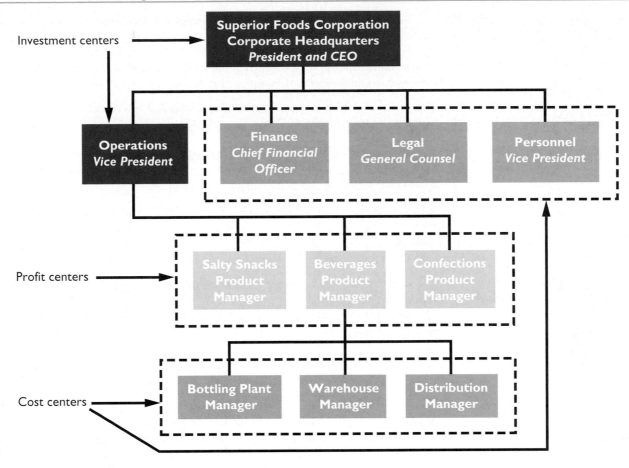

A partial organization chart for Superior Foods Corporation, a company in the snack food and beverage industry, appears in Exhibit 10–1. This partial organization chart indicates how the various business segments of the company are classified in terms of responsibility. Note that the departments and work centers that do not generate significant revenues by themselves are classified as cost centers. These are staff departments such as finance, legal, and personnel, and operating units such as the bottling plant, warehouse, and beverage distribution center. The profit centers are business segments that generate revenues and include the beverage, salty snacks, and confections product segments. The vice president of operations oversees allocation of investment funds across the product segments and is responsible for revenues and costs and so it is treated as an investment center. And finally, corporate headquarters is an investment center, since it is responsible for all revenues, costs, and investments.

Meeting Targets the Wrong Way

IN BUSINESS

Putting too much emphasis on meeting financial targets can lead to undesirable behavior. Michael C. Jensen reports, "I once watched the management of a manufacturing company struggle to reach their year-end targets. In late fall, they announced a price increase of 10% effective January 2. Now it may be that a price increase was needed, but it was not in line with the competition, nor was it likely that January 2, of all dates, was the best time for the increase. A price increase on January 2, would, however, cause customers to order before year-end and thereby help managers reach their targets." The short-term boost in sales comes at the cost of lost future sales and possible customer ill will.

Source: Michael C. Jensen, "Why Pay People to Lie?" *The Wall Street Journal*, January 8, 2001, p. A32.

Traceable and Common Fixed Costs

Performance reports are often compiled for a part of the organization, or segment, such as an investment center. In such segment reports, a distinction should be drawn between *traceable fixed costs* and *common fixed costs*. A **traceable fixed cost** of a segment is a fixed cost that is incurred because of the existence of the segment and if the segment were eliminated, the fixed cost would disappear. Examples of traceable fixed costs include the following:

- The salary of the Fritos product manager at PepsiCo is a traceable fixed cost of the Fritos business segment of PepsiCo.
- The maintenance cost for the building in which Boeing 747s are assembled is a traceable fixed cost of the 747 business segment of Boeing.
- The liability insurance at Disney World is a traceable fixed cost of the Disney World business segment of the Disney Corporation.

A **common fixed cost** is a fixed cost that supports the operations of more than one segment, but is not traceable in whole or in part to any one segment. Even if the segment were entirely eliminated, there would be no change in a common fixed cost. Examples of common fixed costs include the following:

- The salary of the CEO of General Motors is a common fixed cost of the various divisions of General Motors.
- The cost of the checkout equipment at a Safeway or Kroger grocery store is a common fixed cost of the various departments—such as groceries, produce, bakery—in the store.
- The cost of the receptionist's salary at an office shared by a number of doctors is a common fixed cost of the doctors. The cost is traceable to the office, but not to any one of the doctors individually.

In general, traceable costs should be assigned to segments, but common fixed costs should not. Assigning common fixed costs to segments would overstate the costs that are actually caused by the segments and that could be avoided by eliminating the segments. The details of how to deal with traceable and common fixed costs in segment reports are covered in more advanced texts. For example, see Chapter 12 of Ray Garrison and Eric Noreen, *Managerial Accounting*, 10th edition, McGraw-Hill/Irwin, 2003.

IN BUSINESS

Stopping the Bickering

AT&T Power Systems, a subsidiary of AT&T, makes electronic power supplies and components for the data processing and telecommunications industries. Independent business units (i.e., segments) at AT&T Power Systems are evaluated as profit centers; however, "more time was being spent debating the appropriate overhead-allocation scheme than was being spent on strategies to increase contribution margins." If, in fact, no cause-and-effect relation exists between an overhead expense and the activity in any particular segment, then any allocation of this overhead expense to the segments is completely arbitrary and can be endlessly debated by segment managers. Consequently, a change was made to evaluate the segments on the basis of just contribution margin and controllable expenses—eliminating arbitrary allocations of overhead from the performance measure.

Source: Richard L. Jenson, James W. Brackner, and Clifford R. Skousen, *Managerial Accounting in Support of Manufacturing Excellence*, The IMA Foundation for Applied Research, Inc., Montvale, NJ, 1996, pp. 97–101.

CONCEPT CHECK

1. Managers in which of the following responsibility centers are held responsible for profits? (You may select more than one answer.)

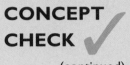

CONCEPT CHECK ✓

(continued)

RATE OF RETURN FOR MEASURING MANAGERIAL PERFORMANCE

When a company is truly decentralized, managers are given a great deal of autonomy. Profit and investment centers are often virtually independent businesses, with their managers having about the same control over decisions as if they were in fact running their own independent firms. With this autonomy, fierce competition often develops among managers, with each striving to make his or her segment the "best" in the company.

Competition between investment centers is particularly keen for investment funds. How do top managers in corporate headquarters go about deciding who gets new investment funds as they become available, and how do these managers decide which investment centers are most profitably using the funds that have already been entrusted to their care? One of the most popular ways of making these judgments is to measure the rate of return that investment center managers are able to generate on their assets. This rate of return is called the *return on investment (ROI)*.

The Return on Investment (ROI) Formula

The **return on investment (ROI)** is defined as net operating income divided by average operating assets:

$$ROI = \frac{\text{Net operating income}}{\text{Average operating assets}}$$

There are some issues about how to measure net operating income and average operating assets, but this formula seems clear enough. The higher the return on investment (ROI) of a business segment, the greater the profit generated per dollar invested in the segment's operating assets.

Concept 10–1

Net Operating Income and Operating Assets Defined

Note that *net operating income,* rather than net income, is used in the ROI formula. **Net operating income** is income before interest and taxes and is sometimes referred to as EBIT (earnings before interest and taxes). Net operating income is used in the formula because the base (i.e., denominator) consists of *operating assets.* Thus, to be consistent we use net operating income in the numerator.

Operating assets include cash, accounts receivable, inventory, plant and equipment, and all other assets held for productive use in the organization. Examples of assets that would not be included in the operating assets category (i.e., examples of nonoperating assets) would include land held for future use, an investment in another company, or a building rented to someone else. The operating assets base used in the formula is typically computed as the average of the operating assets between the beginning and the end of the year.

Plant and Equipment: Net Book Value or Gross Cost?

Determining the dollar amount of plant and equipment that should be included in the operating assets base is a major issue in the use of ROI. To illustrate the problem, assume that a company reports the following amounts for plant and equipment on its balance sheet:

Plant and equipment	$3,000,000
Less accumulated depreciation	900,000
Net book value	$2,100,000

What dollar amount of plant and equipment should the company include with its operating assets in computing ROI? One widely used approach is to include only the plant and equipment's *net book value*—that is, the plant's original cost less accumulated depreciation ($2,100,000 in the example above). A second approach is to ignore depreciation and include the plant's entire *gross cost* in the operating assets base ($3,000,000 in the example above). Both of these approaches are used in actual practice, even though they will obviously yield very different operating asset and ROI figures.

The following arguments can be raised for using net book value to measure operating assets and for using gross cost to measure operating assets in ROI computations:

Arguments for Using Net Book Value to Measure Operating Assets in ROI Computations:

1. The net book value method is consistent with how plant and equipment are reported on the balance sheet (i.e., cost less accumulated depreciation to date).
2. The net book value method is consistent with the computation of operating income, which includes depreciation as an operating expense.

Arguments for Using Gross Cost to Measure Operating Assets in ROI Computations:

1. The gross cost method eliminates both the age of equipment and the method of depreciation as factors in ROI computations. (Under the net book value method, ROI will tend to increase over time as net book value declines due to depreciation.)
2. The gross cost method does not discourage replacement of old, worn-out equipment. (Under the net book value method, replacing fully depreciated equipment with new equipment can have a dramatic, adverse effect on ROI.)

Managers generally view consistency as the most important consideration. As a result, most companies use the net book value approach in ROI computations. In this text, we will also use the net book value approach unless a specific exercise or problem directs otherwise.

CONTROLLING THE RATE OF RETURN

When we first defined the return on investment, we used the following formula:

$$\text{ROI} = \frac{\text{Net operating income}}{\text{Average operating assets}}$$

We can modify this formula slightly by introducing sales as follows:

$$\text{ROI} = \frac{\text{Net operating income}}{\text{Sales}} \times \frac{\text{Sales}}{\text{Average operating assets}}$$

These two equations are equivalent because the sales terms cancel out in the second equation.

The first term on the right-hand side of the equation is the *margin*, which is defined as follows:

$$\text{Margin} = \frac{\text{Net operating income}}{\text{Sales}}$$

The **margin** is a measure of management's ability to control operating expenses in relation to sales. The lower the operating expenses per dollar of sales, the higher the margin earned.

The second term on the right-hand side of the preceding equation is *turnover,* which is defined as follows:

$$\text{Turnover} = \frac{\text{Sales}}{\text{Average operating assets}}$$

Turnover is a measure of the sales that are generated for each dollar invested in operating assets.

The following alternative form of the ROI formula, which we will use most frequently, combines margin and turnover:

$$\text{ROI} = \text{Margin} \times \text{Turnover}$$

Which formula for ROI should be used—the original one stated in terms of net operating income and average operating assets or this one stated in terms of margin and turnover? Either can be used—they will always give the same answer. However, the margin and turnover formulation provides some additional insights.

Some managers tend to focus too much on margin and ignore turnover. To some degree at least, the margin can be a valuable indicator of a manager's performance. Standing alone, however, it overlooks one very crucial area of a manager's responsibility—the investment in operating assets. Excessive funds tied up in operating assets, which depresses turnover, can be just as much of a drag on profitability as excessive operating expenses, which depresses margin. One of the advantages of ROI as a performance measure is that it forces the manager to control the investment in operating assets as well as to control expenses and the margin.

Du Pont pioneered the ROI concept and recognized the importance of looking at both margin and turnover in assessing the performance of a manager. The ROI formula is now widely used as the key measure of the performance of an investment center. The ROI formula blends together many aspects of the manager's responsibilities into a single performance measure that can be compared to the returns of competing investment centers, the returns of other firms in the industry, and to the past returns of the investment center itself.

Du Pont also developed the diagram that appears in Exhibit 10–2. This exhibit helps managers understand how they can control ROI. An investment center manager can increase ROI in basically three ways:

1. Increase sales.
2. Reduce expenses.
3. Reduce assets.

To illustrate how the rate of return can be improved by each of these three actions, consider how the manager of the Monthaven Burger Grill is evaluated. Burger Grill is a small chain of upscale casual restaurants that has been rapidly adding outlets via franchising. The Monthaven franchise is owned by a group of local surgeons who have little time to devote to management and little expertise in business matters. Therefore, they delegate operating decisions—including decisions concerning investment in operating assets such as inventories—to a professional manager they have hired. The manager is evaluated largely based on the ROI the franchise generates.

The following data represent the results of operations for the most recent month:

Net operating income	$10,000
Sales	$100,000
Average operating assets	$50,000

EXHIBIT 10–2   Elements of Return on Investment (ROI)

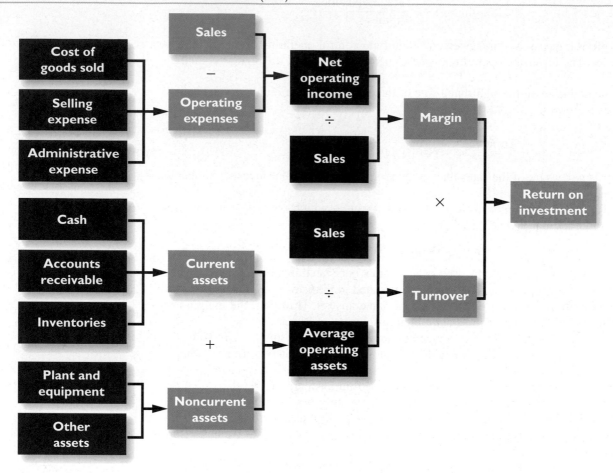

The rate of return generated by the Monthaven Burger Grill investment center is as follows:

$$\text{ROI} = \text{Margin} \times \text{Turnover}$$

$$\frac{\text{Net operating income}}{\text{Sales}} \times \frac{\text{Sales}}{\text{Average operating assets}}$$

$$\frac{\$10,000}{\$100,000} \times \frac{\$100,000}{\$50,000}$$

$$10\% \times 2 = 20\%$$

As we stated above, to improve the ROI figure, the manager can (1) increase sales, (2) reduce expenses, or (3) reduce the operating assets.

Approach 1: Increase Sales   Assume that the manager of the Monthaven Burger Grill is able to increase sales from $100,000 to $110,000. Assume further that either because of good cost control or because some costs in the company are fixed, the net operating income increases even more rapidly, going from $10,000 to $12,000 per period. Assume that the operating assets remain constant. Then the new ROI would be:

$$\text{ROI} = \frac{\$12,000}{\$110,000} \times \frac{\$110,000}{\$50,000}$$

$$10.91\% \times 2.2 = 24\% \text{ (as compared to 20\% above)}$$

Approach 2: Reduce Expenses   Assume that the manager of the Monthaven Burger Grill is able to reduce expenses by $1,000 so that net operating income increases from \$10,000 to \$11,000. Assume that both sales and operating assets remain constant. Then the new ROI would be:

$$ROI = \frac{\$11,000}{\$100,000} \times \frac{\$100,000}{\$50,000}$$

$$11\% \quad \times \quad 2 \quad = 22\% \text{ (as compared to 20\% above)}$$

Approach 3: Reduce Assets   Assume that the manager of the Monthaven Burger Grill is able to reduce operating assets from \$50,000 to \$40,000, but that sales and net operating income remain unchanged. Then the new ROI would be:

$$ROI = \frac{\$10,000}{\$100,000} \times \frac{\$100,000}{\$40,000}$$

$$10\% \quad \times \quad 2.5 \quad = 25\% \text{ (as compared to 20\% above)}$$

A clear understanding of these three approaches to improving the ROI figure is critical to the effective management of an investment center. We will now look at each approach in more detail.

Increase Sales

When first looking at the ROI formula, one is inclined to think that the sales figure is neutral, since it appears as the denominator in the margin computation and as the numerator in the turnover computation. We *could* cancel out the sales figure, but we don't do so for two reasons. First, this would tend to draw attention away from the fact that the rate of return is a function of *two* variables, margin and turnover. And second, it would tend to conceal the fact that a change in sales can affect both the margin and the turnover in an organization. A change in sales can affect the *margin* if expenses increase or decrease at a different rate than sales. For example, a company may be able to keep a tight control on its costs as its sales go up, with the result that net operating income increases more rapidly than sales and increases the margin. Or a company may have fixed expenses that remain constant as sales go up, resulting in an increase in the net operating income and in the margin. Either (or both) of these factors could have been responsible for the increase in the margin percentage from 10% to 10.91% illustrated in approach 1 above.

Further, a change in sales can affect the *turnover* if sales either increase or decrease without a proportionate increase or decrease in the operating assets. In the first approach above, for example, sales increased from \$100,000 to \$110,000, but the operating assets remained unchanged. As a result, the turnover increased from 2 to 2.2 for the period.

Reduce Expenses

Often the easiest route to increased profitability and to a stronger ROI is to simply cut the "fat" out of an organization through a concerted effort to control expenses. When margins begin to be squeezed, this is generally the first line of attack by a manager. Discretionary fixed costs (that is, fixed costs that arise from annual decisions by management to spend in certain fixed cost areas) usually come under scrutiny first, and various programs are either curtailed or eliminated in an effort to cut costs. Managers must be careful, however, not to cut out muscle and bone along with the fat. Also, they must remember that frequent cost-cutting binges can destroy morale. Most managers now agree that it is best to stay "lean and mean" all of the time.

Reduce Operating Assets

Managers have always been sensitive to the need to control sales, operating expenses, and operating margins. However, they have not always been equally sensitive to the need to control investment in operating assets. Firms that have adopted the ROI approach to measuring managerial performance report that one of the first reactions of investment center managers is to trim their investment in operating assets. Managers soon realize that an excessive investment in operating assets reduces turnover and hurts the ROI. As these managers reduce their investment in operating assets, funds are released that can be used elsewhere in the organization.

How can an investment center manager control the investment in operating assets? One approach is to eliminate unneeded inventory. JIT purchasing and JIT manufacturing have been extremely helpful in reducing inventories of all types. Another approach is to devise various methods of speeding up the collection of receivables. For example, many firms use the lockbox technique in which customers in distant states send their payments directly to post office boxes in their area. The funds are received and deposited by a local bank on behalf of the payee firm. This speeds up the collection process, since the payments are not delayed in the postal system. As a result of the speedup in collection, the accounts receivable balance is reduced and the asset turnover is increased.

IN BUSINESS

Insuring the Bottom Line

Insurance companies have begun to offer managers a radical way to avoid some of the risk of having to report bad financial results. For example, the Reliance Group has created a product called Enterprise Earnings Protection Insurance that covers any operating earnings shortfall due to events beyond management's control. If a company buys an insurance policy guaranteeing $5 million in profits, but it posted only a $3 million profit, then Reliance would have to make up the difference of $2 million. Reliance reports that a company may have to pay as little as 5% of its estimated profit to insure against a 20% shortfall.

Source: Diane Brady, "Is Your Bottom Line Covered?" *Business Week*, February 8, 1999, pp. 85–86.

ROI and the Balanced Scorecard

Simply exhorting managers to increase ROI is not sufficient. Managers who are told to increase ROI will naturally wonder how this is to be accomplished. The Du Pont scheme, which is illustrated in Exhibit 10–2, provides managers with *some* guidance. Generally speaking, ROI can be increased by increasing sales, decreasing costs, and/or decreasing investments in operating assets. However, it may not be obvious to managers how they are supposed to increase sales, decrease costs, and decrease investments in a way that is consistent with the company's strategy. For example, a manager who is given inadequate guidance may cut back on investments that are critical to implementing the company's strategy.

For that reason, as discussed in Chapter 8, when managers are evaluated based on ROI, a balanced scorecard approach is advised. And indeed, ROI, or residual income (discussed below), is typically included as one of the financial performance measures on a company's balanced scorecard. As briefly discussed in Chapter 8, the balanced scorecard provides a way of communicating a company's strategy to managers throughout the organization. The scorecard indicates *how* the company intends to improve its financial performance. A well-constructed balanced scorecard should answer questions like: "What internal business processes should be improved?" and "Which customer should be targeted and how will they be attracted and retained at a profit?" In short, a well-constructed balanced scorecard can provide managers with a road map that indicates how the company intends to increase its ROI. In the absence of such a road map of the company's strategy, managers may have difficulty understanding what they are supposed to do to increase ROI and they may work at cross-purposes rather than in harmony with the overall strategy of the company.

Criticisms of ROI

Although ROI is widely used in evaluating performance, it is not a perfect tool. The method is subject to the following criticisms:

1. Just telling managers to increase ROI may not be enough. Managers may not know how to increase ROI; they may increase ROI in a way that is inconsistent with the company's strategy; or they may take actions that increase ROI in the short run but harm the company in the long run (such as cutting back on research and development). This is why ROI is best used as part of a balanced scorecard as discussed above. A balanced scorecard can provide concrete guidance to managers, making it more likely that actions taken are consistent with the company's strategy, and reducing the likelihood that short-run performance will be enhanced at the expense of long-term performance.
2. A manager who takes over a business segment typically inherits many committed costs over which the manager has no control. These committed costs make it difficult to fairly assess the performance of the manager relative to other managers.
3. As discussed in the next section, a manager who is evaluated based on ROI may reject investment opportunities that are profitable for the company as a whole but that would negatively impact the division's ROI.

Putting Too Much Pressure on Meeting Targets

IN BUSINESS

Business Week reports that the CEO of Tyco International, Ltd., puts unrelenting pressure on his managers to deliver growth. "Each year, [the CEO] sets targets for how much each manager must increase his or her unit's earnings in the coming year. The targets are coupled with a powerful incentive system. If they meet or exceed these targets, managers are promised a bonus that can be many times their salary. But if they fall even a bit short, the bonus plummets." This sounds good, but "to many accounting experts, the sort of all-or-nothing bonus structure set up at Tyco is a warning light. If top executives set profit targets too high or turn a blind eye to how managers achieve them, the incentives for managers to cut corners is enormous. Indeed, a blue-ribbon panel of accounting experts who were trying to improve corporate auditing standards several years ago in the wake of such well-known corporate failures as Phar-Mor and Leslie Fay identified just such extreme incentives as a red flag. 'If you're right under the target, there's a tremendous economic interest to accelerate earnings,' says David F. Larcker, a professor of accounting at the Wharton School. 'If you're right over it, there is an incentive to push earnings into the next period.'"

Source: William C. Symonds, Diane Brady, Geoffrey Smith, and Lorraine Woellert, "Tyco: Aggressive or Out of Line?" *Business Week*, November 1, 1999, pp. 160–165.

Jewelry Store Manager

DECISION MAKER

LS

You were recently hired as the manager of a chain of jewelry stores that are located in downtown Chicago. You are excited about the high level of autonomy that you have been given to run the stores but are nervous because you've heard rumors that the previous manager was let go because the return on investment (ROI) of the stores was unacceptable. What steps should you consider to improve ROI?

RESIDUAL INCOME—ANOTHER MEASURE OF PERFORMANCE

Another approach to measuring an investment center's performance focuses on a concept known as *residual income*. **Residual income** is the net operating income that an investment

LEARNING OBJECTIVE 2

Compute residual income and understand the strengths and weaknesses of this method of measuring performance.

Concept 10–2

center earns above the minimum required return on its operating assets. **Economic Value Added (EVA®)** is an adaptation of residual income that has recently been adopted by many companies.[3] Under EVA, companies often modify their accounting principles in various ways. For example, funds used for research and development are often treated as investments rather than as expenses under EVA.[4] These complications are best dealt with in a more advanced course; in this text we will focus on the basics and will not draw any distinction between residual income and EVA.

When residual income or EVA is used to measure performance, the objective is to maximize the total amount of residual income or EVA, not to maximize ROI. If the objective were to maximize ROI, then every company should divest all of its products except the single product with the highest ROI. A wide variety of organizations have embraced some version of residual income or EVA, including Bausch & Lomb, Best Buy, Boise Cascade, Coca-Cola, Dun and Bradstreet, Eli Lilly, Federated Mogul, Georgia-Pacific, Guidant Corporation, Hershey Foods, Husky Injection Molding, J.C. Penney, Kansas City Power & Light, Olin, Quaker Oats, Silicon Valley Bank, Sprint, Toys "R" Us, Tupperware, and the United States Postal Service. In addition, financial institutions such as Credit Suisse First Boston now use EVA—and its allied concept, market value added—to evaluate potential investments in other companies.

IN BUSINESS

Rankings Based on EVA

Economic Value Added (EVA) can be used to evaluate the performance of entire companies as well as segments of companies, such as divisions. *Fortune* magazine publishes an annual ranking of companies based on EVA. In the 2001 ranking, the companies with the largest EVA were Microsoft, Philip Morris, General Electric, Intel, and Exxon-Mobil—each with economic value added in excess of $5 billion for the year. In contrast, the biggest wealth destroyer was AT&T, with a *negative* economic value added for the year of almost $10 billion. A similar study carried out by *CFO Asia* magazine for Asian companies found that EVA ranged from a high of $764 million at CLP Holdings to a low of negative $988 million at Cheung Kong Holdings.

Sources: David Stires, "America's Best & Worst Wealth Creators," *Fortune*, December 10, 2001, pp. 137–142; and Tom Leander, "Value Champs," *CFO Asia*, November 1999, pp. 26–37.

For purposes of illustration, consider the following data for an investment center—the Ketchican Division of Alaskan Marine Services Corporation.

ALASKAN MARINE SERVICES CORPORATION Ketchican Division Basic Data for Performance Evaluation	
Average operating assets	$100,000
Net operating income..............................	$20,000
Minimum required rate of return.....................	15%

---

[3]The basic idea underlying residual income and economic value added has been around for over 100 years. In recent years, economic value added has been popularized and trademarked by the consulting firm Stern, Stewart & Co.

[4]Over 100 different adjustments could be made for deferred taxes, LIFO reserves, provisions for future liabilities, mergers and acquisitions, gains or losses due to changes in accounting rules, operating leases, and other accounts, but most companies make only a few. For further details, see John O'Hanlon and Ken Peasnell, "Wall Street's Contribution to Management Accounting: The Stern Stewart EVA® Financial Management System," *Management Accounting Research* 9 (1998), pp. 421–444.

Alaskan Marine Services Corporation has long had a policy of evaluating investment center managers based on ROI, but it is considering a switch to residual income. The controller of the company, who is in favor of the change to residual income, has provided the following table that shows how the performance of the division would be evaluated under each of the two methods:

ALASKAN MARINE SERVICES CORPORATION Ketchican Division		
	Alternative Performance Measures	
	ROI	Residual Income
Average operating assets (a)...................	$100,000	$100,000
Net operating income (b).....................	$ 20,000	$ 20,000
ROI, (b) ÷ (a)...............................	20%	
Minimum required return (15% × $100,000).......		15,000
Residual income		$ 5,000

The reasoning underlying the residual income calculation is straightforward. The company is able to earn a rate of return of at least 15% on its investments. Since the company has invested $100,000 in the Ketchican Division in the form of operating assets, the company should be able to earn at least $15,000 (15% × $100,000) on this investment. Since the Ketchican Division's net operating income is $20,000, the residual income above and beyond the minimum required return is $5,000. If residual income is adopted as the performance measure to replace ROI, the manager of the Ketchican Division would be evaluated based on the growth in residual income from year to year.

Reacting to the Use of EVA

One study found that, relative to companies that did not adopt EVA, a sample of companies adopting Economic Value Added as a performance measure "(1) increased their dispositions of assets and decreased their new investment, (2) increased their payouts to shareholders through share repurchases, and (3) used their assets more intensively. These actions are consistent with the strong rate of return discipline associated with the capital charge in residual income-based measures."

Source: James S. Wallace, "Adopting Residual Income-Based Compensation Plans: Do You Get What You Pay For?" *Journal of Accounting and Economics* 24, 1997, pp. 275–300.

Motivation and Residual Income

One of the primary reasons why the controller of Alaskan Marine Services Corporation would like to switch from ROI to residual income has to do with how managers view new investments under the two performance measurement schemes. The residual income approach encourages managers to make investments that are profitable for the entire company but that would be rejected by managers who are evaluated by the ROI formula.

To illustrate this problem with ROI, suppose that the manager of the Ketchican Division is considering purchasing a computerized diagnostic machine to aid in servicing marine diesel engines. The machine would cost $25,000 and is expected to generate additional operating income of $4,500 a year. From the standpoint of the company, this would be a good investment since it promises a rate of return of 18% ($4,500 ÷ $25,000), which is in excess of the company's minimum required rate of return of 15%.

If the manager of the Ketchican Division is evaluated based on residual income, she would be in favor of the investment in the diagnostic machine as shown below:

ALASKAN MARINE SERVICES CORPORATION Ketchican Division Performance Evaluated Using Residual Income	Present	New Project	Overall
Average operating assets............	$100,000	$25,000	$125,000
Net operating income..............	$ 20,000	$ 4,500	$ 24,500
Minimum required return...........	15,000	3,750*	18,750
Residual income...................	$ 5,000	$ 750	$ 5,750

*$25,000 × 15% = $3,750.

Since the project would increase the residual income of the Ketchican Division, the manager would want to invest in the new diagnostic machine.

Now suppose that the manager of the Ketchican Division is evaluated based on ROI. The effect of the diagnostic machine on the division's ROI is computed below:

ALASKAN MARINE SERVICES CORPORATION Ketchican Division Performance Evaluated Using ROI	Present	New Project	Overall
Average operating assets (a).........	$100,000	$25,000	$125,000
Net operating income (b)...........	$20,000	$4,500	$24,500
ROI, (b) ÷ (a)....................	20%	18%	19.6%

The new project reduces the division's ROI from 20% to 19.6%. This happens because the 18% rate of return on the new diagnostic machine, while above the company's 15% minimum rate of return, is below the division's present ROI of 20%. Therefore, the new diagnostic machine would drag the division's ROI down even though it would be a good investment from the standpoint of the company as a whole. If the manager of the division is evaluated based on ROI, she will be reluctant to even propose such an investment.

Basically, a manager who is evaluated based on ROI will reject any project whose rate of return is below the division's current ROI even if the rate of return on the project is above the minimum required rate of return for the entire company. In contrast, any project whose rate of return is above the minimum required rate of return for the company will result in an increase in residual income. Since it is in the best interests of the company as a whole to accept any project whose rate of return is above the minimum required rate of return, managers who are evaluated based on residual income will tend to make better decisions concerning investment projects than managers who are evaluated based on ROI.

IN BUSINESS

Shoring Up Return on Capital

Manitowic Co. is located in Manitowic, Wisconsin, on the shores of Lake Michigan. The company makes construction cranes, ice machines, and Great Lakes shipping vessels. Over the past four years, the company's share price has increased over 500%. Part of this increase is attributed to the company's adoption of EVA. The company has slashed headquarters staff from 127 to 30 people. Inventories have been cut by $50 million—from $84 million down to $34 million. Divisions that fail to cut excess assets get no bonus. Before the adoption of EVA, the company's return on total capital was 10.5%. It is now 22%.

Source: Michelle Conlin, "Hoisting Job," *Forbes*, April 19, 1999, pp. 152, 156.

Shoe Store Manager

You are the manager of a shoe store in a busy shopping mall. The store is part of a national chain that evaluates its store managers on the basis of return on investment (ROI). As the manager of the store, you have control over costs, pricing, and the inventory you carry. The ROI of your store was 17.21% last year and is projected to be 17.00% this year unless some action is taken. The projected ROI has been computed as follows:

Average operating assets (a)	$2,000,000
Net operating income (b)	$340,000
ROI, (b) ÷ (a)	17.00%

Your bonus this year will depend on improving your ROI performance over last year. The minimum required rate of return on investment for the national chain is 15%.

You are considering two alternatives for improving this year's ROI:

a. Cut inventories (and average operating assets) by $500,000. This will unfortunately result in a reduction in sales, with a negative impact on net operating income of $79,000.
b. Add a new product line that would increase average operating inventories by $200,000, but would increase net operating income by $33,000.

Which alternative would result in you earning a bonus for the year? Which alternative is in the best interests of the national chain?

Divisional Comparison and Residual Income

The residual income approach has one major disadvantage. It can't be used to compare the performance of divisions of different sizes. You would expect larger divisions to have more residual income than smaller divisions, not necessarily because they are better managed but simply because they are bigger.

As an example, consider the following residual income computations for Division X and Division Y:

	Division	
	X	Y
Average operating assets (a)	$1,000,000	$250,000
Net operating income	$ 120,000	$ 40,000
Minimum required return: 10% × (a)	100,000	25,000
Residual income	$ 20,000	$ 15,000

Observe that Division X has slightly more residual income than Division Y, but that Division X has $1,000,000 in operating assets as compared to only $250,000 in operating assets for Division Y. Thus, Division X's greater residual income is probably more a result of its size than the quality of its management. In fact, it appears that the smaller division is better managed, since it has been able to generate nearly as much residual income with only one-fourth as much in operating assets to work with. This problem can be reduced by focusing on the percentage change in residual income from year to year rather than on the absolute amount of the residual income.

3. Last year sales were $300,000, net operating income was $75,000, and average operating assets were $500,000. If sales next year remain the same as last year and

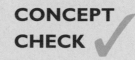

CONCEPT
CHECK ✓

CONCEPT CHECK ✓

(continued)

expenses and average operating assets are reduced by 5%, what will be the return on investment next year?

   a. 12.2%
   b. 18.2%
   c. 20.2%
   d. 25.2%

4. Referring to the facts in question 3 above, if the minimum required return is 12%, what will be the residual income next year?

   a. $26,250
   b. $27,250
   c. $28,250
   d. $29,250

Transfer Prices

A problem arises in evaluating segments of a company when one segment provides a good or service to another segment. For example, the truck division of Ford provides trucks to other Ford divisions to use in their operations such as the division that markets passenger cars. If both the truck and passenger car divisions are evaluated based on their profits, disputes are likely to arise over the *transfer price* charged for the trucks used by the passenger car division. A **transfer price** is the price charged when one segment of an organization provides a good or service to another segment in the organization. The selling segment, in this case the truck division, would naturally like the transfer price to be as high as possible whereas the buying segment, in this case the passenger car division, would like the price to be as low as possible.

The question of what transfer price to charge is one of the most difficult problems in managerial accounting. The objective in transfer pricing should be to motivate the segment managers to do what is in the best interests of the overall organization. For example, if we want the manager of the passenger car division of Ford to make decisions that are in the best interests of the overall organization, the transfer price charged to the passenger car division for trucks must be the cost incurred by the entire organization up to the point of transfer—including any opportunity costs. If the transfer price is less than this cost, then the manager of the passenger car division will think that the cost of the trucks is lower than it really is and will tend to demand more trucks than would be optimal for the entire company. If the transfer price is greater than the cost incurred by the entire organization up to the point of the transfer, then the passenger car division manager will think the cost of the trucks is higher than it really is and will tend to demand fewer trucks than would be optimal for the entire organization. While this principle may seem clear-cut, as a practical matter, implementing it is very difficult for a variety of reasons. In practice, companies usually adopt a simplified transfer pricing policy based on variable cost, absorption cost, or market prices. All of these approaches have flaws, which are covered in more advanced texts.

SUMMARY

LO1 Compute the return on investment (ROI) and show how changes in sales, expenses, and assets affect an organization's ROI.

Return on investment (ROI) is defined to be net operating income divided by average operating assets. Alternatively, it can be defined as the product of margin and turnover, where margin is net operating income divided by sales and turnover is sales divided by average operating assets.

The relations among sales, expenses, assets, and ROI are complex. The effect of a change in any one variable on the others will depend on the specific circumstances. Nevertheless, an increase in sales often leads to an increase in ROI via the effect of sales on net operating income. If the organization has significant fixed costs, then a given percentage increase in sales is likely to have an even larger percentage effect on net operating income.

LO2 Compute residual income and understand the strengths and weaknesses of this method of measuring performance.

Residual income is the difference between net operating income and the minimum required return on average operating assets. The minimum required return on average operating assets is computed by applying the minimum rate of return to the average operating assets.

The major advantage of residual income over ROI is that it does not discourage investment in projects whose rates of return are above the minimum required rate of return for the entire organization, but below the segment's current ROI.

GUIDANCE ANSWERS TO *DECISION MAKER* AND *YOU DECIDE*

Jewelry Store Manager (p. 435)

Three approaches can be used to increase ROI:

1. Increase sales—An increase in sales will positively impact the margin if expenses increase proportionately less than sales. An increase in sales will also affect turnover if there is not a proportionate increase in operating assets.
2. Reduce expenses—This approach is often the first path selected by managers to increase profitability and ROI. You should start by reviewing the stores' discretionary fixed costs (such as advertising). It may be possible to cut some discretionary fixed costs with minimal damage to the long-run goals of the organization. You should also investigate whether there are adequate physical controls over the inventory of jewelry items. Thefts result in an increase in cost of goods sold without a corresponding increase in sales!
3. Reduce operating assets—An excessive investment in operating assets (such as inventory) reduces turnover and hurts ROI. Given the nature of the operations of retail jewelry stores, inventory must be in sufficient quantities at specific times during the year (such as Christmas, Valentine's Day, and Mother's Day) or sales will suffer. However, those levels do not need to be maintained throughout the year.

Shoe Store Manager (p. 439)

The effects of the two alternatives on your store's ROI for the year can be computed as follows:

	Present	Alternative (a)	Overall
Average operating assets (a)	$2,000,000	$(500,000)	$1,500,000
Net operating income (b)	$340,000	$(79,000)	$261,000
ROI, (b) ÷ (a).	17.00%	15.80%	17.40%

	Present	Alternative (b)	Overall
Average operating assets (a)	$2,000,000	$200,000	$2,200,000
Net operating income (b)	$340,000	$33,000	$373,000
ROI, (b) ÷ (a).	17.00%	16.50%	16.95%

Alternative (a) would increase your store's ROI to 17.40%—beating last year's ROI and hence earning you a bonus. Alternative (b) would actually decrease your store's ROI and would result in no bonus for the year. So to earn the bonus, you would select Alternative (a). However, this alternative is not in the best interests of the national chain since the ROI of the lost sales is 15.8%, which exceeds the national chain's minimum required rate of return of 15%. Rather, it would be in the national chain's interests to adopt Alternative (b)—the addition of a new product line. The ROI on these sales would be 16.5%, which exceeds the minimum required rate of return of 15%.

GUIDANCE ANSWERS TO CONCEPT CHECKS

1. **Choices c and d.** Both profit and investment center managers are held responsible for profits. In addition, an investment center manager is held responsible for earning an adequate return on investment or residual income.

2. **Choices b and d.** Common fixed costs should not be assigned to segments. Common fixed costs will not decrease if a segment is discontinued.
3. **Choice b.** The profit would be $300,000 − ($225,000 × 95%) = $86,250. The return on investment would be ($86,250 ÷ ($500,000 × 95%) = 18.2%.
4. **Choice d.** The residual income would be $86,250 − ($475,000 × 12%) = $29,250.

REVIEW PROBLEM: RETURN ON INVESTMENT (ROI) AND RESIDUAL INCOME

The Magnetic Imaging Division of Medical Diagnostics, Inc., has reported the following results for last year's operations:

Sales............................	$25 million
Net operating income.............	$3 million
Average operating assets	$10 million

Required:
1. Compute the margin, turnover, and ROI for the Magnetic Imaging Division.
2. Top management of Medical Diagnostics, Inc., has set a minimum required rate of return on average operating assets of 25%. What is the Magnetic Imaging Division's residual income for the year?

Solution to Review Problem
1. The required calculations appear below:

$$\text{Margin} = \frac{\text{Net operating income, \$3,000,000}}{\text{Sales, \$25,000,000}}$$

$$= 12\%$$

$$\text{Turnover} = \frac{\text{Sales, \$25,000,000}}{\text{Average operating assets, \$10,000,000}}$$

$$= 2.5$$

$$\text{ROI} = \text{Margin} \times \text{Turnover}$$

$$= 12\% \times 2.5$$

$$= 30\%$$

2. The residual income for the Magnetic Imaging Division is computed as follows:

Average operating assets.................................	$10,000,000
Net operating income	$ 3,000,000
Minimum required return (25% × $10,000,000)	2,500,000
Residual income.......................................	$ 500,000

GLOSSARY

Common fixed cost   A fixed cost that supports more than one business segment, but is not traceable in whole or in part to any one of the business segments. (p. 428)

Cost center   A business segment whose manager has control over cost but has no control over revenue or the use of investment funds. (p. 425)

Decentralized organization   An organization in which decision making is not confined to a few top executives but rather is spread throughout the organization. (p. 424)

Economic value added (EVA)   A concept similar to residual income in which a variety of adjustments may be made to GAAP financial statements for performance evaluation purposes. (p. 436)

Investment center   A business segment whose manager has control over cost, revenue, and the use of investment funds. (p. 426)

Margin   Net operating income divided by sales. (p. 431)

Net operating income   Income before interest and income taxes have been deducted. (p. 429)

Operating assets   Cash, accounts receivable, inventory, plant and equipment, and all other assets held for productive use in an organization. (p. 429)

Profit center   A business segment whose manager has control over cost and revenue but has no control over the use of investment funds. (p. 426)

Residual income   The net operating income that an investment center earns above the required return on its operating assets. (p. 435)

Responsibility center   Any business segment whose manager has control over cost, revenue, or the use of investment funds. (p. 426)

Return on investment (ROI)   Net operating income divided by average operating assets. It also equals margin multiplied by turnover. (p. 429)

Segment   Any part or activity of an organization about which the manager seeks cost, revenue, or profit data. (p. 425)

Traceable fixed cost   A fixed cost that is incurred because of the existence of a particular business segment. (p. 428)

Transfer price   The price charged when one division or segment provides goods or services to another division or segment of an organization. (p. 440)

Turnover   The amount of sales generated in an investment center for each dollar invested in operating assets. It is computed by dividing sales by the average operating assets figure. (p. 431)

QUESTIONS

10–1   What is meant by the term *decentralization?*

10–2   What benefits result from decentralization?

10–3   Distinguish between a cost center, a profit center, and an investment center.

10–4   Define a segment of an organization. Give several examples of segments.

10–5   What is meant by the terms *margin* and *turnover?*

10–6   What are the three basic approaches to improving return on investment (ROI)?

10–7   What is meant by residual income?

10–8   In what way can the use of ROI as a performance measure for investment centers lead to bad decisions? How does the residual income approach overcome this problem?

10–9   What is meant by the term *transfer price,* and why are transfer prices needed?

BRIEF EXERCISES

BRIEF EXERCISE 10–1   Compute the Return on Investment (ROI)   (LO1)

Tundra Services Company, a division of a major oil company, provides various services to the operators of the North Slope oil field in Alaska. Data concerning the most recent year appear below:

Sales............................	$18,000,000
Net operating income.............	$5,400,000
Average operating assets	$36,000,000

Required:
1. Compute the margin for Tundra Services Company.
2. Compute the turnover for Tundra Services Company.
3. Compute the return on investment (ROI) for Tundra Services Company.

BRIEF EXERCISE 10–2   Effects of Changes in Sales, Expenses, and Assets on ROI   (LO1)

BusServ.com Corporation provides business-to-business services on the Internet. Data concerning the most recent year appear below:

Sales.........................	$8,000,000
Net operating income...........	$800,000
Average operating assets	$3,200,000

Required:
Consider each question below independently. Carry out all computations to two decimal places.

1. Compute the company's return on investment (ROI).
2. The entrepreneur who founded the company is convinced that sales will increase next year by 150% and that net operating income would increase as a result by 400%, with no increase in average operating assets. What would be the company's ROI?
3. The Chief Financial Officer of the company believes a more realistic scenario would be a $2 million increase in sales, requiring an $800,000 increase in average operating assets, with a resulting $250,000 increase in net operating income. What would be the company's ROI in this scenario?

BRIEF EXERCISE 10–3   Residual Income   (LO2)
Midlands Design Ltd. of Manchester, England, is a company specializing in providing design services to residential developers. Last year the company had net operating income of £400,000 on sales of £2,000,000. The company's average operating assets for the year were £2,200,000 and its minimum required rate of return was 16%.

Required:
Compute the company's residual income for the year.

EXERCISES

EXERCISE 10–4   Computing and Interpreting Return on Investment (ROI)   (LO1)
Selected operating data on the two divisions of York Company are given below:

	Division	
	Eastern	**Western**
Sales.............................	$1,000,000	$1,750,000
Average operating assets	$500,000	$500,000
Net operating income.................	$90,000	$105,000
Property, plant, and equipment..........	$250,000	$200,000

Required:
1. Compute the rate of return for each division using the return on investment (ROI) formula stated in terms of margin and turnover.
2. So far as you can tell from the available data, which divisional manager seems to be doing the better job? Why?

EXERCISE 10–5   Contrasting Return on Investment (ROI) and Residual Income   (LO1, LO2)
Rains Nickless Ltd. of Australia has two engineering consulting divisions that operate in Perth and Darwin. Selected data on the two divisions follow:

	Division	
	Perth	**Darwin**
Sales.............................	$9,000,000	$20,000,000
Net operating income.................	$630,000	$1,800,000
Average operating assets	$3,000,000	$10,000,000

Required:
1. Compute the return on investment (ROI) for each division.
2. Assume that the company evaluates performance by use of residual income and that the minimum required return for any division is 16%. Compute the residual income for each division.
3. Is the Darwin Division's greater residual income an indication that it is better managed? Explain.

EXERCISE 10–6 Evaluating New Investments Using Return on Investment (ROI) and Residual Income (LO1, LO2)

Selected sales and operating data for three divisions of three different service companies are given below:

	Division A	Division B	Division C
Sales....................................	$6,000,000	$10,000,000	$8,000,000
Average operating assets	$1,500,000	$5,000,000	$2,000,000
Net operating income...................	$300,000	$900,000	$180,000
Minimum required rate of return..........	15%	18%	12%

Required:

1. Compute the return on investment (ROI) for each division, using the formula stated in terms of margin and turnover.
2. Compute the residual income for each division.
3. Assume that each division is presented with an investment opportunity that would yield a rate of return of 17%.
   a. If performance is being measured by ROI, which division or divisions will probably accept the opportunity? Reject? Why?
   b. If performance is being measured by residual income, which division or divisions will probably accept the opportunity? Reject? Why?

EXERCISE 10–7 Effects of Changes in Profits and Assets on Return on Investment (ROI) (LO1)

The Abs Shoppe is a regional chain of health clubs. The managers of the clubs, who have authority to make investments as needed, are evaluated based largely on return on investment (ROI). The Abs Shoppe reported the following results for the past year:

Sales.............................	$800,000
Net operating income..............	$16,000
Average operating assets...........	$100,000

Required:

The following questions are to be considered independently. Carry out all computations to two decimal places.

1. Compute the club's return on investment (ROI).
2. Assume that the manager of the club is able to increase sales by $80,000 and that as a result net operating income increases by $6,000. Further assume that this is possible without any increase in operating assets. What would be the club's return on investment (ROI)?
3. Assume that the manager of the club is able to reduce expenses by $3,200 without any change in sales or operating assets. What would be the club's return on investment (ROI)?
4. Assume that the manager of the club is able to reduce operating assets by $20,000 without any change in sales or net operating income. What would be the club's return on investment (ROI)?

EXERCISE 10–8 Cost-Volume-Profit Analysis and Return on Investment (ROI) (LO1)

Images.com is a small Internet retailer of high-quality posters. The company has $800,000 in operating assets and fixed expenses of $160,000 per year. With this level of operating assets and fixed expenses, the company can support sales of up to $5 million per year. The company's contribution margin ratio is 10%, which means that an additional dollar of sales results in additional contribution margin, and net operating income, of 10 cents.

Required:

1. Complete the following table showing the relationship between sales and return on investment (ROI).

Sales	Net Operating Income	Average Operating Assets	ROI
$4,500,000	$290,000	$800,000	?
$4,600,000	?	$800,000	?
$4,700,000	?	$800,000	?

(continued)

(concluded) Sales	Net Operating Income	Average Operating Assets	ROI
$4,800,000	?	$800,000	?
$4,900,000	?	$800,000	?
$5,000,000	?	$800,000	?

2. What happens to the company's return on investment (ROI) as the sales increase? Explain.

PROBLEMS

CHECK FIGURE
Kodiak: 2.0 turnover

PROBLEM 10–9   Return on Investment (ROI) Relations   (LO1)
Provide the missing data in the following table for the divisions of a service company:

	Division		
	Juneau	Kodiak	Leafton
Sales	?	$11,750,000	?
Net operating income	?	$940,000	$210,000
Average operating assets	$650,000	?	?
Margin...........................	4.0%	?	7.0%
Turnover.........................	4.0	?	?
Return on investment (ROI)	?	16.0%	14.0%

CHECK FIGURE
Company B residual
income: $(65,000)

PROBLEM 10–10   Return on Investment (ROI) and Residual Income Relations   (LO1, LO2)
A family friend has asked for your help in analyzing the operations of three anonymous service companies.
Supply the missing data in the below table:

	Company		
	A	B	C
Sales	$9,400,000	$6,800,000	$4,600,000
Net operating income	?	$260,000	?
Average operating assets	$3,100,000	?	$1,900,000
Return on investment (ROI)	19%	16%	?
Minimum required rate of return:			
Percentage	15%	?	13%
Dollar amount	?	$325,000	?
Residual income.................	?	?	$95,000

CHECK FIGURE
(2) Company A margin:
      13.0%

PROBLEM 10–11   Cost Comparison of Performance Using Return on Investment (ROI)   (LO1)
Comparative data on three companies in the same service industry are given below:

	Company		
	A	B	C
Sales	$650,000	$580,000	?
Net operating income	$84,500	$75,400	?
Average operating assets	$325,000	?	$725,000
Margin...........................	?	?	4.0%
Turnover.........................	?	?	2.6
Return on investment (ROI)	?	10.4%	?

Required:
1. What advantages can you see in breaking down the ROI computation into two separate elements, margin and turnover?

2. Fill in the missing information above and comment on the relative performance of the three companies in as much detail as the data permit. Make specific recommendations on steps to be taken to improve the return on investment, where needed.

(Adapted from National Association of Accountants, *Research Report No. 35*, p. 34)

PROBLEM 10–12 Return on Investment (ROI) and Residual Income (LO1, LO2)

Financial data for Pierce Industries for last year follow:

CHECK FIGURE
(1) ROI, 16.0%

PIERCE INDUSTRIES Balance Sheet		
	Ending Balance	Beginning Balance
Assets		
Cash	$ 140,000	$ 170,000
Accounts receivable.	360,000	330,000
Inventory	360,000	350,000
Plant and equipment, net	610,000	680,000
Investment in Salem Service Corp.	270,000	230,000
Land (undeveloped)	180,000	190,000
Total assets.	$1,920,000	$1,950,000
Liabilities and Stockholders' Equity		
Accounts payable	$ 446,000	$ 200,000
Long-term debt	1,400,000	1,700,000
Stockholders' equity	74,000	50,000
Total liabilities and stockholders' equity	$1,920,000	$1,950,000

PIERCE INDUSTRIES Income Statement		
Sales		$6,000,000
Less operating expenses		5,760,000
Net operating income		240,000
Less interest and taxes:		
Interest expense.	$170,000	
Tax expense	30,000	200,000
Net income		$ 40,000

The company paid dividends of $16,000 last year. The "Investment in Salem Service Corp.," on the balance sheet represents an investment in the stock of another company.

Required:

1. Compute the company's margin, turnover, and ROI for last year.
2. The board of directors of Pierce Industries has set a minimum required return of 14%. What was the company's residual income last year?

PROBLEM 10–13 Return on Investment (ROI) and Residual Income (LO1, LO2)

"I know headquarters wants us to add that new product line," said Clem Baker, manager of Westwood Inc.'s Office Products Division. "But I want to see the numbers before I make any move. Our division has led the company for three years, and I don't want any letdown."

Westwood Inc. is a decentralized organization with five autonomous divisions. The divisions are evaluated on the basis of the return that they are able to generate on invested assets, with year-end bonuses given to the divisional managers who have the highest ROI figures. Operating results for the company's Office Products Division for the most recent year are given below:

CHECK FIGURE
(1) Total ROI: 23.8%

Sales.............................	$9,000,000
Less variable expenses.................	5,400,000
Contribution margin	3,600,000
Less fixed expenses....................	2,520,000
Net operating income.................	$1,080,000
Divisional operating assets	$4,500,000

The company had an overall ROI of 18% last year (considering all divisions). The Office Products Division has an opportunity to add a new product line that would require an additional investment in operating assets of $250,000. The cost and revenue characteristics of the new product line per year would be:

Sales.........................	$1,000,000
Variable expenses	60% of sales
Fixed expenses	$350,000

Required:

1. Compute the Office Products Division's ROI for the most recent year; also compute the ROI as it will appear if the new product line is added.
2. If you were in Clem Baker's position, would you be inclined to accept or reject the new product line? Explain.
3. Why do you suppose headquarters is anxious for the Office Products Division to add the new product line?
4. Suppose that the company views a return of 15% on invested assets as being the minimum that any division should earn and that performance is evaluated by the residual income approach.
    a. Compute the Office Products Division's residual income for the most recent year; also compute the residual income as it would appear if the new product line were added.
    b. Under these circumstances, if you were in Clem Baker's position, would you accept or reject the new product line? Explain.

CHECK FIGURE
(3) ROI: 21.2%
(6) ROI: 18.4%

PROBLEM 10–14   Return on Investment Analysis   (LO1)

The income statement for Williamson Inc. for last year is given below:

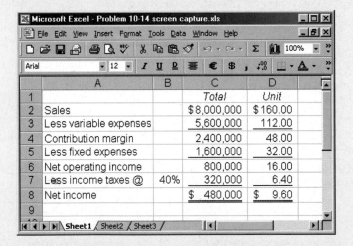

The company had average operating assets of $4 million during the year.

Required:

1. Compute the company's ROI for the period using the ROI formula stated in terms of margin and turnover.

For each of the following questions, indicate whether the margin and turnover will increase, decrease, or remain unchanged as a result of the events described and then compute the new ROI. Consider each question separately, starting in each case from the data used to compute the original ROI in (1) above.

2. Using just-in-time (JIT), the company is able to reduce the average level of inventory by $800,000. (The released funds are used to pay off short-term creditors.)

3. The company achieves a cost savings of $48,000 per year by using less costly materials.

4. The company issues bonds and uses the proceeds to purchase $1 million in machinery and equipment. Interest on the bonds is $120,000 per year. Sales remain unchanged. The new, more efficient equipment reduces production costs by $160,000 per year.

5. As a result of a more intense effort by salespeople, sales are increased by 10%; operating assets remain unchanged.

6. Obsolete items of inventory carried on the records at a cost of $80,000 are scrapped and written off as a loss.

7. The company uses $180,000 of cash (received on accounts receivable) to repurchase and retire some of its common stock.

PROBLEM 10–15   Return on Investment (ROI); Residual Income; Decentralization   (LO1, LO2)

CHECK FIGURE
(1b) Residual income: $656,000

Kramer Industries produces tool and die machinery for manufacturers. The company expanded vertically several years ago by acquiring Douglas Steel Company, one of its suppliers of alloy steel plates. Kramer Industries decided to maintain Douglas's separate identity and therefore established the Douglas Steel Division as one of its investment centers.

Kramer Industries evaluates its divisions on the basis of ROI. Management bonuses are also based on ROI. All investments in operating assets are expected to earn a minimum rate of return of 16%.

Douglas's ROI has ranged from 19% to 22% since it was acquired by Kramer Industries. During the past year, Douglas had an investment opportunity that would yield an estimated rate of return of 18%. Douglas's management decided against the investment because it believed the investment would decrease the division's overall ROI.

Last year's income statement for Douglas Steel Division is given below. The division's operating assets were $16.8 million at the end of the year, which represents an increase of 5% over the previous year-end balance.

DOUGLAS STEEL DIVISION Divisional Income Statement For the Year Ended December 31		
Sales...		$41,000,000
Cost of goods sold		20,863,000
Gross margin...........................		20,137,000
Less operating expenses:		
Selling expenses....................	$7,385,000	
Administrative expenses.............	9,472,000	16,857,000
Net operating income.................		$ 3,280,000

Required:

1. Compute the following performance measures for the Douglas Steel Division:
   a. ROI. (Remember, ROI is based on the average operating assets, computed from the beginning-of-year and end-of-year balances.) State ROI in terms of margin and turnover.
   b. Residual income.

2. Would the management of Douglas Steel Division have been more likely to accept the investment opportunity it had last year if residual income instead of ROI were used as a performance measure? Explain.

3. The Douglas Steel Division is a separate investment center within Kramer Industries. Identify the items Douglas must be free to control if it is to be evaluated fairly by either the ROI or residual income performance measures.

(CMA, adapted)

BUILDING YOUR SKILLS

ANALYTICAL THINKING   (LO1, LO2)

CHECK FIGURE
(1a) Margin: 5%
(3) Total ROI: 15.73%

The Bearing Division of Timkin Company produces a small bearing that is used by a number of companies as a component part in the manufacture of their products. Timkin Company operates its divisions as autonomous units, giving its divisional managers great discretion in pricing and other decisions. Each division is expected to generate a return on its operating assets of at least 12%. The Bearing Division has operating assets of $300,000. The bearings are sold for $4 each. Variable costs are $2.50 per bearing, and fixed costs total $234,000 each period. The division's capacity is 200,000 bearings each period.

Required:

1. How many bearings must be sold each period for the division to obtain the desired rate of return on its assets?
   a. What is the margin earned at this sales level?
   b. What is the turnover at this sales level?

2. The divisional manager is considering two ways of increasing the ROI figure:
   a. Market studies suggest that an increase in price to $4.25 per bearing would result in sales of 160,000 units each period. The decrease in units sold would allow the division to reduce its investment in assets by $10,000, due to the lower level of inventories and receivables that would be needed to support sales. Compute the margin, turnover, and ROI if these changes are made.
   b. Other market studies suggest that a reduction in price to $3.75 per bearing would result in sales of 200,000 units each period. However, this would require an increase in total assets of $10,000, due to the somewhat larger inventories and receivables that would be carried. Compute the margin, turnover, and ROI if these changes are made.

3. Refer to the original data. Assume that the normal volume of sales is 180,000 bearings each period at a price of $4 per bearing. Another division of Timkin Company is currently purchasing 20,000 bearings each period from an overseas supplier at $3.25 per bearing. The manager of the Bearing Division says that this price is "ridiculous" and refuses to meet it, since doing so would result in a loss of $0.42 per bearing for her division:

Selling price		$3.25
Cost per bearing:		
Variable cost	$2.50	
Fixed cost ($234,000 ÷ 200,000 bearings)	1.17	3.67
Loss per bearing		$(0.42)

You may assume that sales to the other division would require an increase of $25,000 in the total assets carried by the Bearing Division. If the manager of the Bearing Division accepts the transfer price of $3.25 for 20,000 bearings per period, what impact would that decision have on the Bearing Division's ROI? Should the manager of the Bearing Division accept the price of $3.25 per bearing? Why or why not?

TEAMWORK IN ACTION   (LO2)

Divide your team into two groups—one will play the part of the managers of the Consumer Products Division of Highstreet Enterprises, Inc., and the other will play the part of the managers of the Industrial Products Division of the same company.

The Consumer Products Division would like to acquire an advanced electric motor from the Industrial Products Division that would be used to make a state-of-the-art sorbet maker. At the expected selling price of $89, the Consumer Products Division would sell 50,000 sorbet makers per year. Each sorbet maker would require one of the advanced electric motors. The only possible source for the advanced electric motor is the Industrial Products Division, which holds a critical patent. The variable cost of the sorbet maker (not including the cost of the electric motor) would be $54. The sorbet maker project would require additional fixed costs of $180,000 per year and additional operating assets of $3 million.

The Industrial Products Division has plenty of spare capacity to make the electric motors requested by the Consumer Products Division. The variable cost of producing the motors would be $13 per unit. The additional fixed costs that would have to be incurred to fill the order from the Consumer Products Division would amount to $30,000 per year and the additional operating assets would be $400,000.

The division managers of Highstreet Enterprises are evaluated based on residual income, with a minimum required rate of return of 20%.

Required:

The two groups—those representing the managers of the Consumer Products Division and those representing the managers of the Industrial Products Division—should negotiate concerning the transfer price for the 50,000 advanced electric motors per year. (The groups may or may not be able to come to an agreement.) Whatever the outcome of the negotiations, each group should write a memo to the instructor justifying the outcome in terms of what would be in the best interests of their division.

COMMUNICATING IN PRACTICE (LO1, LO2)

How do the performance measurement and compensation systems of service firms compare with those of manufacturers? Ask the manager of your local McDonald's, Wendy's, Burger King, or other fast-food chain if he or she could spend some time discussing the performance measures that the company uses to evaluate store managers and how the performance measures tie in with their compensation.

Required:

After asking the following questions, write a brief memorandum to your instructor that summarizes what you discovered during your interview with the manager of the franchise.

1. What are the national chain's goals, that is, the broad, long-range plans of the company (e.g., to increase market share)?
2. What performance measures are used to help motivate the store managers and monitor progress toward achieving the corporation's goals?
3. Are the performance measures consistent with the store manager's compensation plan?

TAKING IT TO THE NET

As you know, the World Wide Web is a medium that is constantly evolving. Sites come and go, and change without notice. To enable periodic update of site addresses, this problem has been posted to the textbook website (www.mhhe.com/bgn2e). After accessing the site, enter the Student Center and select this chapter. Select and complete the Taking It to the Net problem.

CHAPTER ELEVEN

Relevant Costs for Decision Making

Faking Out Taxpayers

Owners of sports teams almost always succeed in tapping the general taxpayer to help build fancy new stadiums that include luxurious skyboxes for wealthy fans. How do they do this? Partly by paying consultants to produce studies that purport to show the new stadium's big favorable economic impact on the area. The trouble is that these studies are bogus. Voters in the state of Washington turned down public funding for the new Safeco baseball field in Seattle, but the state legislature went into special session to pass a tax bill to fund construction anyway. And shortly thereafter, taxpayers were asked to pay $325 million to tear down the old Kingdome football stadium to build a new stadium for the Seattle Seahawks. When asked why public funds should finance private facilities for professional sports, the response was: "Even if you aren't a football fan, the high level of economic activity generated by the Seahawks does affect you ...The Seahawks' total annual economic impact in Washington State is $129 million." Sounds impressive, but the argument contains a fallacy. Most of this money would have been spent in Washington State anyway even if the Seahawks had left Seattle for another city. If a local fan did not have a Seahawks game to attend, what would he/she have done with the money? Burn it? Hardly. Almost all of this money would have been spent locally anyway. An independent estimate of the *additional* spending that would come to Washington State as a result of keeping the Seahawks in Seattle put the total economic impact at less than half that erroneously claimed by proponents of the stadium. To put this in perspective, Seattle's Fred Hutchinson Cancer Research Center alone has over twice the economic impact of professional sports teams in Seattle.

Source: Tom Griffin, "Only a Game," *Columns—The University of Washington Alumni Magazine,* June 1997, pp. 15–17. An online version of this article is available at www.washington.edu/alumni/columns/june97/gamel.html.

After studying Chapter 11, you should be able to:

LO1 Identify relevant and irrelevant costs and benefits in a decision situation.

LO2 Prepare an analysis showing whether a product line or other organizational segment should be dropped or retained.

LO3 Prepare a make or buy analysis.

LO4 Prepare an analysis showing whether a special order should be accepted.

LO5 Determine the most profitable use of a constrained resource and the value of obtaining more of the constrained resource.

Making decisions is one of the basic functions of a manager. Managers are constantly faced with problems of deciding what products to sell, whether to make or buy component parts, what prices to charge, what channels of distribution to use, whether to accept special orders at special prices, and so forth. Decision making is often a difficult task that is complicated by numerous alternatives and massive amounts of data, only some of which may be relevant.

Every decision involves choosing from among at least two alternatives. In making a decision, the costs and benefits of one alternative must be compared to the costs and benefits of other alternatives. Costs that differ between alternatives are called **relevant costs.** Distinguishing between relevant and irrelevant cost and benefit data is critical for two reasons. First, irrelevant data can be ignored and need not be analyzed. This can save decision makers tremendous amounts of time and effort. Second, bad decisions can easily result from erroneously including irrelevant costs and benefits when analyzing alternatives. To be successful in decision making, managers must be able to tell the difference between relevant and irrelevant data and must be able to correctly use the relevant data in analyzing alternatives. The purpose of this chapter is to develop these skills by illustrating their use in a wide range of decision-making situations. We hasten to add that these decision-making skills are as important in your personal life as they are to managers in business. After completing your study of this chapter, you should be able to think more clearly about decisions in many facets of your life.

COST CONCEPTS FOR DECISION MAKING

Four cost terms discussed in Chapter 1 are particularly applicable to this chapter. These terms are *differential costs, incremental costs, opportunity costs,* and *sunk costs.* You may find it helpful to turn back to Chapter 1 and refresh your memory concerning these terms before reading on.

Identifying Relevant Costs and Benefits

LEARNING OBJECTIVE 1

Identify relevant and irrelevant costs and benefits in a decision situation.

Only those costs and benefits that differ in total between alternatives are relevant in a decision. If a cost will be the same regardless of the alternative selected, then the decision has no effect on the cost and it can be ignored. For example, if you are trying to decide whether to go to a movie or to rent a videotape for the evening, the rent on your apartment is irrelevant. Whether you go to a movie or rent a videotape, the rent on your apartment will be exactly the same and is therefore irrelevant in the decision. On the other hand, the cost of the movie ticket and the cost of renting the videotape would be relevant in the decision since they are *avoidable costs.*

An **avoidable cost** is a cost that can be eliminated in whole or in part by choosing one alternative over another. By choosing the alternative of going to the movie, the cost of renting the videotape can be avoided. By choosing the alternative of renting the videotape, the cost of the movie ticket can be avoided. Therefore, the cost of the movie ticket and the cost of renting the videotape are both avoidable costs. On the other hand, the rent on the apartment is not an avoidable cost of either alternative. You would continue to rent your apartment under either alternative. Avoidable costs are relevant costs. Unavoidable costs are irrelevant costs.

Two broad categories of costs are never relevant in decisions. These irrelevant costs are:

1. Sunk costs.
2. Future costs that do not differ between the alternatives.

As we learned in Chapter 1, a **sunk cost** is a cost that has already been incurred and that cannot be avoided regardless of what a manager decides to do. Sunk costs are always the same, no matter what alternatives are being considered, and they are therefore always irrelevant and should be ignored. On the other hand, future costs that do differ between alternatives *are* relevant. For example, when deciding whether to go to a movie or rent a videotape, the cost of buying a movie ticket and the cost of renting a videotape have not yet been incurred. These are future costs that differ between alternatives when the decision is being made and therefore are relevant.

Along with sunk cost, the term **differential cost** was introduced in Chapter 1. In managerial accounting, the terms *avoidable cost, differential cost, incremental cost,* and *relevant cost* are often used interchangeably. To identify the costs that are avoidable (differential) in a particular decision situation and are therefore relevant, these steps can be followed:

1. Eliminate costs and benefits that do not differ between alternatives. These irrelevant costs consist of (a) sunk costs and (b) future costs that do not differ between alternatives.
2. Use the remaining costs and benefits that do differ between alternatives in making the decision. The costs that remain are the differential, or avoidable, costs.

It Isn't Easy to Be Smart about Money

Most of us suffer from psychological quirks that make it very difficult for us to actually ignore irrelevant costs when making decisions. As Dan Seligman puts it: "Higher primates do not like to admit, even to themselves, that they have screwed up." Humans have "the deep-seated, egoistic human need—evidenced in numerous psychological experiments—to justify the sunk costs in one's life . . . Many people do not feel liberated by the news that sunk costs are irrelevant. Quite the contrary—they wish to resist the news."

What's the evidence? A lot of it comes from psychology labs, but much of it is recognizable in daily life. Homeowners commonly refuse to sell their homes for less than they paid for them even though the original price they paid is a sunk cost that is wholly irrelevant in the pricing decision. No matter what price they charge now, they will have paid exactly the same price when they originally bought the house and hence the original cost of the house is completely irrelevant. So why do people refuse to sell houses for less than they paid? Probably to avoid admitting to themselves that they made a mistake.

One of the authors of this text knows about this quirk from personal experience. He sold all of the mutual funds in his retirement accounts and transferred the funds into safe money market funds when the Dow-Jones Industrial stock market average was at 7200. The market subsequently climbed to over 10000, but he has refused to buy back into the stock market until it falls back below 7200. However, this is irrational. The fact that he bailed out of the market when it was at 7200 should be completely irrelevant in the decision of whether and when to buy back into the market. However, buying back at a price above 7200 would be an admission that it was a mistake to sell at that level, so he refuses to do it.

Sources: Dan Seligman, "Of Mice and *Economics,*" *Forbes,* August 24, 1998, p. 62; Brian O'Reilley, "Why Johnny Can't Invest," *Fortune,* November 9, 1998, pp. 173–178; John S. Hammond, Ralph L. Keeney, and Howard Raiffa, "The Hidden Traps in Decision Making," *Harvard Business Review,* September–October 1998, pp. 47–58; and one of the authors' personal investment portfolio records.

Different Costs for Different Purposes

We need to recognize from the outset of our discussion that costs that are relevant in one decision situation are not necessarily relevant in another. Simply put, this means that *the manager needs different costs for different purposes.* For one purpose, a particular group of costs may be relevant; for another purpose, an entirely different group of costs may be relevant. Thus, in *each* decision situation the manager must examine the data at hand and isolate the relevant costs. Otherwise, the manager runs the risk of being misled by irrelevant data.

The concept of "different costs for different purposes" is basic to managerial accounting; we shall see its application frequently in the pages that follow.

What Is Cost Anyway?

The wine newsletter *Liquid Assets* sent out a survey to its readers posing the following question:

> Suppose you bought a case of good 1982 Bordeaux [wine] for $20 a bottle and it now sells for $75. You give the bottle to a friend. Which of the following best captures your feeling of the cost to you as a gift?

The responses were:

		Gift	Drop
Nothing	I paid for the bottle already..	30%	8%
$20	The amount I paid for the bottle.	16%	24%
$20+	The amount I paid for the bottle plus interest.	9%	11%
$75	The amount it would take to replace the bottle.	30%	54%
($55)	I am saving $55. I only paid $20 for a $75 gift.	15%	2%
		100%	100%

The last column in the above table reports the responses to a slightly different question in which readers were asked what they would feel about the cost of the bottle of wine if they had dropped it. From a economist's viewpoint—and the correct viewpoint for making decisions about the wine—the cost of the bottle is $75 whether given as a gift or dropped. Interestingly, only 30% of the respondents gave the correct response when the bottle was given as a gift, but 54% gave the correct response when the bottle was dropped.

Source: Samuel Brittan, "Glad Tidings of Dear Joy," *Financial Times (U.K.),* December 1995.

An Example of Identifying Relevant Costs and Benefits

Cynthia is currently a student in an MBA program in Boston and would like to visit a friend in New York City over the weekend. She is trying to decide whether to drive or take the train. Because she is on a tight budget, she wants to carefully consider the costs of the two alternatives. If one alternative is far less expensive than the other, that may be decisive in her choice. By car, the distance between her apartment in Boston and her friend's apartment in New York City is 230 miles. Cynthia has compiled the following list of items to consider:

Automobile Costs		
Item	Annual Cost of Fixed Items	Cost per Mile (based on 10,000 miles per year)
(a) Annual straight-line depreciation on car [($18,000 original cost − $4,000 estimated resale value in 5 years)/5 years]	$2,800	$0.280
(b) Cost of gasoline ($1.60 per gallon ÷ 32 miles per gallon)		0.050
(c) Annual cost of auto insurance and license	$1,380	0.138
		(continued)

(concluded)	Automobile Costs		
Item		Annual Cost of Fixed Items	Cost per Mile (based on 10,000 miles per year)
(d)	Maintenance and repairs		0.065
(e)	Parking fees at school ($45 per month × 8 months). . . .	$360	0.036
(f)	Total average cost per mile		$0.569
(g)	Reduction in the resale value of car due solely to wear and tear.	$0.026 per mile	
(h)	Cost of round-trip Amtrak ticket from Boston to New York City	$104	
(i)	Benefit of relaxing and being able to study during the train ride rather than having to drive	?	
(j)	Cost of putting the dog in a kennel while gone	$40	
(k)	Benefit of having a car available in New York City	?	
(l)	Hassle of parking the car in New York City	?	
(m)	Cost of parking the car in New York City	$25 per day	

Which costs and benefits are relevant in this decision? Remember, only those costs and benefits that differ between alternatives are relevant. Everything else is irrelevant and can be ignored.

Start at the top of the list with item (a): the original cost of the car is a sunk cost. This cost has already been incurred and therefore can never differ between alternatives. Consequently, it is irrelevant and can be ignored. The same is true of the accounting depreciation of $2,800 per year, which simply spreads the sunk cost across a number of years.

Move down the list to item (b): the cost of gasoline consumed by driving to New York City. This would clearly be a relevant cost in this decision. If Cynthia takes the train, this cost would not be incurred. Hence, the cost differs between alternatives and is therefore relevant.

Item (c), the annual cost of auto insurance and license, is not relevant. Whether Cynthia takes the train or drives on this particular trip, her annual auto insurance premium and her auto license fee will remain the same.[1]

Item (d), the cost of maintenance and repairs, is relevant. While maintenance and repair costs have a large random component, over the long run they should be more or less proportional to the amount the car is driven. Thus, the average cost of $0.065 per mile is a reasonable estimate to use.

Item (e), the monthly fee that Cynthia pays to park at her school during the academic year, would not be relevant in the decision of how to get to New York City. Regardless of which alternative she selects—driving or taking the train—she will still need to pay for parking at school.

Item (f) is the total average cost of $0.569 per mile. As discussed above, some elements of this total are relevant, but some are not relevant. Since it contains some irrelevant costs, it would be incorrect to estimate the cost of driving to New York City and back by simply multiplying the $0.569 by 460 miles (230 miles each way × 2). This erroneous approach would yield a cost of driving of $261.74. Unfortunately, such mistakes are often made in both personal life and in business. Since the total cost is stated on a per-mile basis, people are easily misled. Often people think that if the cost is stated as $0.569 per mile, the cost of driving 100 miles is $56.90. But it is not. Many of the costs included in the $0.569 cost per mile are sunk and/or fixed and will not increase if the car is driven

---

[1]If Cynthia has an accident while driving to New York City or back, this might affect her insurance premium when the policy is renewed. The increase in the insurance premium would be a relevant cost of this particular trip, but the normal amount of the insurance premium is not relevant in any case.

another 100 miles. The $0.569 is an average cost, not an incremental cost. Beware of such unitized costs (i.e., costs stated in terms of a dollar amount per unit, per mile, per direct labor-hour, per machine-hour, and so on)—they are often misleading.

Item (g), the decline in the resale value of the car that occurs as a consequence of driving it more miles, is relevant in the decision. Because she uses the car, its resale value declines. Eventually, she will be able to get less for the car when she sells it or trades it in on another car. This reduction in resale value is a real cost of using the car that should be taken into account. Cynthia estimates this cost by accessing the *Kelly Blue Book* website at www.kbb.com. The reduction in resale value of an asset through use or over time is often called *real* or *economic depreciation.* This is different from accounting depreciation, which attempts to match the sunk cost of the asset with the periods that benefit from that cost.

Item (h), the $104 cost of a round-trip ticket on Amtrak, is clearly relevant in this decision. If she drives, she would not have to buy the ticket.

Item (i) is relevant to the decision, even if it is difficult to put a dollar value on relaxing and being able to study while on the train. It is relevant because it is a benefit that is available under one alternative but not under the other.

Item (j), the cost of putting Cynthia's dog in the kennel while she is gone, is clearly irrelevant in this decision. Whether she takes the train or drives to New York City, she will still need to put her dog in a kennel.

Like item (i), items (k) and (l) are relevant to the decision even if it is difficult to measure their dollar impacts.

Item (m), the cost of parking in New York City, is relevant to the decision.

Bringing together all of the relevant data, Cynthia would estimate the relative costs of driving and taking the train as follows:

Relevant financial cost of driving to New York City:	
Gasoline (460 miles at $0.050 per mile)	$23.00
Maintenance and repairs (460 miles @ $0.065 per mile)	29.90
Reduction in the resale value of car due solely to wear and tear (460 miles @ $0.026 per mile)	11.96
Cost of parking the car in New York City (2 days @ $25 per day)	50.00
Total	$114.86

Relevant financial cost of taking the train to New York City:	
Cost of round-trip Amtrak ticket from Boston to New York City	$104.00

What should Cynthia do? From a purely financial standpoint, it would be cheaper by $10.86 ($114.86 − $104.00) to take the train than to drive. Cynthia has to decide if the convenience of having a car in New York City outweighs the additional cost and the disadvantages of being unable to relax and study on the train and the hassle of finding parking in the city.

In this example, we focused on identifying the relevant costs and benefits—everything else was ignored. In the next example, we will begin the analysis by including all of the costs and benefits—relevant or not. We will see that if we are very careful, we will still get the correct answer because the irrelevant costs and benefits will cancel out when we compare the alternatives.

IN BUSINESS

Cruising on the Cheap

Cruise ship operators such as Princess Cruises sometimes offer deep discounts on popular cruises. Recently, a 10-day Mediterranean cruise on the Norwegian Dream was being offered at up to 75% off the list price. A seven-day cruise to Alaska could be booked for a $499–$700 discount. The cause? "An ambitious fleet expansion left the cruise industry grappling with a tidal wave of capacity . . . Most cruise costs are fixed whether all the ship's berths are filled or not, so it is better to sell cheap than not at all . . . In the current glut, discounting has made it possible for the cruise lines to keep berths nearly full."

Source: Martin Brannigan, *The Wall Street Journal*, July 17, 2000, pp. B1 and B4.

Reconciling the Total and Differential Approaches

Oak Harbor Woodworks is considering a new labor-saving machine that rents for $3,000 per year. The machine will be used on the company's butcher block production line. Data concerning the company's annual sales and costs of butcher blocks with and without the new machine are shown below:

	Current Situation	Situation with the New Machine
Units produced and sold.	5,000	5,000
Selling price per unit	$40	$40
Direct materials cost per unit.	$14	$14
Direct labor cost per unit.	$8	$5
Variable overhead cost per unit	$2	$2
Fixed costs, other	$62,000	$62,000
Fixed costs, new machine	—	$3,000

Given the annual sales and the price and cost data above, the net operating income for the product under the two alternatives can be computed as shown in Exhibit 11–1.

Note that the net operating income is higher by $12,000 with the new machine, so that is the better alternative. Note also that the $12,000 advantage for the new machine can be obtained in two different ways. It is the difference between the $30,000 net operating income with the new machine and the $18,000 net operating income for the current situation. It is also the sum of the differential costs and benefits as shown in the last column of Exhibit 11–1. A positive number in the Differential Costs and Benefits column indicates that the difference between the alternatives favors the new machine; a negative number indicates that the difference favors the current situation. A zero in that column

	Current Situation	Situation with New Machine	Differential Costs and Benefits
Sales (5,000 units @ $40 per unit).	$200,000	$200,000	$ 0
Less variable expenses:			
Direct materials (5,000 units @ $14 per unit)	70,000	70,000	0
Direct labor (5,000 units @ $8 and $5 per unit) .	40,000	25,000	15,000
Variable overhead (5,000 units @ $2 per unit) .	10,000	10,000	0
Total variable expenses .	120,000	105,000	
Contribution margin .	80,000	95,000	
Less fixed expenses:			
Other.	62,000	62,000	0
Rent of new machine	0	3,000	(3,000)
Total fixed expenses	62,000	65,000	
Net operating income.	$ 18,000	$ 30,000	$12,000

EXHIBIT 11–1

Total and Differential Costs

simply means that the total amount for the item is exactly the same for both alternatives. Thus, since the difference in the net operating incomes equals the sum of the differences for the individual items, any cost or benefit that is the same for both alternatives will have no impact on which alternative is preferred. This is the reason that costs and benefits that do not differ between alternatives are irrelevant and can be ignored. If we properly account for them, they will cancel out when we compare the alternatives.

We could have arrived at the same solution much more quickly by ignoring altogether the irrelevant costs and benefits.

- The selling price per unit and the number of units sold do not differ between the alternatives. Therefore the total sales revenues are exactly the same for the two alternatives as shown in Exhibit 11–1. Since the sales revenues are exactly the same, they have no effect on the difference in net operating income between the two alternatives. That is shown in the last column in Exhibit 11–1, which shows a $0 differential benefit.
- The direct materials cost per unit, the variable overhead cost per unit, and the number of units produced and sold do not differ between the alternatives. Consequently, the direct materials cost and the variable overhead cost will be the same for the two alternatives and can be ignored.
- The "other" fixed expenses do not differ between the alternatives, so they can be ignored as well.

Indeed, the only costs that do differ between the alternatives are direct labor costs and the fixed rental cost of the new machine. Hence, these are the only relevant costs. The two alternatives can be compared based on just these relevant costs:

Net advantage to renting the new machine:	
Decrease in direct labor costs (5,000 units at a cost savings of $3 per unit)	$15,000
Increase in fixed expenses	(3,000)
Net annual cost savings from renting the new machine	$12,000

Thus, if we focus on just the relevant costs and benefits, we get exactly the same answer that we got when we listed all of the costs and benefits—including those that do not differ between the alternatives and hence are irrelevant. We get the same answer because the only costs and benefits that matter in the final comparison of the net operating incomes are those that differ between the two alternatives and hence are not zero in the last column of Exhibit 11–1. Those two relevant costs are both listed in the above analysis showing the net advantage to renting the new machine.

Why Isolate Relevant Costs?

In the preceding example, we used two different approaches to analyze the alternatives. First, we considered all costs, both those that were relevant and those that were not; and second, we considered only the relevant costs. We obtained the same answer under both approaches. It would be natural to ask, "Why bother to isolate relevant costs when total costs will do the job just as well?" Isolating relevant costs is desirable for at least two reasons.

First, only rarely will enough information be available to prepare a detailed income statement for both alternatives. Assume, for example, that you are called on to make a decision relating to just a portion of a *single operation* of a multidepartmental, multiproduct firm. Under these circumstances, it would be virtually impossible to prepare an income statement of any type. You would have to rely on your ability to recognize which costs are relevant and which are not in order to assemble that data necessary to make a decision.

Second, mingling irrelevant costs with relevant costs may cause confusion and distract attention from the matters that are really critical. Furthermore, the danger always exists that an irrelevant piece of data may be used improperly, resulting in an incorrect decision. The best approach is to ignore irrelevant data and base the decision entirely on the relevant data.

Relevant cost analysis, combined with the contribution approach to the income statement, provides a powerful tool for making decisions. We will investigate various uses of this tool in the remaining sections of this chapter.

Environmental Costs Add Up

A decision analysis can be flawed by incorrectly including irrelevant costs such as sunk costs and future costs that do not differ between alternatives. It can also be flawed by omitting future costs that *do* differ between alternatives. This is particularly a problem with environmental costs that have dramatically increased in recent years and about which many managers have little knowledge.

Consider the environmental complications posed by a decision of whether to install a solvent-based or powder-based system for spray-painting parts. In a solvent painting system, parts are sprayed as they move along a conveyor. The paint that misses the part is swept away by a wall of water, called a water curtain. The excess paint accumulates in a pit as sludge that must be removed each month. Environmental regulations classify this sludge as hazardous waste. As a result, the company must obtain a permit to produce the waste and must maintain meticulous records of how the waste is transported, stored, and disposed of. The annual costs of complying with these regulations can easily exceed $140,000 in total for a painting facility that initially costs only $400,000 to build. The costs of complying with environmental regulations include the following:

- The waste sludge must be hauled to a special disposal site. The typical disposal fee is about $300 per barrel, or $55,000 per year for a modest solvent-based painting system.
- Workers must be specially trained to handle the paint sludge.
- The company must carry special insurance.
- The company must pay substantial fees to the state for releasing pollutants (i.e., the solvent) into the air.
- The water in the water curtain must be specially treated to remove contaminants. This cost can run into tens of thousands of dollars per year.

In contrast, a powder-based painting system avoids almost all of these environmental costs. Excess powder used in the painting process can be recovered and reused without creating a hazardous waste. Additionally, the powder-based system does not release contaminants into the atmosphere. Therefore, even though the cost of building a powder-based system may be higher than the cost of building a solvent-based system, over the long run the costs of the powder-based system may be far lower due to the high environmental costs of a solvent-based system. Managers need to be aware of such environmental costs and take them fully into account when making decisions.

Source: Germain Böer, Margaret Curtin, and Louis Hoyt, "Environmental Cost Management," *Management Accounting*, September 1998, pp. 28–38.

1. Which of the following statements is false? (You may select more than one answer.)
   a. Under some circumstances, a sunk cost may be a relevant cost.
   b. Future costs that do not differ between alternatives are irrelevant.
   c. The same cost may be relevant or irrelevant depending on the decision context.
   d. Only variable costs are relevant costs. Fixed costs cannot be relevant costs.
2. Assume that in October you bought a $450 nonrefundable airline ticket to Telluride, Colorado, for a 5-day/4-night Christmas ski vacation. You now have an opportunity

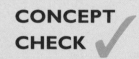

CONCEPT CHECK

to buy an airline ticket for a 5-day/4-night Christmas ski vacation in Stowe, Vermont, for $200 that includes a free ski lift ticket. The price of your lift ticket for the Telluride vacation would be $100. The price of a hotel room in Telluride is $180 per night. The price of a hotel room in Stowe is $150 per night. Which of the following costs is not relevant in a decision of whether to proceed with the planned trip to Telluride or to change to a trip to Stowe?
a. The $450 airline ticket to Telluride.
b. The $200 airline ticket to Stowe.
c. The $100 lift ticket for the Telluride vacation.
d. The $180 per night hotel room in Telluride.
3. Based on the facts in question 2 above, does a differential cost analysis favor Telluride or Stowe, and by how much?
a. Stowe by $470.
b. Stowe by $20.
c. Telluride by $70.
d. Telluride $20.

ADDING AND DROPPING PRODUCT LINES AND OTHER SEGMENTS

LEARNING OBJECTIVE 2

Prepare an analysis showing whether a product line or other organizational segment should be dropped or retained.

Decisions relating to whether old product lines or other segments of a company should be dropped and new ones added are among the most difficult that a manager has to make. In such decisions, many qualitative and quantitative factors must be considered. Ultimately, however, any final decision to drop an old segment or to add a new one is going to hinge primarily on the impact the decision will have on net operating income. To assess this impact, it is necessary to carefully analyze the costs.

An Illustration of Cost Analysis

Concept 11–1

Consider the three major product lines of the Discount Drug Company—drugs, cosmetics, and housewares. Sales and cost information for the preceding month for each separate product line and for the store in total are given in Exhibit 11–2.

What can be done to improve the company's overall performance? One product line—housewares—shows a net operating loss for the month. Perhaps dropping this line would increase the company's profits. However, the report in Exhibit 11–2 may be misleading. No attempt has been made in Exhibit 11–2 to distinguish between fixed expenses

EXHIBIT 11–2

Discount Drug Company
Product Lines

		Product Line		
	Total	**Drugs**	**Cosmetics**	**Housewares**
Sales....................	$250,000	$125,000	$75,000	$50,000
Less variable expenses	105,000	50,000	25,000	30,000
Contribution margin..........	145,000	75,000	50,000	20,000
Less fixed expenses:				
Salaries	50,000	29,500	12,500	8,000
Advertising	15,000	1,000	7,500	6,500
Utilities	2,000	500	500	1,000
Depreciation—fixtures.......	5,000	1,000	2,000	2,000
Rent.....................	20,000	10,000	6,000	4,000
Insurance................	3,000	2,000	500	500
General administrative	30,000	15,000	9,000	6,000
Total fixed expenses	125,000	59,000	38,000	28,000
Net operating income (loss).....	$ 20,000	$ 16,000	$12,000	$ (8,000)

that may be avoidable if a product line is dropped and fixed expenses that cannot be avoided by dropping any particular product line. The alternatives under consideration are keeping the housewares product line and dropping the housewares product line. Only those costs that differ between the two alternatives (i.e., that can be avoided by dropping the housewares product line) are relevant. In deciding whether to drop a product line, it is crucial for managers to clearly identify which costs can be avoided, and hence are relevant to the decision, and which costs cannot be avoided, and hence are irrelevant. The decision should be approached as follows:

If the housewares line is dropped, then the company will lose $20,000 per month in contribution margin, but by dropping the line it may be possible to avoid some fixed costs. It may be possible, for example, to discharge certain employees, or it may be possible to reduce advertising costs. If by dropping the housewares line the company is able to avoid more in fixed costs than it loses in contribution margin, then it will be better off if the product line is eliminated, since overall net operating income should improve. On the other hand, if the company is not able to avoid as much in fixed costs as it loses in contribution margin, then the housewares line should be retained. In short, the manager should ask, "What costs can I avoid if I drop this product line?"

As we have seen from our earlier discussion, not all costs are avoidable. For example, some of the costs associated with a product line may be sunk costs. Other costs may be allocated fixed costs that will not differ in total regardless of whether the product line is dropped or retained.

To show how one should proceed in a product-line analysis, suppose that the management of the Discount Drug Company has analyzed the fixed costs being charged to the three product lines and has determined the following:

1. The salaries expense represents salaries paid to employees working directly on the product. All of the employees working in housewares would be discharged if the product line is dropped.
2. The advertising expense represents product advertising specific to each product line and is avoidable if the line is dropped.
3. The utilities expense represents utilities costs for the entire company. The amount charged to each product line is an allocation based on space occupied and is not avoidable if the product line is dropped.
4. The depreciation expense represents depreciation on fixtures used for display of the various product lines. Although the fixtures are nearly new, they are custom-built and will have no resale value if the housewares line is dropped.
5. The rent expense represents rent on the entire building housing the company; it is allocated to the product lines on the basis of sales dollars. The monthly rent of $20,000 is fixed under a long-term lease agreement.
6. The insurance expense represents insurance carried on inventories within each of the three product lines.
7. The general administrative expense represents the costs of accounting, purchasing, and general management, which are allocated to the product lines on the basis of sales dollars. Total administrative costs will not change if the housewares line is dropped.

With this information, management can identify fixed costs that can and cannot be avoided if the product line is dropped:

Fixed Expenses	Total Cost Assigned to Housewares	Not Avoidable*	Avoidable
Salaries	$ 8,000		$ 8,000
Advertising	6,500		6,500
Utilities	1,000	$ 1,000	
Depreciation—fixtures.	2,000	2,000	

(continued)

(concluded) Fixed Expenses	Total Cost Assigned to Housewares	Not Avoidable*	Avoidable
Rent.	4,000	4,000	
Insurance.	500		500
General administrative	6,000	6,000	
Total	$28,000	$13,000	$15,000

*These fixed costs represent either (1) sunk costs or (2) future costs that will not change whether the housewares line is retained or discontinued.

To determine how dropping the line will affect the overall profits of the company, we can compare the contribution margin that will be lost to the costs that can be avoided if the line is dropped:

Contribution margin lost if the housewares line is discontinued (see Exhibit 11–2)	$(20,000)
Less fixed costs that can be avoided if the housewares line is discontinued (see above)	15,000
Decrease in overall company net operating income	$ (5,000)

In this case, the fixed costs that can be avoided by dropping the product line are less than the contribution margin that will be lost. Therefore, based on the data given, the housewares line should not be discontinued unless a more profitable use can be found for the floor and counter space that it is occupying.

A Comparative Format

Some managers prefer to approach decisions of this type by preparing comparative income statements showing the effects on the company as a whole of either keeping or dropping the product line in question as we did in Exhibit 11–1. A comparative analysis of this type for the Discount Drug Company is shown in Exhibit 11–3.

EXHIBIT 11–3

A Comparative Format for Product-Line Analysis

	Keep Housewares	Drop Housewares	Difference: Net Operating Income Increase (or Decrease)
Sales	$50,000	$ 0	$(50,000)
Less variable expenses	30,000	0	30,000
Contribution margin	20,000	0	(20,000)
Less fixed expenses:			
Salaries	8,000	0	8,000
Advertising	6,500	0	6,500
Utilities	1,000	1,000	0
Depreciation—fixtures	2,000	2,000	0
Rent	4,000	4,000	0
Insurance	500	0	500
General administrative	6,000	6,000	0
Total fixed expenses	28,000	13,000	15,000
Net operating income (loss)	$ (8,000)	$(13,000)	$ (5,000)

As shown in the last column in the exhibit, overall company net operating income will decrease by $5,000 each period if the housewares line is dropped. This is the same answer, of course, as we obtained when we focused just on the lost contribution margin and avoidable fixed costs.

Beware of Allocated Fixed Costs

Our conclusion that the housewares line should not be dropped seems to conflict with the data shown earlier in Exhibit 11–2. Recall from the exhibit that the housewares line is showing a loss rather than a profit. Why keep a product line that is showing a loss? The explanation for this apparent inconsistency lies at least in part with the *common fixed costs* that are being allocated to the product lines. A **common fixed cost** is a fixed cost that supports the operations of more than one segment of an organization and that is not avoidable in whole or in part by eliminating any one segment. For example, the salary of the CEO of a company ordinarily would not be cut if any one product line were dropped, so it is a common fixed cost of the product lines. In fact, if dropping a product line is a good idea that results in higher profits for the company, the compensation of the CEO is likely to increase, rather than decrease. One of the great dangers in allocating common fixed costs is that such allocations can make a product line (or other segment of a business) *look* less profitable than it really is. By allocating the common fixed costs among all product lines, the housewares line has been made to *look* as if it were unprofitable, whereas, in fact, dropping the line would result in a decrease in overall company net operating income. This point can be seen clearly if we recast the data in Exhibit 11–2 and eliminate the allocation of the common fixed costs. This recasting of data is shown in Exhibit 11–4.

Notice that the common fixed expenses have not been allocated to the product lines in Exhibit 11–4. Only the fixed expenses that are traceable to the product lines and that could be avoided by dropping the product lines are assigned to them. For example, the fixed expenses of advertising the housewares product line can be traced to that product line and can be eliminated if that product line is dropped. However, the general administrative

EXHIBIT 11–4

Discount Drug Company Product Lines—Recast in Contribution Format (from Exhibit 11–2)

| | Total | | Product Line | |
		Drugs	Cosmetics	Housewares
Sales	$250,000	$125,000	$75,000	$50,000
Less variable expenses..........	105,000	50,000	25,000	30,000
Contribution margin	145,000	75,000	50,000	20,000
Less traceable fixed expenses:				
Salaries...................	50,000	29,500	12,500	8,000
Advertising................	15,000	1,000	7,500	6,500
Depreciation—fixtures	5,000	1,000	2,000	2,000
Insurance	3,000	2,000	500	500
Total traceable fixed expenses....	73,000	33,500	22,500	17,000
Product-line segment margin.....	72,000	$ 41,500	$27,500	$ 3,000*
Less common fixed expenses:				
Utilities....................	2,000			
Rent	20,000			
General administrative........	30,000			
Total common fixed expenses....	52,000			
Net operating income	$ 20,000			

*If the housewares line is dropped, this $3,000 in segment margin will be lost to the company. In addition, we have seen that the $2,000 depreciation on the fixtures is a sunk cost that cannot be avoided. The sum of these two figures ($3,000 + $2,000 = $5,000) would be the decrease in the company's overall profits if the housewares line were discontinued.

expenses, such as the CEO's salary, cannot be traced to the individual product lines and would not be eliminated if any one product line were dropped. Consequently, these common fixed expenses are not allocated to the product lines in Exhibit 11–4 as they were in Exhibit 11–2. The allocations in Exhibit 11–2 provide a misleading picture that suggests that portions of the fixed common expenses can be eliminated by dropping individual product lines—which is not the case.

Exhibit 11–4 gives us a much different perspective of the housewares line than does Exhibit 11–2. As shown in Exhibit 11–4, the housewares line is covering all of its own traceable fixed costs and is generating a $3,000 *segment margin* toward covering the common fixed costs of the company. The **segment margin** is the difference between the revenue generated by a segment and its own traceable costs. Unless another product line can be found that will generate more than a $3,000 segment margin, the company would be better off keeping the housewares line. By keeping the line, the company's overall net operating income will be higher than if the product line were dropped.

Additionally, we should note that managers may choose to retain an unprofitable product line if the line is necessary to the sale of other products or if it serves as a "magnet" to attract customers. Bread, for example, is not an especially profitable line in some food stores, but customers expect it to be available, and many would undoubtedly shift their buying elsewhere if a particular store decided to stop carrying it.

IN BUSINESS

The Trap Laid by Fully Allocated Costs

A bakery distributed its products through route salespersons, each of whom loaded a truck with an assortment of products in the morning and spent the day calling on customers in an assigned territory. Believing that some items were more profitable than others, management asked for an analysis of product costs and sales. The accountants to whom the task was assigned allocated all manufacturing and marketing costs to products to obtain a net profit for each product. The resulting figures indicated that some of the products were being sold at a loss, and management discontinued these products. However, when this change was put into effect, the company's overall profit declined. It was then seen that by dropping some products, sales revenues had been reduced without commensurate reduction in costs because the common manufacturing costs and route sales costs had to be continued in order to make and sell the remaining products.

THE MAKE OR BUY DECISION

LEARNING OBJECTIVE 3

Prepare a make or buy analysis.

Concept 11–2

A decision whether to produce a part internally or to buy the part externally from a supplier is called a **make or buy decision.** To provide an illustration of a make or buy decision, consider Mountain Goat Cycles. The company is now producing the heavy-duty gear shifters used in its most popular line of mountain bikes. The company's Accounting Department reports the following costs of producing 8,000 units of the shifter internally each year:

	Per Unit	8,000 Units
Direct materials	$6	$ 48,000
Direct labor	4	32,000
Variable overhead	1	8,000
Supervisor's salary	3	24,000
Depreciation of special equipment	2	16,000
Allocated general overhead	5	40,000
Total cost	$21	$168,000

An outside supplier has offered to sell 8,000 shifters a year to Mountain Goat Cycles at a price of only $19 each. Should the company stop producing the shifters internally and start purchasing them from the outside supplier? To approach the decision from a financial point of view, the manager should again focus on the relevant costs. As we have seen, relevant (i.e., differential or avoidable) costs can be obtained by eliminating those costs that are not avoidable—that is, by eliminating (1) the sunk costs and (2) the future costs that will continue regardless of whether the shifters are produced internally or purchased outside. The costs that remain after making these eliminations are the costs that are avoidable to the company by purchasing outside. If these avoidable costs are less than the outside purchase price, then the company should continue to manufacture its own shifters and reject the outside supplier's offer. That is, the company should purchase outside only if the outside purchase price is less than the costs that can be avoided internally as a result of stopping production of the shifters.

Looking at the cost data for producing the shifter internally, note first that depreciation of special equipment is listed as one of the costs of producing the shifters internally. Since the equipment has already been purchased, this depreciation is a sunk cost and is therefore irrelevant. If the equipment could be sold, its salvage value would be relevant. Or if the machine could be used to make other products, this could be relevant as well. However, we will assume that the equipment has no salvage value and that it has no other use except making the heavy-duty gear shifters.

Also note that the company is allocating a portion of its general overhead costs to the shifters. Any portion of this general overhead cost that would actually be eliminated if the gear shifters were purchased rather than made would be relevant in the analysis. However, it is likely that the general overhead costs allocated to the gear shifters are in fact common to all items produced in the factory and would continue unchanged even if the shifters are purchased from the outside. Such allocated common costs are not relevant costs (since they do not differ between the make or buy alternatives) and should be eliminated from the analysis along with the sunk costs.

The variable costs of producing the shifters (materials, labor, and variable overhead) are relevant costs, since they can be avoided by buying the shifters from the outside supplier. If the supervisor can be discharged and his or her salary avoided by buying the shifters, then it too will be relevant to the decision. Assuming that both the variable costs and the supervisor's salary can be avoided by buying from the outside supplier, then the analysis takes the form shown in Exhibit 11–5.

Since it costs $40,000 less to continue to make the shifters internally, Mountain Goat Cycles should reject the outside supplier's offer. However, management may wish to consider one additional factor before coming to a final decision. This factor is the opportunity cost of the space now being used to produce the shifters.

EXHIBIT 11–5

Mountain Goat Cycles Make or Buy Analysis

	Production "Cost" per Unit	Per Unit Differential Costs		Total Differential Costs—8,000 Units	
		Make	Buy	Make	Buy
Direct materials	$ 6	$ 6		$ 48,000	
Direct labor	4	4		32,000	
Variable overhead.	1	1		8,000	
Supervisor's salary	3	3		24,000	
Depreciation of special equipment.	2	—		—	
Allocated general overhead	5	—		—	
Outside purchase price			$19		$152,000
Total cost	$21	$14	$19	$112,000	$152,000
Difference in favor of continuing to make.			$5		$40,000

OPPORTUNITY COST

If the space now being used to produce the shifters *would otherwise be idle,* then Mountain Goat Cycles should continue to produce its own shifters and the supplier's offer should be rejected, as stated above. Idle space that has no alternative use has an opportunity cost of zero.

But what if the space now being used to produce shifters could be used for some other purpose? In that case, the space would have an opportunity cost that should be considered in assessing the desirability of the supplier's offer. What would this opportunity cost be? It would be the segment margin that could be derived from the best alternative use of the space.

To illustrate, assume that the space now being used to produce shifters could be used to produce a new cross-country bike that would generate a segment margin of $60,000 per year. Under these conditions, Mountain Goat Cycles would be better off to accept the supplier's offer and to use the available space to produce the new product line:

	Make	Buy
Total annual cost (see Exhibit 11–5)	$112,000	$152,000
Opportunity cost—segment margin forgone on a potential new product line	60,000	
Total cost	$172,000	$152,000
Difference in favor of purchasing from the outside supplier		$20,000

Opportunity costs are not recorded in the organization's formal accounts since they do not represent actual dollar outlays. Rather, they represent economic benefits that are *forgone* as a result of pursuing some course of action. The opportunity costs of Mountain Goat Cycles are sufficiently large in this case to change the decision.

DECISION MAKER

Vice President of Production

You are faced with a make or buy decision. The company currently makes a component for one of its products but is considering whether it should instead purchase the component. If the offer from an outside supplier were accepted, the company would no longer need to rent the machinery that is currently being used to manufacture the component. You realize that the annual rental cost is a fixed cost, but recall some sort of warning about fixed costs. Is the annual rental cost relevant to this make or buy decision?

SPECIAL ORDERS

Managers must often evaluate whether a *special order* should be accepted, and if the order is accepted, the price that should be charged. A **special order** is a one-time order that is not considered part of the company's normal ongoing business. To illustrate, Mountain Goat Cycles has just received a request from the Seattle Police Department to produce 100 specially modified mountain bikes at a price of $179 each. The bikes would be used to patrol some of the more densely populated residential sections of the city. Mountain Goat Cycles can easily modify its City Cruiser model to fit the specifications of the Seattle Police. The normal selling price of the City Cruiser bike is $249, and its unit product cost is $182 as shown below:

Direct materials.	$ 86
Direct labor	45
Manufacturing overhead	51
Unit product cost	$182

The variable portion of the above manufacturing overhead is $6 per unit. The order would have no effect on the company's total fixed manufacturing overhead costs.

The modifications requested by the Seattle Police Department consist of welded brackets to hold radios, nightsticks, and other gear. These modifications would require $17 in incremental variable costs. In addition, the company would have to pay a graphics design studio $1,200 to design and cut stencils that would be used for spray-painting the Seattle Police Department's logo and other identifying marks on the bikes.

This order should have no effect on the company's other sales. The production manager says that she can handle the special order without disrupting any of the company's regular scheduled production.

What effect would accepting this order have on the company's net operating income?

Only the incremental costs and benefits are relevant. Since the existing fixed manufacturing overhead costs would not be affected by the order, they are not relevant. The incremental net operating income can be computed as follows:

	Per Unit	Total 100 Bikes
Incremental revenue	$179	$17,900
Incremental costs:		
Variable costs:		
Direct materials.	86	8,600
Direct labor	45	4,500
Variable manufacturing overhead	6	600
Special modifications	17	1,700
Total variable cost	$154	15,400
Fixed cost:		
Purchase of stencils		1,200
Total incremental cost.		16,600
Incremental net operating income		$ 1,300

Therefore, even though the $179 price on the special order is below the normal $182 unit product cost and the order would require incurring additional costs, the order would result in an increase in net operating income. In general, a special order is profitable as long as the incremental revenue from the special order exceeds the incremental costs of the order. We must note, however, that it is important to make sure that there is indeed idle capacity and that the special order does not cut into normal sales or undercut normal prices. If the company was operating at capacity, opportunity costs would have to be taken into account as well as the incremental costs that have already been detailed above.

IN BUSINESS

Flying the Friendly Aisles

Shoppers at Safeway can now earn United Airlines frequent flier miles when they buy their groceries. Airlines charge marketing partners such as Safeway about 2¢ per mile. Since airlines typically require 25,000 frequent flier miles for a domestic round-trip ticket, United is earning about $500 per frequent flier ticket issued to Safeway customers. This income to United is higher than many discounted fares. Moreover, United carefully manages its frequent flier program so that few frequent flier passengers displace regular fare-paying customers. The only costs of adding a frequent flier passenger to a flight may be food, a little extra fuel, and some administrative costs. All of the other costs of the flight would be incurred anyway. Thus, the miles that United sells to Safeway are almost pure profit.

Source: Wendy Zellner, *Business Week*, March 6, 2000, pp. 152–154.

PRICING NEW PRODUCTS

When offering a new product or service for the first time, a company must decide on its selling price. A cost-based approach has often been followed in practice. In this approach, the product is first designed and produced, then its cost is determined and its price is computed by adding a mark-up to the cost. This *cost-plus* approach to pricing suffers from a number of drawbacks—the most obvious being that customers may not be willing to pay the price set by the company. If the price is too high, customers may decide to purchase a similar product from a competitor or, if no similar competing product exists, they may decide not to buy the product at all.

Target costing provides an alternative, market-based approach to pricing new products. In the **target costing** approach, management estimates how much the market will be willing to pay for the new product even before the new product has been designed. The company's required profit margin is subtracted from the estimated selling price to determine the target cost for the new product. A cross-functional team consisting of designers, engineers, cost accountants, marketing personnel, and production personnel is charged with the responsibility of ensuring that the cost of the product is ultimately less than the target cost. If at some point in the product development process it becomes clear that it will not be possible to meet the target cost, the new product is abandoned.

The target costing approach to pricing has a number of advantages over the cost-plus approach. First, the target costing approach is focused on the market and the customer. A product is not made unless the company is reasonably confident that customers will be willing to buy the product at a price that provides the company with an adequate profit. Second, the target costing approach instills a much higher level of cost-consciousness than the cost-plus approach and probably results in less expensive products that are more attractive to customers. The target cost lid creates relentless pressure to drive out unnecessary costs. In the cost-plus approach, there is little pressure to control costs since whatever the costs turn out to be, the price will be higher. This allows designers and engineers

Target Costing

Step 1: What will customers pay for this product?	Step 2: What is our target cost?	Step 3: How can we design the product to meet the target cost?	Step 4: Let's manufacture the product!
 Market Research Department	 Finance Department	 Project Engineering Department	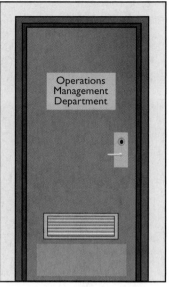 Operations Management Department

to create products with expensive features that customers may not actually be willing to pay for. Because of these advantages, more and more companies are abandoning the cost-plus approach to new product pricing in favor of the target costing approach.

Tutor

Your financial accounting instructor has suggested that you should consider working with selected students in her class as a tutor. Should you adopt a cost-plus or target costing approach to setting your hourly fee?

YOU DECIDE

UTILIZATION OF A CONSTRAINED RESOURCE

Managers are routinely faced with the problem of deciding how constrained resources are going to be utilized. A department store, for example, has a limited amount of floor space and therefore cannot stock every product that may be available. A manufacturer has a limited number of machine-hours and a limited number of direct labor-hours at its disposal. When a limited resource of some type restricts the company's ability to satisfy demand, the company is said to have a **constraint.** Since the company cannot fully satisfy demand, the manager must decide how the constrained resource should be used. Fixed costs are usually unaffected by such choices, so the course of action that will maximize the firm's *total* contribution margin should usually be selected.

LEARNING OBJECTIVE 5

Determine the most profitable use of a constrained resource and the value of obtaining more of the constrained resource.

Contribution in Relation to a Constrained Resource

To maximize total contribution margin, a company should not necessarily promote those products that have the highest *unit* contribution margins. Rather, total contribution margin will be maximized by promoting those products or accepting those orders that provide the highest unit contribution margin *in relation to the constrained resource.* To illustrate, Mountain Goat Cycles makes a line of paniers—a saddlebag for bicycles. There are two models of paniers—a touring model and a mountain model. Cost and revenue data for the two models of paniers are given below:

| | Model | |
	Mountain Panier	Touring Panier
Selling price per unit.	$25	$30
Variable cost per unit	10	18
Contribution margin per unit.	$15	$12
Contribution margin (CM) ratio	60%	40%

The mountain panier appears to be much more profitable than the touring panier. It has a $15 per unit contribution margin as compared to only $12 per unit for the touring model, and it has a 60% CM ratio as compared to only 40% for the touring model.

But now let us add one more piece of information—the plant that makes the paniers is operating at capacity. This does not mean that every machine and every person in the plant is working at the maximum possible rate. Because machines have different capacities, some machines will be operating at less than 100% of capacity. However, if the plant as a whole cannot produce any more units, some machine or process must be operating at capacity. The machine or process that is limiting overall output is called the **bottleneck**—it is the constraint.

At Mountain Goat Cycles, the bottleneck is a stitching machine. The mountain panier requires 2 minutes of stitching time, and the touring panier requires 1 minute of stitching time. Since the stitching machine already has more work than it can handle, something will have to be cut back. In this situation, which product is more profitable? To answer this question, the manager should look at the *contribution margin per unit of the constrained resource*. This figure is computed by dividing the contribution margin by the amount of the constrained resource a unit of product requires. These calculations are carried out below for the mountain and touring paniers.

| | Model | |
	Mountain Panier	Touring Panier
Contribution margin per unit (above) (a)	$15.00	$12.00
Time on the stitching machine required to produce one unit (b)	2 minutes	1 minute
Contribution margin per unit of the constrained resource, (a) ÷ (b)	$7.50 per minute	$12.00 per minute

It is now easy to decide which product is less profitable and should be deemphasized. Each minute of processing time on the stitching machine that is devoted to the touring panier results in an increase of $12 in contribution margin and profits. The comparable figure for the mountain panier is only $7.50 per minute. Therefore, the touring model should be emphasized. Even though the mountain model has the larger per unit contribution margin and the larger CM ratio, the touring model provides the larger contribution margin in relation to the constrained resource.

To verify that the touring model is indeed the more profitable product, suppose an hour of additional stitching time is available and that unfilled orders exist for both products. The additional hour on the stitching machine could be used to make either 30 mountain paniers (60 minutes ÷ 2 minutes per mountain panier) or 60 touring paniers (60 minutes ÷ 1 minute per touring panier), with the following consequences:

| | Model | |
	Mountain Panier	Touring Panier
Contribution margin per unit (above)	$ 15	$ 12
Additional units that can be processed in one hour	× 30	× 60
Additional contribution margin	$450	$720

Since the additional contribution margin would be $720 for the touring paniers and only $450 for the mountain paniers, the touring paniers are the more profitable product given the current situation in which the stitching machine is the company's constraint.

This example clearly shows that looking at unit contribution margins alone is not enough; the contribution margin must be viewed in relation to the amount of the constrained resource each product requires.

Coping with Power Shortages

Tata Iron and Steel Company Ltd. is one of the largest companies in India, employing about 75,000 people. The company has had to cope with electrical power shortages severe enough to force it to shut down some of its mills. But which ones? In these situations, electrical power is the company's constraint and it became imperative to manage this constraint effectively. The first step was to estimate the electrical loads of running each of the company's mills using least-squares regression. These data were then used to compute the contribution margin per KWH (kilowatt-hour) for each mill. The model indicated which mills should be shut down, and in what order, and which products should be cut back. The model also indicated that it would be profitable for the company to install its own diesel generating units—the contribution margin from the additional output more than paid for the costs of buying and running the diesel generators.

Source: "How Tata Steel Optimized Its Results," *The Management Accountant (India)*, July 1997, pp. 372–375.

Managing Constraints

Profits can be increased by effectively managing the organization's constraints. One aspect of managing constraints is to decide how to best utilize them. As discussed above, if the constraint is a bottleneck in the production process, the manager should select the product mix that maximizes the total contribution margin. In addition, the manager should take an active role in managing the constraint itself. Management should focus efforts on increasing the efficiency of the bottleneck operation and on increasing its capacity. Such efforts directly increase the output of finished goods and will often pay off in an almost immediate increase in profits.

It is often possible for a manager to effectively increase the capacity of the bottleneck, which is called **relaxing (or elevating) the constraint.** For example, the stitching machine operator could be asked to work overtime. This would result in more available stitching time and hence more finished goods that can be sold. The benefits from relaxing the constraint in such a manner are often enormous and can be easily quantified. The manager should first ask, "What would I do with additional capacity at the bottleneck if it were available?" In the example, if unfilled orders exist for both the touring and mountain paniers, the additional capacity would be used to process more touring paniers, since that would be a better use of the additional capacity. In that situation, the additional capacity would be worth $12 per minute or $720 per hour. This is because adding an hour of capacity would generate an additional $720 of contribution margin if it were used solely to process more touring paniers. Since overtime pay for the operator is likely to be much less than $720 per hour, running the stitching machine on overtime would be an excellent way to increase the profits of the company while at the same time satisfying customers.

To reinforce this concept, suppose that making touring paniers has already been given top priority and consequently there are only unfilled orders for the mountain panier. How much would it be worth to the company to run the stitching machine overtime in this situation? Since the additional capacity would be used to make the mountain panier, the value of that additional capacity would drop to $7.50 per minute or $450 per hour. Nevertheless, the value of relaxing the constraint would still be quite high.

These calculations indicate that managers should pay great attention to bottleneck operations. If a bottleneck machine breaks down or is ineffectively utilized, the losses to the company can be quite large. In our example, for every minute the stitching machine is down due to breakdowns or setups, the company loses between $7.50 and $12.00. The losses on an hourly basis are between $450 and $720! In contrast, there is no such loss of contribution margin if time is lost on a machine that is not a bottleneck—such machines have excess capacity anyway.

The implications are clear. Managers should focus much of their attention on managing bottlenecks. As we have discussed, managers should emphasize products that most profitably utilize the constrained resource. They should also make sure that products are processed smoothly through the bottlenecks, with minimal lost time due to breakdowns and setups. And they should try to find ways to increase the capacity at the bottlenecks.

The capacity of a bottleneck can be effectively increased in a number of ways, including:

- Working overtime on the bottleneck.
- Subcontracting some of the processing that would be done at the bottleneck.
- Investing in additional machines at the bottleneck.
- Shifting workers from processes that are not bottlenecks to the process that is a bottleneck.
- Focusing business process improvement efforts such as TQM and Business Process Reengineering on the bottleneck.
- Reducing defective units. Each defective unit that is processed through the bottleneck and subsequently scrapped takes the place of a good unit that could be sold.

The last three methods of increasing the capacity of the bottleneck are particularly attractive, since they are essentially free and may even yield additional cost savings.

The methods and ideas discussed in this section are all part of the Theory of Constraints, which was introduced in the Prologue. A number of organizations have successfully used the Theory of Constraints to improve their performance, including Avery Dennison, Bethlehem Steel, Boeing, Champion International, General Motors, ITT, National Semiconductor, Pratt and Whitney Canada, Procter and Gamble, Texas Instruments, United Airlines, United Electrical Controls, the United States Air Force Logistics Command, and the United States Navy Transportation Corps.

CONCEPT CHECK ✓

4. A company has received a special order from a customer to make 5,000 units of a customized product. The direct material cost per unit of the customized product is $15, the direct labor cost per unit is $5, and the manufacturing overhead per unit is $18. The predetermined manufacturing overhead rate is $12 per machine-hour. The variable portion of the manufacturing overhead rate is $4 per machine-hour. If the company has sufficient available manufacturing capacity, what is the minimum price that can be accepted for the special order?
   a. $24
   b. $26

c. $32
d. $38

5. Refer to the facts from question 4 above; however, in answering this question assume that the company is operating at 100% of its capacity before considering the special order. If the company normally manufactures only one product that has a contribution margin of $20 per unit and that consumes 2 machine-hours per unit, what is the opportunity cost (stated in terms of forgone contribution margin) of taking the special order?
   a. $25,000
   b. $50,000
   c. $75,000
   d. $100,000

IN BUSINESS

The Real Cost of Setups

The bottleneck at Southwestern Ohio Steel is the blanking line, on which large rolls of steel up to 60 inches wide are cut into flat sheets. Setting up the blanking line between jobs takes an average of 2.5 hours, and during this time, the blanking line is shut down.

Management estimates the opportunity cost of lost sales at $225 per hour, which is the contribution margin per hour of the blanking line for a typical order. Under these circumstances, a new loading device with an annual fixed cost of $36,000 that would save 720 setup hours per year looked like an excellent investment. The new loading device would have an average cost of only $50 per hour ($36,000 ÷ 720 hours = $50) compared to the $225 per hour the company would generate in added contribution margin.

Source: Robert J. Campbell, "Steeling Time with ABC or TOC," *Management Accounting,* January 1995, pp. 31–36.

IN BUSINESS

Solving the Real Problem

It is often possible to elevate the constraint at very low cost. Western Textile Products makes pockets, waistbands, and other clothing components. The constraint at the company's plant in Greenville, South Carolina, was the slitting machines. These large machines slit huge rolls of textiles into appropriate widths for use on other machines. Management was contemplating adding a second shift to elevate the constraint. However, investigation revealed that the slitting machines were actually being run only one hour in a nine-hour shift. "The other eight hours were required to get materials, load and unload the machine, and do setups. Instead of adding a second shift, a second person was assigned to each machine to fetch materials and do as much of the setting up as possible offline while the machine was running." This approach resulted in increasing the run time to four hours. If another shift had been added without any improvement in how the machines were being used, the cost would have been much higher and there would have been only a one-hour increase in run time.

Source: Eric Noreen, Debra Smith, and James T. Mackey, *The Theory of Constraints and Its Implications for Management Accounting* (Croton-on-Hudson, NY: The North River Press, 1995), pp. 84–85.

SUMMARY

LO1   Identify relevant and irrelevant costs and benefits in a decision situation.

Every decision involves a choice from among at least two alternatives. Only those costs and benefits that differ between alternatives are relevant; costs and benefits that are the same for all alternatives are not affected by the decision and can be ignored. Only future costs that differ between alternatives are relevant. Costs that have already been incurred are sunk costs and are always irrelevant. Future costs that do not differ between alternatives are not relevant.

LO2   Prepare an analysis showing whether a product line or other organizational segment should be dropped or retained.

A decision of whether a product line or other segment should be dropped should focus on the differences in the costs and benefits between dropping or retaining the product line or segment. Caution should be exercised when using reports in which common fixed costs have been allocated among segments. If these common fixed costs are unaffected by the decision of whether to drop or retain the segment, they are irrelevant and should be removed before determining the real profitability of a segment.

LO3   Prepare a make or buy analysis.

A make or buy decision should focus on the costs and benefits that differ between the alternatives of making or buying a component. As in other decisions, sunk costs—such as the depreciation on old equipment—should be ignored. Future costs that do not differ between alternatives—such as allocations of common fixed costs like general overhead—should be ignored.

LO4   Prepare an analysis showing whether a special order should be accepted.

When deciding whether to accept or reject a special order, focus on the benefits and costs that differ between those two alternatives. Specifically, a special order should be accepted when the incremental revenue from the sale exceeds the incremental cost. As always, sunk costs and future costs that do not differ between the alternatives are irrelevant.

LO5   Determine the most profitable use of a constrained resource and the value of obtaining more of the constrained resource.

When demand for a company's products and services exceeds its ability to supply them, the company has a bottleneck. The bottleneck, whether it is a particular material, skilled labor, or a specific machine, is a constrained resource. Since the company is unable to make everything it could sell, managers must decide what the company will make and what the company will not make. In this situation, the profitability of a product is best measured by its contribution margin per unit of the constrained resource. The products with the highest contribution margin per unit of the constrained resource should be favored.

Managers should focus their attention on effectively managing the constraint. This involves making the best use possible of the constrained resource and increasing the amount of the constrained resource that is available. The value of relaxing the constraint is determined by the contribution margin per unit of the constrained resource for the work that would be done if more of the resource were available.

GUIDANCE ANSWERS TO *DECISION MAKER* AND *YOU DECIDE*

Vice President of Production (p. 468)

The warning that you recall about fixed costs in decisions relates to *allocated* fixed costs. Allocated fixed costs often make a product line or other segment of a business appear less profitable than it really is. However, in this situation, the annual rental cost for the machinery is an *avoidable* fixed cost rather than an allocated fixed cost. An avoidable fixed cost is a cost that can be eliminated in whole or in part by choosing one alternative over another. Because the annual rental cost of the machinery can be avoided if the company purchases the components from an outside supplier, it is relevant to this decision.

Tutor (p. 471)

Individuals who provide services to others often struggle to decide how to charge for their services. As a tutor, you probably will not incur any significant costs, unless you agree to provide supplies (such as paper, pencils, calculators, or study guides) or software. As such, a cost-plus approach may not be a practical way to set the hourly fee (or price) for your services. On the other hand, if you use a target costing approach, you would estimate how much students would be willing to pay for the tutoring services. If your institution offers tutoring services to its students, you should inquire about the fee and you should check the student newspaper (or local newspapers) to determine the going rate for tutors. If you plan to tutor instead of working at a part-time job, you should consider the opportunity cost (that is, the hourly rate that you will be forgoing).

GUIDANCE ANSWERS TO CONCEPT CHECKS

1. **Choices a and d.** Sunk costs are always irrelevant. Fixed costs can be relevant costs.
2. **Choice a.** The cost of the airline ticket to Telluride is a sunk cost; it has already been incurred and the ticket is nonrefundable.
3. **Choice b.** The cost of going to Stowe would be $800 [$200 + ($150 per night × 4 nights)] whereas the incremental cost of going to Telluride would be $820 [$100 + ($180 per night × 4 nights)]. Note that the $450 cost of flying to Telluride is irrelevant at this point since it is a sunk cost. The analysis favors Stowe by $20.
4. **Choice b.** The minimum price would be $15 direct materials + $5 direct labor + ($4 per machine-hour overhead rate × 1.5 machine-hours per unit) = $26.
5. **Choice c.** The special order requires 7,500 machine-hours (5,000 units × 1.5 machine-hours per unit). Taking the special order would require sacrificing 3,750 units (7,500 hours ÷ 2 hours per unit) of the regular product. The forgone contribution margin would be 3,750 units × $20 per unit = $75,000.

REVIEW PROBLEM: RELEVANT COSTS

Charter Sports Equipment manufactures round, rectangular, and octagonal trampolines. Data on sales and expenses for the past month follow:

| | Total | Trampoline | | |
		Round	Rectangular	Octagonal
Sales	$1,000,000	$140,000	$500,000	$360,000
Less variable expenses.	410,000	60,000	200,000	150,000
Contribution margin	590,000	80,000	300,000	210,000
Less fixed expenses:				
Advertising—traceable	216,000	41,000	110,000	65,000
Depreciation of special				
equipment	95,000	20,000	40,000	35,000
Line supervisors' salaries.	19,000	6,000	7,000	6,000
General factory overhead*	200,000	28,000	100,000	72,000
Total fixed expenses.	530,000	95,000	257,000	178,000
Net operating income (loss)	$ 60,000	$ (15,000)	$ 43,000	$ 32,000

*A common fixed cost that is allocated on the basis of sales dollars.

Management is concerned about the continued losses shown by the round trampolines and wants a recommendation as to whether or not the line should be discontinued. The special equipment used to produce the trampolines has no resale value. If the round trampoline model is dropped, the two line supervisors assigned to the model would be discharged.

Required:
1. Should production and sale of the round trampolines be discontinued? You may assume that the company has no other use for the capacity now being used to produce the round trampolines. Show computations to support your answer.
2. Recast the above data in a format that would be more usable to management in assessing the long-run profitability of the various product lines.

Solution to Review Problem
1. No, production and sale of the round trampolines should not be discontinued. Computations to support this answer follow:

Contribution margin lost if the round trampolines are discontinued	$(80,000)
Less fixed costs that can be avoided:	
Advertising—traceable $41,000	
Line supervisors' salaries 6,000	47,000
Decrease in net operating income for the company as a whole	$(33,000)

The depreciation of the special equipment represents a sunk cost, and therefore it is not relevant to the decision. The general factory overhead is allocated and will presumably continue regardless of whether or not the round trampolines are discontinued; thus, it is not relevant.

2. If management wants a clear picture of the profitability of the segments, the general factory overhead should not be allocated. It is a common fixed cost and therefore should be deducted from the total product-line segment margin, as shown in Exhibit 11–4. A more useful income statement format would be as follows:

			Trampoline	
	Total	**Round**	**Rectangular**	**Octagonal**
Sales	$1,000,000	$140,000	$500,000	$360,000
Less variable expenses	410,000	60,000	200,000	150,000
Contribution margin	590,000	80,000	300,000	210,000
Less traceable fixed expenses:				
Advertising—traceable	216,000	41,000	110,000	65,000
Depreciation of special				
equipment	95,000	20,000	40,000	35,000
Line supervisors' salaries	19,000	6,000	7,000	6,000
Total traceable fixed expenses	330,000	67,000	157,000	106,000
Product-line segment margin	260,000	$ 13,000	$143,000	$104,000
Less common fixed expenses	200,000			
Net operating income (loss)	$ 60,000			

GLOSSARY

Avoidable cost   A cost that can be eliminated (in whole or in part) by choosing one alternative over another in a decision-making situation. This term is synonymous with *relevant cost* and *differential cost*. (p. 454)

Bottleneck   A machine or some other part of a process that limits the output of the entire process. (p. 472)

Common fixed cost   A fixed cost that supports the operations of more than one segment of an organization and is not avoidable in whole or in part by eliminating any one segment. (p. 465)

Constraint   A limitation under which a company must operate, such as limited available machine time or limited raw materials available that restricts the company's ability to satisfy demand. (p. 471)

Differential cost   Any cost that differs between alternatives in a decision-making situation. This term is synonymous with *avoidable cost* and *relevant cost*. (p. 455)

Make or buy decision   A decision concerning whether an item should be produced internally or purchased from an outside supplier. (p. 466)

Relaxing (or elevating) the constraint   An action that increases the amount of a constrained resource. (p. 473)

Relevant cost   A cost that differs between alternatives in a particular decision. This term is synonymous with *avoidable cost* and *differential cost*. (p. 454)

Segment margin   The difference between the revenue generated by a segment and its own traceable cost. (p. 466)

Special order   A one-time order that is not considered part of the company's normal ongoing business. (p. 469)

Sunk cost   Any cost that has already been incurred and that cannot be changed by any decision made now or in the future. (p. 454)

Target costing   Before launching a new product, management estimates how much the market will be willing to pay for the product and then takes steps to ensure that the cost of the product will be low enough to provide an adequate profit margin. (p. 470)

QUESTIONS

11–1   What is a *relevant cost?*

11–2   Define the following terms: *incremental cost, opportunity cost,* and *sunk cost.*

11–3   Are variable costs always relevant costs? Explain.

11–4   The original cost of a machine the company already owns is irrelevant in decision making. Explain why this is so.

11–5   "Sunk costs are easy to spot—they're simply the fixed costs associated with a decision." Do you agree? Explain.

11–6   "Variable costs and differential costs mean the same thing." Do you agree? Explain.

11–7   "All future costs are relevant in decision making." Do you agree? Why?

11–8   Prentice Company is considering dropping one of its product lines. What costs of the product line would be relevant to this decision? Irrelevant?

11–9   "If a product line is generating a loss, then that's pretty good evidence that the product line should be discontinued." Do you agree? Explain.

11–10   What is the danger in allocating common fixed costs among product lines or other segments of an organization?

11–11   How does opportunity cost enter into the make or buy decision?

11–12   Give four examples of possible constraints.

11–13   How will relating product contribution margins to the constrained resource they require help a company ensure that profits will be maximized?

11–14   Airlines sometimes offer reduced rates during certain times of the week to members of a businessperson's family if they accompany him or her on trips. How does the concept of relevant costs enter into the decision to offer reduced rates of this type?

BRIEF EXERCISES

BRIEF EXERCISE 11–1   Identifying Relevant Costs   (LO1)

A number of costs are listed below that may be relevant in decisions faced by the management of Poulsen & Sonner A/S, a Danish furniture manufacturer:

Item	Case 1 Relevant	Case 1 Not Relevant	Case 2 Relevant	Case 2 Not Relevant
a. Sales revenue				
b. Direct materials				
c. Direct labor				
d. Variable manufacturing overhead				
e. Book value—Model A3000 machine				
f. Disposal value—Model A3000 machine.				
g. Depreciation—Model A3000 machine.				
h. Market value—Model B3800 machine (cost)				
i. Fixed manufacturing overhead (general)				
j. Variable selling expense				
k. Fixed selling expense				
l. General administrative overhead				

Required:

Copy the information above onto your answer sheet and place an X in the appropriate column to indicate whether each item is relevant or not relevant in the following situations. Requirement 1 relates to Case 1 above, and requirement 2 relates to Case 2. Consider the two cases independently.

1. The company chronically runs at capacity and the old Model A3000 machine is the company's constraint. Management is considering the purchase of a new Model B3800 machine to use in addition to the company's present Model A3000 machine. The old Model A3000 machine will continue to be used to capacity as before, with the new Model B3800 being used to expand production. The increase in volume will be large enough to require increases in fixed selling expenses and in general administrative overhead, but not in the general fixed manufacturing overhead.

2. The old Model A3000 machine is not the company's constraint, but management is considering replacing it with a new Model B3800 machine because of the potential savings in direct materials cost with the new machine. The Model A3000 machine would be sold. This change will have no effect on production or sales, other than some savings in direct materials costs due to less waste.

BRIEF EXERCISE 11–2   Dropping or Retaining a Segment   (LO2)
Boyle's Home Center has two departments, Bath and Kitchen. The most recent income statement for the company follows:

	Total	Department Bath	Department Kitchen
Sales	$5,000,000	$1,000,000	$4,000,000
Less variable expenses	1,900,000	300,000	1,600,000
Contribution margin	3,100,000	700,000	2,400,000
Less fixed expenses	2,700,000	900,000	1,800,000
Net operating income (loss)	$ 400,000	$ (200,000)	$ 600,000

A study indicates that $370,000 of the fixed expenses being charged to the Bath Department are sunk costs or allocated costs that will continue even if the Bath Department is dropped. In addition, the elimination of the Bath Department would result in a 10% decrease in the sales of the Kitchen Department. If the Bath Department is dropped, what will be the effect on the net operating income of the company as a whole?

BRIEF EXERCISE 11–3   Make or Buy a Component   (LO3)
For many years, Diehl Company has produced a small electrical part that it uses in the production of its standard line of diesel tractors. The company's unit product cost, based on a production level of 60,000 parts per year, is as follows:

	Per Part	Total
Direct materials	$ 4.00	
Direct labor	2.75	
Variable manufacturing overhead	0.50	
Fixed manufacturing overhead, traceable	3.00	$180,000
Fixed manufacturing overhead, common (allocated on the basis of labor-hours)	2.25	$135,000
Unit product cost	$12.50	

An outside supplier has offered to supply the electrical parts to the Diehl Company for only $10 per part. One-third of the traceable fixed manufacturing costs represent supervisory salaries and other costs that can be eliminated if the parts are purchased. The other two-thirds of the traceable fixed manufacturing costs represent depreciation of special equipment that has no resale value. Economic depreciation on this equipment is due to obsolescence rather than wear and tear. The decision would have no effect on the common fixed costs of the company, and the space being used to produce the parts would otherwise be idle. Show the dollar advantage or disadvantage of accepting the supplier's offer.

BRIEF EXERCISE 11–4   Special Order   (LO4)
Glade Company produces a single product. The cost of producing and selling a single unit of this product at the company's current activity level of 8,000 units per month is as follows:

Direct materials.	$2.50
Direct labor.	$3.00
Variable manufacturing overhead	$0.50
Fixed manufacturing overhead	$4.25
Variable selling and administrative expenses	$1.50
Fixed selling and administrative expenses.	$2.00

The normal selling price is $15 per unit. The company's capacity is 10,000 units per month. An order has been received from an overseas source for 2,000 units at a price of $12 per unit. This order would not affect regular sales.

Required:
1. If the order is accepted, by how much will monthly profits be increased or decreased? (The order would not change the company's total fixed costs.)
2. Assume the company has 500 units of this product left over from last year that are inferior to the current model. The units must be sold through regular channels at reduced prices. What unit cost is relevant for establishing a minimum selling price for these units? Explain.

BRIEF EXERCISE 11–5   Utilization of a Constrained Resource   (LO5)

Shelby Company produces three products, X, Y, and Z. Data concerning the three products follow (per unit):

	Product		
	X	**Y**	**Z**
Selling price	$80	$56	$70
Less variable expenses:			
Direct materials	24	15	9
Labor and overhead.	24	27	40
Total variable expenses	48	42	49
Contribution margin	$32	$14	$21
Contribution margin ratio	40%	25%	30%

Demand for the company's products is very strong, with far more orders each month than the company can produce with the available raw materials. The same material is used in each product. The material costs $3 per pound, with a maximum of 5,000 pounds available each month. Which orders would you advise the company to accept first, those for X, for Y, or for Z? Which orders second? Third?

EXERCISES

EXERCISE 11–6   Identification of Relevant Costs   (LO1)

Steve has just returned from salmon fishing. He was lucky on this trip and brought home two salmon. Steve's wife, Wendy, disapproves of fishing, and to discourage Steve from further fishing trips, she has presented him with the following cost data. The cost per fishing trip is based on an average of 10 fishing trips per year.

Cost per fishing trip:	
Depreciation on fishing boat* (annual depreciation of	
$1,500 ÷ 10 trips)	$150
Boat moorage fees (annual rental of $1,200 ÷ 10 trips).	120
Expenditures on fishing gear, except for snagged lures	
(annual expenditures of $200 ÷ 10 trips)	20
Snagged fishing lures	7
	(continued)

(concluded)

Fishing license (yearly license of $40 ÷ 10 trips)	4
Fuel and upkeep on boat per trip.................................	25
Junk food consumed during trip..................................	8
Total cost per fishing trip	$334
Cost per salmon ($334 ÷ 2 salmon)...............................	$167

*The original cost of the boat was $15,000. It has an estimated useful life of 10 years, after which it will have no resale value. The boat does not wear out through use, but it does become less desirable for resale as it becomes older.

Required:

1. Assuming that the salmon fishing trip Steve has just completed is typical, what costs are relevant to a decision as to whether he should go on another trip this year?
2. Suppose that on Steve's next fishing trip he gets lucky and catches three salmon in the amount of time it took him to catch two salmon on his last trip. How much would the third salmon have cost him to catch? Explain.
3. Discuss the costs that are relevant in a decision of whether Steve should give up fishing.

EXERCISE 11–7   Identification of Relevant Costs   (LO1)

Samantha Ringer purchased a used automobile for $10,000 at the beginning of last year and incurred the following operating costs:

Depreciation ($10,000 ÷ 5 years).....	$2,000
Insurance	$960
Garage rent	$480
Automobile tax and license	$60
Variable operating cost	8¢ per mile

The variable operating costs consist of gasoline, oil, tires, maintenance, and repairs. Samantha estimates that at her current rate of usage the car will have zero resale value in five years, so the annual straight-line depreciation is $2,000. The car is kept in a garage for a monthly fee.

Required:

1. Samantha drove the car 10,000 miles last year. Compute the average cost per mile of owning and operating the car.
2. Samantha is unsure about whether she should use her own car or rent a car to go on an extended cross-country trip for two weeks during spring break. What costs above are relevant in this decision? Explain.
3. Samantha is thinking about buying an expensive sports car to replace the car she bought last year. She would drive the same number of miles irrespective of which car she owns and would rent the same parking space. The sports car's variable operating costs would be roughly the same as the variable operating costs of her old car. However, her insurance and automobile tax and license costs would go up. What costs are relevant in estimating the incremental cost of owning the more expensive car? Explain.

EXERCISE 11–8   Dropping or Retaining a Segment   (LO2)

Dexter Products, Inc., manufactures and sells a number of items, including an overnight case. The company has been experiencing losses on the overnight case for some time, as shown on the following income statement:

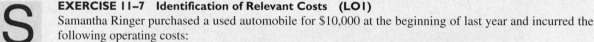

DEXTER PRODUCTS, INC.
Income Statement—Overnight Cases
For the Quarter Ended June 30

Sales		$450,000
Less variable expenses:		
Variable manufacturing expenses................	$130,000	

(continued)

(concluded)	**DEXTER PRODUCTS, INC.** **Income Statement—Overnight Cases** **For the Quarter Ended June 30**	
Sales commissions	48,000	
Shipping	12,000	
Total variable expenses		190,000
Contribution margin		260,000
Less fixed expenses:		
Salary of product line manager	21,000	
General factory overhead	104,000*	
Depreciation of equipment (no resale value)	36,000	
Advertising—traceable	110,000	
Insurance on inventories	9,000	
Purchasing department expenses	50,000†	
Total fixed expenses.		330,000
Net operating loss		$ (70,000)

*Allocated on the basis of machine-hours.
†Allocated on the basis of sales dollars.

Discontinuing the overnight cases would not affect sales of other product lines and would have no noticeable effect on the company's total general factory overhead or total purchasing department expenses.

Required:
Would you recommend that the company discontinue the manufacture and sale of overnight cases? Support your answer with appropriate computations.

EXERCISE 11–9   Make or Buy a Component   (LO3)
Royal Company manufactures 20,000 units of part R-3 each year for use on its production line. The cost per unit for part R-3 follows:

Direct materials.	$ 4.80
Direct labor.	7.00
Variable manufacturing overhead	3.20
Fixed manufacturing overhead	10.00
Total cost per part	$25.00

An outside supplier has offered to sell 20,000 units of part R-3 each year to Royal Company for $23.50 per part. If Royal Company accepts this offer, the facilities now being used to manufacture part R-3 could be rented to another company at an annual rental of $150,000. However, Royal Company has determined that $6 of the fixed manufacturing overhead being applied to part R-3 would continue even if part R-3 were purchased from the outside supplier.

Required:
Prepare computations to show the net dollar advantage or disadvantage of accepting the outside supplier's offer.

EXERCISE 11–10   Evaluating a Special Order   (LO4)
Miyamoto Jewelers is considering a special order for 10 handcrafted gold bracelets for a major upscale wedding. The gold bracelets are to be given as gifts to members of the wedding party. The normal selling price of a gold bracelet is $389.95 and its unit product cost is $264.00 as shown below:

Materials.	$143.00
Direct labor	86.00
Manufacturing overhead.	35.00
Unit product cost.	$264.00

The manufacturing overhead is largely fixed and unaffected by variations in how much jewelry is produced in any given period. However, $7.00 of the overhead is variable with respect to the number of bracelets produced. The customer who is interested in the special bracelet order would like special filigree applied to the bracelets. This filigree would require additional materials costing $6.00 per bracelet and would also require acquisition of a special tool costing $465 that would have no other use once the special order is completed. This order would have no effect on the company's regular sales and the order could be fulfilled using the company's existing capacity without affecting any other order.

Required:

What effect would accepting this order have on the company's net operating income if a special price of $349.95 is offered per bracelet for this order? Should the special order be accepted at this price?

EXERCISE 11–11   Utilization of a Constrained Resource   (LO5)

Banner Company produces three products: A, B, and C. The selling price, variable costs, and contribution margin for one unit of each product follow:

	Product		
	A	**B**	**C**
Selling price	$60	$90	$80
Less variable costs:			
Direct materials	27	14	40
Direct labor	12	32	16
Variable manufacturing overhead....	3	8	4
Total variable cost	42	54	60
Contribution margin	$18	$36	$20
Contribution margin ratio	30%	40%	25%

Due to a strike in the plant of one of its competitors, demand for the company's products far exceeds its capacity to produce. Management is trying to determine which product(s) to concentrate on next week in filling its backlog of orders. The direct labor rate is $8 per hour, and only 3,000 hours of labor time are available each week.

Required:

1. Compute the amount of contribution margin that will be obtained per hour of labor time spent on each product.
2. Which orders would you recommend that the company work on next week—the orders for product A, product B, or product C? Show computations.
3. By paying overtime wages, more than 3,000 hours of direct labor time can be made available next week. Up to how much should the company be willing to pay per hour in overtime wages as long as there is unfilled demand for the three products? Explain.

PROBLEMS

CHECK FIGURE
(1) Discontinuing the bicycling shoes would decrease net operating income by $57,000

PROBLEM 11–12   Dropping or Retaining a Product   (LO2)

The Montlake Shoe Company manufactures three types of shoes—hiking shoes, running shoes, and bicycling shoes. Data on sales and expenses for the past quarter follow:

	Total	Hiking Shoes	Running Shoes	Bicycling Shoes
Sales	$800,000	$220,000	$300,000	$280,000
Less variable manufacturing and				
selling expenses	450,000	95,000	180,000	175,000
Contribution margin.	350,000	125,000	120,000	105,000

(continued)

(concluded)	Total	Hiking Shoes	Running Shoes	Bicycling Shoes
Less fixed expenses:				
Advertising, traceable......................	88,000	26,000	32,000	30,000
Depreciation of special equipment	64,000	18,000	20,000	26,000
Salaries of product-line managers	49,000	14,000	17,000	18,000
Common allocated costs*	100,000	27,500	37,500	35,000
Total fixed expenses........................	301,000	85,500	106,500	109,000
Net operating income (loss)	$ 49,000	$ 39,500	$ 13,500	$ (4,000)

*Allocated on the basis of sales dollars.

Management is concerned about the continued losses shown by the bicycling shoes and wants a recommendation as to whether or not the line should be discontinued. The special equipment used to produce bicycling shoes has no resale value and does not wear out.

Required:

1. Should production and sale of the bicycling shoes be discontinued? Show computations to support your answer.
2. Recast the above data in a format that would be more usable to management in assessing the long-run profitability of the various product lines.

PROBLEM 11–13 Discontinuing a Flight (LO2)

Profits have been decreasing for several years at Wright Airlines. In an effort to improve the company's performance, consideration is being given to dropping several flights that appear to be unprofitable.

A typical income statement for one such flight (flight 581) is given below (per flight):

CHECK FIGURE
(1) Decrease in net operating income if the flight is dropped: $9,300

Ticket revenue (150 passengers × 40% occupancy × $400 per passenger)	$24,000
Less variable expenses (150 passengers × 40% occupancy × $10 per passenger).........................	600
Contribution margin	23,400
Less flight expenses:	
Salaries, flight crew	1,400
Flight promotion	2,000
Depreciation of aircraft....................................	5,000
Fuel for aircraft	8,000
Liability insurance	6,000
Salaries, flight assistants...................................	1,200
Baggage loading and flight preparation	800
Overnight costs for flight crew and assistants at destination	900
Total flight expenses	25,300
Net operating loss...	$ (1,900)

The following additional information is available about flight 581:

a. Members of the flight crew are paid fixed annual salaries, whereas the flight assistants are paid by the flight.

b. One-third of the liability insurance is a special charge assessed against flight 581 because in the opinion of the insurance company, the destination of the flight is in a "high-risk" area. The remaining two-thirds would be unaffected by a decision to drop flight 581.

c. The baggage loading and flight preparation expense is an allocation of ground crews' salaries and depreciation of ground equipment. Dropping flight 581 would have no effect on the company's total baggage loading and flight preparation expenses.

d. If flight 581 is dropped, Wright Airlines has no authorization at present to replace it with another flight.

e. Depreciation of aircraft is due entirely to obsolescence. Depreciation due to wear and tear is negligible.

f. Dropping flight 581 would not allow Wright Airlines to reduce the number of aircraft in its fleet or the number of flight crew on its payroll.

Required:

1. Prepare an analysis showing what impact dropping flight 581 would have on the airline's profits.
2. The airline's scheduling officer has been criticized because only about 50% of the seats on Wright Airlines flights are being filled compared to an average of 60% for the industry. The scheduling officer has explained that Wright Airlines average seat occupancy could be improved considerably by eliminating about 10% of the flights, but that doing so would reduce profits. Explain how this could happen.

CHECK FIGURE
(1) The part can be made inside the company for $7 less per unit.

PROBLEM 11–14   Make or Buy a Component   (LO3)

Strausser Automotive manufactures a variety of engines for use in heavy equipment. The company has always produced most of the parts for its engines, including all of the pistons. An outside supplier has offered to produce and sell one type of piston to Strausser Automotive at a price of $41 per unit. To evaluate this offer, Strausser Automotive has gathered the following information relating to its own cost of producing the piston internally:

	Per Unit	45,000 Units per Year
Direct materials	$13	$ 585,000
Direct labor..................................	16	720,000
Variable manufacturing overhead	4	180,000
Fixed manufacturing overhead, traceable*	3	135,000
Fixed manufacturing overhead, allocated	10	450,000
Total cost....................................	$46	$2,070,000

*One-third supervisory salaries; two-thirds depreciation of special equipment (no resale value).

Required:

1. Assuming that the company has no alternative use for the facilities that are now being used to produce the pistons, should the outside supplier's offer be accepted? Show all computations.
2. Suppose that if the pistons were purchased, Strausser Automotive could use the freed capacity to launch a new product. The segment margin of the new product would be $400,000 per year. Should Strausser Automotive accept the offer to buy the pistons for $41 per unit? Show all computations.

CHECK FIGURE
(1) Net increase in profits: $39,000

PROBLEM 11–15   Accept or Reject a Special Order   (LO4)

Arther & Smith Corporation manufactures and sells a single product called a ret. Operating at capacity, the company can produce and sell 20,000 rets per year. Costs associated with this level of production and sales are given below:

	Unit	Total
Direct materials.............................	$12.00	$240,000
Direct labor................................	10.00	200,000
Variable manufacturing overhead	2.00	40,000
Fixed manufacturing overhead.................	4.00	80,000
Variable selling expense......................	6.00	120,000
Fixed selling expense........................	4.00	80,000
Total cost..................................	$38.00	$760,000

The rets normally sell for $45 each. Fixed manufacturing overhead is constant at $80,000 per year within the range of 15,000 through 20,000 rets per year.

Required:

1. Assume that due to a recession, Arther & Smith Corporation expects to sell only 15,000 rets through regular channels next year. A large retail chain has offered to purchase 5,000 rets if Arther & Smith Corporation is willing to accept a 20% discount off the regular price. There would be no sales commissions on this order; thus, variable selling expenses would be slashed by 70%. However, Arther & Smith Corporation would have to purchase a special machine to engrave the retail chain's name on

the 5,000 units. This machine would cost $12,000. This would be a one-time order that would have no effect on regular sales. Determine the impact on profits next year if this special order is accepted.

2. Refer to the original data. Assume again that Arther & Smith Corporation expects to sell only 15,000 rets through regular channels next year. The U.S. Army would like to make a one-time-only purchase of 5,000 rets. The Army would pay a fixed fee of $6 per ret, and in addition it would reimburse Arther & Smith Corporation for all costs of production (variable and fixed) associated with the units. There would be no variable selling expenses of any type associated with this order. If Arther & Smith Corporation accepts the order, by how much will profits be increased or decreased for the year?

3. Assume the same situation as that described in (2) above, except that the company expects to sell 20,000 rets through regular channels next year. Thus, accepting the U.S. Army's order would require giving up regular sales of 5,000 rets. If the Army's order is accepted, by how much will profits be increased or decreased from what they would be if the 5,000 rets were sold through regular channels?

PROBLEM 11–16   Utilization of a Constrained Resource   (LO5)

The Brandilyn Evans Toy Company manufactures a line of dolls and a doll dress sewing kit. Demand for the dolls is increasing, and management requests assistance from you in determining an economical sales and production mix for the coming year. The company has provided the following information:

CHECK FIGURE
(2) Hours required:
      161,900 DLHs

	Product	Estimated Demand Next Year (Units)	Selling Price per Unit	Direct Materials	Direct Labor
2	Debbie	26,000	$ 35.00	$ 3.50	$ 4.80
3	Trish	42,000	$ 24.00	$ 2.30	$ 3.00
4	Sarah	40,000	$ 22.00	$ 4.50	$ 8.40
5	Mike	46,000	$ 18.00	$ 3.10	$ 6.00
6	Sewing kit	450,000	$ 14.00	$ 1.50	$ 2.40

(Handwritten notes: D.L. 12 per hr; Fixed cost 356,000; VOH $4 per DLHr)

The following additional information is available:

a. The company's plant has a capacity of 150,000 direct labor-hours per year on a single-shift basis. The company's present employees and equipment can produce all five products.

b. The direct labor rate is $12.00 per hour; this rate is expected to remain unchanged during the coming year.

c. Fixed costs total $356,000 per year. Variable overhead costs are $4.00 per direct labor-hour.

d. All of the company's nonmanufacturing costs are fixed.

e. The company's present inventory of finished products is negligible and can be ignored.

Required:

1. Determine the contribution margin per direct labor-hour expended on each product.

2. Prepare a schedule showing the total direct labor-hours that will be required to produce the units estimated to be sold during the coming year.

3. Examine the data you have computed in (1) and (2) above. Indicate how much of each product should be made so that total production time is equal to the 150,000 direct labor-hours available.

4. What is the highest price, in terms of a rate per hour, that Brandilyn Evans Toy Company should be willing to pay for additional capacity (that is, for added direct labor time)?

5. Identify ways in which the company might be able to obtain additional output so that it would not have to leave some demand for its products unsatisfied.

(CPA, adapted)

PROBLEM 11–17   Dropping or Retaining a Segment   (LO2)

Adams County Senior Services is a nonprofit organization devoted to providing essential services to seniors who live in their own homes within the Adams County area. Three services are provided for seniors—home nursing, meals on wheels, and housekeeping. In the home nursing program, nurses visit seniors on a regular basis to check on their general health and to perform tests ordered by their physicians. The meals on wheels

CHECK FIGURE
(1) Dropping housekeeping
      would decrease overall
      net operating income
      by $10,000.

program delivers a hot meal once a day to each senior enrolled in the program. The housekeeping service provides weekly housecleaning and maintenance services. Data on revenue and expenses for the past year follow:

	Total	Home Nursing	Meals on Wheels	House-keeping
Revenues.............................	$900,000	$310,000	$380,000	$210,000
Less variable expenses..................	500,000	130,000	220,000	150,000
Contribution margin.....................	400,000	180,000	160,000	60,000
Less fixed expenses:				
Depreciation.........................	42,000	9,000	18,000	15,000
Liability insurance.....................	43,000	22,000	9,000	12,000
Program administrators' salaries.........	123,000	42,000	43,000	38,000
General administrative overhead*........	180,000	62,000	76,000	42,000
Total fixed expenses....................	388,000	135,000	146,000	107,000
Net operating income (loss)	$ 12,000	$ 45,000	$ 14,000	$ (47,000)

*Allocated on the basis of program revenues.

The head administrator of Adams County Senior Services, Mariam Santoya, is concerned about the organization's finances and considers the net operating income of $12,000 last year to be razor thin. (Last year's results were very similar to the results for previous years and are representative of what would be expected in the future.) She feels that the organization should be building its financial reserves at a more rapid rate in order to prepare for the next inevitable recession. After seeing the above report, Ms. Santoya asked for more information about the financial advisability of perhaps discontinuing the housekeeping program.

The depreciation in housekeeping is for a small van that is used to carry the housekeepers and their equipment from job to job. If the program were discontinued, the van would be donated to a charitable organization. None of the general administrative overhead would be avoided if the housekeeping program were dropped, but the liability insurance and the salary of the program administrator would be avoided.

Required:
1. Should the housekeeping program be discontinued? Explain. Show computations to support your answer.
2. Recast the above data in a format that would be more useful to management in assessing the long-run financial viability of the various services.

CHECK FIGURE
(1) $14,000 advantage to buy

PROBLEM 11–18   Make or Buy Analysis   (LO3)
"That old equipment for producing subassemblies is worn out," said Kari Warner, president of Harleq Corporation. "We need to make a decision quickly." The company is trying to decide whether it should rent new equipment and continue to make its subassemblies internally or whether it should discontinue production of its subassemblies and purchase them from an outside supplier. The alternatives follow:

Alternative 1. New equipment for producing the subassemblies can be rented for $63,000 per year.
Alternative 2. The subassemblies can be purchased from an outside supplier who has offered to provide them for $5.31 each under a five-year contract.

Harleq Corporation's present costs per unit for producing the subassemblies internally (with the old equipment) are given below. These costs are based on a current activity level of 50,000 subassemblies per year:

Direct materials	$2.30
Direct labor	1.90
Variable overhead....................................	0.40
Fixed overhead ($0.42 supervision, $0.90 depreciation, and $1.75 general company overhead)	3.07
Total cost per unit	$7.67

The new equipment would be more efficient and, according to the manufacturer, would reduce direct labor costs and variable overhead costs by 30%. Supervision cost ($21,000 per year) and direct materials cost per unit would not be affected by the new equipment. The new equipment's capacity would be 70,000 subassemblies per year.

The total general company overhead would be unaffected by this decision.

Required:
1. The president is unsure what the company should do and would like an analysis showing what unit costs and what total costs would be under each of the two alternatives given above. Assume that 50,000 subassemblies are needed each year. Which course of action would you recommend to the president?
2. Would your recommendation in (1) above be the same if the company's needs were (a) 60,000 subassemblies per year, or (b) 70,000 subassemblies per year? Show computations in good form.
3. What other factors would you recommend that the company consider before making a decision?

PROBLEM 11–19 Shutting Down or Continuing to Operate a Plant   (LO2)
(Note: This type of decision is similar to that of dropping a product line.)

CHECK FIGURE
(1) $11,800 disadvantage to close

Pritker Devices normally produces and sells 40,000 units of RG-6 each month. RG-6 is a small electrical relay used in the automotive industry as a component part in various products. The selling price is $26 per unit, variable costs are $22 per unit, fixed manufacturing overhead expenses total $300,000 per month, and fixed selling expenses total $66,000 per month.

Strikes in the companies that purchase the bulk of the RG-6 units have caused Pritker Devices' sales to temporarily drop to only 18,000 units per month. Pritker Devices estimates that the strikes will last for about two months, after which sales of RG-6 should return to normal. Due to the current low level of sales, however, Pritker Devices is thinking about closing down its own plant during the strike. If Pritker Devices does close down its plant, it is estimated that fixed manufacturing overhead expenses can be reduced to $240,000 per month and that fixed selling expenses can be reduced by 10%. Start-up expenses at the end of the two-month shutdown period would total $1,000. Since Pritker Devices uses just-in-time (JIT) production methods, no inventories are on hand.

Required:
1. Assuming that the strikes continue for two months, as estimated, would you recommend that Pritker Devices close its own plant? Show computations in good form.
2. At what level of sales (in units) for the two-month period should Pritker Devices be indifferent between closing the plant or keeping it open? Show computations. (Hint: This is a type of break-even analysis, except that the fixed cost portion of your break-even computation should include only those fixed costs that are relevant [i.e., avoidable] over the two-month period.)

PROBLEM 11–20 Relevant Cost Analysis in a Variety of Situations   (LO2, LO3, LO4)

CHECK FIGURE
(1) $19,400 incremental net operating income
(2) $17.90 break-even price

Lucy 'N Pals Corporation has a single product called Pups. The company normally produces and sells 54,000 Pups each year at a selling price of $20.00 per unit. The company's unit costs at this level of activity are given below:

Direct materials	$ 8.00	
Direct labor	3.50	
Variable manufacturing overhead	1.80	
Fixed manufacturing overhead	2.50	($135,000 total)
Variable selling expense	1.20	
Fixed selling expense	2.00	($108,000 total)
Total cost per unit	$19.00	

A number of questions relating to the production and sale of Pups follow. Each question is independent.

Required:
1. Assume that Lucy 'N Pals Corporation has sufficient capacity to produce 70,000 Pups each year without any increase in fixed manufacturing overhead costs. The company could increase its sales by 20% above the present 54,000 units each year if it were willing to increase the fixed selling expenses by $40,000. Would the increase fixed expenses be justified?

2. Assume again that Lucy 'N Pals Corporation has sufficient capacity to produce 70,000 Pups each year. A customer in a foreign market wants to purchase 10,000 Pups. Import duties on the Pups would be $1.50 per unit, and costs for permits and licenses would be $5,000. The only selling costs that would be associated with the order would be $2.60 per unit shipping cost. You have been asked by the president to compute the per unit break-even price on this order.

3. The company has 2,000 Pups on hand that have some irregularities and are therefore considered to be "seconds." Due to the irregularities, it will be impossible to sell these units at the normal price through regular distribution channels. What unit cost figure is relevant for setting a minimum selling price?

4. Due to a strike in its supplier's plant, Lucy 'N Pals Corporation is unable to purchase more material for the production of Pups. The strike is expected to last for two months. Lucy 'N Pals Corporation has enough material on hand to continue to operate at 40% of normal levels for the two-month period. As an alternative, Lucy 'N Pals Corporation could close its plant down entirely for the two months. If the plant were closed, fixed overhead costs would continue at 60% of their normal level during the two-month period; the fixed selling costs would be reduced by 30% while the plant was closed. What would be the dollar advantage or disadvantage of closing the plant for the two-month period?

5. An outside manufacturer has offered to produce Pups for Lucy 'N Pals Corporation and to ship them directly to Lucy 'N Pals Corporation customers. If Lucy 'N Pals Corporation accepts this offer, the facilities that it uses to produce Pups would be idle; however, fixed overhead costs would be reduced by 70%. Since the outside manufacturer would pay for all the costs of shipping, the variable selling costs would be only two-thirds of their present amount. Compute the unit cost that is relevant for comparison to whatever quoted price is received from the outside manufacturer.

BUILDING YOUR SKILLS

ETHICS CHALLENGE CASE   (LO2)

Marvin Braun had just been appointed vice president of the Great Basin Region of the Financial Services Corporation (FSC). The company provides check processing services for small banks. The banks send checks presented for deposit or payment to FSC, which then records the data on each check in a computerized database. FSC sends the data electronically to the nearest Federal Reserve Bank check-clearing center where the appropriate transfers of funds are made between banks. The Great Basin Region consists of three check processing centers in Eastern Idaho—Pocatello, Idaho Falls, and Ashton. Prior to his promotion to vice president, Mr. Braun had been manager of a check processing center in Indiana.

Immediately upon assuming his new position, Mr. Braun requested a complete financial report for the just-ended fiscal year from the region's controller, Lance Whiting. Mr. Braun specified that the financial report should follow the standardized format required by corporate headquarters for all regional performance reports. That report appears below:

Financial Performance Great Basin Region				
		Check Processing Centers		
	Total	Pocatello	Idaho Falls	Ashton
Revenues.	$20,000,000	$7,000,000	$8,000,000	$5,000,000
Operating expenses:				
Direct labor	12,200,000	4,400,000	4,700,000	3,100,000
Variable overhead.	400,000	150,000	160,000	90,000
Equipment depreciation.	2,100,000	700,000	800,000	600,000
Facility expenses.	2,000,000	600,000	500,000	900,000
Local administrative expenses*	450,000	150,000	180,000	120,000
Regional administrative expenses†	400,000	140,000	160,000	100,000
Corporate administrative expenses‡	1,600,000	560,000	640,000	400,000

(continued)

(concluded)	Financial Performance Great Basin Region			
		Check Processing Centers		
	Total	**Pocatello**	**Idaho Falls**	**Ashton**
Total operating expense............	19,150,000	6,700,000	7,140,000	5,310,000
Net operating income	$ 850,000	$ 300,000	$ 860,000	$ (310,000)

*Local administrative expenses are the administrative expenses incurred at the check processing centers.

†Regional administrative expenses are allocated to the check processing centers based on revenues.

‡Corporate administrative expenses represent a standard 8% charge against revenues.

Upon seeing this report, Mr. Braun summoned Lance Whiting for an explanation.

Braun: What's the story on Ashton? It didn't have a loss the previous year, did it?

Whiting: No, the Ashton facility has had a nice profit every year since it was opened six years ago, but Ashton lost a big contract this year.

Braun: Why?

Whiting: One of our national competitors entered the local market and bid very aggressively on the contract. We couldn't afford to meet the bid. Ashton's costs—particularly their facility expenses—are just too high. When Ashton lost the contract, we had to lay off a lot of employees, but we could not reduce the fixed costs of the Ashton facility.

Braun: Why is Ashton's facility expense so high? It's a smaller facility than either Pocatello or Idaho Falls and yet its facility expense is higher.

Whiting: The problem is that we are able to rent suitable facilities very cheaply at Pocatello and Idaho Falls. No such facilities were available at Ashton, so we had them built. Unfortunately, there were big cost overruns. The contractor we hired was inexperienced at this kind of work and in fact went bankrupt before the project was completed. After hiring another contractor to finish the work, we were way over budget. The large depreciation charges on the facility didn't matter at first because we didn't have much competition at the time and could charge premium prices.

Braun: Well, we can't do that anymore. The Ashton facility will obviously have to be shut down. Its business can be shifted to the other two check processing centers in the region.

Whiting: I would advise against that. The $900,000 in depreciation charges at the Ashton facility are misleading. That facility should last indefinitely with proper maintenance. And it has no resale value; there is no other commercial activity around Ashton.

Braun: What about the other costs at Ashton?

Whiting: If we shifted Ashton's business over to the other two processing centers in the region, we wouldn't save anything on direct labor or variable overhead costs. We might save $60,000 or so in local administrative expenses, but we would not save any regional administrative expense. And corporate headquarters would still charge us 8% of our revenues as corporate administrative expenses.

In addition, we would have to rent more space in Pocatello and Idaho Falls to handle the work transferred from Ashton; that would probably cost us at least $400,000 a year. And don't forget that it will cost us something to move the equipment from Ashton to Pocatello and Idaho Falls. And the move will disrupt service to customers.

Braun: I understand all of that, but a money-losing processing center on my performance report is completely unacceptable.

Whiting: And if you do shut down Ashton, you are going to throw some loyal employees out of work.

Braun: That's unfortunate, but we have to face hard business realities.

Whiting: And you would have to write off the investment in the facilities at Ashton.

Braun: I can explain a write-off to corporate headquarters; hiring an inexperienced contractor to build the Ashton facility was my predecessor's mistake. But they'll have my head at headquarters if I show operating losses every year at one of my processing centers. Ashton has to go. At the next corporate board meeting, I am going to recommend that the Ashton facility be closed.

Required:

1. From the standpoint of the company as a whole, should the Ashton processing center be shut down and its work redistributed to the other processing centers in the region? Explain.
2. Do you think Marvin Braun's decision to shut down the Ashton facility is ethical? Explain.

3. What influence should the depreciation on the facilities at Ashton have on prices charged by Ashton for its services?

TEAMWORK IN ACTION   (LO1, LO3, LO5)

Storage Systems, Inc., sells a wide range of drums, bins, boxes, and other containers that are used in the chemical industry. One of the company's products is a very heavy-duty corrosion-resistant metal drum, called the XSX drum, used to store toxic wastes. Production is constrained by the capacity of an automated welding machine that is used to make precision welds. A total of 2,000 hours of welding time are available annually on the machine. Since each drum requires 0.8 hours of welding time, annual production is limited to 2,500 drums. At present, the welding machine is used exclusively to make the XSX drums. The accounting department has provided the following financial data concerning the XSX drums:

		XSX Drums
Selling price per drum................		$154.00
Cost per drum:		
Materials	$44.50	
Direct labor ($18 per hour).........	4.50	
Manufacturing overhead	3.15	
Selling and administrative cost	15.40	67.55
Margin per drum....................		$ 86.45

Management believes 3,000 XSX drums could be sold each year if the company had sufficient manufacturing capacity. As an alternative to adding another welding machine, management has looked into the possibility of buying additional drums from an outside supplier. Metal Products, Inc., a supplier of quality products, would be able to provide up to 1,800 XSX-type drums per year at a price of $120 per drum.

Jasmine Morita, Storage Systems' production manager, has suggested that the company could make better use of the welding machine by manufacturing premium mountain bike frames, which would require only 0.2 hours of welding time per frame. Jasmine believes that Storage Systems could sell up to 3,500 mountain bike frames per year to mountain bike manufacturers at a price of $65 per frame. The accounting department has provided the following data concerning the proposed new product:

		Mountain Bike Frames
Selling price per frame.................		$65.00
Cost per frame:		
Materials..........................	$17.50	
Direct labor ($18 per hour)	22.50	
Manufacturing overhead	15.75	
Selling and administrative cost..........	6.50	62.25
Margin per frame......................		$ 2.75

The mountain bike frames could be produced with existing equipment and personnel. Manufacturing overhead is allocated to products on the basis of direct labor-hours. Most of the manufacturing overhead consists of fixed common costs such as rent on the factory building, but some of it is variable. The variable manufacturing overhead has been estimated at $1.05 per XSX drum and $0.60 per mountain bike frame. The variable manufacturing overhead cost would not be incurred on drums acquired from the outside supplier.

Selling and administrative costs are allocated to products on the basis of revenues. Almost all of the selling and administrative costs are fixed common costs, but it has been estimated that variable selling and administrative costs amount to $0.85 per XSX drum and would be $0.40 per mountain bike frame. The variable selling and administrative costs of $0.85 per drum would be incurred when drums acquired from the outside supplier are sold to the company's customers.

All of the company's employees—direct and indirect—are paid for full 40-hour workweeks and the company has a policy of laying off workers only in major recessions.

Required:

Your team should discuss and then respond to each of the following questions. All team members should understand the answers and be prepared to report to the class.

1. Given the margins of the two products as indicated in the reports submitted by the accounting department, does it make any sense to even consider producing the mountain bike frames? Explain.

2. Compute the contribution margin per unit for:
   a.   Purchased XSX drums.
   b.   Manufactured XSX drums.
   c.   Manufactured mountain bike frames.
3. Determine the number of XSX drums (if any) that should be purchased and the number of XSX drums and/or mountain bike frames (if any) that should be manufactured. What is the improvement in net income that would result from this plan over current operations?

As soon as your analysis was shown to the top management team at Storage Systems, several managers got into an argument concerning how direct labor costs should be treated when making this decision. One manager argued that direct labor is always treated as a variable cost in textbooks and in practice and has always been considered a variable cost at Storage Systems. After all, "direct" means you can directly trace the cost to products. If direct labor is not a variable cost, what is? Another manager argued just as strenuously that direct labor should be considered a fixed cost at Storage Systems. No one had been laid off in over a decade, and for all practical purposes, everyone at the plant is on a monthly salary. Everyone classified as direct labor works a regular 40-hour workweek and overtime has not been necessary since the company adopted just-in-time techniques. Whether the welding machine is used to make drums or frames, the total payroll would be exactly the same. There is enough slack, in the form of idle time, to accommodate any increase in total direct labor time that the mountain bike frames would require.

4. Redo requirements (2) and (3) above, making the opposite assumption about direct labor from the one you originally made. In other words, if you treated direct labor as a variable cost, redo the analysis treating it as a fixed cost. If you treated direct labor as a fixed cost, redo the analysis treating it as a variable cost.
5. What do you think is the correct way to treat direct labor in this situation—as a variable cost or as a fixed cost?

ANALYTICAL THINKING   (LO2)

Mrs. Agatha Spencer-Atwood is managing director of the British company, Imperial Reflections, Ltd. The company makes reproductions of antique dressing room mirrors. Mrs. Spencer-Atwood would like guidance on the advisability of eliminating the Kensington line of mirrors. These mirrors have never been among the company's best-selling products, although their sales have been stable for many years.

Below is a condensed statement of operating income for the company and for the Kensington product line for the quarter ended June 30:

CHECK FIGURE
(2) Minimum sales:
    £198,000

	Total Company	Kensington Product Line
Sales	£5,000,000	£480,000
Cost of sales:		
Direct materials	420,000	32,000
Direct labor	1,600,000	200,000
Fringe benefits (30% of labor)	480,000	60,000
Variable manufacturing overhead	340,000	30,000
Building rent and maintenance	120,000	15,000
Depreciation	80,000	10,000
Royalties (5% of sales)	250,000	24,000
Total cost of sales	3,290,000	371,000
Gross margin	1,710,000	109,000
Selling and administrative expenses:		
Product-line managers' salaries	75,000	8,000
Sales commissions (10% of sales)	500,000	48,000
Fringe benefits (30% of salaries and commissions)	172,500	16,800
Shipping	120,000	10,000
Advertising	350,000	15,000
General administrative expenses	250,000	24,000
Total selling and administrative expenses	1,467,500	121,800
Net operating income (loss)	£ 242,500	£ (12,800)

The following additional data have been supplied by the company:

a.   The company pays royalties to the owners of the original pieces of furniture from which the reproductions are copied.

b.   All of the company's products are manufactured in the same facility and use the same equipment.
The building rent and maintenance and the depreciation are allocated to products on the basis of direct labor dollars. The equipment does not wear out through use; rather it eventually becomes
obsolete.

c.   Ample capacity exists to fill all orders.

d.   Dropping the Kensington product line would have little (if any) effect on sales of other product
lines.

e.   All products are made to order, so there are no inventories.

f.   Shipping costs are traced to the product lines.

g.   Advertising costs are for ads to promote specific product lines. These costs have been traced directly
to the product lines.

h.   General administrative expenses are allocated to products on the basis of sales dollars. There would
be no effect on the total general administrative expenses if the Kensington product line were
dropped.

Required:

1.   Would you recommend that the Kensington product line be dropped, given the current level of sales?
Prepare appropriate computations to support your answer.

2.   What would sales of the Kensington product line have to be, at a minimum, to justify retaining the
product line? Explain your answer. (Hint: Set this up as a break-even problem, but include only the
relevant costs.)

CHECK FIGURE
(1) $0.05 savings per box
    to make

COMMUNICATING IN PRACTICE   (LO3)

Bronson Company manufactures a variety of ballpoint pens. The company has just received an offer from
an outside supplier to provide the ink cartridge for the company's Zippo pen line, at a price of $0.48 per
dozen cartridges. The company is interested in this offer, since its own production of cartridges is at
capacity.

Bronson Company estimates that if the supplier's offer were accepted, the direct labor and variable
overhead costs of the Zippo pen line would be reduced by 10% and the direct materials cost would be reduced by 20%.

Under present operations, Bronson Company manufactures all of its own pens from start to finish. The
Zippo pens are sold through wholesalers at $4 per box. Each box contains one dozen pens. Fixed overhead
costs charged to the Zippo pen line total $50,000 each year. (The same equipment and facilities are used to
produce several pen lines.) The present cost of producing one dozen Zippo pens (one box) is given below:

Direct materials..............	$1.50
Direct labor.................	1.00
Manufacturing overhead	0.80*
Total cost..................	$3.30

*Includes both variable and fixed manu-
facturing overhead, based on production
of 100,000 boxes of pens each year.

Required:

Write a memorandum to the president of Bronson Company that answers the following questions. Include
computations to support your answer as appropriate.

1.   Should Bronson Company accept the outside supplier's offer?

2.   What is the maximum price that Bronson Company should be willing to pay the outside supplier per
dozen cartridges?

3.   Due to the bankruptcy of a competitor, Bronson Company could sell as many as 150,000 boxes of
Zippo pens next year. As stated above, the company presently has enough capacity to produce the
cartridges for only 100,000 boxes of Zippo pens annually. By incurring $30,000 in added fixed cost
each year, the company could expand its production of cartridges to satisfy the anticipated demand

for Zippo pens. The variable cost per unit to produce the additional cartridges would be the same as at present. Under these circumstances, how many boxes of cartridges should be purchased from the outside supplier and how many should be made by Bronson?

4. What qualitative factors should Bronson Company consider in this make or buy decision?

(CMA, adapted)

TAKING IT TO THE NET

As you know, the World Wide Web is a medium that is constantly evolving. Sites come and go and change without notice. To enable periodic update of site addresses, this problem has been posted to the textbook website (www.mhhe.com/bgn2e). After accessing the site, enter the Student Center and select this chapter. Select and complete the Taking It to the Net problem.

CHAPTER TWELVE

Capital Budgeting Decisions

Invest Less, Make More

S

Steven Burd became the CEO of Safeway, one of the largest food and drug retailers in North America, in 1992. At the time, Safeway was operating approximately 1,100 stores, which occupied approximately 39 million square feet of retail space. Burd immediately slashed annual capital spending from $550 million to $290 million. He justified the decision as follows: "We had projects that were not returning the cost of money. So we cut spending back, which made the very best projects come to the surface."

Safeway set a minimum 22.5% pretax return on investment in all new store and remodeling projects. In addition to opening new stores, Burd felt that the company should emphasize expanding existing stores that are in excellent locations so as to pump up sales. With its new approach to capital budgeting firmly in place, Safeway started to steadily increase its capital spending on both new stores and remodeling projects. Ten years after implementing the new decision-making process, Safeway's 1,782 stores occupied 78.8 million square feet of retail space.

Sources: Safeway, Inc., website; and Robert Berner, "Safeway's Resurgence Is Built on Attention to Detail," *The Wall Street Journal*, October 2, 1998, p. B4.

LEARNING OBJECTIVES

After studying Chapter 12, you should be able to:

LO1 Evaluate the acceptability of an investment project using the net present value method.

LO2 Rank investment projects in order of preference.

LO3 Determine the payback period for an investment.

LO4 Compute the simple rate of return for an investment.

LO5 (Appendix 12A) Understand present value concepts and the use of present value tables.

The term **capital budgeting** is used to describe how managers plan significant outlays on projects that have long-term implications, such as the purchase of new equipment and the introduction of new products. Most companies have many more potential projects than can actually be funded. Hence, managers must carefully select those projects that promise the greatest future return. How well managers make these capital budgeting decisions is a critical factor in the long-run profitability of the company.

Capital budgeting involves *investment*—a company must commit funds now in order to receive a return in the future. Investments are not limited to stocks and bonds. Purchase of inventory or equipment is also an investment. For example, Tri-Con Global Restaurants Inc. makes an investment when it opens a new Pizza Hut restaurant. L. L. Bean makes an investment when it installs a new computer to handle customer billing. DaimlerChrysler makes an investment when it redesigns a product such as the Jeep Eagle and must retool its production lines. Merck & Co. invests in medical research. Amazon.com makes an investment when it redesigns its website. All of these investments are characterized by a commitment of funds today in the expectation of receiving a return in the future in the form of additional cash inflows or reduced cash outflows.

CAPITAL BUDGETING—PLANNING INVESTMENTS

Typical Capital Budgeting Decisions

Virtually any decision that involves an outlay now in order to obtain some return (increase in revenue or reduction in costs) in the future is a capital budgeting decision. Typical capital budgeting decisions include:

1. Cost reduction decisions: Should new equipment be purchased to reduce costs?
2. Expansion decisions: Should a new plant, warehouse, or other facility be acquired to increase capacity and sales?
3. Equipment selection decisions: Which of several available machines should be purchased?
4. Lease or buy decisions: Should new equipment be leased or purchased?
5. Equipment replacement decisions: Should old equipment be replaced now or later?

The Yukon Goes Online

Canada's Yukon Territory, which is two-thirds the size of Texas, has only 31,000 residents. Two-thirds of those live in Whitehorse, the territory's capital. All are about to get higher-speed Internet access as part of an ambitious Canadian government program to connect the Yukon with the rest of the world. To date, the Yukon's physical isolation has precluded economic growth in the area. The Internet may change all that. In some ways, it already has. A variety of organizations in the Yukon have made significant outlays on Internet projects that will have long-term implications.

After struggling to stay in business with annual sales of only $10,000, Herbie Croteau, the founder of Midnight Sun Plant Food, spent $1,600 to build a website for the company. Just two years later, sales are expected to exceed $65,000. Croteau is in the process of spending another $2,000 to redesign the company's website.

The town of Haines Junction is spending $10,000 to redesign its website. The town's chief administrative officer estimates that printing costs for tourist brochures will drop by 75% since tourist information can now be obtained online.

Capital budgeting decisions tend to fall into two broad categories—*screening decisions* and *preference decisions*. **Screening decisions** relate to whether a proposed project passes a preset hurdle. For example, a company may have a policy of accepting projects only if they promise a return of, say, 20% on the investment. The required rate of return is the minimum rate of return a project must yield to be acceptable.

Preference decisions, by contrast, relate to selecting from among several *competing* courses of action. To illustrate, a company may be considering several different machines to replace an existing machine on the assembly line. The choice of which machine to purchase is a *preference* decision.

In this chapter, we initially discuss ways of making screening decisions. Preference decisions are discussed toward the end of the chapter.

The Time Value of Money

As stated earlier, investments commonly involve returns that extend over fairly long periods of time. Therefore, in approaching capital budgeting decisions, it is necessary to employ techniques that recognize the *time value of money*. A dollar today is worth more than a dollar a year from now. The same concept applies in choosing between investment projects. Those projects that promise earlier returns are preferable to those that promise later returns.

The capital budgeting techniques that recognize the above two characteristics of business investments most fully are those that involve *discounted cash flows*. We will spend most of this chapter illustrating the use of discounted cash flow methods in making capital budgeting decisions. If you are not already familiar with discounting and the use of present value tables, you should read Appendix 12A, The Concept of Present Value, at the end of this chapter before proceeding any further.

Screening versus Preference Decisions

Screening Decisions   **Preference Decisions**

Several approaches can be used to evaluate investments using discounted cash flows. The easiest method to use is the *net present value method*, which is the subject of the next several sections.

THE NET PRESENT VALUE METHOD

Under the net present value method, the present value of a project's cash inflows is compared to the present values of the project's cash outflows. The difference between the present values of these cash flows, called the **net present value,** determines whether or not the project is an acceptable investment. To illustrate, consider the following data:

Example A

Harper Company is contemplating the purchase of a machine capable of performing certain operations that are now performed manually. The machine will cost $5,000, and it will last for five years. At the end of the five-year period, the machine will have a zero scrap value. Use of the machine will reduce labor costs by $1,800 per year. Harper Company requires a minimum return of 20% on all investment projects.[1]

Should the machine be purchased? Harper Company must determine whether a cash investment now of $5,000 can be justified if it will result in an $1,800 reduction in cost each year over the next five years. It may appear that the answer is obvious since the total cost savings is $9,000 (5 years × $1,800 per year). However, the company can earn a 20% return by investing its money elsewhere. It is not enough that the cost reductions cover just the original cost of the machine; they must also yield a return of at least 20% or the company would be better off investing the money elsewhere.

To determine whether the investment is desirable, the stream of annual $1,800 cost savings should be discounted to its present value and then compared to the cost of the new machine. Since Harper Company requires a minimum return of 20% on all investment projects, this rate is used in the discounting process and is called the *discount rate*. Exhibit 12–1 shows how this analysis is done.

According to the analysis, Harper Company should purchase the new machine. The present value of the cost savings is $5,384, as compared to a present value of only $5,000 for the required investment (cost of the machine). Deducting the present value of the required investment from the present value of the cost savings gives a *net present value* of $384. Whenever the net present value is zero or greater, as in our example, an investment project is acceptable. Whenever the net present value is negative (the present value of the

EXHIBIT 12–1

Net Present Value Analysis of a Proposed Project

Initial cost	$5,000
Life of the project (years)	5
Annual cost savings	$1,800
Salvage value	$0
Required rate of return	20%

Item	Year(s)	Amount of Cash Flow	20% Factor	Present Value of Cash Flows
Annual cost savings	1–5	$1,800	2.991*	$5,384
Initial investment	Now	(5,000)	1.000	(5,000)
Net present value				$ 384

*From Table 12B-4 in Appendix 12B at the end of this chapter.

---

[1]For simplicity, we ignore taxes and inflation throughout this chapter.

cash outflows exceeds the present value of the cash inflows), an investment project is not acceptable. In sum:

If the Net Present Value Is ...	Then the Project Is ...
Positive	Acceptable, since it promises a return greater than the required rate of return.
Zero.	Acceptable, since it promises a return equal to the required rate of return.
Negative.	Not acceptable, since it promises a return less than the required rate of return.

A full interpretation of the solution would be as follows: The new machine promises more than the required 20% rate of return. This is evident from the positive net present value of $384. Harper Company could spend up to $5,384 for the new machine and still obtain the minimum required 20% rate of return. The net present value of $384, therefore, shows the amount of "cushion" or "margin of error." One way to look at this is that the company could underestimate the cost of the new machine by up to $384, or overestimate the net present value of the future cash savings by up to $384, and the project would still be financially attractive.

Emphasis on Cash Flows

In capital budgeting decisions, the focus is on cash flows and not on accounting net income. The reason is that accounting net income is based on accrual concepts that ignore the timing of cash flows into and out of an organization. From a capital budgeting standpoint, the timing of cash flows is important, since a dollar received today is more valuable than a dollar received in the future. Therefore, even though accounting net income is useful for many things, it is not ordinarily used in discounted cash flow analysis.[2] Instead of focusing on accounting net income, the analyst concentrates on identifying the specific cash flows of the investment project.

What kinds of cash flows should the analyst look for? Although they will vary from project to project, certain types of cash flows tend to recur as explained in the following paragraphs.

Typical Cash Outflows   Most projects will have an immediate cash outflow in the form of an initial investment in equipment or other assets. Any salvage value realized from the sale of old equipment can be recognized as a cash inflow or as a reduction in the required investment. In addition, some projects require that a company expand its working capital. **Working capital** is current assets (cash, accounts receivable, and inventory) less current liabilities. When a company takes on a new project, the balances in the current asset accounts will often increase. For example, opening a new Nordstrom's department store would require additional cash in sales registers, increased accounts receivable for new customers, and more inventory on shelves. These additional working capital needs should be treated as part of the initial investment in a project. Also, many projects require periodic outlays for repairs and maintenance and for additional operating costs. These should all be treated as cash outflows for capital budgeting purposes.

Typical Cash Inflows   On the cash inflow side, a project will normally either increase revenues or reduce costs. Either way, the amount involved should be treated as a cash inflow for capital budgeting purposes. Notice that as far as cash inflows are concerned, *a reduction in costs is equivalent to an increase in revenues.* Cash inflows are also frequently

---

[2]Under certain conditions, capital budgeting decisions can be correctly made by discounting appropriately defined accounting net income. However, this approach requires advanced techniques that are beyond the scope of this book.

realized from salvage of equipment when a project ends, although in some cases the company may actually have to pay to dispose of low-value or hazardous items. In addition, any working capital that was tied up in the project can be released for use elsewhere at the end of the project and should be treated as a cash inflow. Working capital is released, for example, when a company sells off its inventory or collects its receivables.

In summary, the following types of cash flows are common in business investment projects:

Cash outflows:
  Initial investment (including installation costs).
  Increased working capital needs.
  Repairs and maintenance.
  Incremental operating costs.
Cash inflows:
  Incremental revenues.
  Reduction in costs.
  Salvage value.
  Release of working capital.

Hazardous PCs

Disposing of old equipment can be difficult—particularly when environmental regulations are involved. For example, computer equipment often contains lead and other substances that could contaminate the air, soil, or groundwater. Cindy Brethauer, the network administrator for 1st Choice Bank, in Greeley, Colorado, was faced with the mounting problem of storing old monitors, printers, and personal computers that could not be simply thrown away. These bulky items were constantly being shuttled back and forth from one storage space to another. For help, she turned to Technology Recycling LLC, which hauls away old computers and peripherals for $35 per component. Technology LLC employs disabled people to strip the machines. Many of the materials taken from the machines are recycled, while the environmentally sensitive materials are taken to disposal facilities approved by the Environmental Protection Agency. Technology LLC handles the complicated paperwork for its customers.

Source: Jill Hecht Maxwell, *Inc. Tech*, 2000, 1, p. 25.

Simplifying Assumptions

Two simplifying assumptions are usually made in net present value analysis.

The first assumption is that all cash flows other than the initial investment occur at the end of periods. This is somewhat unrealistic in that cash flows typically occur *throughout* a period rather than just at its end. The purpose of this assumption is just to simplify computations.

The second assumption is that all cash flows generated by an investment project are immediately reinvested at a rate of return equal to the discount rate. Unless these conditions are met, the net present value computed for the project will not be accurate.

A Return on Investment of 100%

During negotiations to build a replacement for the old Fenway Park in Boston, the Red Sox offered the city approximately $2 million per year over 30 years in exchange for an investment of $150 million by the city for land acquisition and cleanup. In May 2000, after denying his lack of support for the project, Boston Mayor Thomas M. Menino stated that his goal is a 100% rate of return on any investment that is made by the city. Some doubt that the Red Sox would be able to pay players' salaries if the team were required to meet the mayor's goal. The mayor has countered with a list of suggestions for raising private funds (such as selling shares to the public, as the Celtics did in 1986). Private funds would reduce the investment that would need to be made by the city and, as a result, reduce the future payments made to the city by the Red Sox. Negotiations continue.

Source: Meg Vaillancourt, "Boston Mayor Wants High Return on Investment in New Ballpark," *Knight-Ridder/Tribune Business News,* May 11, 2000, pITEM00133018.

Choosing a Discount Rate

A positive net present value indicates that the project's return exceeds the discount rate. A negative net present value indicates that the project's return is less than the discount rate. Therefore, if the company's minimum required rate of return is used as the discount rate, a project with a positive net present value is acceptable and a project with a negative net present value is unacceptable.

What is a company's minimum required rate of return? The company's *cost of capital* is usually regarded as the minimum required rate of return. The **cost of capital** is the average rate of return the company must pay to its long-term creditors and to shareholders for the use of their funds. The cost of capital is the minimum required rate of return because if a project's rate of return is less than the cost of capital, the company does not earn enough of a return to compensate its creditors and shareholders. Therefore, any project with a rate of return less than the cost of capital should not be accepted.

The cost of capital serves as a *screening device* in net present value analysis. When the cost of capital is used as the discount rate, any project with a negative net present value does not cover the company's cost of capital and should be discarded as unacceptable.

Negotiator for the Red Sox

DECISION MAKER

As stated above, Boston Mayor Thomas M. Menino's goal is a 100% rate of return on any investment that is made by the city to build a new park for the Red Sox. How would you respond to the mayor?

An Extended Example of the Net Present Value Method

To conclude our discussion of the net present value method, we present below an extended example of how it is used to analyze an investment proposal. This example will also help to tie together (and to reinforce) many of the ideas developed thus far.

Example B

Under a special licensing arrangement, Swinyard Company has an opportunity to market a new product in the western United States for a five-year period. The product would be purchased from the manufacturer, with Swinyard Company responsible for promotion and distribution costs. The licensing arrangement could be renewed at the end of the five-year period. After careful study, Swinyard Company has estimated the following costs and revenues for the new product:

Cost of equipment needed	$60,000
Working capital needed	$100,000
Overhaul of the equipment in four years	$5,000

(continued)

503

(concluded)	
Salvage value of the equipment in five years..........	$10,000
Annual revenues and costs:	
Sales revenues...............................	$200,000
Cost of goods sold	$125,000
Out-of-pocket operating costs (for salaries,	
advertising, and other direct costs)	$35,000

At the end of the five-year period, the working capital would be released for investment elsewhere if Swinyard decides not to renew the licensing arrangement. Swinyard Company uses a 14% discount rate. Would you recommend that the new product be introduced?

This example involves a variety of cash inflows and cash outflows. The solution is given in Exhibit 12–2.

Notice particularly how the working capital is handled in this exhibit. It is counted as a cash outflow at the beginning of the project and as a cash inflow when it is released at the end of the project. Also notice how the sales revenues, cost of goods sold, and out-of-pocket costs are handled. **Out-of-pocket costs** are actual cash outlays for salaries, advertising, and other operating expenses. Depreciation would not be an out-of-pocket cost, since it involves no current cash outlay.

Since the overall net present value is positive, the new product should be added assuming the company has no better use for the investment funds.

EXPANDING THE NET PRESENT VALUE METHOD

So far, our examples have involved only a single investment alternative. We will now expand the net present value method to include two alternatives. In addition, we will integrate the concept of relevant costs into the discounted cash flow analysis.

The net present value method can be used to compare competing investment projects in two ways. One is the *total-cost approach,* and the other is the *incremental-cost approach.* Each approach is illustrated below.

EXHIBIT 12–2   The Net Present Value Method—An Extended Example

Sales revenues..........................	$200,000
Less cost of goods sold...................	125,000
Less out-of-pocket costs for	
salaries, advertising, etc.	35,000
Annual net cash inflows	$ 40,000

Item	Year(s)	Amount of Cash Flows	14% Factor	Present Value of Cash Flows
Purchase of equipment...........................	Now	$ (60,000)	1.000	$ (60,000)
Working capital needed..........................	Now	(100,000)	1.000	(100,000)
Overhaul of equipment	4	(5,000)	0.592*	(2,960)
Annual net cash inflows from sales				
of the product line...........................	1–5	40,000	3.433†	137,320
Salvage value of the equipment	5	10,000	0.519*	5,190
Working capital released	5	100,000	0.519*	51,900
Net present value................................				$ 31,450

*From Table 12B–3 in Appendix 12B.
†From Table 12B–4 in Appendix 12B.

The Total-Cost Approach

The total-cost approach is the most flexible method for comparing projects. To illustrate the mechanics of the approach, consider the following data:

Example C

Harper Ferry Company provides a ferry service across the Mississippi River. One of its small ferryboats is in poor condition. This ferry can be renovated at an immediate cost of $200,000. Further repairs and an overhaul of the motor will be needed five years from now at a cost of $80,000. In all, the ferry will be usable for 10 years if this work is done. At the end of 10 years, the ferry will have to be scrapped at a salvage value of approximately $60,000. The scrap value of the ferry right now is $70,000. It will cost $300,000 each year to operate the ferry, and revenues will total $400,000 annually.

As an alternative, Harper Ferry Company can purchase a new ferryboat at a cost of $360,000. The new ferry will have a life of 10 years, but it will require some repairs at the end of 5 years. It is estimated that these repairs will amount to $30,000. At the end of 10 years, it is estimated that the ferry will have a scrap value of $60,000. It will cost $210,000 each year to operate the ferry, and revenues will total $400,000 annually.

Harper Ferry Company requires a return of at least 14% before taxes on all investment projects.

Should the company purchase the new ferry or renovate the old ferry? Exhibit 12–3 gives the solution using the total-cost approach.

Two points should be noted from the exhibit. First, observe that *all* cash inflows and *all* cash outflows are included in the solution under each alternative. No effort has been made to isolate those cash flows that are relevant to the decision and those that are not

EXHIBIT 12–3   The Total-Cost Approach to Project Selection

	New Ferry	Old Ferry
Annual revenues	$400,000	$400,000
Annual cash operating costs.	210,000	300,000
Net annual cash inflows	$190,000	$100,000

Item	Year(s)	Amount of Cash Flows	14% Factor*	Present Value of Cash Flows
Buy the new ferry:				
Initial investment	Now	$(360,000)	1.000	$(360,000)
Salvage of the old ferry	Now	70,000	1.000	70,000
Repairs in five years	5	(30,000)	0.519	(15,570)
Net annual cash inflows ($400,000 − $210,000)	1–10	190,000	5.216	991,040
Salvage of the new ferry.	10	60,000	0.270	16,200
Net present value.				701,670
Keep the old ferry:				
Renovation.	Now	$(200,000)	1.000	(200,000)
Repairs in five years	5	(80,000)	0.519	(41,520)
Net annual cash inflows ($400,000 − $300,000)	1–10	100,000	5.216	521,600
Salvage of the old ferry	10	60,000	0.270	16,200
Net present value.				296,280
Net present value in favor of buying the new ferry				$ 405,390

*All present value factors are from Tables 12B–3 and 12B–4 in Appendix 12B.

relevant. The inclusion of all cash flows associated with each alternative gives the approach its name—the *total-cost* approach.

Second, notice that the net present value is computed for each of the two alternatives. This is a distinct advantage of the total-cost approach in that an unlimited number of alternatives can be compared side by side to determine the best action. For example, another alternative for Harper Ferry Company would be to get out of the ferry business entirely. If management desired, the net present value of this alternative could be computed to compare with the alternatives shown in Exhibit 12–3. Still other alternatives might be open to the company. Once management has determined the net present value of each alternative, it can select the course of action that promises to be the most profitable. In the case at hand, given only the two alternatives, the best alternative is to purchase the new ferry.[3]

IN BUSINESS

Does It Really Need to Be New?

Tom Copeland, the director of Corporate Finance Practice at the consulting firm Monitor Group, observes: "If they could afford it, most people would like to drive a new car. Managers are no different . . . [I]n my experience, . . . [managers] routinely spend millions of dollars on new machines years earlier than they need to. In most cases, the overall cost (including the cost of breakdowns) is 30% to 40% lower if a company continues servicing an existing machine for five more years instead of buying a new one. In order to fight impulsive acquisitions of new machinery, companies should require unit managers to run the numbers on all alternative investment options open to them—including maintaining the existing assets or buying used ones."

Source: Tom Copeland, "Cutting Costs Without Drawing Blood," *Harvard Business Review*, September–October 2000, pp. 3–7.

The Incremental-Cost Approach

When only two alternatives are being considered, the incremental-cost approach offers a simpler and more direct route to a decision. Unlike the total-cost approach, it focuses only on differential costs.[4] The procedure is to include in the discounted cash flow analysis only those costs and revenues that *differ* between the two alternatives being considered. To illustrate, refer again to the data in Example C relating to Harper Ferry Company. The solution using only differential costs is presented in Exhibit 12–4.

Two things should be noted from the data in this exhibit. First, notice that the net present value in favor of buying the new ferry of $405,390 shown in Exhibit 12–4 agrees with the net present value shown under the total-cost approach in Exhibit 12–3. This agreement should be expected, since the two approaches are just different roads to the same destination.

Second, notice that the costs used in Exhibit 12–4 are just the differences between the costs shown for the two alternatives in the prior exhibit. For example, the $160,000 incremental investment required to purchase the new ferry in Exhibit 12–4 is the difference between the $360,000 cost of the new ferry and the $200,000 cost required to renovate the old ferry from Exhibit 12–3. The other figures in Exhibit 12–4 have been computed in the same way.

---

[3]The alternative with the highest net present value is not always the best choice, although it is the best choice in this case. For further discussion, see the section Preference Decisions—The Ranking of Investment Projects.

[4]Technically, the incremental-cost approach is misnamed, since it focuses on differential costs (that is, on both cost increases and decreases) rather than just on incremental costs. As used here, the term *incremental costs* should be interpreted broadly to include both cost increases and cost decreases.

EXHIBIT 12–4   The Incremental-Cost Approach to Project Selection

Item	Year(s)	Amount of Cash Flows	14% Factor*	Present Value of Cash Flows
Incremental investment to buy the new ferry..........	Now	$(160,000)	1.000	$(160,000)
Salvage of the old ferry now	Now	70,000	1.000	70,000
Difference in repairs in five years	5	50,000	0.519	25,950
Increase in net annual cash inflows	1–10	90,000	5.216	469,440
Difference in salvage value in 10 years	10	0	0.270	0
Net present value in favor of buying the new ferry				$ 405,390

*All present value factors are from Tables 12B–3 and 12B–4 in Appendix 12B.

Least-Cost Decisions

Revenues (and cash inflows) are not directly involved in some decisions. For example, a company that does not charge for delivery service may need to replace an old delivery truck, or a company may be trying to decide whether to lease or to buy its fleet of company cars. In situations such as these, where no revenues are involved, the most desirable alternative will be the one that promises the *least total cost* from the present value perspective. Hence, these are known as least-cost decisions. To illustrate a least-cost decision, assume the following data:

Example D

Val-Tek Company is considering replacing an old threading machine. A new threading machine is available that could substantially reduce annual operating costs. Selected data relating to the old and the new machines are presented below:

	Old Machine	New Machine
Purchase cost when new	$200,000	$250,000
Salvage value now................	$30,000	—
Annual cash operating costs	$150,000	$90,000
Overhaul needed immediately......	$40,000	—
Salvage value in six years	$0	$50,000
Remaining life....................	6 years	6 years

Val-Tek Company uses a 10% discount rate.

Exhibit 12–5 provides an analysis of the alternatives using the total-cost approach.

As shown in the exhibit, the new machine has the lowest total cost when the present value of the net cash outflows is considered. An analysis of the two alternatives using the incremental-cost approach is presented in Exhibit 12–6. As before, the data in this exhibit represent the differences between the alternatives as shown under the total-cost approach.

1. Which of the following statements is false? (You may select more than one answer.)
   a. The total-cost and incremental-cost approaches to net present value analysis can occasionally lead to conflicting results.
   b. The cost of capital is a screening mechanism for net present value analysis.
   c. The present value of a dollar increases as the time of receipt extends further into the future.
   d. The higher the cost of capital, the lower the present value of a dollar received in the future.

CONCEPT CHECK ✓

EXHIBIT 12–5   The Total-Cost Approach (Least-Cost Decision)

Item	Year(s)	Amount of Cash Flows	10% Factor*	Present Value of Cash Flows
Buy the new machine:				
Initial investment	Now	$(250,000)	1.000	$(250,000)†
Salvage of the old machine........................	Now	30,000	1.000	30,000†
Annual cash operating costs	1–6	(90,000)	4.355	(391,950)
Salvage of the new machine.......................	6	50,000	0.564	28,200
Present value of net cash outflows				(583,750)
Keep the old machine:				
Overhaul needed now	Now	(40,000)	1.000	(40,000)
Annual cash operating costs	1–6	(150,000)	4.355	(653,250)
Present value of net cash outflows				(693,250)
Net present value in favor of				
buying the new machine........................				$ 109,500

*All factors are from Tables 12B-3 and 12B-4 in Appendix 12B.
†These two items could be netted into a single $220,000 incremental-cost figure ($250,000 − $30,000 = $220,000).

EXHIBIT 12–6   The Incremental-Cost Approach (Least-Cost Decision)

Item	Year(s)	Amount of Cash Flows	10% Factor*	Present Value of Cash Flows
Incremental investment required to				
purchase the new machine	Now	$(210,000)	1.000	$(210,000)†
Salvage of the old machine........................	Now	30,000	1.000	30,000†
Savings in annual cash operating costs................	1–6	60,000	4.355	261,300
Difference in salvage value in six years	6	50,000	0.564	28,200
Net present value in favor of buying				
the new machine				$ 109,500

*All factors are from Tables 12B-3 and 12B-4 in Appendix 12B.
†These two items could be netted into a single $180,000 incremental-cost figure ($210,000 −$30,000 = $180,000).

IN BUSINESS

Trading In That Old Car?

Consumer Reports magazine provides the following data concerning the alternatives of keeping a four-year-old Ford Taurus for three years or buying a similar new car to replace it. The illustration assumes the car would be purchased and used in suburban Chicago.

	Keep the Old Taurus	Buy a New Taurus
Annual maintenance	$1,180	$650
Annual insurance......................	$370	$830
Annual license	$15	$100
Trade-in value in three years............	$605	$7,763
Purchase price, including sales tax		$17,150

Consumer Reports is ordinarily extremely careful in its analysis, but it has omitted in this case one financial item that would clearly differ substantially between the alternatives and

hence would be relevant. What is it? To check your answer, go to the textbook website at
www.mhhe.com/bgn2e. After accessing the site, click on the link to the Internet Exercises
and then the link to this chapter.

Source: "When to Give Up on Your Clunker," *Consumer Reports*, August 2000, pp. 12–16.

IN BUSINESS

(continued)

PREFERENCE DECISIONS—THE RANKING OF INVESTMENT PROJECTS

Recall that when considering investment opportunities, managers must make two types of decisions—screening decisions and preference decisions. Screening decisions, which come first, pertain to whether or not some proposed investment is basically acceptable. Preference decisions come *after* screening decisions and attempt to answer the following question: "How do the remaining investment proposals, all of which have been screened and provide an acceptable rate of return, rank in terms of preference? That is, which one(s) would be *best* for the firm to accept?"

LEARNING OBJECTIVE 2
Rank investment projects in order of preference.

Preference decisions are more difficult to make than screening decisions because investment funds are usually limited. This often requires that some (perhaps many) otherwise very profitable investment opportunities must be passed up.

Sometimes preference decisions are called rationing decisions or ranking decisions because they ration limited investment funds among many competing alternatives. Hence, the alternatives must be ranked.

Unfortunately, the net present value of one project cannot be directly compared to the net present value of another project unless the investments in the projects are of equal size. For example, assume that a company is considering two competing investments, as shown below:

	Investment A	Investment B
Investment required.	$(80,000)	$(5,000)
Present value of cash inflows.	81,000	6,000
Net present value	$ 1,000	$ 1,000

Each project has a net present value of $1,000, but the projects are not equally desirable when funds are limited. The project requiring an investment of only $5,000 is much more desirable than the project requiring an investment of $80,000. To compare the two projects on a more valid basis, the present value of the cash inflows should be divided by the investment required. The result is called the **profitability index.** The formula for the profitability index follows:

$$\text{Profitability index} = \frac{\text{Present value of cash inflows}}{\text{Investment required}} \tag{1}$$

The profitability indexes for the two investments above would be computed as follows:

	Investment A	Investment B
Present value of cash inflows (a). . . .	$81,000	$6,000
Investment required (b).	$80,000	$5,000
Profitability index, (a) ÷ (b).	1.01	1.20

509

When using the profitability index to rank competing investment projects, the preference rule is: *The higher the profitability index, the more desirable the project.*[5] Applying this rule to the two investments above, investment B should be chosen over investment A.

The profitability index is an application of the techniques for utilizing scarce resources discussed in Chapter 11. In this case, the scarce resource is the limited funds available for investment, and the profitability index is similar to the contribution margin per unit of the scarce resource.

A few details should be clarified with respect to the computation of the profitability index. The "Investment required" refers to any cash outflows that occur at the beginning of the project, reduced by any salvage value recovered from the sale of old equipment. The "Investment required" also includes any investment in working capital that the project may need. Finally, we should note that the "Present value of cash inflows" is net of all *out*flows that occur after the project starts.

THE INTERNAL RATE OF RETURN METHOD

The *internal rate of return* method is a popular alternative to the net present value method. The **internal rate of return** is the rate of return promised by an investment over its useful life. It is computed by finding the discount rate at which the net present value of the investment is zero. The internal rate of return can be used either to screen projects or to rank them. Any project whose internal rate of return is less than the cost of capital is rejected and in general, the higher the rate of return of a project, the more desirable it is considered to be.

For technical reasons that are discussed in more advanced texts, the net present value method is generally considered to be more reliable than the internal rate of return method for both screening and ranking projects.

THE NET PRESENT VALUE METHOD AND INCOME TAXES

Our discussion of the net present value method has assumed that there are no income taxes. In most countries—including the United States—income taxes, both on individual income and on business income, are a fact of life.

Income taxes affect net present value analysis in two ways. First, income taxes affect the cost of capital in that the cost of capital should reflect the *after-tax* cost of long-term debt and of equity. Second, net present value analysis should focus on *after-tax cash flows*. The effects of income taxes on both revenues and expenses should be fully reflected in the analysis. This includes taking into account the tax deductibility of depreciation. Whereas depreciation is not itself a cash flow, it reduces taxable income and therefore income taxes, which *are* a cash flow. The techniques for adjusting the cost of capital and cash flows for income taxes are beyond the scope of this book and are covered in more advanced texts.

OTHER APPROACHES TO CAPITAL BUDGETING DECISIONS

The net present value and internal rate of return methods are widely used as decision-making tools. Other methods of making capital budgeting decisions are also used, however, and are preferred by some managers. In this section, we discuss two such methods known as *payback* and *simple rate of return*. Both methods have been in use for many years, but have been declining in popularity as primary tools for project evaluation.

---

[5]Because of the "lumpiness" of projects, the ranking provided by the profitability index may not be perfect. Nevertheless, it is a good starting point.

The Payback Method

The payback method focuses on the *payback period*. The **payback period** is the length of time that it takes for a project to recoup its initial cost out of the cash receipts that it generates. This period is sometimes referred to as "the time that it takes for an investment to pay for itself." The basic premise of the payback method is that the more quickly the cost of an investment can be recovered, the more desirable is the investment.

The payback period is expressed in years. *When the net annual cash inflow is the same every year,* the following formula can be used to compute the payback period:

$$\text{Payback period} = \frac{\text{Investment required}}{\text{Net annual cash inflow*}} \qquad (2)$$

*If new equipment is replacing old equipment, this becomes incremental net annual cash inflow.

LEARNING OBJECTIVE 3
Determine the payback period for an investment.

Concept 12–2

To illustrate the payback method, consider the following data:

Example E
York Company needs a new milling machine. The company is considering two machines: machine A and machine B. Machine A costs $15,000 and will reduce operating costs by $5,000 per year. Machine B costs only $12,000 but will also reduce operating costs by $5,000 per year.

Required:
Which machine should be purchased according to the payback method?

$$\text{Machine A payback period} = \frac{\$15,000}{\$5,000} = 3.0 \text{ years}$$

$$\text{Machine B payback period} = \frac{\$12,000}{\$5,000} = 2.4 \text{ years}$$

According to the payback calculations, York Company should purchase machine B, since it has a shorter payback period than machine A.

Investing in an MBA

IN BUSINESS

The financial benefit of earning an MBA degree is enhanced earning power; the costs include both tuition and the opportunity cost of lost salary for two years. *Forbes* magazine computed both the net present value and the payback period for 80 full-time MBA programs. *Forbes* looked at the first five years of enhanced earnings after the degree is granted and the costs of getting the degree. The net present value of an MBA varies a great deal—ranging from over $100,000 at Harvard to $1,000 or less at some institutions. The payback periods show less variation. The quickest paybacks are at Harvard and Ohio State—3.3 years. The slowest payback is about five years. Earnings that extend beyond the five-year horizon are ignored in the *Forbes* analysis. If these earnings had been included, the net present values of degrees at even the lowest-ranked schools would have increased substantially.

Source: Kurt Brandenhausen, "The Bottom Line on B-Schools," *Forbes*, February 7, 2000, pp. 100–104.

Evaluation of the Payback Method

The payback method is not a true measure of the profitability of an investment. Rather, it simply tells the manager how many years will be required to recover the original investment. Unfortunately, a shorter payback period does not always mean that one investment is more desirable than another.

To illustrate, consider again the two machines used in the example above. Since machine B has a shorter payback period than machine A, it *appears* that machine B is more desirable than machine A. But if we add one more piece of information, this illusion quickly disappears. Machine A has a projected 10-year life, and machine B has a projected 5-year life. It would take two purchases of machine B to provide the same length of service as would be provided by a single purchase of machine A. Under these circumstances, machine A would be a much better investment than machine B, even though machine B has a shorter payback period. Unfortunately, the payback method has no inherent mechanism for highlighting differences in useful life between investments. Such differences can be very important, and relying on payback alone may result in incorrect decisions.

A further criticism of the payback method is that it does not consider the time value of money. A cash inflow to be received several years in the future is weighed equally with a cash inflow to be received right now. To illustrate, assume that for an investment of $8,000 you can purchase either of the two following streams of cash inflows:

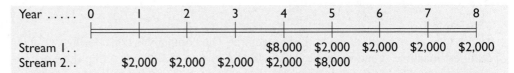

Year	0	1	2	3	4	5	6	7	8
Stream 1. .					$8,000	$2,000	$2,000	$2,000	$2,000
Stream 2. .	$2,000	$2,000	$2,000	$2,000	$8,000				

Which stream of cash inflows would you prefer to receive in return for your $8,000 investment? Each stream has a payback period of 4.0 years. Therefore, if payback alone were relied on in making the decision, you would be forced to say that the streams are equally desirable. However, from the point of view of the time value of money, stream 2 is much more desirable than stream 1.

On the other hand, under certain conditions the payback method can be very useful. For one thing, it can help identify which investment proposals are in the "ballpark." That is, it can be used as a screening tool to help answer the question, "Should I consider this proposal further?" If a proposal doesn't provide a payback within some specified period, it can be dropped without further analysis. In addition, the payback period is often of great importance to new firms that are "cash poor." When a firm is cash poor, a project with a short payback period but a low rate of return might be preferred over another project with a high rate of return but a long payback period. The reason is that the company may simply need a faster return of its cash investment. And finally, the payback method is sometimes used in industries where products become obsolete very rapidly—such as consumer electronics. Since products may last only a year or two, the payback period on investments must be very short.

Capital Budgeting in Academia

Capital budgeting techniques are widely used in large nonprofit organizations. A survey of universities in the United Kingdom revealed that 41% use the net present value method, 23% use the internal rate of return method, 29% use the payback method, and 11% use the accounting rate of return method. (Some universities use more than one method.) Furthermore, the central Funding Council of the United Kingdom requires that the net present value method be used for projects whose lifespans exceed 20 years.

Source: Paul Cooper, "Management Accounting Practices in Universities," *Management Accounting (U.K.)*, February 1996, pp. 28–30.

An Extended Example of Payback

As shown by formula (2) given earlier, the payback period is computed by dividing the investment in a project by the net annual cash inflows that the project will generate. If new equipment is replacing old equipment, then any salvage to be received on disposal of the old equipment should be deducted from the cost of the new equipment, and only the *incremental* investment should be used in the payback computation. In addition, any depreciation deducted in arriving at the project's net operating income must be added back to obtain the project's expected net annual cash inflow. To illustrate, consider the following data:

Example F

Goodtime Fun Centers, Inc., operates amusement parks. Some of the vending machines in one of its parks provide very little revenue, so the company is considering removing the machines and installing equipment to dispense soft ice cream. The equipment would cost $80,000 and have an eight-year useful life. Incremental annual revenues and costs associated with the sale of ice cream would be as follows:

Sales......................	$150,000
Less cost of ingredients	90,000
Contribution margin..........	60,000
Less fixed expenses:	
Salaries	27,000
Maintenance	3,000
Depreciation.............	10,000
Total fixed expenses	40,000
Net operating income........	$ 20,000

The vending machines can be sold for a $5,000 scrap value. The company will not purchase equipment unless it has a payback of three years or less. Should the equipment to dispense ice cream be purchased?

An analysis of the payback period of the proposed equipment is given in Exhibit 12–7. Several things should be noted from this exhibit. First, notice that depreciation is added back to net operating income to obtain the net annual cash inflow from the new equipment. Depreciation is not a cash outlay; thus, it must be added back to net operating income to adjust it to a cash basis. Second, notice in the payback computation that the salvage value from the old machines has been deducted from the cost of the new equipment, and that only the incremental investment has been used in computing the payback period.

Since the proposed equipment has a payback period of less than three years, the company's payback requirement has been met.

EXHIBIT 12–7

Computation of the Payback Period

Step 1:	*Compute the net annual cash inflow.* Since the net annual cash inflow is not given, it must be computed before the payback period can be determined:

Net operating income (given above).............	$20,000
Add: Noncash deduction for depreciation	10,000
Net annual cash flow.........................	$30,000

Step 2:	*Compute the payback period.* Using the net annual cash inflow figure from above, the payback period can be determined as follows:

Cost of the new equipment	$80,000
Less salvage value of old equipment.............	5,000
Investment required	$75,000

$$\text{Payback period} = \frac{\text{Investment required}}{\text{Net annual cash inflow}}$$

$$= \frac{\$75,000}{\$30,000} = 2.5 \text{ years}$$

Rapid Obsolescence

Intel Corporation invests a billion to a billion and a half dollars in plants to fabricate computer processor chips. But the fab plants can only be used to make state-of-the-art chips for about two years. By the end of that time, the equipment is obsolete and the plant must be converted to making less complicated chips. Under such conditions of rapid obsolescence, the payback method may be the most appropriate way to evaluate investments. If the project does not pay back within a few years, it may never pay back its initial investment.

Source: "Pentium at a Glance," *Forbes ASAP,* February 26, 1996, p. 66.

Payback and Uneven Cash Flows

When the cash flows associated with an investment project change from year to year, the simple payback formula that we outlined earlier cannot be used. Consider the following data:

Year	Investment	Cash Inflow
1	$4,000	$1,000
2		$0
3		$2,000
4	$2,000	$1,000
5		$500
6		$3,000
7		$2,000
8		$2,000

What is the payback period on this investment? The answer is 5.5 years, but to obtain this figure it is necessary to track the unrecovered investment year by year. The steps involved in this process are shown in Exhibit 12–8. By the middle of the sixth year, sufficient cash inflows will have been realized to recover the entire investment of $6,000 ($4,000 + $2,000).

The Simple Rate of Return Method

The **simple rate of return** method is another capital budgeting technique that does not involve discounting cash flows. The simple rate of return is also known as the accounting rate of return or the unadjusted rate of return.

EXHIBIT 12–8

Payback and Uneven Cash Flows

Year	(1) Beginning Unrecovered Investment	(2) Investment	(3) Cash Inflow	(4) Ending Unrecovered Investment (1) + (2) − (3)
1	$0	$4,000	$1,000	$3,000
2	$3,000		$0	$3,000
3	$3,000		$2,000	$1,000
4	$1,000	$2,000	$1,000	$2,000
5	$2,000		$500	$1,500
6	$1,500		$3,000	$0
7	$0		$2,000	$0
8	$0		$2,000	$0

Unlike the other capital budgeting methods that we have discussed, the simple rate of return method does not focus on cash flows. Rather, it focuses on accounting net operating income. The approach is to estimate the revenues that will be generated by a proposed investment and then to deduct from these revenues all of the projected operating expenses associated with the project. This net operating income is then related to the initial investment in the project, as shown in the following formula:

$$
\text{Simple rate of return} = \frac{\begin{array}{c}\text{Incremental} \\ \text{revenues}\end{array} - \begin{array}{c}\text{Incremental expenses,} \\ \text{including depreciation}\end{array} = \begin{array}{c}\text{Incremental net} \\ \text{operating income}\end{array}}{\text{Initial investment*}} \quad (3)
$$

*The investment should be reduced by any salvage from the sale of old equipment.

Or, if a cost reduction project is involved, formula (3) becomes:

$$
\text{Simple rate of return} = \frac{\begin{array}{c}\text{Cost} \\ \text{savings}\end{array} - \begin{array}{c}\text{Depreciation on} \\ \text{new equipment}\end{array}}{\text{Initial investment*}} \quad (4)
$$

*The investment should be reduced by any salvage
from the sale of old equipment.

Example G

Brigham Tea, Inc., is a processor of a low acid tea. The company is contemplating purchasing equipment for an additional processing line. The additional processing line would increase revenues by $90,000 per year. Incremental cash operating expenses would be $40,000 per year. The equipment would cost $180,000 and have a nine-year life. No salvage value is projected.

Required:
Compute the simple rate of return.

Solution:
By applying the formula for the simple rate of return found in equation (3), we can compute the simple rate of return:

$$
\text{Simple rate of return} = \frac{\left[\begin{array}{c}\$90,000 \\ \text{Incremental} \\ \text{revenues}\end{array}\right] - \left[\begin{array}{c}\$40,000 \text{ Cash operating expenses} \\ + \$20,000 \text{ Depreciation}\end{array}\right]}{\$180,000 \text{ Initial investment}}
$$

$$
= \frac{\$30,000}{\$180,000}
$$

$$
= 16.7\%
$$

Example H

Midwest Farms, Inc., hires people on a part-time basis to sort eggs. The cost of this hand-sorting process is $30,000 per year. The company is investigating the purchase of an egg-sorting machine that would cost $90,000 and have a 15-year useful life. The machine would have negligible salvage value, and it would cost $10,000 per year to operate and maintain. The egg-sorting equipment currently being used could be sold now for a scrap value of $2,500.

Required:
Compute the simple rate of return on the new egg-sorting machine.

Solution:
A cost reduction project is involved in this situation. By applying equation (4), we can compute the simple rate of return as follows:

$$\text{Simple rate} \atop \text{of return} = \frac{\$20{,}000\text{* Cost} \atop \text{savings} - \$6{,}000\text{† Depreciation} \atop \text{on new equipment}}{\$90{,}000 - \$2{,}500}$$

$$= 16.0\%$$

*\$30,000 − \$10,000 = \$20,000 cost savings.
†\$90,000 ÷ 15 years = \$6,000 depreciation.

Criticisms of the Simple Rate of Return

The most damaging criticism of the simple rate of return method is that it does not consider the time value of money. The simple rate of return method considers a dollar received 10 years from now as just as valuable as a dollar received today. Thus, the simple rate of return method can be misleading if the alternatives being considered have different cash flow patterns. Additionally, many projects do not have constant incremental revenues and expenses over their useful lives. As a result, the simple rate of return will fluctuate from year to year, with the possibility that a project may appear to be desirable in some years and undesirable in other years. In contrast, the net present value method provides a single number that summarizes all of the cash flows over the entire useful life of the project.

CONCEPT CHECK ✓

2. If a $300,000 investment has a profitability index of 1.25, what is the net present value of cash inflows associated with the investment?
   a. $375,000
   b. $240,000
   c. $325,000
   d. $300,000
3. Which of the following statements is false? (You may select more than one answer.)
   a. The payback period increases as the cost of capital decreases.
   b. The simple rate of return will be the same for two alternatives that have identical cash flow patterns even if the pattern of accounting net income differs between the alternatives.
   c. The internal rate of return will be higher than the cost of capital for projects that have positive net present values.
   d. If two alternatives have the same present value of cash inflows, the alternative that requires the higher investment will have the higher profitability index.

IN BUSINESS

Watching the Really Long Term

Forest product companies have some of the longest horizons in industry—trees they plant today may not reach their peak for decades. Of the 29 forest product companies that responded to a questionnaire, 9% use the simple rate of return as the primary criterion to evaluate timber investments, 15% use the payback period, 38% use the internal rate of return, and 38% use the net present value. None of the largest forest products firms use either the simple rate of return or the payback method to evaluate timber projects. For other investment decisions—that typically have shorter horizons—the method used shifted away from net present value and toward the payback period.

Source: Jack Bailes, James Nielsen, and Stephen Lawton, "How Forest Product Companies Analyze Capital Budgets," *Management Accounting*, October 1998, pp. 24–30.

POSTAUDIT OF INVESTMENT PROJECTS

After an investment project has been approved and implemented, a *postaudit* should be conducted. A **postaudit** involves checking whether or not expected results are actually realized. This is a key part of the capital budgeting process. It helps to keep managers honest in their investment proposals. Any tendency to inflate the benefits or downplay the costs in a proposal should become evident after a few postaudits have been conducted. The postaudit also provides an opportunity to reinforce and possibly expand successful projects and to cut losses on floundering projects.

The same technique should be used in the postaudit as was used in the original approval process. That is, if a project was approved on the basis of a net present value analysis, then the same procedure should be used in performing the postaudit. However, the data used in the postaudit analysis should be *actual observed data* rather than estimated data. This gives management an opportunity to make a side-by-side comparison to see how well the project has worked out. It also helps ensure that estimated data received on future proposals will be carefully prepared, since the persons submitting the data will know that their estimates will be given careful scrutiny in the postaudit process. Actual results that are far out of line with original estimates should be carefully reviewed.

Counting the Environmental Costs

IN BUSINESS

Companies often grossly underestimate how much they are spending on environmental costs. Many of these costs are buried in broad cost categories such as manufacturing overhead. Kestrel Management Services, LLC, a management consulting firm specializing in environmental matters, found that one chemical facility was spending five times as much on environmental expenses as its cost system reported. At another site, a small manufacturer with $840,000 in pretax profits thought that its annual safety and environmental compliance expenses were about $50,000 but, after digging into the accounts, found that the total was closer to $300,000. Alerted to this high cost, management of the company invested about $125,000 in environmental improvements, anticipating a three- to six-month payback period. By taking steps such as more efficient dust collection, the company improved its product quality, reduced scrap rates, decreased its consumption of city water for cooling, and reduced the expense of discharging wastewater into the city's sewer system. Further analysis revealed that spending $50,000 to improve energy efficiency would reduce annual energy costs by about $45,000. Few of these costs were visible in the company's traditional cost accounting system.

Source: Thomas P. Kunes, "A Green and *Lean* Workplace?" *Strategic Finance*, February 2001, pp. 71–73, 83.

Financing the Sports Car

YOU DECIDE

You would like to buy a new Mazda Miata sports car. The car can be purchased for $21,495 in cash or it can be acquired from the dealer via a leasing arrangement. Under the terms of the lease, you would have to make a payment of $2,078 when the lease is signed and then monthly payments of $300 for 24 months. At the end of the 24-month lease, you can choose to buy the car you have leased for an additional payment of $13,776. If you do not make that final payment, the car reverts to the dealer.

You have enough cash to make the initial payment on the lease, but not enough to buy the car for cash. However, you could borrow the additional cash from a credit union for 1% per month. Do you think you should pay cash, borrowing the amount from a credit union, or should you sign the lease with the dealer?

Hints: The net present value of the cash purchase option, including any payments to the credit union, is $21,495. (Accept this latter statement as true; don't try to do the computations to verify it.) Determine the net present value of the lease, using 1% per month as the discount rate in your analysis. The present value of an annuity of $1 for 24 periods at 1% per period is 21.243 and the present value of a single payment of $1 at the end of 24 periods at 1% per period is 0.788.

SUMMARY

LO1   Evaluate the acceptability of an investment project using the net present value method.
Investment decisions should take into account the time value of money since a dollar today is more valuable than a dollar received in the future. In the net present value method, future cash flows are discounted to their present value so that they can be compared on a valid basis with current cash outlays. The difference between the present value of the cash inflows and the present value of the cash outflows is called the project's net present value. If the net present value of the project is negative, the project is rejected. The company's cost of capital is often used as the discount rate in the net present value method.

LO2   Rank investment projects in order of preference.
After screening out projects whose net present values are negative, the company may still have more projects than can be supported with available funds. The remaining projects can be ranked using the profitability index, which is computed by dividing the present value of the project's future net cash inflows by the required initial investment.

LO3   Determine the payback period for an investment.
The payback period is the number of periods that are required to recover the investment in a project from the project's cash inflows. The payback period is most useful for projects whose useful lives are short and uncertain. It is not, however, a generally reliable method for evaluating investment opportunities since it ignores the time value of money and all cash flows that occur after the investment has been recovered.

LO4   Compute the simple rate of return for an investment.
The simple rate of return is determined by dividing a project's accounting net operating income by the initial investment in the project. The simple rate of return is not a reliable guide for evaluating potential projects since it ignores the time value of money and its value may fluctuate from year to year.

GUIDANCE ANSWERS TO *DECISION MAKER* AND *YOU DECIDE*

Negotiator for the Red Sox (p. 503)
Apparently, the mayor is suggesting that 100% is the appropriate rate of return for discounting the cash flows that would be received by the city to their net present value. You might respond by pointing out that an organization's cost of capital is usually regarded as the minimum required rate of return. Because the City of Boston does not have shareholders, its cost of capital might be considered the average rate of return that must be paid to its long-term creditors. It is highly unlikely that the city pays interest of 100% on its long-term debt.

Note that it is very possible that the term *return on investment* is being misused either by the mayor, the media, or both in this situation. The mayor's goal might actually be a 100% recovery of the city's investment from the Red Sox. Rather than expecting a 100% return *on* investment, the mayor may simply want a 100% return *of* investment. Taking the time to clarify the mayor's intent might change the course of negotiations.

Financing the Sports Car (p. 517)
The formal analysis, using the least-cost approach, appears below:

Item	Month(s)	Amount of Cash Flows	1% Factor	Present Value of Cash Flows
Pay cash for the car:				
Cash payment	Now	$(21,495)	1.000	$(21,495)
Net present value				$(21,495)
Lease the car:				
Cash payment on lease signing	Now	$ (2,078)	1.000	$ (2,078)
Monthly lease payment	1–24	(300)	21.243	(6,373)
Final payment.	24	(13,776)	0.788	(10,855)
Net present value				$(19,306)
Net present value in favor of leasing				$ 2,189

The leasing alternative is $2,189 less costly, in terms of net present value, than the cash purchase alternative. In addition, the leasing alternative has the advantage that you can choose to not make the final payment of $13,776 at the end of 24 months if for some reason you decide you do not want to keep the car. For example, if the resale value of the car at that point is far less than $13,776, you may choose to turn the car back over to the dealer and you can save the $13,776. If, however, you had purchased the car outright, you would not have this option—you could only realize the resale value. Because of this "real option," the leasing alternative is even more valuable than the net present value calculations indicate. Therefore, you should lease the car rather than pay cash (and borrow from the credit union).

GUIDANCE ANSWERS TO CONCEPT CHECKS

1. **Choices a and c.** The total-cost and incremental-cost approaches always provide identical results. The present value of a dollar decreases as the time of receipt extends further into the future.
2. **Choice a.** The net present value of cash flows is $300,000 × 1.25 = $375,000.
3. **Choices a, b, and d.** The payback period does not consider the time value of money; the cost of capital is ignored. The simple rate of return is based on accounting income, not cash flows. If two alternatives have the same present value of cash inflows, the alternative that requires the lower investment, as opposed to the higher investment, will have the higher profitability index.

REVIEW PROBLEM: COMPARISON OF CAPITAL BUDGETING METHODS

Lamar Company is studying a project that would have an eight-year life and require a $2,400,000 investment in equipment. At the end of eight years, the project would terminate and the equipment would have no salvage value. The project would provide net operating income each year as follows:

Sales		$3,000,000
Less variable expenses.		1,800,000
Contribution margin		1,200,000
Less fixed expenses:		
Advertising, salaries, and other		
fixed out-of-pocket costs	$700,000	
Depreciation	300,000	
Total fixed expenses		1,000,000
Net operating income.		$ 200,000

The company's discount rate is 12%.

Required:

1. Compute the net annual cash inflow from the project.
2. Compute the project's net present value. Is the project acceptable?
3. Compute the project's payback period.
4. Compute the project's simple rate of return.

Solution to Review Problem

1. The net annual cash inflow can be computed by deducting the cash expenses from sales:

Sales	$3,000,000
Less variable expenses	1,800,000
Contribution margin.	1,200,000
Less advertising, salaries, and	
other fixed out-of-pocket costs	700,000
Net annual cash inflow	$ 500,000

Or it can be computed by adding depreciation back to net operating income:

Net operating income.	$200,000
Add: Noncash deduction	
for depreciation.	300,000
Net annual cash inflow	$500,000

2. The net present value can be computed as follows:

Item	Year(s)	Amount of Cash Flows	12% Factor	Present Value of Cash Flows
Cost of new equipment	Now	$(2,400,000)	1.000	$(2,400,000)
Net annual cash inflow	1–8	500,000	4.968	2,484,000
Net present value.				$ 84,000

Yes, the project is acceptable since it has a positive net present value.

3. The formula for the payback period is:

$$\text{Payback period} = \frac{\text{Investment required}}{\text{Net annual cash inflow}}$$

$$= \frac{\$2,400,000}{\$500,000}$$

$$= 4.8 \text{ years}$$

4. The formula for the simple rate of return is:

$$\text{Simple rate of return} = \frac{\begin{array}{c}\text{Incremental}\\ \text{revenues}\end{array} - \begin{array}{c}\text{Incremental expenses,}\\ \text{including depreciation}\end{array}}{\text{Initial investment}} = \frac{\text{Incremental net operating}}{\text{income}}$$

$$= \frac{\$200,000}{\$2,400,000}$$

$$= 8.3\%$$

GLOSSARY

Capital budgeting   The process of planning significant outlays on projects that have long-term implications such as the purchase of new equipment or the introduction of a new product. (p. 498)

Cost of capital   The average rate of return the company must pay to its long-term creditors and shareholders for the use of their funds. (p. 503)

Internal rate of return   The discount rate at which the net present value of an investment project is zero; thus, the internal rate of return represents the return promised by a project over its useful life. (p. 510)

Net present value   The difference between the present value of the cash inflows and the present value of the cash outflows of an investment project. (p. 500)

Out-of-pocket costs   Actual cash outlays for salaries, advertising, repairs, and similar costs. (p. 504)

Payback period   The length of time that it takes for a project to fully recover its initial cost out of the cash receipts that it generates. (p. 511)

Postaudit   The follow-up after a project has been approved and implemented to determine whether expected results are actually realized. (p. 517)

Preference decision   A decision as to which of several competing acceptable investment proposals is best. (p. 499)

Profitability index   The ratio of the present value of a project's cash inflows to the investment required. (p. 509)

Screening decision   A decision as to whether a proposed investment passes a preset hurdle. (p. 499)

Simple rate of return   The rate of return computed by dividing a project's annual accounting net operating income by the initial investment required. (p. 514)

Working capital   The excess of current assets over current liabilities. (p. 501)

The Concept of Present Value

A dollar received today is more valuable than a dollar received a year from now for the simple reason that if you have a dollar today, you can put it in the bank and have more than a dollar a year from now. Since dollars today are worth more than dollars in the future, we need some means of weighting cash flows that are received at different times so that they can be compared. Mathematics provides us with the means of making such comparisons. With a few simple calculations, we can adjust the value of a dollar received any number of years from now so that it can be compared with the value of a dollar in hand today.

The Mathematics of Interest

If a bank pays 5% interest, then a deposit of $100 today will be worth $105 one year from now. This can be expressed in mathematical terms by means of the following equation:

$$F_1 = P(1 + r) \tag{5}$$

where F_1 = the balance at the end of one period, P = the amount invested now, and r = the rate of interest per period.

If the investment made now is $100 deposited in a savings account that is to earn interest at 5%, then $P = \$100$ and $r = 0.05$. Under these conditions, $F_1 = \$105$, the amount to be received in one year.

The $100 present outlay is called the **present value** of the $105 amount to be received in one year. It is also known as the *discounted value* of the future $105 receipt. The $100 figure represents the value in present terms of $105 to be received a year from now when the interest rate is 5%.

Compound Interest   What if the $105 is left in the bank for a second year? In that case, by the end of the second year the original $100 deposit will have grown to $110.25:

Original deposit.	$100.00
Interest for the first year: $100 × 0.05	5.00
Balance at the end of the first year.	105.00
Interest for the second year: $105 × 0.05.	5.25
Balance at the end of the second year	$110.25

Notice that the interest for the second year is $5.25, as compared to only $5.00 for the first year. The reason for the greater interest earned during the second year is that during the second year, interest is being paid *on interest*. That is, the $5.00 interest earned during the first year has been left in the account and has been added to the original $100 deposit when computing interest for the second year. This is known as **compound interest.** In this case, the compounding is annual. Interest can be compounded on a semiannual, quarterly, monthly, or even more frequent basis. The more frequently compounding is done, the more rapidly the balance will grow.

We can determine the balance in an account after n periods of compounding using the following equation:

$$F_n = P(1 + r)^n \tag{6}$$

where n = the number of periods of compounding.

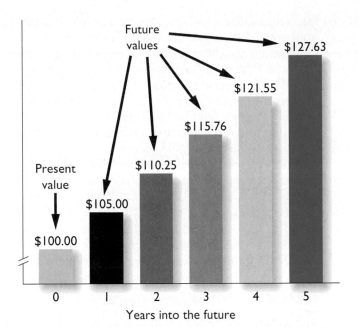

If $n = 2$ years and the interest rate is 5% per year, then the balance in two years will be as follows:

$$F_2 = \$100(1 + 0.05)^2$$

$$F_2 = \$110.25$$

Present Value and Future Value   Exhibit 12A–1 shows the relationship between present value and future value. As shown in the exhibit, if $100 is deposited in a bank at 5% interest, it will grow to $127.63 by the end of five years if interest is compounded annually.

Computation of Present Value

An investment can be viewed in two ways. It can be viewed either in terms of its future value or in terms of its present value. We have seen from our computations above that if we know the present value of a sum (such as our $100 deposit), it is a relatively simple task to compute the sum's future value in n years by using equation (6). But what if the tables are reversed and we know the *future* value of some amount but we do not know its present value?

For example, assume that you are to receive $200 two years from now. You know that the future value of this sum is $200, since this is the amount that you will be receiving in two years. But what is the sum's present value—what is it worth *right now?* The present value of any sum to be received in the future can be computed by turning equation (6) around and solving for P:

$$P = \frac{F_n}{(1 + r)^n} \tag{7}$$

In our example, $F_n = \$200$ (the amount to be received in the future), $r = 0.05$ (the annual rate of interest), and $n = 2$ (the number of years in the future that the amount is to be received).

$$P = \frac{\$200}{(1 + 0.05)^2}$$

$$P = \frac{\$200}{1.1025}$$

$$P = \$181.40$$

As shown by the computation above, the present value of a $200 amount to be received two years from now is $181.40 if the interest rate is 5%. In effect, $181.40 received *right now* is equivalent to $200 received two years from now if the rate of return is 5%. The $181.40 and the $200 are just two ways of looking at the same thing.

The process of finding the present value of a future cash flow, which we have just completed, is called **discounting.** We have *discounted* the $200 to its present value of $181.40. The 5% interest that we have used to find this present value is called the **discount rate.** Discounting future sums to their present value is a common practice in business, particularly in capital budgeting decisions.

If you have a power key (y^x) on your calculator, the above calculations are fairly easy. However, some of the present value formulas we will be using are more complex and difficult to use. Fortunately, tables are available in which many of the calculations have already been done for you. For example, Exhibit 12B–3 in Appendix 12B shows the discounted present value of $1 to be received at various periods in the future at various interest rates. The table indicates that the present value of $1 to be received two periods from now at 5% is 0.907. Since in our example we want to know the present value of $200 rather than just $1, we need to multiply the factor in the table by $200:

$$\$200 \times 0.907 = \$181.40$$

This answer is the same as we obtained earlier using the formula in equation (7).

Present Value of a Series of Cash Flows

Although some investments involve a single sum to be received (or paid) at a single point in the future, other investments involve a *series* of cash flows. A series (or stream) of identical cash flows is known as an **annuity.** To provide an example, assume that a firm has just purchased some government bonds in order to temporarily invest funds that are being held for future plant expansion. The bonds will yield interest of $15,000 each year and will be held for five years. What is the present value of the stream of interest receipts from the bonds? As shown in Exhibit 12A–2, the present value of this stream is $54,075 if we assume a discount rate of 12% compounded annually. The discount factors used in this exhibit were taken from Exhibit 12B–3 in Appendix 12B.

Two points are important in connection with Exhibit 12A–2. First, notice that the present value of the $15,000 interest declines the further it is received in the future. The present value of $15,000 received a year from now is $13,395, as compared to only $8,505 for the $15,000 interest payment to be received five years from now. This point simply underscores the fact that money has a time value.

The second point is that the computations in Exhibit 12A–2 involved unnecessary work. The same present value of $54,075 could have been obtained more easily by referring to Exhibit 12B–4 in Appendix 12B. Exhibit 12B–4 contains the present value of $1

EXHIBIT 12A–2

Present Value of a Series of Cash Receipts

Year	Factor at 12% (Table 12B–3)	Interest Received	Present Value
1	0.893	$15,000	$13,395
2	0.797	15,000	11,955
3	0.712	15,000	10,680
4	0.636	15,000	9,540
5	0.567	15,000	8,505
			$54,075

to be received each year over a *series* of years at various interest rates. Exhibit 12B–4 has been derived by simply adding together the factors from Exhibit 12B–3, as follows:

Year	Exhibit 12B–3 Factors at 12%
1	0.893
2	0.797
3	0.712
4	0.636
5	0.567
	3.605

The sum of the five factors above is 3.605. Notice from Exhibit 12B–4 that the factor for $1 to be received each year for five years at 12% is also 3.605. If we use this factor and multiply it by the $15,000 annual cash inflow, then we get the same $54,075 present value that we obtained earlier in Exhibit 12A–2:

$$\$15,000 \times 3.605 = \$54,075$$

Therefore, when computing the present value of a series (or stream) of equal cash flows that begins at the end of period 1, Exhibit 12B–4 should be used.

To summarize, the present value tables in Appendix 12B should be used as follows:

Exhibit 12B–3: This table should be used to find the present value of a single cash flow (such as a single payment or receipt) occurring in the future.

Exhibit 12B–4: This table should be used to find the present value of a series (or stream) of identical cash flows beginning at the end of the current period and continuing into the future.

The use of both of these tables is illustrated in various exhibits in the main body of the chapter. *When a present value factor appears in an exhibit, you should take the time to trace it back into either Exhibit 12B–3 or Exhibit 12B–4 to get acquainted with the tables and how they work.*

GLOSSARY (APPENDIX 12A)

Annuity   A series, or stream, of identical cash flows. (p. 524)
Compound interest   The process of paying interest on interest in an investment. (p. 522)
Discount rate   The rate of return that is used to find the present value of a future cash flow. (p. 524)
Discounting   The process of finding the present value of a future cash flow. (p. 524)
Present value   The value now of an amount that will be received in some future period. (p. 522)

Future Value and Present Value Tables

EXHIBIT 12B–1 Future Value of $1. $F_n = P(1 + r)^n$

Periods	4%	5%	6%	7%	8%	9%	10%	11%	12%	13%	14%	15%	16%	17%	18%	19%	20%
1	1.040	1.050	1.060	1.070	1.080	1.090	1.100	1.110	1.120	1.130	1.140	1.150	1.160	1.170	1.180	1.190	1.200
2	1.082	1.103	1.124	1.145	1.166	1.188	1.210	1.232	1.254	1.277	1.300	1.323	1.346	1.369	1.392	1.416	1.440
3	1.125	1.158	1.191	1.225	1.260	1.295	1.331	1.368	1.405	1.443	1.482	1.521	1.561	1.602	1.643	1.685	1.728
4	1.170	1.216	1.262	1.311	1.360	1.412	1.464	1.518	1.574	1.630	1.689	1.749	1.811	1.874	1.939	2.005	2.074
5	1.217	1.276	1.338	1.403	1.469	1.539	1.611	1.685	1.762	1.842	1.925	2.011	2.100	2.192	2.288	2.386	2.488
6	1.265	1.340	1.419	1.501	1.587	1.677	1.772	1.870	1.974	2.082	2.195	2.313	2.436	2.565	2.700	2.840	2.986
7	1.316	1.407	1.504	1.606	1.714	1.828	1.949	2.076	2.211	2.353	2.502	2.660	2.826	3.001	3.185	3.379	3.583
8	1.369	1.477	1.594	1.718	1.851	1.993	2.144	2.305	2.476	2.658	2.853	3.059	3.278	3.511	3.759	4.021	4.300
9	1.423	1.551	1.689	1.838	1.999	2.172	2.358	2.558	2.773	3.004	3.252	3.518	3.803	4.108	4.435	4.785	5.160
10	1.480	1.629	1.791	1.967	2.159	2.367	2.594	2.839	3.106	3.395	3.707	4.046	4.411	4.807	5.234	5.695	6.192
11	1.539	1.710	1.898	2.105	2.332	2.580	2.853	3.152	3.479	3.836	4.226	4.652	5.117	5.624	6.176	6.777	7.430
12	1.601	1.796	2.012	2.252	2.518	2.813	3.138	3.498	3.896	4.335	4.818	5.350	5.936	6.580	7.288	8.064	8.916
13	1.665	1.886	2.133	2.410	2.720	3.066	3.452	3.883	4.363	4.898	5.492	6.153	6.886	7.699	8.599	9.596	10.699
14	1.732	1.980	2.261	2.579	2.937	3.342	3.797	4.310	4.887	5.535	6.261	7.076	7.988	9.007	10.147	11.420	12.839
15	1.801	2.079	2.397	2.759	3.172	3.642	4.177	4.785	5.474	6.254	7.138	8.137	9.266	10.539	11.974	13.590	15.407
16	1.873	2.183	2.540	2.952	3.426	3.970	4.595	5.311	6.130	7.067	8.137	9.358	10.748	12.330	14.129	16.172	18.488
17	1.948	2.292	2.693	3.159	3.700	4.328	5.054	5.895	6.866	7.986	9.276	10.761	12.468	14.426	16.672	19.244	22.186
18	2.026	2.407	2.854	3.380	3.996	4.717	5.560	6.544	7.690	9.024	10.575	12.375	14.463	16.879	19.673	22.901	26.623
19	2.107	2.527	3.026	3.617	4.316	5.142	6.116	7.263	8.613	10.197	12.056	14.232	16.777	19.748	23.214	27.252	31.948
20	2.191	2.653	3.207	3.870	4.661	5.604	6.727	8.062	9.646	11.523	13.743	16.367	19.461	23.106	27.393	32.429	38.338
30	3.243	4.322	5.743	7.612	10.063	13.268	17.449	22.892	29.960	39.116	50.950	66.212	85.850	111.065	143.371	184.675	237.376

EXHIBIT 12B–2 Future Value of an Annuity of $1 in Arrears.

$$F_n = \frac{(1+r)^n - 1}{r}$$

Periods	4%	5%	6%	7%	8%	9%	10%	11%	12%	13%	14%	15%	16%	17%	18%	19%	20%
1	1.000	1.000	1.000	1.000	1.000	1.000	1.000	1.000	1.000	1.000	1.000	1.000	1.000	1.000	1.000	1.000	1.000
2	2.040	2.050	2.060	2.070	2.080	2.090	2.100	2.110	2.120	2.130	2.140	2.150	2.160	2.170	2.180	2.190	2.200
3	3.122	3.153	3.184	3.215	3.246	3.278	3.310	3.342	3.374	3.407	3.440	3.473	3.506	3.539	3.572	3.606	3.640
4	4.246	4.310	4.375	4.440	4.506	4.573	4.641	4.710	4.779	4.850	4.921	4.993	5.066	5.141	5.215	5.291	5.368
5	5.416	5.526	5.637	5.751	5.867	5.985	6.105	6.228	6.353	6.480	6.610	6.742	6.877	7.014	7.154	7.297	7.442
6	6.633	6.802	6.975	7.153	7.336	7.523	7.716	7.913	8.115	8.323	8.536	8.754	8.977	9.207	9.442	9.683	9.930
7	7.898	8.142	8.394	8.654	8.923	9.200	9.487	9.783	10.089	10.405	10.730	11.067	11.414	11.772	12.142	12.523	12.916
8	9.214	9.549	9.897	10.260	10.637	11.028	11.436	11.859	12.300	12.757	13.233	13.727	14.240	14.773	15.327	15.902	16.499
9	10.583	11.027	11.491	11.978	12.488	13.021	13.579	14.164	14.776	15.416	16.085	16.786	17.519	18.285	19.086	19.923	20.799
10	12.006	12.578	13.181	13.816	14.487	15.193	15.937	16.722	17.549	18.420	19.337	20.304	21.321	22.393	23.521	24.709	25.959
11	13.486	14.207	14.972	15.784	16.645	17.560	18.531	19.561	20.655	21.814	23.045	24.349	25.733	27.200	28.755	30.404	32.150
12	15.026	15.917	16.870	17.888	18.977	20.141	21.384	22.713	24.133	25.650	27.271	29.002	30.850	32.824	34.931	37.180	39.581
13	16.627	17.713	18.882	20.141	21.495	22.953	24.523	26.212	28.029	29.985	32.089	34.352	36.786	39.404	42.219	45.244	48.497
14	18.292	19.599	21.015	22.550	24.215	26.019	27.975	30.095	32.393	34.883	37.581	40.505	43.672	47.103	50.818	54.841	59.196
15	20.024	21.579	23.276	25.129	27.152	29.361	31.772	34.405	37.280	40.417	43.842	47.580	51.660	56.110	60.965	66.261	72.035
16	21.825	23.657	25.673	27.888	30.324	33.003	35.950	39.190	42.753	46.672	50.980	55.717	60.925	66.649	72.939	79.850	87.442
17	23.698	25.840	28.213	30.840	33.750	36.974	40.545	44.501	48.884	53.739	59.118	65.075	71.673	78.979	87.068	96.022	105.931
18	25.645	28.132	30.906	33.999	37.450	41.301	45.599	50.396	55.750	61.725	68.394	75.836	84.141	93.406	103.740	115.266	128.117
19	27.671	30.539	33.760	37.379	41.446	46.018	51.159	56.939	63.440	70.749	78.969	88.212	98.603	110.285	123.414	138.166	154.740
20	29.778	33.066	36.786	40.995	45.762	51.160	57.275	64.203	72.052	80.947	91.025	102.444	115.380	130.033	146.628	165.418	186.688
30	56.085	66.439	79.058	94.461	113.283	136.308	164.494	199.021	241.333	293.199	356.787	434.745	530.312	647.439	790.948	966.712	1181.882

EXHIBIT 12B–3 Present Value of $1.

$$P = \frac{F_n}{(1 + r)^n}$$

Periods	4%	5%	6%	7%	8%	9%	10%	11%	12%	13%	14%	15%	16%	17%	18%	19%	20%	21%	22%	23%	24%	25%
1	0.962	0.952	0.943	0.935	0.926	0.917	0.909	0.901	0.893	0.885	0.877	0.870	0.862	0.855	0.847	0.840	0.833	0.826	0.820	0.813	0.806	0.800
2	0.925	0.907	0.890	0.873	0.857	0.842	0.826	0.812	0.797	0.783	0.769	0.756	0.743	0.731	0.718	0.706	0.694	0.683	0.672	0.661	0.650	0.640
3	0.889	0.864	0.840	0.816	0.794	0.772	0.751	0.731	0.712	0.693	0.675	0.658	0.641	0.624	0.609	0.593	0.579	0.564	0.551	0.537	0.524	0.512
4	0.855	0.823	0.792	0.763	0.735	0.708	0.683	0.659	0.636	0.613	0.592	0.572	0.552	0.534	0.516	0.499	0.482	0.467	0.451	0.437	0.423	0.410
5	0.822	0.784	0.747	0.713	0.681	0.650	0.621	0.593	0.567	0.543	0.519	0.497	0.476	0.456	0.437	0.419	0.402	0.386	0.370	0.355	0.341	0.328
6	0.790	0.746	0.705	0.666	0.630	0.596	0.564	0.535	0.507	0.480	0.456	0.432	0.410	0.390	0.370	0.352	0.335	0.319	0.303	0.289	0.275	0.262
7	0.760	0.711	0.665	0.623	0.583	0.547	0.513	0.482	0.452	0.425	0.400	0.376	0.354	0.333	0.314	0.296	0.279	0.263	0.249	0.235	0.222	0.210
8	0.731	0.677	0.627	0.582	0.540	0.502	0.467	0.434	0.404	0.376	0.351	0.327	0.305	0.285	0.266	0.249	0.233	0.218	0.204	0.191	0.179	0.168
9	0.703	0.645	0.592	0.544	0.500	0.460	0.424	0.391	0.361	0.333	0.308	0.284	0.263	0.243	0.225	0.209	0.194	0.180	0.167	0.155	0.144	0.134
10	0.676	0.614	0.558	0.508	0.463	0.422	0.386	0.352	0.322	0.295	0.270	0.247	0.227	0.208	0.191	0.176	0.162	0.149	0.137	0.126	0.116	0.107
11	0.650	0.585	0.527	0.475	0.429	0.388	0.350	0.317	0.287	0.261	0.237	0.215	0.195	0.178	0.162	0.148	0.135	0.123	0.112	0.103	0.094	0.086
12	0.625	0.557	0.497	0.444	0.397	0.356	0.319	0.286	0.257	0.231	0.208	0.187	0.168	0.152	0.137	0.124	0.112	0.102	0.092	0.083	0.076	0.069
13	0.601	0.530	0.469	0.415	0.368	0.326	0.290	0.258	0.229	0.204	0.182	0.163	0.145	0.130	0.116	0.104	0.093	0.084	0.075	0.068	0.061	0.055
14	0.577	0.505	0.442	0.388	0.340	0.299	0.263	0.232	0.205	0.181	0.160	0.141	0.125	0.111	0.099	0.088	0.078	0.069	0.062	0.055	0.049	0.044
15	0.555	0.481	0.417	0.362	0.315	0.275	0.239	0.209	0.183	0.160	0.140	0.123	0.108	0.095	0.084	0.074	0.065	0.057	0.051	0.045	0.040	0.035
16	0.534	0.458	0.394	0.339	0.292	0.252	0.218	0.188	0.163	0.141	0.123	0.107	0.093	0.081	0.071	0.062	0.054	0.047	0.042	0.036	0.032	0.028
17	0.513	0.436	0.371	0.317	0.270	0.231	0.198	0.170	0.146	0.125	0.108	0.093	0.080	0.069	0.060	0.052	0.045	0.039	0.034	0.030	0.026	0.023
18	0.494	0.416	0.350	0.296	0.250	0.212	0.180	0.153	0.130	0.111	0.095	0.081	0.069	0.059	0.051	0.044	0.038	0.032	0.028	0.024	0.021	0.018
19	0.475	0.396	0.331	0.277	0.232	0.194	0.164	0.138	0.116	0.098	0.083	0.070	0.060	0.051	0.043	0.037	0.031	0.027	0.023	0.020	0.017	0.014
20	0.456	0.377	0.312	0.258	0.215	0.178	0.149	0.124	0.104	0.087	0.073	0.061	0.051	0.043	0.037	0.031	0.026	0.022	0.019	0.016	0.014	0.012
21	0.439	0.359	0.294	0.242	0.199	0.164	0.135	0.112	0.093	0.077	0.064	0.053	0.044	0.037	0.031	0.026	0.022	0.018	0.015	0.013	0.011	0.009
22	0.422	0.342	0.278	0.226	0.184	0.150	0.123	0.101	0.083	0.068	0.056	0.046	0.038	0.032	0.026	0.022	0.018	0.015	0.013	0.011	0.009	0.007
23	0.406	0.326	0.262	0.211	0.170	0.138	0.112	0.091	0.074	0.060	0.049	0.040	0.033	0.027	0.022	0.018	0.015	0.012	0.010	0.009	0.007	0.006
24	0.390	0.310	0.247	0.197	0.158	0.126	0.102	0.082	0.066	0.053	0.043	0.035	0.028	0.023	0.019	0.015	0.013	0.010	0.008	0.007	0.006	0.005
25	0.375	0.295	0.233	0.184	0.146	0.116	0.092	0.074	0.059	0.047	0.038	0.030	0.024	0.020	0.016	0.013	0.010	0.009	0.007	0.006	0.005	0.004
26	0.361	0.281	0.220	0.172	0.135	0.106	0.084	0.066	0.053	0.042	0.033	0.026	0.021	0.017	0.014	0.011	0.009	0.007	0.006	0.005	0.004	0.003
27	0.347	0.268	0.207	0.161	0.125	0.098	0.076	0.060	0.047	0.037	0.029	0.023	0.018	0.014	0.011	0.009	0.007	0.006	0.005	0.004	0.003	0.002
28	0.333	0.255	0.196	0.150	0.116	0.090	0.069	0.054	0.042	0.033	0.026	0.020	0.016	0.012	0.010	0.008	0.006	0.005	0.004	0.003	0.002	0.002
29	0.321	0.243	0.185	0.141	0.107	0.082	0.063	0.048	0.037	0.029	0.022	0.017	0.014	0.011	0.008	0.006	0.005	0.004	0.003	0.002	0.002	0.002
30	0.308	0.231	0.174	0.131	0.099	0.075	0.057	0.044	0.033	0.026	0.020	0.015	0.012	0.009	0.007	0.005	0.004	0.003	0.003	0.002	0.002	0.001
40	0.208	0.142	0.097	0.067	0.046	0.032	0.022	0.015	0.011	0.008	0.005	0.004	0.003	0.002	0.001	0.001	0.001	0.000	0.000	0.000	0.000	0.000

EXHIBIT 12B-4 Present Value of an Annuity of $1 in Arrears.

$$P_n = \frac{1}{r}\left[1 - \frac{1}{(1+r)^n}\right]$$

Periods	4%	5%	6%	7%	8%	9%	10%	11%	12%	13%	14%	15%	16%	17%	18%	19%	20%	21%	22%	23%	24%	25%
1	0.962	0.952	0.943	0.935	0.926	0.917	0.909	0.901	0.893	0.885	0.877	0.870	0.862	0.855	0.847	0.840	0.833	0.826	0.820	0.813	0.806	0.800
2	1.886	1.859	1.833	1.808	1.783	1.759	1.736	1.713	1.690	1.668	1.647	1.626	1.605	1.585	1.566	1.547	1.528	1.509	1.492	1.474	1.457	1.440
3	2.775	2.723	2.673	2.624	2.577	2.531	2.487	2.444	2.402	2.361	2.322	2.283	2.246	2.210	2.174	2.140	2.106	2.074	2.042	2.011	1.981	1.952
4	3.630	3.546	3.465	3.387	3.312	3.240	3.170	3.102	3.037	2.974	2.914	2.855	2.798	2.743	2.690	2.639	2.589	2.540	2.494	2.448	2.404	2.362
5	4.452	4.329	4.212	4.100	3.993	3.890	3.791	3.696	3.605	3.517	3.433	3.352	3.274	3.199	3.127	3.058	2.991	2.926	2.864	2.803	2.745	2.689
6	5.242	5.076	4.917	4.767	4.623	4.486	4.355	4.231	4.111	3.998	3.889	3.784	3.685	3.589	3.498	3.410	3.326	3.245	3.167	3.092	3.020	2.951
7	6.002	5.786	5.582	5.389	5.206	5.033	4.868	4.712	4.564	4.423	4.288	4.160	4.039	3.922	3.812	3.706	3.605	3.508	3.416	3.327	3.242	3.161
8	6.733	6.463	6.210	5.971	5.747	5.535	5.335	5.146	4.968	4.799	4.639	4.487	4.344	4.207	4.078	3.954	3.837	3.726	3.619	3.518	3.421	3.329
9	7.435	7.108	6.802	6.515	6.247	5.995	5.759	5.537	5.328	5.132	4.946	4.772	4.607	4.451	4.303	4.163	4.031	3.905	3.786	3.673	3.566	3.463
10	8.111	7.722	7.360	7.024	6.710	6.418	6.145	5.889	5.650	5.426	5.216	5.019	4.833	4.659	4.494	4.339	4.192	4.054	3.923	3.799	3.682	3.571
11	8.760	8.306	7.887	7.499	7.139	6.805	6.495	6.207	5.938	5.687	5.453	5.234	5.029	4.836	4.656	4.486	4.327	4.177	4.035	3.902	3.776	3.656
12	9.385	8.863	8.384	7.943	7.536	7.161	6.814	6.492	6.194	5.918	5.660	5.421	5.197	4.988	4.793	4.611	4.439	4.278	4.127	3.985	3.851	3.725
13	9.986	9.394	8.853	8.358	7.904	7.487	7.103	6.750	6.424	6.122	5.842	5.583	5.342	5.118	4.910	4.715	4.533	4.362	4.203	4.053	3.912	3.780
14	10.563	9.899	9.295	8.745	8.244	7.786	7.367	6.982	6.628	6.302	6.002	5.724	5.468	5.229	5.008	4.802	4.611	4.432	4.265	4.108	3.962	3.824
15	11.118	10.380	9.712	9.108	8.559	8.061	7.606	7.191	6.811	6.462	6.142	5.847	5.575	5.324	5.092	4.876	4.675	4.489	4.315	4.153	4.001	3.859
16	11.652	10.838	10.106	9.447	8.851	8.313	7.824	7.379	6.974	6.604	6.265	5.954	5.668	5.405	5.162	4.938	4.730	4.536	4.357	4.189	4.033	3.887
17	12.166	11.274	10.477	9.763	9.122	8.544	8.022	7.549	7.120	6.729	6.373	6.047	5.749	5.475	5.222	4.990	4.775	4.576	4.391	4.219	4.059	3.910
18	12.659	11.690	10.828	10.059	9.372	8.756	8.201	7.702	7.250	6.840	6.467	6.128	5.818	5.534	5.273	5.033	4.812	4.608	4.419	4.243	4.080	3.928
19	13.134	12.085	11.158	10.336	9.604	8.950	8.365	7.839	7.366	6.938	6.550	6.198	5.877	5.584	5.316	5.070	4.843	4.635	4.442	4.263	4.097	3.942
20	13.590	12.462	11.470	10.594	9.818	9.129	8.514	7.963	7.469	7.025	6.623	6.259	5.929	5.628	5.353	5.101	4.870	4.657	4.460	4.279	4.110	3.954
21	14.029	12.821	11.764	10.836	10.017	9.292	8.649	8.075	7.562	7.102	6.687	6.312	5.973	5.665	5.384	5.127	4.891	4.675	4.476	4.292	4.121	3.963
22	14.451	13.163	12.042	11.061	10.201	9.442	8.772	8.176	7.645	7.170	6.743	6.359	6.011	5.696	5.410	5.149	4.909	4.690	4.488	4.302	4.130	3.970
23	14.857	13.489	12.303	11.272	10.371	9.580	8.883	8.266	7.718	7.230	6.792	6.399	6.044	5.723	5.432	5.167	4.925	4.703	4.499	4.311	4.137	3.976
24	15.247	13.799	12.550	11.469	10.529	9.707	8.985	8.348	7.784	7.283	6.835	6.434	6.073	5.746	5.451	5.182	4.937	4.713	4.507	4.318	4.143	3.981
25	15.622	14.094	12.783	11.654	10.675	9.823	9.077	8.422	7.843	7.330	6.873	6.464	6.097	5.766	5.467	5.195	4.948	4.721	4.514	4.323	4.147	3.985
26	15.983	14.375	13.003	11.826	10.810	9.929	9.161	8.488	7.896	7.372	6.906	6.491	6.118	5.783	5.480	5.206	4.956	4.728	4.520	4.328	4.151	3.988
27	16.330	14.643	13.211	11.987	10.935	10.027	9.237	8.548	7.943	7.409	6.935	6.514	6.136	5.798	5.492	5.215	4.964	4.734	4.524	4.332	4.154	3.990
28	16.663	14.898	13.406	12.137	11.051	10.116	9.307	8.602	7.984	7.441	6.961	6.534	6.152	5.810	5.502	5.223	4.970	4.739	4.528	4.335	4.157	3.992
29	16.984	15.141	13.591	12.278	11.158	10.198	9.370	8.650	8.022	7.470	6.983	6.551	6.166	5.820	5.510	5.229	4.975	4.743	4.531	4.337	4.159	3.994
30	17.292	15.372	13.765	12.409	11.258	10.274	9.427	8.694	8.055	7.496	7.003	6.566	6.177	5.829	5.517	5.235	4.979	4.746	4.534	4.339	4.160	3.995
40	19.793	17.159	15.046	13.332	11.925	10.757	9.779	8.951	8.244	7.634	7.105	6.642	6.233	5.871	5.548	5.258	4.997	4.760	4.544	4.347	4.166	3.999

QUESTIONS

12–1   What is the difference between capital budgeting screening decisions and capital budgeting preference decisions?

12–2   What is meant by the term *time value of money?*

12–3   What is meant by the term *discounting?*

12–4   Why is the net present value method of making capital budgeting decisions superior to other methods such as the payback and simple rate of return methods?

12–5   What is net present value? Can it ever be negative? Explain.

12–6   If a firm has to pay interest of 14% on long-term debt, then its cost of capital is 14%. Do you agree? Explain.

12–7   What is meant by an investment project's internal rate of return? How is the internal rate of return computed?

12–8   Explain how the cost of capital serves as a screening tool when dealing with the net present value method.

12–9   As the discount rate increases, the present value of a given future cash flow also increases. Do you agree? Explain.

12–10   Refer to Exhibit 12–2. Is the return on this investment proposal exactly 14%, more than 14%, or less than 14%? Explain.

12–11   Why are preference decisions sometimes called *rationing* decisions?

12–12   How is the profitability index computed, and what does it measure?

12–13   What is the preference rule for ranking investment projects under the net present value method?

12–14   Can an investment with a profitability index of less than 1.00 be an acceptable investment? Explain.

12–15   What is meant by the term *payback period?* How is the payback period determined?

12–16   How can the payback method be useful to the manager?

12–17   What is the major criticism of the payback and simple rate of return methods of making capital budgeting decisions?

BRIEF EXERCISES

BRIEF EXERCISE 12–1   Net Present Value Method   (LO1)
The management of Opry Company, a wholesale distributor of suntan products, is considering the purchase of a machine that would reduce operating costs in its warehouse. The machine will cost $25,000, and it will last for 10 years. At the end of the 10-year period, the machine will have zero scrap value. Use of the machine will reduce operating costs by $4,000 per year. The company requires a minimum return of 14% before taxes on all investment projects.

Required:
1. Determine the net present value of the investment in the machine.
2. What is the difference between the total, undiscounted, cash inflows and cash outflows over the entire life of the machine?

BRIEF EXERCISE 12–2   Comparison of Projects Using Net Present Value   (LO1)
Service Temps, a company that supplies temporary workers for restaurants and other service industries, has $15,000 to invest. Management is trying to decide between two alternative uses of the funds. The alternatives are as follows:

	Invest in Project A	Invest in Project B
Investment required	$15,000	$15,000
Annual cash inflows.	$4,000	$0
Single cash inflow at the end of 10 years	—	$60,000
Life of the project	10 years	10 years

Service Temps uses a 16% discount rate.

Required:
Which investment would you recommend that the company accept? Show all computations using net present value. Prepare a separate computation for each investment.

BRIEF EXERCISE 12–3   Preference Ranking   (LO2)

Information on four investment proposals at El Torrito, a chain of Mexican restaurants, is given below:

	Investment Proposal			
	A	**B**	**C**	**D**
Investment required	$(85,000)	$(200,000)	$(90,000)	$(170,000)
Present value of cash inflows	119,000	184,000	135,000	221,000
Net present value	$ 34,000	$ (16,000)	$ 45,000	$ 51,000
Life of the project	5 years	7 years	6 years	6 years

Required:
1. Compute the profitability index for each investment proposal.
2. Rank the proposals in terms of preference.

BRIEF EXERCISE 12–4   Payback Method   (LO3)

The management of Weimar Inc., a civil engineering design company, is considering an investment in a high-quality blueprint printer with the following characteristics:

Year	Investment	Cash Inflow
1.	$38,000	$2,000
2.	$6,000	$4,000
3.	—	$8,000
4.	—	$9,000
5.	—	$12,000
6.	—	$10,000
7.	—	$8,000
8.	—	$6,000
9.	—	$5,000
10.	—	$5,000

Required:
1. Determine the payback period of the investment.
2. Would the payback period be affected if the cash inflow in the last year were several times larger?

BRIEF EXERCISE 12–5   Simple Rate of Return Method   (LO4)

The management of Wallingford MicroBrew is considering the purchase of an automated bottling machine for $80,000. The machine would replace an old piece of equipment that costs $33,000 per year to operate. The new machine would have a useful life of 10 years with no salvage value. The new machine would cost $10,000 per year to operate. The old machine currently in use could be sold now for a scrap value of $5,000.

Required:
Compute the simple rate of return on the new automated bottling machine.

BRIEF EXERCISE 12–6   (Appendix 12A) Basic Present Value Concepts   (LO5)

Each of the following parts is independent.

1. Largo Freightlines plans to build a new garage in three years to have more space for repairing its trucks. The garage will cost $400,000. What lump-sum amount should the company invest now to have the $400,000 available at the end of the three-year period? Assume that the company can invest money at:
   a.   Eight percent.
   b.   Twelve percent.

2. Martell Products, Inc., can purchase a new copier that will save $5,000 per year in copying costs. The copier will last for six years and have no salvage value. What is the maximum purchase price that Martell Products would be willing to pay for the copier if the company's required rate of return is:

    a.   Ten percent.

    b.   Sixteen percent.

3. Sally has just won the million-dollar Big Slam jackpot at a gambling casino. The casino will pay her $50,000 per year for 20 years as the payoff. If Sally can invest money at a 10% rate of return, what is the present value of her winnings? Did she really win a million dollars? Explain.

EXERCISES

EXERCISE 12–7 Basic Net Present Value Analysis (LO1)

Renfree Mines, Inc., owns the mining rights to a large tract of land in a mountainous area. The tract contains a mineral deposit that the company believes might be commercially attractive to mine and sell. An engineering and cost analysis has been made, and it is expected that the following cash flows would be associated with opening and operating a mine in the area:

Cost of equipment required.	$850,000
Net annual cash receipts	$230,000*
Working capital required	$100,000
Cost of road repairs in three years	$60,000
Salvage value of equipment in five years.	$200,000

*Receipts from sales of ore, less out-of-pocket costs for salaries, utilities, insurance, and so forth.

It is estimated that the mineral deposit would be exhausted after five years of mining. At that point, the working capital would be released for reinvestment elsewhere. The company's required rate of return is 14%.

Required:

Determine the net present value of the proposed mining project. Should the project be accepted? Explain.

EXERCISE 12–8 Net Present Value Analysis of Two Alternatives (LO1)

Wriston Legacies, a retailer of fine estate jewelry, has $300,000 to invest. The company is trying to decide between two alternative uses of the funds. The alternatives are as follows:

	A	B
Cost of equipment required	$300,000	$0
Working capital investment required	$0	$300,000
Annual cash inflows	$80,000	$60,000
Salvage value of equipment in seven years	$20,000	$0
Life of the project	7 years	7 years

The working capital needed for project B will be released for investment elsewhere at the end of seven years. Wriston Legacies uses a 20% discount rate.

Required:

Which investment alternative (if either) would you recommend that the company accept? Show all computations using the net present value format. Prepare a separate computation for each project.

EXERCISE 12–9 Preference Ranking of Investment Projects (LO2)

Lake Union Yacht Brokers is investigating five different investment opportunities. Information on the five projects under study is given on the next page:

		Project Number			
	1	2	3	4	5
Investment required..............	$(480,000)	$(360,000)	$(270,000)	$(450,000)	$(400,000)
Present value of cash inflows at a 10% discount rate	567,270	433,400	336,140	522,970	379,760
Net present value................	$ 87,270	$ 73,400	$ 66,140	$ 72,970	$ (20,240)
Life of the project..............	6 years	12 years	6 years	3 years	5 years

Since the company's required rate of return is 10%, a 10% discount rate has been used in the present value computations above. Limited funds are available for investment, so the company can't accept all of the available projects.

Required:
1. Compute the profitability index for each investment project.
2. Rank the five projects according to preference, in terms of:
    a.   Net present value.
    b.   Profitability index.
3. Which ranking do you prefer? Why?

EXERCISE 12–10   Basic Payback Period and Simple Rate of Return Computations   (LO3, LO4)

Martin Landscaping Company is considering the purchase of a new piece of equipment for laying sprinkler systems. Relevant information concerning the equipment follows:

Purchase cost	$180,000
Annual cost savings that will be provided by the equipment...............	$37,500
Life of the equipment	12 years

Required:
1. Compute the payback period for the equipment. If the company rejects all proposals with a payback period of more than four years, would the equipment be purchased?
2. Compute the simple rate of return on the equipment. Use straight-line depreciation based on the equipment's useful life. Would the equipment be purchased if the company requires a rate of return of at least 14%?

EXERCISE 12–11   Basic Present Value Analysis   (LO1)

On January 2, Fred Critchfield paid $18,000 for 900 shares of the common stock of Acme Company. Mr. Critchfield received an $0.80 per share dividend on the stock at the end of each year for four years. At the end of four years, he sold the stock for $22,500. Mr. Critchfield has a goal of earning a minimum return of 12% on all of his investments.

Required:
Did Mr. Critchfield earn a 12% return on the stock? Use the net present value method. (Round all computations to the nearest whole dollar.)

PROBLEMS

PROBLEM 12–12   Basic Net Present Value Analysis   (LO1)

The Confectioner's Corner Inc. would like to buy a new Italian-made machine that automatically dips chocolates. The dipping operation is currently done by hand. The machine the company is considering costs $100,000. The machine would be usable for 10 years but would require the replacement of several key parts at the end of the fifth year. These parts would cost $7,000, including installation. After 10 years, the machine would be sold for $6,000.

CHECK FIGURE
(2) $28,638 net present value

Management estimates that the cost to operate the machine will be only $6,500 per year. The present method of dipping chocolates costs $24,000 per year. In addition to reducing costs, the new machine will increase production by 5,500 boxes of chocolates per year. The company realizes a contribution margin of $2.10 per box. An 18% rate of return is required on all investments.

Required:

1. What are the net annual cash inflows that will be provided by the new dipping machine?
2. Compute the new machine's net present value. Use the incremental cost approach and round all dollar amounts to the nearest whole dollar.

PROBLEM 12–13   Net Present Value Analysis   (LO1)

In 10 years, Jerry Cantrell will retire. He is exploring the possibility of opening a self-service car wash. The car wash could be managed in the free time he has available from his regular occupation, and it could be closed easily when he retires. After careful study, Jerry has determined the following:

a.   A building in which a car wash could be installed is available under a 10-year lease at a cost of $1,200 per month.

b.   Purchase and installation costs of equipment would total $110,000. In 10 years the equipment could be sold for 10% of its original cost.

c.   An investment of an additional $1,800 would be required to cover working capital needs for cleaning supplies, change funds, and so forth. After 10 years, this working capital would be released for investment elsewhere.

d.   Both an auto wash and a vacuum service would be offered with a wash costing $1.50 and the vacuum costing $0.25 per use.

e.   The only variable costs associated with the operation would be $0.23 per wash for water and $0.10 per use of the vacuum for electricity.

f.   In addition to rent, monthly costs of operation would be: cleaning, $780; insurance, $60; and maintenance, $510.

g.   Gross receipts from the auto wash would be about $1,110 per week. According to the experience of other self-service car washes, 70% of the customers using the wash would also use the vacuum.

Jerry will not open the car wash unless it provides at least a 12% return, since he could earn this rate of return on high-grade securities.

Required:

1. Assuming that the car wash will be open 52 weeks a year, compute the expected net annual cash receipts (gross cash receipts less cash disbursements) from its operation. (Do not include the cost of the equipment, the working capital, or the salvage value in these computations.)
2. Would you advise Jerry to open the car wash? Show computations using the net present value method of investment analysis. Round all dollar figures to the nearest whole dollar.

PROBLEM 12–14   Total Cost and Incremental Cost Approaches   (LO1)

San Jose Flights, S.A., of Panama, has a small truck that it uses for intracity deliveries. The truck is in bad repair and must be either overhauled or replaced with a new truck. The company has assembled the following information (Panama uses the U.S. dollar as its currency):

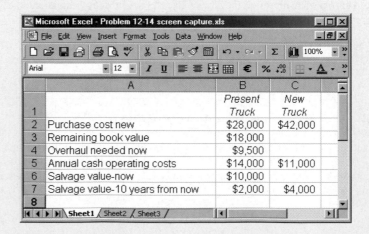

	Present Truck	New Truck
Purchase cost new	$28,000	$42,000
Remaining book value	$18,000	
Overhaul needed now	$9,500	
Annual cash operating costs	$14,000	$11,000
Salvage value-now	$10,000	
Salvage value-10 years from now	$2,000	$4,000

If the company keeps and overhauls its present delivery truck, then the truck will be usable for 10 more years. If a new truck is purchased, it will be used for 10 years, after which it will be traded in on another truck. The new truck would be diesel operated, resulting in a substantial reduction in annual operating costs, as shown above.

The company computes depreciation on a straight-line basis. All investment projects are evaluated using a 16% discount rate.

Required:
1. Should San Jose Flights, S.A., keep the old truck or purchase the new one? Use the total-cost approach to net present value in making your decision. Round to the nearest whole dollar.
2. Redo (1) above, this time using the incremental-cost approach.

PROBLEM 12–15   Keep or Sell Property   (LO1)

CHECK FIGURE
PV of cash flows for the
alternative of keeping
the property: $251,543

Ben Ryatt, professor of languages at Southern University, owns a small office building adjacent to the university campus. He acquired the property 12 years ago at a total cost of $560,000—$52,000 for the land and $508,000 for the building. He has just received an offer from a realty company that wants to purchase the property; however, the property has been a good source of income over the years, so Professor Ryatt is unsure whether he should keep it or sell it. His alternatives are:

1. **Keep the property.** Professor Ryatt's accountant has kept careful records of the income realized from the property over the past 10 years. These records indicate the following annual revenues and expenses:

Rental receipts........................		$150,000
Less building expenses:		
Utilities............................	$28,600	
Depreciation of building	17,800	
Property taxes and insurance	19,500	
Repairs and maintenance...............	10,500	
Custodial help and supplies.............	43,500	119,900
Net operating income...................		$ 30,100

Professor Ryatt makes a $12,600 mortgage payment each year on the property. The mortgage will be paid off in 10 more years. He has been depreciating the building by the straight-line method, assuming a salvage value of $9,600 for the building, which he still thinks is an appropriate figure. He feels sure that the building can be rented for another 16 years. He also feels sure that 16 years from now the land will be worth 2.5 times what he paid for it.

2. **Sell the property.** A realty company has offered to purchase the property by paying $150,000 immediately and $23,000 per year for the next 16 years. Control of the property would go to the realty company immediately. To sell the property, Professor Ryatt would need to pay the mortgage off, which could be done by making a lump-sum payment of $71,000.

Required:
Professor Ryatt requires a 14% rate of return. Would you recommend he keep or sell the property? Show computations using the total-cost approach to net present value analysis.

PROBLEM 12–16   Ranking of Projects   (LO2)

CHECK FIGURE
(1) Project B profitability
index: 1.26

Oxford Company has limited funds available for investment and must ration the funds among five competing projects. Selected information on the five projects follows:

Project	Investment Required	Net Present Value	Life of the Project (years)
A	$140,000	$42,000	8
B............	$190,000	$49,400	14
C	$175,000	$49,000	9
D	$132,000	$ (2,640)	6
E............	$138,000	$31,740	3

The company wants your assistance in ranking the desirability of the projects.

Required:
1. Compute the profitability index for each project.
2. In order of preference, rank the five projects in terms of:
   a. Net present value
   b. Profitability index
3. Which ranking do you prefer? Why?

PROBLEM 12–17   Simple Rate of Return and Payback Methods   (LO3, LO4)
Otthar's Amusement Center contains a number of electronic games as well as a miniature golf course and various rides located outside the building. Otthar Luvinson, the owner, would like to construct a water slide on one portion of his property. Otthar has gathered the following information about the slide:

a. Water slide equipment could be purchased and installed at a cost of $500,000. The slide would be usable for 10 years, after which it would have no salvage value.
b. Otthar would use straight-line depreciation on the slide equipment.
c. To make room for the water slide, several rides would be dismantled and sold. These rides are fully depreciated, but they could be sold for $40,000 to an amusement park in a nearby city.
d. Otthar has concluded that water slides would increase ticket sales by $320,000 per year.
e. Based on experience at other water slides, Otthar estimates that incremental operating expenses each year for the slide would be: salaries, $115,000; insurance, $28,200; utilities, $12,000; and mainte-nance, $32,000.

Required:
1. Prepare an income statement showing the expected net operating income each year from the water slide.
2. Compute the simple rate of return expected from the water slide. Based on this computation, would the water slide be constructed if Otthar requires a simple rate of return of at least 15% on all investments?
3. Compute the payback period for the water slide. If Otthar requires a payback period of 5 years or less, would the water slide be constructed?

PROBLEM 12–18   Simple Rate of Return and Payback Analysis of Two Machines   (LO3, LO4)
Blue Ridge Furniture is considering the purchase of two different items of equipment, as described below:

1. **Machine A.** A compacting machine has just come onto the market that would permit Blue Ridge Furniture to compress sawdust into various shelving products. At present the sawdust is disposed of as a waste product. The following information is available about the machine:
   a. The machine would cost $780,000 and would have a 25% salvage value at the end of its 10-year useful life. The company uses straight-line depreciation and considers salvage value in computing depreciation deductions.
   b. The shelving products manufactured from use of the machine would generate revenues of $350,000 per year. Variable manufacturing costs would be 20% of sales.
   c. Fixed expenses associated with the new shelving products would be (per year): advertising, $42,000; salaries, $86,000; utilities, $9,000; and insurance, $13,000.
2. **Machine B.** A second machine has come onto the market that would allow Blue Ridge Furniture to automate a sanding process that is now done largely by hand. The following information is available:
   a. The new sanding machine would cost $220,000 and would have no salvage value at the end of its 10-year useful life. The company would use straight-line depreciation on the new machine.
   b. Several old pieces of sanding equipment that are fully depreciated would be disposed of at a scrap value of $7,200.
   c. The new sanding machine would provide substantial annual savings in cash operating costs. It would require an operator at an annual salary of $26,000 and $3,000 in annual maintenance costs. The current, hand-operated sanding procedure costs the company $85,000 per year in total.

Blue Ridge Furniture requires a simple rate of return of 16% on all equipment purchases. Also, the com-pany will not purchase equipment unless the equipment has a payback period of 4 years or less.

Required:
1. For machine A:
   a. Prepare an income statement showing the expected net operating income each year from the new shelving products. Use the contribution format.
   b. Compute the simple rate of return.
   c. Compute the payback period.

2. For machine B:
   a. Compute the simple rate of return.
   b. Compute the payback period
3. According to the company's criteria, which machine, if either, should the company purchase?

PROBLEM 12–19   Net Present Value Analysis of Securities   (LO1)
Anita Vasquez received $160,000 from her mother's estate. She placed the funds into the hands of a broker, who purchased the following securities on Anita's behalf:

a. Common stock was purchased at a cost of $80,000. The stock paid no dividends, but it was sold for $180,000 at the end of 4 years.
b. Preferred stock was purchased at its par value of $30,000. The stock paid a 6% dividend (based on par value) each year for 4 years. At the end of 4 years, the stock was sold for $24,000.
c. Bonds were purchased at a cost of $50,000. The bonds paid $3,000 in interest every six months. After 4 years, the bonds were sold for $58,500. (Note: In discounting a cash flow that occurs semi-annually, the procedure is to halve the discount rate and double the number of periods. Use the same procedure in discounting the proceeds from the sale.)

CHECK FIGURE
(1) $6,760 NPV of common stock

The securities were all sold at the end of four years so that Anita would have funds available to start a new business venture. The broker stated that the investments had earned more than a 20% return, and he gave Anita the following computation to support his statement:

Common stock:	
Gain on sale ($180,000 − $80,000)	$100,000
Preferred stock:	
Dividends paid (6% × $30,000 × 4 years)	7,200
Loss on sale ($24,000 − $30,000).	(6,000)
Bonds:	
Interest paid ($3,000 × 8 periods)	24,000
Gain on sale ($58,500 − $50,000)	8,500
Net gain on all investments	$133,700

$$\frac{\$133,700 \div 4 \text{ years}}{\$160,000} = 20.9\%$$

Required:
1. Using a 20% discount rate, compute the net present value of each of the three investments. On which investment(s) did Anita earn a 20% rate of return? (Round computations to the nearest whole dollar.)
2. Considering all three investments together, did Anita earn a 20% rate of return? Explain.
3. Anita wants to use the $262,500 proceeds ($180,000 + $24,000 + $58,500 = $262,500) from sale of the securities to open a fast-food franchise under a 10-year contract. What net annual cash inflow must the store generate for Anita to earn a 16% return over the 10-year period? Assume that Anita will not receive back her original investment at the end of the contract. (Round computations to the nearest whole dollar.)

BUILDING YOUR SKILLS

ANALYTICAL THINKING   (LO1)
Wyndham Stores operates a regional chain of upscale department stores. The company is going to open another store soon in a prosperous and growing suburban area. In discussing how the company can acquire the desired building and other facilities needed to open the new store, Harry Wilson, the company's marketing vice president, stated, "I know most of our competitors are starting to lease facilities, rather than buy, but I just can't see the economics of it. Our development people tell me that we can buy the building site, put a building on it, and get all the store fixtures we need for $14 million. They also say that property taxes, insurance, maintenance, and repairs would run $200,000 a year. When you figure that we plan to keep a site for 20 years, that's a total cost of $18 million. But then when you realize that the building and property will be worth at least $5 million in 20 years, that's a net cost to us of only $13 million. Leasing costs a lot more than that."

"I'm not so sure," replied Erin Reilley, the company's executive vice president. "Guardian Insurance Company is willing to purchase the building site, construct a building and install fixtures to our specifications, and then lease the facility to us for 20 years for an annual lease payment of only $1 million."

CHECK FIGURE
(1) $3,949,950 NPV in favor of leasing

"That's just my point," said Harry. "At $1 million a year, it would cost us $20 million over the 20 years instead of just $13 million. And what would we have left at the end? Nothing! The building would belong to the insurance company! I'll bet they would even want the first lease payment in advance."

"That's right," replied Erin. "We would have to make the first payment immediately and then one payment at the beginning of each of the following 19 years. However, you're overlooking a few things. For one thing, we would have to tie up a lot of our funds for 20 years under the purchase alternative. We would have to put $6 million down immediately if we buy the property, and then we would have to pay the other $8 million off over four years at $2 million a year."

"But that cost is nothing compared to $20 million for leasing," said Harry. "Also, if we lease, I understand we would have to put up a $400,000 security deposit that we wouldn't get back until the end. And besides that, we would still have to pay all the repair and maintenance costs just like we owned the property. No wonder those insurance companies are so rich if they can swing deals like this."

"Well, I'll admit that I don't have all the figures sorted out yet," replied Erin. "But I do have the operating cost breakdown for the building, which includes $90,000 annually for property taxes, $60,000 for insurance, and $50,000 for repairs and maintenance. If we lease, Guardian will handle its own insurance costs and will pay the property taxes, but we'll have to pay for the repairs and maintenance. I need to put all this together and see if leasing makes any sense with our 12% before-tax required rate of return. The president wants a presentation and recommendation in the executive committee meeting tomorrow."

Required:

1. Using the net present value approach, determine whether Wyndham Stores should lease or buy the new store. Assume that you will be making your presentation before the company's executive committee and remember that the president detests sloppy, disorganized reports.

2. What reply will you make in the meeting if Harry Wilson brings up the issue of the building's future sales value?

CHECK FIGURE
(1) $24,640 NPV in favor of Alternative 2

TEAMWORK IN ACTION   (LO1)

Woolrich Company's market research division has projected a substantial increase in demand over the next several years for one of the company's products. To meet this demand, the company will need to produce units as follows:

Year	Production in Units
1	20,000
2	30,000
3	40,000
4–10	45,000

At present, the company is using a single model 2600 machine to manufacture this product. To increase its productive capacity, the company is considering two alternatives:

Alternative 1. The company could purchase another model 2600 machine that would operate along with the one it now owns. The following information is available on this alternative:

a.   The model 2600 machine now in use was purchased for $165,000 four years ago. Its present book value is $99,000, and its present market value is $90,000.

b.   A new model 2600 machine costs $180,000 now. The old model 2600 machine will have to be replaced in six years at a cost of $200,000. The replacement machine will have a market value of about $100,000 when it is four years old.

c.   The variable cost required to produce one unit of product using the model 2600 machine is given under the "general information" on the next page.

d.   Repairs and maintenance costs each year on a single model 2600 machine total $3,000.

Alternative 2. The company could purchase a model 5200 machine and use the old model 2600 machine as standby equipment. The model 5200 machine is a high-speed unit with double the capacity of the model 2600 machine. The following information is available on this alternative:

a.   The cost of a new model 5200 machine is $250,000.

b.   The variable cost required to produce one unit of product using the model 5200 machine is given under the "general information" on the next page.

c. The model 5200 machine is more costly to maintain than the model 2600 machine. Repairs and maintenance on a model 5200 machine and on a model 2600 machine used as standby would total $4,600 per year.

The following general information is available on the two alternatives:

a. Both the model 2600 machine and the model 5200 machine have a 10-year life from the time they are first used in production. The scrap value of both machines is negligible and can be ignored. Straight-line depreciation is used by the company.

b. The two machine models are not equally efficient. Comparative variable costs per unit of product are as follows:

	Model 2600	Model 5200
Direct materials per unit..................	$0.36	$0.40
Direct labor per unit.....................	0.50	0.22
Supplies and lubricants per unit	0.04	0.08
Total variable cost per unit................	$0.90	$0.70

c. No other factory costs would change as a result of the decision between the two machines.

d. Woolrich Company uses an 18% discount rate.

Required:

Your team should discuss and then respond to the following questions. All team members should agree with and understand the answers and be prepared to present them in class.

1. Which alternative should the company choose? Use the net present value approach. (Round to the nearest whole dollar.)

2. Suppose that the cost of materials increases by 50%. Would this make the model 5200 machine more or less desirable? Explain. No computations are needed.

3. Suppose that the cost of labor increases by 25%. Would this make the model 5200 machine more or less desirable? Explain. No computations are needed.

COMMUNICATING IN PRACTICE   (LO1, LO3, LO4)

Use an online yellow pages directory such as www.comfind.com or www.athand.com to find a manufacturer in your area that has a website. Make an appointment with the controller or chief financial officer of the company. Before your meeting, find out as much as you can about the organization's operations from its website.

Required:

After asking the following questions about a capital budgeting decision that was made by the management of the company, write a brief memorandum to your instructor that summarizes the information obtained from the company's website and addresses what you found out during your interview.

1. What was the nature of the capital project?
2. What was the total cost of the capital project?
3. Did the project costs stay within budget (or estimate)?
4. What financial criteria were used to evaluate the project?

TAKING IT TO THE NET

As you know, the World Wide Web is a medium that is constantly evolving. Sites come and go and change without notice. To enable periodic update of site addresses, this problem has been posted to the textbook website (www.mhhe.com/bgn2e). After accessing the site, enter the Student Center and select this chapter. Select and complete the Taking It to the Net problem.

CHAPTER THIRTEEN

"How Well Am I Doing?" Statement of Cash Flows

DECISION FEATURE

Is the Party Over?

There was a time when many thought that e-tailers (e-retailers) might wipe out traditional retailers. Now investors wonder if any e-tailers will be able to survive. It all boils down to cash flows. Unable to generate the cash needed to support their ongoing operations, the dot.coms are having a hard time raising money. The traditional sources of funds are venture capitalists, Wall Street investors, and banks. Venture capitalists, who often made the initial cash investments required to finance the start-up operations of many e-tailers, are unwilling to invest additional cash. After snatching up the initial public offering of almost any dot.com during the late 1990s, Wall Street investors are now guarded. Banks, quite willing to provide financing to established companies with histories of profitability, are reluctant to loan money to e-tailers because the risk of default is high.

Typically, a potential investor would start with a company's financial statements. The balance sheet provides information about the company's financial condition, and the income statement indicates whether or not a company is profitable, but neither helps to predict whether a company will generate cash. Users of financial statements look to the statement of cash flows for that information.

Market Guide, a Wall Street research firm, analyzes the statements of cash flows of selected e-tailers. Their approach estimates how long it will take for a given company to burn through its available cash. Matt Krantz, a *USA Today* reporter, updated the information and warned that 5 of the 15 companies included in the *USA Today* "Internet 100" could run out of cash by mid-2001. The five companies cited were Drugstore.com, Egghead.com, EMusic, eToys, and Travelocity. Krantz was on target. Shortly thereafter, Egghead.com and eToys went bankrupt and EMusic laid off more than one-third of its staff.

Sources: Matt Krantz, "Dot-Coms Could Run Out of Cash," *USA Today,* August 18, 2000, 1B; Matt Krantz, "E-Retailers Run Low on Fuel," *USA Today,* April 26, 2000, 1B; News.com website; and ecommercetimes website.

LEARNING OBJECTIVES

After studying Chapter 13, you should be able to:

LO1 Know how to classify changes in noncash balance sheet accounts as sources or uses of cash.

LO2 Classify transactions as operating activities, investing activities, or financing activities.

LO3 Prepare a statement of cash flows using the indirect method to determine the net cash provided by operating activities.

LO4 (Appendix 13A) Use the direct method to determine the net cash provided by operating activities.

LO5 (Appendix 13B) Prepare a statement of cash flows using the T-account approach.

Three major financial statements are ordinarily required for external reports—an income statement, a balance sheet, and a statement of cash flows. The **statement of cash flows** highlights the major activities that directly and indirectly impact cash flows and hence affect the overall cash balance. Managers focus on cash for a very good reason—without sufficient cash at the right times, a company may miss golden opportunities or may even fall into bankruptcy.

The statement of cash flows answers questions that cannot be easily answered by the income statement and balance sheet alone. For example, the statement of cash flows can be used to answer questions like the following: Where did Delta Airlines get the cash to pay a dividend of nearly $140 million in a year in which, according to its income statement, it lost more than $1 billion? How was The Walt Disney Company able to invest nearly $800 million in expansion of its theme parks, including a major renovation of Epcot Center, despite a loss of more than $500 million on its investment in EuroDisney? Where did Wendy's International, Inc., get $125 million to expand its chain of fast-food restaurants in a year in which its net income was only $79 million and it did not raise any new debt? To answer such questions, familiarity with the statement of cash flows is required.

The statement of cash flows is a valuable analytical tool for managers as well as for investors and creditors, although managers tend to be more concerned with forecasted statements of cash flows that are prepared as part of the budgeting process. The statement of cash flows can be used to answer crucial questions such as the following:

1. Is the company generating sufficient positive cash flows from its ongoing operations to remain viable?
2. Will the company be able to repay its debts?
3. Will the company be able to pay its usual dividend?
4. Why do net income and net cash flow differ for the year?
5. To what extent will the company have to borrow money in order to make needed investments?

In this chapter, our focus is on preparing the statement of cash flows and on its use as a tool for assessing the finances of a company.

THE BASIC APPROACH TO A STATEMENT OF CASH FLOWS

LEARNING OBJECTIVE 1

Know how to classify changes in noncash balance sheet accounts as sources or uses of cash.

For the statement of cash flows to be useful to managers and others, it is important that companies employ a common definition of cash. It is also important that the statement be constructed using consistent guidelines for identifying activities that are *sources* of cash and *uses* of cash. The proper definition of cash and the guidelines to use in identifying sources and uses of cash are discussed in this section.

Definition of Cash

In a statement of cash flows, *cash* is broadly defined to include both cash and cash equivalents. **Cash equivalents** consist of short-term, highly liquid investments such as Treasury bills, commercial paper, and money market funds that are made solely for the purpose of generating a return on temporarily idle funds. Instead of simply holding cash, most companies invest their excess cash reserves in these types of interest-bearing assets that can be easily converted into cash. These short-term, liquid assets are usually included in *marketable securities* on the balance sheet. Since such assets are equivalent to cash, they are included with cash in a statement of cash flows.

Constructing the Statement of Cash Flows Using Changes in Noncash Balance Sheet Accounts

While not the recommended procedure, a type of statement of cash flows could be constructed by simply summarizing all of the debits and credits to the Cash and Cash Equivalents accounts during a period. However, this approach would overlook all of the transactions that involved an implicit exchange of cash. For example, when a company purchases inventory on credit, cash is implicitly exchanged. In essence, the supplier loans the company cash, which the company then uses to acquire inventory from the supplier. Rather than just looking at the transactions that explicitly involve cash, financial statement users are interested in all of the transactions that implicitly or explicitly involve cash. When inventory is purchased on credit, the Inventory account increases, which is an implicit *use* of cash. At the same time, Accounts Payable increases, which is an implicit *source* of cash. In general, increases in the Inventory account are classified as uses of cash and increases in the Accounts Payable account are classified as sources of cash. This suggests that analyzing changes in balance sheet accounts, such as Inventory and Accounts Payable, will uncover both the explicit and implicit sources and uses of cash. And this is indeed the basic approach taken in the statement of cash flows. The logic underlying this approach is demonstrated in Exhibit 13–1.

Exhibit 13–1 requires some explanation. The exhibit shows how net cash flow can be explained in terms of net income, dividends, and changes in balance sheet accounts. The first line in the exhibit consists of the balance sheet equation: Assets = Liabilities + Stockholders' Equity. The first step is to recognize that assets consist of cash and noncash assets. This is shown in the second line of the exhibit. The third line in the exhibit recognizes that if the account balances are always equal, then the changes in the account balances must be equal too. The next step is simply to note that the change in cash for a period is by definition the company's net cash flow, which yields line 4 in the exhibit. The only difference between line 4 and line 5 is that the changes in noncash assets is moved

EXHIBIT 13–1 Explaining Net Cash Flow by Analysis of the Noncash Balance Sheet Accounts

1. Assets = Liabilities + Stockholders' Equity
2. Cash + Noncash Assets = Liabilities + Stockholders' Equity
3. Change in Cash + Changes in Noncash Assets = Changes in Liabilities + Changes in Stockholders' Equity
4. Net Cash Flow + Changes in Noncash Assets = Changes in Liabilities + Changes in Stockholders' Equity
5. Net Cash Flow = Changes in Liabilities − Changes in Noncash Assets + Changes in Stockholders' Equity
6. Net Cash Flow = Changes in Liabilities − Changes in Noncash Assets + Net Income − Dividends + Changes in Capital Stock
7. Net Cash Flow = Net Income − Changes in Noncash Assets + Changes in Liabilities − Dividends + Changes in Capital Stock

EXHIBIT 13–2

Classifications of Sources and
Uses of Cash

	Sources	Uses
Net income	Always	
Net loss		Always
Changes in noncash assets	Decreases	Increases
Changes in liabilities*	Increases	Decreases
Changes in capital stock accounts	Increases	Decreases
Dividends paid to stockholders		Always
	Total sources	− Total uses = Net cash flow

*Contra asset accounts, such as the Accumulated Depreciation and Amortization account, follow the rules for liabilities.

from the left-hand side of the equation to the right-hand side. This is done because we are attempting to explain net cash flow, so it should be by itself on the left-hand side of the equation. To get from line 5 to line 6, we need to remember that stockholders' equity is affected by net income, dividends, and changes in capital stock. Net income increases stockholders' equity, while dividends reduce stockholders' equity. To get from line 6 of the exhibit to line 7, a few terms on the right-hand side of the equation are rearranged.

According to equation 7 in Exhibit 13–1, the net cash flow for a period can be determined by starting with net income, then deducting changes in noncash assets, adding changes in liabilities, deducting dividends paid to stockholders, and finally adding changes in capital stock. It is important to realize that changes in accounts can be either increases (positive) or decreases (negative), and this affects how we should interpret equation 7 in Exhibit 13–1. For example, increases in liabilities are added back to net income, whereas decreases in liabilities are deducted from net income to arrive at the net cash flow. On the other hand, increases in noncash assets are deducted from net income while decreases in noncash assets are added back to net income. Exhibit 13–2 summarizes the appropriate classifications—in terms of sources and uses—of net income, dividends, and changes in the noncash balance sheet accounts.

The classifications in Exhibit 13–2 seem to make sense. Positive net income generates cash, whereas a net loss consumes cash. Decreases in noncash assets, such as sale of inventories or property, are a source of cash. Increases in noncash assets, such as purchase of inventories or property, are a use of cash. Increases in liabilities, such as taking out a loan, are a source of cash. Decreases in liabilities, such as paying off a loan, are a use of cash. Increases in capital stock accounts, such as sale of common stock, are a source of cash. And payments of dividends to stockholders use cash.

Constructing a simple statement of cash flows is a straightforward process. Begin with net income (or net loss) and then add to it everything listed as sources in Exhibit 13–2 and subtract from it everything listed as uses. This will be illustrated with an example in the next section.

IN BUSINESS

What's Up at Amazon?

Amazon.com, the online retailer of books and other merchandise, may have the best chance of eventually succeeding of any Internet retailer. Even so, "[I]t's no news that Amazon has had troubles, but the numbers are worse than many on Wall Street have admitted." Robert Tracy, a CPA and an analyst on the staff of grantsinvestor.com, took a close look at Amazon's financial statements and found that the company was holding its bills longer than it used to, especially at year-end. The cash flow from this increase in accounts payable exceeded the cash flow from all other operating sources combined. "Bulls [i.e., those who are positive about Amazon.com stock] will commend the company on imaginative cash management. Bears [i.e., those who are skeptical about the stock] will

AN EXAMPLE OF A SIMPLIFIED STATEMENT OF CASH FLOWS

To illustrate the ideas introduced in the preceding section, we construct in this section a *simplified* statement of cash flows for Nordstrom, Inc., one of the leading fashion retailers in the United States. This simplified statement does not follow the format required by the Financial Accounting Standards Board (FASB) for external financial reports, but it shows where the numbers come from in a statement of cash flows and how they fit together. In later sections, we will show how the same basic data can be used to construct a full-fledged statement of cash flows that would be acceptable for external reports.

Constructing a Simplified Statement of Cash Flows

According to Exhibit 13–2, to construct a statement of cash flows we need the company's net income or loss, the changes in each of its balance sheet accounts, and the dividends paid to stockholders for the year. We can obtain this information from the Nordstrom financial statements that appear in Exhibits 13–3, 13–4, and 13–5. In a few instances, the actual statements have been simplified for ease of computation and discussion.

Note that changes between the beginning and ending balances have been computed for each of the balance sheet accounts in Exhibit 13–4, and each change has been classified as a source or use of cash. For example, accounts receivable decreased by $17 million. And, according to Exhibit 13–2, a decrease in such an asset account is classified as a source of cash.

A *simplified* statement of cash flows appears in Exhibit 13–6. This statement was constructed by gathering together all of the entries listed as sources in Exhibit 13–4 and all of the entries listed as uses. The sources exceeded the uses by $62 million. This is the net cash flow for the year and is also, by definition, the change in cash and cash equivalents for the year. (Trace this $62 million back to Exhibit 13–4.)

EXHIBIT 13–3

NORDSTROM, INC.* Income Statement (dollars in millions)	
Net sales	$3,638
Less cost of sales	2,469
Gross margin	1,169
Less operating expenses.	941
Net operating income	228
Nonoperating items:	
Gain on sale of store	3
Income before taxes.	231
Less income taxes.	91
Net income.	$ 140

*This statement is loosely based on an actual income statement published by Nordstrom. Among other differences, there was no "Gain on sale of store" in the original statement. This "gain" has been included here to illustrate how to handle gains and losses on a statement of cash flows.

EXHIBIT 13–4

NORDSTROM, INC.*
Comparative Balance Sheet
(dollars in millions)

	Ending Balance	Beginning Balance	Change	Source or Use?
Assets				
Current assets:				
Cash and cash equivalents	$ 91	$ 29	$+62	
Accounts receivable	637	654	−17	Source
Merchandise inventory	586	537	+49	Use
Total current assets	1,314	1,220		
Property, buildings, and equipment . . .	1,517	1,394	+123	Use
Less accumulated depreciation and amortization	654	561	+93	Source
Net property, buildings, and equipment	863	833		
Total assets	$2,177	$2,053		
Liabilities and Stockholders' Equity				
Current liabilities:				
Accounts payable	$ 264	$ 220	+44	Source
Accrued wages and salaries payable	193	190	+3	Source
Accrued income taxes payable	28	22	+6	Source
Notes payable	40	38	+2	Source
Total current liabilities	525	470		
Long-term debt	439	482	−43	Use
Deferred income taxes	47	49	−2	Use
Total liabilities	1,011	1,001		
Stockholders' equity:				
Common stock	157	155	+2	Source
Retained earnings	1,009	897	+112	†
Total stockholders' equity	1,166	1,052		
Total liabilities and stockholders' equity	$2,177	$2,053		

*This statement differs from the actual statement published by Nordstrom.
†The change in retained earnings of $112 million equals the net income of $140 million less the cash dividends paid to stockholders of $28 million. Net income is classified as a source and dividends as a use.

EXHIBIT 13–5

NORDSTROM, INC.*
Statement of Retained Earnings
(dollars in millions)

Retained earnings, beginning balance	$ 897
Add: Net income	140
	1,037
Deduct: Dividends paid	28
Retained earnings, ending balance	$1,009

*This statement differs in a few details from the actual statement published by Nordstrom.

EXHIBIT 13–6

NORDSTROM, INC.
Simplified **Statement of Cash Flows**
(dollars in millions)

Note: This simplified statement is for illustration purposes only. It should *not* be used to complete end-of-chapter homework assignments or for preparing an actual statement of cash flows. See Exhibit 13–12 for the proper format for a statement of cash flows.

Sources

Net income	$140	
Decreases in noncash assets:		
Decrease in accounts receivable	17	
Increases in liabilities (and contra asset accounts):		
Increase in accumulated depreciation and amortization	93	
Increase in accounts payable	44	
Increase in accrued wages and salaries	3	
Increase in accrued income taxes	6	
Increase in notes payable	2	
Increases in capital stock accounts:		
Increase in common stock	2	
Total sources		$307

Uses

Increases in noncash assets:		
Increase in merchandise inventory	49	
Increase in property, buildings, and equipment	123	
Decreases in liabilities:		
Decrease in long-term debt	43	
Decrease in deferred income taxes	2	
Dividends	28	
Total uses		245
Net cash flow		$ 62

The Need for a More Detailed Statement

While the simplified statement of cash flows in Exhibit 13–6 is not difficult to construct, it is not acceptable for external financial reports and is not as useful as it could be for internal reports. The FASB requires that the statement of cash flows follow a different format and that a few of the entries be modified. Nevertheless, almost all of the entries on a full-fledged statement of cash flows are the same as the entries on the simplified statement of cash flows—they are just in a different order.

In the following sections, we will discuss the modifications to the simplified statement that are necessary to conform to external reporting requirements.

1. Which of the following is considered a source of cash on the statement of cash flows? (You may select more than one answer.)
   a. A decrease in the accounts payable account.
   b. An increase in the inventory account.
   c. A decrease in the accounts receivable account.
   d. An increase in the property, plant, and equipment account.

CONCEPT CHECK ✓

Plugging the Cash Flow Leak

Modern synthetic fabrics such as polyester fleece and Gore-Tex have almost completely replaced wool in ski clothing. John Fernsell started Ibex Outdoor Clothing in Woodstock, Vermont, to buck this trend. Fernsell's five-person firm designs and sells jackets made of high-grade wool from Europe.

Fernsell quickly discovered an unfortunate fact of life about the wool clothing business—he faces a potentially ruinous cash crunch every year. Ibex orders wool from Europe in February but does not pay the mills until June when they ship fabric to the garment makers in California. The garment factories send finished goods to Ibex in July and August, and Ibex pays them on receipt. Ibex ships to retailers in September and October, but doesn't get paid until November, December, or even January. That means from June to December the company spends like crazy—and takes in virtually nothing. Fernsell tried to get by with a line of credit, but it was insufficient. To survive, he had to ask his suppliers to let him pay late, which was not a long-term solution. To reduce this cash flow problem, Fernsell is introducing a line of wool *summer* clothing so that some cash will be flowing in from May through July, when he must pay his suppliers for the winter clothing.

Source: Daniel Lyons, "Wool Gatherer," *Forbes*, April 16, 2001, p. 310.

ORGANIZATION OF THE FULL-FLEDGED STATEMENT OF CASH FLOWS

LEARNING OBJECTIVE 2

Classify transactions as operating activities, investing activities, or financing activities.

Concept 13–1

To make it easier to compare statements of cash flows from different companies, the Financial Accounting Standards Board (FASB) requires that companies follow prescribed rules for preparing the statement of cash flows. Most companies follow these rules for internal reports as well as for external financial statements.

The FASB requires that the statement of cash flows be divided into three sections: *operating activities, investing activities,* and *financing activities.* The guidelines to be followed in classifying transactions under these three heads are summarized in Exhibit 13–7 and discussed below.

Operating Activities

Generally, **operating activities** are those activities that enter into the determination of net income. Technically, however, the FASB defines operating activities as all the transactions that are not classified as investing or financing activities. Generally speaking, this

EXHIBIT 13–7

Guidelines for Classifying Transactions as Operating, Investing, and Financing Activities

---

Operating activities:
- Net income
- Changes in current assets
- Changes in noncurrent assets that affect net income (e.g., depreciation)
- Changes in current liabilities (except for debts to lenders and dividends payable)
- Changes in noncurrent liabilities that affect net income

Investing activities:
- Changes in noncurrent assets that are not included in net income

Financing activities:
- Changes in the current liabilities that are debts to lenders rather than obligations to suppliers, employees, or the government
- Changes in noncurrent liabilities that are not included in net income
- Changes in capital stock accounts
- Dividends

Operating, Investing, and Financing Activities

Operating Activities   **Investing Activities**   **Financing Activities**

includes all transactions affecting current assets. It also includes all transactions affecting current liabilities except for issuing and repaying a note payable. Operating activities also include changes in noncurrent balance sheet accounts that directly affect net income such as the Accumulated Depreciation and Amortization account.

Investing Activities

Generally speaking, transactions that involve acquiring or disposing of noncurrent assets are classified as **investing activities.** These transactions include acquiring or selling property, plant, and equipment; acquiring or selling securities held for long-term investment, such as bonds and stocks of other companies; and lending money to another entity (such as a subsidiary) and the subsequent collection of the loan. However, as previously discussed, changes in noncurrent assets that directly affect net income such as depreciation and amortization charges are classified as operating activities.

Financing Activities

As a general rule, borrowing from creditors or repaying creditors as well as transactions with the company's owners are classified as **financing activities.** For example, when a company borrows money by issuing a bond, the transaction is classified as a financing activity. However, transactions with creditors that affect net income are classified as operating activities. For example, interest on the company's debt is included in operating activities rather than financing activities because interest is deducted as an expense in computing net income. In contrast, dividend payments to owners do not affect net income and therefore are classified as financing rather than operating activities.

Most changes in current liabilities are considered to be operating activities unless the transaction involves borrowing money directly from a lender, as with a note payable, or repaying such a debt. Transactions involving accounts payable, wages payable, and taxes payable are included in operating activities rather than financing activities, since these transactions occur on a routine basis and involve the company's suppliers, employees, and the government rather than lenders.

Warning Signs on the Statement of Cash Flows   IN BUSINESS

Herb Greenberg, a columnist for *Fortune* magazine, emphasizes the importance of monitoring a company's cash flows:

> [S]tick with two basic indicators: cash flow from operations (how much money the company's core business generates day to day) and total cash flow (which includes the core business, financing, and any investments). Are these two numbers going up

or down? Up, it almost goes without saying, is better than down. A slide in both suggested to Bill Fleckenstein of Fleckenstein Capital that Gateway was headed for earnings trouble back in June. Sure enough, in November the company warned of a profit shortfall. "If earnings are growing and the company is consuming cash, that's one of the largest red lights on the balance sheet decoder ring," Fleckenstein says.

Source: Herb Greenberg, "Minding Your K's and Q's," *Fortune*, January 8, 2001, p. 180.

OTHER ISSUES IN PREPARING THE STATEMENT OF CASH FLOWS

We must consider several other issues before we can illustrate the preparation of a statement of cash flows that would be acceptable for external financial reports. These issues are (1) whether amounts on the statement should be presented gross or net, (2) whether operating activities should be presented using the direct or indirect method, and (3) whether direct exchanges should be reported on the statement.

Cash Flows: Gross or Net?

For both financing and investing activities, items on the statement of cash flows should be presented in gross amounts rather than in net amounts. To illustrate, suppose that Macy's Department Stores purchases $50 million in property during the year and sells other property for $30 million. Instead of showing the net change of $20 million, the company must show the gross amounts of both the purchases and the sales. The purchases would be recorded as a use of cash, and the sales would be recorded as a source of cash. In like manner, if Alcoa receives $80 million from the issue of long-term bonds and then pays out $30 million to retire other bonds, the two transactions must be reported separately on the statement of cash flows rather than being netted against each other.

The gross method of reporting does *not* extend to operating activities, where debits and credits to an account are ordinarily netted against each other on the statement of cash flows. For example, if Sears adds $600 million to its accounts receivable as a result of sales during the year and $520 million of receivables is collected, only the net increase of $80 million would be reported on the statement of cash flows.

Operating Activities: Direct or Indirect Method?

The net result of the cash inflows and outflows arising from operating activities is known formally as the **net cash provided by operating activities.** This figure can be computed by either the direct or the indirect method.

Under the **direct method,** the income statement is reconstructed on a cash basis from top to bottom. For example, in the direct method, cash collected from customers is used instead of revenue, and payments to suppliers is used instead of cost of sales. In essence, cash receipts are counted as revenues and cash disbursements are counted as expenses. The difference between the cash receipts and cash disbursements is the net cash provided by operating activities for the period.

Under the **indirect method,** the operating activities section of the statement of cash flows is constructed by starting with net income and adjusting it to a cash basis. That is, rather than directly computing cash sales, cash expenses, and so forth, these amounts are arrived at *indirectly* by removing from net income any items that do not affect cash flows. The indirect method has an advantage over the direct method in that it shows the reasons for any differences between net income and the net cash provided by operating activities. The indirect method is also known as the **reconciliation method.**

Which method should be used for constructing the operating activities section of the statement of cash flows—the direct method or the indirect method? Both methods will result in exactly the same amount for the net cash provided by operating activities. However, for external reporting purposes, the FASB *recommends* and *encourages* the use of the direct method. But there is a catch. If the direct method is used, there must be a supplementary reconciliation of net income with operating cash flows. In essence, if a company chooses to use the direct method, it must also go to the trouble to construct a statement in which a form of the indirect method is used. However, if a company chooses to use the indirect method for determining the net cash flows from operating activities, there is no requirement that it also report the results of using the direct method.

The Popularity of the Indirect Method

A survey of 600 companies revealed that only 7, or 1.2%, use the direct method to construct the statement of cash flows for external reports. The remaining 98.8% probably use the indirect method because it is simply less work.

Source: American Institute of Certified Public Accountants, *Accounting Trends and Techniques: 2000*, Jersey City, NJ, 2000, p. 523.

While there are some good reasons for using the direct method, we use the indirect method in this chapter because it is by far the most popular method. The direct method is discussed and illustrated in Appendix 13A at the end of the chapter.

Direct Exchange Transactions

Companies sometimes enter into **direct exchange transactions** in which noncurrent balance sheet items are swapped. For example, a company might issue common stock in a direct exchange for property. Or creditors might swap their long-term debt for common stock of the company. Or a company might acquire equipment under a long-term lease contract offered by the seller.

Direct exchange transactions are not reported on the statement of cash flows. However, such direct exchanges are disclosed in a separate schedule that accompanies the statement.

2. Which of the following statements is false? (You may select more than one answer.)
   a. Purchasing a new manufacturing plant would be classified as an investing activity.
   b. Paying off accounts payable balances would be classified as a financing activity.
   c. Dividend payments would be classified as a financing activity.
   d. Either the direct or the indirect method can be used to calculate the net cash provided by financing activities.

CONCEPT CHECK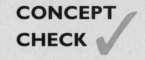

AN EXAMPLE OF A FULL-FLEDGED STATEMENT OF CASH FLOWS

In this section, we apply the FASB rules to construct a statement of cash flows for Nordstrom that would be acceptable for external reporting. The approach we take is based on an analysis of changes in balance sheet accounts, as in our earlier discussion of the simplified statement of cash flows. Indeed, as you will see, the full-fledged statement of cash flows is for the most part just a reorganized form of the simplified statement that appears in Exhibit 13–6.

The format for the operating activities part of the statement of cash flows is shown in Exhibit 13–8. For example, consider the effect of an increase in the Accounts Receivable

LEARNING OBJECTIVE 3

Prepare a statement of cash flows using the indirect method to determine the net cash provided by operating activities.

EXHIBIT 13–8

General Model: Indirect Method
of Determining the "Net Cash
Provided by Operating Activities"

	Add (+) or Deduct (−) to Adjust Net Income
Net income	$XXX
Adjustments needed to convert net income to a cash basis:	
Depreciation, depletion, and amortization charges	+
Add (deduct) changes in current asset accounts affecting revenue or expense:*	
Increase in the account	−
Decrease in the account	+
Add (deduct) changes in current liability accounts affecting revenue or expense:†	
Increase in the account	+
Decrease in the account	−
Add (deduct) gains or losses on sales of assets:	
Gain on sales of assets	−
Loss on sales of assets.	+
Add (deduct) changes in the Deferred Income Taxes account:	
Increase if a liability; decrease if an asset	+
Decrease if a liability; increase if an asset	−
Net cash provided by operating activities.	$XXX

*Examples include accounts receivable, accrued receivables, inventory, and prepaid expenses.
†Examples include accounts payable, accrued liabilities, and taxes payable.

account on the net cash provided by operating activities. Since the Accounts Receivable account is a noncash asset, we know from Exhibit 13–2 that increases in this account are treated as *uses* of cash. In other words, increases in Accounts Receivable are deducted when determining net cash flows. Intuitive explanations for this and other adjustments are sometimes slippery, but commonly given explanations are listed in Exhibit 13–9 for some of these adjustments. For example, Exhibit 13–9 suggests that an increase in Accounts Receivable is deducted from net income because sales have been recorded for which no cash has been collected. Therefore, to adjust net income to a cash basis, the increase in the Accounts Receivable account must be deducted from net income to show that cash-basis sales are less than reported sales. However, we can more simply state that an increase in Accounts Receivable is deducted when computing net cash flows because, according to the logic of Exhibits 13–1 and 13–2, increases in all noncash assets must be deducted.

Eight Basic Steps to Preparing the Statement of Cash Flows

A number of techniques have been developed to help prepare the statement of cash flows. Preparing a statement of cash flows can be confusing, and important details can be easily overlooked without such aids. We recommend that you use a worksheet, such as the one in Exhibit 13–10, to prepare a statement of cash flows. Another technique relies on the use of T-accounts, which is discussed in Appendix 13B at the end of the chapter.

As noted above, we will use the worksheet approach to illustrate the preparation of the statement of cash flows in this chapter. The statement of cash flows can be prepared using the eight steps that follow. This brief summary of the steps will be followed by more detailed explanations later.

1. Copy the title of each account appearing on the comparative balance sheet onto the worksheet except for cash and cash equivalents and retained earnings. Contra asset

EXHIBIT 13–9 Explanation of Adjustments for Changes in Current Asset and Current Liability Accounts (see Exhibit 13–8)

	Change in the Account	This Change Means That ...	Therefore, to Adjust to a Cash Basis under the Indirect Method, We Must ...
Accounts Receivable and Accrued Receivables	Increase	Sales (revenues) have been reported for which no cash has been collected.	Deduct the amount from net income to show that cash-basis sales are less than reported sales (revenues).
	Decrease	Cash has been collected for which no sales (revenues) have been reported for the current period.	Add the amount to net income to show that cash-basis sales are greater than reported sales (revenues).
Inventory	Increase	Goods have been purchased that are not included in cost of goods sold (COGS).	Deduct the amount from net income to show that cash-basis COGS is greater than reported COGS.
	Decrease	Goods have been included in COGS that were purchased in a prior period.	Add the amount to net income to show that cash-basis COGS is less than reported COGS.
Prepaid Expenses	Increase	More cash has been paid out for services than has been reported as expense.	Deduct the amount from net income to show that cash-basis expenses are greater than reported expenses.
	Decrease	More has been reported as expense for services than has been paid out in cash.	Add the amount to net income to show that cash-basis expenses are less than reported expenses.
Accounts Payable and Accrued Liabilities	Increase	More has been reported as expense for goods and services than has been paid out in cash.	Add the amount to net income to show that cash-based expenses for goods and services are less than reported expenses.
	Decrease	More cash has been paid out for goods and services than has been reported as expense.	Deduct the amount from net income to show that cash-basis expenses for goods and services are greater than reported expenses.
Taxes Payable	Increase	More income tax expense has been reported than has been paid out in cash.	Add the amount to net income to show that cash-basis expenses are less than reported expenses.
	Decrease	More cash has been paid to the tax authorities than has been reported as income tax expense.	Deduct the amount from net income to show that cash-basis expenses are greater than reported expenses.

accounts such as the Accumulated Depreciation and Amortization account should be listed with the liabilities. Contra asset accounts are treated the same way as liabilities on the statement of cash flows.

2. Compute the change from the beginning balance to the ending balance in each balance sheet account. Break the change in retained earnings down into net income and dividends paid to stockholders.

3. Using Exhibit 13–2 as a guide, code each entry on the worksheet as a source or a use.

4. Under the Cash Flow Effect column, write sources as positive numbers and uses as negative numbers.

5. Make any necessary adjustments to reflect gross, rather than net, amounts involved in transactions—including adjustments for gains and losses. Some of these adjustments may require adding new entries to the bottom of the worksheet. The net effect of all such adjusting entries must be zero.

6. Classify each entry on the worksheet as an operating activity, investing activity, or financing activity according to the FASB's criteria, as given in Exhibit 13–7.

EXHIBIT 13–10

	(1) Change	(2) Source or Use?	(3) Cash Flow Effect	(4) Adjust-ments	(5) Adjusted Effect (3) + (4)	(6) Classi-fication*
NORDSTROM, INC. Statement of Cash Flows Worksheet (dollars in millions)						
Assets (except cash and cash equivalents)						
Current assets:						
Accounts receivable.................	$−17	Source	$+17		$+17	Operating
Merchandise inventory..............	+49	Use	−49		−49	Operating
Noncurrent assets:						
Property, buildings, and equipment	+123	Use	−123	$−15	−138	Investing
Contra Assets, Liabilities, and Stockholders' Equity						
Contra assets:						
Accumulated depreciation and amortization ..	+93	Source	+93	+10	+103	Operating
Current liabilities:						
Accounts payable.....................	+44	Source	+44		+44	Operating
Accrued wages and salaries payable	+3	Source	+3		+3	Operating
Accrued income taxes payable	+6	Source	+6		+6	Operating
Notes payable	+2	Source	+2		+2	Financing
Noncurrent liabilities:						
Long-term debt	−43	Use	−43		−43	Financing
Deferred income taxes	−2	Use	−2		−2	Operating
Stockholders' equity:						
Common stock	+2	Source	+2		+2	Financing
Retained earnings:						
Net income	+140	Source	+140		+140	Operating
Dividends.........................	−28	Use	−28		−28	Financing
Additional Entries						
Proceeds from sale of store..............				+8	+8	Investing
Gain on sale of store...................				−3	−3	Operating
Total (net cash flow)			$+62	$ 0	$+62	

*See Exhibit 13–11 (page 557) for the reasons for these classifications.

7. Copy the data from the worksheet to the statement of cash flows section by section, starting with the operating activities section.

8. At the bottom of the statement of cash flows prepare a reconciliation of the beginning and ending balances of cash and cash equivalents. The net change in cash and cash equivalents shown at the bottom of this statement should equal the change in the Cash and Cash Equivalents accounts during the year.

On the following pages we will apply these eight steps to the data contained in the comparative balance sheet for Nordstrom, Inc., found in Exhibit 13–4. *As we discuss each step, refer to Exhibit 13–4 and trace the data from this exhibit into the worksheet in Exhibit 13–10.*

Setting Up the Worksheet (Steps 1–4)

As indicated above, step 1 in preparing the worksheet is to simply list all of the relevant account titles from the company's balance sheet. Note that we have done this for Nordstrom, Inc., on the worksheet in Exhibit 13–10. (The titles of Nordstrom's accounts have been taken from the company's comparative balance sheet, which is found in Exhibit 13–4.) The only significant differences between Nordstrom's balance sheet accounts and the worksheet listing are that (1) the Accumulated Depreciation and Amortization account has been moved down with the liabilities on the worksheet, (2) the Cash and Cash Equivalents accounts have been omitted, and (3) the change in retained earnings has been broken down into net income and dividends.

As stated in step 2, the change in each account's balance during the year is listed in the first column of the worksheet. We have entered these changes for Nordstrom's accounts onto the worksheet in Exhibit 13–10. (Refer to Nordstrom's comparative balance sheet in Exhibit 13–4 to see how these changes were computed.)

Then, as indicated in step 3, each change on the worksheet is classified as either a source or a use of cash. Whether a change is a source or a use can be determined by referring back to Exhibit 13–2, where we first discussed these classifications. For example, Nordstrom's Merchandise Inventory account increased by $49 million during the year. According to Exhibit 13–2, increases in noncash asset accounts are classified as uses of cash, so an entry has been made to that effect in the second column of the worksheet for the Merchandise Inventory account.

So far, nothing is new. All of this was done already in Exhibit 13–4 in preparation for constructing the simplified statement of cash flows. Step 4 is mechanical, but it helps prevent careless errors. Sources are coded as positive changes and uses as negative changes in the Cash Flow Effect column on the worksheet.

Adjustments to Reflect Gross, Rather than Net, Amounts (Step 5)

As discussed earlier, the FASB requires that gross, rather than net, amounts be disclosed in the investing and financing sections. This rule requires special treatment of gains and losses. To illustrate, suppose that Nordstrom decided to sell an old store and move its retail operations to a new location. Assume that the original cost of the old store was $15 million, its accumulated depreciation was $10 million, and that it was sold for $8 million in cash. The journal entry to record this transaction (in millions) appears below:

Cash	8	
Accumulated Depreciation and Amortization	10	
Property, Buildings, and Equipment		15
Gain on Sale		3

The $3 million gain is reflected in the income statement in Exhibit 13–3.

We can reconstruct the gross additions to the Property, Buildings, and Equipment account and the gross charges to the Accumulated Depreciation and Amortization account with the help of T-accounts:

Property, Buildings, and Equipment				Accumulated Depreciation and Amortization			
Bal.	1,394					561	Bal.
Additions (plug*)	138	15	Disposal of store	Disposal of store	10	103	Depreciation charges (plug)
Bal.	1,517					654	Bal.

*By *plug* we mean the balancing figure in the account.

According to the FASB rules, the gross additions of $138 million to the Property, Buildings, and Equipment account should be disclosed on the statement of cash flows rather than the net change in the account of $123 million ($1,517 million − $1,394 million = $123 million). Likewise, the gross depreciation charges of $103 million should be disclosed rather than the net change in the Accumulated Depreciation and Amortization account of $93 million ($654 million − $561 million = $93 million). And the cash proceeds of $8 million from sale of the building should also be disclosed on the statement of cash flows. All of this is accomplished, while preserving the correct overall net cash flows on the statement, by using the above journal entry to make adjusting entries on the worksheet. As indicated in Exhibit 13–2, the debits are recorded as positive adjustments, and the credits are recorded as negative adjustments. These adjusting entries are recorded under the Adjustments column in Exhibit 13–10.

It may not be clear why the gain on the sale is *deducted* in the operating activities section of the statement of cash flows. The company's $140 million net income, which is part of the operating activities section, includes the $3 million gain on the sale of the store. But this $3 million gain must be reported in the *investing* activities section of the statement of cash flows as part of the $8 million proceeds from the sale transaction. Therefore, to avoid double counting, the $3 million gain is deducted from net income in the operating activities section of the statement. The adjustments we have made on the worksheet accomplish this. The $3 million gain will be deducted in the operating activities section, and all $8 million of the sale proceeds will be shown as an investing item. As a result, all of the gain will be included in the investing section of the statement of cash flows and none of it will be in the operating activities section. There will be no double counting of the gain.

In the case of a loss on the sale of an asset, we do the opposite. The loss is added back to the net income figure in the operating activities section of the statement of cash flows. Whatever cash proceeds are received from the sale of the asset are reported in the investing activities section.

Before turning to step 6 in the process of building the statement of cash flows, one small step is required. Add the Adjustments in column (4) to the Cash Flow Effect in column (3) to arrive at the Adjusted Effect in column (5).

Classifying Entries as Operating, Investing, or Financing Activities (Step 6)

In step 6, each entry on the worksheet is classified as an operating, investing, or financing activity using the guidelines in Exhibit 13–7. These classifications are entered directly on the worksheet in Exhibit 13–10 and are explained in Exhibit 13–11. Most of these classifications are straightforward, but the classification of the change in the Deferred Income Taxes account may require some additional explanation. Because of the way income tax expense is determined for financial reporting purposes, the expense that appears on the income statement often differs from the taxes that are actually owed to the government. Usually, the income tax expense overstates the company's actual income tax liability for the year. When this happens, the journal entry to record income taxes includes a credit to Deferred Income Taxes:

Income Tax Expense.............................	XXX	
Income Taxes Payable.........................		XXX
Deferred Income Taxes (plug)		XXX

Since deferred income taxes arise directly from the computation of an expense, the change in the Deferred Income Taxes account is included in the operating activities section of the statement of cash flows.

In the case of Nordstrom, the Deferred Income Taxes account decreased during the year, so income tax expense was apparently less than the company's income tax liability for the year by $2 million. In other words, for some reason Nordstrom had to pay the government $2 million more than the income tax expense recorded on the income statement, and therefore this additional cash outflow must be deducted to convert net income to a cash basis. Or, looking back again to Exhibit 13–2, Deferred Income Taxes is a liability account for Nordstrom. Since this liability account decreased during the year, the change is counted as a use of cash and is deducted in determining net cash flow for the year.

EXHIBIT 13–11   Classifications of Entries on Nordstrom's Statement of Cash Flows

Entry	Classification	Reason
• Changes in Accounts Receivable and Merchandise Inventory	Operating activity	Changes in current assets are included in operating activities.
• Change in Property, Buildings, and Equipment	Investing activity	Changes in noncurrent assets that do not directly affect net income are included in investing activities.
• Change in Accumulated Depreciation and Amortization	Operating activity	Depreciation and amortization directly affect net income and are therefore included in operating activities.
• Changes in Accounts Payable, Accrued Wages and Salaries Payable, and Accrued Income Taxes Payable	Operating activity	Changes in current liabilities (except for notes payable) are included in operating activities.
• Change in Notes Payable	Financing activity	Issuing or repaying notes payable is classified as a financing activity.
• Change in Long-Term Debt	Financing activity	Changes in noncurrent liabilities that do not directly affect net income are included in financing activities.
• Change in Deferred Income Taxes	Operating activity	Deferred income taxes result from income tax expense that directly affects net income. Therefore, this entry is included in operating activities.
• Change in Common Stock	Financing activity	Changes in capital stock accounts are always included in financing activities.
• Net Income	Operating activity	Net income is always included in operating activities.
• Dividends	Financing activity	Dividends paid to stockholders are always included in financing activities.
• Proceeds from sale of store	Investing activity	The gross amounts received on disposal of noncurrent assets are included in investing activities.
• Gains from sale of store	Operating activity	Gains and losses directly affect net income and are therefore included in operating activities.

Owner

DECISION MAKER

You are the owner of a small manufacturing company. The company started selling its products internationally this year, which has resulted in a very significant increase in sales revenue and net income during the last two months of the year. The operating activities section of the company's statement of cash flows shows a negative number (that is, cash was *used* rather than *provided* by operations). Would you be concerned?

The Completed Statement of Cash Flows (Steps 7 and 8)

Once the worksheet is completed, the actual statement of cash flows is easy to complete. Nordstrom's statement of cash flows appears in Exhibit 13–12. Trace each item from the worksheet into this statement.

EXHIBIT 13–12

NORDSTROM, INC.* Statement of Cash Flows—Indirect Method (dollars in millions)	
Operating Activities	
Net income.	$140
Adjustments to convert net income to a cash basis:	
Depreciation and amortization charges.	103
Decrease in accounts receivable	17
Increase in merchandise inventory	(49)
Increase in accounts payable	44
Increase in accrued wages and salaries payable.	3
Increase in accrued income taxes payable	6
Decrease in deferred income taxes	(2)
Gain on sale of store	(3)
Net cash provided by operating activities	259
Investing Activities	
Additions to property, buildings, and equipment	(138)
Proceeds from sale of store.	8
Net cash used in investing activities.	(130)
Financing Activities	
Increase in notes payable	2
Decrease in long-term debt.	(43)
Increase in common stock	2
Cash dividends paid	(28)
Net cash used in financing activities.	(67)
Net increase in cash and cash equivalents.	62
Cash and cash equivalents at beginning of year.	29
Cash and cash equivalents at end of year	$ 91

*This statement differs from the actual statement published by Nordstrom.

Reconciliation of the beginning and ending cash balances →

Concept 13–2

The operating activities section of the statement follows the format laid out in Exhibit 13–8, beginning with net income. The other entries in the operating activities section are considered to be adjustments required to convert net income to a cash basis. The sum of all of the entries under the operating activities section is called the "net cash provided by operating activities."

The investing activities section comes next on the statement of cash flows. The worksheet entries that have been classified as investing activities are recorded in this section in any order. The sum of all the entries in this section is called the "net cash used for investing activities."

The financing activities section of the statement follows the investing activities section. The worksheet entries that have been classified as financing activities are recorded in this section in any order. The sum of all of the entries in this section is called the "net cash provided by financing activities."

Finally, for step 8, the bottom of the statement of cash flows contains a reconciliation of the beginning and ending balances of cash and cash equivalents.

Interpretation of the Statement of Cash Flows

The completed statement of cash flows in Exhibit 13–12 provides a very favorable picture of Nordstrom's cash flows. The net cash flow from operations is a healthy $259 million. This positive cash flow permitted the company to make substantial additions to its property, buildings, and equipment and to pay off a substantial portion of its long-term debt. If similar conditions prevail in the future, the company can continue to finance substantial growth from its own cash flows without the necessity of raising debt or selling stock.

When interpreting a statement of cash flows, it is particularly important to examine the net cash provided by operating activities. This figure provides a measure of how successful the company is in generating cash on a continuing basis. A negative cash flow from operations would usually be a sign of fundamental difficulties. A positive cash flow from operations is necessary to avoid liquidating assets or borrowing money just to sustain day-to-day operations.

What's Wrong with This Picture?

IN BUSINESS

Getty Images is the world's biggest stock photo company—owning the rights to over 70 million images and 30,000 hours of film. The company gets its revenues from licensing the use of these images. The stock market is impressed with the potential in this market—despite losses of $63 million in the first six months of the year, the company's stock was worth $1.8 billion. "What is there for a growth company to talk about if earnings are so rotten? Anything but earnings . . . Getty Images declared victory in its cash from operations, which it said had swelled to a robust $17.1 million in the second quarter, up from a deficit of $2.6 million in the first. Does that mean Getty collected its bills and whittled down its inventory? Nope. Both receivables and inventory are rising. The cash flow from operations, rather, comes from not paying bills."

Source: Elizabeth MacDonald, "Image Problem," *Forbes*, October 16, 2000, pp. 104–106.

Depreciation, Depletion, and Amortization

A few pitfalls can trap the unwary when reading a statement of cash flows. Perhaps the most common pitfall is to misinterpret the nature of the depreciation charges on the statement of cash flows. Since depreciation is added back to net income, one might think that all you have to do to increase net cash flow is to increase depreciation charges. This is false. In a merchandising company like Nordstrom, increasing the depreciation charge by X dollars would decrease net income by X dollars because of the added expense. Adding back the depreciation charge to net income on the statement of cash flows simply cancels out the reduction in net income caused by the depreciation charge. Referring back to Exhibit 13–2, depreciation, depletion, and amortization charges are added back to net income on the statement of cash flows because they are a decrease in an asset (or, an increase in a contra asset)—not because they generate cash.

Portfolio Manager

YOU DECIDE

You work for a mutual fund with the responsibility of selecting stocks to include in its investment portfolio. You have been analyzing the financial statements of a chain of retail clothing stores and noticed that the company's cash flow from operations for the quarter ending on December 31 was negative even though the company had a small positive net operating income for the quarter. Further analysis indicated that most of the negative cash flow was due to a large increase in inventories. Should you be concerned?

SUMMARY

LO1 Know how to classify changes in noncash balance sheet accounts as sources or uses of cash.
The statement of cash flows is one of the three major financial statements prepared by organizations. It explains how cash was generated and how it was used during the period. The statement of cash flows is widely used as a tool for assessing the financial health of organizations. In general, sources of cash include net income, decreases in assets, increases in liabilities, and increases in stockholders' capital accounts. Uses of cash include increases in assets, decreases in liabilities, decreases in stockholders' capital accounts, and dividends. A simplified form of the statement of cash flows can be easily constructed using just these definitions and a comparative balance sheet.

LO2 Classify transactions as operating activities, investing activities, or financing activities.
For external reporting purposes, the statement of cash flows must be organized in terms of operating, investing, and financing activities. While there are some exceptions, operating activities include net income and changes in current assets and current liabilities. And, with a few exceptions, changes in noncurrent assets are generally included in investing activities and changes in noncurrent liabilities are generally included in financing activities.

LO3 Prepare a statement of cash flows using the indirect method to determine the net cash provided by operating activities.
The operating activities section of the statement of cash flows can be constructed using the indirect method (discussed in the main body of the chapter) or the direct method (discussed in Appendix 13A). Although the FASB prefers the use of the direct method, most companies use the indirect method. Both methods report the same amount of net cash provided by operating activities.

    When the indirect method is used, the operating activities section of the statement of cash flows starts with net income and shows the adjustments required to adjust net income to a cash basis. A worksheet can be used to construct the statement of cash flows. After determining the change in each balance sheet account, adjustments are made to reflect gross, rather than net, amounts involved in selected transactions, and each entry on the worksheet is labeled as an operating, investing, or financing activity. The data from the worksheet are then used to prepare each section of the statement of cash flows, beginning with the operating activities section.

GUIDANCE ANSWERS TO *DECISION MAKER* AND *YOU DECIDE*

Owner (p. 557)
Even though the company reported positive net income, the net effect of the company's operations was to *consume* rather than *generate* cash during the year. Cash disbursements relating to the company's operations exceeded the amount of cash receipts from operations. If the company generated a significant amount of sales just before the end of the year, it is quite possible that cash has not yet been received from the customers. In fact, given that the additional sales were international, a longer collection period would be expected. Nevertheless, as owner, you probably would want to ensure that the company's credit-granting policies and procedures were adhered to when these sales were made, and you should also monitor the trend in the average collection period.

Portfolio Manager (p. 559)
The low profit (i.e., net operating income) and negative cash flow for the quarter ending December 31 should definitely be of concern for a clothing retailer. Due to the Christmas and Hanukkah holidays, this is traditionally the best quarter of the year for retailers. Furthermore, the increase in inventories is very troubling. This may indicate that sales fell below expectations and that the goods in inventory may have to be deeply discounted in the new year to clear the shelves for new merchandise. At minimum, some very hard questions should be directed to the executives of the clothing chain before buying any of its stock.

GUIDANCE ANSWERS TO CONCEPT CHECKS

1. **Choice c.** A decrease in a noncash asset, such as accounts receivable, is a source of cash.
2. **Choices b and d.** Paying suppliers is an operating activity. The direct and indirect methods are used to calculate cash from operating activities, not financing activities.

REVIEW PROBLEM

Rockford Company's comparative balance sheet and income statement for the year 2004 follow:

ROCKFORD COMPANY
Comparative Balance Sheet
December 31, 2004, and 2003
(dollars in millions)

	2004	2003
Assets		
Cash.	$ 26	$ 10
Accounts receivable.	180	270
Inventory	205	160
Prepaid expenses.	17	20
Plant and equipment	430	309
Less accumulated depreciation	(218)	(194)
Long-term investments	60	75
Total assets.	$700	$650
Liabilities and Stockholders' Equity		
Accounts payable.	$230	$310
Accrued liabilities.	70	60
Bonds payable	135	40
Deferred income taxes	15	8
Common stock	140	140
Retained earnings.	110	92
Total liabilities and stockholders' equity	$700	$650

ROCKFORD COMPANY
Income Statement
For the Year Ended December 31, 2004
(dollars in millions)

Sales	$1,000
Less cost of sales	530
Gross margin	470
Less operating expenses	352
Net operating income	118
Nonoperating items:	
Loss on sale of equipment	(4)
Income before taxes.	114
Less income taxes	48
Net income.	$ 66

Notes: Dividends of $48 million were paid in 2004. The loss on sale of
equipment of $4 million reflects a transaction in which equipment
with an original cost of $12 million and accumulated depreciation of
$5 million was sold for $3 million in cash.

Required:

Using the indirect method, determine the net cash provided by operating activities for 2004 and construct
a statement of cash flows for the year.

Solution to Review Problem

A worksheet for Rockford Company appears below. Using the worksheet, it is a simple matter to construct the statement of cash flows, including the net cash provided by operating activities.

ROCKFORD COMPANY Statement of Cash Flows Worksheet For the Year Ended December 31, 2004 (dollars in millions)						
	(1) Change	(2) Source or Use?	(3) Cash Flow Effect	(4) Adjust- ments	(5) Adjusted Effect (3) + (4)	(6) Classi- fication
Assets (except cash and cash equivalents)						
Current assets:						
Accounts receivable	$ −90	Source	$+90		$+90	Operating
Inventory.	+45	Use	−45		−45	Operating
Prepaid expenses.	−3	Source	+3		+3	Operating
Noncurrent assets:						
Property, buildings, and equipment . . .	+121	Use	−121	$−12	−133	Investing
Long-term investments	−15	Source	+15		+15	Investing
Contra Assets, Liabilities, and Stockholders' Equity						
Contra assets:						
Accumulated depreciation	+24	Source	+24	+5	+29	Operating
Current liabilities:						
Accounts payable	−80	Use	−80		−80	Operating
Accrued liabilities	+10	Source	+10		+10	Operating
Noncurrent liabilities:						
Bonds payable	+95	Source	+95		+95	Financing
Deferred income taxes	+7	Source	+7		+7	Operating
Stockholders' equity:						
Common stock	+0	—	+0		+0	Financing
Retained earnings:						
Net income	+66	Source	+66		+66	Operating
Dividends.	−48	Use	−48		−48	Financing
Additional Entries						
Proceeds from sale of equipment.				+3	+3	Investing
Loss on sale of equipment				+4	+4	Operating
Total (net cash flow)			$+16	$ 0	$+16	

ROCKFORD COMPANY Statement of Cash Flows—Indirect Method For the Year Ended December 31, 2004 (dollars in millions)	
Operating Activities	
Net income	$66
Adjustments to convert net income to a cash basis:	
Depreciation and amortization charges	29
Decrease in accounts receivable.	90
Increase in inventory.	(45)
Decrease in prepaid expenses	3
	(continued)

(concluded)   **ROCKFORD COMPANY**
Statement of Cash Flows—Indirect Method
For the Year Ended December 31, 2004
(dollars in millions)

Decrease in accounts payable.........................	(80)
Increase in accrued liabilities.........................	10
Increase in deferred income taxes	7
Loss on sale of equipment	4
Net cash provided by operating activities	84

Investing Activities:

Additions to property, buildings, and equipment	(133)
Decrease in long-term investments	15
Proceeds from sale of equipment........................	3
Net cash used in investing activities	(115)

Financing Activities:

Increase in bonds payable	95
Cash dividends paid....................................	(48)
Net cash provided by financing activities	47
Net increase in cash and cash equivalents	16
Cash and cash equivalents at beginning of year	10
Cash and cash equivalents at end of year..................	$ 26

Note that the $16 increase in cash and cash equivalents agrees with the $16 increase in the company's Cash account shown in the balance sheet, and it agrees with the total in column (5) in the above worksheet.

GLOSSARY

Cash equivalents   Short-term, highly liquid investments such as Treasury bills, commercial paper, and money market funds that are made solely for the purpose of generating a return on temporarily idle funds. (p. 542)

Direct exchange transactions   Transactions involving only noncurrent balance sheet accounts. For example, a company might issue common stock that is directly exchanged for property. (p. 551)

Direct method   A method of computing the cash provided by operating activities in which the income statement is reconstructed on a cash basis from top to bottom. (p. 550)

Financing activities   All transactions (other than payment of interest) involving borrowing from creditors or repaying creditors as well as transactions with the company's owners (except stock dividends and stock splits). (p. 549)

Indirect method   A method of computing the cash provided by operating activities that starts with net income and adjusts it to a cash basis. It is also known as the *reconciliation method.* (p. 550)

Investing activities   Transactions that involve acquiring or disposing of noncurrent assets. (p. 549)

Net cash provided by operating activities   The net result of the cash inflows and outflows arising from day-to-day operations. (p. 550)

Operating activities   Transactions that enter into the determination of net income. (p. 548)

Reconciliation method   See *Indirect method.* (p. 550)

Statement of cash flows   A financial statement that highlights the major activities that directly and indirectly impact cash flows and hence affect the overall cash balance. (p. 542)

The Direct Method of Determining the Net Cash Provided by Operating Activities

LEARNING OBJECTIVE 4

Use the direct method to determine the net cash provided by operating activities.

To compute the net cash provided by operating activities under the direct method, we must reconstruct the income statement on a cash basis from top to bottom. A model is presented in Exhibit 13A–1 that shows the adjustments that must be made to adjust sales, expenses, and so forth, to a cash basis. To illustrate, we have included in the exhibit the Nordstrom data from the chapter.

Note that the "net cash provided by operating activities" ($259 million) agrees with the amount computed in the chapter by the indirect method. The two amounts agree, since the direct and indirect methods are just different roads to the same destination. The investing and financing activities sections of the statement will be exactly the same as shown for the indirect method in Exhibit 13–12. The only difference between the indirect and direct methods is in the operating activities section.

Similarities and Differences in the Handling of Data

Although we arrive at the same destination under either the direct or the indirect method, not all data are handled in the same way in the adjustment process. Stop for a moment, flip back to the general model for the indirect method in Exhibit 13–8, and compare the adjustments made in that exhibit to the adjustments made for the direct method in Exhibit 13A–1. The adjustments for accounts that affect revenue are the same in the two methods. In either case, increases in the account are deducted and decreases in the accounts are added. The adjustments for accounts that affect expenses, however, are handled in *opposite* ways in the indirect and direct methods. This is because under the indirect method the adjustments are made to *net income,* whereas under the direct method the adjustments are made to the *expense accounts* themselves.

To illustrate this difference, note the handling of prepaid expenses and depreciation in the indirect and direct methods. Under the indirect method (Exhibit 13–8), an increase in the Prepaid Expenses account is *deducted* from net income in computing the amount of cash provided by operations. Under the direct method (Exhibit 13A–1), an increase in Prepaid Expenses is *added* to operating expenses. The reason for the difference can be explained as follows: An increase in Prepaid Expenses means that more cash has been paid out for items such as insurance than has been included as expense for the period. Therefore, to adjust net income to a cash basis, we must either deduct this increase from net income (indirect method) or we must add this increase to operating expenses (direct method). Either way, we will end up with the same figure for cash provided by operations. In like manner, depreciation is added to net income under the indirect method to cancel out its effect (Exhibit 13–8), whereas it is deducted from operating expenses under the direct method to cancel out its effect (Exhibit 13A–1). These differences in the handling of data are true for all other expense items in the two methods.

In the matter of gains and losses on sales of assets, no adjustments are needed at all under the direct method. These gains and losses are simply ignored, since they are not part of sales, cost of goods sold, operating expenses, or income taxes. Observe that in Exhibit 13A–1, Nordstrom's $3 million gain on the sale of the store is not listed as an adjustment in the operating activities section.

Special Rules—Direct and Indirect Methods

As stated earlier, when the direct method is used, the FASB requires a reconciliation between net income and the net cash provided by operating activities, as determined by the

Revenue or Expense Item	Add (+) or Deduct (−) to Adjust to a Cash Basis	Illustration—Nordstrom (in millions)
Sales revenue (as reported)...............		$3,638
Adjustments to a cash basis:		
1. Increase in accounts receivable.......	−	
2. Decrease in accounts receivable......	+	+17
Total.................................		$3,655
Cost of goods sold (as reported)...........		2,469
Adjustments to a cash basis:		
3. Increase in merchandise inventory	+	+49
4. Decrease in merchandise inventory ...	−	
5. Increase in accounts payable.........	−	−44
6. Decrease in accounts payable........	+	_____
Total.................................		2,474
Operating expenses (as reported)		941
Adjustments to a cash basis:		
7. Increase in prepaid expenses.........	+	
8. Decrease in prepaid expenses........	−	
9. Increase in accrued liabilities.........	−	−3
10. Decrease in accrued liabilities........	+	
11. Period's depreciation, depletion, and amortization charges...............	−	−103
Total.................................		835
Income tax expense (as reported)		91
Adjustments to a cash basis:		
12. Increase in accrued taxes payable......	−	−6
13. Decrease in accrued taxes payable.....	+	
14. Increase in deferred income taxes......	−	
15. Decrease in deferred income taxes.....	+	+2
Total.................................		87
Net cash provided by operating activities.....		$ 259

indirect method. Thus, *when a company elects to use the direct method, it must also present the indirect method* in a separate schedule accompanying the statement of cash flows.

On the other hand, if a company elects to use the indirect method to compute the net cash provided by operating activities, then it must also provide a special breakdown of data. The company must provide a separate disclosure of the amount of interest and the amount of income taxes paid during the year. The FASB requires this separate disclosure so that users can take the data provided by the indirect method and make estimates of what the amounts for sales, income taxes, and so forth, would have been if the direct method had been used instead.

SUMMARY

LO4 (Appendix 13A) Use the direct method to determine the net cash provided by operating activities.

When the direct method is used to determine the net cash provided by operating activities, the income statement is reconstructed on a cash basis. A worksheet, which starts with the major components of the company's income statement (such as sales revenue, cost of goods sold, operating expenses, and income tax expense), can be used to organize the data. Each of the income statement components is adjusted to a cash basis by reference to the changes in the related balance sheet account. (For example, the amount of sales revenue reported on the income statement is converted to the amount of cash received from customers by subtracting the increase, or adding the decrease, in accounts receivable during the period.) Special disclosure rules apply when a company uses the direct method.

The T-Account Approach to Preparing the Statement of Cash Flows

LEARNING OBJECTIVE 5

Prepare a statement of cash flows using the T-account approach.

A worksheet approach was used to prepare the statement of cash flows in the chapter. The T-account approach is an alternative technique that is sometimes used to prepare the statement of cash flows. To illustrate the T-account approach, we will again use the data for Nordstrom, Inc., that was used to illustrate the worksheet approach.

The T-Account Approach

Note from Nordstrom's comparative balance sheet in Exhibit 13–4 that cash and cash equivalents increased from $29 million to $91 million, an increase of $62 million during the year. To determine the reasons for this change we will again prepare a statement of cash flows. As before, our basic approach will be to analyze the changes in the various balance sheet accounts. However, in this appendix we will use T-accounts rather than a worksheet.

Exhibit 13B–1 contains a T-account, titled "Cash," which we will use to accumulate the cash "Provided" and the cash "Used." The exhibit also includes T-accounts with the beginning and ending account balances for each of the other accounts on Nordstrom's balance sheet. *Before proceeding, refer to Nordstrom's comparative balance sheet in Exhibit 13–4 in the main body of the chapter, and trace the data from this exhibit to the T-accounts in Exhibit 13B–1.*

As we analyze each balance sheet account, we will post the related entry(s) directly to the T-accounts. To the extent that these changes have affected cash, we will also post an appropriate entry to the T-account representing Cash. *As you progress through this appendix, trace each entry to the T-accounts in Exhibit 13B–2. Pay special attention to the placement and description of the entries affecting the T-account representing Cash.*

Observe that in the Cash T-account in Exhibit 13B–2, all operating items are near the top of the Cash T-account, below the net income figure. Also note that the T-account includes a subtotal titled "Net cash provided by operating activities." If the amounts in the "Used" column exceeded the amounts in the "Provided" column, the subtotal would be on the credit side of the T-account and would be labeled "Net cash *used* in operating activities." Also note that all investing and financing items have been placed below the subtotal in the lower portion of the Cash T-account. At the bottom of the T-account is a total titled "Net increase in cash and cash equivalents." If the amounts in the "Used" column exceeded the amounts in the "Provided" column, this total would be on the credit side of the T-account and would be labeled "Net *decrease* in cash and cash equivalents." The entries in the Cash T-account contain all of the entries needed for the statement of cash flows.

Retained Earnings The Retained Earnings account is generally the most useful starting point when developing a statement of cash flows. Details of the change in Nordstrom's Retained Earnings account are presented in Exhibit 13–5. Note from the exhibit that net income was $140 million and dividends were $28 million. The entries to record these changes and their effects on Cash are shown below. (The dollar amounts are in millions.)

The entry to record net income and the effect on Cash would be:

	(1)		
Cash—Provided		140	
Retained Earnings—Net Income			140

EXHIBIT 13B–1   T-Accounts Showing Changes in Account Balances—Nordstrom, Inc. (in millions)

Cash		
	Provided	**Used**
Net cash provided by operating activities		
Net increase in cash and cash equivalents		

Accounts Receivable			Merchandise Inventory			Property, Buildings, and Equipment			Accumulated Depreciation		
Bal.	654		Bal.	537		Bal.	1,394			561	Bal.
Bal.	637		Bal.	586		Bal.	1,517			654	Bal.

Accounts Payable			Accrued Wages and Salaries Payable			Accrued Income Taxes Payable			Notes Payable		
	220	Bal.		190	Bal.		22	Bal.		38	Bal.
	264	Bal.		193	Bal.		28	Bal.		40	Bal.

Long-Term Debt			Deferred Income Taxes			Common Stock			Retained Earnings		
	482	Bal.		49	Bal.		155	Bal.		897	Bal.
	439	Bal.		47	Bal.		157	Bal.		1,009	Bal.

Recall that net income is converted to a cash basis when the indirect method is used to prepare the operating activities section of the statement of cash flows. Since net income is the starting point, the cash effect is included at the top of the Cash T-account.

    The entry to record the dividends paid and the effect on Cash would be:

	(2)		
Retained Earnings—Dividends....................		28	
Cash—Used			28

Since the payment of cash dividends is classified as an investing activity, the cash effect is included in the lower portion of the Cash T-account along with the other investing and financing items.

    Once posted to the Retained Earnings T-account in Exhibit 13B–2, these two entries fully explain the change that took place in the Retained Earnings account during the year. We can now proceed through the remainder of the balance sheet accounts in Exhibit 13B–1, analyzing the change between the beginning and ending balances in each account, and recording the appropriate entries in the T-accounts.

Current Asset Accounts   Each of the current asset accounts is examined to determine the change that occurred during the year. The change is then recorded as a debit if the account balance increased or as a credit if the account balance decreased. The offsetting entry in the case of an increase in the account balance is "Cash—Used"; the offsetting entry in the case of a decrease in the account balance is "Cash—Provided."

EXHIBIT 13B–2 T-Accounts after Posting of Account Changes—Nordstrom, Inc. (in millions)

Cash					
		Provided	**Used**		
Net income	(1)	140	49	(4)	Increase in merchandise inventory
Decrease in accounts receivable	(3)	17	3	(5)	Gain on sale of store
Depreciation and amortization charges	(7)	103	2	(13)	Decrease in deferred income taxes
Increase in accounts payable	(8)	44			
Increase in accrued wages and salaries payable	(9)	3			
Increase in accrued income taxes payable	(10)	6			
Net cash provided by operating activities		259			
Proceeds from sale of store	(5)	8	28	(2)	Cash dividends paid
Increase in notes payable	(11)	2	138	(6)	Additions to property, buildings, and equipment
Increase in common stock	(14)	2	43	(12)	Decrease in long-term debt
Net increase in cash and cash equivalents		62			

Accounts Receivable				Merchandise Inventory				Property, Buildings, and Equipment				Accumulated Depreciation			
Bal.	654			Bal.	537			Bal.	1,394					561	Bal.
		17	(3)	(4)	49			(6)	138	15	(5)	(5)	10	103	(7)
Bal.	637			Bal.	586			Bal.	1,517					654	Bal.

Accounts Payable				Accrued Wages and Salaries Payable				Accrued Income Taxes Payable				Notes Payable			
		220	Bal.			190	Bal.			22	Bal.			38	Bal.
		44	(8)			3	(9)			6	(10)			2	(11)
		264	Bal.			193	Bal.			28	Bal.			40	Bal.

Long-Term Debt				Deferred Income Taxes				Common Stock				Retained Earnings			
		482	Bal.			49	Bal.			155	Bal.			897	Bal.
(12)	43			(13)	2					2	(14)	(2)	28	140	(1)
		439	Bal.			47	Bal.			157	Bal.			1,009	Bal.

To demonstrate, note that Nordstrom's Accounts Receivable decreased by $17 million during the year. The entry to record this change and its effect on Cash would be:

	(3)		
Cash—Provided		17	
Accounts Receivable			17

The merchandise inventory account increased by $49 million during the year. The entry to record this change and its effect on Cash would be:

	(4)		
Merchandise Inventory		49	
Cash—Used			49

Note that these two entries result in the correct adjusting entries in the current asset T-accounts so as to reconcile the beginning and ending balances. Also note that the changes in these two current asset accounts are included in the upper portion of the Cash T-account. This is because changes in current assets are considered part of operations and therefore are used to convert net income to a cash basis in the operating activities section of the statement of cash flows.

Property, Buildings, and Equipment and Accumulated Depreciation

The activity in the Property, Buildings, and Equipment account and the Accumulated Depreciation account is analyzed in the chapter beginning on page 555. *Reread the analysis of these accounts before proceeding.* Nordstrom sold a store, purchased property, buildings, and equipment, and recorded depreciation expense during the year. The entries in this case for the T-account analysis are more complex than for current assets. These entries are presented below. You should carefully trace each of these entries to the T-accounts in Exhibit 13B–2.

The entry to record the sale of the store and its effect on Cash would be:

(5)		
Cash—Provided	8	
Accumulated Depreciation.	10	
Property, Buildings, and Equipment		15
Gain on Sale		3

Since the sale of property, buildings, and equipment is classified as an investing activity, the cash effect is included in the lower portion of the Cash T-account along with the other investing and financing items. The proceeds from the sale, which will be reported in the investing activities section of the statement of cash flows, includes the gain that was recognized on the sale of the store. However, this gain was reported on Nordstrom's income statement in Exhibit 13–3 as part of net income, which is the starting point for the operating activities section. As a result, to avoid double counting, the gain must be subtracted (or removed) from net income in the operating activities section of the statement of cash flows. Accordingly, the gain is recorded in the "Used" column in the upper portion of the Cash T-account along with the other operating items.

The entry to record the purchase of property, buildings, and equipment and its effect on Cash would be:

(6)		
Property, Buildings, and Equipment	138	
Cash—Used		138

Since the purchase of property, buildings, and equipment is classified as an investing activity, the cash effect is included in the lower portion of the Cash T-account along with the other investing and financing items. Entry (6), along with entry (5) above, explains the change in the Property, Buildings, and Equipment account during the year.

The entry to record depreciation and amortization expense for the year would be:

(7)		
Cash—Provided	103	
Accumulated Depreciation.		103

Note that depreciation and amortization expense does not involve an actual cash outflow. Consequently, depreciation and amortization expense must be added to net income to convert it to a cash basis in the operating activities section of the statement of cash flows. Note that the depreciation and amortization expense is recorded in the "Provided" column in the upper portion of the Cash T-account along with the other operating items. Entry (7), along with entry (5) above, explains the change in the Accumulated Depreciation account during the year.

Current Liabilities   The T-accounts in Exhibit 13B–1 show that Nordstrom has four current liability accounts. Three of the four current liability accounts (Accounts Payable, Accrued Wages and Salaries Payable, and Accrued Income Taxes Payable) relate to the company's operating activities. In the entries that follow, increases in current liabilities are recorded as credits, with the offsetting entry being "Cash—Provided." Decreases in current liabilities are recorded as debits, with the offsetting entry being "Cash—Used."

Accounts Payable increased by $44 million during the year. The entry to record this change and its effect on Cash would be:

	(8)		
Cash—Provided		44	
Accounts Payable			44

The Accrued Wages and Salaries Payable account increased by $3 million during the year. The entry to record this change and its effect on Cash would be:

	(9)		
Cash—Provided		3	
Accrued Wages and Salaries Payable			3

The Accrued Income Taxes Payable account increased by $6 million during the year. The entry to record this change and its effect on Cash would be:

	(10)		
Cash—Provided		6	
Accrued Income Taxes Payable.			6

Since the changes in these three current liability accounts are considered to be part of operations, their cash effects are included in the upper portion of the Cash T-account along with the other operating items.

The Notes Payable account increased by $2 million during the year. The entry to record this would be:

	(11)		
Cash—Provided		2	
Notes Payable.			2

Since transactions involving notes payable are classified as financing activities, their cash effects are included in the lower portion of the Cash T-account along with the other investing and financing items.

Long-Term Debt   Nordstrom's Long-Term Debt account decreased by $43 million during the year. The entry to record this would be:

	(12)		
Long-Term Debt.		43	
Cash—Used			43

Since transactions involving long-term debt are classified as financing activities, their cash effects are included in the lower portion of the Cash T-account along with the other investing and financing items.

Deferred Income Taxes   The activity in Deferred Income Taxes is analyzed in the chapter beginning on page 556. *Reread the analysis of this account before proceeding.* The entry to record the activity in this account and its effect on Cash would be:

	(13)		
Deferred Income Taxes		2	
Cash—Used			2

Since changes in the Deferred Income Taxes account are classified as part of operations, its cash effects are included in the upper portion of the Cash T-account along with the other operating items.

Common Stock　　The Common Stock account increased by $2 million. The entry to record this would be:

	(14)		
Cash—Provided		2	
Common Stock			2

With this entry, our analysis of changes in Nordstrom's balance sheet accounts is complete. At this point, the subtotal titled "Net cash provided by operating activities" can be computed. To ensure that all activity has been properly recorded in the Cash T-account, the total titled "Net increase in cash and cash equivalents" should also be computed (by adding the investing and financing items in the lower portion of the Cash T-account to the subtotal of the upper portion). The $62 million net increase in cash and cash equivalents that is detailed in the Cash T-account in Exhibit 13A–2 equals the increase in cash and cash equivalents shown on Nordstrom's comparative balance sheet in Exhibit 13–4.

Preparing the Statement of Cash Flows from the Completed T-Accounts

The Cash T-account in Exhibit 13B–2 now contains the entries for those transactions that have affected Nordstrom's cash position during the year. Our only remaining task is to organize these data into a formal statement of cash flows. The statement is easy to prepare since the data relating to the operating activities are grouped in the upper portion of the Cash T-account and the data relating to investing and financing activities are grouped in the lower portion of the account.

　　The technique used to gather and organize data for the preparation of a statement of cash flows does not affect the preparation of the statement itself. The end result is the same. The statement of cash flows for Nordstrom, Inc., is presented in the chapter in Exhibit 13–12. *Refer to the Cash T-account in Exhibit 13B–2, and trace the entries in this T-account to Nordstrom's statement of cash flows in Exhibit 13–12.* Note that the subtotal, "Net cash provided by operating activities," and the total, "Net increase in cash and cash equivalents," in the Cash T-account match the amounts reported on Nordstrom's statement of cash flows.

SUMMARY

LO5　(Appendix 13B) Prepare a statement of cash flows using the T-account approach.
The T-account approach is an alternative technique that can be used to gather and organize the data required to prepare a statement of cash flows. T-accounts are created for each balance sheet account. Each of these accounts is analyzed, and the related entries are posted directly to the T-accounts. The offsetting entry in most cases is Cash. Debits to Cash are labeled "Cash—Provided" and credits are labeled "Cash—Used." Operating items are listed near the top of the Cash T-account and investing and financing items are listed in the lower portion of the Cash T-account. The completed Cash T-account is used to prepare each section of the statement of cash flows, beginning with the operating activities section.

QUESTIONS

13–1   What is the purpose of a statement of cash flows?

13–2   What are *cash equivalents,* and why are they included with cash on a statement of cash flows?

13–3   What are the three major sections on a statement of cash flows, and what are the general rules that determine the transactions that should be included in each section?

13–4   Why is interest paid on amounts borrowed from banks and other lenders considered to be an operating activity when the amounts borrowed are financing activities?

13–5   If an asset is sold at a gain, why is the gain deducted from net income when computing the cash provided by operating activities under the indirect method?

13–6   Why aren't transactions involving accounts payable considered to be financing activities?

13–7   Give an example of a direct exchange and explain how such exchanges are handled when preparing a statement of cash flows.

13–8   Assume that a company repays a $300,000 loan from its bank and then later in the same year borrows $500,000. What amount(s) would appear on the statement of cash flows?

13–9   How do the direct and the indirect methods differ in their approach to computing the cash provided by operating activities?

13–10 A business executive once stated, "Depreciation is one of our biggest sources of cash." Do you agree that depreciation is a source of cash? Explain.

13–11 If the balance in Accounts Receivable increases during a period, how will this increase be handled under the indirect method when computing the cash provided by operating activities?

13–12 (Appendix 13A) If the balance in Accounts Payable decreases during a period, how will this decrease be handled under the direct method in computing the cash provided by operating activities?

13–13 During the current year, a company declared and paid a $60,000 cash dividend and a 10% stock dividend. How will these two items be treated on the current year's statement of cash flows?

13–14 Would a sale of equipment for cash be considered a financing activity or an investing activity? Why?

13–15 (Appendix 13A) A merchandising company showed $250,000 in cost of goods sold on its income statement. The company's beginning inventory was $75,000, and its ending inventory was $60,000. The accounts payable balance was $50,000 at the beginning of the year and $40,000 at the end of the year. Using the direct method, adjust the company's cost of goods sold to a cash basis.

BRIEF EXERCISES

BRIEF EXERCISE 13–1   Classifying Transactions as Sources or Uses   (LO1)
Below are certain events that took place at Hazzard, Inc., last year:

a.   Short-term investment securities were purchased.
b.   Equipment was purchased.
c.   Accounts payable increased.
d.   Deferred taxes decreased.
e.   Long-term bonds were issued.
f.   Common stock was sold.
g.   A cash dividend was declared and paid.
h.   Interest was paid to long-term creditors.
i.   A long-term mortgage was entirely paid off.
j.   Inventories decreased.
k.   The company recorded net income of $1 million for the year.
l.   Depreciation charges totaled $200,000 for the year.
m.   Accounts receivable increased.

Required:
For each of the above transactions, indicate whether it would be classified as a source or a use (or neither) on a simplified statement of cash flows.

BRIEF EXERCISE 13–2   Classifying Transactions as Operating, Investing, or Financing   (LO2)
Refer to the transactions for Hazzard, Inc., listed in Brief Exercise 13–1.

Required:

For each of the transactions in Brief Exercise 13–1, indicate whether it would be classified as an operating, investing, or financing activity (or would not be reported) on the statement of cash flows.

BRIEF EXERCISE 13–3   Net Cash Provided by Operating Activities (Indirect Method)   (LO3)

For the year ended December 31, 2002, Strident Company, an office equipment wholesaler, reported a net income of $84,000. Balances in the company's current asset and current liability accounts at the beginning and end of the year were as follows:

	December 31	
	2002	**2001**
Current assets:		
Cash......................	$60,000	$80,000
Accounts receivable	$250,000	$190,000
Inventory..................	$437,000	$360,000
Prepaid expenses............	$12,000	$14,000
Current liabilities:		
Accounts payable............	$420,000	$390,000
Accrued liabilities	$8,000	$12,000

The Deferred Income Taxes Liability account on the balance sheet increased by $6,000 during the year, and depreciation charges were $50,000 during the year.

Required:

Using the indirect method, determine the cash provided by operating activities for the year.

BRIEF EXERCISE 13–4   (Appendix 13A) Net Cash Provided by Operating Activities (Direct Method)   (LO4)

Refer to the data for Strident Company in Brief Exercise 13–3. The company's income statement for the most recent year was as follows:

Sales	$1,000,000
Less cost of goods sold	580,000
Gross margin	420,000
Less operating expenses...................	300,000
Income before taxes.......................	120,000
Less income taxes (30%)	36,000
Net income..............................	$ 84,000

Required:

Using the direct method (and the data from Brief Exercise 13–3), convert the company's income statement to a cash basis.

BRIEF EXERCISE 13–5   (Appendix 13B) Posting Account Changes to a Cash T-Account   (LO5)

Refer to the data for Strident Company in Brief Exercise 13–3.

Required:

Using the indirect method (and the data from Brief Exercise 13–3), post the account changes to a Cash T-account to determine the cash provided by operating activities for the year.

EXERCISES

EXERCISE 13–6   Net Cash Provided by Operating Activities (Indirect Method)   (LO3)

Changes in various accounts and gains and losses on sales of assets during the year for Weston Company, an industrial air conditioning sales and installation company, are given below:

Item	Amount
Accounts Receivable	$70,000 decrease
Accrued Interest Receivable	$6,000 increase
Inventory	$110,000 increase
Prepaid Expenses	$3,000 decrease
Accounts Payable	$40,000 decrease
Accrued Liabilities	$9,000 increase
Deferred Income Taxes Liability.	$15,000 increase
Sale of equipment.	$8,000 gain
Sale of long-term investments	$12,000 loss

Required:

For each item, place an *X* in the Add or Deduct column to indicate whether the dollar amount should be added to or deducted from net income under the indirect method when computing the cash provided by operating activities for the year. Use the following column headings in preparing your answers:

Item	Amount	Add	Deduct

EXERCISE 13–7   Prepare a Statement of Cash Flows (Indirect Method)   (LO2, LO3)

Comparative financial statement data for Holly Company are given below:

	December 31	
	2002	2001
Cash.	$ 4	$ 7
Accounts receivable	36	29
Inventory	75	61
Plant and equipment	210	180
Accumulated depreciation.	(40)	(30)
Total assets	$285	$247
Accounts payable.	$ 45	$ 39
Common stock	90	70
Retained earnings	150	138
Total liabilities and stockholders' equity	$285	$247

For 2002, the company reported net income as follows:

Sales	$500
Less cost of goods sold	300
Gross margin	200
Less operating expenses	180
Net income	$ 20

Dividends of $8 were declared and paid during 2002. There were no sales of plant and equipment during the year.

Required:

Using the indirect method, prepare a statement of cash flows for 2002.

EXERCISE 13–8   (Appendix 13A) Net Cash Provided by Operating Activities (Direct Method) (LO4)

Refer to the data for Holly Company in Exercise 13–7.

Required:

Using the direct method, convert the company's income statement to a cash basis.

EXERCISE 13–9   Prepare a Statement of Cash Flows (Indirect Method)   (LO2, LO3)

The following changes took place last year in Herald Company's balance sheet accounts:

Debit Balance Accounts		Credit Balance Accounts	
Cash	$20 I	Accumulated Depreciation	$40 I
Accounts Receivable.	$10 D	Accounts Payable	$20 I
Inventory....................	$30 I	Accrued Liabilities	$10 D
Prepaid Expenses	$5 D	Taxes Payable	$10 I
Long-Term Investments	$30 D	Bonds Payable.................	$20 D
Plant and Equipment...........	$150 I	Deferred Income Taxes	$5 I
Land	$30 D	Common Stock	$40 I
		Retained Earnings.............	$40 I

D = Decrease; I = Increase.

Long-term investments that had cost the company $50 were sold during the year for $45, and land that had cost $30 was sold for $70. In addition, the company declared and paid $35 in cash dividends during the year. No sales or retirements of plant and equipment took place during the year.

The company's income statement for the year follows:

Sales...................................		$600
Less cost of goods sold.................		250
Gross margin.........................		350
Less operating expenses................		280
Net operating income..................		70
Nonoperating items:		
Loss on sale of investments	$(5)	
Gain on sale of land	40	35
Income before taxes...................		105
Less income taxes.....................		30
Net income...........................		$ 75

The company's cash balance at the beginning of the year was $100, and its balance at the end of the year was $120.

Required:

1. Use the indirect method to determine the cash provided by operating activities for the year.
2. Prepare a statement of cash flows for the year.

EXERCISE 13–10   (Appendix 13A) Adjust Net Income to a Cash Basis (Direct Method)   (LO4)

Refer to the data for Herald Company in Exercise 13–9.

Required:

Use the direct method to convert the company's income statement to a cash basis.

PROBLEMS

PROBLEM 13–11   Classifying Transactions on a Statement of Cash Flows   (LO1, LO2)

Below are a number of transactions that took place in Maplewood Corporation, a company involved in residential construction, during the past year:

a.   Preferred stock was converted into common stock.
b.   Bonds were retired.
c.   A long-term loan was made to a subsidiary.
d.   Interest was received on the loan in (c) above, reducing Interest Receivable.
e.   Common stock was sold for cash.
f.   A stock dividend was declared and issued on common stock.
g.   A building was acquired by issuing shares of common stock.

h. Interest was paid on a note, decreasing Interest Payable.
i. Equipment was sold for cash.
j. Short-term investments were sold.
k. Cash dividends were declared and paid.
l. Equipment was purchased by giving a long-term note to the seller.
m. Deferred Income Taxes, a long-term liability, was reduced.
n. Dividends were received on stock of another company held as an investment.

Required:
Prepare an answer sheet with the following column headings:

Transaction	Source, Use, or Neither	Activity			Reported in Separate Schedule?	Not on the Statement
		Operating	Investing	Financing		

Enter the letter of the transaction in the left column and indicate whether the transaction would be a source, use, or neither. Then place an X in the appropriate column to show the proper classification of the transaction on the statement of cash flows, or to show if it would not appear on the statement at all.

CHECK FIGURE
(1) Net cash used for
    investing activities:
    $194,000

PROBLEM 13–12   Prepare a Statement of Cash Flows (Indirect Method)   (LO2, LO3)
Balance sheet accounts for Schmidt, Inc., contained the following amounts at the end of Years 1 and 2:

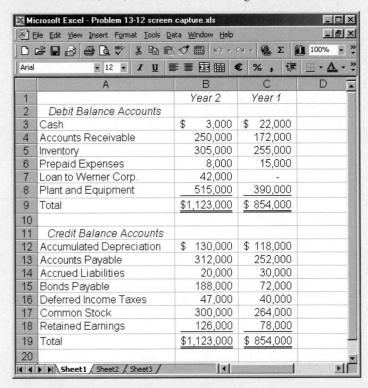

	A	B	C
1		Year 2	Year 1
2	*Debit Balance Accounts*		
3	Cash	$ 3,000	$ 22,000
4	Accounts Receivable	250,000	172,000
5	Inventory	305,000	255,000
6	Prepaid Expenses	8,000	15,000
7	Loan to Werner Corp.	42,000	-
8	Plant and Equipment	515,000	390,000
9	Total	$1,123,000	$ 854,000
10			
11	*Credit Balance Accounts*		
12	Accumulated Depreciation	$ 130,000	$ 118,000
13	Accounts Payable	312,000	252,000
14	Accrued Liabilities	20,000	30,000
15	Bonds Payable	188,000	72,000
16	Deferred Income Taxes	47,000	40,000
17	Common Stock	300,000	264,000
18	Retained Earnings	126,000	78,000
19	Total	$1,123,000	$ 854,000
20			

The company's income statement for Year 2 follows:

Sales	$945,000
Less cost of goods sold	535,000
Gross margin	410,000
Less operating expenses..........	326,000
Net operating income	84,000
Gain on sale of equipment........	3,000
Income before taxes.............	87,000
Less income taxes..............	28,000
Net income....................	$ 59,000

Equipment that had cost $45,000 and on which there was accumulated depreciation of $30,000 was sold during Year 2 for $18,000. Cash dividends totaling $11,000 were declared and paid during Year 2.

Required:
1. Using the indirect method, compute the cash provided by operating activities for Year 2.
2. Prepare a statement of cash flows for Year 2.
3. Prepare a brief explanation as to why cash declined so sharply during the year.

PROBLEM 13–13   (Appendix 13A) Prepare and Interpret a Statement of Cash Flows (Direct Method)   (LO2, LO4)

Refer to the financial statement data for Schmidt, Inc., in Problem 13–12. Brian Young, president of the company, considers $20,000 to be the minimum cash balance for operating purposes. As can be seen from the balance sheet data, only $3,000 in cash was available at the end of the current year. The sharp decline is puzzling to Brian Young particularly since sales and profits are at a record high.

Required:
1. Using the direct method, adjust the company's income statement to a cash basis for Year 2.
2. Using the data from (1) above and other data from the problem as needed, prepare a statement of cash flows for Year 2.
3. Explain to Brian Young why cash declined so sharply during the year.

PROBLEM 13–14   Prepare a Statement of Cash Flows (Indirect Method)   (LO2, LO3)

Comparative financial statements for Shores Inc. follow:

CHECK FIGURE
(1) Net cash provided by operating activities: $34,000

CHECK FIGURE
(1) Net cash provided by operating activities: $91

SHORES INC. **Comparative Balance Sheet** **December 31, Year 2 and Year 1**		
	Year 2	**Year 1**
Assets		
Cash...............................	$ 8	$ 18
Accounts receivable...................	355	233
Inventory...........................	120	168
Prepaid expenses.....................	12	5
Plant and equipment..................	612	475
Less accumulated depreciation.........	(97)	(88)
Long-term investments................	17	22
Total assets........................	$1,027	$833
Liabilities and Stockholder's Equity		
Accounts payable.....................	$ 321	$225
Accrued liabilities....................	62	74
Bonds payable.......................	288	174
Deferred income taxes................	45	36
Common stock.......................	205	254
Retained earnings....................	106	70
Total liabilities and stockholders' equity.........	$1,027	$833

SHORES INC. **Income Statement** **For the Year Ended December 31, Year 2**	
Sales..................................	$805
Less cost of goods sold...................	502
Gross margin...........................	303
Less operating expenses..................	215

(continued)

(concluded)	SHORES INC. Income Statement For the Year Ended December 31, Year 2	
Net operating income		88
Nonoperating items:		
Gain on sale of investment	$7	
Loss on sale of equipment.	(4)	3
Income before taxes		91
Less income taxes		24
Net income		$ 67

During Year 2, the company sold some equipment for $10 that had cost $20 and on which there was accumulated depreciation of $6. In addition, the company sold long-term investments for $12 that had cost $5 when purchased several years ago. Cash dividends totaling $31 were paid during Year 2.

Required:
1. Using the indirect method, determine the cash provided by operating activities for Year 2.
2. Use the information in (1) above, along with an analysis of the remaining balance sheet accounts, to prepare a statement of cash flows for Year 2.

CHECK FIGURE
(1) Net cash provided by operating activities: $91

PROBLEM 13–15   (Appendix 13A) Prepare a Statement of Cash Flows (Direct Method)   (LO2, LO4)

Refer to the financial statement data for Shores Inc. in Problem 13–14.

Required:
1. Using the direct method, adjust the company's income statement for Year 2 to a cash basis.
2. Use the information obtained in (1) above, along with an analysis of the remaining balance sheet accounts, to prepare a statement of cash flows for Year 2.

CHECK FIGURE
(1) Net cash provided by operating activities: $3,000

PROBLEM 13–16   Prepare and Interpret a Statement of Cash Flows (Indirect Method)   (LO2, LO3)

Marisa Thalmer, president of Becker Products, considers $14,000 to be the minimum cash balance for operating purposes. As can be seen from the statements below, only $3,000 in cash was available at the end of Year 2. Since the company reported a large net income for the year, and also issued both bonds and common stock, the sharp decline in cash is puzzling to Ms. Thalmer.

BECKER PRODUCTS Comparative Balance Sheet December 31, Year 2 and Year 1		
	Year 2	Year 1
Assets		
Current assets:		
Cash	$ 3,000	$ 22,000
Accounts receivable	120,000	82,000
Inventory.	108,000	85,000
Prepaid expenses	5,000	8,000
Total current assets.	236,000	197,000
Long-term investments.	54,000	74,000
Plant and equipment.	436,000	280,000
Less accumulated depreciation.	60,000	50,000
Net plant and equipment	376,000	230,000
Total assets	$666,000	$501,000
		(continued)

(concluded)	**BECKER PRODUCTS** **Comparative Balance Sheet** **December 31, Year 2 and Year 1**		
		Year 2	**Year 1**
Liabilities and Stockholders' Equity			
Current liabilities:			
Accounts payable		$ 72,000	$ 60,000
Accrued liabilities		19,000	18,000
Total current liabilities		91,000	78,000
Bonds payable..........................		130,000	
Deferred income taxes...................		12,000	10,000
Stockholders' equity:			
Preferred stock.......................		82,000	95,000
Common stock........................		265,000	238,000
Retained earnings		86,000	80,000
Total stockholders' equity		433,000	413,000
Total liabilities and stockholders' equity.......		$666,000	$501,000

BECKER PRODUCTS **Income Statement** **For the Year Ended December 31, Year 2**		
Sales.....................................		$502,000
Less cost of goods sold....................		310,000
Gross margin.............................		192,000
Less operating expenses...................		156,000
Net operating income.....................		36,000
Nonoperating items:		
Gain on sale of investments	$10,000	
Gain on sale of equipment	3,000	13,000
Income before taxes......................		49,000
Less income taxes........................		18,000
Net income..............................		$ 31,000

The following additional information is available for Year 2.

a. Dividends totaling $25,000 were declared and paid in cash.
b. Equipment was sold during the year for $10,000. The equipment had originally cost $25,000 and had accumulated depreciation of $18,000.
c. The decrease in the Preferred Stock account is the result of a conversion of preferred stock into an equal dollar amount of common stock.
d. Long-term investments that had cost $20,000 were sold during the year for $30,000.

Required:
1. Using the indirect method, compute the cash provided by operating activities for Year 2.
2. Using the data from (1) above, and other data from the problem as needed, prepare a statement of cash flows for Year 2.
3. Explain to the president the major reasons for the decline in the company's cash position.

PROBLEM 13–17 (Appendix 13A) Prepare and Interpret a Statement of Cash Flows (Direct Method) (LO2, LO4)
Refer to the financial statements for Becker Products in Problem 13–16. Since the Cash account decreased so dramatically during Year 2, the company's executive committee is anxious to see how the income statement would appear on a cash basis.

CHECK FIGURE
(2) Net cash used for
     investing activities:
     $141,000

Required:

1. Using the direct method, adjust the company's income statement for Year 2 to a cash basis.
2. Using the data from (1) above, and other data from the problem as needed, prepare a statement of cash flows for Year 2.
3. Prepare a brief explanation for the executive committee setting forth the major reasons for the sharp decline in cash during the year.

CHECK FIGURE
(2) Net cash used for investing activities: $567,000

PROBLEM 13–18   Worksheet; Prepare and Interpret Statement of Cash Flows (Indirect Method) (LO2, LO3)

"See, I told you things would work out," said Nick Cranmer, president of LaPerna Inc. "We expanded sales from $1,500,000 to $2,015,000 in Year 2, nearly doubled our warehouse space, and ended the year with more cash in the bank than we started with. A few more years of expansion like this and we'll be the industry leaders."

"Yes, I'll admit our statements look pretty good," replied Robin Melloy, the company's vice president. "But we're doing business with a lot of companies we don't know much about and that worries me. I'll admit, though, that we're certainly moving a lot of merchandise; our inventory is actually down from last year."

A comparative balance sheet for LaPerna Inc. containing data for the last two years follows:

LAPERNA INC.
Comparative Balance Sheet
December 31, Year 2 and Year 1

	Year 2	Year 1
Assets		
Current assets:		
Cash	$ 44,000	$ 28,000
Marketable securities	20,000	14,000
Accounts receivable	562,000	532,000
Inventory	846,000	858,000
Prepaid expenses	11,000	6,000
Total current assets	1,483,000	1,438,000
Long-term investments	57,000	112,000
Loans to subsidiaries	132,000	76,000
Plant and equipment	3,172,000	2,597,000
Less accumulated depreciation	810,000	755,000
Net plant and equipment	2,362,000	1,842,000
Goodwill	85,000	92,000
Total assets	$4,119,000	$3,560,000
Liabilities and Stockholders' Equity		
Current liabilities:		
Accounts payable	$ 310,000	$ 168,000
Accrued liabilities	76,000	84,000
Total current liabilities	386,000	252,000
Long-term notes	800,000	575,000
Deferred income taxes	86,000	77,000
Total liabilities	1,272,000	904,000
Stockholders' equity:		
Common stock	1,740,000	1,648,000
Retained earnings	1,107,000	1,008,000
Total stockholders' equity	2,847,000	2,656,000
Total liabilities and stockholders' equity	$4,119,000	$3,560,000

The following additional information is available about the company's activities during Year 2.

a. Cash dividends declared and paid to the common stockholders totaled $70,000.
b. Long-term notes with a value of $390,000 were repaid during the year.
c. Equipment was sold during the year for $74,000. The equipment had cost $125,000 and had $30,000 in accumulated depreciation on the date of sale.
d. Long-term investments were sold during the year for $115,000. These investments had cost $55,000 when purchased several years ago.
e. The company's income statement for Year 2 follows:

Sales.		$2,015,000
Less cost of goods sold.		1,302,000
Gross margin.		713,000
Less operating expenses.		500,000
Net operating income.		213,000
Nonoperating items:		
Gain on sale of investments	$ 60,000	
Loss on sale of equipment	(21,000)	39,000
Income before taxes.		252,000
Less income taxes.		83,000
Net income.		$ 169,000

Required:
1. Prepare a worksheet like Exhibit 13–10 for LaPerna Inc.
2. Using the indirect method, prepare a statement of cash flows for Year 2.
3. What problems relating to the company's activities are revealed by the statement of cash flows that you have prepared?

PROBLEM 13–19   (Appendix 13A) Adjust Income Statement to Cash Basis (Direct Method) (LO4)

Refer to the data for the LaPerna Inc. in Problem 13–18. All of the long-term notes issued during Year 2 are being held by LaPerna Inc.'s bank. The bank's management wants the income statement adjusted to a cash basis so that it can compare the cash basis statement to the accrual basis statement.

CHECK FIGURE
Net cash provided by operating activities: $342,000

Required:
Use the direct method to convert LaPerna Inc.'s Year 2 income statement to a cash basis.

BUILDING YOUR SKILLS

ANALYTICAL THINKING   (LO2, LO3)

Listed below are the *changes* that have taken place in Luang Corporation's balance sheet accounts as a result of the past year's activities:

CHECK FIGURE
Net cash provided by operating activities: $255,000

Debit Balance Accounts	Net Increase (Decrease)
Cash	$(30,000)
Accounts Receivable.	20,000
Inventory.	(60,000)
Prepaid Expenses	10,000
Long-Term Investments	50,000
Plant and Equipment.	120,000
Net increase	$110,000

(continued)

(concluded) Credit Balance Accounts	Net Increase (Decrease)
Accumulated Depreciation................	$40,000
Accounts Payable	30,000
Accrued Liabilities......................	10,000
Taxes Payable	10,000
Bonds Payable..........................	(40,000)
Deferred Income Taxes..................	(5,000)
Common Stock.........................	20,000
Retained Earnings	45,000
Net increase	$110,000

The following additional information is available about last year's activities:

a.   The company sold equipment during the year for $40,000. The equipment had cost the company $120,000 when purchased, and it had $70,000 in accumulated depreciation at the time of sale.

b.   Net income for the year was $___?___.

c.   The balance in the Cash account at the beginning of the year was $100,000; the balance at the end of the year was $___?___.

d.   The company declared and paid $35,000 in cash dividends during the year.

e.   Long-term investments that had cost $60,000 were sold during the year for $80,000.

f.   The beginning and ending balances in the Plant and Equipment and Accumulated Depreciation accounts for the past year are given below:

	Ending	Beginning
Plant and Equipment..............	$620,000	$500,000
Accumulated Depreciation	$240,000	$200,000

g.   If data are not given explaining the change in an account, make the most reasonable assumption as to the cause of the change.

Required:
Using the indirect method, prepare a statement of cash flows for the past year.

COMMUNICATING IN PRACTICE   (LO3, LO4)
Use an online yellow pages directory such as www.athand.com to find a company in your area that has a website on which it has an annual report, including a statement of cash flows. Make an appointment with the controller or chief financial officer of the company. Before your meeting, find out as much as you can about the organization's operations from its website.

Required:
After asking the following questions, write a brief memorandum to your instructor that summarizes the information obtained from the company's website and addresses what you found out during your interview.

1.   Does the company use the direct method or the indirect method to determine the cash flows from operating activities when preparing its statement of cash flows? Why?

2.   How is the information reported on the statement of cash flows used for decision-making purposes?

TAKING IT TO THE NET
As you know, the World Wide Web is a medium that is constantly evolving. Sites come and go and change without notice. To enable periodic update of site addresses, this problem has been posted to the textbook website (www.mhhe.com/bgn2e). After accessing the site, enter the Student Center and select this chapter. Select and complete the Taking It to the Net problem.

"How Well Am I Doing?" Financial Statement Analysis

LEARNING
OBJECTIVES

*After studying Chapter 14,
you should be able to:*

LO1 Prepare and interpret
financial statements in
comparative and common-size
form.

LO2 Compute and interpret
financial ratios that would be
most useful to a common
stockholder.

LO3 Compute and interpret
financial ratios that would be
most useful to a short-term
creditor.

LO4 Compute and interpret
financial ratios that would be
most useful to a long-term
creditor.

DECISION FEATURE

Biotech Companies Go Out of Favor

A venture capitalist invests in a start-up company with the hope of recognizing a significant profit when the start-up company goes public by selling shares of its stock on the open market. During the 1980s and early 1990s, investments by venture capitalists in biotechnology companies helped fund the development of drugs used to treat a variety of diseases that were previously considered untreatable (e.g., cancer, kidney failure, heart attacks, arthritis, and the AIDS virus, among others). However, in 1997, a reallocation of funds took place in the venture capital market. Software vendors, health care service providers, and Internet-based businesses came into favor, and biotech companies went out of fashion. Instead of waiting for returns on biotech investments that took years to realize because of the length of time required to get drugs to market, venture capitalists opted for the quicker payoffs in other industries. Payoffs were especially rapid on investments in dot.com companies, which were managing to go public long before they reached profitability. By 1999, even biotech companies with experienced management teams and well-conceived development plans for a multitude of drugs were finding it difficult, if not impossible, to raise money.

Cynthia Robbins-Roth, the founding partner of Bio Venture Consultants, believes that the venture capitalists' decision-making model was flawed. Part of the problem is the tendency for investors to jump on board when a hot new fad (such as the dot.com one) surfaces. She emphasizes the need to separately analyze each company, rather than analyzing just one and then investing in similar companies. Robbins-Roth is also critical of the technical expertise of the analysts that were working for venture capital firms. She highlights the mounting need for new drugs as the population ages and the opportunities provided by recent leaps in biotechnology that will make possible the development of those drugs.

Source: Cynthia Robbins-Roth, "Seduced & Abandoned," *Forbes ASAP,* May 29, 2000, pp. 153–154.

All financial statements are essentially historical documents. They tell what *has happened* during a particular period of time. However, most users of financial statements are concerned about what *will happen* in the future. Stockholders are concerned with future earnings and dividends. Creditors are concerned with the company's future ability to repay its debts. Managers are concerned with the company's ability to finance future expansion. Despite the fact that financial statements are historical documents, they can still provide valuable information bearing on all of these concerns.

Financial statement analysis involves careful selection of data from financial statements for the primary purpose of forecasting the financial health of the company. This is accomplished by examining trends in key financial data, comparing financial data across companies, and analyzing key financial ratios. In this chapter, we consider some of the more important ratios and other analytical tools that financial analysts use.

Managers are also vitally concerned with the financial ratios discussed in this chapter. First, the ratios provide indicators of how well the company and its business units are performing. Some of these ratios might be used in a balanced scorecard approach as discussed in Chapter 8. The specific ratios selected depend on the company's strategy. For example, a company that wants to emphasize responsiveness to customers may closely monitor the inventory turnover ratio discussed later in this chapter. Second, since managers must report to shareholders and may wish to raise funds from external sources, managers must pay attention to the financial ratios used by external investors to evaluate the company's investment potential and creditworthiness.

Those AOL Disks You Received

During the late 1990s, investors seemed to eagerly embrace any dot.com company that was losing money. However, there was a time when investors were more cautious, and start-up companies were under a lot of pressure to report positive earnings. This was the case in the mid-1990s as America Online was building its base of online customers.

AOL recorded the costs that it incurred to advertise its online services and mail disks to millions of potential subscribers as assets. Accounting professors and stock analysts were critical of the practice; these costs did not meet the asset criteria. Finally, in 1996, the company agreed that the costs should instead be expensed as incurred and wrote off $385 million of assets that were on its balance sheet.

AOL would have reported losses rather than earnings during six separate quarters in 1994, 1995, and 1996 if the company had expensed the costs as they were incurred. Some wonder whether the millions of online customers who subscribed to AOL would have flocked to the company if it had been reporting losses at that time. They also wonder if AOL would have been able to pull off its $160 billion deal to acquire Time-Warner in June if it had not been so successful in signing up online customers during the mid-1990s.

The SEC ultimately charged that the company should have been expensing the costs as incurred. During May 2000, the agency levied a fine of $3.5 million against AOL. Even though the SEC's investigation took years to complete, analysts agree that it sends a message to Internet-based businesses. Stock analysts will be taking a closer look at accounting policies, and they can react more quickly than the SEC can.

Source: David Henry, "AOL Pays $3.5M to Settle SEC Case," *USA Today,* May 16, 2000, p. 3B.

LIMITATIONS OF FINANCIAL STATEMENT ANALYSIS

Although financial statement analysis is a highly useful tool, it has two limitations that we must mention before proceeding any further. These two limitations involve the comparability of financial data between companies and the need to look beyond ratios.

Comparison of Financial Data

Comparisons of one company with another can provide valuable clues about the financial health of an organization. Unfortunately, differences in accounting methods between companies sometimes make it difficult to compare the companies' financial data. For example, if one company values its inventories by the LIFO method and another company by the average cost method, then direct comparisons of financial data such as inventory valuations and cost of goods sold between the two companies may be misleading. Sometimes enough data is presented in footnotes to the financial statements to restate data to a comparable basis. Otherwise, the analyst should keep in mind the lack of comparability of the data before drawing any definite conclusions. Nevertheless, even with this limitation in mind, comparisons of key ratios with other companies and with industry averages often suggest avenues for further investigation.

The Need to Look beyond Ratios

An inexperienced analyst may assume that ratios are sufficient in themselves as a basis for judgments about the future. Nothing could be further from the truth. Conclusions based on ratio analysis must be regarded as tentative. Ratios should not be viewed as an end, but rather they should be viewed as a *starting point,* as indicators of what to pursue in greater depth. They raise many questions, but they rarely answer any questions by themselves.

In addition to ratios, other sources of data should be analyzed in order to make judgments about the future of an organization. The analyst should look, for example, at industry trends, technological changes, changes in consumer tastes, changes in broad economic factors, and changes within the company itself. A recent change in a key management position, for example, might provide a basis for optimism about the future, even though the past performance of the company (as shown by its ratios) may have been mediocre.

STATEMENTS IN COMPARATIVE AND COMMON-SIZE FORM

Few figures appearing on financial statements have much significance standing by themselves. It is the relationship of one figure to another and the amount and direction of change over time that are important in financial statement analysis. How does the analyst key in on significant relationships? How does the analyst dig out the important trends and changes in a company? Three analytical techniques are widely used:

1. Dollar and percentage changes on statements.
2. Common-size statements.
3. Ratios.

The first and second techniques are discussed in this section; the third technique is discussed in the remainder of the chapter. To illustrate these analytical techniques, we analyze the financial statements of Brickey Electronics, a producer of computer components.

Concept 14–1

Dollar and Percentage Changes on Statements

A good place to begin in financial statement analysis is to put statements in comparative form. This consists of little more than putting two or more years' data side by side. Statements cast in comparative form underscore movements and trends and may give the analyst valuable clues as to what to expect.

Examples of financial statements placed in comparative form are given in Exhibits 14–1 and 14–2. These statements of Brickey Electronics reveal the company has been experiencing substantial growth. The data on these statements are used as a basis for discussion throughout the remainder of the chapter.

EXHIBIT 14–1

BRICKEY ELECTRONICS
Comparative Balance Sheet
December 31, 2004, and 2003
(dollars in thousands)

	2004	2003	Increase (Decrease) Amount	Increase (Decrease) Percent
Assets				
Current assets:				
Cash	$ 1,200	$ 2,350	$(1,150)	(48.9)%*
Accounts receivable, net	6,000	4,000	2,000	50.0%
Inventory	8,000	10,000	(2,000)	(20.0)%
Prepaid expenses	300	120	180	150.0%
Total current assets	15,500	16,470	(970)	(5.9)%
Property and equipment:				
Land	4,000	4,000	0	0%
Buildings and equipment, net	12,000	8,500	3,500	41.2%
Total property and equipment	16,000	12,500	3,500	28.0%
Total assets	$31,500	$28,970	$ 2,530	8.7%
Liabilities and Stockholders' Equity				
Current liabilities:				
Accounts payable	$ 5,800	$ 4,000	$ 1,800	45.0%
Accrued payables	900	400	500	125.0%
Notes payable, short term	300	600	(300)	(50.0)%
Total current liabilities	7,000	5,000	2,000	40.0%
Long-term liabilities:				
Bonds payable, 8%	7,500	8,000	(500)	(6.3)%
Total liabilities	14,500	13,000	1,500	11.5%
Stockholders' equity:				
Preferred stock, $100 par, 6%,				
$100 liquidation value	2,000	2,000	0	0%
Common stock, $12 par	6,000	6,000	0	0%
Additional paid-in capital	1,000	1,000	0	0%
Total paid-in capital	9,000	9,000	0	0%
Retained earnings	8,000	6,970	1,030	14.8%
Total stockholders' equity	17,000	15,970	1,030	6.4%
Total liabilities and stockholders' equity	$31,500	$28,970	$ 2,530	8.7%

*Since we are measuring the amount of change between 2003 and 2004, the dollar amounts for 2003 become the base figures for expressing these changes in percentage form. For example, Cash decreased by $1,150 between 2003 and 2004. This decrease expressed in percentage form is computed as follows: $1,150 ÷ $2,350 = 48.9%. Other percentage figures in this exhibit and Exhibit 14–2 are computed in the same way.

Horizontal Analysis   Comparison of two or more years' financial data is known as **horizontal analysis** or **trend analysis.** Horizontal analysis is facilitated by showing changes between years in both dollar *and* percentage form, as has been done in Exhibits 14–1 and 14–2. Showing changes in dollar form helps the analyst focus on key factors that have affected profitability or financial position. For example, observe in Exhibit 14–2 that sales for 2004 were up $4 million over 2003, but that this increase in sales was more than negated by a $4.5 million increase in cost of goods sold.

EXHIBIT 14–2

BRICKEY ELECTRONICS
Comparative Income Statement and Reconciliation of Retained Earnings
For the Years Ended December 31, 2004, and 2003
(dollars in thousands)

	2004	2003	Increase (Decrease) Amount	Percent
Sales	$52,000	$48,000	$4,000	8.3%
Cost of goods sold.	36,000	31,500	4,500	14.3%
Gross margin	16,000	16,500	(500)	(3.0)%
Operating expenses:				
Selling expenses	7,000	6,500	500	7.7%
Administrative expenses	5,860	6,100	(240)	(3.9)%
Total operating expenses	12,860	12,600	260	2.1%
Net operating income	3,140	3,900	(760)	(19.5)%
Interest expense.	640	700	(60)	(8.6)%
Net income before taxes	2,500	3,200	(700)	(21.9)%
Less income taxes (30%)	750	960	(210)	(21.9)%
Net income	1,750	2,240	$ (490)	(21.9)%
Dividends to preferred				
stockholders, $6 per share				
(see Exhibit 14–1)	120	120		
Net income remaining for				
common stockholders	1,630	2,120		
Dividends to common				
stockholders, $1.20 per share	600	600		
Net income added to				
retained earnings	1,030	1,520		
Retained earnings, beginning				
of year.	6,970	5,450		
Retained earnings, end of year	$ 8,000	$ 6,970		

Showing changes between years in percentage form helps the analyst to gain *perspective* and to gain a feel for the *significance* of the changes that are taking place. A $1 million increase in sales is much more significant if the prior year's sales were $2 million than if the prior year's sales were $20 million. In the first situation, the increase would be 50%—undoubtedly a significant increase for any company. In the second situation, the increase would be only 5%—perhaps just a reflection of normal growth.

Trend Percentages Horizontal analysis of financial statements can also be carried out by computing *trend percentages*. **Trend percentages** state several years' financial data in terms of a base year. The base year equals 100%, with all other years stated as some percentage of this base. To illustrate, consider McDonald's Corporation, the largest global food service retailer, with more than 26,000 restaurants worldwide. McDonald's enjoyed tremendous growth during the 1990s, as evidenced by the following data:

	2000	1999	1998	1997	1996	1995	1994	1993	1992	1991	1990
Sales (millions). . .	$14,243	$13,259	$12,421	$11,409	$10,687	$9,795	$8,321	$7,408	$7,133	$6,695	$6,640
Net income (millions)	$1,977	$1,948	$1,550	$1,642	$1,573	$1,427	$1,224	$1,083	$959	$860	$802

By simply looking at these data, one can see that sales increased every year. But how rapidly have sales been increasing, and have the increases in net income kept pace with the increases in sales? It is difficult to answer these questions by looking at the raw data alone. The increases in sales and the increases in net income can be put into better perspective by stating them in terms of trend percentages, with 1990 as the base year. These percentages (all rounded) appear as follows:

	2000	1999	1998	1997	1996	1995	1994	1993	1992	1991	1990
Sales*	215%	200%	187%	172%	161%	148%	125%	112%	107%	101%	100%
Net income	247%	243%	193%	205%	196%	178%	153%	135%	120%	107%	100%

*For 2000, $14,243 ÷ $6,640 = 215%; for 1999, $13,259 ÷ $6,640 = 200%, and so on.

The trend analysis is particularly striking when the data are plotted as in Exhibit 14–3. McDonald's sales growth was impressive throughout the entire 11-year period, but it was outpaced by even higher growth in the company's net income. A review of the company's income statement reveals that the dip in net income growth in 1998 was attributable, in part, to the $161.6 million that McDonald's spent to implement its "Made for You" program and a special charge of $160 million that related to a home office productivity initiative.

Common-Size Statements

Key changes and trends can also be highlighted by the use of *common-size statements.* A **common-size statement** is one that shows the items appearing on it in percentage form as well as in dollar form. Each item is stated as a percentage of some total of which that item is a part. The preparation of common-size statements is known as **vertical analysis.**

Common-size statements are particularly useful when comparing data from different companies. For example, in one year, Wendy's net income was about $110 million, whereas McDonald's was $1,427 million. This comparison is somewhat misleading because of the dramatically different sizes of the two companies. To put this in better perspective, the net income figures can be expressed as a percentage of the sales revenues of each company. Since Wendy's sales revenues were $1,746 million and McDonald's were $9,794 million, Wendy's net income as a percentage of sales was about 6.3% and McDonald's was about 14.6%. While the comparison still favors McDonald's, the contrast between the two companies has been placed on a more comparable basis.

The Balance Sheet   One application of the vertical analysis idea is to state the separate assets of a company as percentages of total assets. A common-size statement of this type is shown in Exhibit 14–4 for Brickey Electronics.

EXHIBIT 14–3   McDonald's Corporation: Trend Analysis of Sales and Net Income

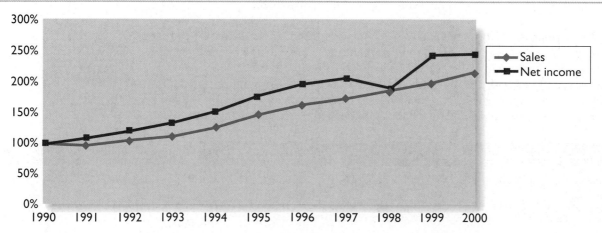

Notice from Exhibit 14–4 that placing all assets in common-size form clearly shows the relative importance of the current assets as compared to the noncurrent assets. It also shows that significant changes have taken place in the *composition* of the current assets over the last year. Notice, for example, that the receivables have increased in relative importance and that both cash and inventory have declined in relative importance. Judging from the sharp increase in receivables, the deterioration in the cash position may be a result of inability to collect from customers.

EXHIBIT 14–4

BRICKEY ELECTRONICS
Common-Size Comparative Balance Sheet
December 31, 2004, and 2003
(dollars in thousands)

	2004	2003	Common-Size Percentages 2004	2003
Assets				
Current assets:				
Cash	$ 1,200	$ 2,350	3.8%*	8.1%
Accounts receivable, net	6,000	4,000	19.0	13.8
Inventory	8,000	10,000	25.4	34.5
Prepaid expenses	300	120	1.0	0.4
Total current assets	15,500	16,470	49.2	56.9
Property and equipment:				
Land	4,000	4,000	12.7	13.8
Buildings and equipment, net	12,000	8,500	38.1	29.3
Total property and equipment.	16,000	12,500	50.8	43.1
Total assets.	$31,500	$28,970	100.0%	100.0%
Liabilities and Stockholders' Equity				
Current liabilities:				
Accounts payable	$ 5,800	$ 4,000	18.4%	13.8%
Accrued payables	900	400	2.9	1.4
Notes payable, short term	300	600	1.0	2.1
Total current liabilities	7,000	5,000	22.2	17.3
Long-term liabilities:				
Bonds payable, 8%	7,500	8,000	23.8	27.6
Total liabilities.	14,500	13,000	46.0	44.9
Stockholders' equity:				
Preferred stock, $100, 6%,				
$100 liquidation value	2,000	2,000	6.3	6.9
Common stock, $12 par	6,000	6,000	19.0	20.7
Additional paid-in capital	1,000	1,000	3.2	3.5
Total paid-in capital.	9,000	9,000	28.6	31.1
Retained earnings.	8,000	6,970	25.4	24.1
Total stockholders' equity	17,000	15,970	54.0	55.1
Total liabilities and stockholders' equity.	$31,500	$28,970	100.0%	100.0%

*Each asset account on a common-size statement is expressed in terms of total assets, and each liability and equity account is expressed in terms of total liabilities and stockholders' equity. For example, the percentage figure above for Cash in 2004 is computed as follows: $1,200 ÷ $31,500 = 3.8%.

EXHIBIT 14–5

BRICKEY ELECTRONICS Common-Size Comparative Income Statement For the Years Ended December 31, 2004, and 2003 (dollars in thousands)			Common-Size Percentages	
	2004	2003	2004	2003
Sales	$52,000	$48,000	100.0%	100.0%
Cost of goods sold	36,000	31,500	69.2	65.6
Gross margin	16,000	16,500	30.8	34.4
Operating expenses:				
Selling expenses	7,000	6,500	13.5	13.5
Administrative expenses	5,860	6,100	11.3	12.7
Total operating expenses	12,860	12,600	24.7	26.2
Net operating income	3,140	3,900	6.0	8.1
Interest expense	640	700	1.2	1.5
Net income before taxes	2,500	3,200	4.8	6.7
Income taxes (30%)	750	960	1.4	2.0
Net income	$ 1,750	$ 2,240	3.4%	4.7%

*The percentage figures for each year are expressed in terms of total sales for the year. For example, the percentage figure for cost of goods sold in 2004 is computed as follows: $36,000 ÷ $52,000 = 69.2%

The Income Statement Another application of the vertical analysis idea is to place all items on the income statement in percentage form in terms of sales. A common-size statement of this type is shown in Exhibit 14–5.

By placing all items on the income statement in common size in terms of sales, it is possible to see at a glance how each dollar of sales is distributed among the various costs, expenses, and profits. And by placing successive years' statements side by side, it is easy to spot interesting trends. For example, as shown in Exhibit 14–5, the cost of goods sold as a percentage of sales increased from 65.6% in 2003 to 69.2% in 2004. Or looking at this from a different viewpoint, the *gross margin percentage* declined from 34.4% in 2003 to 30.8% in 2004. Managers and investment analysts often pay close attention to the gross margin percentage since it is considered a broad gauge of profitability. The **gross margin percentage** is computed as follows:

$$\text{Gross margin percentage} = \frac{\text{Gross margin}}{\text{Sales}}$$

The gross margin percentage tends to be more stable for retailing companies than for other service companies and for manufacturers since the cost of goods sold in retailing excludes fixed costs. When fixed costs are included in the cost of goods sold figure, the gross margin percentage tends to increase and decrease with sales volume. With increases in sales volume, the fixed costs are spread across more units and the gross margin percentage improves.

While a higher gross margin percentage is generally considered to be better than a lower gross margin percentage, there are exceptions. Some companies purposely choose a strategy emphasizing low prices (and hence low gross margins). An increasing gross margin in such a company might be a sign that the company's strategy is not being effectively implemented.

Common-size statements are also very helpful in pointing out efficiencies and inefficiencies that might otherwise go unnoticed. To illustrate, in 2004, Brickey Electronics' selling expenses increased by $500,000 over 2003. A glance at the common-size income statement shows, however, that on a relative basis, selling expenses were no higher in 2004 than in 2003. In each year they represented 13.5% of sales.

Gross Margins Can Make the Difference

IN BUSINESS

After announcing a 42% increase in quarterly profits, Dell Computer Corp.'s shares fell over 6%. Why? According to *The Wall Street Journal,* investors focused on the company's eroding profit margins. "Analysts . . . said that a decline in gross margins was larger than they had expected and indicated a difficult pricing environment. Gross margins fell nearly a full percentage point to 21.5% of sales, from 22.4%." Dell had cut its prices to increase its market share, which worked, but at the cost of lowered profitability.

Source: Gary McWilliams, "Dell Net Rises, but Margins Spur Worries," *The Wall Street Journal,* May 19, 1999, p. A3.

RATIO ANALYSIS—THE COMMON STOCKHOLDER

A number of financial ratios are used to assess how well the company is doing from the standpoint of the stockholders. These ratios naturally focus on net income, dividends, and stockholders' equities.

LEARNING OBJECTIVE 2

Compute and interpret financial ratios that would be most useful to a common stockholder.

Earnings per Share

An investor buys a share of stock in the hope of realizing a return in the form of either dividends or future increases in the value of the stock. Since earnings form the basis for dividend payments, as well as the basis for future increases in the value of shares, investors are always interested in a company's reported *earnings per share.* Probably no single statistic is more widely quoted or relied on by investors than earnings per share, although it has some inherent limitations, as discussed below.

Concept 14–2

Earnings per share is computed by dividing net income available for common stockholders by the average number of common shares outstanding during the year. "Net income available for common stockholders" is net income less dividends paid to the owners of the company's preferred stock.[1]

$$\text{Earnings per share} = \frac{\text{Net income} - \text{Preferred dividends}}{\text{Average number of common shares outstanding}}$$

Using the data in Exhibits 14–1 and 14–2, we see that the earnings per share for Brickey Electronics for 2004 would be computed as follows:

$$\frac{\$1,750,000 - \$120,000}{(500,000 \text{ shares*} + 500,000 \text{ shares})/2} = \$3.26$$

*$6,000,000 ÷ 12 = 500,000 shares.

Price-Earnings Ratio

The relationship between the market price of a share of stock and the stock's current earnings per share is often quoted in terms of a **price-earnings ratio.** If we assume that the

---

[1]Another complication can arise when a company has issued securities such as executive stock options or warrants that can be converted into shares of common stock. If these conversions were to take place, the same earnings would have to be distributed among a greater number of common shares. Therefore, a supplemental earnings per share figure, called diluted earnings per share, may have to be computed. Refer to a current intermediate financial accounting text for details.

current market price for Brickey Electronics' stock is $40 per share, the company's price-earnings ratio would be computed as follows:

$$\text{Price-earnings ratio} = \frac{\text{Market price per share}}{\text{Earnings per share}}$$

$$\frac{\$40}{\$3.26} = 12.3$$

The price-earnings ratio is 12.3; that is, the stock is selling for about 12.3 times its current earnings per share.

The price-earnings ratio is widely used by investors as a general guideline in gauging stock values. A high price-earnings ratio means that investors are willing to pay a premium for the company's stock—presumably because the company is expected to have higher than average future earnings growth. Conversely, if investors believe a company's future earnings growth prospects are limited, the company's price-earnings ratio will be relatively low. For example, not long ago, the stock prices of some dot.com companies—particularly those with little or no earnings—were selling at levels that gave rise to unprecedented price-earnings ratios. However, these price-earnings ratios were unsustainable in the long run and the companies' stock prices eventually fell.

IN BUSINESS

Stickiness?

The Internet stock market bubble of the late 1990s resulted in financial ratios for dot.com companies that were way out of line with traditional standards. Price-earnings ratios, in particular, reached dizzying heights. Investment analysts and dot.com enthusiasts developed new measures of performance in an attempt to justify the very high market valuations of these companies—most of whom had never earned a dime of profit. Thomas A. Weber of *The Wall Street Journal* has this to say about one measure that was widely used to evaluate the performance of dot.com companies: "Remember 'stickiness'? At the height of the dot.com hype, this cloyingly named concept set a new standard for buzzword-driven exuberance. Websites sought it, and investors swooned over it. Everybody wanted to get sticky. Now the truth can be told: Sticky was stupid. Internet companies took a simple notion—namely, that products that engage customers for long stretches of time must be valuable—and elevated it into a cult . . . If you want to gauge success, accountants have a much more useful number to obsess over. It's called net income."

Source: Thomas E. Weber, "A 'Sticky' Situation: How a Web Buzzword Spun Out of Control," *The Wall Street Journal*, March 5, 2001, p. B1.

Dividend Payout and Yield Ratios

Investors hold shares in a company because they anticipate an attractive return. The return sought isn't always dividends. Many investors prefer not to receive dividends. Instead, they prefer to have the company retain all earnings and reinvest them internally in order to support growth. The stocks of companies that adopt this approach, loosely termed *growth stocks,* may enjoy higher stock prices. Other investors prefer to have a dependable, current source of income through regular dividend payments. Such investors seek stocks with consistent dividend records and payout ratios.

The Dividend Payout Ratio   The **dividend payout ratio** gauges the portion of current earnings being paid out in dividends. Investors who seek market-price growth would like this ratio to be small, whereas investors who seek dividends prefer it to be large. This ratio is computed by relating dividends per share to earnings per share for common stock:

$$\text{Dividend payout ratio} = \frac{\text{Dividends per share}}{\text{Earnings per share}}$$

For Brickey Electronics, the dividend payout ratio for 2004 is computed as follows:

$$\frac{\$1.20 \text{ (see Exhibit 14–2)}}{\$3.26} = 36.8\%$$

There is no such thing as a "right" payout ratio, even though it should be noted that the ratio tends to be similar for companies within a particular industry. Industries with ample opportunities for growth at high rates of return on assets tend to have low payout ratios, whereas payout ratios tend to be high in industries with limited reinvestment opportunities.

The Dividend Yield Ratio   The **dividend yield ratio** is obtained by dividing the current dividends per share by the current market price per share:

$$\text{Dividend yield ratio} = \frac{\text{Dividends per share}}{\text{Market price per share}}$$

The market price for Brickey Electronics' stock is $40 per share so the dividend yield is computed as follows:

$$\frac{\$1.20}{\$40} = 3.0\%$$

The dividend yield ratio measures the rate of return (in the form of cash dividends only) that would be earned by an investor who buys the common stock at the current market price. A low dividend yield ratio is neither bad nor good by itself. As discussed above, a company may pay out very little dividends because it has ample opportunities for reinvesting funds within the company at high rates of return.

Return on Total Assets

Managers have both *financing* and *operating* responsibilities. Financing responsibilities relate to how one *obtains* the funds needed to provide for the assets in an organization. Operating responsibilities relate to how one *uses* the assets once they have been obtained. Both are vital to a well-managed company. However, care must be taken not to confuse or mix the two when assessing the performance of a manager. That is, whether funds have been obtained from creditors or from stockholders should not be allowed to influence one's assessment of *how well* the assets have been employed since being received by the company.

The **return on total assets** is a measure of operating performance that shows how well assets have been employed. It is defined as follows:

$$\text{Return on total assets} = \frac{\text{Net income} + [\text{Interest expense} \times (1 - \text{Tax rate})]}{\text{Average total assets}}$$

Adding interest expense back to net income results in an adjusted earnings figure that shows what earnings would have been if the assets had been acquired solely by selling shares of stock. With this adjustment, the return on total assets can be compared for companies with differing amounts of debt or over time for a single company that has changed its mix of debt and equity. Thus, the measurement of how well the assets have been employed is not influenced by how the assets were financed. Notice that the interest expense is placed on an after-tax basis by multiplying it by the factor $(1 - \text{Tax rate})$.

The return on total assets for Brickey Electronics for 2004 would be computed as follows (from Exhibits 14–1 and 14–2):

Net income	$ 1,750,000
Add back interest expense: $640,000 \times (1 - 0.30).	448,000
Total (a)	$ 2,198,000
Assets, beginning of year	$28,970,000
Assets, end of year.	31,500,000
Total	$60,470,000
Average total assets: $60,470,000 \div 2 (b)	$30,235,000
Return on total assets, (a) \div (b)	7.3%

Brickey Electronics earned a return of 7.3% on average assets employed over the last year.

Return on Common Stockholders' Equity

One of the primary reasons for operating a corporation is to generate income for the benefit of the common stockholders. One measure of a company's success in this regard is the **return on common stockholders' equity,** which divides the net income remaining for common stockholders by the average common stockholders' equity for the year. The formula is as follows:

$$\frac{\text{Return on common}}{\text{stockholders' equity}} = \frac{\text{Net income} - \text{Preferred dividends}}{\text{Average common stockholders' equity}}$$

$$\text{where} \quad \frac{\text{Average common}}{\text{stockholders' equity}} = \frac{\text{Average total stockholders' equity}}{-\text{Average preferred stock}}$$

For Brickey Electronics, the return on common stockholders' equity is 11.3% for 2004 as shown below:

Net income	$ 1,750,000
Deduct preferred dividends	120,000
Net income remaining for common stockholders (a)	$ 1,630,000
Average stockholders' equity	$16,485,000*
Deduct average preferred stock.	2,000,000†
Average common stockholders' equity (b)	$14,485,000
Return on common stockholders' equity, (a) \div (b).	11.3%

*$15,970,000 + $17,000,000 = $32,970,000; $32,970,000 \div 2 = $16,485,000.
†$2,000,000 + $2,000,000 = $4,000,000; $4,000,000 \div 2 = $2,000,000.

Compare the return on common stockholders' equity above (11.3%) with the return on total assets computed in the preceding section (7.3%). Why is the return on common stockholders' equity so much higher? The answer lies in the principle of *financial leverage.* Financial leverage is discussed in the following paragraphs.

IN BUSINESS

Comparing Banks

Deutsche Bank, the German banking giant, fares poorly in comparisons with its global rivals. Its net-income-to-assets ratio (i.e., return on assets) is only 0.26%, while its peers such as Citigroup and Credit Suisse have ratios of up to 0.92%. Its return on equity is only 10%, whereas the return on equity of almost all its peers is in the 14% to 16% range. One reason for Deutsche Bank's anemic performance is the bank's bloated and expensive payroll. Deutsche Bank's earnings average about $23,000 per employee. At HSBC (Hong

Kong and Shanghai Banking Corporation) the figure is $32,000 per employee and at Credit Suisse it is $34,000.

Source: Justin Doebele, "Best Bank Bargain?" *Forbes,* August 9, 1999, pp. 89–90.

IN BUSINESS

(continued)

Financial Leverage

Financial leverage (often called *leverage* for short) involves acquiring assets with funds that have been obtained from creditors or from preferred stockholders at a fixed rate of return. If the assets in which the funds are invested are able to earn a rate of return *greater* than the fixed rate of return required by the funds' suppliers, then the company has **positive financial leverage** and the common stockholders benefit.

For example, suppose that CBS is able to earn an after-tax return of 12% on its broadcasting assets. If the company can borrow from creditors at a 10% interest rate to expand its assets, then the common stockholders can benefit from positive leverage. The borrowed funds invested in the business will earn an after-tax return of 12%, but the after-tax interest cost of the borrowed funds will be only 7% [10% interest rate × (1 − 0.30) = 7%]. The difference will go to the common stockholders.

We can see this concept in operation in the case of Brickey Electronics. Notice from Exhibit 14–1 that the company's bonds payable bear a fixed interest rate of 8%. The after-tax interest cost of these bonds is only 5.6% [8% interest rate × (1 − 0.30) = 5.6%]. The company's assets are generating an after-tax return of 7.3%, as we computed earlier. Since this return on assets is greater than the after-tax interest cost of the bonds, leverage is positive, and the difference accrues to the benefit of the common stockholders. This explains in part why the return on common stockholders' equity (11.3%) is greater than the return on total assets (7.3%).

Unfortunately, leverage is a two-edged sword. If assets are unable to earn a high enough rate to cover the interest costs of debt and preferred dividends (**negative financial leverage**), *the common stockholder suffers.*

The Impact of Income Taxes   Debt and preferred stock are not equally efficient in generating positive leverage. The reason is that interest on debt is tax deductible, whereas preferred dividends are not. This usually makes debt a much more effective source of positive leverage than preferred stock.

Financial Leverage

| Creditors/Preferred Stockholders | Common Stockholders | Creditors/Preferred Stockholders | Common Stockholders |

Positive Financial Leverage   **Negative Financial Leverage**

EXHIBIT 14–6   Leverage from Preferred Stock and Long-Term Debt

	Alternative 1: $100,000,000 Common Stock	Alternative 2: $50,000,000 Common Stock; $50,000,000 Preferred Stock	Alternative 3: $50,000,000 Common Stock; $50,000,000 Bonds
		Alternatives: $100,000,000 Issue of Securities	
Earnings before interest and taxes	$ 15,000,000	$15,000,000	$15,000,000
Deduct interest expense (8% × $50,000,000)	—	—	4,000,000
Net income before taxes................................	15,000,000	15,000,000	11,000,000
Deduct income taxes (30%)	4,500,000	4,500,000	3,300,000
Net income	10,500,000	10,500,000	7,700,000
Deduct preferred dividends (8% × $50,000,000)............	—	4,000,000	—
Net income remaining for common (a)	$ 10,500,000	$ 6,500,000	$ 7,700,000
Common stockholders' equity (b)	$100,000,000	$50,000,000	$50,000,000
Return on common stockholders' equity (a) ÷ (b)	10.5%	13.0%	15.4%

To illustrate this point, suppose that the Hospital Corporation of America is considering three ways of financing a $100 million expansion of its chain of hospitals:

1. $100 million from an issue of common stock.
2. $50 million from an issue of common stock, and $50 million from an issue of preferred stock bearing a dividend rate of 8%.
3. $50 million from an issue of common stock, and $50 million from an issue of bonds bearing an interest rate of 8%.

Assuming that the Hospital Corporation of America can earn an additional $15 million each year before interest and taxes as a result of the expansion, the operating results under each of the three alternatives are shown in Exhibit 14–6.

If the entire $100 million is raised from an issue of common stock, then the return to the common stockholders will be only 10.5%, as shown under alternative 1 in the exhibit. If half of the funds are raised from an issue of preferred stock, then the return to the common stockholders increases to 13%, due to the positive effects of leverage. However, if half of the funds are raised from an issue of bonds, then the return to the common stockholders jumps to 15.4%, as shown under alternative 3. Thus, long-term debt is much more efficient in generating positive leverage than is preferred stock. The reason is that the interest expense on long-term debt is tax deductible, whereas the dividends on preferred stock are not.

The Desirability of Leverage   Because of leverage, having some debt in the capital structure can substantially benefit the common stockholder. For this reason, most companies today try to maintain a level of debt that is considered to be normal within the industry. Many companies, such as commercial banks and other financial institutions, rely heavily on leverage to provide an attractive return on their common shares.

Book Value per Share

Another statistic frequently used in attempting to assess the well-being of the common stockholder is book value per share. The **book value per share** measures the amount that would be distributed to holders of each share of common stock if all assets were sold at their balance sheet carrying amounts (i.e., book values) and if all creditors were paid off. Thus, book value per share is based entirely on historical costs. The formula for computing it is as follows:

$$\text{Book value per share} = \frac{\text{Common stockholders' equity (Total stockholders' equity } - \text{ Preferred stock)}}{\text{Number of common shares outstanding}}$$

Total stockholders' equity (see Exhibit 14–1).	$17,000,000
Deduct preferred stock (see Exhibit 14–1)	2,000,000
Common stockholders' equity	$15,000,000

The book value per share of Brickey Electronics' common stock is computed as follows:

$$\frac{\$15,000,000}{500,000 \text{ shares}} = \$30 \text{ per share}$$

If this book value is compared with the $40 market value of Brickey Electronics stock, then the stock appears to be somewhat overpriced. However, as we discussed earlier, market prices reflect expectations about future earnings and dividends, whereas book value largely reflects the results of events that occurred in the past. Ordinarily, the market value of a stock exceeds its book value. For example, in a recent year, Microsoft's common stock often traded at over 4 times its book value, and Coca-Cola's market value was over 17 times its book value.

Looking at McDonald's Financials

McDonald's Corporation provides an interesting illustration of the use of financial ratios. The data below relate to the year ended December 31, 2000. (Averages were computed by adding together the beginning and end of year amounts reported on the balance sheet and dividing the total by two.)

Net income	$1,977 million
Interest expense.	$430 million
Tax rate	31.4%
Average total assets.	$21,334 million
Preferred stock dividends	$0 million
Average common stockholders' equity.	$9,422 million
Common stock dividends per share	$0.22
Earnings per share	$1.49
Market price per share—end of year	$34.00
Book value per share—end of year.	$7.05

Some key financial ratios from the standpoint of the common stockholder are computed below:

$$\text{Return on total assets} = \frac{\$1,977 + [\$430 \times (1 - 0.314)]}{\$21,334} = 10.6\%$$

$$\text{Return on common stockholders' equity} = \frac{\$1,977 - \$0}{\$9,422} = 21.0\%$$

$$\text{Dividend payout ratio} = \frac{\$0.22}{\$1.49} = 14.8\%$$

$$\text{Dividend yield ratio} = \frac{\$0.22}{\$34.00} = 0.65\%$$

The return on common stockholders' equity of 21.0% is higher than the return on total assets of 10.6%, and therefore the company has positive financial leverage. (Creditors provide about half of the company's financing; stockholders provide the remainder.)

According to the management discussion in the annual report, "Given the Company's returns on equity and assets, management believes it is prudent to invest a significant portion of earnings back into the business and to use free cash flow for share repurchases. Accordingly, the common stock dividend is modest." Indeed, only 14.8% of earnings are paid out in dividends. In relation to the stock price, this is a dividend yield of less than 1%. Finally, note that the market value per share is over four times as large as the book value per share. This premium over book value reflects the market's perception that McDonald's earnings will continue to grow in the future.

Source: McDonald's Corporation annual report for the year 2000.

CONCEPT CHECK

1. Which of the following statements is false? (You may select more than one answer.)
   a. The price-earnings ratio will increase if the earnings per share increases and the market price per share remains the same.
   b. The return on common stockholders' equity will decrease if the preferred dividend payment increases and all else stays constant.
   c. The dividend payout ratio will increase if the market price per share decreases.
   d. The return on total assets will increase if the investment in assets increases and all else stays constant.

RATIO ANALYSIS—THE SHORT-TERM CREDITOR

LEARNING OBJECTIVE 3

Compute and interpret financial ratios that would be most useful to a short-term creditor.

Short-term creditors, such as suppliers, want to be repaid on time. Therefore, they focus on the company's cash flows and on its working capital since these are the company's primary sources of cash in the short run.

Working Capital

The excess of current assets over current liabilities is known as **working capital.** The working capital for Brickey Electronics is computed below:

$$\text{Working capital} = \text{Current assets} - \text{Current liabilities}$$

	2004	2003
Current assets	$15,500,000	$16,470,000
Current liabilities	7,000,000	5,000,000
Working capital	$ 8,500,000	$11,470,000

The amount of working capital available to a company is of considerable interest to short-term creditors, *since it represents assets financed from long-term capital sources that do not require near-term repayment.* Therefore, the greater the working capital, the greater is the cushion of protection available to short-term creditors and the greater is the assurance that short-term debts will be paid when due.

Although it is always comforting to short-term creditors to see a large working capital balance, a large balance by itself is no assurance that debts will be paid when due. Rather than being a sign of strength, a large working capital balance may simply mean that obsolete inventory is being accumulated. Therefore, to put the working capital figure into proper perspective, it must be supplemented with other analytical work. The following four ratios (the current ratio, the acid-test ratio, the accounts receivable turnover, and the inventory turnover) should all be used in connection with an analysis of working capital.

Bringing in the Cash

Burlington Northern Santa Fe, the second largest railroad system in the United States, goes to great lengths to minimize its investment in working capital. In fact, the company has negative working capital—its current assets are less than its current liabilities. To achieve this enviable record, the company has worked hard to improve many things—including its collections of receivables. A lot of the problems in collecting accounts receivable had to do with untimely billing and errors in bills, so the company automated and redesigned its billing process. As a result, the number of bills waiting to be processed and sent to customers dropped from about 50,000 to about 15,000. Once the bills had been sent out, the customer still might not pay—sometimes because of a dispute. The company's CFO Tom Hund explains: "Our average bill is a little over $1,000, so we have a lot of them. With some of our larger customers, we found that if they had a dispute with any of our bills, they wouldn't pay the whole batch. We said that was unreasonable, and started having the marketing arms of our business units work on why we had disputed bills and how we could correct them. We got great support from those folks. At the time, our days sales outstanding . . . was about 50. Now we've got it down to 29."

Source: Randy Myers, "Cash Crop," *CFO*, August 2000, pp. 58–81.

Current Ratio

The elements involved in the computation of working capital are frequently expressed in ratio form. A company's current assets divided by its current liabilities is known as the **current ratio:**

$$\text{Current ratio} = \frac{\text{Current assets}}{\text{Current liabilities}}$$

For Brickey Electronics, the current ratios for 2003 and 2004 would be computed as follows:

2004	2003
$\dfrac{\$15,500,000}{\$7,000,000} = 2.21 \text{ to } 1$	$\dfrac{\$16,470,000}{\$5,000,000} = 3.29 \text{ to } 1$

Although widely regarded as a measure of short-term debt-paying ability, the current ratio must be interpreted with great care. A *declining* ratio, as above, might be a sign of a deteriorating financial condition. On the other hand, it might be the result of eliminating obsolete inventories or other stagnant current assets. An *improving* ratio might be the result of an unwise stockpiling of inventory, or it might indicate an improving financial situation. In short, the current ratio is useful, but tricky to interpret. To avoid a blunder, the analyst must take a hard look at the individual assets and liabilities involved.

The general rule of thumb calls for a current ratio of 2 to 1. This rule is subject to many exceptions, depending on the industry and the company involved. Some industries can operate quite successfully with a current ratio of slightly over 1 to 1. The adequacy of a current ratio depends heavily on the *composition* of the assets. For example, as we see in the following table, both Worthington Corporation and Greystone, Inc., have current ratios of 2 to 1. However, they are not in comparable financial condition. Greystone is likely to have difficulty meeting its current financial obligations, since almost all of its current assets consist of inventory rather than more liquid assets such as cash and accounts receivable.

	Worthington Corporation	Greystone, Inc.
Current assets:		
Cash	$ 25,000	$ 2,000
Accounts receivable, net	60,000	8,000
Inventory	85,000	160,000
Prepaid expenses	5,000	5,000
Total current assets (a)	$175,000	$175,000
Current liabilities (b)	$ 87,500	$ 87,500
Current ratio, (a) ÷ (b)	2 to 1	2 to 1

Acid-Test (Quick) Ratio

The **acid-test (quick) ratio** is a much more rigorous test of a company's ability to meet its short-term debts than the current ratio. Inventories and prepaid expenses are excluded from total current assets, leaving only the more liquid (or "quick") assets to be divided by current liabilities.

$$\text{Acid-test ratio} = \frac{\text{Cash} + \text{Marketable securities} + \text{Current receivables*}}{\text{Current liabilities}}$$

*Current receivables include both accounts receivable and any short-term notes receivable.

The acid-test ratio is designed to measure how well a company can meet its obligations without having to liquidate or depend too heavily on its inventory. Since inventory may be difficult to sell in times of economic stress, it is generally felt that to be properly protected, each dollar of liabilities should be backed by at least $1 of quick assets. Thus, an acid-test ratio of 1 to 1 is usually viewed as adequate.

The acid-test ratios for Brickey Electronics for 2003 and 2004 are computed below:

	2004	2003
Cash (see Exhibit 14–1)	$1,200,000	$2,350,000
Accounts receivable (see Exhibit 14–1)	6,000,000	4,000,000
Total quick assets (a)	$7,200,000	$6,350,000
Current liabilities (see Exhibit 14–1) (b)	$7,000,000	$5,000,000
Acid-test ratio, (a) ÷ (b)	1.03 to 1	1.27 to 1

Although Brickey Electronics has an acid-test ratio for 2004 that is within the acceptable range, an analyst might be concerned about several disquieting trends revealed in the company's balance sheet. Notice in Exhibit 14–1 that short-term debts are rising, while the cash position seems to be deteriorating. Perhaps the weakened cash position is a result of the greatly expanded volume of accounts receivable. One wonders why the accounts receivable have been allowed to increase so rapidly in so brief a time.

In short, as with the current ratio, the acid-test ratio should be interpreted with one eye on its basic components.

Accounts Receivable Turnover

The **accounts receivable turnover** is a rough measure of how many times a company's accounts receivable have been turned into cash during the year. It is frequently used in conjunction with an analysis of working capital, since a smooth flow from accounts receivable into cash is an important indicator of the "quality" of a company's working capital and is critical to the company's ability to operate. The accounts receivable turnover is computed by dividing sales on account (i.e., credit sales) by the average accounts receivable balance for the year.

$$\text{Accounts receivable turnover} = \frac{\text{Sales on account}}{\text{Average accounts receivable balance}}$$

Assuming that all sales for the year were on account, the accounts receivable turnover for Brickey Electronics for 2004 would be computed as follows:

$$\frac{\text{Sales on account}}{\text{Average accounts receivable balance}} = \frac{\$52,000,000}{\$5,000,000^*} = 10.4 \text{ times}$$

*$4,000,000 + $6,000,000 = $10,000,000; $10,000,000 ÷ 2 = $5,000,000 average.

The turnover figure can then be divided into 365 to determine the average number of days being taken to collect an account (known as the **average collection period**).

$$\text{Average collection period} = \frac{365 \text{ days}}{\text{Accounts receivable turnover}}$$

The average collection period for Brickey Electronics for 2004 is computed as follows:

$$\frac{365}{10.4 \text{ times}} = 35 \text{ days}$$

This simply means that on average it takes 35 days to collect on a credit sale. Whether the average of 35 days taken to collect an account is good or bad depends on the credit terms Brickey Electronics is offering its customers. If the credit terms are 30 days, then a 35-day average collection period would usually be viewed as very good. Most customers will tend to withhold payment for as long as the credit terms will allow and may even go over a few days. This factor, added to ever-present problems with a few slow-paying customers, can cause the average collection period to exceed normal credit terms by a week or so and should not cause great alarm.

On the other hand, if the company's credit terms are 10 days, then a 35-day average collection period is worrisome. The long collection period may result from many old unpaid accounts of doubtful collectibility, or it may be a result of poor day-to-day credit management. The company may be making sales with inadequate credit checks on customers, or perhaps no follow-ups are being made on slow accounts.

Inventory Turnover

The **inventory turnover ratio** measures how many times a company's inventory has been sold and replaced during the year. It is computed by dividing the cost of goods sold by the average level of inventory on hand:

$$\text{Inventory turnover} = \frac{\text{Cost of goods sold}}{\text{Average inventory balance}}$$

The average inventory figure is the average of the beginning and ending inventory figures. Since Brickey Electronics has a beginning inventory of $10,000,000 and an ending inventory of $8,000,000, its average inventory for the year would be $9,000,000. The company's inventory turnover for 2004 would be computed as follows:

$$\frac{\text{Cost of goods sold}}{\text{Average inventory balance}} = \frac{\$36,000,000}{\$9,000,000} = 4 \text{ times}$$

The number of days being taken to sell the entire inventory one time (called the **average sale period**) can be computed by dividing 365 by the inventory turnover figure:

$$\text{Average sale period} = \frac{365 \text{ days}}{\text{Inventory turnover}}$$

$$\frac{365 \text{ days}}{4 \text{ times}} = 91\frac{1}{4} \text{ days}$$

The average sale period varies from industry to industry. Grocery stores tend to turn their inventory over very quickly, perhaps as often as every 12 to 15 days. On the other hand, jewelry stores tend to turn their inventory over very slowly, perhaps only a couple of times each year.

If a company has a turnover that is much slower than the average for its industry, then it may have obsolete goods on hand, or its inventory stocks may be needlessly high. Excessive inventories tie up funds that could be used elsewhere in operations. Managers sometimes argue that they must buy in very large quantities to take advantage of the best discounts being offered. But these discounts must be carefully weighed against the added costs of insurance, taxes, financing, and risks of obsolescence and deterioration that result from carrying added inventories.

Inventory turnover has been increasing in recent years as companies have adopted just-in-time (JIT) methods. Under JIT, inventories are purposely kept low, and thus a company utilizing JIT methods may have a very high inventory turnover as compared to other companies. Indeed, one of the goals of JIT is to increase inventory turnover by systematically reducing the amount of inventory on hand.

CONCEPT CHECK ✓

2. Total sales at a store are $1,000,000 and 80% of those sales are on credit. The beginning and ending accounts receivable balances are $100,000 and $140,000, respectively. What is the accounts receivable turnover?
   a. 3.33 times
   b. 6.67 times
   c. 8.33 times
   d. 10.67 times

3. A retailer's total sales are $1,000,000 and the gross margin percentage is 60%. The beginning and ending inventory balances are 240,000 and 260,000, respectively. What is the inventory turnover?
   a. 1.60 times
   b. 2.40 times
   c. 3.40 times
   d. 3.60 times

YOU DECIDE

Portfolio Manager

You work for a mutual fund and have the responsibility of selecting stocks to include in its investment portfolio. You have been analyzing the financial statements of a chain of retail clothing stores and noticed that the company's current ratio has increased, but its acid-test quick ratio has decreased. In addition, the company's accounts receivable turnover has decreased and its inventory turnover ratio has decreased. Finally, the company's price-earnings ratio is at an all-time high. Would you recommend buying stock in the retailer to include in the mutual fund's investment portfolio?

DECISION MAKER

Vice President of Sales

Although its credit terms require payment within 30 days, your company's average collection period is 33 days. A major competitor has an average collection period of 27 days.

You have been asked to explain why your company is not doing as well as the competitor. You have investigated your company's credit policies and procedures and have concluded that they are reasonable and adequate under the circumstances. What rationale would you consider to explain why (1) the average collection period of your company exceeds the credit terms, and (2) the average collection period of the company is higher than that of its competitor?

Watch Those Receivables and Inventories!

Herb Greenberg, an investment columnist for *Fortune* magazine, warns investors to look out for two "sure warning signs: receivables and inventory that rise faster than sales . . . A fast rise in receivables could mean that the company is pulling out all the stops to get customers to take its products. That's good, *unless* it means stealing sales from future quarters. As for a rise in inventory: If finished goods are piling up in warehouses—absent some reasonable explanation, like a looming product launch—they must not be selling." To monitor these possibilities, watch the accounts receivable turnover or average collection period for the receivables and the inventory turnover or average sale period for the inventories.

Source: Herb Greenberg, "Minding Your K's and Q's," *Fortune*, January 8, 2001, p. 180.

Warning Signs at Amazon.com

Ravi Suria, a debt analyst at Lehman Brothers, sounded an early warning about Amazon.com's finances. Amazon's inventory turnover plummeted from 8.5 times to 2.9 times within two years. And in a year in which its sales grew 170%, its inventories skyrocketed by 650%. Suria points out that "When a company manages inventory properly, it should grow along with its sales growth rate." When inventory grows faster than sales, "it means simply that they're not selling as much as they are buying."

Source: Robert Hof, Debra Sparks, Ellen Neuborne, and Wendy Zellner, "Can Amazon Make It?" *Business Week*, July 10, 2000, pp. 38–43.

RATIO ANALYSIS—THE LONG-TERM CREDITOR

The position of long-term creditors differs from that of short-term creditors in that they are concerned with both the near-term *and* the long-term ability of a company to meet its commitments. They are concerned with the near term since the interest they are entitled to is normally paid on a current basis. They are concerned with the long term since they want to be fully repaid on schedule.

Since the long-term creditor is usually faced with greater risks than the short-term creditor, companies are often required to agree to various restrictive covenants, or rules, for the long-term creditor's protection. Examples of such restrictive covenants include the maintenance of minimum working capital levels and restrictions on payment of dividends to common stockholders. Although these restrictive covenants are in widespread use, they are a poor second to adequate future *earnings* from the point of view of assessing protection and safety. Creditors do not want to go to court to collect their claims; they would much prefer staking the safety of their claims for interest and eventual repayment of principal on an orderly and consistent flow of funds from operations.

Times Interest Earned Ratio

The most common measure of the ability of a company's operations to provide protection to the long-term creditor is the **times interest earned ratio.** It is computed by dividing earnings *before* interest expense and income taxes (i.e., net operating income) by the yearly interest charges that must be met:

$$\text{Times interest earned} = \frac{\text{Earnings before interest expense and income taxes}}{\text{Interest expense}}$$

For Brickey Electronics, the times interest earned ratio for 2004 would be computed as follows:

$$\frac{\$3,140,000}{\$640,000} = 4.9 \text{ times}$$

Earnings before income taxes must be used in the computation, since interest expense deductions come *before* income taxes are computed. Creditors have first claim on earnings. Only those earnings remaining after all interest charges have been provided for are subject to income taxes.

Generally, earnings are viewed as adequate to protect long-term creditors if the times interest earned ratio is 2 or more. Before making a final judgment, however, it would be necessary to look at a company's long-run *trend* of earnings and evaluate how vulnerable the company is to cyclical changes in the economy.

Debt-to-Equity Ratio

Long-term creditors are also concerned with keeping a reasonable balance between the portion of assets provided by creditors and the portion of assets provided by the stockholders of a company. This balance is measured by the **debt-to-equity ratio:**

$$\text{Debt-to-equity ratio} = \frac{\text{Total liabilities}}{\text{Stockholders' equity}}$$

	2004	2003
Total liabilities (a)	$14,500,000	$13,000,000
Stockholders' equity (b)	$17,000,000	$15,970,000
Debt-to-equity ratio, (a) ÷ (b)	0.85 to 1	0.81 to 1

The debt-to-equity ratio indicates the amount of assets being provided by creditors for each dollar of assets being provided by the owners of a company. In 2003, creditors of Brickey Electronics were providing 81 cents of assets for each $1 of assets being provided by stockholders; the figure increased only slightly to 85 cents by 2004.

Creditors would like the debt-to-equity ratio to be relatively low. The lower the ratio, the greater the amount of assets being provided by the owners of a company and the greater is the buffer of protection to creditors. By contrast, common stockholders would like the ratio to be relatively high, since through leverage, common stockholders can benefit from the assets being provided by creditors.

In most industries, norms have developed over the years that serve as guides to companies in their decisions as to the "right" amount of debt to include in the capital structure. Different industries face different risks. For this reason, the level of debt that is appropriate for companies in one industry is not necessarily a guide to the level of debt that is appropriate for companies in a different industry.

4. Total assets are $1,500,000 and stockholder's equity is $900,000. What is the debt-to-equity ratio?
   a. 0.33 to 1
   b. 0.50 to 1
   c. 0.60 to 1
   d. 0.67 to 1

CONCEPT CHECK

SUMMARY OF RATIOS AND SOURCES OF COMPARATIVE RATIO DATA

Exhibit 14–7 contains a summary of the ratios discussed in this chapter. The formula for each ratio and a summary comment on each ratio's significance are included in the exhibit.

Exhibit 14–8 contains a listing of published sources that provide comparative ratio data organized by industry. These sources are used extensively by managers, investors, and analysts in doing comparative analyses and in attempting to assess the well-being of companies. The World Wide Web also contains a wealth of financial and other data. A search engine such as Google can be used to track down information on individual companies. Many companies have their own websites on which they post their latest financial reports and news of interest to potential investors. The *EDGAR* database listed in Exhibit 14–8 is a particularly rich source of data. It contains copies of all reports filed by companies with the SEC since about 1995—including annual reports filed as form 10-K.

More Information about Segments

IN BUSINESS

Comparisons of one company with others in its industry often help an analyst better interpret financial data about the company. As companies have become more diversified, it has become more difficult to select competitors for comparison.

The Financial Accounting Standards Board issued *SFAS No. 131* in response to analysts' demands for additional information about a company's segments. The Statement requires broader disclosure of segment information than previously reported under *SFAS No. 14* and may help to overcome some of the limitations otherwise inherent in comparing one company to another. For example, Wal-Mart did not report any segments under *SFAS No. 14;* but it now discloses information about three operating segments (its U.S. discount stores, its U.S. warehouse membership-club stores, and its international operations) under *SFAS No. 131.* Likewise, IBM, which did not report any segments under the prior rules, now discloses information about seven different operating segments.

Critics of the new reporting standards note that the beneficiaries of the enhanced reporting requirements include not only investors and creditors but also competitors, and worry that too much information is being provided.

Source: Joe Sanders, Sherman Alexander, and Stan Clark, "New Segment Reporting—Is It Working?" *Strategic Finance,* December 1999, p. 35.

EXHIBIT 14–7 Summary of Ratios

Ratio	Formula	Significance
Gross margin percentage	Gross margin ÷ Sales	A broad measure of profitability
Earnings per share (of common stock)	(Net income − Preferred dividends) ÷ Average number of common shares outstanding	Tends to have an effect on the market price per share, as reflected in the price-earnings ratio
Price-earnings ratio	Market price per share ÷ Earnings per share	An index of whether a stock is relatively cheap or relatively expensive in relation to current earnings
Dividend payout ratio	Dividends per share ÷ Earnings per share	An index showing whether a company pays out most of its earnings in dividends or reinvests the earnings internally
Dividend yield ratio	Dividends per share ÷ Market price per share	Shows the return in terms of cash dividends being provided by a stock
Return on total assets	{Net income + [Interest expense × (1 − Tax rate)]} ÷ Average total assets	Measure of how well assets have been employed by management
Return on common stockholders' equity	(Net income − Preferred dividends) ÷ Average common stockholders' equity (Average total stockholders' equity − Average preferred stock)	When compared to the return on total assets, measures the extent to which financial leverage is working for or against common stockholders
Book value per share	Common stockholders' equity (Total stockholders' equity − Preferred stock) ÷ Number of common shares outstanding	Measures the amount that would be distributed to holders of common stock if all assets were sold at their balance sheet carrying amounts and if all creditors were paid off
Working capital	Current assets − Current liabilities	Measures the company's ability to repay current liabilities using only current assets
Current ratio	Current assets ÷ Current liabilities	Test of short-term debt-paying ability
Acid-test (quick) ratio	(Cash + Marketable securities + Current receivables) ÷ Current liabilities	Test of short-term debt-paying ability without having to rely on inventory
Accounts receivable turnover	Sales on account ÷ Average accounts receivable balance	A rough measure of how many times a company's accounts receivable have been turned into cash during the year
Average collection period (age of receivables)	365 days ÷ Accounts receivable turnover	Measure of the average number of days taken to collect an account receivable
Inventory turnover ratio	Cost of goods sold ÷ Average inventory balance	Measure of how many times a company's inventory has been sold during the year
Average sale period (turnover in days)	365 days ÷ Inventory turnover	Measure of the average number of days taken to sell the inventory one time
Times interest earned ratio	Earnings before interest expense and income taxes ÷ Interest expense	Measure of the company's ability to make interest payments
Debt-to-equity ratio	Total liabilities ÷ Stockholders' equity	Measure of the amount of assets being provided by creditors for each dollar of assets being provided by the stockholders

EXHIBIT 14–8   Sources of Financial Ratios

Source	Content
Almanac of Business and Industrial Financial Ratios, Prentice-Hall; published annually	An exhaustive source that contains common-size income statements and financial ratios by industry and by size of companies within each industry.
Annual Statement Studies, Robert Morris Associates; published annually. See www.rmahq.org/Ann_Studies/asstudies.html for definitions and explanations of ratios and balance sheet and income statement data that are contained in the *Annual Statement Studies.*	A widely used publication that contains common-size statements and financial ratios on individual companies; companies arranged by industry.
Business & Company ASAP; database that is continually updated	Exhaustive database of business articles in periodicals for both industry and company information. Many of the articles are available in full text. Directory listings for over 150,000 companies are also included in the database.
EDGAR, Securities and Exchange Commission; website that is continually updated; www.sec.gov	An exhaustive database accessible on the World Wide Web that contains reports filed by companies with the SEC; these reports can be downloaded.
EBSCOhost (Business Source Elite index), EBSCO publishing; database that is continually updated	Exhaustive database of business articles in periodicals useful for both industry and company information. Full text is included from nearly 970 journals; indexing and abstracts are offered for over 1,650 journals.
FreeEdgar, EDGAR Online, Inc.; website that is continually updated; www.freeedgar.com	A site that allows you to search SEC filings; financial information can be downloaded directly into Excel worksheets.
Hoover's Online, Hoovers, Inc.; website that is continually updated; www.hoovers.com	A site that provides capsule profiles for 10,000 U.S. companies with links to company websites, annual reports, stock charts, news articles, and industry information.
Key Business Ratios, Dun & Bradstreet; published annually	Fourteen commonly used financial ratios are computed for over 800 major industry groupings.
Moody's Industrial Manual and Moody's Bank and Finance Manual, Dun & Bradstreet; published annually	An exhaustive source that contains financial ratios on all companies listed on the New York Stock Exchange, the American Stock Exchange, and regional American exchanges.
PricewaterhouseCoopers website that is continually updated; www.edgarscan.tc.pw.com	This source of financial statement data has an easier-to-use interface than other sources.
Standard & Poor's Industry Survey, Standard & Poor's; published annually	Various statistics, including some financial ratios, are given by industry and for leading companies within each industry grouping.

SUMMARY

LO1   Prepare and interpret financial statements in comparative and common-size form.
It is difficult to interpret raw data from financial statements without standardizing the data in some way so that it can be compared over time and across companies. For example, all of the financial data for a company can be expressed as a percentage of the data in some base year. This makes it easier to spot trends over time. To make it easier to compare companies, common-size financial statements are often used in which income statement data are expressed as a percentage of sales and balance sheet data are expressed as a percentage of total assets.

LO2   Compute and interpret financial ratios that would be most useful to a common stockholder.
Common stockholders are most concerned with the company's earnings per share, price-earnings ratio, dividend payout and yield ratios, return on total assets, book value per share, and return on common stockholders' equity. Generally speaking, the higher these ratios, the better it is for common stockholders.

LO3 **Compute and interpret financial ratios that would be most useful to a short-term creditor.**
Short-term creditors are most concerned with the company's ability to repay its debt in the near future.
Consequently, these investors focus on the relation between current assets and current liabilities and the
company's ability to generate cash. Specifically, short-term creditors monitor working capital, the current
ratio, the acid-test (quick) ratio, accounts receivable turnover, and inventory turnover.

LO4 **Compute and interpret financial ratios that would be most useful to a long-term creditor.**
Long-term creditors have many of the same concerns as short-term creditors, but also monitor the times interest earned ratio and the debt-to-equity ratio. These ratios indicate the company's ability to pay interest
out of operations and how heavily the company is financially leveraged.

GUIDANCE ANSWERS TO *DECISION MAKER* AND *YOU DECIDE*

Portfolio Manager   (p. 604)
All of the ratios—current ratio, acid-test quick ratio, accounts receivable turnover, and inventory turnover
ratio—indicate deteriorating operations. And yet the company's price-earnings ratio is at an all-time high,
suggesting that the stock market is optimistic about the company's future and its stock price is at a lofty
level. It would be very risky to invest in this company without digging deeper and finding out what has
caused the deteriorating operating ratios.

Vice President of Sales   (p. 604)
An average collection period of 33 days means that on average it takes 33 days to collect on a credit sale.
Whether the average of 33 days is acceptable or not depends on the credit terms that your company is offering to its customers. In this case, an average collection period of 33 days is good because the credit terms
offered by your company are net 30 days. Why might the average collection period exceed the credit terms?
Some customers may misjudge the amount of time that it takes mail to reach the company's offices. Certain customers may experience temporary cash shortages and delay payment for short periods of time. Others might be in the process of returning goods and have not paid for the goods that will be returned because
they realize that a credit will be posted to their account. Still others may be in the process of resolving disputes regarding the goods that were shipped.

    Turning to the competitor's average collection period of 27 days, it is possible that the competitor's
credit terms are 25 days rather than 30 days. Or, the competitor might be offering sales discounts to its customers (e.g., 2/10, n/30) for paying early. You should recall from your financial accounting course that sales
discounts are offered as an incentive to customers to motivate them to pay invoices well in advance of the
due date. If enough customers take advantage of the sales discounts, the average collection period will drop
below 30 days.

GUIDANCE ANSWERS TO CONCEPT CHECKS

1. **Choices a, c, and d.** The price-earnings ratio will decrease, rather than increase, if the earnings per
   share increases and the market price per share remains the same. The dividend payout ratio is not affected by the market price per share. The return on total assets will decrease if the investment in assets increases and all else stays constant.
2. **Choice b.** The accounts receivable turnover is $800,000 of credit sales ÷ $120,000 average accounts receivable balance = 6.67 times.
3. **Choice a.** First, calculate the cost of goods sold as follows: $1,000,000 × (1 − 0.60) = $400,000.
   Next, the inventory turnover is calculated as follows: $400,000 of cost of goods sold ÷ $250,000 average inventory = 1.60 times.
4. **Choice d.** Total assets of $1,500,000 − $900,000 of stockholders' equity = $600,000 of total liabili-
   ties. The debt-to-equity ratio is $600,000 ÷ $900,000 = 0.67 to 1.

REVIEW PROBLEM: SELECTED RATIOS AND FINANCIAL LEVERAGE

Starbucks Coffee Company is the leading retailer and roaster of specialty coffee in North America with
over 1,000 stores offering freshly brewed coffee, pastries, and coffee beans. Data from its financial statements are given below:

STARBUCKS COFFEE COMPANY
Comparative Balance Sheet
(dollars in thousands)

	End of Year	Beginning of Year
Assets		
Current assets:		
Cash	$126,215	$ 20,944
Marketable securities	103,221	41,507
Accounts receivable	17,621	9,852
Inventories	83,370	123,657
Other current assets	9,114	9,390
Total current assets	339,541	205,350
Property and equipment, net	369,477	244,728
Other assets	17,595	18,100
Total assets	$726,613	$468,178
Liabilities and Stockholders' Equity		
Current liabilities:		
Accounts payable	$ 38,034	$ 28,668
Short-term bank loans	16,241	13,138
Accrued payables	18,005	13,436
Other current liabilities	28,811	15,804
Total current liabilities	101,091	71,046
Long-term liabilities:		
Bonds payable	165,020	80,398
Other long-term liabilities	8,842	4,503
Total liabilities	274,953	155,947
Stockholders' equity:		
Preferred stock	0	0
Common stock and additional paid-in capital	361,309	265,679
Retained earnings	90,351	46,552
Total stockholders' equity	451,660	312,231
Total liabilities and stockholders' equity	$726,613	$468,178

Note: The effective interest rate on the bonds payable was about 5%.

STARBUCKS COFFEE COMPANY
Comparative Income Statement
(dollars in thousands)

	Current Year	Prior Year
Revenue	$696,481	$465,213
Cost of goods sold	335,800	211,279
Gross margin	360,681	253,934
Operating expenses:		
Store operating expenses	210,693	148,757
Other operating expenses	19,787	13,932
Depreciation and amortization	35,950	22,486
General and administrative expenses	37,258	28,643
Total operating expenses	303,688	213,818

(continued)

(concluded)	**STARBUCKS COFFEE COMPANY** **Comparative Income Statement** **(dollars in thousands)**		
		Current Year	Prior Year
Net operating income		56,993	40,116
Gain on sale of investment.		9,218	0
Plus interest income.		11,029	6,792
Less interest expense		8,739	3,765
Net income before taxes		68,501	43,143
Less income taxes (about 38.5%).		26,373	17,041
Net income.		$ 42,128	$ 26,102

Required:

For the current year:

1. Compute the return on total assets.
2. Compute the return on common stockholders' equity.
3. Is Starbucks' financial leverage positive or negative? Explain.
4. Compute the current ratio.
5. Compute the acid-test (quick) ratio.
6. Compute the inventory turnover.
7. Compute the average sale period.
8. Compute the debt-to-equity ratio.

Solution to Review Problem:

1. Return on total assets:

$$\text{Return on total assets} = \frac{\text{Net Income} + [\text{Interest expense} \times (1 - \text{Tax rate})]}{\text{Average total assets}}$$

$$\frac{\$42,128 + [\$8,739 \times (1 - 0.385)]}{(\$726,613 + \$468,178)/2} = 8.0\% \text{ (rounded)}$$

2. Return on common stockholders' equity:

$$\text{Return on common stockholders' equity} = \frac{\text{Net income} - \text{Preferred dividends}}{\text{Average common stockholders' equity}}$$

$$\frac{\$42,128 - \$0}{(\$451,660 + \$312,231)/2} = 11.0\% \text{ (rounded)}$$

3. The company has positive financial leverage, since the return on common stockholders' equity (11%) is greater than the return on total assets (8%). The positive financial leverage was obtained from current liabilities and the bonds payable. The interest rate on the bonds is substantially less than the return on total assets.

4. Current ratio:

$$\text{Current ratio} = \frac{\text{Current assets}}{\text{Current liabilities}}$$

$$\frac{\$339,541}{\$101,091} = 3.36 \text{ (rounded)}$$

5. Acid-test (quick) ratio:

$$\text{Acid-test ratio} = \frac{\text{Cash} + \text{Marketable securities} + \text{Current receivables}}{\text{Current liabilities}}$$

$$\frac{\$126,215 + \$103,221 + \$17,621}{\$101,091} = 2.44 \text{ (rounded)}$$

This acid-test ratio is quite high and provides Starbucks with the ability to fund rapid expansion.

6. Inventory turnover:

$$\text{Inventory turnover} = \frac{\text{Cost of goods sold}}{\text{Average inventory balance}}$$

$$\frac{\$335,800}{(\$83,370 + \$123,657)/2} = 3.24 \text{ (rounded)}$$

7. Average sale period:

$$\text{Average sale period} = \frac{365 \text{ days}}{\text{Inventory turnover}}$$

$$\frac{365 \text{ days}}{3.24} = 113 \text{ days (rounded)}$$

8. Debt-to-equity ratio:

$$\text{Debt-to-equity ratio} = \frac{\text{Total liabilities}}{\text{Stockholders' equity}}$$

$$\frac{\$274,953}{\$451,660} = 0.61 \text{ (rounded)}$$

GLOSSARY

(Note: Definitions and formulas for all financial ratios are shown in Exhibit 14–7. These definitions and formulas are not repeated here.)

Common-size statements A statement that shows the items appearing on it in percentage form as well as in dollar form. On the income statement, the percentages are based on total sales revenue; on the balance sheet, the percentages are based on total assets. (p. 590)

Financial leverage Acquiring assets with funds that have been obtained from creditors or from preferred stockholders at a fixed rate of return. (p. 597)

Horizontal analysis A side-by-side comparison of two or more years' financial statements. (p. 588)

Negative financial leverage A situation in which the fixed return to a company's creditors and preferred stockholders is greater than the return on total assets. In this situation, the return on common stockholders' equity will be *less* than the return on total assets. (p. 597)

Positive financial leverage A situation in which the fixed return to a company's creditors and preferred stockholders is less than the return on total assets. In this situation, the return on common stockholders' equity will be *greater* than the return on total assets. (p. 597)

Trend analysis See *horizontal analysis*. (p. 588)

Trend percentages The expression of several years' financial data in percentage form in terms of a base year. (p. 589)

Vertical analysis The presentation of a company's financial statements in common-size form. (p. 590)

QUESTIONS

14–1 Distinguish between horizontal and vertical analysis of financial statement data.

14–2 What is the basic purpose for examining trends in a company's financial ratios and other data? What other kinds of comparisons might an analyst make?

14–3 Assume that two companies in the same industry have equal earnings. Why might these companies have different price-earnings ratios?

14–4 Armcor, Inc., is in a rapidly growing technological industry. Would you expect the company to have a high or low dividend payout ratio?

14–5 Distinguish between a manager's *financing* and *operating* responsibilities. Which of these responsibilities is the return on total assets ratio designed to measure?

14–6 What is meant by the dividend yield on a common stock investment?

14–7 What is meant by the term *financial leverage?*

14–8 The president of a medium-size plastics company was quoted in a business journal as stating, "We haven't had a dollar of interest-paying debt in over 10 years. Not many companies can say that." As a stockholder in this company, how would you feel about its policy of not taking on interest-paying debt?

14–9 Why is it more difficult to obtain positive financial leverage from preferred stock than from long-term debt?

14–10 If a stock's market value exceeds its book value, then the stock is overpriced. Do you agree? Explain.

14–11 Weaver Company experiences a great deal of seasonal variation in its business activities. The company's high point in business activity is in June; its low point is in January. During which month would you expect the current ratio to be highest?

14–12 A company seeking a line of credit at a bank was turned down. Among other things, the bank stated that the company's 2 to 1 current ratio was not adequate. Give reasons why a 2 to 1 current ratio might not be adequate.

BRIEF EXERCISES

BRIEF EXERCISE 14–1   Trend Percentages   (LO1)

Starkey Office Products' sales, current assets, and current liabilities (all in thousands of dollars) have been reported as follows over the last five years (Year 5 is the most recent year):

	Year 5	Year 4	Year 3	Year 2	Year 1
Sales	$5,625	$5,400	$4,950	$4,725	$4,500
Current assets:					
Cash	$ 64	$ 72	$ 84	$ 88	$ 80
Accounts receivable	560	496	432	416	400
Inventory	896	880	816	864	800
Total current assets	$1,520	$1,448	$1,332	$1,368	$1,280
Current liabilities	$ 390	$ 318	$ 324	$ 330	$ 300

Required:

1. Express all of the asset, liability, and sales data in trend percentages. (Show percentages for each item.) Use Year 1 as the base year, and carry computations to one decimal place.
2. Comment on the results of your analysis.

BRIEF EXERCISE 14–2   Common-Size Income Statement   (LO1)

A comparative income statement is given below for Ryder Hardwoods, a retailer of hardwood flooring materials:

RYDER HARDWOODS Comparative Income Statement For the Years Ended June 30, 2002, and 2001		
	2002	**2001**
Sales	$5,000,000	$4,000,000
Less cost of goods sold	3,160,000	2,400,000
Gross margin	1,840,000	1,600,000
Selling expenses	900,000	700,000
Administrative expenses	680,000	584,000
Total expenses	1,580,000	1,284,000
Net operating income	260,000	316,000
Interest expense	70,000	40,000
Net income before taxes	$ 190,000	$ 276,000

The president is concerned that net income is down in 2002 even though sales have increased during the year. The president is also concerned that administrative expenses have increased, since the company made a concerted effort during 2002 to pare "fat" out of the organization.

Required:

1. Express each year's income statement in common-size percentages. Carry computations to one decimal place.
2. Comment briefly on the changes between the two years.

BRIEF EXERCISE 14–3   Financial Ratios for Common Stockholders   (LO2)

Comparative financial statements for Heritage Antiquing Services for the fiscal year ending December 31 appear below. The company did not issue any new common or preferred stock during the year. A total of 600 thousand shares of common stock were outstanding. The interest rate on the bond payable was 14.0%, the income tax rate was 40%, and the dividend per share of common stock was $0.75. The market value of the company's common stock at the end of the year was $26. All of the company's sales are on account.

HERITAGE ANTIQUING SERVICES Comparative Balance Sheet (dollars in thousands)		
	2003	**2002**
Assets		
Current assets:		
Cash	$ 1,080	$ 1,210
Accounts receivable, net	9,000	6,500
Inventory....................................	12,000	10,600
Prepaid expenses	600	500
Total current assets	22,680	18,810
Property and equipment:		
Land	9,000	9,000
Buildings and equipment, net	36,800	38,000
Total property and equipment....................	45,800	47,000
Total assets	$68,480	$65,810
Liabilities and Stockholders' Equity		
Current liabilities:		
Accounts payable	$18,500	$17,400
Accrued payables	900	700
Notes payable, short term......................	—	100
Total current liabilities	19,400	18,200
Long-term liabilities:		
Bonds payable................................	8,000	8,000
Total liabilities................................	27,400	26,200
Stockholders' equity:		
Preferred stock...............................	1,000	1,000
Common stock................................	2,000	2,000
Additional paid-in capital	4,000	4,000
Total paid-in capital...........................	7,000	7,000
Retained earnings.............................	34,080	32,610
Total stockholders' equity	41,080	39,610
Total liabilities and stockholders' equity	$68,480	$65,810

HERITAGE ANTIQUING SERVICES Comparative Income Statement and Reconciliation (dollars in thousands)		
	2003	**2002**
Sales	$66,000	$64,000
Cost of goods sold.............................	43,000	42,000
		(continued)

(concluded) **HERITAGE ANTIQUING SERVICES** **Comparative Income Statement and Reconciliation** **(dollars in thousands)**		
	2003	**2002**
Gross margin	23,000	22,000
Operating expenses:		
Selling expenses	11,500	11,000
Administrative expenses	7,400	7,000
Total operating expenses	18,900	18,000
Net operating income	4,100	4,000
Interest expense................................	800	800
Net income before taxes	3,300	3,200
Less income taxes................................	1,320	1,280
Net income......................................	1,980	1,920
Dividends to preferred stockholders................	60	400
Net income remaining for common stockholders	1,920	1,520
Dividends to common stockholders	450	450
Net income added to retained earnings	1,470	1,070
Retained earnings, beginning of year	32,610	31,540
Retained earnings, end of year	$34,080	$32,610

Required:
Compute the following financial ratios for common stockholders for the year 2003:

1. Gross margin percentage.
2. Earnings per share of common stock.
3. Price-earnings ratio.
4. Dividend payout ratio.
5. Dividend yield ratio.
6. Return on total assets.
7. Return on common stockholders' equity.
8. Book value per share.

BRIEF EXERCISE 14–4   Financial Ratios for Short-Term Creditors   (LO3)
Refer to the data in Brief Exercise 14–3 for Heritage Antiquing Services.

Required:
Compute the following financial data for short-term creditors for the year 2003:

1. Working capital.
2. Current ratio.
3. Acid-test ratio.
4. Accounts receivable turnover. (Assume that all sales are on account.)
5. Average collection period.
6. Inventory turnover.
7. Average sale period.

BRIEF EXERCISE 14–5   Financial Ratios for Long-Term Creditors   (LO4)
Refer to the data in Brief Exercise 14–3 for Heritage Antiquing Services.

Required:
Compute the following financial ratios for long-term creditors for the year 2003:

1. Times interest earned ratio.
2. Debt-to-equity ratio.

EXERCISE 14–6   Selected Financial Ratios for Common Stockholders   (LO2)

Selected financial data from the September 30 year-end statements of Kosanka Marine Services Company are given below:

Total assets	$5,000,000
Long-term debt (12% interest rate)	$750,000
Preferred stock, $100 par, 7%	$800,000
Total stockholders' equity	$3,100,000
Interest paid on long-term debt	$90,000
Net income	$470,000

Total assets at the beginning of the year were $4,800,000; total stockholders' equity was $2,900,000. There has been no change in the preferred stock during the year. The company's tax rate is 30%.

Required:
1. Compute the return on total assets.
2. Compute the return on common stockholders' equity.
3. Is the company's financial leverage positive or negative? Explain.

EXERCISE 14–7   Selected Financial Measures for Short-Term Creditors   (LO3)

Rightway Gutter Installers had a current ratio of 2.5 to 1 on June 30 of the current year. On that date, the company's assets were as follows:

Cash		$ 80,000
Accounts receivable	$530,000	
Less allowance for doubtful accounts	70,000	460,000
Inventory		750,000
Prepaid expenses		10,000
Equipment, net		1,900,000
Total assets		$3,200,000

Required:
1. What was the company's working capital on June 30?
2. What was the company's acid-test ratio on June 30?
3. The company paid an account payable of $100,000 immediately after June 30.
   a.   What effect did this transaction have on working capital? Show computations.
   b.   What effect did this transaction have on the current ratio? Show computations.

EXERCISE 14–8   Selected Financial Ratios   (LO3, LO4)

Recent financial statements for Madison Corporation, a company that sells drilling equipment, are given below:

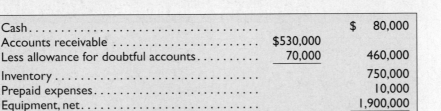

MADISON CORPORATION
Balance Sheet
June 30

Assets	
Current assets:	
Cash	$ 21,000
Accounts receivable, net	160,000
Merchandise inventory	300,000
Prepaid expenses	9,000

(continued)

(concluded)	**MADISON CORPORATION** **Balance Sheet** **June 30**	
Total current assets..........................		490,000
Property and equipment, net..................		810,000
Total assets		$1,300,000
Liabilities and Stockholders' Equity		
Liabilities:		
Current liabilities..........................		$ 200,000
Bonds payable, 10%........................		300,000
Total liabilities		500,000
Stockholders' equity:		
Common stock, $5 par value	$100,000	
Retained earnings	700,000	
Total stockholders' equity....................		800,000
Total liabilities and stockholders' equity.........		$1,300,000

MADISON CORPORATION **Income Statement** **For the Year Ended June 30**	
Sales..	$2,100,000
Less cost of goods sold.....................................	1,260,000
Gross margin..	840,000
Less operating expenses.....................................	660,000
Net operating income.......................................	180,000
Less interest expense.......................................	30,000
Net income before taxes	150,000
Less income taxes...	45,000
Net income..	$ 105,000

Account balances at the beginning of the company's fiscal year were: accounts receivable, $140,000; and inventory, $260,000. All sales were on account.

Required:

Compute financial ratios as follows:

1. Gross margin percentage.
2. Current ratio.
3. Acid-test (quick) ratio.
4. Accounts receivable turnover in days.
5. Inventory turnover in days.
6. Debt-to-equity ratio.
7. Times interest earned.
8. Book value per share.

EXERCISE 14–9   Selected Financial Ratios for Common Stockholders   (LO2)

Refer to the financial statements for Madison Corporation in Exercise 14–8. In addition to the data in these statements, assume that Madison Corporation paid dividends of $3.15 per share during the year. Also assume that the company's common stock had a market price of $63 per share on June 30 and there was no change in the number of outstanding shares of common stock during the fiscal year.

Required:

Compute the following:

1. Earnings per share.
2. Dividend payout ratio.
3. Dividend yield ratio.
4. Price-earnings ratio.

EXERCISE 14–10   Selected Financial Ratios for Common Stockholders   (LO2)

Refer to the financial statements for Madison Corporation in Exercise 14–8. Assets at the beginning of the year totaled $1,100,000, and the stockholders' equity totaled $725,000.

Required:

Compute the following:

1. Return on total assets.
2. Return on common stockholders' equity.
3. Was financial leverage positive or negative for the year? Explain.

PROBLEMS

PROBLEM 14–11   Common-Size Statements and Financial Ratios for Creditors   (LO1, LO3, LO4)

Vicki Newport organized Newport Industry 10 years ago in order to produce and sell several electronic devices on which she had secured patents. Although the company has been fairly profitable, it is now experiencing a severe cash shortage. For this reason, it is requesting a $500,000 long-term loan from San Juan Bank, $80,000 of which will be used to bolster the Cash account and $420,000 of which will be used to modernize certain key items of equipment. The company's financial statements for the two most recent years follow:

CHECK FIGURE

(1e) Inventory turnover this year: 5.0 times

(1g) Times interest earned last year: 6.0 times

NEWPORT INDUSTRY Comparative Balance Sheet		
	This Year	**Last Year**
Assets		
Current assets:		
Cash......................................	$ 60,000	$ 140,000
Marketable securities......................	0	30,000
Accounts receivable, net	470,000	290,000
Inventory	940,000	590,000
Prepaid expenses.........................	35,000	40,000
Total current assets	1,505,000	1,090,000
Plant and equipment, net..................	1,410,000	1,300,000
Total assets..............................	$2,915,000	$2,390,000
Liabilities and Stockholders' Equity		
Liabilities:		
Current liabilities........................	$ 703,000	$ 371,000
Bonds payable, 12%	500,000	500,000
Total liabilities.	1,203,000	871,000
Stockholders' equity:		
Preferred stock, $25 par, 8%	300,000	300,000
Common stock, $10 par	550,000	550,000
Retained earnings.........................	862,000	669,000
Total stockholders' equity	1,712,000	1,519,000
Total liabilities and equity..................	$2,915,000	$2,390,000

NEWPORT INDUSTRY		
Comparative Income Statement		
	This Year	**Last Year**
Sales	$4,960,000	$4,380,000
Less cost of goods sold	3,839,000	3,470,000
Gross margin	1,121,000	910,000
Less operating expenses	651,000	550,000
Net operating income	470,000	360,000
Less interest expense	60,000	60,000
Net income before taxes.	410,000	300,000
Less income taxes (30%)	123,000	90,000
Net income	287,000	210,000
Dividends paid:		
Preferred dividends	24,000	24,000
Common dividends	70,000	60,000
Total dividends paid	94,000	84,000
Net income retained	193,000	126,000
Retained earnings, beginning of year	669,000	543,000
Retained earnings, end of year.	$ 862,000	$ 669,000

During the past year, the company introduced several new product lines and raised the selling prices on a number of old product lines in order to improve its profit margin. The company also hired a new sales manager, who has expanded sales into several new territories. Sales terms are 2/10, n/30. All sales are on account. The following ratios are typical of firms in this industry:

Current ratio	2.5 to 1
Acid-test (quick) ratio	1.3 to 1
Average age of receivables.	17 days
Inventory turnover in days.	60 days
Debt-to-equity ratio.	0.90 to 1
Times interest earned	6.00 times
Return on total assets	13%
Price-earnings ratio	12

Required:

1. To assist the San Juan Bank in making a decision about the loan, compute the following ratios for both this year and last year:
   a. The amount of working capital.
   b. The current ratio.
   c. The acid-test (quick) ratio.
   d. The average age of receivables. (The accounts receivable at the beginning of last year totaled $240,000.)
   e. The inventory turnover in days. (The inventory at the beginning of last year totaled $490,000.)
   f. The debt-to-equity ratio.
   g. The number of times interest was earned.
2. For both this year and last year:
   a. Present the balance sheet in common-size format.
   b. Present the income statement in common-size format down through net income.
3. Comment on the results of your analysis in (1) and (2) above and make a recommendation as to whether or not the loan should be approved.

CHECK FIGURE
(1a) EPS this year: $4.78
(1c) Dividend payout ratio
     last year: 32.2%

PROBLEM 14–12   Financial Ratios for Common Stockholders   (LO2)
Refer to the financial statements and other data in Problem 14–11. Assume that you are an account executive for a large brokerage house and that one of your clients has asked for a recommendation about the

possible purchase of Newport Industry stock. You are not acquainted with the stock and for this reason wish to do certain analytical work before making a recommendation.

Required:
1. You decide first to assess the well-being of the common stockholders. For both this year and last year, compute:
   a. The earnings per share. There has been no change in preferred or common stock over the last two years.
   b. The dividend yield ratio for common. The company's stock is currently selling for $38 per share; last year it sold for $35 per share.
   c. The dividend payout ratio for common.
   d. The price-earnings ratio. How do investors regard Newport Industry as compared to other companies in the industry? Explain.
   e. The book value per share of common. Does the difference between market value and book value suggest that the stock is overpriced? Explain.
2. You decide next to assess the company's rate of return. Compute the following for both this year and last year:
   a. The return on total assets. (Total assets at the beginning of last year were $2,230,000.)
   b. The return on common equity. (Stockholders' equity at the beginning of last year was $1,418,000.)
   c. Is the company's financial leverage positive or negative? Explain.
3. Would you recommend that your client purchase shares of Newport Industry stock? Explain.

PROBLEM 14–13   Effects of Financial Leverage   (LO2)

Several investors are in the process of organizing a new company offering barge services in the Puget Sound area. The investors believe that $3,000,000 will be needed to finance the new company's operations, and they are considering three methods of raising this amount of money.

CHECK FIGURE
(2) Return on common equity method A: 12.5%

1. **Method A:** All $3,000,000 would be obtained through issue of common stock.
2. **Method B:** $1,500,000 would be obtained through issue of common stock and the other $1,500,000 would be obtained through issue of $100 par value, 10% preferred stock.
3. **Method C:** $1,500,000 would be obtained through issue of common stock, and the other $1,500,000 would be obtained through issue of bonds carrying an interest rate of 10%.

The investors organizing the new company are confident that it can earn $500,000 each year before interest and taxes. The tax rate will be 25%.

Required:
1. Assuming that the investors are correct in their earnings estimate, compute the net income that would go to the common stockholders under each of the three financing methods listed above.
2. Using the income data computed in (1) above, compute the return on common equity under each of the three methods.
3. Why do methods B and C provide a greater return on common equity than does method A? Why does method C provide a greater return on common equity than method B?

PROBLEM 14–14   Effects of Transactions on Financial Ratios   (LO3)

Cribbit Inc. operates a self-storage facility and sells storage supplies. The company's working capital accounts at the beginning of the year are given below:

CHECK FIGURE
(1c) Acid-test ratio: 1.6 to 1

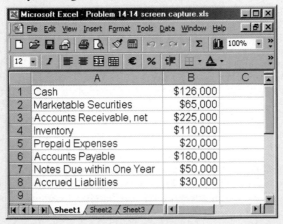

	A	B	C
1	Cash	$126,000	
2	Marketable Securities	$65,000	
3	Accounts Receivable, net	$225,000	
4	Inventory	$110,000	
5	Prepaid Expenses	$20,000	
6	Accounts Payable	$180,000	
7	Notes Due within One Year	$50,000	
8	Accrued Liabilities	$30,000	
9			

During the year, Cribbit completed the following transactions:

x.   Paid a cash dividend previously declared, $15,000.
a.   Issued additional shares of capital stock for cash, $120,000.
b.   Sold inventory costing $60,000 for $90,000, on account.
c.   Wrote off uncollectible accounts in the amount of $12,000. The company uses the allowance method
     of accounting for bad debts.
d.   Declared a cash dividend, $18,000.
e.   Paid accounts payable, $65,000.
f.   Borrowed cash on a short-term note with the bank, $40,000.
g.   Sold inventory costing $25,000 for $15,000 cash.
h.   Purchased inventory on account, $70,000.
i.   Paid off all short-term notes due, $45,000.
j.   Purchased equipment for cash, $22,000.
k.   Sold marketable securities costing $24,000 for cash, $21,000.
l.   Collected cash on accounts receivable, $100,000.

Required:
1. Compute the following amounts and ratios as of the beginning of the year:
   a.   Working capital.
   b.   Current ratio.
   c.   Acid-test (quick) ratio.
2. Indicate the effect of each of the transactions given above on working capital, the current ratio, and
   the acid-test (quick) ratio. Give the effect in terms of increase, decrease, or none. Item (x) is given
   below as an example of the format to use:

	The Effect on		
Transaction	**Working Capital**	**Current Ratio**	**Acid-Test Ratio**
(x) Paid a cash dividend previously declared	None	Increase	Increase

PROBLEM 14–15   Interpretation of Financial Ratios   (LO1, LO2, LO3)
Shannon Michaels is interested in the stock of Acelicom, a company that sells building materials to the construction industry. Before purchasing the stock, Shannon would like to learn as much as possible about the
company. However, all he has to go on is the current year's (Year 3) annual report, which contains no comparative data other than the summary of ratios given below:

	Year 3	Year 2	Year 1
Sales trend	132	118	108
Current ratio	2.7:1	2.4:1	2.3:1
Acid-test (quick) ratio	0.6:1	0.8:1	1.0:1
Accounts receivable turnover	9.8 times	10.7 times	12.8 times
Inventory turnover	6.4 times	7.8 times	8.4 times
Dividend yield	7.4%	6.8%	5.7%
Dividend payout ratio	42%	52%	62%
Return on total assets	12.8%	11.5%	9.8%
Return on common equity	15.1%	10.5%	8.6%
Dividends paid per share*	$1.40	$1.40	$1.40

*There have been no changes in common stock outstanding over the three-year period.

Shannon would like answers to a number of questions about the trend of events in Acelicom over the
last three years. His questions are:

a.   Is it becoming easier for the company to pay its bills as they come due?
b.   Are customers paying their accounts at least as fast now as they were in Year 1?
c.   Is the total of accounts receivable increasing, decreasing, or remaining constant?
d.   Is the level of inventory increasing, decreasing, or remaining constant?
e.   Is the market price of the company's stock going up or down?

f. Is the amount of earnings per share increasing or decreasing?
g. Is the price-earnings ratio going up or down?
h. Is the company employing financial leverage to the advantage of the common stockholders?

Required:
Answer each of Shannon's questions using the data given above. In each case, explain how you arrived at your answer.

PROBLEM 14–16 Comprehensive Ratio Analysis (LO2, LO3, LO4)
You have just been hired as a loan officer at Wamamish Bank. Your supervisor has given you a file containing a request from SafeT Corp., a manufacturer of safety helmets, for a $4,000,000, five-year loan. Financial statement data on the company for the last two years follow:

CHECK FIGURE
(2a) EPS this year: $8.08
(2b) Dividend yield ratio last year: 5.5%

SafeT Corp. Comparative Balance Sheet	This Year	Last Year
Assets		
Current assets:		
Cash	$ 158,000	$ 360,000
Marketable securities	0	200,000
Accounts receivable, net	2,590,000	1,950,000
Inventory	4,610,000	3,320,000
Prepaid expenses	340,000	280,000
Total current assets	7,698,000	6,110,000
Plant and equipment, net	9,500,000	8,840,000
Total assets	$17,198,000	$14,950,000
Liabilities and Stockholders' Equity		
Liabilities:		
Current liabilities	$ 3,900,000	$ 2,560,000
Note payable, 10%	4,000,000	3,600,000
Total liabilities	7,900,000	6,160,000
Stockholders' equity:		
Preferred stock, 8%, $100 par value	2,500,000	2,500,000
Common stock, $50 par value	5,000,000	5,000,000
Retained earnings	1,798,000	1,290,000
Total stockholders' equity	9,298,000	8,790,000
Total liabilities and stockholders' equity	$17,198,000	$14,950,000

SafeT Corp. Comparative Income Statement For the Years Ended December 31	This Year	Last Year
Sales (all on account)	$15,200,000	$12,800,000
Less cost of goods sold	9,270,000	7,420,000
Gross margin	5,930,000	5,380,000
Less operating expenses	4,090,000	4,060,000
Net operating income	1,840,000	1,320,000
Less interest expense	400,000	360,000
Net income before taxes	1,440,000	960,000

(continued)

(concluded)	SafeT Corp. Comparative Income Statement For the Years Ended December 31		
		This Year	Last Year
Less income taxes (30%).................		432,000	288,000
Net income		1,008,000	672,000
Dividends paid:			
Preferred dividends.....................		200,000	200,000
Common dividends.....................		300,000	250,000
Total dividends paid.......................		500,000	450,000
Net income retained......................		508,000	222,000
Retained earnings, beginning of year...........		1,290,000	1,068,000
Retained earnings, end of year		$ 1,798,000	$ 1,290,000

Vanna Cho, who just a year ago was appointed president of SafeT Corp., argues that although the company has had a "spotty" record in the past, it has "turned the corner," as evidenced by a 19% jump in sales and by a greatly improved earnings picture between last year and this year. Ms. Cho also points out that investors generally have recognized the improving situation at SafeT Corp., as shown by the increase in market value of the company's common stock, which is currently selling for $63.80 per share (up from $45.80 per share last year). Ms. Cho feels that with her leadership and with the modernized equipment that the $4,000,000 loan will permit the company to buy, profits will be even stronger in the future. Ms. Cho has a reputation in the industry for being a good manager who runs a "tight" ship.

Not wanting to botch your first assignment, you decide to generate all the information that you can about the company. You determine that the following ratios are typical of firms in SafeT Corp.'s industry:

Current ratio	2.3 to 1
Acid-test (quick) ratio	1.0 to 1
Average age of receivables.......	33 days
Inventory turnover.............	126 days
Return on assets	10.7%
Debt-to-equity ratio...........	0.72 to 1
Times interest earned	6.0
Price-earnings ratio	10.9

Required:

1. You decide first to assess the rate of return that the company is generating. Compute the following for both this year and last year:
    a. The return on total assets. (Total assets at the beginning of last year were $14,384,000.)
    b. The return on common equity. (Stockholders' equity at the beginning of last year totaled $8,568,000.) There has been no change in preferred or common stock over the last two years.)
    c. Is the company's financial leverage positive or negative? Explain.
2. You decide next to assess the well-being of the common stockholders. For both this year and last year, compute:
    a. The earnings per share.
    b. The dividend yield ratio for common.
    c. The dividend payout ratio for common.
    d. The price-earnings ratio. How do investors regard SafeT Corp. as compared to other firms in the industry? Explain.
    e. The book value per share of common. Does the difference between market value per share and book value per share suggest that the stock at its current price is a bargain? Explain.
    f. The gross margin percentage.
3. You decide, finally, to assess creditor ratios to determine both short-term and long-term debt-paying ability. For both this year and last year, compute:
    a. Working capital.
    b. The current ratio.

c. The acid-test ratio.

d. The average age of receivables. (The accounts receivable at the beginning of last year totaled $1,660,000.)

e. The inventory turnover. (The inventory at the beginning of last year totaled $1,800,000.) Also compute the number of days required to turn the inventory one time (use a 365-day year).

f. The debt-to-equity ratio.

g. The number of times interest was earned.

4. Would you recommend that the loan be granted?

PROBLEM 14–17   Common-Size Financial Statements   (LO1)

Refer to the financial statement data for SafeT Corp. given in Problem 14–16.

CHECK FIGURE
none

Required:

For both this year and last year:

1. Present the balance sheet in common-size format.
2. Present the income statement in common-size format down through net income.
3. Comment on the results of your analysis.

PROBLEM 14–18   Effects of Transactions on Financial Ratios   (LO2, LO3, LO4)

In the right-hand column below, certain financial ratios are listed. To the left of each ratio is a business transaction or event relating to the operating activities of Stuen Inc., an importer of marble and other fine building stones.

CHECK FIGURE
none

Business Transaction or Event	Ratio
1. The company declared a cash dividend.	Current ratio
2. The company sold inventory on account at cost.	Acid-test (quick) ratio
3. The company issued bonds with an interest rate of 12%. The company's return on assets is 16%.	Return on common stockholders' equity
4. The company's net income decreased by 3% between last year and this year. Long-term debt remained unchanged.	Times interest earned
5. A previously declared cash dividend was paid.	Current ratio
6. The market price of the company's common stock dropped from $27.50 to $21.00. The dividend paid per share remained unchanged.	Dividend payout ratio
7. Obsolete inventory totaling $85,000 was written off as a loss.	Inventory turnover ratio
8. The company sold inventory for cash at a profit.	Debt-to-equity ratio
9. The company changed customer credit terms from 2/10, n15 to 2/15, n/30 to comply with a change in industry practice.	Accounts receivable turnover ratio
10. The company issued a common stock dividend on common stock.	Book value per share
11. The market price of the company's common stock increased from $27.50 to $33.00.	Book value per share
12. The company paid $60,000 on accounts payable.	Working capital
13. The company issued a common stock dividend to common stockholders.	Earnings per share
14. The company paid accounts payable.	Debt-to-equity ratio
15. The company purchased inventory on credit terms.	Acid-test (quick) ratio
16. An uncollectible account was written off against the Allowance for Bad Debts.	Current ratio
17. The market price of the company's common stock increased from $27.50 to $33.00. Earnings per share remained unchanged.	Price-earnings ratio
18. The market price of the company's common stock increased from $27.50 to $33.00. The dividend paid per share remained unchanged.	Dividend yield ratio

Required:

Indicate the effect that each business transaction or event would have on the ratio listed opposite to it. State the effect in terms of increase, decrease, or no effect on the ratio involved, and give the reason for your answer. In all cases, assume that the current assets exceed the current liabilities both before and after the event or transaction. Use the following format for your answers:

Effect on Ratio	Reason for Increase, Decrease, or No Effect
1.	
Etc....	

CHECK FIGURE
(1a) EPS this year: $3.88
(2a) Return on total assets
    this year: 15.9%

PROBLEM 14–19   Financial Ratios for Common Stockholders   (LO2)
(Problem 14–20 and Problem 14–21 delve more deeply into the data presented below. Each problem is independent.) Farizon Labs was organized several years ago to produce and market several new "miracle drugs." The company is small but growing, and you are considering the purchase of some of its common stock as an investment. The following data on the company are available for the past two years:

FARIZON LABS
Comparative Income Statement
For the Years Ended December 31

	This Year	Last Year
Sales.....................................	$20,600,000	$15,500,000
Less cost of goods sold.....................	13,184,000	9,145,000
Gross margin.............................	7,416,000	6,355,000
Less operating expenses....................	5,400,000	4,700,000
Net operating income......................	2,016,000	1,655,000
Less interest expense	240,000	240,000
Net operating income before taxes	1,776,000	1,415,000
Less income taxes (30%)....................	532,800	424,500
Net income	$ 1,243,200	$ 990,500

FARIZON LABS
Comparative Retained Earnings Statement
For the Years Ended December 31

	This Year	Last Year
Retained earnings, January 1....................	$2,390,500	$1,900,000
Add net income (above)......................	1,243,200	990,500
Total	3,633,700	2,890,500
Deduct cash dividends paid:		
Preferred dividends	80,000	80,000
Common dividends	540,000	420,000
Total dividends paid	620,000	500,000
Retained earnings, December 31................	$3,013,700	$2,390,500

FARIZON LABS
Comparative Balance Sheet
December 31

	This Year	Last Year
Assets		
Current assets:		
Cash	$ 153,700	$ 190,500
Accounts receivable, net	1,440,000	680,000
Inventory..................................	2,810,000	1,240,000
Prepaid expenses	210,000	190,000

(continued)

(concluded)	**FARIZON LABS** **Comparative Balance Sheet** **December 31**	
	This Year	**Last Year**
Total current assets	4,613,700	2,300,500
Plant and equipment, net	5,330,000	5,560,000
Total assets	$9,943,700	$7,860,500
Liabilities and Stockholders' Equity		
Liabilities:		
Current liabilities	$2,430,000	$970,000
Bonds payable, 12%.	2,000,000	2,000,000
Total liabilities	4,430,000	2,970,000
Stockholders' equity:		
Preferred stock, 8%, $10 par value.	1,000,000	1,000,000
Common stock, $5 par value.	1,500,000	1,500,000
Retained earnings	3,013,700	2,390,500
Total stockholders' equity	5,513,700	4,890,500
Total liabilities and stockholders' equity	$9,943,700	$7,860,500

After some research, you have determined that the following ratios are typical of firms in the industry in which Farizon Labs operates.

Dividend yield ratio	3.3%
Dividend payout ratio	47.7%
Price-earnings ratio	17.3
Return on total assets	15.8%
Return on common equity	22.5%

The company's common stock is currently selling for $55 per share. Last year the stock sold for $40 per share.

There has been no change in the preferred or common stock outstanding over the last three years.

Required:

1. In analyzing the company, you decide first to compute the earnings per share and related ratios. For both last year and this year, compute:
   a. The earnings per share.
   b. The dividend yield ratio.
   c. The dividend payout ratio.
   d. The price-earnings ratio.
   e. The book value per share of common stock.
   f. The gross margin percentage.
2. You decide next to determine the rate of return that the company is generating. For both last year and this year, compute:
   a. The return on total assets. (Total assets were $6,349,500 at the beginning of last year.)
   b. The return on common stockholders' equity. (Common stockholders' equity was $3,279,500 at the beginning of last year.)
   c. Is financial leverage positive or negative? Explain.
3. Based on your work in (1) and (2) above, does the company's common stock seem to be an attractive investment? Explain.

PROBLEM 14–20   Financial Ratios for Creditors   (LO3, LO4)

Refer to the data in Problem 14–19. Although Farizon Labs has been very profitable since it was organized several years ago, the company is beginning to experience some difficulty in paying its bills as they come due. Management has approached First Trust Bank requesting a two-year, $800,000 loan to bolster the cash account.

CHECK FIGURE
(1b) Current ratio this year:
    1.9 to 1
(1g) Debt-to-equity ratio
    last year: 0.61 to 1

First Trust Bank has assigned you to evaluate the loan request. You have gathered the following data relating to firms in the pharmaceutical industry:

Current ratio	2.4 to 1
Acid-test (quick) ratio	1.2 to 1
Average age of receivables.	13.8 days
Inventory turnover in days.	37.3 days
Time interest earned	8.1 times
Debt-to-equity ratio.	0.68 to 1

The following additional information is available about Farizon Labs.

a.   All sales are on account.
b.   At the beginning of last year, the accounts receivable balance was $640,000 and the inventory balance was $910,000.

Required:

1. Compute the following amounts and ratios for both last year and this year:
   a.   The working capital.
   b.   The current ratio.
   c.   The acid-test ratio.
   d.   The accounts receivable turnover in days.
   e.   The inventory turnover in days.
   f.   The times interest earned.
   g.   The debt-to-equity ratio.
2. Comment on the results of your analysis in (1) above.
3. Would you recommend that the loan be approved? Explain.

CHECK FIGURE
none

PROBLEM 14–21   Common-Size Financial Statements   (LO1)
Refer to the data in Problem 14–19. The president of Farizon Labs is deeply concerned. Sales increased by $5,100,000 from last year to this year, yet the company's net operating income increased by only a small amount. Also, the company's operating expenses went up this year, even though a major effort was launched during the year to cut costs.

Required:

1. For both last year and this year, prepare the income statement and the balance sheet in common-size format. Round computations to one decimal place.
2. From your work in (1) above, explain to the president why the increase in profits was so small this year. Were any benefits realized from the company's cost-cutting efforts? Explain.

BUILDING YOUR SKILLS

ANALYTICAL THINKING   (LO2, LO3, LO4)
Incomplete financial statements for Tanner Corporation are given below:

TANNER CORPORATION Income Statement For the Year Ended December 31	
Sales.	$2,700,000
Less cost of goods sold.	?
Gross margin.	?
Less operating expenses	?
Net operating income.	?
Less interest expense	45,000
Net income before taxes	?
Less income taxes (40%).	?
Net income	$?

TANNER CORPORATION
Balance Sheet
December 31

Current assets:

Cash.	$	?
Accounts receivable, net.		?
Inventory		?
Total current assets.		?
Plant and equipment, net.		?
Total assets	$	?
Current liabilities.	$250,000	
Bonds payable, 10%		?
Total liabilities		?
Stockholders' equity:		
Common stock, $2.50 par value.		?
Retained earnings		?
Total stockholders' equity.		?
Total liabilities and stockholders' equity.	$	?

The following additional information is available about the company:

a. Selected financial ratios computed from the statements above are given below:

Current ratio	2.40 to 1
Acid-test (quick) ratio	1.12 to 1
Accounts receivable turnover	15.0 times
Inventory turnover	6.0 times
Debt-to-equity ratio	0.875 to 1
Times interest earned	7.0 times
Earnings per share	$4.05
Return on total assets	14%

b. All sales during the year were on account.
c. The interest expense on the income statement relates to the bonds payable; the amount of bonds outstanding did not change throughout the year.
d. There were no changes in the number of shares of common stock outstanding during the year.
e. Selected balances at the *beginning* of the current year (January 1) were as follows:

Accounts receivable	$160,000
Inventory.	$280,000
Total assets	$1,200,000

Required:
Compute the missing amounts on the company's financial statements. (Hint: You may find it helpful to think about the difference between the current ratio and the acid-test ratio.)

ETHICS CHALLENGE   (LO3)

Mountain Aerosport was founded by Jurgen Prinz to produce a ski he had designed for doing aerial tricks. Up to this point, Jurgen has financed the company from his own savings and from retained profits. However, Jurgen now faces a cash crisis. In the year just ended, an acute shortage of a vital tungsten steel alloy had developed just as the company was beginning production for the Christmas season. Jurgen had been assured by his suppliers that the steel would be delivered in time to make Christmas shipments, but the suppliers had been unable to fully deliver on this promise. As a consequence, Mountain Aerosport had large stocks of unfinished skis at the end of the year and had been unable to fill all of the orders that had come in from retailers for the Christmas season. Consequently, sales were below expectations for the year, and Jurgen does not have enough cash to pay his creditors.

Well before the accounts payable were to become due, Jurgen visited a local bank and inquired about obtaining a loan. The loan officer at the bank assured Jurgen that there should not be any problem getting a loan to pay off his accounts payable—providing that on his most recent financial statements the current ratio was above 2.0, the acid-test ratio was above 1.0, and net operating income was at least four times the interest on the proposed loan. Jurgen promised to return later with a copy of his financial statements.

Jurgen would like to apply for a $120 thousand six-month loan bearing an interest rate of 10% per year. The unaudited financial reports of the company appear below.

MOUNTAIN AEROSPORT
Comparative Balance Sheet
As of December 31, This Year and Last Year
(in thousands of dollars)

	This Year	Last Year
Assets		
Current assets:		
Cash	$105	$225
Accounts receivable, net	75	60
Inventory	240	150
Prepaid expenses	15	18
Total current assets	435	453
Property and equipment	405	270
Total assets	$840	$723
Liabilities and Stockholders' Equity		
Current liabilities:		
Accounts payable	$231	$135
Accrued payables	15	15
Total current liabilities	246	150
Long-term liabilities	0	0
Total liabilities	246	150
Stockholders' equity:		
Common stock and additional		
paid-in capital	150	150
Retained earnings	444	423
Total stockholders' equity	594	573
Total liabilities and stockholders' equity	$840	$723

MOUNTAIN AEROSPORT
Income Statement
For the Year Ended December 31, This Year
(in thousands of dollars)

Sales (all on account)	$630
Cost of goods sold	435
Gross margin	195
Operating expenses:	
Selling expenses	63
Administrative expenses	102
Total operating expenses	165
Net operating income	30
Interest expense	0
Net income before taxes	30
Less income taxes (30%)	9
Net income	$ 21

Required:

1. Based on the above unaudited financial statements and the statement made by the loan officer, would the company qualify for the loan?
2. Last year Jurgen purchased and installed new, more efficient equipment to replace an older heat-treating furnace. Jurgen had originally planned to sell the old equipment but found that it is still needed whenever the heat-treating process is a bottleneck. When Jurgen discussed his cash flow problems with his brother-in-law, he suggested to Jurgen that the old equipment be sold or at least reclassified as inventory on the balance sheet since it could be readily sold. At present, the equipment is carried in the Property and Equipment account and could be sold for its net book value of $68 thousand. The bank does not require audited financial statements. What advice would you give to Jurgen concerning the machine?

TEAMWORK IN ACTION   (LO1, LO2, LO3, LO4)

Obtain the most recent annual report or SEC filing 10-K of a publicly traded company that interests you. It may be a local company or it may be a company in an industry that you would like to know more about. Using the annual report, compute as many of the financial ratios covered in this chapter as you can for at least the past two years. This may pose some difficulties—particularly since companies often use different terms for many income statement and balance sheet items than were shown in the chapter. Nevertheless, do the best that you can. After you have computed the financial ratios, summarize the company's performance for the current year. Has it improved, gotten worse, or remained about the same? Do the ratios indicate any potential problems or any areas that have shown significant improvement? What recommendations, if any, would you make to a bank about extending short-term credit to this company? What recommendations, if any, would you make to an insurance company about extending long-term credit to this company? What recommendations, if any, would you make to an investor about buying or selling this company's stock?

COMMUNICATING IN PRACTICE   (LO1, LO2, LO3, LO4)

Typically, the market price of shares of a company's stock takes a beating when the company announces that it has not met analysts' expectations. As a result, many companies are under a lot of pressure to meet analysts' revenue and earnings projections. To manage (that is, to inflate or smooth) earnings, managers sometimes record revenue that has not yet been earned by the company, delay the recognition of expenses that have been incurred or employ other accounting tricks.

A wave of accounting scandals related to earnings management swept over the capital markets in the wake of the collapse of Enron in 2002. Some earlier examples illustrate how companies have attempted to manage their earnings. On March 20, 2000, MicroStrategy announced that it was forced to restate its 1999 earnings; revenue from multiyear contracts had been recorded in the first year instead of being spread over the lives of the related contracts as required by GAAP. On April 3, 2000, Legato Systems Inc. announced that it had restated its earnings; $7 million of revenue had been improperly recorded because customers had been promised that they could return the products purchased. As further discussed in this chapter, America Online overstated its net income during 1994, 1995, and 1996. In May 2000, upon completing its review of the company's accounting practices, the SEC levied a fine of $3.5 million against AOL. Just prior to the announcement of the fine levied on AOL, Helane Morrison, head of the SEC's San Francisco office, reemphasized that the investigation of misleading financial statements is a top priority for the agency. [Sources: Jeff Shuttleworth, "Investors Beware: Dot.Coms Often Use Accounting Tricks," *Business Journal Serving San Jose & Silicon Valley,* April 14, 2000, p. 16; David Henry, "AOL Pays $3.5M to Settle SEC Case," *USA Today,* May 16, 2000, p. 3B.]

Required:

Write a memorandum to your instructor that answers the following questions. Use headings to organize the information presented in the memorandum. Include computations to support your answers, when appropriate.

1. Why would companies be tempted to manage earnings?
2. If the earnings that are reported by a company are misstated, how might this impact business decisions made about that company (such as the acquisition of the company by another business)?
3. What ethical issues, if any, arise when a company manages its earnings?
4. How would investors and financial analysts tend to view the financial statements of a company that has been known to manage its earnings in the past?

TAKING IT TO THE NET

As you know, the World Wide Web is a medium that is constantly evolving. Sites come and go and change without notice. To enable periodic update of site addresses, this problem has been posted to the textbook website (www.mhhe.com/bgn2e). After accessing the site, enter the Student Center and select this chapter. Select and complete the Taking It to the Net problem.

PHOTO CREDITS

INDEX